ALL ABOUT LAW

Exploring the Canadian Legal System

FOURTH EDITION

DWIGHT L. GIBSON

Head of Administration
West Carleton Secondary School
Dunrobin, Ontario

TERRY G. MURPHY

Head, Business Studies
Frontenac Secondary School
Kingston, Ontario

FREDERICK E. JARMAN

Head, History Department
Central High School of Commerce
Toronto, Ontario

DEREK GRANT

Vice Principal
Kitsilano Secondary School
Vancouver, British Columbia

Nelson Canada

I(T)P An International Thomson Publishing Company

Toronto • Albany • Bonn • Boston • Cincinnati • Detroit • London • Madrid • Melbourne
• Mexico City • New York Pacific Grove • Paris • San Francisco • Singapore • Tokyo • Washington

To Michael and Corrie,
and to Kit, Jamie, and Karen
and in memory of Jean Lagacé

ITP™

International Thomson Publishing
The ITP logo is used under licence

©Nelson Canada,
A division of Thomson Canada Limited, 1996
Third edition copyright ©1990 by John Wiley & Sons
Canada Limited
Second edition copyright ©1984 by John Wiley & Sons Canada Limited
First edition copyright ©1977 by John Wiley & Sons Canada Limited

Published in 1996 by
Nelson Canada,
A division of Thomson Canada Limited
1120 Birchmount Road
Scarborough, Ontario M1K 5G4

Every reasonable effort to trace the copyright holders of materials appearing in this book has been made. Information that will enable the publisher to rectify any error or omission will be welcomed.

∞

This book is printed on acid-free paper, approved under Environment Canada's "Environmental Choice Program." The choice of paper reflects Nelson Canada's goal of using, within the publishing process, the available resources, technology, and suppliers that are as environment friendly as possible.

Canadian Cataloguing in Publication Data

Gibson, Dwight L., 1944—
    All about law: exploring the Canadian legal system

4th ed.
For use in secondary schools.

Includes index.
ISBN 0-17-604752-2

1. Law - Canada.   I. Murphy, Terry G., 1940—
II. Title

KE444.G62 1996   349.71   C96-930630-X
KF385.ZA2G62 1996

Readers wishing further information on data provided through the cooperation of Statistics Canada may obtain copies of related publications by mail from: Publications Sales, Statistics Canada, Ottawa, Ontario K1A 0T6, by calling 1-613-951-7277 or toll-free 1-800-267-6677. Readers may also facsimile their order by dialing 1-613-951-1584.

Disclaimer
This text has been prepared for use in a high school curriculum as a source of information. It has not been written by lawyers and does not, nor does it purport to, convey legal advice. Under no circumstances should you use information from the text to address or resolve actual legal problems. We strongly recommend that you seek the advice of a lawyer if you have a legal problem.

Printed and bound in Canada by Bryant Press
    4 5 6 7 8 9 0 BP 4 3 2 1 0 9 8

**All About Law
Project Team**

Project Coordinators:
Carolyn Madonia
Kathryn Lye

Developmental Editor:
Geraldine Kikuta

Copy Editor:
Sandra Manley

Editorial Consultant:
Ruth Chernia

Publishing Consultant:
Sylvia Gilchrist

Art Director:
Liz Harasymczuk

**Cover and Interior
Design/Technical Art:**
Sylvia Vander Schee

**Senior Composition
Analyst/Designer:**
Suzanne Peden

Manuscript Processor:
Elaine Andrews

Senior Composition Analyst:
Alicja Jamorski

Illustrators:
Allan Moon
Andrew Woodhouse

Production Coordinator:
Renate McCloy

Photo Researcher:
Ann Ludbrook

Permissions:
Siobhan Dooley

Team Leader and Publisher:
Lynn Fisher

REVIEWERS

Ernie Armitage

L.V. Rogers Secondary School
Nelson, British Columbia

J. Timothy Buehner

Henry Wise Wood Senior High School
Calgary, Alberta

Karen Clark

Barrister & Solicitor
Toronto, Ontario

Robert W. d'Arras

Laurentian High School
Ottawa, Ontario

Tita De Rousseau

Andrew, Donahoe & Oake
Edmonton, Alberta

Shirley Douglas

Black Gold Regional School Division
Leduc, Alberta

Eileen E. English

New Glasgow High School
New Glasgow, Nova Scotia

Wayne Enns

Dakota Collegiate
Winnipeg, Manitoba

Margaret Ferguson

Consultant, Law-related Education
Fort Langley, British Columbia

Susan M. Hare

Barrister & Solicitor, Ojibway Nation
West Bay First Nation, Ontario

Sandra Hawkins

Columneetza Senior Secondary School
Williams Lake, British Columbia

Allan C. Hutchinson

Osgoode Hall Law School,
York University, Toronto, Ontario

Stan Kopciuch

Miller Comprehensive High School
Regina, Saskatchewan

Rod Lis

Beaumont Composite High School
Beaumont, Alberta

Lynda Raven Lyons

Dr. F.J. Donevan Collegiate
Oshawa, Ontario

Bruce E. Machon, B.A., LL.B

Stong, Blackburn, Machon, Bohm
Richmond Hill, Ontario

William G. McLean

Barrister & Solicitor
Orillia, Ontario

Mary E. Mouat

Quadra Legal Centre
Victoria, British Columbia

Peter Otten

North Surrey Learning Center
Surrey, British Columbia

David G. Perry

Quadra Legal Centre
Victoria, British Columbia

Colin Robinson

Quadra Legal Centre
Victoria, British Columbia

Michael Schultz

Chinguacousy Secondary School
Brampton, Ontario

Kimberley Smith Maynard

Barrister & Solicitor
Trenton, Ontario

Murray W. Stenton

St. Patrick's High School
Halifax, Nova Scotia

TABLE OF CONTENTS

PREFACE

Introduction

Law is an essential part of Canada's culture; without it, we cannot function effectively in our daily lives. A broad knowledge and understanding of law is not only a vital part of a student's education, but is also an important factor in the operation of a democratic and orderly society. Students who understand, appreciate, and respect the concept of the rule of law and the operation, benefits, and limitations of our legal system are more likely to be productive, informed, and law-abiding citizens. In turn, they will have the knowledge, skills, and understanding to be effective members of our society. They will also recognize that our legal system must adapt to complex social changes while balancing majority values with individual rights.

Nowhere is this more evident than in the impact of the Canadian Constitution and the *Charter of Rights and Freedoms*. Since the *Charter* was enacted in 1982, the Supreme Court of Canada has issued many judgments that comment on values believed to be reflective of our country. The range of judgments varies from the weight drunkenness will be given when determining intent in a criminal case to a civil matter such as the age of retirement. The significance of many of these judgments is not that they provided precedents, but that governments were required to make changes to various laws. About 36 percent of the cases in this text represent Supreme Court of Canada decisions.

In Unit 2, students are introduced to criminal law and the major legislative amendments that have been made to the *Criminal Code* in the 1990s. The chapter dealing with the *Young Offenders Act* is of special interest to students. This fourth edition includes the 1992 and 1995 amendments to the *Act* made in response to society's concerns for greater safety and protection.

Aspects of civil law, family law, and employment law are important to students as this is the area of law that will most likely affect them throughout their lives. Units 3, 4, and 5 provide in-depth coverage of these areas.

As we head into the twenty-first century, environmental law concerns, the issues of aboriginal rights and Native land claims, and immigration law are being debated by all levels of government and involved citizens. Unit 6 provides some background on these ongoing legal concerns so that students will be able to help promote social action through legal means as they become leaders of tomorrow.

Features of the Fourth Edition

Each of the six units in this new edition begins with a **Careers** profile that provides information about varied occupations related to the law.

A feature new to this edition is the use of newspaper and magazine articles to begin each chapter. These articles have been selected to generate student interest in the material that is to follow. The articles and the Something to Think About questions are revisited at the end of the chapter. Other new features include **Looking Back**, which provides a historical perspective on certain aspects of the law, and **Did You Know**, which offers relevant and interesting facts corresponding with the main text.

This edition retains the study aids for students that were so successful in the third edition. The **Chapter at a Glance** provides a preview of the main topics discussed in the chapter, while the **Learning Outcomes** outline the key concepts that students should know by the time they have completed the chapter.

To assist students in learning the "language of law," key terms are now previewed at the beginning of each chapter and appear printed in **bold** type within the chapter. These words can be used to review key concepts within the chapter. All of these terms are defined in the **Glossary**.

Each section within the chapter is followed by a series of recall questions in **Reviewing Your Reading**. These questions are designed to enable students to check their understanding and comprehension of the new material just presented.

Within each chapter there is an extensive collection of recent and relevant case studies from across Canada. Of the 220 cases presented, a concerted effort was made to use as many current cases as possible to show how the law is being applied to issues relevant today. Precedent setting and historically valuable cases have also been included from the third edition. These are identified by a ⚖ icon.

All cases have been identified by their complete citation to make students aware of how current, or how old, the decision is and its appropriateness to their lives today. Further, it is important for students to know the last court in which the case was heard as the higher the court, the more binding the decision. Cases from provincial courts of appeal or the Supreme Court of Canada have a more significant impact on all Canadians than lower court decisions.

All in-chapter cases are followed with relevant questions to illustrate the points of law covered and to give students the opportunity to analyze the reasons for the judgments. In answering these questions, students are expected to consider the information they have learned in the chapter along with the details presented in the case itself. As well, students will recognize that concepts they have learned in other chapters will have an application to case questions.

Each chapter features an issue related to the chapter content. These objective discussions of controversial current issues present arguments for two sides and are followed by thought-provoking questions. Students may investigate these arguments in greater detail or they may wish to use the focus of the issue as a springboard to explore alternative aspects of the topic.

In response to input we have received from teachers at conferences and workshops across the country, the **Chapter Review** at the end of each chapter has been changed significantly to include a variety of questions and activities under the following five features:

- **Reviewing Key Terms** tests student comprehension of the "language of law," listed at the beginning of each chapter.
- **Exploring Legal Concepts** contains questions that require students to develop their

legal knowledge by analyzing the concepts presented within the chapter.
- **Applying Legal Concepts** contains case situations with questions designed to develop critical thinking and decision-making skills.
- **Extending Legal Concepts** is activity-focused to encourage cooperative learning situations. Conducting interviews, debating, brainstorming, role playing, using information technology, and preparing reports are a sample of the type of activities included in this section.
- **Researching an Issue** presents an issue topic related to the chapter and challenges students to research and prepare arguments to support the Point and Counterpoint positions.

An important new feature of this edition is an **Appendix** in which the *Canadian Charter of Rights and Freedoms* is reproduced in its entirety to facilitate student reference.

Learning Outcomes

The ability of students to reason logically and make informed decisions is an important goal of education. The study of law is an important step to achieving this goal. The cases, questions, and activities in this new edition provide students with opportunities to develop their legal knowledge, as well as their skills in critical thinking, organization, research, analysis, and decision-making. Through interaction with others and sharing of ideas, students learn to apply the law they have studied to resolve conflict as presented in courtroom cases and in their personal and professional lives. The text and the activities are designed to create a sensitivity and tolerance toward others and an appreciation of other opinions and attitudes that may be based on different value systems.

Acknowledgements

We are very grateful to a number of people who assisted us in the preparation of this fourth edition. Besides those teachers across Canada who made us feel welcome at conferences and provided suggestions for changes in this edition, we must thank our students. Many of them are our best critics, as they bring clarity to concepts in a way that only those for whom a text is written are able to do. As a result, many of the case studies and activities in this text have been class-tested over the past years and are, hopefully, free of error and ambiguity. Many of their recommendations were followed throughout the development of this text, although we alone are responsible for the final content. To all the lawyers, teachers, and students who have made their mark on this book, we extend our thanks.

We would also like to recognize the staff at Nelson Canada, both in-house and freelance, for providing us with a positive and supportive working relationship and without whom this text would not have been possible. In particular, we would like to thank Geraldine Kikuta and Kathryn Lye, who helped shape the final version of this book significantly.

Finally, we would like to thank our families, who sacrificed much of their time with us in the evenings and on weekends so that we could complete this text and reach the goal of publishing our fourth edition. We cannot replace the time, but we do hope they feel, as we do, that the end result was well worth the lost time and effort. Thank you for your love, understanding, and patience.

Dwight L. Gibson & Terry G. Murphy
April 1996

CITATION REFERENCES

The information below provides the full names of the sources listed in abbreviated form in the Table of Cases citations:

A.C.	Appeal Cases
Alta. L.R.	Alberta Law Reports
A.R.	Alberta Reports
B.C.L.R.	British Columbia Law Reports
B.L.R.	Business Law Reports
C.C.L.T.	Canadian Cases on the Law of Torts
C.C.C.	Canadian Criminal Cases
C.H.R.R.	Canadian Human Rights Reporter
C.L.L.C.	Canadian Labour Law Cases
C.L.R.B.R. (NS)	Canadian Labour Relations Boards Reports (New Series)
C.P.R.	Canadian Patent Reporter
C.R.	Criminal Reports
D.L.R.	Dominion Law Reports
E.R.	English Reports
H.R.T.	Human Rights Tribunal
I.A.B.	Immigration Appeal Board
L.A.C.	Labour Arbitration Cases
L.R.B.	Labour Relations Board
L.R.H.L.	Law Reports House of Lords
Man. R.	Manitoba Reports
Nfld. & P.E.I.R.	Newfoundland & Prince Edward Island Reports
N.B.R.	New Brunswick Reports
N.R.	National Reporter
N.S.R.	Nova Scotia Reports
O.A.C.	Ontario Appeal Cases
O.L.R.	Ontario Law Reports
O.R.	Ontario Reports
Q.B.	Queen's Bench
Q.B.D.	Queen's Bench Division
Sask. R.	Saskatchewan Reports
R.F.L.	Reports on Family Law
R.P.R.	Real Property Reports
S.C.R.	Supreme Court Reports
W.W.R.	Western Weekly Reports

TABLE OF CASES

AN INTRODUCTION TO LAW

CAREERS

Introduction

As Canadians we believe that to "judge" well one must form an opinion objectively and wisely and use good critical sense to arrive at a decision in accordance with law which will be regarded with respect. It is no surprise, then, that we demand the highest standards of our court judges and confer upon them great honour and respect.

In Focus: COURT JUDGE

Judges are appointed by federal or provincial governments to adjudicate civil and criminal cases and administer justice in a court of law. At the lowest level are the justices of the peace who try minor offences, commit more serious cases for trial in the higher courts, administer oaths and perform marriages. At the highest level are the nine judges of the Supreme Court of Canada. Judges earn between $76 000 and $132 000 per year.

Education and Other Qualifications

If it is your ambition to be a judge, you must acquire extensive experience as a lawyer or as a professor of law. You must be a member in good standing of a provincial law society or bar association. Persons appointed to senior court positions, such as Chief Justice, usually have had experience as a judge in that court.

Responsibilities

As a judge, you will be responsible for interpreting the law, including the *Charter of Rights and Freedoms*, and enforcing rules of procedure and deciding on the admissibility of evidence. In jury trials, you will instruct juries on the laws which apply to the case they are deciding. In non-jury trials, you will render the decisions. You will also determine damages or provide other remedies in civil cases, and pass sentence on persons convicted in criminal cases. In family law matters, you will hear divorce petitions, divide assets between spouses, and determine custody of children and the terms of access for the non-custodial parents.

Work Environment

You will spend most of your time in courtrooms hearing cases and making extensive notes for immediate or later reference. With some cases, you will have to write carefully reasoned judgments which you will read in court. Although you will work closely with many court officers and be in contact with many kinds of people, you must not discuss cases nor offer political opinions at any time.

Do You Fit the Job?

As a judge, you must be able to remain objective and composed at all times. You must be able to reason well, think on your feet, be a good listener, and an effective public speaker. Above all, you must be a capable decision maker.

PROFILE: Julius Isaac

Julius Alexander Isaac, Chief Justice of the Federal Court of Canada, was born in Grenada, West Indies in 1928. He attended the University of Toronto where he earned his law degree in 1958.

His long and distinguished career in the Canadian legal system includes private and public sector practice in Ontario, Saskatchewan, Alberta, and Ontario, where he worked as Assistant Deputy Attorney General (Criminal Law). In 1989, he was appointed Justice of the Supreme Court of Ontario and in 1991 Chief Justice of the Federal Court of Canada.

Chief Justice Isaac has received many awards, including the Canadian Black Achievement Award for Law and the Honorary Degree of Doctor of Civil Laws from the University of Windsor in 1994. He has been a guest lecturer at conferences and seminars across Canada and in 1994 was a speaker at the Continuing Education Series for the Legal Education Society of Alberta. He is very active in community work and is Co-Chair of the Johnston Chair in Black Studies at Dalhousie University in Nova Scotia.

Chief Justice Isaac's advice to high school students who are contemplating a career in law is that they should be well motivated, acquire a good understanding of the nature of Canadian society and the laws governing them. Above all, you must learn at an early stage of your career that success comes only with diligence and dedication.

Questions and Activities

1. Visit a courtroom and observe a judge conducting a trial. Make a mental note of the skills and personal qualities which the judge must draw on while presiding.

2. Interview a judge. Find out about the judge's educational background and career prior to appointment to the bench. Ask the judge which aspects of his or her work are the most challenging and rewarding.

3. Locate and read a book or magazine article on the career of a famous Canadian judge. Decide what experiences or qualities were critical to that judge's success.

Chapter

1

LAW: ITS PURPOSE AND HISTORY

These are the key terms introduced in this chapter:

accused
administrative law
amending formula
assizes
bill
British North America Act
bylaws
Cabinet
case law
citation
civil law
Code of Hammurabi
codification
common law
Constitution Act, 1867
Constitution Act, 1982
constitutional law
contract law

criminal law
Crown attorney
defendant
employment law
family law
feudalism
French *Civil Code*
House of Commons
jurisdiction
Justinian Code
labour law
law
Mosaic Law
Napoleonic Code
Parliament
patriation
plaintiff
precedent

private law
procedural law
proclamation date
property law
public law
regulations
restitution
retribution
Royal Assent
Rule of Law
Senate
stare decisis
Statute of Westminster
statute law
substantive law
Ten Commandments
tort law

Chapter at a Glance

Learning Outcomes

At the end of this chapter, you will be able to

1. explain what law is and the need for laws;
2. list and explain the four main functions of law;
3. distinguish between substantive and procedural law;
4. identify public law and private law, the key divisions of substantive law, and the various categories within each;
5. outline the contributions of early law systems to today's Canadian law;
6. describe the development of English common law and explain the rule of precedent and the Rule of Law;
7. explain how Canadian laws are applied and interpreted;
8. state the components of Canada's Constitution;
9. distinguish between key areas of federal and provincial jurisdiction;
10. describe how a bill becomes a law.

Three teens in Quebec are accused of bludgeoning an elderly couple to death for kicks.

A 15-year-old in British Columbia stomps a man to death, leaving a footprint on his forehead.

A 17-year-old in Calgary mows down a policeman in a stolen car, cutting him in half.

Horrific crimes like these seem to scream from headlines every day and have helped foster the impression that teens are maiming and murdering like never before. And their law-abiding peers say they're paying the price.

"Older people think all kids are like that," says 14-year-old

Bum Rap on Crime Rankles Law-abiding Kids

Claudio Presutti as he hangs out with friends in a Halifax shopping mall. "If we're walking down the street, they'll move away or they'll hold their bag tighter like we're going to steal it or something like that. It's stereotyping."

Contrary to public concern that youth crime is widespread, federal statistics reveal there has

been no increase in youth violence in recent years. The Canadian Centre for Justice Statistics reports that the number of youth charges of homicide (first- and second-degree murder and manslaughter) fell to 36 in 1993 from 53 in 1992.

Figures suggest adults are much likelier to kill than teens. In 1993, there were a total of 630 homicides in Canada.

A professor at St. Mary's University blames the media for sensationalizing crime.

From: Steve MacLeod, "Bum rap on crime rankles law-abiding kids." *Canadian Press*, reported in *The Toronto Star*, May 30, 1995. Reprinted with permission—The Toronto Star Syndicate.

Something to Think About

- **Do you think youth crime is increasing in your community?**
- **Does the media sensationalize youth crime?**
- **Do you feel, like Claudio Presutti, that you are being stereotyped by older people as a potential young offender?**

1.1 INTRODUCTION

Society is fascinated with the law. Movies and news reports on radio and television highlight sensational trials. You read about law in novels, newspapers, magazines, and on the Internet. Even judgments of the Supreme Court of Canada are available on the Internet. Many of you know people who have appeared as witnesses at a trial, served on a trial jury, or been victims of a crime. Some of you may know people who have been sued for some reason or charged with breaking the law. We expect the law to be fair and just, but sometimes we question an offender's sentence as being too lenient or too harsh.

Studying a nation's legal system is very much like studying its language. Law tells a great deal about the nation's past. It also reveals current values and beliefs.

Just as the study of science and mathematics requires a specialized vocabulary, so does law. In this chapter you will learn the language of law. You will explore the differences between laws and rules. You will also begin to distinguish divisions and types of law.

The roots of Canadian law will be outlined. Some emphasis is placed on the development of English common law, in particular, and the emergence of the rule of precedent, still closely followed in our courts.

The *Constitution Act, 1867*, and the *Constitution Act, 1982*, important statutes that divide law-making powers between the federal and provincial levels of government, will be considered. As well, how laws are made at the federal, provincial, and municipal levels of government will be described briefly.

1.2 $\mathcal{L}$AW AND ITS FUNCTIONS

When people get together in groups—at school, at work, at home, or in a country—some rules and laws are necessary to keep peace and order. It is unlikely that everyone will get along with everyone else all of the time. Without clearly defined rules, the only law that would exist might be the survival of the fittest or the strongest.

Many of you probably belong to sports teams or organizations that require rules for a smooth and orderly operation. Imagine playing soccer, baseball, hockey, or any other sport without rules. The results would be chaos and injuries. For instance, aggressive players would know they would not be penalized for their rough or violent actions during the game. Referees would also be unnecessary as they could not keep order without rules.

Similarly, clubs and organizations need rules to run meetings, to encourage open and honest debate among members, and to reach agreement, by voting or a show of hands, on important decisions.

Rules of a game or an organization apply only to the participants of the game or to the members of the organization. Laws, on the other hand, apply to all members of society at all times.

Thus, all laws are rules, but not all rules are laws. Although rules are optional, laws are mandatory. As a member of society, you must obey, accept, and abide by the law or be prepared to be punished for breaking the law. **Law**, then, is a set of rules of conduct, established by government, for all members of society to obey and follow. As an individual, you are free to do what you want, except for those things the law prohibits.

Although most people willingly accept those laws that impose speed limits on highways, restrict the use of drugs and alcohol, and control environmental pollution, some do not. As soon as Canadians do not agree with the laws in this country, they have a great many options available to them. They can organize into groups to raise public awareness about the laws that concern them. They can lobby government for change; they can litigate; they can organize peaceful protests. Some protests—such as the Clayoquot

Sound protests in British Columbia in 1993—result in arrests; some protests—such as the 1990 Oka blockade—result in deaths. However, it is still a dominant characteristic of our democracy that people can oppose laws in a number of ways.

The Need for Laws

Consider an individual alone on an otherwise deserted island. Janelle's plane has crashed and she is the sole survivor. She makes her own rules. She sleeps, gets up, swims, works, and does whatever she wants whenever she wants. There is no need for law. Janelle's actions do not interfere with the needs or concerns of anyone else.

If Stacie is shipwrecked during a storm and lands on Janelle's island, the situation must change. Janelle will have to adjust her needs, desires, and actions to accommodate Stacie. Discussion and compromise will occur. Rules will develop. For example, one day, Janelle catches a rabbit to eat. Stacie cannot find food. They share. In the evening, Janelle cannot sleep due to Stacie's singing. Specific arrangements, or rules, begin to develop.

The fact that Janelle and Stacie make specific arrangements or rules on certain occasions does not mean that they have established laws. However, there are ways for them to do so. Laws will be established if the two agree that certain rules will always govern their conduct. For example, the agreement, "We will always share all our food, so that each of us gets an equal portion," is a law, and so is "Neither of us will sing after the other has gone to sleep." Laws are necessary for people to live together peacefully in society. It is one thing to agree that no one should sing after the other has gone to sleep, but it is quite another matter to have agreement on what happens to the singer if that rule is violated.

Another way for Janelle and Stacie to make law is to repeat the same arrangements over an extended period. If each shares her food with the other on every occasion, a law governing the sharing of food will come into being. After sharing many times, Janelle couldn't suddenly decide not to do so any more; she would be breaking this law. Likewise, after refraining from singing late at night for a very long period, Stacie couldn't decide to show off her singing voice in the middle of the night without reason. She, too, would be breaking the law.

If the number of people on the island increases, so will the need for more, and increasingly complex, rules of conduct and the need to record or write down the laws for the information of everyone. The more people there are, the more varied are the interests and requirements of the group. Therefore, the need to restrict, within reason, the complete freedom each person claims will be greater.

Increasingly complex societies have applied various laws to limit the behaviour of the members of those societies. For example, taking someone else's property or life is considered "against the rules" in every society. So is swindling someone in a business deal or speeding on a highway. Parking overnight on the street in winter and thus hindering a snowplough is against the law in many communities. For each of these antisocial acts, various sanctions or punishments are prescribed. These rules, and many others, form the basis of the law.

The Functions of Law

Law provides a framework within which all members of society must behave. Laws give us the ability to do what we want, as long as our activities do not interfere illegally or unreasonably with the activities of others. By setting out what cannot be done, the law infers that all other actions are legal. Laws reflect a society's values. As you study law, try to uncover those values. Consider the following: What sorts of behaviours are criminalized? What defences are allowed? What punishments are imposed? Which are treated more seriously—property offences or personal injury offences? How are family relationships and behaviours enforced?

One of the law's most important functions is providing the basis for settling disputes or disagreements. If a dispute arises between two opposing teams during a sports event, the game's rules will usually settle the dispute. Similarly, laws help resolve disputes peacefully through discussion and negotiation, or through the courts as a last resort.

LOOKING BACK

Over one thousand years ago in England, trial by ordeal was commonly used to determine innocence or guilt or to resolve disputes. An accused man might be asked to hold a red-hot brand in his hand. If his wound healed quickly, he was innocent; if he lost his hand or died, he was obviously guilty.

Another trial by ordeal involved binding the accused's hands and throwing her into a pond or lake. If she sank, she was innocent and pulled to safety; if she floated, she was guilty.

Trial by combat, which involved a duel arranged between the two disputing parties, was a dispute-resolution method used by nobility. Both trial by ordeal and by combat were based on the belief that God would protect the innocent and expose the guilty.

Establishing Rules of Conduct

As a society, we live in close contact with other people. Laws are needed to minimize or reduce possible conflicts. The laws outlined in provincial and territorial *Highway Traffic Acts*, for example, indicate such concerns as minimum driving ages, speed limits for city and highway driving, mandatory wearing of seat belts, procedures for signalling and passing other vehicles, and so on. All of these laws are intended to assist an orderly flow of traffic and to reduce the risk of injury or accident to others.

Protecting Rights and Freedoms

Laws by themselves serve little purpose without a means or process to enforce them. For this, we have the police and our system of courts. The RCMP, provincial police, and local police forces exist to ensure public safety and the protection of life and property. Criminal law outlines prohibited actions and appropriate penalties. In that way it limits the rights of the individual. Constitutional law ensures that those limitations of individual rights are not taken too far. The *Charter of Rights and Freedoms* limits law makers and law enforcers.

Providing Protection for Society

Laws are needed to protect you and others from people or groups who might take advantage of you. For example, contract law protects you and other young people from unscrupulous retailers who may take advantage of your age or inexperience. Labour law requires employers to pay you a minimum wage for hours of work and to provide safe and clean working conditions. Laws have also been established to protect developmentally or physically challenged persons and to provide them with the basic necessities of life. The various divisions of the law are discussed in greater detail in section 1.3 of this chapter.

The following fictitious case is provided to familiarize you with case analysis, which you will encounter throughout the text in your study of real cases.

Did You Know

Challenging a person to a duel is still a criminal offence in Canada, with a maximum jail sentence of up to two years for a convicted offender.

While on an Environmental Studies field trip, Jamie, Kirk, and Greg, three students from Crestview Secondary School, became trapped in a cave by a landslide. The three began to examine their situation. They noticed a trickle of water on the wall of the cave. Greg said that he learned in a science class that, as long as there was water, they could live without food for about 30 days. They all noted that there was no animal or vegetable matter in the cave. However, Greg mentioned that if two of them reached a state of desperation and killed the third and ate his flesh, they could survive for nearly another two weeks. As Jamie had a calendar watch with a luminous dial, keeping track of time was no problem.

On the 27th day, Kirk suggested that they draw lots to determine who would be killed for the benefit of the other two. When lots were drawn later that day, Kirk lost. He pleaded with Jamie and Greg to reconsider, but they pointed out that he had proposed this arrangement and that they had all agreed on it. Just as they were about to strangle Kirk, a rescue team broke through to save them.

1. **What is a society comprised of? Did the boys in the cave constitute a society?**

2. **Were the boys still a part of the outside society from which they came? Why or why not?**

3. **Did the boys pass a law? Explain.**

4. **If Jamie and Greg had strangled Kirk, would they have been found guilty of any crime after their rescue? If so, what? If not, why not?**

5. **Would there be any difference in your decision if**

   a) **they could have escaped from the cave by exploring a few metres farther?**

   b) **they were stranded on a lifeboat in the ocean? Explain.**

6. **Suppose Jamie and Greg were found guilty of killing Kirk, and their lawyer pleaded for mercy. What would your decision be if you were the judge?**

Reviewing Your Reading

1. **Why are laws necessary in society?**

2. **Distinguish between a rule and a law.**

3. **What causes law to change?**

4. **What was trial by ordeal? Why did its use disappear?**

5. **List the four main functions of law.**

6. **What is enforcement? How does it distinguish laws from rules?**

1.3 DIVISIONS OF THE LAW

Today's law can first be divided into two basic types: substantive law and procedural law. **Substantive law** consists of all laws that set out the rights and obligations or duties of each person in society. For example, substantive law allows Canadians to own property and enjoy certain rights that arise from ownership. These include the right to expel trespassers, the right to use property in any way so long as it does not interfere with others, and the right to enter into legally enforceable contracts. Substantive law provides individuals with the legal right to go to court to seek remedies against violations of their property or breaches of the contracts they make.

Procedural law outlines the steps and procedures involved in protecting and enforcing the rights given under substantive law. The procedures for legal arrest and jury selection and the steps involved in preparing a legally binding contract or a legal will are examples of procedural law.

Substantive law is further divided into public law and private law, and these categories have further subdivisions. Each is discussed below.

Public Law

Public law regulates relationships between governments and society. It represents laws that apply to all individuals. The main types of public law are criminal, constitutional, and administrative law.

Criminal Law

Canada's **criminal law** is a series of rules passed by the federal Parliament that prohibit or prevent certain actions, such as murder, kidnapping, sexual assault, break and enter, theft, and so on. Most of Canada's criminal law is found in the *Criminal Code* where certain criminal acts and their punishments are described. The *Narcotic Control Act* and the *Young Offenders Act* are other examples. Criminal law's main purposes are to punish offenders and to protect society. You may come in contact with criminal law as a victim, a witness, a juror, or an accused.

In criminal actions, society is represented by a **Crown attorney** who attempts to prove the charges, beyond a reasonable doubt, against the **accused**, or defendant, to determine whether that person is "guilty" or "not guilty." Criminal law is examined in greater detail in Unit 2.

Constitutional Law

The laws that set out the structure of our federal government and outline the division of powers between the federal and provincial governments are represented in **constitutional law**. Since the *Charter of Rights and Freedoms* was added to our *Constitution Act, 1982*, the Constitution also protects the rights of citizens in their contracts with government. This information is found in the *Constitution Act, 1867*, the *Constitution Act, 1982*, and the *Charter of Rights and Freedoms*. It is discussed later in this chapter.

Administrative Law

One of the fastest-growing areas of law, which governs the relationship between citizens and government and public agencies is **administrative law**. For example, legal disputes over such issues as the sale and consumption of alcoholic beverages, cable television service, telephone rates and competition, labour relations, employment insurance, and immigration would be resolved by special boards created by law for this purpose.

The federal and provincial governments have delegated the right to make decisions, such as the granting of licences or social assistance benefits and fee increases, to various boards, such as the Liquor Control Boards, the Canadian Radio-television and Telecommunications Commission (CRTC), the Employment Insurance Commission, and the Canadian Transport Commission, which regulates all interprovincial transportation. The decisions of these agencies effectively take the form of precedents and often have a major impact on our lives.

Private Law

Private law, commonly called **civil law**, outlines the personal and private relationships between two persons or between persons and organizations. Civil law's main purposes are to regulate the conduct between disputing parties and to compensate individuals or organizations for wrongs done to them by others.

There is no Crown attorney involved in civil actions. Each of the parties is usually represented by a lawyer. The person launching the action is the **plaintiff**, while the person being sued is the **defendant**. Usually, the defendant's conduct has resulted in harm, loss, or injury to the other person or to that person's property. However, unlike criminal law where the Crown must prove the

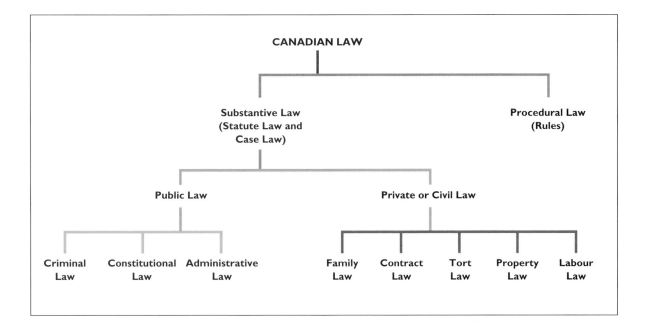

```
                          CANADIAN LAW

         Substantive Law                           Procedural Law
         (Statute Law and                          (Rules)
          Case Law)

      Public Law                      Private or Civil Law

Criminal   Constitutional   Administrative   Family   Contract   Tort   Property   Labour
  Law         Law             Law             Law      Law       Law      Law       Law
```

charges against the accused beyond a reasonable doubt, the plaintiff in a civil action must prove his or her claim on the balance of probabilities. The judge must determine whose story is more believable—the plaintiff's or the defendant's. Civil law is examined in greater detail in Units 3 to 6.

It is possible for the same incident to result in both a criminal and civil action. Suppose Chernesky was driving on the highway when an accident ahead forced her to put on her brakes suddenly. Because her brakes needed relining, however, she couldn't stop quickly enough and hit the car in front, damaging it severely and injuring both the driver and a passenger. Breath samples taken by police also indicated that Chernesky was intoxicated at the time of the accident. Thus, from this single accident, Chernesky could be charged with the crime of impaired driving and sued in a civil action for negligence because she didn't keep her brakes in proper repair. There is no particular order in which these two cases would be tried. Usually whichever case is ready first will be tried first.

Private (civil) law can be further subdivided. The categories of family law, contract law, tort law, property law, and labour law are described briefly below and are discussed in greater detail later in this text.

Family Law

Family law deals with the relationships between individuals living together as spouses, whether or not they are legally married, and between parents and children. This area of law is constantly changing. Many recent issues deal with the increasing numbers of common-law and same-sex relationships, unpaid support payments to spouses and children, division of property, child custody, and a parent's right to move, among others. Family law is discussed in greater detail in Unit 4.

Contract Law

The requirements for legally binding agreements that impose rights and responsibilities on the parties involved are outlined in **contract law**. It may be something as simple as buying a CD—you offer to pay for it, and the store accepts your money—or as complicated as agreeing to build new aircraft for hundreds of millions of dollars. If there is a violation or breach of this agreement, the injured party can seek a remedy through legal action in the courts. Contract law is discussed in greater detail in Unit 5.

Tort Law

Tort law is a wrong, other than a breach of contract, that one person commits against another person. For instance, in the earlier example, those injured in the car hit by Chernesky could sue her for money for such things as pain and suffering and for the injuries suffered, as well as damage to the car. A patient could sue a surgeon for malpractice, for negligence that occurred during an operation. Negligence, or carelessness, is the major cause of action in tort law. Tort law is discussed in greater detail in Unit 3.

Property Law

Property law governs the relationships between individuals regarding such issues as the buying or renting of land or buildings, or the use of a person's property and its effect on neighbouring lands. Many of the laws affecting property were established by the English courts hundreds of years ago. Much of the case law concerning property has been put into statute form, such as the *Landlord and Tenant Acts* of the various provinces and territories. Property law is discussed in greater detail in Chapter 19.

Labour Law

Labour law, or **employment law**, refers to the body of law that affects relations between employers and employees. Such concerns as minimum wages, pay equity, hours of work, working conditions, dismissal procedures, and workers' compensation are key issues in labour law, discussed in greater detail in Chapter 20.

Reviewing Your Reading

1. Using examples, distinguish between substantive and procedural law.

2. Into what two classes of law is substantive law divided, and what does each of these classes regulate?

3. Name and describe briefly three types of public law.

4. In criminal law, who are the parties involved at trial?

5. Name and describe briefly five types of private law.

6. In civil law, who are the parties involved at trial?

7. How does the burden of proof differ between criminal and civil trials?

8. Some incidents may result in both criminal and civil actions. Give an example. Why is it necessary that this option is available?

1.4 *T*HE EARLY HISTORY OF LAW

The laws of ancient civilizations have had a great influence on the development of Canadian law. In early societies, local customs and beliefs were the law. Customs were traditionally accepted and were usually based on sound common sense. It was not necessary to write them down, because everyone was aware of them and passed them on by word of mouth to future generations. As societies grew more complex, the rules also became more complex. It became too difficult for many citizens to know and understand them. Yet, for justice to be served, people had to be aware of the laws. It finally became necessary for existing laws to be written down in a permanent form.

The Code of Hammurabi

Hammurabi was a famous king who lived in Babylon (now Iraq) about 3800 years ago. He recognized the need to take nearly 300 laws and present them in a recorded form understandable to all citizens. This set of laws, known as the **Code of Hammurabi**, is one of the most important and earliest records we have of written laws. Hammurabi had these laws carved in columns of stone. Some of these columns were unearthed by archaeologists in Susa, Iran, in 1901 and are now displayed in the Louvre Museum in Paris, France.

A code is simply a written collection of a country's laws, clearly arranged so that they can be used and understood. This process of preparing a code is called **codification**. The Code of Hammurabi was organized under such headings as family, criminal, labour, property, trade, and business. Babylonian judges could match a person's offence and punishment by looking at the written law rather than deciding for themselves what punishment to pass. Crimes punishable by death required a trial by a panel of judges. The following are some provisions from the Code of Hammurabi.

3.	If a man has borne false witness in a trial, or has not established the statement that he has made, if that case be a capital [very serious] trial, that man shall be put to death.
46.	If a man neglect to strengthen his dike, and a break be made in his dike, and he let water carry away farmland, the man in whose dike the break has been made shall restore grain which he has damaged.
195.	If a man has struck his father, his hands shall be cut off.
196.	If a man destroy the eye of another man, they shall destroy his eye.
218.	If a surgeon has operated with the bronze lancet on a patrician for a serious injury, and has caused his death, or has removed a cataract for a patrician with a bronze lancet, and has made him lose his eye, his hands shall be cut off.

Hammurabi's laws made no distinction between criminal and civil law. Many legal concerns that existed in Hammurabi's time are still major issues, for example, not telling the truth at trial, negligence and causing damage to another's property, hitting another person, and causing injury or death during surgery. The Code followed the principle that the strong should not injure the weak, and that the punishment should fit the crime, prescribing "an eye for an eye, a tooth for a tooth"—the concept of **retribution**.

Moses and Mosaic Law

About 800 years after Hammurabi died, Moses gave his laws to the Hebrew people. Many of these laws were patterned on the Code of Hammurabi. This **Mosaic law** is set out in the first five books of the Old Testament. The Bible tells the story of Moses climbing Mount Sinai to receive the **Ten Commandments** engraved on two stone tablets from God. The Ten Commandments, which forbid such things as killing, adultery, and bearing false witness, continue to hold a central position in the teachings of both the Jewish and Christian faiths.

To punish those guilty of worshipping idols or adultery, Mosaic law ordered execution by stoning. The condemned person was killed by being pelted with stones. The *Penal Code of Iran* still prescribes stoning as a punishment for adultery and other sexual offences.

The Mosaic laws show some significant differences from Babylonian law. Again, assault of one's father was considered a very serious offence, but the severity of the punishment increased from cutting off the offender's hands to death. As well, mothers were recognized under the law, and cursing one's parents became a major offence with the potential of the death penalty. These very harsh penalties indicate the high regard that the society gave to parents.

In our society, theft has usually been punished by a fine paid to the court system or a jail term. Mosaic law, on the other hand, required **restitution**—the offender repaying the victim for goods stolen. In recent years, some form of restitution has become a more common punishment and is discussed further in Chapter 6. The following are some provisions from Mosaic law.

Exodus	
21:15–16	Whoever strikes his father or his mother shall be put to death . . . Whoever curses his father or his mother shall be put to death . . .
21:29	When an ox has been accustomed to gore in the past, and its owner has been warned but has not kept it in, and it kills a man or a woman, the ox shall be stoned, and its owner shall also be put to death.
22:1	If a man steals an ox or a sheep, and kills it or sells it, he shall pay five oxen for an ox, and four sheep for a sheep. He shall make restitution; if he has nothing, he shall be sold for his theft.
23:1	You shall not utter a false report. You shall not join hands with a wicked man, to be a malicious witness.

Roman Law

Roman law, the system that originated in early Rome, became the basis of law for most of western Europe, except England. As the Roman Empire grew, the number of laws increased and they became more complex. The Romans found it necessary to establish a profession devoted to the study of legal matters; this was the beginning of law as we know it today and the role of modern lawyers.

By A.D. 100, the Roman Empire had spread over much of Europe, and remained intact until the fifth century. As a result, Roman laws influenced most European countries. These laws were strengthened when the Roman emperor Justinian codified 1000 years of Roman laws and produced what is known as the **Justinian Code**. The Code was a collection of past laws, opinions from leading Roman legal experts, and new laws enacted by Justinian.

In 1804, after the French Revolution, Emperor Napoleon Bonaparte revised French law, originally based on Roman law and the Justinian Code. As Bonaparte conquered much of Europe, his *Napoleonic Code*, or **French *Civil Code***, served as the model for much of European law. As French immigrants settled in parts of the New World, the French *Civil Code* became the basis of the law in Quebec and in the American state of Louisiana. Similarly, legal systems today in such countries as Mexico and Thailand are based on the civil law of Spain and France.

As you learned in the last section, law that applies to disputes between private individuals is called civil law and is distinct from public law and criminal law. The term "civil law" as it is used in the rest of Canada is sometimes confused with the French *Civil Code* on which law in Quebec is based. Throughout the rest of the text, the term "civil law" refers to private law in all Canadian provinces and territories except Quebec.

Reviewing Your Reading

1. **What is the importance of the Code of Hammurabi in legal history?**

2. **How did Mosaic law differ from the Code of Hammurabi?**

3. **Define the concepts of retribution and restitution. How do they differ?**

4. **By examining the laws and punishments during Hammurabi's time, Moses' time, and the present, what observations can you make about the values of each society?**

5. **What is the Justinian Code? How does it influence Canadian law?**

6. **What is another name for the French *Civil Code*? How did it get to Canada? Why is it significant in Canada today?**

1.5 THE DEVELOPMENT OF CANADIAN LAW

Canadian law is based upon the laws of France and England, the countries that colonized Canada. The legal systems of the two countries differ considerably. As you have just learned, French law was codified and written down, and today's civil laws in Quebec are based on the French *Civil Code*.

English law, on the other hand, was not codified or written down until quite late in England's history, and much of it still has not been codified. It is simply accepted as existing over hundreds of years.

Before A.D. 1066, centuries of invasions by conquerors, like the Romans, the Anglo-Saxons and the Danes, had resulted in counties with different rules and customs. There were no laws common to England. The Norman invasion under William, Duke of Normandy, marked the beginning of a distinctive system of English law.

Feudalism and Common Law

As King of England, William introduced a system of government, already established in western Europe, called **feudalism**. The feudal system was based on a series of rights, duties and obligations. The king was at the top of the feudal structure and owned all of the land. He parcelled out large pieces, or manors, to his lords and barons, who thereby became the king's vassals, owing him allegiance and military service. They also helped in local administration. The lord's vassals were the freemen, who served in the lord's army, and serfs. Both worked the lord's lands and their own and gave shares of all they produced to the lord and the church. The feudal system in England was the basis for our modern property laws.

The lord of each manor was the sole judge in trials involving any of his vassals. Inequity resulted from this system of justice. One lord might have found a vassal guilty of theft of another vassal's property and sentenced him to death, while another lord's vassal, guilty of the same offence, might only have been sentenced to make restitution. In response to this inequity, the king appointed a number of judges who travelled the countryside and held hearings, or **assizes**. These judges would meet regularly in London to share their experiences. Common agreement slowly arose from these discussions. By the twelfth and thirteenth centuries there was more consistency. The consistency of decisions became the basis of English **common law**, common to all people throughout England. Only when no custom existed did judges make their own decisions.

This common-law system was introduced to North America by the colonists who first settled here, and today, judges from the highest courts in many Canadian provinces still travel to the provincial counties. There they hold regional assizes to deal with the most serious criminal and civil offences.

Precedent

Common law is based upon the very important principle known as **stare decisis**, or the rule of **precedent**. *Stare decisis* is Latin, meaning "to stand by earlier decisions."

At one time in England, after a certain case and the resulting decision were common knowledge in the legal community, all judges who had cases with similar facts brought before the court would give similar decisions. By treating similar cases alike, judges established a standard and common system of judging offences throughout the country. (At first, these case decisions existed only in the judges' memories and were known as "unwritten law.")

The rigid following of precedent resulted in the law failing many people and producing unfair results. The king remained the "fountainhead of justice" to whom persons could turn or appeal when they felt the common law had failed them. The king had the authority to overrule judges' decisions when he felt it was necessary to do so.

Following precedent too closely may still be a problem if the precedent is not a recent one. An extreme example would be if today's judges used precedents dealing with horse-drawn carriages to reach decisions in cases dealing with impaired driving and automobile negligence.

Nonetheless, the rule of precedent is important for two reasons. First, it introduces a degree of certainty into the law. A person, or his or her lawyer, going before the courts, can examine previous similar cases and the arguments that were used, and expect a somewhat similar result. Second, it causes the courts to act impartially, rather than favour any of the parties in an action. One of the more important aspects of trials is that lawyers present reports of earlier cases to persuade judges to reach similar decisions arrived at in those cases.

Many of the older cases in this text are landmark judgments that set precedents that are still followed by the courts when reaching decisions in new cases. These landmark cases are identified by a logo of the scales of justice.

Case Law

As the number of judges and cases increased, recording decisions became more essential. Thus, common law is often called **case law** also.

Many cases decided in court are recorded and published in volumes of reports, which are available in law libraries.

There are many such reports. Some, including *Canadian Criminal Cases* (C.C.C.) and *Reports on Family Law* (R.F.L.), report on specific areas of the law. Others report on cases decided in particular courts: *Ontario Appeal Cases* (O.A.C.) and *Supreme Court Reports* (S.C.R.). Still other reports relate to cases heard in particular provinces only: *Alberta Law Reports* (Alta. L.R.), *British Columbia Law Reports* (B.C.L.R.), and *Newfoundland & Prince Edward Island Reports* (Nfld. & P.E.I.R.). A list of common report series appears in the Key to Citation References near the front of this book.

Each recorded case is given a title or a **citation**. It lists basic information on who is involved in the case, whether the case is public or private law, the year the court decision was reached, which court heard the case, and specific information on the law report in which the decision appears. This information enables interested persons to locate the case easily in a law library. Here are examples of criminal and civil law citations, with explanations.

With this information on how to read citations, you should be able to determine the type of law involved in all of the cases in this text before you even read the details of the case. A consolidated list of all of the cases in this text appears in the Table of Cases near the front of the text.

In summary, while the term "common law" has other meanings, the most significant one for us is that it is the law based on judges' trial decisions, precedent, and reported case law. It serves as a major part of Canadian law today and is distinct from the statute law made by governments and discussed below.

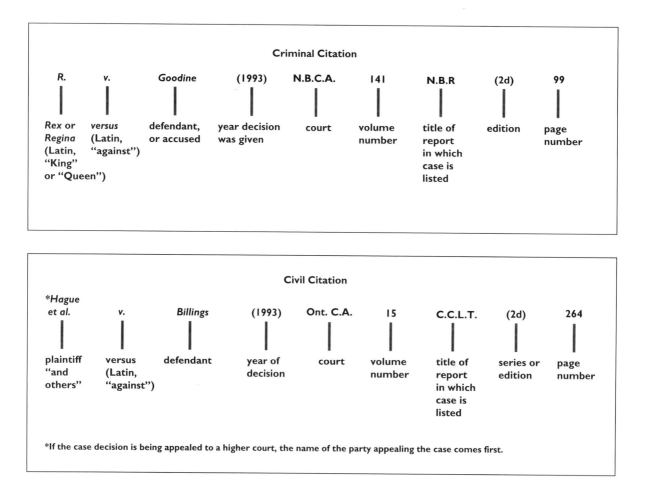

Criminal Citation

R.	v.	Goodine	(1993)	N.B.C.A.	141	N.B.R	(2d)	99
Rex or Regina (Latin, "King" or "Queen")	versus (Latin, "against")	defendant, or accused	year decision was given	court	volume number	title of report in which case is listed	edition	page number

Civil Citation

*Hague et al.	v.	Billings	(1993)	Ont. C.A.	15	C.C.L.T.	(2d)	264
plaintiff "and others"	versus (Latin, "against")	defendant	year of decision	court	volume number	title of report in which case is listed	series or edition	page number

*If the case decision is being appealed to a higher court, the name of the party appealing the case comes first.

One Friday evening the accused, Marlene Davis, and four female friends were partying at Eddy's Lounge in Edmonton, Alberta. They arrived about 10:30 p.m. and shared pitchers of beer until 2:00 a.m., by which time the accused and some of her friends were well under the influence of alcohol.

About this time, Davis left her table with a mug of beer in hand, and walked toward the bar where she became involved in an argument with Darrin Huculak, a former boyfriend of one of her friends. In an attempt to prevent this argument from escalating, a third person, Wayne Grant, at the bartender's request, stepped between the accused and Huculak. Davis spat at Huculak over Grant's shoulder and then threw the contents of her beer mug at Huculak. However, the mug slipped and hit Grant in the mouth, causing him serious cuts and injuries.

The accused was charged with assault with a weapon but was found guilty of the lesser charge of common assault.

1. **What type of law is involved in this case?**
2. **Explain the citation and what it means.**
3. **What is an assault?**
4. **Why was Davis charged with assault with a weapon?**
5. **Do you think Davis intended to injure Grant? Why or why not?**
6. **Why do you think Davis was convicted of the less serious charge of common assault? Do you agree? Explain.**

R. v. Davis
(1995)

Alberta Provincial Court
30 Alta. L.R. (3d) 361

The parties in this action were playing golf together. The plaintiff had about 20 years' experience playing golf; the defendant was a novice. The plaintiff was aware of his partner's inexperience and offered him the benefit of his experience.

Ropponen hit the ball into the rough, and Finnie went to help him find it. When the defendant found his ball, he took two practice swings and the plaintiff started to walk behind him. When the plaintiff was about 7 metres away, the defendant hit the ball, which veered off at a 75-degree angle and struck the plaintiff. Ropponen did not know where Finnie was when he hit the ball, and Finnie did not know Ropponen was about to hit the ball, although both men could see each other. The defendant did not give any verbal warning that he was about to hit the ball, and the plaintiff did not call out to indicate his position. The defendant's ball struck the plaintiff in the eye, causing injury. Finnie brought an action for damages for personal injury.

The British Columbia Supreme Court court ruled that each of the parties was at fault in varying degrees.

Finnie v. Ropponen
(1987)

British Columbia Supreme Court
40 C.C.L.T. 155

1. **Is this a criminal or a civil action? How can you tell?**
2. **In this action who is the plaintiff? Who is the defendant?**
3. **What does the plaintiff want?**
4. **As lawyer for the plaintiff, explain what your arguments would be.**
5. **As lawyer for the defendant, explain what your defence would be.**
6. **Why did the court find both parties at fault? Who do you think was more at fault? Why?**

The Rule of Law

During the reign of England's King John (1199–1216), an important development in the history of English law occurred. The king considered himself above the law and abused the power of his position. Eventually, the most powerful groups in the land—the nobility, the clergy, and free men—united and forced King John to sign the Magna Carta, the "Great Charter," at Runnymede in 1215. This famous document recognized and instituted the principle of the Rule of Law.

The results were twofold. First, King John and all subsequent rulers were to be subject to the law. Equality became an important concept in law for the first time. Second, no ruler could impose restrictions on the people arbitrarily or without reason. The legal rights of the people could not be touched by the king and the king was responsible for maintaining these rights. The Magna Carta expressed this most famous achievement, the Writ of Habeas Corpus, which stated that any person who was held and imprisoned without an explanation was entitled to appear before the courts within a reasonable time. Then he or she would either be released if the detention was unlawful, or tried by his or her peers or equals if it was lawful.

In Canada we are governed by the **Rule of Law**. This means that every dispute will be settled by peaceful means, either by discussion and negotiation or by due process in the courts as a last resort. Disputes are not to be settled by violent means in which the strongest always win, nor by government officials making rules on their own for their benefit only.

The Rule of Law exists because our society believes that might is not right. Resolving disputes by peaceful means is better, not only for the individuals involved, but also for society itself. The Rule of Law brings order to our lives by preventing the use of violence or arbitrary conduct in conflict resolution.

Parliament and Statute Law

Although subject to the law, King John and his successors still struggled with the barons for power. Around 1265, a group of barons again revolted against the king to force him to reform the English legal process. Representatives were called together from all parts of England, forming the first **Parliament**.

Parliament's first role was to correct the injustices resulting from the application of strict rules of precedent established by the common-law courts. Later, Parliament worked to reduce the power of the barons and the clergy. However, its most important function was passing **statute law** or Acts of Parliament.

As society progressed, common and case law were no longer totally adequate; new situations occurred not covered by existing law. As a result, Parliament made new laws to deal with these situations. Also, many of the common-law decisions were codified and became statute law.

Furthermore, Parliament made the law available to citizens in statute books. When the federal government in Ottawa passes an Act, it becomes part of the *Revised Statutes of Canada* (R.S.C.), volumes of federal statute law that give Canadians access to a current version of the law. Many public libraries have these volumes in their reference sections. Each of the provincial governments follows a similar procedure for its own statutes. Examples of provincial statute books include the *Revised Statutes of Ontario* (R.S.O.) and the *Revised Statutes of New Brunswick* (R.S.N.B.).

In making a decision in any case, courts must consider both the common law and the statute law. Canada's substantive law represents common-law decisions and statute laws passed by government.

Reviewing Your Reading

1. **Why does Canada have two legal systems today? What are they?**
2. **Why were the king's courts, the local assizes, preferred to the manor courts?**
3. **What is the rule of precedent?**
4. **List two advantages and one disadvantage of following precedent in reaching court decisions.**
5. **What is a citation? How do you distinguish between a criminal and a civil citation?**
6. **What is common law?**
7. **What are the characteristics of the Rule of Law?**
8. **What is statute law? Where can you locate it?**

1.6 CANADA'S CONSTITUTION

When the present-day provinces of Ontario, Quebec, New Brunswick, and Nova Scotia formed the Dominion of Canada on July 1, 1867, the British Parliament passed the *British North America Act* (*BNA Act*) to establish Canada as a nation, independent of Great Britain. Thus, the *BNA Act* was Canada's first Constitution, passed by the British Parliament since it retained the power to pass laws applying to Canada.

The *Statute of Westminster*, passed in Great Britain in 1931, was of major constitutional importance, since it allowed Canada to pass its own laws. Canada could also make agreements with other countries without Britain's involvement or interference. Finally, Canada was no longer subject to the laws of Great Britain. Canada was on its way to greater independence as a nation.

On April 17, 1982, Queen Elizabeth II signed the *Constitution Act, 1982*, making it the supreme law of the land.

Nonetheless, as a British statute, the *BNA Act* could only be amended by the British Parliament. Canada did not have complete legislative independence to change its own constitution. Over the years since 1867, Britain was more than willing to give the Constitution to Canada, but the federal and provincial governments could not agree on procedures to amend or change the Constitution or determine a new division of law-making powers between the levels of governments. Until these procedures were formalized, Britain retained custody of the *BNA Act*.

After 115 years, many meetings, and much negotiation, Canada finally devised a method of amending the *BNA Act*. With an **amending formula** in place that requires consent of the Canadian Parliament and seven provinces comprising at least 50 percent of the population, the Constitution was transferred to Canada. This **patriation** occurred on April 17, 1982. The *BNA Act* was renamed the *Constitution Act, 1867*. For consistency, this text will refer to the *BNA Act* as the *Constitution Act, 1867*, hereafter.

Although the *Constitution Act, 1867*, is still the main part of the Constitution, key elements of the **Constitution Act, 1982**, include the amending formula and a new *Charter of Rights and Freedoms*. This statute, which is the main focus of Chapter 2, has had a major impact on all Canadians since its passage.

The Division of Powers

The *Constitution Act, 1867,* lists which level of government has **jurisdiction,** authority or control, over which powers. This division of power is not a power hierarchy, however. The federal government's 29 areas of jurisdiction are outlined in section 91. The 16 areas of provincial jurisdiction are outlined in section 92. Section 93 gave the provinces control over education because of the differing linguistic and ethnic backgrounds of their people.

Although the *Constitution Act, 1867,* established two levels of government only, the provinces have delegated some of their power to the third level of government, the local municipality. Municipalities include cities, towns, townships, villages, and counties. They operate and pass **bylaws** to regulate their activities, such as household garbage quotas, noise pollution, store-closing hours, lawn-watering restrictions, building regulations, and so on.

You might think that such a comprehensive outline of powers would leave no room for disputes about which level of government has jurisdiction over a particular matter. However, disagreements have existed for many years. When the makers of the Constitution originally divided these powers, they could not have foreseen many of the changes in society.

For example, the growing reliance of nations on natural resources has brought the issue of control over offshore resources—along with the possibilities for tax revenue—to the forefront. Communications have expanded from a simple telegraph system in the 1860s to the various modern media, from satellites to computer links. Communications were placed under federal jurisdiction by the *Constitution Act, 1867.* However, the provinces feel that they should have control over this matter to meet local needs.

When disputes arise, they are referred to the courts for resolution if discussion and negotiation do not work. In many instances, the courts have sided with the federal government because section 91 specifies that it has the residual (remaining) power to make laws for the "peace, order, and good government of Canada." The time may never come when the various governments in Canada agree entirely on the issue of jurisdiction. The *Constitution Act, 1982,* is certainly not the final

Constitution Act, 1867
Division of Power

Federal Government Powers (Section 91)	Provincial Government Powers (Section 92)
• peace, order, and good government • criminal law • unemployment insurance • banking, currency, and coinage • federal penitentiaries • marriage and divorce • postal services • Indians and their lands	• property and civil rights • marriage ceremonies • police forces and provincial courts • highways and roads • provincial jails • hospitals

form of the Canadian Constitution. However, it has made it possible for any further amendments to be made within Canada, without referral to Great Britain.

Reviewing Your Reading

1. What is the significance of the *British North America Act,* and on what date was it passed?

2. Discuss the significance of the *Statute of Westminster.*

3. Explain what it means to patriate a Constitution. Why did it take so long to patriate our Constitution?

4. Distinguish between the *Constitution Act, 1867,* and the *Constitution Act, 1982.*

5. Distinguish between sections 91 and 92 of the *Constitution Act, 1867,* and list three important powers contained in each section.

6. What is the third level of government? What type of laws does it pass? How does it get jurisdiction to pass those laws?

7. What happens when disputes arise between governments over the issue of jurisdiction?

1.7 How laws are made

Before any piece of proposed legislation reaches Parliament or a provincial legislature, much time, money, study, and effort has taken place researching it. Proposed legislation is called a **bill**. Once a bill is passed, it becomes an Act or statute law.

Passage of Federal Legislation

A bill is usually introduced into Parliament or the House of Commons in Ottawa by the government. The **House of Commons** is the major law-making body in Canada with members elected by people living in ridings (political divisions) all across Canada. The political party that has the largest number of elected members forms the government. The other parties are the opposition parties.

The leader of the party in power is the Prime Minister. He or she appoints elected members of his or her party to the **Cabinet**. Cabinet members have titles or portfolios and are in charge of various departments or ministries. Usually, Cabinet ministers introduce bills into the House of Commons.

Three readings are required for a bill to become law. The first reading introduces the bill and its general purpose. A second reading follows in which the bill is debated in principle. It is then usually sent to one of a number of government committees for a detailed examination; all political parties are represented on each committee. It is therefore unnecessary for all members of the House of Commons to examine every bill in detail. This would be too time-consuming.

After the appropriate committee has concluded its work, the bill returns to the House. Often, proposed changes are suggested, and a third reading, debate, and a vote then take place.

When a bill passes through the House of Commons, it is forwarded to the **Senate** for approval. The Senate reviews bills in a similar three-stage process. It has the power to reject a bill and send it back to the House of Commons for further discussion, but this seldom happens. Also, bills may start in the Senate and then be sent down to the House of Commons for debate, but this also hardly ever happens.

Once a bill passes through the Senate, it is ready to go to the Governor General, the Queen's federal representative. His or her signature gives **Royal Assent** to the bill, at which time it becomes an Act. Most bills do not become law on the day of Royal Assent. They usually have a **proclamation date**, the date on which they actually come into effect. This delay is needed to give the government time to publicize the new law and to prepare the details or regulations to support the workings of the new law.

Passage of Provincial Legislation

The passage of a bill through a provincial legislature is similar to the procedure followed in the federal Parliament. However, provincial and territorial governments do not have a Senate. Once a bill passes through three readings in the provincial legislative assembly, it goes to the Lieutenant-Governor, the Queen's provincial representative, for his or her signature.

Regulations for Statutes

Once a federal or provincial bill becomes a statute law, the department responsible for administering the legislation is empowered to draw up the necessary **regulations** to accompany it. Each statute specifies the general intent of the law, while the regulations set out its details and how the law will operate. The regulations are often more lengthy and important than the statute itself. Once the regulations have been finalized, they are published to give the public access to them.

Passage of Municipal Bylaws

The procedure for passing bylaws varies from one municipality to another. In general, bylaws are enacted by elected councils with reeves or mayors at the head. Large urban areas may have an executive body, such as a Board of Control.

Reviewing Your Reading

1. **What is the purpose for each of the three readings of a bill?**

2. **How does the passage of provincial legislation differ from that of federal legislation?**

3. **Why do most bills not become law until their proclamation date?**

Traditionally, courts have handled violations of our laws. However, in recent years, overcrowding of the courts has created a backlog of cases and a need to seek alternatives to traditional methods for solving disputes.

Mediation: Can it replace the courts?

Alternative dispute resolution (ADR) has become familiar as a method of settling conflicts in non-traditional ways. ADR methods involve *negotiation*, where two parties communicate with each other, *mediation*, where a third party helps the two parties make a decision, and *arbitration*, where a third party listens to the two parties and makes the decision regarding their dispute. The most prevalent ADR method is mediation.

Mediators are neutral parties who are trained to help disputants come up with solutions to their own problems. It is believed that any solution that comes from the disputants themselves is more effective than one imposed by authority figures.

Mediation is not new. It has long been used successfully to resolve disputes between labour and management. However, ADR programs are now finding their way into other areas of business. Even the legal community has recognized the importance of ADR. The Canadian Bar Association is counselling its members to become experts in ADR methods, and its journal recently referred to ADR as a "growth industry."

On One Side

Those who support the implementation of mediation programs in most conflict situations argue that the court system takes too long, is too expensive, and does not guarantee satisfaction.

They suggest that if people are educated and trained in ADR, including anger and stress management, they will come to accept and even expect to settle their differences through the vari-ous conflict resolution programs that ADR offers. Since the majority of crimes in Canada are non-violent, many of these cases could be settled through mediation. This would relieve the criminal and civil courts of a tremendous burden.

Such programs would be faster and cheaper than litigation and would bring closure through a win-win solution where both parties gain something. Other benefits include avoiding possible courtroom trauma.

On the Other Side

Critics of ADR believe that, while mediation may be used successfully in neighbourhood spats, it cannot be used effectively in legal situations. Disputants, they argue, have a win-lose mentality and prefer to gamble on winning the case and the damages that go with it in the courts.

Opponents maintain that ADR methods would not necessarily be cheaper since the same lawyers who litigate are now offering their services as mediators. ADR will just create another layer of bureaucracy and expense for disputants.

Instead of ADR, they advocate speeding up the legal system and making it more efficient by creating more courts and appointing more judges to handle the backlog of cases.

The Bottom Line

The long delays in dealing with cases in Canada's justice system is a serious problem. *Charter* rights mean that charges against criminal suspects are being dropped because of long delays. Something has to be done. Should ADR methods be implemented as a solution? Should the number of courts and judges be increased to handle the backlog? You be the judge!

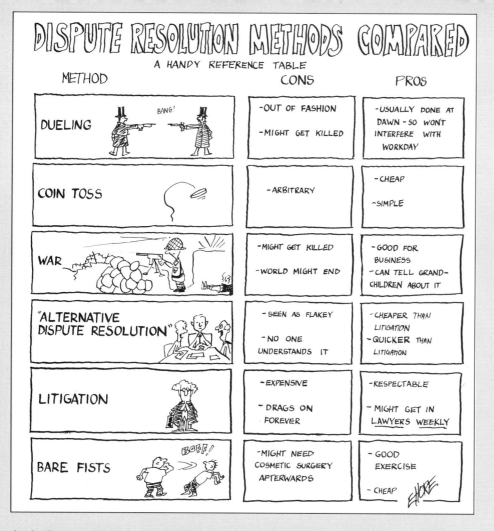

DISPUTE RESOLUTION METHODS COMPARED

A HANDY REFERENCE TABLE

METHOD	CONS	PROS
DUELING	- OUT OF FASHION - MIGHT GET KILLED	- USUALLY DONE AT DAWN - SO WON'T INTERFERE WITH WORKDAY
COIN TOSS	- ARBITRARY	- CHEAP - SIMPLE
WAR	- MIGHT GET KILLED - WORLD MIGHT END	- GOOD FOR BUSINESS - CAN TELL GRAND-CHILDREN ABOUT IT
"ALTERNATIVE DISPUTE RESOLUTION"	- SEEN AS FLAKEY - NO ONE UNDERSTANDS IT	- CHEAPER THAN LITIGATION - QUICKER THAN LITIGATION
LITIGATION	- EXPENSIVE - DRAGS ON FOREVER	- RESPECTABLE - MIGHT GET IN LAWYERS WEEKLY
BARE FISTS	- MIGHT NEED COSMETIC SURGERY AFTERWARDS	- GOOD EXERCISE - CHEAP

1. **Indicate whether you would recommend mediation or the court system to resolve each of the following disputes and give reasons for your choice.**

   a) divorced parents both want custody of their child
   b) a woman identifies a man as the person stalking her
   c) a divorcing couple can't agree on who should get what property
   d) a university student wants to move out of his apartment, but he has signed a lease
   e) a woman is charged with killing her spouse
   f) a teen is caught shoplifting a pair of jeans
   g) a man believes he has been wrongly dismissed from his job

2. **Create an organizer and list the advantages and disadvantages of each of the alternative dispute resolution methods—negotiation, mediation, and arbitration—in resolving disputes.**

3. **Use your resource centre to research information about the operation of criminal and civil courts in your province. Find out the approximate annual cost of operation, the number of cases handled annually, the average length of time it takes for a case to come to trial, and the average length of a trial.**

CHAPTER REVIEW

Reviewing Key Terms

For each of the following statements, indicate the key term being defined:

a) all law dealing with relations between an individual and the state

b) all laws passed by a legislature or parliament

c) all law relating to interaction between individuals

d) that part of law that creates, defines, and regulates rights and obligations

e) the body of law that prescribes or outlines methods of enforcing rights

f) the date on which a statute comes into force

g) the collection of legal principles and law into one body of statutes

h) the fundamental principle that neither the individual nor the government is above the law

i) the act of making good; having the offender pay back the victim for injury or loss

j) a court decision used as the authority for deciding a similar case

k) a person who launches or begins a civil action

l) the prosecutor or person who represents society in a criminal action

Exploring Legal Concepts

1. List five activities in which you have participated since you woke up this morning that are regulated by different rules or laws. For each activity, state whether it is a rule or a law, and describe how your conduct was regulated as a result.

2. Why are the rules of a school not considered law? Briefly describe other types of rules that govern our conduct but are not considered law.

3. Some people believe that laws increase an individual's freedom in a democratic society. Do you agree or disagree? Give examples.

4. State whether each of the following is an example of substantive or procedural law:
   a) a law that makes it illegal to ring a false fire alarm
   b) a law that outlines the steps to follow in making a legal arrest
   c) a law that makes it illegal to drink alcohol under the age of majority
   d) a law that outlines the rules for jury selection
   e) a law that outlines the steps in obtaining a legal search warrant
   f) a law that outlines the differences between first- and second-degree murder

5. Indicate whether each of the following is an example of public or private law:
   a) Revenue Canada brings an action against a tax evader.
   b) Henry Lafratta brings an action against his school board and teacher for injuries suffered during a physical education class.
   c) Kyle Anstey takes his employer to court in an attempt to obtain lost wages due to wrongful dismissal.
   d) The federal government takes the City of Vancouver to court over a bylaw that the city has passed.
   e) The provincial Attorney General brings an action against an alleged murderer.

6. For each of the following, indicate the type of private law involved:
   a) Kevin Vowles rents an apartment for one year from Jamie Paterson.
   b) Dan Atack and Elizabeth VanDalen get married.
   c) Chris Hall lends his car to Oichi Okimoto who is involved in a careless driving accident.
   d) Marco Estrada is awarded custody of his children.
   e) Amanda Garfield and Valerie Gauthier agree to sell goods to each other.

7. Briefly outline two significant contributions to today's Canadian law that developed in and emerged from the English feudal system.

8. Hardeep has been charged with break and enter, and theft over $5000. After his lawyer hears the facts, she suggests that he will likely be found guilty. As well, she predicts a possible sentence. How is she able to make such predictions?

Applying Legal Concepts

1. Feldthusen's barn was old and in disrepair. He decided to burn it down and collect the insurance money so that he could build a new one. He set fire to it and it burned to the ground. Feldthusen was charged with arson and fraud.
   - **What type of law is involved? How would the case citation begin?**

2. After a big argument over a family matter, a teenage son strikes his father, causing serious injury.
   - **Under Babylonian law, has the son committed an offence? If so, what would have been the punishment?**
   - **Under Mosaic law, what penalty would the son have received?**
   - **Under current Canadian law, what penalty might the son receive?**

3. Joshua steals some farm animals from a neighbouring farmer, Rafia, but is caught in the act and brought to trial.
   - **Under Mosaic law, what would happen to Joshua?**
   - **Under current Canadian law, what would likely happen to him?**

4. Your community institutes a voluntary "blue box" recycling program. In a television interview Gina Sidoli states that she does not intend to recycle, because she does not have time to rinse her metal cans and plastic containers.
   - **Is Sidoli breaking the law? Why or why not?**
   - **Is it right that she should ignore an issue that society considers very important? Explain.**

5. In the 1930s, William Aberhart, Premier of Alberta, proposed that the government of Alberta issue its own money. He felt that this would allow his government to carry out its policies without Ottawa's intervention and overcome the effects of the Depression.
   - **Did the province of Alberta have the right to issue its own money? Explain, using the Constitution Act, 1867, as a guide.**

6. Two residents of the United States purchased property in Prince Edward Island and applied to have their deed registered. Their request was refused. Provincial legislation stated that non-residents cannot own land in the province if the property exceeds 10 acres [4 ha] or is shore frontage of a particular length. The two Americans took court action to declare the law invalid.

- **Did the province of Prince Edward Island have the right to pass such a law?**

- **Did the Americans succeed in having the law declared invalid? Explain, using the *Constitution Act, 1867*, as a guide.**

7. The defendant, Les-Mark Investments, was convicted for failing to maintain a fire-alarm system in violation of bylaw 300-68. It had been established that the fire-alarm system defects were the result either of the defendant's negligence or the acts of vandals. The defendant appealed the conviction, but the appeal court dismissed the appeal.

- **What level of government is responsible for passing bylaws?**

- **What arguments could the company use in its appeal?**

- **Why do the authorities consider it extremely important for fire regulations to be followed so strictly?**

8. *R. v. Dudley and Stephens* (1884) England 14 Q.B.D. 273

The accused, Dudley and Stephens, along with Brooks and a 17-year-old boy, Parker, were shipwrecked some 2500 kilometres from the Cape of Good Hope in an open boat. They had only two tins of turnip and no water. On the fourth day, they caught a turtle. After that, they had no more food. They managed to catch some rainwater in their oilskin caps.

On the eighteenth day, Dudley and Stephens spoke to Brooks about what should be done if no more food was obtained. They suggested that Parker, who was suffering the most and had no family, should be sacrificed to save the rest. Brooks disagreed.

On the twentieth day, while Parker was asleep, Dudley made signs to Stephens and Brooks indicating the youth should be killed. Stephens agreed; Brooks dissented. Dudley offered a prayer and killed Parker. The three men then fed on the remains of the youth for four days, at which time a passing vessel picked them up. They were returned to England, where Dudley and Stephens were put on trial for murder.

The accused were found guilty of the charge, since the facts were found to be no legal justification for their killing of Parker. However, Queen Victoria granted them Royal Mercy and commuted (changed) their death sentence to one of life imprisonment because of public sentiment and concern. The legal authorities then took further action and released Dudley and Stephens after six months' imprisonment.

- **Why wasn't Brooks charged with murder? Do you agree? Why or why not?**

- **Could Brooks have done anything to prevent Parker's death? Explain.**

- **Should Dudley and Stephens have been charged with murder? Why or why not?**

- **As the Crown attorney, outline your case against the accused.**

- **Five judges tried this case. The argument presented by the defence dealt mainly with the necessity of the actions of the accused for their survival. Is this a valid argument or defence? Explain.**

- **Is it ever necessary to take another's life? If so, when? If not, why not?**

Extending Legal Concepts

1. Now that you have completed this chapter, review the opening article and Something to Think About. Have your answers or opinions changed? Why or why not?

2. Consider all the rules that exist in your school. Brainstorm which of these rules you would like to see changed or dropped and provide reasons for your decisions. Describe the steps you would follow to try to have these rules dropped or changed.

3. With a partner, research answers to the following questions about the federal government and prepare a report to share with your peers.

   a) What is the size of the federal Cabinet?

   b) Who is the current person in each of the following positions?

   - Prime Minister
   - Minister of Finance
   - Minister of Justice
   - Solicitor General
   - Minister of Health
   - Minister of the Environment
   - Secretary of State for External Affairs
   - Minister of National Defence

   c) Who is your federal Member of Parliament, and what constituency or riding does he or she represent?

   d) Who is Canada's Governor General?

4. With a partner, research answers to the following questions about your provincial government and prepare a report to share with your peers.

   a) What is the size of the provincial Cabinet?

   b) Who is the current person in each of the following positions?

   - Premier
   - Minister of Finance
   - Attorney General
   - Minister of Health
   - Minister of the Environment
   - Solicitor General

   c) Who is your provincial member of the legislative assembly, and what constituency or riding does he or she represent?

   d) Who is your province's Lieutenant-Governor?

5. Prepare a flow chart to show the steps involved in the passage of federal legislation.

6. Using reference material in your resource centre, including CD-ROM and the Internet, and texts from your school's History/Social Sciences department, research and prepare a report describing the effect on Canadian law of each of the following. In your report, provide the background and the reasons for the passage of each statute, and the impact of each on Canadian law. Make certain that you simply don't repeat the information presented in this chapter.

   a) the *British North America Act, 1867*

   b) the *Statute of Westminster, 1931*

Researching an Issue

The Democratic Process

The political context of society is one factor that affects how laws are made. In a legislative or representative democracy, individuals are freely elected by a majority of citizens to make decisions, which includes passing laws on their behalf. In a direct democracy, citizens make decisions themselves by voting at public meetings.

Statement

Canada's legislative democracy is the best type of democratic system.

Point

Owing to the geographic size of the country, the interests of Canadians are better served through a legislative democracy.

Counterpoint

Having more direct input into making decisions and passing laws through a direct democracy would better serve the interests of Canadians.

- **With a partner, research this issue and reflect on your findings.**
- **Prepare points on this statement that could be used for a class debate.**
- **Discuss your findings with others in your class.**

Chapter 2

THE RIGHTS AND FREEDOMS OF CANADIANS

These are the key terms introduced in this chapter:

adverse effect discrimination

amelioration

civil rights

conciliation

differential treatment

discrimination

entrenched

franchise

freedom

genocide

human rights

notwithstanding clause

prejudice

read down

respondent

riots

stereotyping

strike down

supremacy

unlawful assembly

Chapter at a Glance

Learning Outcomes

At the end of this chapter, you will be able to

1. distinguish between rights and freedoms;
2. compare the *Canadian Bill of Rights* and the *Canadian Charter of Rights and Freedoms*;
3. outline the matters governed by the *Charter*;
4. identify the rights and freedoms guaranteed by the *Charter*;
5. describe situations when a right may be justifiably limited by law;
6. discuss the enforcement of *Charter* rights;
7. distinguish between stereotyping, prejudice, and discrimination;
8. discuss two types of discrimination;
9. describe the intent of human rights legislation;
10. outline the procedure for hearing complaints in cases involving violations of human rights.

The Charter in Action

Since 1982, the courts have been interpreting the legal meaning of the rights encoded in the *Charter of Rights and Freedoms*. In the past few years, a number of widely publicized Supreme Court judgments have exacerbated our fears that criminals have too many rights.

Typical of these cases is the Askov decision in 1990. When the Supreme Court of Ontario dismisses criminal charges against a group of accused extortionists on the grounds that the two-year delay of their trial violates the right to justice "within a reasonable amount of time," this leads to the dismissal of over 50 000 other criminal cases that fail this test of reasonable time.

Whether or not the court's interpretations of the *Charter* has furthered the cause of justice is still a matter of debate among members of the legal community. Our system of justice is constantly evolving. History is still to be written about the long-term changes the *Charter* will wreak on our society, or whether, in our fervour to combat our fear of crime, we will throw away the rights we have worked so hard to uphold.

From: Jason Ziedenberg, "& justice for all – The Charter in Action." *why* magazine, Winter 1996. Reprinted with permission.

Something to Think About

1. **Are most Canadians aware of the rights guaranteed by the *Charter of Rights and Freedoms*?**
2. **How has the *Charter of Rights and Freedoms* affected Canadians?**
3. **Do you think the *Charter* has furthered the cause of justice?**

2.1 INTRODUCTION

Canada is considered one of the best countries in the world in which to live. There are a variety of reasons for this, but one of them is the value that Canadians place on civil and human rights. We have enacted laws that acknowledge and confer rights that we think every person should have. Canada has a mosaic of races, creeds, and nationalities, and we have enacted laws designed to preserve this diversity and prevent prejudiced behaviour.

Although civil and human rights have always been a part of our social fabric, neither were specified in our law until recently. **Civil rights** and **freedoms** control the power that the government has over its citizens in various areas of their lives. For example, the government, generally, cannot interfere with freedom of religion or freedom of speech. Civil rights were first given recognition in statute form in the federal *Bill of Rights* of 1960, and then in the *Charter of Rights and Freedoms* in 1982 (reproduced in its entirety in the Appendix). As part of our Constitution, the *Charter* **entrenched** our rights and freedoms. They can therefore only be changed by an amendment to the Constitution, which is not an easy process.

Human rights have been legislated by the federal and provincial governments only in recent years. They protect us from discrimination by other individuals in certain areas of our lives. Human rights are discussed later in this chapter, and in the respective chapters in which they apply.

2.2 THE CANADIAN BILL OF RIGHTS

The aftermath of World War II focused world attention on the issue of civil and human rights. The limitation and withdrawal of individual rights (what one can do) and freedoms (acts that are free of coercion and constraints), and the atrocities committed against particular groups of people during the war provided a lasting example of the power of the state, and of how it can be abused. It also made people aware, not only of the worth of humanity as a whole, but also of the worth of individual human beings.

The movement toward legislation guaranteeing the rights of Canadians was introduced into Parliament in 1945 by John Diefenbaker, a member of Parliament at that time. The next decade saw controversy over the matter: One group favoured the tradition of depending on the common law and the courts to protect citizens' rights; the other side believed that formal written legislation would be more effective.

During the general election campaigns of 1957 and 1958, Diefenbaker, by then leader of the Progressive Conservatives, promised Canadians a federal *Bill of Rights* if his party formed the next government. As Prime Minister, Diefenbaker kept his promise. He introduced legislation and the *Canadian Bill of Rights* became law on August 10, 1960.

The *Bill of Rights* was not a revolutionary piece of legislation. It merely set down in writing the rights already recognized under common law. Its significance was that it codified and formally recognized these rights, thereby reminding Canadians of the rights they had and still have.

The *Bill of Rights* gave Canadians, "without discrimination by reason of race, national origin, religion, or sex, the following human rights and fundamental freedoms":

- the right to life, liberty, and security of the person and enjoyment of property, and the right not to be deprived thereof except by due process of law
- the right to equality before the law and its protection
- freedom of religion, speech, assembly and association, and the press
- the right not to be arbitrarily detained, imprisoned, or exiled
- the right not to receive cruel and unusual treatment or punishment
- the right to be informed promptly of the reason for arrest
- the right to retain and instruct counsel without delay
- the right to obtain a writ of habeas corpus to determine the validity of detention
- the right not to give evidence if denied counsel, and protection against self-incrimination
- the right to a fair hearing
- the right to be presumed innocent until proven guilty
- the right to reasonable bail
- the right to an interpreter in any legal proceedings

Although the *Canadian Charter of Rights and Freedoms* was passed in 1982, the *Bill of Rights* is still in force for matters under federal jurisdiction. One item covered in the *Bill* that is not included in the *Charter* is the right to enjoy property and not be deprived thereof except by due process of law. A bill proposing that this right be added to the *Charter* was introduced into Parliament, but was defeated.

John Diefenbaker introduced the legislation for the *Canadian Bill of Rights*.

Reviewing Your Reading

1. **State the opposing views on the enactment of human rights legislation after World War II.**

2. **Who was responsible for the passage of Canada's first human rights legislation, and how did he accomplish his goal?**

3. **Why was the *Bill of Rights* significant?**

4. **What is the current status of the *Bill of Rights*?**

5. **What right is recognized in the *Bill of Rights* that is not part of the *Charter*?**

2.3 CONSTITUTIONAL PROTECTION OF CIVIL RIGHTS

When the *Constitution Act, 1982*, was enacted, many Canadians considered the *Canadian Charter of Rights and Freedoms* its most important part. But why was the *Charter* necessary when the *Bill of Rights* already existed?

The *Bill* had two perceived weaknesses. First, as a federal statute, the *Bill of Rights* applied only to matters falling under federal jurisdiction. Although all the provinces had passed human rights legislation, the provincial statutes did not include many of the matters contained in the federal *Bill of Rights*, especially in the area of legal rights. The *Charter* overcomes this failing. As part of the Constitution, the *Charter* applies to all levels of government, with some exceptions that will be noted later.

The second weakness of the *Bill of Rights* is that it is a statute. Parliament has **supremacy** in making and changing law. Courts merely interpret, apply, and enforce it. All statutes are equal. No statute, including the *Bill of Rights*, could have the effect of negating another.

The *Charter of Rights and Freedoms* is not a statute. It is part of our Constitution. Section 52 underlines the fact that "the Constitution of Canada is the supreme law of Canada, and any law that is inconsistent with the provisions of the Constitution is, to the extent of the inconsistency,

of no force or effect." This clear statement that the Constitution is supreme over law gives the courts greater latitude.

Despite this greater latitude, courts still must work within the constitutional framework. Their role is not to create, rewrite, or amend legislation. Section 52 allows them to declare existing legislation "of no force or effect." Section 24 offers further options.

24.

(1) Anyone whose rights or freedoms, as guaranteed by this Charter, have been infringed or denied may apply to a court of competent jurisdiction to obtain such remedy as the court considers appropriate and just in the circumstances.

(2) Where, in proceedings under subsection (1), a court concludes that evidence was obtained in a manner that infringed or denied any rights or freedoms guaranteed by this Charter, the evidence shall be excluded if it is established that, having regard to all the circumstances, the admission of it in the proceedings would bring the administration of justice into disrepute.

When drafting the *Charter*, the federal and provincial governments of Canada established its wording. The *Charter* gives the right to Parliament to restrict our rights, under section 1:

1.

The Canadian Charter of Rights and Freedoms guarantees the rights and freedoms set out in it subject only to such reasonable limits prescribed by law as can be demonstrably justified in a free and democratic society.

Thus, rights have some limits that can be imposed by the government. Though we have the right to trial by jury, Parliament has specified that it will only be for certain types of cases. Though

The Supreme Court of Canada, top row from left to right: Justices Frank Iacobucci, Peter Cory, Beverley McLachlin, John C. Major; bottom row, Justices John Sopinka, Gerard La Forest, Chief Justice Antonio Lamer, Justices Claire L' Heureux-Dubé, Charles Gonthier.

we have freedom of speech, Parliament or legislatures have specified many limits to that freedom, such as censorship of movies, and not being able to libel anyone. With our rights and freedoms come responsibilities. We cannot show movies that do not meet Canadian moral values. We cannot say things about people that are not true.

The purpose of the *Charter* is to limit government. In *R. v. Therens* (1985) the Supreme Court noted that constitutional protections must, by their nature, be expressed in general terms. Once a protection has been enacted, it becomes the task of the courts, particularly the Supreme Court of Canada, to develop and adapt it.

In another case, *Law Society of Upper Canada v. Skapinker* (1984), the Supreme Court stated that the *Charter* is a constitutional instrument designed to guide and serve the Canadian community, and to reconcile the respective rights of individual and community, over a long period. It must be interpreted with regard to the future, since narrow and technical interpretation can stunt the growth of the law and hence the community it serves.

Flexibility and interpretation must, however, be balanced with certainty. The power of the courts to interpret legislation has both supporters and critics. The Supreme Court of Canada

has become a more visible force in the interpretation of our laws, and thus our value system, since the inception of the *Charter*.

Suppose that a movie producer created a movie that went beyond the bounds of what most people would consider acceptable. In order for the issue to come before the courts, a charge would have to be laid that the movie is obscene. This charge would be laid under the *Criminal Code*. The movie producer could then challenge the *Criminal Code* section being applied to his or her work. The basis of the challenge would be that freedom of expression was being unreasonably limited by the *Code*. Freedom of expression is a right protected in the *Charter*. As you have seen, section 52 provides that the Constitution, including the *Charter*, is the "supreme law." If a provision of the *Criminal Code*, in this case the obscenity section, is inconsistent with a provision of the Constitution, it will be "of no force or effect."

There are two questions to be decided in this case. Whether the movie producer's work is obscene is a criminal question. Criminal law will be discussed in Unit 2. The movie producer is asking a different question. Is the *Criminal Code* section defining and restricting obscenity an unreasonable limitation of the producer's *Charter* rights? The constitutional question must be answered first. If the limitation is unreasonable, then the section will be "of no force or effect" and so it will be irrelevant whether or not the judge believes the work in question is obscene.

The movie producer will therefore bring a preliminary application for a declaration that the section is "of no force or effect." The movie producer, who is the accused in the criminal matter, is the applicant in this matter, and as such must prove that the matter is governed by the *Charter* (see section 32) and that a right or freedom protected by the *Charter* is being limited (see section 2).

The **respondent**, the party who is alleged to have discriminated, will be the Government of Canada, which passed the law in question. In response it can argue that no right or freedom protected by the *Charter* has been limited, or it can argue that there is a limitation, but the limitation is reasonable and justified. As you learned in Chapter 1, all law limits freedom, but our *Charter* cannot make all law "of no force or effect." A challenged law will often be protected by section 1 of our *Charter* even when it has been proven to limit protected rights or freedoms.

Matters Governed by the *Charter*

The first task of the courts when dealing with a case brought on the basis of a section of the *Charter* is to determine whether the matter actually falls under the *Charter*. Section 32 makes it clear that the *Charter* does not apply in all situations:

32.

(1) This Charter applies

   (a) to the Parliament and government of Canada in respect of all matters within the authority of Parliament including all matters relating to the Yukon Territory and Northwest Territories; and

   (b) to the legislature and government of each province in respect of all matters within the authority of the legislature of each province.

Through section 32, the *Charter* protects the rights of the individual with respect to the state by regulating the actions of the federal Parliament, the provincial legislatures, and all organizations that come under governmental authority, such as boards and agencies. The *Charter* regulates only the relationship between the individual and the state—it does not apply to private matters. In most cases, the rights of individuals in private matters are protected by other human rights legislation or by common law.

The Notwithstanding Clause

Section 33 of the *Charter* contains the famous **notwithstanding clause**:

33.

(1) Parliament or legislature of a province may expressly declare in an Act of Parliament or of the legislature, as the case may be, that the Act or a provision thereof shall operate notwithstanding a provision included in section 2 or sections 7 to 15 of this Charter.

This section is called the "notwithstanding clause" because a government can declare legislation to be valid and of effect notwithstanding that it violates a provision of the *Charter*. The section was added to induce some of the provinces to sign the *Charter*. Any legislation that is enacted under section 33 ceases to have effect after five years, or at an earlier date if specified in the legislation. However, it can be reenacted. It is important to note that the section cannot be used to overrule certain rights, such as the right to vote, minority language education rights, and mobility rights.

The notwithstanding clause has been used several times since 1982 by provincial legislatures. Its most notable use was in connection with the Quebec language law issue, which gave rise to the case *Ford v. Attorney General of Quebec.*

Ford was one of five retailers challenging the validity of two sections of the *Charter of the French Language,* a Quebec provincial statute commonly known as Bill 101. Ford carried on business under the company name *Les Lainages du Petit Mouton Enr.* The sign at the entry to her business said "Laine Wool." (*Laine* is French for "wool.") Under Bill 101, public signs, posters, and commercial advertising were required to be in French only, unless health and safety were concerned. Moreover, only the French version of a company's name could be used. Ford had been informed by the Commission responsible for monitoring the law that her sign did not conform with the provisions, and that she was to change it. She challenged the validity of the law on the basis that it infringed her freedom of expression, guaranteed by the *Charter of Rights and Freedoms* and by section 3 of the Quebec *Charter of Human Rights and Freedoms.*

The Quebec Court of Appeal ruled that the two sections of Bill 101 were invalid. The Attorney General of Quebec then appealed to the Supreme Court of Canada, which also ruled the two sections invalid.

Both sections were found to infringe section 3 of the Quebec *Charter of Human Rights and Freedoms,* and the provision concerning the use of the French language in signs and commercial advertising was found to infringe section 2(b) of the *Charter of Rights and Freedoms.* In its ruling, the Supreme Court stated that "freedom of expression" includes the freedom to express oneself in the language of one's choice. The evidence presented by the Attorney General of Quebec did not demonstrate that the requirement of the use of French only was either necessary for the achievement of the legislative purpose or proportionate to it. Hence the two sections of Bill 101 could not be saved by section 1 of the *Charter of Rights and Freedoms* or by the similar section in the Quebec *Charter of Human Rights and Freedoms.*

In response to the Court's ruling, the Quebec Premier introduced Bill C-178. By invoking the notwithstanding clause of the *Charter of Rights and Freedoms,* the original law concerning the use of French only in signs was allowed to stand.

Ford v. Attorney General of Quebec
(1988)

Supreme Court of Canada
2 S.C.R. 712

1. **Why did the Premier invoke section 33 of the *Charter of Rights and Freedoms*?**

2. **When would the Quebec legislature have to reinvoke the notwithstanding clause to continue the use of French only in signs?**

3. **Could the federal Cabinet constitutionally disallow Bill C-178, thereby overriding Quebec's use of the notwithstanding clause?**

4. **Many politicians and political commentators feel that the notwithstanding clause should be removed from the *Charter.* Do you agree or disagree?**

Reviewing Your Reading

1. a) **What are the two perceived weaknesses of the *Canadian Bill of Rights*?**

   b) **How did the *Charter* overcome each of them?**

2. **Why do some critics believe the *Charter* has given the courts too much power?**

3. a) **Briefly outline the matters governed by the *Charter,* as stated in section 32.**

   b) **Give two examples of situations to which the *Charter* would not apply.**

2.4 RIGHTS AND FREEDOMS UNDER THE CHARTER

Once it has been established that a case falls under the *Charter,* the courts must determine whether a right or freedom specified in that document has been infringed. The majority of rights and freedoms fall into seven categories found in sections 2 to 23. The rights of Native people are covered in section 25 of the *Charter* and sections 5 and 35 of the *Constitution Act, 1982,* while multicultural heritage rights are mentioned in section 27 of the *Charter.* These rights and freedoms are described below.

Fundamental Freedoms

Section 2 of the *Charter* states:

> **2.**
>
> Everyone has the following fundamental freedoms:
> **(a)** freedom of conscience and religion;
> **(b)** freedom of thought, belief, opinion, and expression, including freedom of the press and other media of communication;
> **(c)** freedom of peaceful assembly; and
> **(d)** freedom of association.

Freedoms are not created by law. They pre-exist law and are not absolute. They can be limited by statute if the limitation is justifiable. The function of the courts is to make that determination.

Freedom of Conscience and Religion

Freedom of conscience and religion means that one can choose or choose not to have religious beliefs, practise them, and express them without reprisal. This section has resulted in court cases dealing with these freedoms, such as the opening of businesses on Sundays, the education of children according to the religious beliefs of their parents, the closing of public schools on religious holy days, and discrimination on the basis of religion by requiring people of certain faiths to work on their day of worship.

The courts have ruled that the guarantee of freedom of religion does not require governments to refrain from imposing any burden on the practice of religion. Legislation that has a trivial or insubstantial effect on religious practice is not a breach of freedom of religion. To breach freedom of religion, legislation must infringe a fundamental doctrine of some faith, one which the followers of that faith believe to be self-evidently true and not open to debate.

Freedom of Thought, Belief, Opinion, and Expression

The *Charter* clause on "freedom of thought, belief, opinion, and expression" applies to all forms of communication, including speech, writing, pictorial art, sculpture, film, and dance. Court cases based on this freedom have included such matters

CASE

B. (R.) v. Children's Aid Society of Metropolitan Toronto

(1995)

Supreme Court of Canada

1 S.C.R. 315

Sheena B. was born four weeks prematurely. She was transferred to the Hospital for Sick Children in Toronto because of her physical condition. Her parents consented to all the treatments provided during those initial weeks. The physicians avoided using blood transfusions as part of the treatment, because as Jehovah's Witnesses, her parents objected to it for religious reasons, and they claimed it was unnecessary.

A physician believed that Sheena might require a blood transfusion to treat potentially life-threatening heart failure. A judge granted the Children's Aid Society a 72-hour wardship, on the basis that a transfusion might be necessary. Sheena's condition improved marginally, but the physicians wanted to maintain the ability to transfuse in case of an emergency. The temporary wardship order was extended for three weeks.

A few days later, Sheena received a blood transfusion as part of the examination and an operation. Despite the fact that the transfusion had taken place, the parents sought to have their rights in determining their child's medical treatment decided. Specifically, they wanted to know if their rights had been violated under sections 7 and 15 of the *Charter*.

The Supreme Court of Canada ruled that the events relating to Sheena's wardship and transfusion seriously infringed on her parents' freedom to choose medical treatment for her in accordance with the tenets of their faith. However, it also ruled that the infringement was justified under section 1 of the *Charter*.

1. **A temporary wardship order is defined in the glossary. Why would the Children's Aid Society be given wardship of the child?**

2. **In your opinion, should a court be able to overrule the rights of a parent in determining a child's medical treatment?**

3. **The Supreme Court of Canada indicated that while the state may intervene when it considers it necessary to safeguard the child's autonomy or health, such intervention must be justified. In your opinion, was it justified in Sheena's situation?**

4. **Who do you think should have the onus of proof in this case, the parents or the Children's Aid Society? Why?**

5. **In your opinion how could the infringement be justified under section 1?**

as public incitement of hatred against an identifiable group, the printing of obscene material, the use of cartoons to advertise goods to children under 13 years of age, and the reporting of judicial proceedings held in various courts.

The right to free expression has some limits. There is legislation that provides for censorship of materials considered obscene, or regulates communication with prostitutes. The law regarding crimes such as obscenity and soliciting will be examined in Chapter 7. A prohibition is also placed upon communications that wilfully promote hatred against an identifiable group. The press has also found that there is a limit to free expression. The courts have upheld most provisions outlined in the *Criminal Code* that permit a judge to restrict access to courts and to restrict the publication of names or descriptions of events where they will affect the right to a fair trial.

A number of cases have been brought to court regarding public incitement of hatred. The *Criminal Code* specifies that it is an offence to advocate or promote **genocide**. It is also an offence to incite hatred against any identifiable group where it is likely to lead to a breach of peace. An identifiable group means any section of the public distinguished by colour, race, religion, or ethnic origin.

CASE

The Canadian Broadcasting Corporation (CBC) planned to broadcast a miniseries, *The Boys of St. Vincent*, coproduced with the National Film Board. The series was a fictional account of sexual and physical abuse of children in a Newfoundland Catholic orphanage. The CBC had advertised the series nationally. It was to be broadcast in two parts on December 6 and 7, 1992.

Dagenais, Monette, Dugas, and Radford were former or present members of a Catholic religious order known as the Christian Brothers. All were charged with physical and sexual abuse that allegedly took place in Ontario Catholic

Dagenais v. Canadian Broadcasting Corp.
(1994)

Supreme Court of Canada
3 S.C.R. 835

training schools where they were teachers. The victims were young boys in their care. The judge in Dagenais' trial was scheduled to charge the jury on December 7. On December 3, Dagenais brought an application before the court requesting that the judge charge the jury on December 4 instead of December 7, or that he sequester the jury over the weekend so that they could not see the television broadcasts. The judge declined, but he did order the jury not to watch the show.

The four men then sought a court order to block the broadcast in Ontario and parts of Quebec until their trials were over. A judge of the Ontario Court of Justice issued an order that the program not be broadcast anywhere in Canada until the completion of the trials, that there be no publicity about the broadcast, and that there be no publication of the fact of the application, or any material relating to it. The Ontario Court of Appeal upheld the decision not to broadcast, but restricted the order to Ontario and the Montreal CBC television station and removed the other bans.

The CBC and the National Film Board appealed to the Supreme Court of Canada, which allowed the appeal and set aside the publication ban. The Court indicated such a ban should only be ordered when it is necessary to prevent a real and substantial risk to the fairness of the trial, because reasonably available alternative measures will not prevent the risk, and when the helpful effects of the publication ban outweigh the harmful effects to the free expression of those affected by the ban.

1. **What two conflicting *Charter* rights are at issue in this matter?**
2. **Why did the trial judge impose a ban on the broadcast?**
3. **Why did the judge of the Ontario Court of Justice impose a ban on the advertising of the program, and on publication of the fact that the accused had applied to the court for an order banning the broadcast?**
4. **What two factors must be considered when ordering a publication ban according to the Supreme Court of Canada? Relate them to this case.**
5. **In your opinion, what alternatives were available to the Court to ensure that the broadcast did not affect the fairness of the trials?**
6. **Outline the significance of the Supreme Court of Canada decision.**

CASE

R. v. Keegstra
(1990)

Supreme Court
of Canada
117 N.R. 1

James Keegstra was a high school teacher in Eckville, Alberta, from the early 1970s until his dismissal in 1982. In his classes, Keegstra taught his students that the Holocaust, in which six million Jews died during World War II, had not actually happened, and that the fabrication was part of a Jewish conspiracy to rule the world. He described Jews to his students as being "treacherous," "subversive," "sadistic," "money loving," and "power hungry." He further stated that they were responsible for depressions, anarchy, chaos, wars, and revolutions. He expected his students to reproduce his teachings in class and on exams; if they failed to do so, their marks suffered.

In 1984, Keegstra was charged with unlawfully promoting hatred against an identifiable group, contrary to section 319(2) [then section 281(2)] of the *Criminal Code* which states, "Everyone who, by communicating statements in any public place, incites hatred against any identifiable group where such incitement is likely to lead to a breach of the peace is guilty of (a) an indictable offence and is liable to imprisonment for a term not exceeding two years; or (b) an offence punishable on summary conviction."

Keegstra was convicted by a judge and jury in the Alberta Court of Queen's Bench, after the longest trial in Alberta history, and fined $5000. He appealed his conviction to the Alberta Court of Appeal and, in June 1988, the court unanimously accepted his argument. The court held that the *Criminal Code* provision violated his *Charter* right to freedom of expression, that the *Criminal Code* provision was overly broad and not a reasonable limit prescribed by law under section 1 of the *Charter*.

The Crown then appealed that judgment to the Supreme Court of Canada where the appeal was heard in December 1989. In a 4–3 judgment released on December 13, 1990, the Court upheld the Crown's appeal. All seven judges agreed that the hate law violated the *Charter*'s section 2(b) guarantee to freedom of expression. However, only four of them believed that this infringement was a restriction that could be justified under section 1 of the *Charter* to help protect hate propaganda victims. The remaining three judges could not justify the law under section 1.

1. **What was Keegstra's main defence for his actions?**

2. **Did Keegstra take advantage of his position as a teacher and abuse the public trust?**

3. **In 1988, Ontario Justice Samuel Grange wrote: "Freedom of speech has never been absolute." What does this mean, and do you agree? Why or why not?**

4. **Andrew Cardozo of the Canadian Ethnocultural Council called the Supreme Court's decision a victory for people from ethnic and visible minorities who find themselves being targeted by hate mongers. He said: "Minorities can feel a bit reassured after such a decision against hate mongering." Do you agree? Why or why not?**

5. **After the Court's decision, Jim Keegstra said: "If we all have to think the same way, well, then we're just robots ... We were taught in university that you can be sceptical and no, you'll never be taken to court. Well, you see that's not true anymore." Do you agree with Keegstra's opinion? Explain.**

6. **Lorne Shipman, Ontario Regional Director for the League of Human Rights of B'Nai Brith Canada, stated: "This decision serves, as all laws do, as a boundary of reasonable societal behaviour and as a deterrent to those whose intent is to cause hatred and upset our fragile dream of equality for all." Defend or refute this statement in light of the Keegstra decision.**

Freedom of Peaceful Assembly and Freedom of Association

Most cases concerning freedom of peaceful assembly relate to the right to hold or attend a demonstration, and the right to picket. It is significant that the word "peaceful" was included; the right of the state to control **riots** or demonstrations that get out of hand is thereby recognized. The *Criminal Code* prohibits an **unlawful assembly**—a group of three or more persons, having a common purpose, that causes fear in others. If an unlawful assembly begins to disturb the peace tumultuously, it is categorized as a riot. If 12 or more persons are unlawfully and riotously assembled, a person authorized by law may read the "riot act":

> "Her Majesty the Queen charges and commands all persons being assembled immediately to disperse and peaceably to depart to their habitations or to their lawful business on the pain of being guilty of an offence for which, on conviction, they may be sentenced to imprisonment for life. GOD SAVE THE QUEEN."

The right to freedom of association has long been recognized in common law. People could associate as long as they did not have an unlawful objective. This freedom, like others, has government-imposed limitations. Court cases involving freedom of association have centred on the right to collective bargaining with an employer and related issues, which will be discussed more fully in Chapter 20, Employment Law.

Democratic Rights

Before 1982, no guarantee of voting rights existed in law. The right was contained in the various *Election Acts*. However, since these were only statutes, theoretically any government could have withdrawn the right to vote and abolished elections entirely. Indeed, the right to vote was not extended to many groups in Canada.

Sections 3, 4, and 5 of the *Charter* set out the democratic rights of Canadians (see Appendix). The right to vote—**franchise**—is not subject to the notwithstanding clause. However, it is not an absolute right and is therefore subject to reasonable restrictions having to do with age, mental capacity, residence, and registration, among others. Each province, for instance, has a residency requirement; a citizen must be in residence for either 6 or 12 months before being able to vote. In addition, certain groups are excluded from the right to vote. One such group is the judiciary. The Chief Electoral Officer of the federal government has recommended that judges should be given the franchise. They were not given a vote so that they would remain independent of the government. In a 1996 decision, the Supreme Court of Canada ruled that inmates in federal institutions have a right to vote in federal elections. The courts have ruled that these sections of the *Charter* do not apply to municipal elections, in that they specifically refer to federal and provincial governments.

Did You Know
Women did not have the right to vote until 1918, and Native people could not vote in federal elections until 1960!

Mobility Rights

Mobility rights are stated in section 6 of the *Charter*. Note that subsection (1) applies to every citizen of Canada, while subsection (2) applies to every citizen of Canada and every person who has the status of a permanent resident.

6.

(1) Every citizen of Canada has the right to enter, remain in, and leave Canada.

(2) Every citizen of Canada and every person who has the status of a permanent resident of Canada has the right
  (a) to move to and take up residence in any province; and
  (b) to pursue the gaining of a livelihood in any province.

(3) The rights specified in subsection (2) are subject to
  (a) any laws or practices of general application in force in a province other than those that discriminate among persons primarily on the basis of province of present or previous residence; and
  (b) any laws providing for reasonable residency requirements as a qualification for the receipt of publicly provided social services.

(4) Subsection (2) and (3) do not preclude any law, program, or activity that has as its object the amelioration (improvement) in a province of conditions of individuals in that province who are socially or economically disadvantaged if the rate of employment in that province is below the rate of employment in Canada.

This section recognizes the "one Canada" concept, since it opens the doors of every province to any Canadian to pursue his or her livelihood without regard to provincial boundaries. However, some provinces were concerned that, when the economy was good in a particular province, there would be a large influx of people from other provinces. These newcomers would not only gain economic benefits, but would also enjoy the province's social services to which they had not contributed. Moreover, they might take jobs that would otherwise have gone to the local populace. Subsection (3) was added to deal with these concerns.

Subsection (4) allows each province to introduce what might otherwise be considered discriminatory legislation, prohibiting the entry of citizens from other provinces for the purpose of obtaining work if the unemployment rate in the province is below that for the whole of Canada. The right of a government to make laws that, under normal circumstances, might be considered discriminatory is called employment equity. Other examples of the right to pass employment equity legislation will be examined in Chapter 20.

Legal Rights

The legal rights guaranteed by the *Charter* are set out in sections 7 to 14. They will be discussed in detail in Unit 2, Criminal Law.

Equality Rights

Section 15, the equality section of the *Charter*, was considered to be the section that would have the greatest effect on legislation. It prohibits the government from discriminating against individuals. (In some situations discrimination by individuals against individuals is governed by human rights legislation.) As a result, it did not come into effect until three years after the rest of the *Charter*. The delay was intended to allow governments to review their legislation to make it coincide with the requirements of the section.

You must examine the wording of section 15 carefully to understand its intent. It begins with "Every individual," which shows that the section does not apply to corporations. The rights enumerated include equality "before and under the law." Equality "before the law" guarantees every individual access to the courts. Equality "under the law" indicates that the legislation applies equally to every individual. The right to "equal protection and equal benefit" of the law is also specified.

15.

(1) Every individual is equal before and under the law and has the right to the equal protection and equal benefit of the law without discrimination and, in particular, without discrimination based on race, national or ethnic origin, colour, religion, sex, age, or mental or physical disability.

(2) Subsection (1) does not preclude any law, program, or activity that has as its object the amelioration of conditions of disadvantaged individuals or groups including those that are disadvantaged because of race, national or ethnic origin, colour, religion, sex, age, or mental or physical disability.

The phrase "in particular" means that the areas of discrimination identified are merely examples. It is possible to claim discrimination on bases not identified, such as sexual orientation.

Section 15 does not guarantee that equality rights are absolute. For each of the areas of prohibited discrimination, exceptions apply. For example, there are many exceptions under the age category, from drinking age to driving age to retirement age and pension age. These exceptions are considered justifiable in a free and democratic society.

The first significant case on equality rights to appear before the Supreme Court of Canada was *Andrews v. Law Society of British Columbia* (1989). Andrews was a British subject permanently residing in Canada. He met all the requirements for admission to the British Columbia bar under the *Barristers and Solicitors Act*, except that of Canadian citizenship. Thus, following previous equality decisions, he would come under the "similarly situated should be similarly treated" test. This means that he would be treated the same as all other non-citizens who applied for bar admission and be denied entry. No discrimination would then occur. However, the Supreme Court of Canada took a much broader view of the section. It noted that equality would not occur if he were denied access to the British Columbia bar, for section 15 applied to "every individual" and not just Canadian citizens. One justice commented, "If we allow people to come to live in Canada, I cannot see why they should be treated differently from anyone else."

The Court ruled that Andrew's equality rights had been infringed.

Many other significant issues involving equality have come before the Supreme Court of Canada, including the Thibaudeau case regarding maintenance payments.

CASE

Thibaudeau v. Canada
(1995)

Supreme Court of Canada
2 S.C.R. 627

Suzanne Thibaudeau married Jacque Chainé in 1978, and they divorced in 1987. Thibaudeau was awarded custody of their two children. Her ex-husband was ordered to pay her alimony of $1150 a month for the exclusive benefit of the children. No amount was awarded to Thibaudeau who had sufficient financial self-sufficiency. The court recognized that the amount paid to her required that she make a greater contribution to the financial maintenance of the children than would be required by the ratio between the respective incomes of the former spouses.

In 1989, Thibaudeau received $14 490 for the maintenance of the couple's children. For that year she filed three income tax returns: one covered her personal situation and dealt essentially with her employment income; the other two were filed on behalf of the children and reported for each an income totalling half the alimony received by Thibaudeau. The Minister of National Revenue reviewed the tax returns, and included the amounts received as alimony in computing Thibaudeau's income. That was the required way of reporting the income under the *Income Tax Act*. She therefore had to pay $4042.80 more tax. Thibaudeau filed a notice of objection with the Minister of Revenue, which was turned down.

Thibaudeau challenged the constitutionality of the *Income Tax Act* in the Tax Court of Canada. She claimed that imposing a tax burden on her for amounts she was to use solely for the benefit of her children infringed her equality rights as guaranteed by section 15(1) of the *Charter*. She argued that the prejudice that she suffered resulted from her civil status, her gender, and her social status. She was part of a group of whom the great majority are separated or divorced women, who have a certain degree of financial self-sufficiency, who have custody of their children, and who receive taxable alimony from their former spouses for the benefit of their children. Yet those child support payments are tax-deductible for the paying parent.

The Tax Court of Canada dismissed her appeal. A majority of the Federal Court of Appeal reversed that decision and concluded that the applicable section of the *Income Tax Act* infringed her equality rights and could not be justified under section 1 of the *Charter*. The Minister of Justice appealed the decision to the Supreme Court of Canada, which allowed the appeal.

1. **Outline the tax filing rule that was required by the *Income Tax Act*, and the tax filing method that Thibaudeau followed.**

2. **Outline the argument that Thibaudeau presented to show that her equality rights had been infringed.**

3. The Supreme Court of Canada noted that no burden has been created for parents in Thibaudeau's situation. Indeed, Justice Cory noted that the tax rules usually promote the best interests of the children by ensuring that more money is available to provide for their care. In what way is this true?

4. The Supreme Court of Canada noted that the amount of taxable income is determined by the family-law system. What does this statement mean?

5. Justice Gonthier of the Supreme Court of Canada indicated that the right to the equal benefit of the law does not mean that each taxpayer has an equal right to receive the same amounts, deductions, or benefits, but merely that he or she has a right to be equally governed by the law. Explain how this statement relates to Thibaudeau's position.

Section 15(2) provides for affirmative action. For example, it would allow a government to introduce classes in English as a second language for individuals who have another first language, but not require that government to provide similar second language education for people whose first language is English.

Did You Know

Intense lobbying resulted in the addition of subsection 2 of section 15 in the final draft of the *Charter*.

Section 28 was added to the *Charter* to provide specific recognition for equality between the sexes. The "notwithstanding clause" in section 33 does not apply to section 28. However, it does apply to section 15.

Language Rights

Sections 16 to 22 outline the status of English and French as official languages of Canada. The sections provide that both English and French have equal status in Parliament and any institution thereof. Either language can be used in Parliamentary debates, and the laws of Canada must be printed in both English and French. In addition, either language can be used in courts established by the federal government. Canadians therefore have the right to use either language when communicating with and receiving services from federal government offices, where there is sufficient demand for a given service, and it is reasonable to have it.

Minority Language Education Rights

Section 23 provides for minority language education rights in English and French only, and for Canadian citizens only. It is up to the provinces, which have jurisdiction over education, to decide whether to provide education for groups that speak other languages.

Three main criteria determine the right of a Canadian citizen to be educated in English or French, only one of which needs to be met.

The first criterion is the person's mother tongue, the language first learned and still understood. This provision is of most benefit to French-speaking people who live outside Quebec, because it gives them the right to be educated in French. The provision applies in all of Canada except Quebec.

The second provision considers the language in which the parents were educated. This is important to English-speaking Canadians who live in or move to Quebec. For example, if either parent has been educated in English, the parents have the right to have their children educated in English. This provision applies in all provinces and territories.

The third criterion is the language in which other children in the family are receiving or have received their education. If one child is being educated in French, for instance, all children in the family have the right to be educated in that language. This provision, too, applies throughout Canada.

An important condition is imposed on anyone claiming the minority language education right. It is a numbers test. A province has to provide education in the minority language out of public funds only where there is a sufficient number of citizens to warrant the service. The "sufficient number" is not defined; it is up to each province to decide whether the service is warranted. A person who wishes to dispute the decision must appeal to the courts.

Aboriginal Rights

The rights of the aboriginal or Native peoples have been recognized by section 25 of the *Charter* and section 35 of the *Constitution Act, 1982*, which is not part of the *Charter*. Therefore the limitations in section 1 of the *Charter* do not apply.

Section 35 of the *Constitution Act, 1982*, indicates that Indians, Inuit, and Métis constitute Canada's aboriginal population. It also guarantees the "existing rights" of the aboriginal peoples. However, those rights are not spelled out.

A constitutional conference on aboriginal rights was held in 1983, but it failed to resolve all matters being addressed. It was agreed that treaty rights entrenched in the Constitution included any that might be acquired in the future through land claim settlements. Aboriginal rights and treaty rights were also recognized as applying to both genders. One of the main issues of the conference, the desire of the aboriginal peoples to be self-governing, remained unresolved.

This issue, along with that of land titles, will probably take many years to settle. More discussion on the *Charter* and aboriginal rights is found in Chapter 22.

Multicultural Heritage Rights

Section 27 of the *Charter* gives a directive to both the governing bodies and the courts that, when forming legislation and interpreting it, the multicultural heritage of Canada should be considered.

Reviewing Your Reading

1. List and briefly discuss the freedoms guaranteed by section 2 of the *Charter*.

2. What principles does the court follow when resolving cases involving freedom of conscience and religion?

3. Name three situations in which a limit is placed on freedom of expression.

4. Why is it significant that Canadians are granted freedom of peaceful assembly?

5. Name three restrictions that can be placed on the right to vote.

6. Why do Canadian judges not have the right to vote?

7. What condition is put on the right to move, take up residence, and pursue a livelihood in any province?

8. Why did the equality rights section not come into effect until three years after the rest of the *Charter*?

9. a) List six areas of discrimination expressly forbidden by section 15(1) of the *Charter*.

   b) Does the *Charter* permit discrimination on other grounds than these? Explain.

10. What is affirmative action?

11. What principle concerning equality rights was established in *Andrews v. Law Society of British Columbia*?

2.5 *Resolving Infringements of the Charter*

Once it has been established that a particular case is governed by the *Charter*, and that a guaranteed right or freedom has been infringed, the courts must determine whether the infringement is justifiable on the basis of section 1 of the *Charter*. The wording of this section clearly indicates that rights and freedoms are fundamental but not absolute. For instance, you have already seen that the state limits individual expression by forbidding certain types of expression, such as the promotion of hatred against an identifiable group. It is the function of the courts to determine whether the limits prescribed by law are reasonable, and whether they can be demonstrably justified in a free and democratic society. The party claiming that the exception is a reasonable limit that can be demonstrably justified in a free and democratic society must prove that it is. In most cases this onus falls on the state.

Section 1 of the *Charter* recognizes that in some situations rights must be limited. The section requires that limitations be "reasonable," "prescribed by law," and "demonstrably justified."

The Supreme Court of Canada decided in the case *R. v. Oakes* that to be "reasonable" a law must be designed to fulfill an important governmental objective and actually help achieve that objective. The intrusion on protected rights must be minimal and proportionate to the seriousness of the objective.

The requirement that the limitation be "prescribed by law" includes a requirement that the legislation not be overly broad—that it clearly and narrowly address the issue. It must not leave too much room for discretion in its application. For example, in the evaluation of printed material or films, specific guidelines must exist as to what constitutes obscenity.

To be "justified," both the objective and the means must be defensible in terms of values recognized by free and democratic societies.

The case *Irwin Toy Limited v. Attorney General of Quebec* illustrates the application of these three principles in determining whether it is justifiable to limit a right or freedom.

CASE

Irwin Toy Limited sought a declaration that the *Consumer Protection Act* of Quebec, which placed limits on commercial advertising "directed at persons under 13 years of age," was *ultra vires* the Quebec legislature, and that it infringed the Quebec *Charter of Human Rights and Freedoms* and the *Canadian Charter of Rights and Freedoms*.

The *Consumer Protection Act* stated that, in determining whether an advertisement was directed at persons under 13, account had to be taken of the context of its presentation, and particularly of the nature and intended purpose of the goods advertised, the manner of presenting the advertisement, and the time and place of its showing. The regulations provided occasions when advertisements could be aimed at children, for example, to announce a new show. They also provided a long list of what could not be contained in advertisements aimed at children. Before being shown, an advertisement could be submitted for evaluation to determine whether it was acceptable.

The case was heard in the Superior Court of the District of Montreal, then the Quebec Court of Appeal. Evidence was presented at trial that children under the age of 13 are susceptible to media manipulation, since they are unable to differentiate clearly between reality and fiction, or to grasp the persuasive intention behind the message. On final appeal, the Supreme Court of Canada ruled that the law did not infringe unreasonably on Irwin's right to freedom of expression.

Irwin Toy Limited v. Attorney General of Quebec (1989)

Supreme Court of Canada
58 D.L.R. (4th) 577

1. **What do you think is the main objective of Quebec's *Consumer Protection Act* in banning advertisements directed at young children?**

2. **Does discrimination result because the Quebec law can be applied to television programs that originate in Quebec, but not to signals coming from outside the province?**

3. **Does advertising aimed at children fall within the scope of the provision on freedom of expression?**

4. **Was the purpose or effect of the limits in the statute to control attempts to convey meaning through advertising? Explain.**

5. a) What two things had to be shown to have the limit imposed on freedom of expression declared justifiable under section 1 of the *Charter*?

   b) Which party had to prove that the restriction was justified?

6. Did the limit on freedom follow the three principles in section 1 of the *Charter* as interpreted by the Supreme Court?

7. Do you agree or disagree with the Supreme Court's decision? Explain.

Remedies under the *Charter*

There are two methods of enforcing the rights and freedoms guaranteed by the *Charter*. The first, section 52 of the *Constitution Act, 1982*, gives the courts the right to declare a law ineffective, as you read earlier. The courts can either strike down or read down the legislation in question. To **strike down** is to rule that the law is no longer in effect; to **read down** is to rule that the law is generally acceptable, but is unacceptable in the case before the court.

The second method of enforcing *Charter* provisions is to provide the complainant with a remedy as set out in section 24.

Throughout this text, you will encounter cases brought under the *Charter* that illustrate examples of the diverse remedies that may be awarded by the courts.

Reviewing Your Reading

1. What are the three requirements included in section 1 for limiting a right protected in the *Charter*?

2. Which party must show that an infringement is justifiable?

3. What does the word "reasonable" mean as used in section 1?

4. What is a remedy?

5. What remedy does section 52 provide? In what sorts of situations would it be useful?

6. What remedy is available under section 24(2)? In what sorts of situations would it apply?

7. Does section 24(1) provide any specific additional remedies? Explain.

2.6 HUMAN RIGHTS

Human rights involve the relationship between individuals, whereas the above discussion on civil rights and the *Charter* involved relationships between individuals and the government. The government has legislated that certain behaviours are unacceptable in our dealings with each other. Every person living in Canada has the right to be free from discrimination by other individuals, that is, the right to be treated as equal to all other Canadians. But what constitutes discrimination? To answer this question, it might be helpful to distinguish among stereotyping, prejudice, and discrimination. Only the last of these actually contravenes human rights legislation.

Stereotyping

Stereotyping involves making a global judgment by applying the characteristics that are assumed to belong to one member of a group to all members of that group. Examples include saying that all women are poor drivers, that Chinese people are superior at mathematics or sciences, or that teenagers are troublemakers. Any group that experiences stereotyping will find such statements derogatory. Stereotyping fails to recognize the individual and can lead to prejudice.

Prejudice

Prejudice and stereotyping are really two sides of one coin. **Prejudice** involves making a judgment by applying the characteristics that are assumed to belong to a certain group to an individual belonging to that group. Prejudicial views are often learned during youth from others within the individual's environment, especially family and friends. Such attitudes are based in belief, not in objective, factual observation. A person's prejudice toward a group will influence his or her relationship with all members of that group. For instance, suppose that a person believes that women cannot play baseball. If he refuses to play baseball with his friends because they have chosen a woman as the pitcher, he is demonstrating a prejudice. He is extending his beliefs about a group (women) to an individual woman.

Discrimination

Human rights legislation cannot control stereotyping or prejudice. Rather it is intended to address discrimination. **Discrimination** results in certain situations when a person acts on a prejudice. For example, if a man refuses to hire a woman for an engineering position simply because he believes that women do not make good engineers, the law would consider that person guilty of the offence of discrimination. Human rights legislation prohibits discrimination on many bases, which are listed in the next section.

Discrimination may be either intentional or unintentional. If the man in our example has stated flatly, "I'll never hire a woman for an engineering position!" he is discriminating intentionally. However, it is often difficult to prove intentional discrimination. The offender will usually disguise the discrimination to avoid possible court action under human rights legislation. An interviewer may allege that the job was already filled, or that another person had better qualifications, when neither is true. Intentional discrimination is frequently called **differential treatment**.

Much discrimination is unintentional. Suppose that an advertisement to recruit law-enforcement trainees requires applicants to be over a certain height. Although the advertisement does not discriminate intentionally, it effectively eliminates many otherwise qualified people. This is also known as **adverse effect discrimination**. It will be illustrated in *Re Ontario Human Rights Commission and Simpsons-Sears Ltd.*, in Chapter 20.

Reviewing Your Reading

1. Using original examples, describe (a) stereotyping and (b) prejudice.
2. Where do people often learn prejudice?
3. How does discrimination differ from prejudice?
4. a) Describe intentional discrimination, using an example.
   b) What is another term for intentional discrimination?
5. a) Describe unintentional discrimination, using an example.
   b) Give another term for this form of discrimination.

2.7 *H*UMAN RIGHTS LEGISLATION

The rights involved in the interactions between individuals are covered in both federal and provincial legislation. The federal legislation is the *Canadian Human Rights Act*. Examples of provincial statutes include Alberta's *Individual's Rights Protection Act* and Quebec's *Charter of Human Rights and Freedoms*. The federal and provincial statutes apply to matters under each government's jurisdiction.

In each province, the human rights statute has primacy over all other provincial statutes. In other words, if there is a conflict between two statutes, the human rights legislation prevails. Not all matters pertaining to rights in relationships between individuals are necessarily covered in human rights legislation. Some provinces, for example, include employment-related matters in their statute on labour or employment standards.

Human rights legislation is updated continually. Amendments reflect changes in social attitudes and take into account new examples of discrimination. At present, Canadian human rights legislation pertaining to interactions between individuals covers these general areas:

- the provision of services and facilities
- employment, employment agencies, and advertising

- public accommodation
- the rental, purchase, and sale of real estate
- contracts
- publications
- trade unions and employer or occupational associations
- advertisements for accommodation and employment
- signs, notices, and advertisements on public display
- pension plans and funds
- harassment and sexual solicitation

The law as it applies to providing goods, services, facilities, accommodation, and employment will be discussed in Chapters 19 and 20.

Enforcing Human Rights Legislation

Every federal and provincial human rights statute provides for the appointment of a commission to enforce the legislation. The objective of enforcement is to put the complainant in the position that she or he would have occupied had the discrimination not occurred. This objective is reached through the negotiation of a settlement between the complainant and the respondent. The process may involve simply making the respondent aware of the facts of the case and of the applicable law.

The procedure for hearing and resolving complaints of discrimination is basically the same across the country. No fees are involved. A complaint must be made to the appropriate commission within six months of the occurrence of discrimination under provincial legislation or one year under federal legislation. A human rights officer interviews the complainant. If the facts indicate that a violation has occurred, a formal complaint is prepared and signed by the complainant. A copy is sent to the respondent.

If human rights legislation has been violated, the matter is pursued. An investigating officer interviews the complainant, the respondent, and any witnesses for more information. If the officer cannot resolve the matter at this stage, **conciliation** takes place. The investigating officer brings the complainant and the respondent together for a discussion. Any settlement reached during the investigation or conciliation must be approved by the commission.

If no settlement is reached, a board of inquiry or tribunal is appointed by the government. All parties present their views before the board. In most cases, the complainant is represented by the commission. A board of inquiry has greater authority than the conciliator and can make an order to resolve the complaint. If the order is disobeyed, or if one party wishes to appeal the board's decision, the matter can be brought before the courts as a civil case.

CASE

Central Alberta Dairy Pool v. Alberta (Human Rights Commission)

(1990)

Supreme Court of Canada 2 S.C.R. 489

Christie was employed by the Central Alberta Dairy Pool from 1980 to April of 1983. In February of 1983, Christie joined the World Wide Church of God, which observes a Saturday Sabbath, a five-day Fall Feast of the Tabernacle, and five other holy days during the year. Religious adherents were expected not to work on those days. Christie's request that he work the early Friday shift to avoid conflict with the onset of his Sabbath was granted.

In March of 1983, Christie requested permission to take unpaid leave on two holy days, one being Easter Monday. He offered to work alternative days outside his regular schedule in consideration for his absence on the holy day. His supervisor approved the first day but not the Monday, because he was needed at the plant. All milk that arrived on the weekend had to be canned promptly on Monday to prevent spoilage. Mondays were also busy shipping days. The contingency arrangement in case of employee absence on Mondays due to sickness was to adjust work assignments and/or have the supervisor assist in maintaining operations. Christie was advised that if he failed to report for work on the Monday his employment would be terminated.

Christie took a complaint of discrimination to the Alberta Human Rights Commission. Section 7(1)(b) of the *Individual's Rights Protection Act* of Alberta stated, "No employer . . . shall discriminate against any person with regard to employment or any term or condition of employment, because of the race, religious beliefs . . . of that person . . ." Section 7(3) stated that subsection (1) "does not apply with respect to a refusal, limitation, specification, or preference based on a bona fide occupational requirement." The Alberta Human Rights Commission ruled that the employer had discriminated against Christie. The Central Alberta Dairy Pool appealed. The Alberta Court of Queen's Bench reversed the Commission's decision. The Alberta Court of Appeal agreed with the Queen's Bench ruling, but when the Alberta Human Rights Commission further appealed to the Supreme Court of Canada, the original decision was restored.

1. **What procedure would the Alberta Human Rights Commission have followed when Christie brought his complaint of discrimination to it?**

2. **What is a bona fide occupational requirement? Give examples.**

3. **Summarize Christie's argument about how he was discriminated against.**

4. **Summarize the position of the employer, Central Alberta Dairy Pool.**

5. **The Supreme Court of Canada indicated that the employer must accommodate the employee up to the point of undue hardship, and that the onus was on the employer to show that it fulfilled this requirement. Did the employer accommodate Christie up to the point of undue hardship?**

Human rights legislation is intended to compensate the victims. The usual result of a complaint investigation will be the restoration of rights that were denied, along with an ordered apology from the respondent. The board may also order the respondent to make a payment to compensate for loss of self-respect. If the discrimination concerned employment, the order may require the employer to post relevant sections of the human rights legislation, to implement a program familiarizing employees with the legislation, and to promise not to discriminate again. If the discrimination occurred during the hiring process, the employer may be required to hire the complainant or offer him or her the next available job.

Disobeying the order of a board of inquiry carries a criminal penalty. All human rights statutes provide a fine for anyone who intimidates a person who has complained about discrimination or who has given or will give evidence about discrimination.

Reviewing Your Reading

1. **What result is intended by the enforcement of human rights legislation?**

2. **What time limits exist on bringing a complaint of discrimination?**

3. **Outline the procedure for hearing and resolving complaints of discrimination.**

4. **What power does a board of inquiry have that a conciliator does not?**

5. **Name three penalties that may be imposed by a board of inquiry.**

The Supreme Court of Canada and the Charter of Rights and Freedoms: Are they working for Canadians?

When the *Charter of Rights and Freedoms* became law, it gave courts, especially the Supreme Court of Canada, broad new powers to strike down provincial and federal laws that the Court considers to be discriminatory and against the civil rights of Canadians.

Since 1982, the Supreme Court has struck down several important laws, including Canada's abortion law. In recent years, the Court has made several controversial decisions.

- On September 30, 1994, in a 6–3 decision, the Court ruled that extreme drunkenness may be a defence to rape. According to the decision, convicting someone who did not know what he was doing contravenes the *Charter of Rights and Freedoms*.
- On May 18, 1995, in a 6–1 decision, the Supreme Court upheld an appeal, granting a rapist a new trial because police had violated his constitutional rights under section 10(b) of the *Charter.* In the decision, Mr. Justice Frank Iacobucci wrote, "We should never lose sight of the fact that even a person accused of the most heinous crimes, and no matter the likelihood that he actually committed those crimes, is entitled to the full protection of the *Charter.*"

  Yet in that same month, in a 6–1 judgment, the Court upheld a conviction for cocaine trafficking, even though the accused's constitutional rights to be protected against unfair search and seizure had been abused by police. The Court said that because cocaine use has a devastating effect on society, an illegal search would not offend the public.

- On July 20, 1995, in a 3–2 decision, the Supreme Court dismissed murder charges against two men, saying serious errors made by the Crown unfairly denied them their right to a speedy trial.
- In September 1995, in a 5–4 decision, the Court struck down the federal law prohibiting tobacco advertising. The Court ruled that the section of the *Charter of Rights and Freedoms* protecting free speech covers commercial messages as well as political and social discourse.

Decisions like these have bewildered and shocked many Canadians.

On One Side

Many Canadians believe that the Supreme Court of Canada has become too powerful and that it is time to reexamine the role that judges should play. They oppose the idea that nine appointed judges can overrule laws made by the elected representatives of the people.

Some people believe that the Supreme Court of Canada is giving too many rights to individuals through its decisions, and that society as a whole is being ignored and even threatened. These people feel the *Charter* threatens the healthy respect for the law and institutions held by most Canadians by overemphasizing individual rights. They believe that the *Charter* does more to protect those who violate the law than it does to guarantee the liberties of law-abiding citizens.

Opponents of the *Charter* further argue that the large number of *Charter*-related cases is clear evidence that respect for the law is changing. They claim that such cases are causing delays in the Canadian legal system and making law enforcement more difficult.

On the Other Side

Those who support the *Charter* point out that the entrenchment of our rights and freedoms in the Constitution gives individuals protection from interference and infringement by governments. They see the *Charter* as a necessary safeguard for common-law concepts that otherwise may not be recognized by a particular law or government act.

Moreover, because of section 52 of the *Constitution Act*, legislation that was previously beyond the reach of the courts is now subject to constitutional challenge.

Many experts believe that it will take a long time before the effects of the *Charter* can be fully determined. As cases are settled, laws and procedures will change to meet the standards of the *Charter of Rights and Freedoms*. They see law as being in a state of process. As society's views change, public reaction to and repudiation of certain decisions can lead to different decisions down the road.

The Bottom Line

The *Charter* has revolutionized life and law in Canada. The spotlight is on judges and their decisions. This is especially the case in Supreme Court decisions because of their importance and impact across Canada. Are the Supreme Court's interpretations of the *Charter* having a negative or a positive effect on Canadian individuals and society? You be the judge!

1. Research one of the Supreme Court decisions identified above and prepare a summary of the case.

2. Working in groups of four, find out how each justice of the Court voted in the above four decisions. Compare your findings.

3. Gather arguments to support the position that the Supreme Court's interpretations of the *Charter* are having either (a) a positive effect, or (b) a negative effect on Canadian individuals and society.

4. Compile news reports of other cases and verdicts involving the *Charter*. Have these verdicts affected the freedom of Canadians? Explain your answer. What long-term effect do you think they will have on Canadian society?

CHAPTER REVIEW

Reviewing Legal Terms

For each of the following statements, indicate the key term being defined:

a) clause that allows governments to override the *Charter* and declare legislation valid for five years

b) to rule that a law is no longer in effect

c) something granted by legislation

d) rights in the *Charter* that can only be changed by an amendment to the Constitution

e) a judgment that applies the characteristics that are assumed to belong to a certain group to an individual belonging to that group

f) discussion with a third party to try to resolve an issue

g) to rule that a law generally acceptable is unacceptable in the specific case before the court

h) action that effectively eliminates most members of a certain group

i) applying the characteristics that are assumed to belong to one member of a group to all members of that group

j) Parliament has the final say in lawmaking

Exploring Legal Concepts

1. Should all citizens of a country be eligible to vote? If not, which groups should be excluded? Why? At what age should the franchise be given? Explain.

2. Should prisoners have the right to vote? Explain.

3. In your opinion, should public schools be allowed to begin the school day with a Christian prayer? Why or why not?

4. Governments can use the "notwithstanding" clause to protect legislation that would otherwise be found to contravene the *Charter*. Some say that in effect this means that the *Charter* is not worth the paper that it is written on. Comment on this statement.

5. Many people believe that the enactment of the *Charter* resulted in the Supreme Court of Canada having too much control over the values that shape our country. Comment on this statement.

6. Some provinces have suggested that for people moving into the province, there should be a residency requirement of a specified time period to collect welfare. Should provinces be permitted to erect such barriers? Do such provisions violate the mobility rights?

7. Would it be discriminatory for an insurance company to deny benefits to a policy holder suffering from an AIDS-related disease?

8. Rank the fundamental freedoms in descending order from the one that you consider most important to the one you consider least important. Write a one-page summary to defend your ranking.

9. Should the rights to accommodation and employment be included in the *Charter*? Explain.

Applying Legal Concepts

1. *R. v. Squires* (1992) Ontario Court of Appeal 78 C.C.C. (3d) 97

   Squires, a reporter with the CBC, was assigned to cover a preliminary hearing involving the attempted murder of a Turkish diplomat in Ottawa. After the diplomat had testified, he left the courtroom in his wheelchair. In the corridor, Squires had his departure videotaped. The *Judicature Act* of Ontario provides that no person shall take or attempt to take any photograph, motion picture, or other record capable of producing visual representation by electronic means or otherwise of any person entering or leaving the room in which the judicial proceeding is to be or has been convened. The *Act* provides certain exceptions, which did not apply in this case. Squires argued that the section of the *Act* infringed the freedom of expression, including freedom of the press as guaranteed by section 2(b) of the *Charter*.

   - **In your opinion, did the Act infringe Squires rights?**

2. *R. v. S. (R.D.)* (1995) Nova Scotia Supreme Court 98 C.C.C. (3d) 235

   R.D.S., a 16-year old, was tried on two counts of assault and one count of resisting a police officer in the lawful execution of his duty. R.D.S. was acquitted of all three charges. There were no reporters at the trial.

   After the trial, Dorey, a reporter for the *Halifax Herald*, received information that in her closing remarks, the judge had criticized the conduct of the Halifax Police Department in relation to minority youths. Dorey wished to write a story concerning those comments and the police reaction to them. He contacted the Halifax Family Court with a request to listen to the tape recording of the trial proceedings. The *Young Offenders Act* provides that Youth Court may grant access to the record of any case to any person deemed to have a valid interest in the record.

   Dorey indicated that he was advised by Family Court staff that the trial judge had some concerns over allowing him to listen to the tape. A court date was scheduled to deal with the request. In her decision, the trial judge denied the plaintiff access to the tape recording. The newspaper appealed the decision, claiming that the action violated its *Charter* rights to freedom of expression and freedom of the press.

   - **Were the newspaper's rights unreasonably limited?**

3. *Miron v. Trudel* (1995) Supreme Court of Canada 2 S.C.R. 418

   Miron and Valliere had lived together in a common-law relationship since 1983. Miron was father to two of the three children born to Valliere. The Economical Mutual Insurance Company issued a motor vehicle insurance policy to Valliere for the one-year period for December 12, 1986, to December 12, 1987. In August of 1987, Miron sustained injuries while a passenger in a motor vehicle owned by McIsaac and driven by Trudel. Neither McIsaac nor Trudel was insured. Miron therefore claimed accident benefits for loss of income in the policy issued by Economical Mutual Insurance Company to Valliere. The insurance company denied the claim on the basis that Miron was not legally married to Valliere. They sued the company.

   Economical Mutual Insurance Company brought a motion to determine whether Miron was the "spouse" for the purpose of the claim. A judge ruled that for the purposes of the applicable portions of the policy, "spouse" meant a person who is legally married. Thus, Miron was not insured under the policy. Miron and Valliere appealed to the Ontario Court of Appeal, basing their argument on section 15 of the *Charter*. The matter eventually found its way to the Supreme Court of Canada.

- **In your opinion, were the equality rights of Miron and Valliere unreasonably limited? Should they be entitled to their claim?**

4. *Ramsden v. Peterborough (City)* (1993) Supreme Court of Canada 2 S.C.R. 1084

Ramsden advertised two upcoming performances of his band by affixing posters on hydro poles in Peterborough. This contravened Bylaw No. 3270 of the city, which prohibited postering on trees, all types of poles, and all other public property. Ramsden was charged on both occasions. Ramsden took the position that the bylaw was unconstitutional because it violated his section 2 (b) *Charter* right to freedom of expression. He was convicted, and appealed. It was agreed that postering on utility poles can constitute a safety hazard to workers climbing them and a traffic hazard if placed facing traffic. It was also agreed that abandoned posters may constitute visual and aesthetic blight and contribute to litter. His appeal to the Provincial Court was dismissed but was allowed by the Ontario Court of Appeal. The city appealed to the Supreme Court of Canada.

- **Were Ramsden's rights reasonably limited by the bylaw?**

5. *Osborne v. Canada* (1991) Supreme Court of Canada 2 S.C.R. 69

A number of public servants wished to work after hours on behalf of Cassidy, who was a candidate for election to Parliament. Two other people were elected to be delegates to the 1984 leadership convention of the Liberal Party. They were both forced to resign as delegates after being advised by their employers that they would suffer disciplinary action if they failed to do so. They all sought a declaration that section 33 of the *Public Service Employment Act* was of no force and effect as it violated sections 2(b) and 2(d) of the *Charter*. Section 33(1)(a) of the *Act* prohibited public servants from engaging in work for or against a candidate and section 33(1)(b) prohibited work for or against a political party.

- **Did the sections of the *Act* violate the right to freedom of speech, and if so could they be justified under section 1 of the *Charter*?**

6. Nugent was convicted of second-degree murder in the strangling death of a 73-year-old man. An audiotaped confession and a videotaped reconstruction of the killing, performed for the RCMP, aided the conviction. Nugent appealed to the Nova Scotia Court of Appeal. It ruled that the tapes were obtained in violation of Nugent's right to a lawyer. Using section 24(2) of the *Charter*, it found the tapes were inadmissible and overturned the conviction. Months later, Vickery, a CBC producer, requested a copy of the tapes to use on a program about videotaped confessions. The request was denied by the Nova Scotia Court of Appeal and appealed to the Supreme Court of Canada.

- **In your opinion, should the tapes be released?**

7. *R. v. Lawrence* (1992) Alberta Court of Queen's Bench 74 C.C.C. (3d) 495

Lawrence attended a public meeting of about 275 people in Athabasca, Alberta. The meeting had been called by the Alberta government to announce approval of locating the Alberta-Pacific Pulp Mill in the vicinity. A panel comprising the premier of Alberta, the local M.L.A., and the provincial ministers of economic development, environment, and forestry was on stage. Some people supported the mill, but protestors from two environmental organizations, "Friends of the North" and "Friends of the Athabasca" were present. There were heated exchanges between the supporters and opponents.

Heckling started as soon as the meeting began. At one point, Lawrence jumped onto the stage and "gave the finger" to each of the politicians and swore at one of them. A police officer returned him to his seat with a warning. Later, Lawrence jumped up and again swore and gestured to the panel. He then resisted the attempts of two police officers to remove him. He was arrested and charged for causing a disturbance and resisting arrest.

At trial, Lawrence argued that the offence of causing a disturbance and the power in the *Police Act* to arrest for breach of the peace were unconstitutional violations of his *Charter* right to freedom of expression. He was acquitted of causing a disturbance and convicted of resisting arrest. He appealed the decision.

- **In your opinion, why was Lawrence acquitted of causing a disturbance?**

- **Was his guarantee of freedom of expression unreasonably limited?**

8. *Egan v. Canada* (1995) Supreme Court of Canada 2 S.C.R. 513

Egan and Nesbit were a homosexual couple. They had lived together since 1948 in an intimate, caring, mutually supportive relationship. They shared bank accounts, credit cards, and property ownership and appointed each other their respective executors and beneficiaries in their wills. They referred to themselves as partners in relating with their families and friends.

In 1986, 38 years after the relationship began, Egan started to receive old age security and a guaranteed income supplement. Nesbit applied for a spousal allowance, which is given to spouses between the ages of 60 and 65 whose combined income falls below a fixed level. His application was rejected on the basis that his relationship with Egan did not fall within the definition of "spouse," as given in section 2 of the *Old Age Security Act*. That section defined spouse as "a person of the opposite sex who is living with that person, having lived with that person for at least one year, if the two persons have publicly represented themselves as husband and wife."

Egan and Nesbit claimed before the Federal Court that the definition of "spouse" in the *Act* contravenes the equality provisions of section 15(1) of the *Charter*. They claimed that it discriminates on the basis of sexual orientation. They wanted a declaration that the definition should be extended to include "partners in same-sex relationships otherwise akin to a conjugal relationship." The Trial Division dismissed the action, the Federal Court of Appeal upheld that judgment, and Egan and Nesbit appealed to the Supreme Court of Canada.

- **Should Nesbit be entitled to the benefit?**

Extending Legal Concepts

1. Now that you have completed this chapter, review the opening article and Something to Think About. Have your answers or opinions changed? Why or why not?

2. Using the data for 1994 found in the chart "Distribution of Complaints by Ground of Discrimination, 1991 to 1994" in Chapter 20, prepare a bar graph to show the number and percentage of complaints for each ground of discrimination. If possible, use a computer spreadsheet or graphing software.

3. Using reference materials in your resource centre, including CD-ROM and the Internet, obtain current information on any of the following topics, and compare them with the Canadian situation. Write a one-page summary of your findings, and create a poster to display your information.

   a) constitutions of other countries

   b) civil rights in other countries

   c) human rights in other countries

4. Using reference materials in your resource centre, including CD-ROM and the Internet, obtain current information on views concerning the *Charter* and its place in Canadian society. Write a one-page summary of your findings.

5. Write a letter to your local Member of Parliament outlining your position on any issue raised in this chapter.

Researching an Issue

Judicial Independence

In Canada, the chief judges of the 35-member Canadian Judicial Council are appointed by the Prime Minister. Many of these are patronage appointments. Others are appointments made after consultation with other chief judges. Not only does the Prime Minister appoint the chief judges, but the executive branch of the government also supplies judicial funding. Since the government is frequently the chief litigant in the courts, some Canadians believe this is a conflict that may disadvantage some Canadians.

Statement

Chief judges have a growing range of tremendous powers and should be accountable for their decisions. Judicial independence is one step toward that end.

Point

Before appointment, candidates should be reviewed by a committee that comprises judges, lawyers, government officials from all parties, and lay people to ensure their independence.

Counterpoint

The judiciary is exemplary and individual judges would not consciously let personal interests colour their behaviour on the bench. Keep the status quo.

- **With a partner, research this issue and reflect on your findings.**

- **Prepare points on this statement that could be used for a class debate.**

- **Discuss your findings with others in your class.**

CRIMINAL LAW

CAREERS

Introduction

Canada's criminal justice system offers a variety and range of jobs that ensures employment for thousands of people across Canada. The focus in this section is on the position of police officer.

In Focus: POLICE OFFICER

Three groups in Canada provide law enforcement: the federal police force—the Royal Canadian Mounted Police; the provincial police forces, such as the Ontario Provincial Police and the Sûreté du Québec; and the municipal or regional police forces. The starting salary for a constable is approximately $30 000 per year.

Education and Other Qualifications

If you wish to join a police force you must have a high school diploma. However, a post-secondary education is becoming increasingly desirable. Useful high school courses are keyboarding, law, and physical education. You must be of good character, possess a valid driver's licence, and be able to pass a thorough medical examination, a fitness test, and a security check. You may also be required to pass other job-relevant ability tests. Your first rank, after you have passed a training course, will be that of constable.

Responsibilities

As a police officer, you are responsible for maintaining public safety and order and enforcing laws and regulations. You may be assigned to traffic patrol where you will enforce traffic laws, provide emergency roadside assistance, and investigate traffic accident scenes. Another assignment may be to investigate a crime, secure evidence from the crime scene, interview witnesses, make arrests, and provide testimony in court. You may also be asked to provide other community services such as visiting classrooms to talk about crime prevention and safety.

Work Environment

Most of your time while on duty will be spent outdoors. You will probably work on a rotating shift basis which means that sometimes you will be working nights and weekends. Occasionally, your work will be physically and emotionally demanding, and there may be times when your life will be in danger.

Do You Fit the Job?

As a police officer you must combine many attributes: working well alone and in a team, showing good judgement, being observant, assuming responsibility and being able to make quick decisions. You must be honest and reliable, as well as a skilled communicator. You must enjoy working with and learning about people.

PROFILE: Christine Silverberg

In July 1995, Christine Silverberg was appointed Chief of Police of Calgary's 1600-member police service, making her the first female police chief of a major Canadian city. More than 200 candidates from across Canada were considered for the position. Prior to joining the Calgary Police Service, she was the Deputy Chief of the Hamilton-Wentworth Regional Police in Ontario.

Chief Silverberg holds a bachelor's degree in sociology and a master's degree in criminology. She also holds professional accreditation in public relations, and has undertaken courses at Queen's University School of Business. Chief Silverberg has also received numerous certificates in police operations and police management through the Ontario Police College and the Canadian Police College. She started her career as a corrections officer at the Vanier Centre for Women before joining the Peel Regional Police in Ontario in 1972.

Chief Silverberg believes strongly in neighbourhood policing "which engages communities and volunteers as equal partners in problem identification and problem solving." She supports fair and equitable employment practices and believes that when the hiring process is completely free of any form of discrimination, competency will win.

Questions and Activities

1. Make a list of the personal qualities you consider most important in judging candidates for police officer training. Justify your choices. Compare your list with those of your classmates.

2. Prepare a report describing the work and outlining the education requirements and working conditions of one of the following occupations: correctional officer, criminologist, polygraph examiner, probation and parole officer, security guard.

3. Are you in favour of affirmative action programs to encourage the hiring of minority groups as police officers? Support your position.

4. Invite a police officer to visit your classroom to describe his or her work and to discuss the advantages and disadvantages of a career in the police force.

CRIMINAL LAW AND CRIMINAL OFFENCES

These are the key terms introduced in this chapter:

abet	dual procedure offence	omission
absolute liability	due diligence	onus
accessory after the fact	general intent	quasi-criminal law
actus reus	hybrid offence	recklessness
aid	indictable offence	specific intent
attempt	intent	strict liability
civil law	jurisdiction	summary conviction offence
conspiracy	knowledge	wilful blindness
Criminal Code of Canada	*mens rea*	
criminal law	motive	

Chapter at a Glance

Learning Outcomes

At the end of this chapter, you will be able to

1. explain why criminal law is necessary;
2. describe the conditions for an action to be considered a crime;
3. identify the jurisdiction of the federal and the provincial governments over criminal law;
4. compare summary conviction with indictable offences;
5. describe the concept of quasi-criminal offences;
6. describe the elements that must exist for a person to be convicted of a crime;
7. discuss general and specific intent;
8. compare absolute liability with strict liability offences;
9. describe when there may be a party to an offence;
10. describe an attempt and a conspiracy;
11. outline the Criminal Court system.

Some Court Judgments Confound Our Sense of Natural Justice

Amazing, isn't it, that OPP Const. Serge Loranger faces no criminal penalty for killing a teenager with his car?

Loranger's acquittal . . . again illustrates the gap between justice in the courtroom and justice in the eyes of the community.

Although Loranger is not guilty of any crime, we do know these things about his actions on the night of August 22, 1994. After about four hours in a Bells Corners bar and the consumption of approximately seven to nine beers, Loranger felt he was fit to make the short drive home to Kanata. Although the night was clear and the pavement dry, Loranger wasn't able to see 16-year-old cyclist Shayne Norris pedalling on the road. Loranger struck the boy, sending his body hurtling 57 metres. The collision damaged the fender, headlight, windshield, and passenger window of his car.

Despite the impact and the damage to the vehicle, there is no proof that Loranger stopped. Instead, he sped home, racing erratically through suburban streets. He and a friend he had been drinking with returned to the scene to briefly search for what had been hit, then drove back to Bells Corners, where they phoned police from a doughnut shop and reported hitting a deer.

To a reasonable person, Loranger's actions appear suspicious. Provincial Court Judge Geraldine Sparrow described them that way in her judgment.

Unfortunately, in court the test is not what a reasonable person would deduce from the facts, but whether there is a reasonable doubt that the accused committed the crime.

Loranger's trial turned on whether he was aware that he had struck a person. If he was unaware that he had struck Norris, there would be no crime and no need for him to remain at the scene. One would think that a person would have to be blind not to realize that a cyclist had just bounced off his windshield, but this is difficult for a Crown attorney to establish because there is no way to probe what Loranger actually thought.

The Crown might have asked Loranger, but there was no opportunity for that because Loranger didn't testify. No need to, really, when he could have his version of events explained by his drinking buddies . . .

The Loranger acquittal seems to confound natural justice and it leaves us with a desire to lash out, to find someone to blame. We can blame police who fumbled the gathering of evidence, letting Loranger escape trial earlier on the more serious charge of impaired driving. We can blame the law for the curious way it is constructed.

In truth, the blame lies solely with Serge Loranger. He was the one behind the wheel. The one who had too much to drink, smashed up the company car, and sped from the scene of the accident, only to return with a story that seems at best implausible . . .

Some are disappointed that the court didn't deliver retribution, but perhaps the truth that Loranger has to cope with is a greater punishment than any a judge could mete out.

From: Randall Denley, "Some court judgments confound our sense of natural justice." *The Ottawa Citizen*, October 21, 1995. Reprinted with permission of *The Ottawa Citizen*.

Something to Think About

- What is the principle test in a court of law when deciding upon innocence or guilt?
- Who do citizens look to when trying to place blame for a trial decision with which they do not agree?
- "Since the purpose of a trial is to arrive at the truth, an accused should have to testify." Discuss this statement.

3.1 INTRODUCTION

The law exists to protect people as a society and as individuals. **Criminal law** deals with offences committed against society as a whole. Offences against individuals are dealt with under **civil law**. Let us examine this distinction using a criminal example.

Suppose Ronald Fawcett decides to break into Kathy Williston's house, steal her electronic equipment, and sell it. He breaks the door lock with a crowbar and enters the house while no one is home. He leaves with a CD player, a video cassette recorder, and a video camera. The *Criminal Code* describes the offence of break and enter and the penalty for committing the offence as follows:

348.

(1) Every one who
   (a) breaks and enters a place with intent to commit an indictable offence therein,
   (b) breaks and enters a place and commits an indictable offence therein, or
   (c) breaks out of a place after
      (i) committing an indictable offence therein, or
      (ii) entering the place with intent to commit an indictable offence therein,
is guilty of an indictable offence and liable
   (d) to imprisonment for life, if the offence is committed in relation to a dwelling-house, or
   (e) to imprisonment for a term not exceeding fourteen years, if the offence is committed in relation to a place other than a dwelling-house.

Fawcett would be charged under criminal law for he has come into conflict with what society deems acceptable. People have the right to not have their houses broken into and to not have their goods taken. Should Fawcett be found guilty

he may be compelled to pay a fine or be imprisoned. Both of these penalties result in a cost to *him*—either paying money, or being deprived of his freedom. However, neither penalty compensates Williston for the loss that *she* has suffered due to the break-in. She must seek her personal compensation by suing Fawcett under civil law—a case that would be heard at a different time and in a different court.

The Need for Criminal Law

The criminal law offers us order and predictability. It provides a value framework within which to live our lives. But is criminal law really necessary? Would it not be enough for the individual who has been wronged to be compensated by the offender? Civil law offers this possibility. Criminal law does not.

Criminal law focuses more on prevention and on penalty than it does on compensation. It is difficult, if not impossible, to compensate for many criminal offences. The victim of a murder can never be revived. The individual, or society, whose values have been coloured by exposure to obscene material will never be the same. The victim of a penniless thief will not be repaid. The thief can continue to rob with impunity.

Most people believe that criminal law should protect people and property. Some want it to do so by discouraging potential offenders. Others want it to rehabilitate those who have already harmed society. Still others look to it for retribution.

3.2 THE NATURE OF CRIMINAL LAW

It is very difficult to define precisely what constitutes a crime. In this book, a crime will be considered to be any action that the Parliament of Canada has deemed to be criminal. A certain action that is not considered criminal today may be classified as a crime tomorrow if Parliament passes a law making it so. Parliament declares certain actions to be criminal to reflect the values and wishes of society. For instance, Canadian criminal law contains prohibitions against such actions as obtaining body samples for DNA testing and the illegal use of computer data—both developments of the late twentieth century. Penalties for drinking and driving or the use of narcotics likewise reflect the concerns of contemporary society. Criminal law reflects social changes and growth.

Criminal Actions

Due to different values, not all members of society agree on what actions should be considered criminal. Certain laws, such as those dealing with abortion, capital punishment, and gun control, are sources of repeated public debate. Parliament may be called upon to reconsider such laws several times within a short period for a variety of reasons. It may be that a specific incident has brought an issue back into public focus. Another possibility is that an interest group that opposes an existing law will gain enough public support to force Parliament to reconsider it. In such situations it is likely that even though the law passed in Parliament, support for it was far from unanimous. The 1995 gun laws are a good example.

What, then, constitutes a crime within the laws of Canada? The Law Reform Commission of Canada, in its report *Our Criminal Law*, suggested that for an action to be considered a crime, certain conditions must exist:

- the action must be considered wrong;
- the action must cause harm to other people, to society, or to those who need protection (such as minors);
- the harm must be serious in both nature and degree;
- the harm must best be dealt with through the mechanism of criminal law.

Reviewing Your Reading

1. Why does criminal law exist?
2. Name three purposes that Canadians feel can be fulfilled by criminal law.
3. What are some of the possible causes of crime?
4. Why does Parliament decide to make certain actions criminal?

5. Give three examples of laws enacted in the past few years that indicate society's changing values and/or concerns.
6. List the conditions that must exist for an action to be considered a crime according to the Law Reform Commission of Canada.

3.3 JURISDICTION OVER CRIMINAL LAW

The criminal law system inherited by early Canada (except Quebec) was essentially the English case law system with slight modifications by English statutes. At first, each province was free to make its own criminal statutes. In 1867, the first four provinces to enter Confederation gave this **jurisdiction** (law-making authority) to the federal Parliament. Section 91(27) of the *Constitution Act, 1867*, gave the Parliament of Canada exclusive jurisdiction over the criminal law "except the constitution of courts of criminal jurisdiction, but including the procedure in criminal matters." The provinces were to establish the criminal courts, but the federal government was to determine how they operated. The intent was to strengthen the federal government by giving it authority over matters common to the whole country. Thus, a given offence is considered a crime whether committed in British Columbia or in Newfoundland.

Quasi-Criminal Law

The provinces retained the right to enact laws on all matters falling under their jurisdiction. As well, they were given the authority to transfer jurisdiction over any of these matters to the municipalities. Technically, laws passed by the provinces or municipalities are not considered part of criminal law; rather, they are referred to as **quasi-criminal law**. It is these quasi-criminal laws, such as traffic offences that fall under the *Highway Traffic Act* of each province, that citizens are most likely to encounter. Quasi-criminal laws differ from province to province.

The *Criminal Code*

The ***Criminal Code of Canada*** is the main source of our criminal law. It came into effect on July 1, 1893. In 1955, a major revision of the *Criminal Code* eliminated offences contrary to common law, English statutes, and provincial statutes made prior to 1955. After this, it was generally not necessary to refer to criminal laws passed earlier than 1955. Today, most criminal offences are found in the *Criminal Code* and in the many statutes passed by Parliament, such as the *Narcotic Control Act* and the *Official Secrets Act*. As well, all procedures from the time police begin to investigate a crime until a person is released from an institution after serving a sentence are specified in these *Acts*.

The *Criminal Code* is essentially the same in structure, style, and content as it was when the first *Code* was enacted in 1893. It has frequently been recommended that it should be rewritten so that it is clearer and better organized. Changes are constantly being made to the *Code* to ensure that it continues to meet present needs. In 1995, bills before Parliament concerned over one hundred items in the *Criminal Code*.

The judiciary also influences the construction of our criminal law. It is the role of the judiciary to interpret laws passed by Parliament or a provincial legislature and determine how they apply in individual cases. This gives judges the power to determine how the will of Parliament and the legislatures—as embodied in law—will be enacted against criminals. This is their job. Judges also have the power to determine whether laws or procedures followed by the state are consistent with the *Canadian Charter of Rights and Freedoms*. Should a judge find that a law is unconstitutional, that is contrary to the *Charter*, he or she can require a number of different remedies. However, it is the responsibility of Parliament or the legislature to decide whether a law struck down as unconstitutional will be rewritten.

Judiciary influence is also reflected in the many criminal procedures that were decided upon by previous judgments and are still followed according to precedent. The influence of the judiciary over our criminal law is reflected in the following case and others that are examined in this unit.

CASE

R. v. B. (K.G.)

(1993)

Supreme Court of Canada

I S.C.R. 734

Joseph Wright and his brother Steven were walking home in Scarborough. B. and three other young men driving by got into an argument with the Wrights. One of the youths pulled a knife and killed Joseph. The four youths fled the scene.

The police interviewed the three friends separately a few weeks later. Each was accompanied by a parent and advised of his right to counsel. They were told that they were under no obligation to answer questions and that they were not "at this time" charged with any offence. With the youths' consent, the interviews were videotaped. Each youth told the police that B. had said that he thought he had caused the death of the victim by using the knife. B. was subsequently charged with second-degree murder and tried in Youth Court.

At trial, the three youths withdrew their earlier statements, saying that they had lied to avoid being accused of stabbing Wright. Although the trial judge had no doubt that the withdrawals were false, the witnesses' prior statements could not be tendered as proof that B. actually made the admissions. Under the traditional common-law position, they could only be used to impeach (cast doubt on) the witnesses' credibility.

Wright's brother gave evidence identifying the killer, but it was not very positive. The trial judge therefore acquitted B., and the Ontario Court of Appeal upheld the acquittal. The three witnesses pleaded guilty to perjury as a result of their testimony at trial. The Crown subsequently appealed to the Supreme Court of Canada, asking it to reconsider the common-law rule that limits the use of prior inconsistent statements to impeach the credibility of the witness.

The Supreme Court of Canada in its decision stated that "the time has come for the rule limiting the use of prior inconsistent statements to impeach the credibility of the witness to be replaced by a new rule recognizing the changed means and methods of proof in modern society . . . Considering a change to the rule is not a matter better left to Parliament; the rule itself is judge-made and lends itself to judicial reform. A reformed rule must carefully balance the accused's interests in a criminal trial with the interests of society in seeing justice done." The Court therefore changed its earlier precedent and ruled that prior inconsistent statements can be admitted as evidence under certain circumstances, which were outlined in the decision.

1. **What is the criminal offence of perjury?**
2. **Why did the Crown appeal to the Supreme Court of Canada?**
3. **What is a prior inconsistent statement?**
4. **The Supreme Court of Canada refers to a "rule limiting the use of prior inconsistent statements to impeach the credibility of the witness." What does the court mean by the phrase "to impeach the credibility of the witness"? Can prior inconsistent statements be used for this purpose?**
5. **What else could a prior inconsistent statement conceivably be used for in court?**
6. **What was the source of the law of evidence that the witnesses' prior inconsistent statements could not be admitted as proof that the accused actually made the admission?**
7. **Politicians usually make laws. Judges usually interpret them. In your own words, explain why the Supreme Court of Canada ruled that it could change the law on prior inconsistent statements without reference to Parliament.**
8. **What change to the criminal law of evidence did the Supreme Court of Canada make?**
9. **Why did the trial judge have to acquit the accused?**

Ehore

Reprinted with permission of Ed Hore.

Reviewing Your Reading

1. **What is the origin of Canadian criminal law?**

2. **Why was the federal government given jurisdiction over criminal law?**

3. **What are quasi-criminal laws?**

4. **Where can one find the most common crimes and their penalties listed?**

5. **Outline three ways that the judiciary influences our criminal law.**

3.4 TYPES OF CRIMINAL OFFENCES

If you attend a session of a Canadian court, you will hear people being charged with summary conviction offences and indictable offences. Some offences can be either summary or indictable. These are called hybrid offences, or dual procedure offences. For these offences, the Crown decides which type of charge will be laid. It is significant which type of offence has been committed, for it determines

- the power of arrest for a citizen or police;
- the rights of the accused;
- how the trial will proceed;
- what penalty will be imposed.

Summary Conviction Offences

Summary conviction offences are minor offences for which an accused can be arrested or summoned to court without delay.

The maximum penalty for most summary convictions under the *Criminal Code* is $2000 and/or six months' imprisonment. In other statutes, more severe penalties for summary offences are specified. For example, the *Narcotic Control Act* specifies a maximum penalty of a fine of $2000 and/or imprisonment for one year for possession of a narcotic. All provincial offences are summary. Penalties vary from small fines to imprisonment.

Indictable Offences

Indictable offences are serious crimes and incur more severe penalties than summary conviction offences. The *Criminal Code* sets a maximum penalty for each offence, up to life imprisonment for some. The actual penalty is imposed at the discretion of the trial judge.

Some indictable offences incur a minimum penalty instead of relying on the judge's discretion. For example, impaired driving carries a minimum penalty that can range from a $300 fine to three months' imprisonment, depending upon the number of times the accused has committed the offence.

Hybrid Offences

Hybrid offences, or **dual procedure offences**, are those for which the Crown has the right to choose whether to proceed summarily or by indictment. Theft is an example of a hybrid offence, as section 334 of the *Criminal Code* makes clear:

334.

Except where otherwise provided by law, every one who commits theft

(a) is guilty of an indictable offence and liable to imprisonment for a term not exceeding ten years, where the property stolen is a testamentary instrument or where the value of what is stolen exceeds five thousand dollars; or

(b) is guilty

  (i) of an indictable offence and is liable to imprisonment for a term not exceeding two years, or

  (ii) of an offence punishable on summary conviction, where the value of what is stolen does not exceed five thousand dollars.

If a person stole a chocolate bar and it was a first offence, the Crown would probably choose to make the charge a summary offence. The accused may not be considered to have developed a pattern of criminal activity. However, further offences by the same person may result in the Crown proceeding by indictment, where the penalty can be much more severe. Hybrid offences are treated as indictable offences until the charge is laid in court. The accused therefore has to make an appearance, even though there is a possibility that the Crown will proceed summarily. The use of hybrid offences in the *Criminal Code* has been criticized by those who believe that the Crown is, to some degree, deciding on the penalty to be received. Such critics feel the judge should make that decision.

Reviewing Your Reading

1. **How can you tell if an offence is summary or indictable?**
2. **Give three differences in the procedures used for summary and indictable offences.**
3. **How can you tell if an offence is hybrid (dual procedure)?**
4. **What important decision can the Crown attorney make for hybrid offences that she or he does not make for summary or indictable offences?**

3.5 *T*HE ELEMENTS OF A CRIME

For all true criminal offences, it is necessary to prove that two elements existed at the time of the offence: ***actus reus*** and ***mens rea***. *Actus reus* is Latin for "a guilty act or deed." It involves the physical conduct of the accused. For *actus reus* to exist, an individual must commit a prohibited action. *Mens rea* is Latin for "a guilty mind." It focuses on the mental state of the accused and requires proof that the accused intended to commit a criminal wrong. The two elements must exist at the same time. If I have the desire to run you over with my car today—*mens rea*—and then do it accidentally tomorrow—*actus reus*—criminal liability does not result.

The *Charter of Rights and Freedoms* specifies in section 11(d) that a person is "to be presumed innocent until proven guilty according to law in a fair and public hearing by an independent and impartial tribunal." The **onus**, or responsibility for proof of *actus reus* and *mens rea*, is therefore on the

Crown. The Crown must prove its case beyond a reasonable doubt. If there is any doubt in the mind of the judge or jury that the accused committed the crime, the accused will be acquitted.

Actus reus

Most offences contained in the *Criminal Code* specify the wrongful action that must be committed for criminal liability. Section 348 of the *Criminal Code* on p. 62 clearly states that two actions must be proven as the *actus reus* for a break and enter—to break into the place and to enter the place.

Fawcett committed break and enter. You will recall that he broke the door with a crowbar and entered Williston's house. What if he had only broken a window in a door? He has still "broken" but he has not entered. If he reaches an arm through the window to open the door and someone scares him off, he has still entered because a part of his body was in the house.

For some offences, the *actus reus* can result from failure to do something, an **omission**. For example, to withhold necessities from someone you are legally obligated to provide for or to fail to obtain assistance for someone in childbirth, are both wrongful actions. For other offences, neither an action nor failure to act is required, but only a certain state of being. Fawcett, for example, may have been found in possession of break-in instruments before he committed the break and enter. His state of being is the possession of break-in instruments. There is a separate offence in the *Criminal Code* for the possession of break-in instruments under circumstances that "give rise to a reasonable inference that the instrument has been used or is or was intended to be used for any such purpose."

Mens Rea

As mentioned earlier, *mens rea* is the second element that must exist for an accused to be found guilty of most offences. Note that the wording of the offence of break and enter includes "with intent to commit." This is *mens rea*.

The mental state required for *mens rea* to exist falls into two possible categories: intent or knowledge and recklessness.

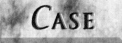

CASE

R. v. Mac
(1995)

**Ontario Court
of Appeal
97 C.C.C. (3d) 115**

Khuan Mac and two companions, Ms. Ng and Mr. Yip, were searched when they returned to Canada from the United States. Each was carrying a large amount of money in denominations of $20 or less: Mac $12 000, Ms. Ng $25 000, and Mr. Yip $2764. When asked where they got the money, each told a story that made it difficult to determine which of the three, if any, actually had possession of it and how it had come into their possession. Mr. Yip also gave a false name when asked to identify himself. The money was seized and the three were permitted to go on their way and no charges were ever laid.

Mac applied to the Provincial Court for the return of his money. The Crown asked the court to have the money forfeited to the government. Mac based his position on section 489(1) of the *Criminal Code,* which states that anything seized by a peace officer should be returned as soon as practicable if there is no dispute as to who is lawfully entitled to possession of it, and if it is not needed for any further proceeding.

The judge indicated that the onus was on Mac to show that he was lawfully entitled to the money. Mac testified that the money had been loaned to him by his relatives to buy a car. Before coming across the border he gave part of it to Ng and Yip to carry. Ng confirmed the story. The peace officer who seized the money indicated that there was no evidence that the money was obtained by criminal or illegal conduct. The Crown made submissions that the money must be a part of a money-laundering scheme or illicit drug money.

The trial judge rejected Mac's evidence as unbelievable and ordered that the money be kept. Mac appealed this ruling to the Ontario Court of Appeal. The court ruled that there was no onus on Mac to prove that the money was not obtained by a criminal act, and that he obtained the money legally. It also ruled that he only had to prove that he was in possession of the money when it was seized. If he did so, the money should be returned to him, which it was. The court stated that the onus is on the Crown to prove that the money is tainted by criminality.

1. **Do you believe that the peace officer had the right to seize the money?**

2. **The court could presume that Mac got the money legally or illegally. Which presumption does section 11(d) of the *Charter* require?**

3. **Whose job would it be to rebut that presumption?**

4. **What section of the *Charter* would Mac rely upon? Why?**

5. **The court also resolved what should be done with the money that was found in Yip's possession. What do you think should be done with it and why?**

Intent or Knowledge

Intent means that a person's state of mind is such that the person desires to carry out a certain action and can foresee its results, as Fawcett did when he broke into Williston's house. The existence of intent is based on the facts, and on what a reason-able person would be thinking in the circumstances. The intent is not, of course, that which is indicated by an accused, who would obviously say that he or she did not intend to commit the wrong.

The intent required to commit an offence can be either **general intent** or **specific intent**. The

Harricharan was awakened in his home at 4:00 a.m. by a loud bang. Through the window he saw smoke and flames coming from the garage. He rushed to the kitchen phone to call for help. In his newly renovated kitchen he could not find the card bearing the seven-digit emergency number; 911 was not available in his area. As the kitchen started to fill with smoke Harricharan ran back upstairs, put some clothing in a suitcase and boxes, threw them through the bedroom window, and jumped out. He then used a ladder to climb back into the house to collect, among other things, important personal papers.

When the smoke started to enter the bedroom he climbed out of the window and walked around the yard a few more times. The trial judge found that Harricharan at this point was totally out of his mind: confused, annoyed, and mad. He was so tired that when he went to put some of his stuff in his barn he collapsed.

Harricharan's house was in a rural area, a five-minute run from the nearest neighbour. At 5:30 a.m., on her way to work, the neighbour noticed that the house was on fire, and phoned the fire department. By the time the fire department arrived, only the brick walls of the house remained. Two vehicles in the garage were destroyed. No cause of the fire was ever determined. Harricharan had put over $100 000 into renovations, doing much of the work himself. The incident was a traumatic experience for him. He gave voluntary statements to the police and an independent insurance adjuster.

Harricharan was charged under section 436(1) of the *Criminal Code* that he "unlawfully did, as a result of a marked departure from the standard of care that a reasonably prudent person would use to prevent or control the spread of fires, cause a fire in a dwelling house." The trial judge found Harricharan guilty, ruling that the applicable section of the *Criminal Code* imposed a duty on him to stop the spread of the fire. He observed that Harricharan should have gone for help rather than returning to the house. Harricharan appealed the trial judge's decision to the Ontario Court of Appeal.

The Appeal Court overturned the conviction. It ruled that for a finding of guilty under section 436(1) bodily harm to another person or damage to property must result from the person's marked departure from the standard of care. It was not sufficient for the person's marked departure from the standard of care merely to have led to the spread of the fire. In addition, even if it was appropriate to include the spread of fire into the *actus reus*, the Crown must still prove that the behaviour was a cause of the fire or its spread.

R. v. Harricharan

(1995)

Ontario Court of Appeal
98 C.C.C. (3d) 145

1. **What duty is imposed upon a person by section 436(1) of the *Criminal Code*?**
2. **What is the *actus reus* of this offence? Must the accused start a fire to be convicted?**
3. **If the accused did not start the fire but knew it was there and did not show the required standard of care, what defence if any does she or he have?**
4. **In your opinion, did Harricharan fulfill the *actus reus* of the offence?**

R. v. Thornton
(1990)

Ontario Court
of Appeal
3 C.R. (4th) 381

Thornton was charged with common nuisance endangering the lives or health of the public. He donated blood to the Red Cross at a time when he knew that he had twice tested positive for HIV antibodies and that he was therefore infectious. He admitted that he deliberately withheld that information from the Red Cross.

According to Red Cross policies and procedures, Thornton was not permitted to give blood. He had read signs and a pamphlet that made those policies clear. Thornton testified that he donated his blood as a form of blood-letting to get rid of some of the contaminated blood, hoping that it would lessen the odds of his developing the fatal disease. He also said that he thought that the Red Cross screening system was foolproof and that his blood would not get through the system. Evidence given at trial indicated that it was 99.3 percent accurate.

Athena Munroe, a friend of Thornton, testified that before he gave his blood she discussed with him the seriousness of what would happen if the blood got into the general population. She said he didn't seem all that concerned about the consequences. She indicated that he said "I just wanted to see if I could get away with it. See if I get caught." She gave evidence that he knew that his blood would be caught by the screening process. She also testified that Thornton made up the story about blood-letting after the event.

Thornton was found guilty at trial and appealed to the Ontario Court of Appeal, one of the grounds being that he did not have the necessary *mens rea*. The appeal was dismissed, and the sentence of 15 months' imprisonment affirmed. The maximum penalty for the offence is two years.

1. **What was the charge? What is the *actus reus* of that offence? Did Thornton have it?**

2. **The trial judge had to determine whether Munroe or Thornton gave the more credible evidence. What factors might he have considered in making that determination?**

3. **In your opinion, did Thornton possess the necessary *mens rea*? Explain.**

4. **Would you consider Thornton's actions to be a serious offence or one of a minor nature?**

wording of the offence in the *Criminal Code* indicates the level of intent that is required for the accused to be found guilty.

General Intent. The Nova Scotia Court of Appeal, in *R. v. Saulnier* (1989), defined a general intent offence as follows: "For a general intent offence the Crown need only prove beyond a reasonable doubt that the accused had the intent to perform the *actus reus* of the offence. This intent can be inferred from the acts of the accused; it is a minimal intent that he consciously did the act that

constitutes the offence." In the case of assault, for example, the Crown need only prove the intent to apply force. That intent can be inferred from the fact that the accused *did* apply force. Similarly, for the charge of trespassing at night, once the Crown has proven that the accused *was* on someone else's property at night, the intent to be there is inferred. No further *mens rea* need be proven.

Specific Intent. Specific intent offences also allow an inference of intent to commit the action in question, but there must be proof of a further intent. For example, the offence for break and enter outlined above is a specific intent offence for it involves an intentional unlawful action (breaking and entering a place), which is committed with the intent to commit a further specific illegal action (an indictable offence).

To prosecute Fawcett for the specific intent offence of break and enter, it is necessary for the prosecution to prove that

1. the *actus reus* existed (that he had the general intent to break and enter), and
2. he had the specific intent to commit an indictable offence therein, such as theft.

Let us compare other crimes to examine the distinction between general intent and specific intent offences. A frustrated hockey player strikes an opponent with his stick, having no intent or purpose other than to "send the opponent a message." The player dies from the blow. Another person, after committing a sexual assault, strikes a person on the head with an axe with intent to kill. In the first situation, the Crown need only prove that the *actus reus*, the act of striking the blow, occurred. The accused will be found guilty of manslaughter—a general intent offence. It would not be necessary to prove that the hockey player had intent to kill. In the latter case, the Crown must prove that the *actus reus*, the striking with an axe, and the *mens rea*, the intent to kill the person, coexisted.

The distinction between general intent offences and specific intent offences is significant, as we will see later when discussing the defence of drunkenness.

The law considers some people to be incapable of forming the intent necessary to commit a wrongful action. Examples are those suffering from mental disorders, minors, or infants, and those who are under the influence of alcohol or drugs to such an extent that they do not understand the nature of their actions. These persons will be considered in Chapter 5 under Defences and in Chapter 9, which deals with the *Young Offenders Act*.

Knowledge. For a conviction, **knowledge** of certain facts can provide the necessary *mens rea*. For example, section 342(1)(d) of the *Criminal Code* says: "every one who uses a credit card that he knows has been revoked or cancelled is guilty" of an offence. Here, it is only necessary to prove that the person had used the credit card, and that he or she knew it had been revoked. No proof of the intent to defraud any person is required.

The *Criminal Code* denies the accused the right to defend himself or herself on the grounds that the accused did not know he or she was committing an offence. In section 19 of the *Code*, it is specifically stated: "Ignorance of the law by a person who commits an offence is not an excuse for committing that offence."

Motive. The rationale for committing an offence is **motive**; it is frequently confused with intent. However, in making a decision upon guilt, motive is irrelevant. The fact that Fawcett's motive was to steal goods to sell and get money has little relevance to his guilt. A person can have a motive and not commit an offence. Suppose that a suspicious fire kills a man whose wife is having a serious affair with another man. The wife may have had a motive to kill, but unless it can be shown that she acted to cause the fire, or failed to act, no offence is deemed to have been committed. Motive may be used as circumstantial evidence, but the elements of the offence must be proven to obtain a conviction. As well, the motive for an offence may be considered by the judge when deciding upon a penalty.

Recklessness or Wilful Blindness

Recklessness is defined as the taking of a risk where the result of the action—committing a crime—is foreseeable. The following case illustrates recklessness that led to a conviction.

In *R. v. Blondin* (1971), the accused returned to Canada from Japan with a scuba-diving outfit. He had been paid to import the outfit, knew that something illegal was inside the tank, but did not know that it contained hashish. Although he had no intent to illegally import narcotics, Blondin was found guilty. The court ruled that he was reckless, for he knew that what he was importing was illegal and he took the risk of importing the tank nonetheless. He saw the risk and took a chance.

Wilful blindness results when a person has become aware of the need for some inquiry but declines to make the inquiry because he or she does not wish to know the truth. The following case illustrates wilful blindness that led to a conviction.

CASE

R. v. Sansregret
(1985)

Supreme Court
of Canada
45 C.R. (3d) 193

Sansregret and the complainant had lived together in the complainant's house for about a year. The complainant decided to end the affair and told Sansregret to leave. He did. Their relationship had been one of contention and discord with violence on the part of Sansregret, which included slappings as described by him, or blows as described by her.

On a September morning at 4:30, Sansregret broke into the complainant's house and terrorized her with a file-like instrument. To calm him she implied that there might be some hope of a reconciliation, and they had intercourse. A report was made to the police, the complainant asserting that she had been raped, but no charges were laid.

In October, Sansregret again broke into the house. He struck the complainant on the mouth, threatened her with a butcher knife, and on three occasions rammed the blade into the wall with great force, once very close to her. He told her that if the police came he would put the knife through her and added that had he found her with a man he would have killed them both. After about an hour of violent behaviour, she tried to calm him. She again held out a hope of reconciliation, if he would settle down and get a job. He calmed down and after some conversation he joined her on the bed, and they had intercourse. She reported the incident to the police, and Sansregret was charged with rape. (This offence is now called sexual assault.)

The complainant swore that her consent to the intercourse was solely for the purpose of calming Sansregret to protect herself from further violence. The trial judge acquitted Sansregret, indicating that the accused had honestly believed that the victim was consenting to sexual intercourse. The Crown's appeal to the Manitoba Court of Appeal succeeded, and Sansregret appealed to the Supreme Court of Canada. The Supreme Court of Canada found Sansregret guilty, based on wilful blindness.

1. **What is the *mens rea* of sexual assault? Be specific about what the accused has to know.**

2. **Sansregret's defence was that he lacked *mens rea*. He stated that he did not know something that he needed to know in order to be found guilty. What did he say he did not know?**

3. **What, if any, evidence is there that Sansregret should have known?**

4. **What does it mean to be wilfully blind? Are you convinced that Sansregret was wilfully blind?**

5. **What does it mean to be reckless? Are you convinced that Sansregret was reckless?**

6. **Distinguish between recklessness and wilful blindness as it relates to this case.**

Strict Liability and Absolute Liability Offences

The above discussion indicates that *mens rea* must exist for an act to be criminal. These offences also have a moral fault attached. However, there is a separate category of offences that are less serious than those found in the *Criminal Code*. These regulatory offences are divided into those with **strict liability** and those with **absolute liability**. These offences can be in violation of federal or provincial laws and they differ from those requiring proof of *mens rea* in two ways. First, they do not require proof of *mens rea*. They are regulatory in nature and have been instituted for the general protection of the public, rather than to punish offenders. Speeding, shortweighting a package of food, and polluting the environment are examples of regulatory offences. The second difference is that regulatory offences have lesser penalties. As a result, they do not carry the stigma associated with the conviction for a criminal offence.

Strict Liability Offences

For strict liability offences, proof that the act was committed is all that is necessary for a conviction. However, the defence of **due diligence** can be put forth by the accused. Due diligence means that the accused took reasonable care not to commit the offence or honestly believed in a mistaken set of facts that would have rendered the act or omission innocent, if they were true.

Absolute Liability Offences

Absolute liability offences are similar to strict liability offences in that the Crown does not have to prove *mens rea*. However, due diligence is not accepted as a defence to committing these offences. If the person committed the *actus reus*, he or she is guilty no matter what precautions were taken to not commit the offence. Since the regulatory offences in the various *Acts* do not indicate whether they are strict liability or absolute liability, it is left to the courts to decide

CASE

The *Motor Vehicle Act* of British Columbia stated in subsection (1) that the driver of a vehicle who (a) was prohibited from driving or (b) had a suspended licence was guilty of an offence and was liable to a fine and imprisonment. Subsection (2) stated that subsection (1) created an absolute liability offence in which guilt was established by proof of driving, whether or not the offender was aware of the prohibition or suspension.

The British Columbia Court of Appeal declared the section to be of no force and effect, since it was inconsistent with section 7 of the *Charter of Rights and Freedoms*. This *Charter* section provides that "everyone has the right to life, liberty and security of the person and the right not to be deprived thereof except in accordance with the principles of fundamental justice." The mandatory imprisonment requirement was seen to be in violation of the right to liberty. Furthermore, the violation could not be saved by the section 7 provision that it could be adopted if it fell within the principles of fundamental justice.

The decision was appealed to the Supreme Court of Canada, which upheld it.

Re B.C. Motor Vehicle Act
(1985)

Supreme Court of Canada
2 S.C.R. 486

1. In this offence, what constitutes *actus reus*?
2. a) How do you know this is an absolute liability offence?
   b) What is the chief purpose of absolute liability offences?
3. Do you think the compulsory imprisonment of offenders could be defended as a "reasonable limit as prescribed by law," thereby making a law valid under section 1 of the *Charter*?
4. Why do you think the Supreme Court of Canada decided that no imprisonment may be imposed for an absolute liability offence and that an offence punishable by imprisonment cannot be an absolute liability offence?

what the government intended. Absolute liability offences provide little opportunity for a successful defence. They are not meant to punish the offender by imprisonment, but rather to protect the public. Consequently, the Supreme Court of Canada ruled in *Re B.C. Motor Vehicle Act* (1985) that an absolute liability offence that provided for a term of imprisonment was unconstitutional.

Attempt

A person who intends to commit a criminal action but fails to carry out the intent is still recognized by the law as a danger to society. It is immaterial that the person found it impossible to carry out the act under the circumstances. In Fawcett's case, a peace officer could have observed him walking around the house at night with a flashlight, trying the doors to see if they were locked. Fawcett would be found guilty of an attempt to break and enter, as indicated under section 24(1) of the *Criminal Code*.

An **attempt**, like any crime, requires proof that there was intent to commit the offence, and *actus reus*. The *actus reus* begins at the moment preparation turns into some step toward the commission of the offence. It is the judge who decides (even in trial by jury) when the preparation stage has ended and the attempt stage has begun. Fawcett prepared by buying housebreaking tools and recording the comings and goings of the occupants of the house. Only when he took his first steps toward the actual break-in, did he have the *actus reus* of an attempt. The *mens rea* is demonstrated by this commencement to act and is witnessed by the possession of the housebreaking tools and the recordings. At trial, if the Crown is unable to prove that the offence was committed, but only that an attempt was made, the accused may be convicted of the attempt. If the accused was originally charged with the attempt, but the evidence indicates that the offence was actually committed, the judge may order the accused to be tried for the offence itself.

Conspiracy

An agreement between two or more persons to carry out an unlawful action or to perform a lawful action by unlawful means is termed a **conspiracy**. There must be a serious intention by both parties to carry out the action—jokes or threats not intended to be taken seriously are not considered conspiracy. But if a serious agreement does exist, then it is not necessary to show that any action fulfilled the agreement. The penalty for conspiracy is generally the same as for the offence that was the object of the conspiracy.

Reviewing Your Reading

1. Name and describe the two elements that must exist for a crime to be committed.
2. Describe the concept of onus.
3. *Actus reus* does not always require an action to be committed. Give an example of such a circumstance.
4. Describe the different categories of *mens rea*.
5. Distinguish between general and specific intent.
6. What is motive? With what is it frequently confused?
7. Compare recklessness with wilful blindness.
8. State the two differences between absolute and strict liability offences and those requiring *mens rea*.
9. Distinguish between absolute liability offences and strict liability offences.
10. What is the defence of due diligence?
11. When does an attempt begin?
12. What is a conspiracy?

3.6 *P*ARTIES TO AN OFFENCE

A person who commits an offence, aids a person to commit an offence, or abets a person in committing an offence is defined as a party to an offence under section 21 of the *Criminal Code*.

Aiding or Abetting

Aid means to assist the principal offender in the commission of the crime. **Abet** means to encourage. Two things must be proved before an accused can be convicted of being a party by aiding or abetting. The first is that the accused had knowledge that the

Cribbin met Ginell at a bar. In a washroom, Ginell grabbed Cribbin in the genital area, but Cribbin indicated he was not a homosexual. Later Ginell joined Cribbin and his friends, and the group left to buy more beer. Following an argument, Cribbin, Ginell, Reid, and a woman drove to a deserted road where they drank. Cribbin testified that Ginell touched him on the shoulder and invited him to go for a walk in the woods. In response, Cribbin punched Ginell in the cheek and kicked him in the leg. According to Cribbin, Reid then hit Ginell over the head with a beer bottle. Ginell fell to the ground and Reid punched and kicked him repeatedly. Cribbin tried to stop Reid. When the beating stopped, Reid pulled something out of Ginell's pocket, and the three quickly left. They went shopping with Ginell's credit cards. Although the injuries sustained were not life-threatening, Ginell was abandoned unconscious, and he drowned in his own blood.

Cribbin and Reid were charged with second-degree murder. Reid pleaded guilty, and Cribbin was convicted of manslaughter. The trial judge indicated to the jury that Cribbin could be found guilty of murder simply on the basis of his knowledge of the co-accused's intention to rob the deceased; or, alternatively, Cribbin could be found guilty of murder if he effectively did anything to assist the co-accused in carrying out his intention to rob, even if he did not know of that plan. Cribbin appealed his conviction to the Ontario Court of Appeal. That court indicated that the jury should have been instructed that Cribbin could only be found guilty of murder as Reid's accomplice if he knew of Reid's intention to kill Ginell or to cause him bodily harm that he knew was likely to cause death and if the accused intended to aid or abet the co-accused. As well, Cribbin could be found guilty of murder if the jury was satisfied beyond a reasonable doubt that he formed an intention with Reid to rob the deceased and that Cribbin knew that the commission of murder would be a probable consequence of carrying out the intent to rob. The jury should also have been told that Cribbin could be found guilty of manslaughter as an aider and abetter to the murder committed by Reid.

R. v. Cribbin
(1994)

Ontario Court of Appeal
28 C.R. (4th) 137

1. **Under what circumstances could Cribbin be found guilty of murder as a principal offender?**

2. **Under what circumstances could Cribbin be found guilty of manslaughter as an aider or abetter?**

3. **Based on the facts given, would the jury find Cribbin guilty? If so, of what? Refer specifically to the *actus reus* and *mens rea* requirements of the offence and to the relevant facts.**

other intended to commit an offence. The second is that the accused aided or abetted the other. Mere presence at the scene is not conclusive evidence of aiding or abetting.

Under section 21(2), a person who plans an offence is just as guilty as a person who actually commits the offence. However, a person is not guilty if his or her action is not intended to assist in the commission of an offence.

To counsel or incite someone to commit a criminal act is also an offence. If a person urges a friend to take an unlocked car with the keys in it for a joyride, that person is inciting or urging another to commit an offence. Even if the

CASE

R. v. Goodine
(1993)

New Brunswick
Court of Appeal
141 N.B.R. (2d) 99

One summer afternoon in 1992, Todd Johnston, his girlfriend, Jason Boyd, and the accused Cory Goodine went for a drive. After driving on some country roads near Arthurette, New Brunswick, Johnston stopped the truck and, without warning, shot Boyd in the head with a revolver. He then dragged Boyd's body a short distance and, still holding the revolver, ordered Goodine to "get off the truck and help me because you're in on this, too." Goodine obeyed Johnston's orders to drag the body into the woods and, when the victim moaned, Johnston shot Boyd again in the back of the head. Medical evidence at trial indicated that either shot would have caused Boyd's death.

A few days later, Goodine told two of his friends about the murder and took them to Boyd's body. The next day, the friends reported the incident to the police who then arrested Goodine and charged him with being an accessory after the fact to murder. The accused was acquitted by a jury at trial. The Crown appealed to the Court of Appeal where the Crown's appeal was dismissed.

1. **Why did the Crown appeal the accused's acquittal?**
2. **What is the *actus reus* of accessory after the fact?**
3. **What did Goodine do that caused him to be charged?**
4. **Why was Goodine not charged with aiding and abetting?**
5. **What reasons or defence would Goodine plead to explain his actions?**
6. **Why did the jury acquit Goodine? Do you agree? Why or why not?**

offence is not completely carried out, the inciter is liable to the same penalty as the person who attempted it.

Accessories after the Fact

The *Criminal Code* provides a penalty for a person who is an **accessory after the fact**, that is, someone who helps a person who has committed a crime to escape detention or capture as outlined in section 23 of the *Criminal Code*.

Assisting a person who has committed a crime to escape capture includes providing food, clothing, and shelter to the offender. One exception to this law is the favoured relationship between a legally married couple. A man or a woman cannot be held responsible for assisting in the escape of a spouse and someone escaping with the spouse. It is assumed that legally married part-

ners have committed the offence together. There may be changes in the near future concerning many of the laws governing spouses and their interaction with the law. Many of the current laws were inherited from the common law, where the wife was considered to be one with her husband. It has been suggested that these laws do not reflect current values in our society. Many *Acts* now recognize common-law spouses. It is only a matter of time before an equality challenge is brought under the *Charter* concerning common-law spouses and aspects of criminal law.

At the trial of an accessory, it must be shown that the principal offender committed an offence, either by proof or by entering the conviction of the principal as evidence. Even if the principal offender has not been found guilty, the accessory can still be convicted.

Reviewing Your Reading

1. Referring to section 21(1) of the *Criminal Code*, state who may be a party to an offence.
2. Distinguish between "aid" and "abet."
3. What is the significance of section 21(2) of the *Criminal Code*?
4. State who may be an accessory after the fact.

3.7 OUR CRIMINAL COURT SYSTEM

One objective in recent years has been to establish methods of resolving conflicts between the accused and the state without having a full trial. However, thousands of cases still go to trial each year. The cost of operating the criminal justice system, which is paid for by the taxpayer, is very high. The court structure and court procedure are changing constantly to improve efficiency and reduce costs.

Jurisdiction over the court system is divided between the federal and provincial governments. The *Constitution Act, 1867,* gave the federal government control over criminal law and the procedure to be followed in criminal matters. The federal government was given the right to establish the Supreme Court of Canada and the Federal Court of Canada and to appoint judges to these courts. The various federal and provincial criminal courts are outlined below.

Federal Courts

The Supreme Court of Canada

The Supreme Court of Canada mainly hears appeals, which may be from any provincial Court of Appeal or from the Federal Court of Canada. The court also hears referral cases from governments, where an important principle of law is involved or an injustice has occurred. *Reference Re Milgaard* is an example of a situation of injustice. The permission of the court must be obtained to have an appeal heard by the Supreme Court unless there is a dissenting opinion in the Court of Appeal judgment. Appeal is then one of right.

The Supreme Court of Canada consists of a Chief Justice and eight other judges. At least three of the nine judges on the Supreme Court of Canada must be appointed from the Province of Quebec, while traditionally the other six have been made up of three from Ontario, one from Atlantic Canada, and two from the West.

Not all the judges need to hear a case, but all nine usually attend for important matters. Every case is heard by an odd number of judges, since a majority is essential for a decision. Each decision is recorded in writing, since it provides case law as a precedent for lower courts. In any split decision, one judge is selected to write the majority decision and another to write the dissenting decision. If there is a significant point of law in the appeal, the court will give the reasoning for its decision in detail so that it can be referred to by others in the legal community.

The Federal Court of Canada

The Federal Court of Canada hears all claims against and by the federal government, disputes between the provinces, and matters that fall under federal jurisdiction as specified by the *Constitution Act, 1867*, except criminal matters. It is divided into a trial and appellate division. The latter hears appeals of cases decided in the trial division and of all decisions made by federal boards and commissions, such as the Canada Labour Board.

Provincial Courts

The provinces were given the power of organization and maintenance of the provincial courts. Each province has a Court of Appeal that hears appeals from all of the trial courts and lower courts in the province. The chief justice in each province appoints judges, usually three for each case, to hear the appeals.

Trial Court

Each province also has a trial court of unlimited jurisdiction, called the Supreme Court (Trial Division) or Court of Queen's Bench, which tries the most important criminal cases. Although these are provincial courts, trial court judges are appointed by the federal government.

CASE

Reference Re Milgaard
(1992)

Supreme Court
of Canada
I S.C.R. 866

David Milgaard was found guilty of the murder of Gail Miller in a trial by judge and jury in 1970. He was sentenced to life imprisonment. His conviction was affirmed by the Saskatchewan Court of Appeal, and his request to appeal to the Supreme Court of Canada was dismissed. He was imprisoned. Later, a key witness, Ronald Wilson, recanted part of his testimony. Additional evidence to a confession made by Milgaard and sexual assaults committed by another person brought into question Milgaard's conviction.

In 1991, the Governor General in Council asked the Supreme Court of Canada to review and consider the judicial record of Milgaard's conviction to determine if a miscarriage of justice had occurred. At the hearing, the court heard several witnesses, including Milgaard, who had not testified at trial. Fresh evidence was presented.

The Supreme Court of Canada ruled that the continued conviction of Milgaard constituted a miscarriage of justice. However, it was not satisfied beyond a reasonable doubt that Milgaard was innocent. It recommended that the conviction be quashed and a new trial ordered. It further recommended that if the Attorney General for the Province of Saskatchewan did not wish to pursue a new trial there should not be one.

1. **What function did the Supreme Court of Canada carry out in this case?**
2. **What is fresh evidence?**
3. **On what basis are cases referred to the Supreme Court of Canada?**
4. **Should cases where there is still some possibility that the original accused is guilty have to be retried so that a jury can make a decision based on the facts?**

Provincial Court, Criminal Division

Each province has a Provincial Court, Criminal Division (Territorial Court in the Yukon Territory and Northwest Territories), in which all criminal cases start. For the more serious cases, dates are set for future proceedings. Trials are held by judge alone for the least serious offences and all provincial offences. (A special court in Ontario, the Provincial Offences Court, handles cases involving strictly provincial offences.) The judges in these courts are appointed by the province. Approximately 90 percent of criminal cases are disposed of by this court. The rest go to higher courts.

Other Courts

Each province is at liberty to establish other courts, or arrange its court structure, to hear other specialized matters. Family and youth courts often combine for administrative purposes.

Criminal Courts and Criminal Offences

As noted earlier, summary conviction offences and indictable offences have different trial procedures. These will be examined in more detail in the following chapters. Each also follows a different path through the court system.

Examples of Categories of Indictable Offences

Least Severe	More Severe	Most Severe
Trial procedure similar to summary offences	Accused selects one of three trial procedures	Trial usually before judge and jury
Theft (under $5000)	Manslaughter	Murder
Mischief (under $5000)	Assault	Treason
Fraud (under $5000)	Sexual Assault	Piracy
Driving while disqualified	Weapon Offences	Bribing a judicial official

Regulatory Offences and Summary Offences Procedure

There is a six-month limitation period for the laying of a charge for a summary offence. The accused may send a representative instead of appearing for trial personally. However, the judge can require the accused to appear.

For some quasi-criminal offences under provincial jurisdiction, such as traffic offences and federal and provincial regulatory offences, a court appearance is not usually necessary. The mere signing of a "guilty" plea on the ticket citation is sufficient. However, entering a plea of "not guilty" in such a situation requires a court appearance.

Indictable Offences Procedure

For indictable offences, there is no time limit for the laying of a charge after an offence has been committed. The accused must appear personally in court.

For procedure purposes, indictable offences are divided into three sub-categories, according to the seriousness of the offence. The least serious are treated very much like summary offences. For more serious indictable offences, the accused is allowed to choose the trial procedure to be followed: by a provincial court judge, a higher court judge, or a judge and jury. This middle category—more severe—contains the greatest number of indictable offences, examples are sexual assault and weapons offences. The most serious indictable offences against society are usually tried by judge and jury. These include murder and treason.

Reviewing Your Reading

1. In two columns, summarize the jurisdiction that the federal and provincial governments have over the criminal court system.

2. Identify the two federal courts, and describe the responsibilities of each.

3. Outline the trial and appeal courts that exist in your province.

Will stricter gun control make Canada a safer place?

In Canada, 1.2 million handguns are registered with the government and are classified as restricted weapons. Canadians also own an estimated 6 million rifles and shotguns for which there are no records. Until 1979, there were few restrictions on anyone who wanted to buy and use a rifle or shotgun. In that year, the government altered the gun laws slightly, requiring those who wanted to purchase a rifle or shotgun to obtain a Firearms Acquisition Certificate (FAC). To obtain a FAC, an application had to be completed so that police could check to see if the applicant had a recent criminal record or a history of mental illness. In 1989, after the massacre of 14 women in Montreal, it became more difficult to obtain a FAC. An applicant had to take a gun course to show competence in gun handling and use, and police conducted a more rigorous background check of the applicant. Then, in the early 1990s, the federal government introduced a bill that would control ownership and use of guns in Canada.

On June 13, 1995, the House of Commons voted 192–63 to adopt Bill C-68, a controversial law known as the *Firearms Act*. This law requires all Canadians, by the year 2001, to obtain a government licence called a Firearms Possession Certificate for any gun they own. The law also requires gun owners to pay $10 to register the make, model, and serial number of each firearm in their possession within five years from January 1, 1998. The maximum penalty for failing to register firearms can result in a 10-year prison sentence. This licensing and registration of firearms will give authorities a computerized record of all gun owners and the weapons in their possession. In effect, this law puts rifles and shotguns in the same category as handguns. The *Firearms Act* also sets a mandatory minimum four-year prison term for anyone convicted of using a gun in a serious crime, such as murder, robbery, or sexual assault.

On One Side

Opponents to this legislation see it as a threat to gun ownership in Canada. Hunters, target shooters, and gun collectors feel threatened. The National Firearms Association (100 000 members) maintains that the new law will make it more difficult for Canadians to defend themselves and their property. The association claims that criminals, who buy their guns illegally, will be encouraged to commit more crime because the new law puts unfair restrictions on law-abiding citizens. They see gun control as good news for criminals and bad news for everyone else.

Other critics view gun ownership as a democratic right and argue that the government has no moral or legal right to limit gun use. They claim that since firearms are used in only 6 percent of adult crimes, restricting the rights of all Canadians is unjustified.

Compulsory registration sparks the fiercest opposition. Gun registration, they argue, is the first step toward the banning of guns altogether, the final step being government confiscation of all registered firearms.

GUNS R'NT US

ALLAN ROCK

BILL C-68 PASSED

Corrigan TORONTO STAR

The Toronto Star Syndicate

On the Other Side

Supporters of the bill include police chiefs, women's organizations, victims' groups, experts in suicide prevention, and emergency room physicians. They believe that stricter gun controls will make Canada a safer place. They note that firearms are responsible for 1400 deaths in Canada each year. Of these, 75 percent are suicides and 15 percent are homicides. Accidents, legal intervention by police, and undetermined reasons make up the balance. Firearms are also a leading cause of death among teens. Tougher gun laws, which will make it more difficult to own guns, may reduce impulsive suicides in this age group.

The most ardent supporters of gun control would prefer the legislation go even further and ban the ownership and use of guns altogether.

They believe that if it were illegal to own guns, there would be a dramatic drop in gun-related crimes and Canada would be a safer country. They point to the high rate of crime and violence in the United States where citizens own an estimated 212 million firearms.

The Bottom Line

Bill C-68 was approved by the Senate on November 23, 1995, after a vote of 64–28 (with seven abstentions). Angry representatives of the firearms community vowed revenge in the next federal election. Clearly, gun control will remain a controversial issue among Canadians.

Will gun control make Canada a safer place or is it a restriction of individual freedom? You be the judge!

1. **Why is the government passing stricter gun laws?**

2. **Is Bill C-68 too strict? Does it violate the civil liberties of Canadians?**

3. **What arguments are presented by both the opponents and supporters of stricter gun laws? Which are most valid in your opinion?**

4. **Should guns be banned totally in Canada? If so, are there particular groups that should be exempt from such a ban?**

CHAPTER REVIEW

Reviewing Key Terms

For each of the following statements, indicate the key term being defined:

a) the thought or feeling that makes one act

b) to actively assist another in the commission of a crime

c) careless of the consequences of one's act

d) the agreement of two or more to do an unlawful act, or to do a lawful act by unlawful means

e) an act that becomes a crime at the moment when preparation turns into the actual attempt

f) offence that may be tried summarily or by indictment

g) a wrong specified under a provincial statute

h) to encourage another in the commission of an offence

i) an unlawful act that is committed with the intent to commit a further illegal action

j) the wrongful action

Exploring Legal Concepts

1. Summarize your views on how criminal law protects our society.

2. Bertha Wilson, a former justice of the Supreme Court of Canada, said shortly after her appointment: "The law responds to changes in society; it seldom initiates them." Discuss this statement in relation to any two criminal laws that have changed in recent years.

3. Make a list of all your activities since you awoke this morning. For each, indicate what criminal or quasi-criminal laws governed each action.

4. Outline reasons why Parliament should be the source of change in Canadian criminal law and not the judiciary.

5. Socrates defined the essential qualities of a judge: "Four things belong to a judge: to hear courteously; to answer wisely; to consider soberly; and to decide impartially." Many people believe that because of the social status of a judge, he or she cannot decide impartially. Comment on this statement.

6. In your opinion, how does the law give order and predictability to our society? Support your answer with examples.

7. In a diverse society such as Canada's, discussion frequently occurs as to whether our laws should have a more federal focus, or whether each province should have jurisdiction over its laws. Outline the advantages and disadvantages to having a common *Criminal Code* for all of Canada.

8. You have agreed to tutor a friend on some areas of law. To assist you in your tutoring, prepare an organizer that would illustrate the differences between each of the items in the following pairs:

a) *mens rea* and *actus reus*

b) specific intent and general intent

c) strict liability and absolute liability

Applying Legal Concepts

1. *R. v. Oommen* (1994) Supreme Court of Canada 2 S.C.R. 507

   In the early morning hours, Oommen killed Beaton as she lay sleeping on a mattress in his apartment. He fired 9 to 13 shots at her from a semi-automatic repeating rifle. The evidence disclosed no rational motive for the killing.

   For a number of years Oommen had been suffering from a mental disorder. As a result, he harboured false and fixed beliefs that he was the butt of conspiracies and situations that endangered him. His disorder had led to hospitalization on a number of occasions.

   At the time of the killing, Oommen believed that the members of a local union were conspiring to destroy him. He became fixated with the notion that his assailants and enemies had commissioned Beaton to kill him. On the evening of the killing he became convinced that members of the conspiracy had surrounded his apartment building with the intention of moving in on him and killing him. He felt that he was obliged to kill Beaton to prevent her from killing him.

   At the trial, Oommen relied on the defence of mental disorder. Psychiatrists testified that Oommen possessed the general capacity to distinguish right from wrong and would know that to kill a person is wrong but that, on the night of the murder, his delusion deprived him of that capacity and led him to believe that killing was necessary and justified under the circumstances as he perceived them. The trial judge rejected the defence of mental disorder, concluding that in view of Oommen's general capacity to know right from wrong, he was not relieved from criminal responsibility. Oommen was convicted of second-degree murder and sentenced to life imprisonment without eligibility of parole for ten years.

   • **What is the *mens rea* requirement of second-degree murder? Did Oommen possess this *mens rea*?**

   • **Did either his motive or his delusion have any effect on your decision? Why or why not?**

2. *R. v. Kirkness* (1990) Supreme Court of Canada 3 S.C.R. 74

   Kirkness had been drinking with his friend Snowbird when they agreed to break into a house at Snowbird's suggestion. Kirkness used the handle of a garden tool to gain entry through a window of the house of an 83-year-old woman. He then let Snowbird in through the door and gave the broken handle to Snowbird as a weapon. Snowbird proceeded to sexually assault and kill the woman. Kirkness was told to leave the room when the assault began. He remained across the hall during the assault. He placed a chair against the outside door of the house and occupied himself with stealing various things. Snowbird dragged the unconscious woman into the hallway and began to choke her. Kirkness asked him "not to do that because he was going to kill her." Snowbird then suffocated the victim.

   • **Is Kirkness a party to the murder? Why or why not?**

3. *R. v. Mills* (1992) Manitoba Court of Appeal 77 C.C.C. (3d) 318

Mills was employed as a grave digger at a cemetery. He used a backhoe to refill the graves. After about 18 months on the job, his procedure for refilling the graves changed. He attempted to complete the job faster by using the downward pressure of the bucket on the backhoe to tamp down the earth. As a result, many of the coffins collapsed. Mills was charged with offering indignities to human remains.

- **Did Mills possess the necessary intent to be found guilty of the charge?**

4. *R. v. Courtaulds Fibres Canada* (1992) Ontario Court (Provincial Division) 76 C.C.C. (3d) 68

Courtaulds Fibres Canada was charged under Ontario's *Environmental Protection Act* and the *Water Resources Act* for 13 spills of chemicals into the St. Lawrence River. The spills occurred as a result of human error or failure of equipment in an aging part of Courtaulds' plant. Mr. Drumer, a chemical engineer, was appointed 11 months before the first of the spills. He took immediate steps to educate the staff concerning environmental matters and began to upgrade the equipment in the plant. Courtaulds had been in discussion with the Ministry of the Environment concerning environmental concerns.

- **Did Courtaulds show due diligence?**

5. *R. v. Jackson* (1977) Ontario Court of Appeal 35 C.C.C. (2d) 331

Deralis was an admitted trafficker in narcotics. Jackson, a friend who lived in the same apartment building as Deralis, agreed to store 3 kilograms of marijuana in a hollow plastic kitchen stool for him. Jackson did it because he knew that Deralis had a record, whereas he did not, and he would be helping Deralis from being detected. The police found the marijuana. Jackson was found guilty of possession, but the Crown appealed to obtain a conviction of trafficking, stating that Jackson had aided and abetted Deralis in his trafficking.

- **Should Jackson be found guilty of trafficking for aiding and abetting Deralis?**

6. *R. v. Wilkins* (1964) Ontario Court of Appeal 44 C.R. 375

A police officer parked his motorcycle, but left it running, while he went to write a ticket. Wilkins drove the motorcycle a short distance to play a joke on the officer. He was charged with the theft of the motorcycle. Theft requires the intent to convert an object to one's own use.

- **What was Wilkins' motive? Can he be found guilty of theft?**

7. *R. v. Paquette* (1977) Supreme Court of Canada 2 S.C.R. 189

Paquette was charged with murder because of a death caused by Simard in the course of a robbery by Simard and Clermont. Paquette was not present during the robbery or the murder. In his statement to the police, Paquette stated that he had been forced at gunpoint to drive the other accused to the scene of the robbery. He drove around the block while they committed the offence, and on his return the two tried unsuccessfully to get into the car.

The Crown based its case against Paquette on section 21(2) of the *Criminal Code.* Section 17 of the *Code* states that a person who commits an offence under compulsion by threat of immediate death is excused from liability unless the offence committed is robbery or murder.

- **Should Paquette be found guilty of murder under section 21(2), or released under Section 17?**

8. *R. v. Nickel City Transport (Sudbury) Ltd.* (1993) Ontario Court of Appeal 82 C.C.C. (3d) 541

   Nickel City Transport (Sudbury) Ltd. was charged with carrying a load on its triple-axle truck in excess of the permissible weight as stated in the *Highway Traffic Act* of Ontario. The company had loaded the cargo on the trailer and sent a driver to visually inspect the load to determine whether the weight was distributed properly. No scales were available. Evidence indicated that it is impossible for a visual inspection to tell whether one axle of a three-axle tractor trailer is overloaded.

   The appeal court found that: (a) the applicable section of the *Highway Traffic Act* does not create an absolute prohibition but allows for exceptions to the prescribed limits; (b) the regulations were complicated and imposed an onerous duty on commercial vehicle operators; (c) the legislation, while important, is not of paramount importance to public safety; (d) the punishments are not trivial.

   - **Should the offence be one of strict liability or absolute liability? Explain.**

   - **If the offence is one of strict liability, did the accused provide sufficient evidence to show due diligence?**

Extending Legal Concepts

1. Now that you have completed this chapter, review the opening article and Something to Think About. Have your answers or opinions changed? Why or why not?

2. With the class, brainstorm a list of questions to elicit people's attitudes toward the causes of crime. Prepare a survey and distribute it to the people in your school and/or community. Collect the survey forms. Prepare a written report that summarizes the results of your data and the attitudes of those you surveyed. Include any visuals that will help to summarize your data.

3. From a newspaper, collect five criminal law cases that have not yet gone to trial.

   a) For each case, indicate the offence committed, the *mens rea,* and the *actus reus* of the offence. Consult the *Criminal Code of Canada* to find the maximum penalty for the offence.

   b) For each case, indicate the evidence that you think the Crown and the defence will present.

   c) Indicate whether you think that the accused will be found guilty or not guilty at trial. Give reasons for your decision.

4. With a partner, brainstorm a list of offences for which the accused is the only person affected by the offence. For each offence that you list, indicate whether or not you think it should be a crime. Compare your findings with another pair of partners. As a class, list the offences that each group has obtained. Discuss whether or not they should be offences. Discuss, negotiate, and attempt to obtain a group consensus.

5. Using a copy of the *Criminal Code of Canada*, find five laws that have changed in the last 10 years. For each of the laws, explain how the law reflects a change in the values of Canadians.

6. Using reference materials in your resource centre, including CD-ROM and the Internet, obtain current information on the court structure of your province, and the costs of the justice system in Canada. Write a summary of your findings, and create a poster to display your information.

Researching an Issue

Supreme Court Appointments

Debates concerning the appointment of judges to the Supreme Court of Canada have received media attention, especially since the Canadian *Charter of Rights and Freedoms* was made law in 1982. At the present time, the judges are appointed by the prime minister. In the United States, judges are appointed by the president but they must go through a hearing process to be approved by Congress.

Statement

Judges appointed to the Supreme Court of Canada should have to go through a hearing process before their appointment is confirmed.

Point

Since the judges of the Supreme Court of Canada make significant decisions that reflect the values of our society, their values should be put before the Canadian people before they are appointed.

Counterpoint

The personal lives of judges appointed to the Supreme Court of Canada should not be dragged through the media before their appointment.

- **With a partner, research this issue and reflect on your findings.**
- **Prepare points on this statement that could be used for a class debate.**
- **Discuss your findings with others in your class.**

BRINGING THE ACCUSED TO TRIAL

These are the key terms introduced in this chapter:

adjournment

appearance notice

arrest

bail

detention

duty counsel

forensic science

habeas corpus

information

line-up

material witness

plea bargain

polygraph test

preliminary hearing

prima facie

recognizance with surety

recognizance without surety

search

search warrant

show-cause hearing

summons

surety

telewarrant

undertaking

venue

warrant for arrest

Learning Outcomes

At the end of this chapter, you will be able to

1. list the steps in a legal arrest;
2. outline the rights of the arresting person;
3. outline the rights of the arrested person;
4. outline the requirements for a legal search;
5. describe the release procedures that can be used instead of arrest, and after arrest;
6. state and describe the steps taken before the trial.

10-year Court Battle Puts Justice on Trial

The acquittal of Guy Paul Morin by the Ontario Court of Appeal leaves behind a justice system wrestling with serious questions about its own guilt.

A three-judge panel acquitted Morin on Monday of killing nine-year-old Christine Jessop in 1984 after both prosecutors and defence lawyers cited the results of DNA tests on semen found on the youngster's underwear.

Ontario Attorney General Marion Boyd has called a public inquiry into the case.

Morin, 35, told reporters he did not kill Jessop and that DNA testing completed Friday proves that once and for all.

"They accused an innocent person for the last 10 years, falsely," he said. Morin said now it's time for prosecutors and police to explain themselves to the public.

"This case was handled horribly. It's pretty pathetic. I think I was just like the fall guy, the person to just put the blame on and appease the public's worries," Morin said.

Boyd said there has to be a public airing of issues surrounding the treatment of Morin in order to shore up public confidence in the justice system. Durham Regional Police and prosecutors have been harshly criticized for their handling of the case.

Boyd appointed former Quebec Superior Court Chief Justice Alan Gold to head the inquiry, noting his first job will be to talk about compensation with Morin and his lawyers.

"While obviously money cannot wipe away the years of pain and turmoil caused to Mr. Morin and his family, I hope Mr. Gold will have the details of a fair and just financial compensation package worked out with Mr. Morin and his lawyer as soon as possible," Boyd said.

Morin said he couldn't imagine any amount of money "could help me or my family for the suffering over the 10 years."

From: Richard Brennan, "10-year court battle puts justice on trial." *The Ottawa Citizen*, January 24, 1995. Reprinted with permission—*The Windsor Star.*

Something to Think About

- **Should the police investigate themselves when there is evidence of mishandling of a case?**
- **Should the state have to compensate someone who is found not guilty due to a case being mishandled?**
- **Should suspects have to provide body samples for DNA testing?**

4.1 INTRODUCTION

Friction between police officers and the public often occurs at the time of arrest, particularly when the accused is innocent or confused. Experience and intuition may lead the police to suspect that an offence was committed. In enforcing their authority to make an arrest, the police may rely on having "reasonable grounds" to believe that an offence has been committed. The accused, on the other hand, naturally wants to make the fullest use of his or her rights available under the law. Thus, conflict may arise.

Many Canadians confuse their rights with those of American citizens. In fact, there are significant differences. Canada's law tries to protect Canadian society by balancing the investigation and arrest rights granted to the police with the *Charter* right of the accused to be considered innocent until proven guilty according to law in a fair and public hearing. As you read this chapter, try to evaluate whether or not this balance truly exists. Make yourself aware of your rights as a citizen and of the rights of law enforcement agents.

4.2 ARREST

Suspicion is not enough cause for an arrest to be made. An officer must determine that an offence has been committed and have reasonable grounds to believe that the suspect committed the offence.

The police have three options available in the apprehension and charging of a suspect. They can issue an appearance notice, arrest the suspect, or obtain a warrant for arrest.

Appearance Notice

For summary conviction offences, hybrid offences, and less serious indictable offences, the police may issue an **appearance notice**. This document indicates the offence with which the accused is being charged, and gives the time and place of his or her court appearance. The accused must sign the document and be given a copy. The officer will then swear an **information** before a judge or justice. This document states that the officer believes on reasonable grounds that the offence was committed by the person who was given the appearance notice.

Arrest

For more serious indictable offences, the police will **arrest** the suspect. The arresting officer must

1. identify himself or herself;
2. advise the accused that he or she is under arrest;
3. inform the accused of the charge(s);
4. touch the accused to signify that he or she is legally in custody.

The purpose of arrest is to lay a charge, preserve evidence, and prevent the accused from committing a further offence. Any officer can arrest without a warrant if there are reasonable grounds to believe that a person has committed an indictable offence, is committing an indictable or a summary offence, or is about to commit an indictable offence. Note that police powers differ depending on whether an indictable or a summary offence is involved. After arrest, the officer must swear an information before a judge or justice.

If the accused resists arrest, a police officer can use as much force as is necessary to prevent an escape. The police are criminally liable for the use of unnecessary force. Even force that is likely to cause death or grievous bodily harm can be used if it protects others from death or bodily harm. In 1994, a bill passed in Parliament provided for the use of deadly force by a peace officer or anyone lawfully assisting the officer in the following situations, when

- the behaviour of a suspect poses a threat of serious harm or death;
- the suspect flees in order to escape arrest;
- no other less violent means exists to prevent escape.

The intent is to ensure that "police response to the threat posed by a fleeing suspect is in proportion to the seriousness of that threat and in keeping with current public values."

Warrant for Arrest

If the accused flees, the police have a third option. The officer can swear an information before a judge or justice, who can then issue a **summons**—a document that requires the accused to appear in court at a certain time and place. A summons is delivered to the accused by a sheriff or a deputy.

If the officer can demonstrate that the accused will not appear in court voluntarily, a **warrant for arrest** will be issued. It names or describes the accused, sets out the offence, and orders that the accused be arrested forthwith and brought before a justice. The warrant is valid within the territorial jurisdiction of the person or court issuing it until the accused is arrested. In the case of immediate pursuit, the warrant is valid everywhere in Canada. A Canada-wide warrant can also be obtained if the police believe that the suspect has escaped to another province.

A judge or justice who does not believe that there are reasonable grounds to believe that the accused has committed the offence can refuse to issue either a summons or a warrant. The most important criterion for laying a charge is "reasonable grounds." However, what is "reasonable" is very often difficult to determine.

**R. v.
Macooh**

(1993)

**Supreme Court
of Canada
2 S.C.R. 802**

An officer saw Macooh drive through a stop sign, a summary offence, at 3:45 a.m. in Spirit River, Alberta. The officer put the cruiser's emergency signals on and followed him. Macooh accelerated, drove through two more stop signs, stopped at an apartment building, and ran toward the back door. The officer yelled at him to stop, but Macooh entered the building. The officer followed him to an apartment and called out at the door, identifying himself as a member of the RCMP. Receiving no answer, he entered the apartment and found Macooh in bed.

Macooh was advised that he was under arrest for failing to stop for a police officer. Macooh, who appeared to be impaired, resisted the officer. He was arrested, but refused a demand for a breath sample. The charges against Macooh were impaired driving, failing to stop for a peace officer, failing to provide a breath sample, and assaulting a peace officer with intent to resist arrest.

At trial, the provincial court judge ruled that the officer's entry into the dwelling house while in hot pursuit of Macooh for a provincial offence was unlawful and that, therefore, his arrest within the premises was unlawful. In addition, since the entry was illegal, all the evidence obtained due to the entry was not admitted. Macooh relied on sections 7 and 9 of the *Charter* as part of his defence. (See Appendix.) Macooh was acquitted on all charges. The summary conviction appeal judge upheld the acquittals.

The Alberta Court of Appeal and the Supreme Court of Canada both ruled that the right of arrest on private property during immediate pursuit was not limited to indictable offences, if the offender can be arrested without a warrant. Macooh's arrest was therefore lawful. The court indicated that immediate or hot pursuit must be continuous pursuit conducted with reasonable diligence so that the pursuit and capture along with the commission of the offence may be considered as forming part of a single transaction. He was therefore convicted.

1. **What indications are there that the officer was in "hot pursuit"?**

2. **What rights do police who are in hot pursuit have to enter a dwelling? Does it matter if the offence is summary or indictable?**

3. **Should the police have more search powers if the offence is indictable? Why or why not?**

4. **Does a warrantless police officer have the right to arrest an individual who fails to stop when requested to do so?**

5. **What rights does Macooh have under sections 7 and 9 of the *Charter*? What did the arresting officer do that limited these rights?**

6. **What arguments would support the officer's position that the limitation of section 7 and 9 rights was reasonable in this situation?**

7. **What reasons can you give for allowing a peace officer to enter the premises when in "hot pursuit"?**

8. **What precedent did the court set in this decision?**

Arrest by Citizens

Citizens can make an arrest under certain circumstances, according to section 494 of the *Criminal Code.*

494.

(1) Any one may arrest without warrant
   (a) a person whom he finds committing an indictable offence; or
   (b) a person who, on reasonable grounds, he believes
       (i) has committed a criminal offence, and
       (ii) is escaping from and freshly pursued by persons who have lawful authority to arrest that person.
(2) Any one who is
   (a) the owner or a person in lawful possession of property, or
   (b) a person authorized by the owner or by a person in lawful possession of property, may arrest without warrant a person whom he finds committing a criminal offence on or in relation to that property.

This gives store detectives, private detectives, and citizens the authority to make arrests. However, citizens' arrests are unusual. A citizen must know whether an offence has been committed or, in the case of a person being chased, whether the peace officer has a legal authority to arrest. The person being arrested may also resist, and the citizen may then find the incident escalates into a physically threatening situation. If the citizen does make an arrest and finds a mistake was made, there can be unpleasant results. The accused may sue the citizen for false arrest or assault.

Citizens may also become involved in preventing crime and/or making an arrest if they are commandeered by an officer to give assistance, as set out in the *Criminal Code.*

The table below summarizes the rights of an officer and a citizen in making arrests in various circumstances.

Reviewing Your Reading

1. Outline in detail the three options available to police when it is believed that an offence has been committed.

2. What is the purpose of an arrest?

3. a) How much force may an officer use when making an arrest?

   b) What liability is associated with the use of excessive force?

4. a) In what circumstances may an officer make an arrest?

   b) What could happen if these circumstances do not exist?

5. Describe the circumstances under which a citizen (a) may make an arrest and (b) is obliged to help make an arrest.

Summaries of a Peace Officer's and a Citizen's Right of Arrest

Summary of Right of Arrest by a Peace Officer

Time of Commission of Offence	ARREST WITHOUT WARRANT* BY A PEACE OFFICER FOR:	
	Summary Offence	*Indictable Offence*
Committed in the past.	May not arrest.	May arrest.
Observed being committed.	May arrest.	May arrest.
About to be committed.	May not arrest.	May arrest.
*Arrest may be made at any time with a warrant.		

Summary of Right of Arrest by a Citizen

Time of Commission of Offence	ARREST BY A CITIZEN FOR:	
	Summary Offence	*Indictable Offence*
Committed in the past.	May arrest, if suspect is immediately pursued by a person with right to arrest.	
Observed being committed.	May not arrest.*	May arrest.
About to be committed.	May not arrest.	May not arrest.
*A citizen may arrest for a summary offence on his or her property if the commission of the offence is observed.		

4.3 DUTIES OF POLICE OFFICERS

The duties of police officers are specified in the *Act* that establishes the force. In Canada, there are three levels of policing: federal, provincial, and municipal. The Royal Canadian Mounted Police (RCMP) is the federal, or national, police force. The provincial police forces in Ontario and Quebec are the Ontario Provincial Police (OPP) and the Sûreté du Québec (SQ), respectively. In all other provinces the RCMP also serve as the provincial police force. Municipal police, such as the Moose Jaw Police Department, enforce municipal laws. The RCMP, the OPP in Ontario, and the SQ in Quebec carry out the duties of the municipal police in localities that do not have their own municipal forces.

Police Conduct

Police officers are responsible for their conduct when carrying out their duties and can be charged under criminal law or sued under civil law for breach of conduct. Each province has a board that reviews complaints from citizens concerning police conduct. In recent years there have been many well-publicized cases admonishing police officers for their conduct. However, police officers have to make frequent value judgments, some of them life threatening, often with little time to evaluate their options. Section 25 of the *Criminal Code* states that a peace officer "is, if he acts on reasonable grounds, justified in doing what he is required or authorized to do and in using as much force as is necessary for that purpose."

The Police Log

A police officer, usually the first person at a crime scene, is responsible for bringing law and order to the situation. The officer must keep an accurate log of what was witnessed. The log, what is remembered, and the conduct of the officer in making an arrest and interrogating the accused are frequently the most important factors in determining the acceptance of evidence by the court.

Reviewing Your Reading

1. What are the three levels of police in Canada?
2. What general power does a police officer have?
3. Why is it important that a police officer keep a good log?

4.4 CITIZENS' RIGHTS

The legal rights of citizens who are detained and or arrested have been clarified in sections 7–11 (see Appendix) of the *Canadian Charter of Rights and Freedoms* enacted under the *Constitution Act, 1982*. Nevertheless, the meaning of many clauses remains open to court interpretation.

Rights on Being Detained

To understand the rights of citizens upon detention or arrest, it is necessary to know the difference between these two terms. The four steps that are necessary for a legal arrest were identified on p. 89. According to the Supreme Court of Canada in *R. v. Therens* (1985), **detention** occurs when a person is stopped by someone, usually a police officer or a store detective, and "submits or acquiesces in the deprivation of liberty and reasonably believes that the choice to do otherwise does not exist."

Thus, if a person is asked to go to the police station and consents, believing that there is no other choice but to submit, detention exists. The person must be informed of the reasons for the detention and, more importantly, must be advised about retaining counsel. A person who goes voluntarily, however, is not being detained and need not be so advised.

A 1993 decision of the Ontario Court of Appeal in *R. v. Simpson* brought into question the right of the police to detain.

Did You Know

Computer software has been developed to carry out data-base searches for possible suspects. When a person is arrested, he or she is video-taped, and details about the individual and the case are entered in a data base.

Dated 5-17-1993. By permission of Johnny Hart and Creators Syndicate, Inc.

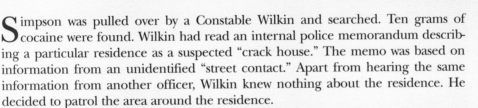

CASE

S impson was pulled over by a Constable Wilkin and searched. Ten grams of
cocaine were found. Wilkin had read an internal police memorandum describing a particular residence as a suspected "crack house." The memo was based on
information from an unidentified "street contact." Apart from hearing the same
information from another officer, Wilkin knew nothing about the residence. He
decided to patrol the area around the residence.

Wilkin saw a woman get out of a car in the driveway, enter the residence, and
return to the vehicle with Simpson. Wilkin did not know either the woman or
Simpson and had no information about either of them. He indicated at trial that he
intended to pull them over for investigative purposes. After following the vehicle for
a short distance, Wilkin directed the vehicle to pull over. While talking to Simpson,
he noticed a bulge in his front pant pocket, reached out and touched it, and felt a
"hard lump." When asked what was in his pocket, Simpson replied, "Nothing."
Wilkin instructed Simpson to remove the object from his pocket "very carefully."
Instead, Simpson removed it very quickly as if trying to throw something away. A
struggle ensued, and Wilkin removed a small plastic bag containing cocaine from
Simpson's hand. The trial judge ruled that Wilkin had a legitimate reason to
embark on the investigative course he undertook, a right to stop the vehicle, and
the right to insist that Simpson empty his pocket. He found Simpson guilty. Simpson
appealed to the Ontario Court of Appeal on the basis that his right not to be arbitrarily detained was infringed.

The Ontario Court of Appeal stated that the detention was a direct result of the
stopping of the motor vehicle. If the officer had no authority to stop the vehicle,
then the detention may have been unlawful and possibly arbitrary. The officer's purpose in effecting the stop is relevant to the lawfulness. Wilkin admitted that his decision to stop the motor vehicle had nothing to do with the enforcement of laws relating to the operation of motor vehicles, nor to the *Narcotic Control Act*. He stopped the
car to seek confirmation about reported activities at the alleged "crack house." By
questioning the occupants and looking into the vehicle, Wilkins hoped to establish
grounds to arrest either or both of the occupants for drug-related offences.

R. v. Simpson
(1993)

**Ontario Court
of Appeal
79 C.C.C. (3d) 482**

The court noted that Wilkin considered anyone who attended the residence subject to detention and questioning by the police. "This dangerous and erroneous perception of the reach of police powers must be emphatically rejected. Judicial acquiescence in such conduct by the reception of evidence obtained through that conduct would bring the administration of justice into disrepute." The court acquitted Simpson.

1. **What does it mean to be "detained"? Was Simpson being detained? Did Wilkin have the right to stop Simpson's vehicle? Why or why not?**

2. **What are the rights of a person under detention?**

3. **Under what circumstances can the police search without a warrant? Did the police have the right to search Simpson?**

4. **Section 24(2) of the *Charter* provides that when "evidence was obtained in a manner that infringed or denied any rights ... guaranteed by this *Charter*, the evidence shall be excluded if ... the admission of it ... would bring the administration of justice into disrepute." What does the phrase "bring into disrepute" mean to you? Do you believe that the behaviour of the police in this situation could bring the administration of justice into disrepute?**

5. **The Ontario Court of Appeal refers to a "dangerous and erroneous perception of the reach of police powers." What is this perception? Why might that perception be "dangerous"?**

6. **Does this decision tend to add to or diminish the search powers of the police? Explain.**

Cooperating with Police

An informed and responsible citizen may want to cooperate with police. An innocent person who is forthcoming often shows his or her innocence by immediately volunteering information. This can save time and money. Despite the presumption of innocence, police do tend to form conclusions on the basis of an individual's behaviour when questioned.

If, however, an officer persists in questioning, detains, or attempts to search a reluctant individual, that person should immediately demand counsel, secure the officer's badge number, and collect names of witnesses.

A citizen who is illegally detained may bring an action for false arrest or detention against the police officer or file a complaint with the police commission. A citizen is allowed to use as much force as necessary to resist an illegal arrest or search, but the force used must be reasonable.

Rights on Being Arrested

A person has the right to be informed promptly of the reason for the arrest and the right to retain counsel. The Supreme Court of Canada has held that this includes being advised of the availability of **duty counsel**, who is a lawyer on duty at the court, and legal aid. The accused can refuse to answer any questions, except those necessary to complete the charge—name, address, occupation, and date of birth—until he or she has obtained counsel.

The police are required to caution the accused concerning these rights by stating, "You have the right to retain and instruct legal counsel without delay. You have the right to telephone any lawyer that you wish. You also have the right to free legal advice from a legal aid lawyer. If you are charged with an offence, you can contact the Legal Aid Plan for legal assistance. Do you understand? Do you wish to telephone a lawyer now?"

The accused must be told of the right in a manner that he or she can understand, and at a time when he or she is capable of understanding and appreciating the right. If the person is intoxicated, the officer must wait until he or she is sober. An officer must find means of having the

The accused, S.G.J. was charged with uttering [passing as genuine] counterfeit money and having in his possession without lawful justification four $100 counterfeit bills. S.G.J. had asked Mr. Bentsclaw, a store clerk employed by Bonanza Books, if he could pay for his items with a $100 bill. Mr. Bentsclaw, who had previously worked for a bank, was trained to spot "funny money." He refused the bill and told S.G.J. that it was not a good bill. S.G.J. did not seem upset and told him that he had got it from his employer, and then left the store.

Bentsclaw phoned the police immediately, giving them an accurate description of S.G.J. The police spotted S.G.J. at once, sitting at a bus stop a few blocks from the book store.

The police told S.G.J. that he was being investigated for counterfeit money. When S.G.J. stood, someone at the bus stop asked him if the wallet sitting on the bench was his. S.G.J. acknowledged that it was. The wallet contained four $100 bills which were clearly counterfeit. After being given the *Charter* warning, S.G.J. said, "I found them, I just found them." One police officer asked whether he knew the bills were phoney. S.G.J. did not respond.

S.G.J. gave evidence that he was in a nightclub when he found a wallet containing the four $100 bills on the top of a urinal. There was no I.D., so he kept the bills. When arrested by police, S.G.J. said that he answered "yes" to the officer's question whether he knew the bills were counterfeit and said, "I didn't know that the bills were counterfeit until the clerk told me." He said it was his intention to check them out with his mother. The officer had no recollection of this conversation.

The court ruled that S.G.J. was not guilty of uttering counterfeit money but was guilty of possession of counterfeit money. The judge indicated that S.G.J. should have taken the opportunity to show the police the counterfeit bills rather than to try to avoid detection. S.G.J. appealed the decision to the British Columbia Court of Appeal.

R. v. J. (S.G.)
(1992)

British Columbia Court of Appeal 77 C.C.C. (3d) 472

1. **What is uttering of counterfeit money?**
2. **For S.G.J. to be acquitted of uttering counterfeit money, what must the judge find concerning the evidence about the bills that S.G.J. gave?**
3. **What evidence is there that S.G.J. tried to conceal the fact that he knew the money was counterfeit?**
4. **Could S.G.J. be found guilty if he was in possession of the money not knowing that it was counterfeit?**
5. **What might S.G.J. have done to immediately acknowledge that he did not know the bills were counterfeit?**

rights explained to a person who lacks mental capacity or who speaks a language other than English or French. Once the accused decides to take advantage of the right to counsel, the police must stop questioning, provide access to a telephone, and allow the accused to make as many calls as are reasonable. The accused must be given privacy to discuss the matter with counsel. The accused could, of course, waive the right to counsel and answer questions.

Police Rights

The police have the right to **search** the accused upon arrest to locate evidence relating to the charge, or to locate any item that may assist the accused to escape custody or cause violence. Any possession can be taken—even items not related to the crime. The police also have the right to take the accused to the police station. Here, a more thorough search is likely to take place, possibly even a strip and skin-frisk, or a body cavity search or probe where drugs are involved. Such involved searches must be justified and done by an officer of the same gender as the accused. The police may wish to fingerprint and photograph the accused at this time, or later. They can only do so, however, if the offence charged is indictable.

The accused does not have to participate in a **line-up**, or show-up, or take a **polygraph test** (lie detector test), or give samples of blood, urine, or breath (except in the case of an impaired driving offence). He or she should, however, consult with counsel about these procedures. It actually might be to the advantage of the accused to permit evidence to be collected. For instance, when a murder has been committed under the influence of alcohol or drugs, the extent of the influence might affect the outcome of the trial. If the accused is greatly influenced by alcohol or drugs, this fact may aid his or her defence.

CASE

R. v. Bartle
(1994)

Supreme Court of Canada
3 S.C.R. 172

Bartle was arrested for impaired driving after failing a roadside breath test in the early hours of a Saturday morning. The officer read Bartle his rights from a pre-printed caution card that mentioned the availability of legal aid. The officer did not indicate that free and immediate preliminary legal advice was available from duty counsel, who could be reached by calling a toll-free number printed on the caution card. Bartle made an incriminating statement shortly after the caution. At the police station Bartle was asked twice whether he wanted to call a lawyer, but he declined. No mention was made of the toll-free number.

At trial, Bartle testified that he thought that he could only contact a lawyer during normal working hours, and that he had indicated to a constable that he did not know who to call at that time of night. The constable contradicted this evidence, stating that Bartle only indicated that he didn't want to contact a lawyer. Bartle was convicted at trial. That conviction was overturned on appeal to the Ontario Court, General Division, but restored by the Court of Appeal. Bartle appealed to the Supreme Court of Canada where he was acquitted. The Court stated: "The fact that a detainee merely indicates that he or she knows his or her rights will not, by itself, provide a reasonable basis for believing that the detainee in fact understands their full extent or the means by which they can be implemented." Since Bartle was not clearly and fully informed of his rights at the outset, he could not make an informed choice and decision about whether or not to contact counsel. A detainee must be given information about access to legal aid and to duty counsel.

1. **What duties do the police have at the time of arrest concerning informing detainees of their rights?**

2. **Why does a detained person need to be fully informed of his or her rights?**

3. **What principle was established by this case?**

Reviewing Your Reading

1. With reference to the *Charter*, summarize the rights of a citizen (a) on arrest or detention and (b) when charged with an offence.

2. For each of the rights of the police, state the corresponding right of a citizen: (a) the right to question before arrest; (b) the right to search a person before arrest; (c) the right to question after arrest; (d) the right to search a person after arrest.

3. Distinguish between arrest and detention.

4. Why is it sometimes advantageous for a suspect to give the police information or to cooperate, or to let them collect evidence?

5. What rights do the police have concerning the arrested person in each of the following: fingerprinting, requesting a line-up, a polygraph test, or a blood sample?

4.5 SEARCH LAWS

The police may want to search the residence of the accused to find evidence related to the charge. To do so they must have a **search warrant**, a legal document issued by the court to increase police authority.

Obtaining the Search Warrant

To apply for a search warrant, an officer must swear before a justice or judge that an offence has been committed and that there are reasonable grounds to believe that evidence of illegal activity is on the premises. The officer then outlines the grounds to the court. If accepted, a search warrant will be issued. If the information about the evidence being on the premises was received from an informer, the officer must outline to the court why the informer is reliable before a warrant will be issued. Since the *Charter* guarantees the right to be secure against unreasonable search or seizure, many warrants have been challenged in court as being defective.

Telewarrants, introduced in 1985, can be obtained by telephone or other telecommunication means, such as by fax. This process allows for the warrant to be obtained quickly where there is a likelihood that evidence may be destroyed. At the end of 1995, telewarrants were in use in all provinces and territories except Nova Scotia, the Northwest Territories, Ontario, Prince Edward Island, and Saskatchewan.

Using the Search Warrant

The warrant can be used to search a residence only on the date indicated and between the hours of six in the morning and nine at night, unless otherwise stated. The search can only involve searching those areas and items outlined in the warrant itself. Only the items shown on the warrant can be seized, unless other illegal items used in or obtained by the commission of a crime are found. These items, however, must be found while carrying out the terms of the warrant, or be in plain view—the police cannot go beyond the terms of the warrant in hopes of finding anything that will justify the laying of a charge. The items seized can be kept for a period of up to three months, or for a longer period if they are needed as evidence at trial.

Search Laws and Rules

When using the search warrant, the police should demand to be admitted. If permission is refused, or no one is home, the police are entitled to break into the premises. They are liable for any excessive force used. Anyone who answers the door can ask the police to show a copy of the search warrant before allowing them entry. If the document is not correct in every detail, entrance can be refused. Once inside, the police can only search a person after arrest, unless they believe that the person possesses illegal drugs, liquor, or weapons.

The 1985 revisions to the *Criminal Code* addressed many concerns about search laws. Because of adverse publicity directed at occupants of searched premises, the *Code* made it a summary offence to publish the location of any place searched, or the names of the occupants, unless a charge was laid or the occupants gave their permission. As well, special rules now apply to documents seized from a lawyer that fall under the solicitor-client privilege. Provisions have also been introduced for the swift return of any items seized that are not needed as evidence.

R. v. Ruiz
(1991)

**New Brunswick
Court of Appeal
10 C.R. (4th) 34**

Ruiz was convicted of conspiring with Zanabria, Manzano-Bustamante, Rodriguez, and Hernandez to break two prisoners out of jail. The prisoners were Colombian nationals awaiting trial on charges of importing a large quantity of cocaine into Canada. Mrs. Thibodeau, who operated a convenience store, noticed three vehicles enter the yard of her store. She saw four men get out of the vehicles. One of the men who entered the store spoke in a "strange . . . unknown" language. Ruiz entered and asked for a public telephone and a map of Edmundston. Mrs. Thibodeau saw the occupants move clothing from one vehicle to another. She became suspicious and made a note of the vehicles and their licence numbers. She telephoned the RCMP to tell them that these men were suspicious.

The same afternoon the three vehicles were stopped and searched. The officers who stopped the van driven by Ruiz saw what they thought were the handles of bolt cutters and a butcher knife or machete inside the van. The three vehicles contained handguns, rifles, ammunition, explosives, backpacks, rain gear, passports for the two prisoners, a generator, a rubber raft, and an electric grinder. The men were arrested, all pleading guilty except for Ruiz. He testified that he was not aware of the activities of his three companions and had only been hired to act as a translator. Ruiz was convicted, however. He appealed his nine-year sentence, claiming that the search of his vehicle was illegal since it was warrantless and the suspicions of Thibodeau were not sufficient to permit the police to conduct the search. Thus the evidence so obtained should not have been admitted.

The New Brunswick Court of Appeal noted that the plain view doctrine permits, within strict limits, the introduction into evidence of items obtained without a search warrant. First, the initial intrusion must be justified. Second, the incriminating evidence must be discovered inadvertently. Third, it must have been immediately apparent to the police that the items observed were evidence of a crime, contraband, or otherwise subject to seizure. The court dismissed Ruiz's appeal.

1. **What were the police looking for when the three vehicles were initially stopped and searched?**

2. **What reason did they have to believe they would find evidence in those vehicles? Was that reason sufficient to stop and look into the vehicles?**

3. **What was in "plain view" when the vehicles were stopped? What did the police believe it was? Did they come upon this evidence "inadvertently"?**

4. **Why was it immediately apparent to the police that the visible material was evidence of a crime?**

5. **Was the evidence referred to in question 3 sufficient, in your view, to form a reasonable basis for a warrantless search?**

6. **What test did the Court of Appeal apply to determine whether or not the evidence was admissible?**

In 1987, James Henry Wise was a prime suspect in two murders, and a suspect in four other murders near the rural community of Monkland, Ontario. Police thought the acts may have been committed by a serial killer, though no one was ever charged. In addition to the murders, police had received a tape of an anonymous telephone call threatening more killings. The voice sounded similar to Wise's. They obtained a warrant to search Wise's home and vehicle, but found nothing. His vehicle had been towed to the local police department for the search to be carried out. While there, a tracking device, a beeper, was installed in the back seat to locate the vehicle when visual surveillance failed.

A month later, the police used the beeper and established surveillance on a vehicle similar to Wise's which was in the area. While surveilling, police heard a Bell Canada microwave communication tower, valued at over two million dollars, crash to the ground. They then saw Wise's vehicle leave a nearby field. The police again obtained a search warrant for the vehicle and found melted pieces of metal, consistent with the metal guy wires of the communications tower. Wise was charged with mischief to property over $1000 [now over $5000].

The trial judge acquitted Wise, holding that there had been a violation of his *Charter* right to protection against unreasonable search and seizure. He ruled that none of the evidence obtained directly or indirectly as a result of the use of the electronic tracking device should be admitted. The Crown appealed, conceding the violation of Wise's *Charter* rights. The Ontario Court of Appeal allowed the appeal on the basis that admission of the evidence would not bring the administration of justice into disrepute under section 24(2) of the *Charter*. It set aside the acquittal and ordered a new trial.

Wise appealed to the Supreme Court of Canada, which agreed with the Ontario Court of Appeal. The Court ruled that Wise's right was violated since the beeper invaded his reasonable expectation of privacy, and that there had been no legal authorization for installing it. However, it also ruled that the search was only minimally intrusive as privacy expectations in a vehicle are not equal to those in one's house. The tracking device was merely an extension of physical surveillance and was attached to Wise's vehicle, not to Wise. The police had a valid belief that they were protecting the public given the murders in the area and that Wise was a suspect. The court also indicated that it would be preferable if the installation of tracking devices and the subsequent monitoring of vehicles were controlled by legislation.

Mr. Justice La Forest of the Supreme Court of Canada, dissented in the ruling. He said, "In a free society the police cannot be permitted to conduct the sort of intrusive search carried on in this case based on mere suspicion, even strong suspicion. That is clearly unacceptable in a free society . . . The long-term consequences of admitting evidence obtained in circumstances like this on the integrity of our system of justice outweighed the harm done by this accused being acquitted. The end did not justify the means."

R. v. Wise
(1992)

Supreme Court of Canada
11 C.R. (4th) 253

1. **Do you think that the police should be able to attach beepers to vehicles (a) at all, or (b) with a warrant?**
2. **Why do you think that the Supreme Court of Canada indicated that the matter should be covered by legislation?**
3. **The Court compared invasion of privacy using the beeper to that of using a video camera or an electronic monitor that intercepts private communications. Do you think that there can be different degrees of invasion of privacy for legal purposes? Refer specifically to an individual's expectation of privacy in various locations, such as a movie theatre, an office, an automobile, and a bedroom.**
4. **Explain what Mr. Justice La Forest means when he refers to the "long-term consequences of admitting evidence obtained in circumstances like this on the integrity of our system of justice."**
5. **In this case, the individual's expectation of privacy as protected by section 8 of the *Charter* must be weighed against "the harm done by this accused being acquitted." Which side do you believe should be given more consideration?**

In 1993, the *Criminal Code* was amended to give police access to the use of more modern technologies in search. Video surveillance, tracking devices, and telephone recorders can now be used with the permission of a judge, so long as they do not interfere with the person's bodily integrity or the person's property. The judge may include terms and conditions that he or she considers advisable. In cases of video surveillance where the person has reasonable expectation of privacy, the warrant must contain terms and conditions to ensure that the privacy of the person is respected.

Exceptions to Search Laws

The major areas of exceptions to search laws have to do with drugs, liquor, and illegal weapons.

Under the *Narcotic Control Act*, any place that is not a residence, as well as the persons inside it, can be searched without a warrant if there is a reasonable belief that the building contains illegal drugs, or the people in the building possess narcotics. However, this should be done only when it is impracticable to obtain a search warrant. The Supreme Court of Canada has also ruled that because of the need for surprise entry in some situations involving drugs, it is not necessary to always give prior announcement of entry. To search a *residence*, a search warrant must be obtained.

Under provincial liquor laws, an automobile can be searched without a warrant if a police officer believes it contains illegal liquor that will be used for an unlawful purpose. The officer can also search land but must have a warrant to search a dwelling. Whether or not a person inside a dwelling can be searched varies from province to province.

The *Criminal Code* provides that any place except a dwelling can be searched without a warrant for illegal weapons. This includes a person or vehicle. The police can seize any restricted weapon if a registration certificate or a possession licence cannot be produced, or any firearm in the possession of a person under 16 years of age who fails to produce a possession permit. A prohibited weapon can, of course, be seized at any time.

Other laws in addition to the *Criminal Code* give government-appointed officers the right to search without a warrant under certain circumstances. The *Fish and Game Laws*, for example, may permit an officer to search cars or land for violations of the law without a warrant. The *Food and Drug Act* also gives officers the right to seize items prescribed in the *Act*.

The following case illustrates the procedures used to get evidence of cultivation of marijuana.

G rant was stopped at a routine roadblock check near Victoria. His truck was found to contain several items consistent with a marijuana-growing operation. The police were told by a reliable informant that Grant had been on his way to set up a marijuana operation when he was stopped. The police conducted two warrantless searches of the perimeter of Grant's residence. They noticed covered windows on the lower floor, heard what they described as the sound of electric motors or fans emanating from inside the residence, and noted two air vents that looked recently installed. They also determined through inquiries of the public utility that electrical consumption at Grant's residence had been unusually high. The police obtained search warrants based on the information collected to search Grant's home and an apartment in which he was living. They seized 80 marijuana plants, growing equipment, drug-related paraphernalia, and documents.

Grant was charged with unlawful cultivation of marijuana and possession of marijuana for the purposes of trafficking. The trial judge acquitted the accused and the Court of Appeal for British Columbia dismissed the Crown's appeal. The ruling indicated that Grant's rights had been violated under section 8 of the *Charter.* The Supreme Court of Canada allowed the Crown's appeal. The Court indicated that the police should have obtained a warrant to conduct the warrantless perimeter searches, as there was no reason to believe that evidence was going to be lost, destroyed, or removed. The officers had acted in good faith. They believed a warrantless perimeter search was valid. Also, there was other evidence that provided valid grounds for the issuance of a search warrant.

In a similar case, *R. v. Kokesch* (1990) Supreme Court of Canada 3 S.C.R. 3, police entered onto Kokesch's property without a warrant and conducted a perimeter search. The search was made without reasonable and probable grounds to believe that an offence had been or was being committed on the property. After the perimeter search, the officers used the information to obtain a search warrant. They seized a number of marijuana plants. Based on the evidence, Kokesch was charged with possession of marijuana for the purpose of trafficking and with cultivating marijuana. The trial judge excluded the evidence, but the Court of Appeal allowed the Crown's appeal and ordered a new trial. It ruled that the perimeter search was not unreasonable, and even if so, the admission of the evidence would not bring the administration of justice into disrepute. Kokesch appealed to the Supreme Court of Canada.

1. **What evidence was there, irrespective of that obtained from the perimeter search, that Grant was engaged in cultivating marijuana?**
2. **Was a warrant necessary for the perimeter search?**
3. **Why did the Court uphold the conviction even though the perimeter search violated Grant's rights?**
4. **Is there any distinction between the facts of the Grant case and the Kokesch case? Based on the information given, how do you think the Supreme Court of Canada ruled in Kokesch's case?**

R. v. Grant
(1993)

Supreme Court of Canada
3 S.C.R. 222

Reviewing Your Reading

1. Define "search warrant," and then describe how one is obtained and used.

2. Discuss three provisions concerning search laws that were included in the 1985 *Criminal Code* amendments.

3. What is a telewarrant?

4. What restrictions are there on the use of video surveillance equipment used under authority of a warrant?

5. Describe the major exceptions to search laws.

4.6 RELEASE PROCEDURES

Most accused persons are not kept locked up at the time of an incident. There are a variety of methods by which the accused can be released. The officer at the scene or the officer in charge of a lockup may release a person charged with a summary conviction offence, a hybrid offence, or an indictable offence, carrying a penalty of five years or less. Of course, if there are grounds to believe that further offences will be committed, or the accused will not appear in court, the accused may be confined until a bail hearing takes place.

For indictable offences carrying a penalty of more than five years' imprisonment, the accused must be brought before a justice within 24 hours, or as soon as possible, for what is referred to as a bail hearing. **Bail** refers to the amount of money or other security that is paid to insure the appearance of the accused at later proceedings. Once bail is posted the accused is released. The *Criminal Code* was amended in 1985 to give less of an emphasis on paying money as a condition of release. If a person pleads not guilty, the justice must release the accused on his or her promise to appear, unless the prosecution can show cause as to why the accused should be detained. Cause must be either that the accused will not attend court or is a threat to the protection and safety of the public.

Judicial Release Procedures

If released, the accused is required to sign an **undertaking**, and to fulfill any of its conditions imposed by the court. These conditions might prevent the accused from communicating with witnesses, require him or her to report to a police station weekly, forbid association with former friends, or require the accused to do whatever the court feels is in his or her best interests. The accused may possibly enter into a **recognizance with surety** or **recognizance without surety**. A recognizance is a document which states that the person recognizes that it is alleged that he or she committed an offence, and that he or she is to attend court at a specified time. A **surety** is a person who is willing to make a payment on behalf of the accused. By signing the recognizance, the surety acknowledges that if the accused does not show up for trial an amount of money will have to be paid, or the deposit forfeited. The accused may also be released without surety on his or her own recognizance, having paid a sum of money.

Show Cause for Release

The accused has the right to a **show-cause hearing**, so that he or she may be released pending trial. In the situations listed below, it is up to the accused to show cause why he or she should *not* be kept in custody until trial where

- the accused is charged with an indictable offence committed while on release for another indictable offence;
- the accused is charged with an indictable offence and is not a Canadian resident;
- the accused is charged with the offence of failing to appear, or with breach of a condition of a release order;
- the charge is importing, possession for the purpose of trafficking, or trafficking a narcotic.

Release Denied

If the accused is not released by the justice, he or she is entitled to appeal the decision to a higher court. If for any reason the accused is kept without being arrested, or is denied a bail hearing, he or she can ask for a writ of **habeas corpus**. Such a writ requires that the body, the accused, be brought before the court to seek a remedy for a right that he or she feels is being denied. A judge rules on the application. Meanwhile, the accused is kept in a local detention centre, awaiting trial.

Every eight days, the accused is brought before a judge and given the opportunity to disclose any mistreatment. The accused can waive this right to appear and can go directly to the next trial date. To decrease the cost and risk involved in transporting the person in custody from the detention centre to court and back every eight days, authorities are piloting a two-way video-conferencing link between detention centres and courthouses. This system allows the inmate to hear the court proceedings and be seen on a television monitor by courtroom officials. The inmate can also communicate privately by phone with his or her lawyer.

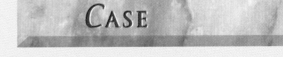

CASE

R. v. Morales
(1992)

Supreme Court of Canada
3 S.C.R. 711

Maximo Morales was charged with trafficking in narcotics, possession of narcotics for the purpose of trafficking, importing narcotics, and conspiracy to import narcotics, contrary to sections 4 and 5 of the *Narcotic Control Act*. He was alleged to have participated in a major network to import cocaine. At the time of his arrest, he was awaiting trial for assault with a weapon, an indictable offence. Morales was denied bail and ordered detained in custody until trial.

Normally bail is granted unless the prosecution can show cause as to why the accused should be detained. However, in the situation where the accused is charged with an indictable offence committed while on release for another indictable offence, or where the charge is importing, possession for the purpose of trafficking, or trafficking a narcotic, the onus is on the accused to show why his or her detention in custody is not justified.

Morales believed that being detained violated his section 11(e) *Charter* right not to be denied reasonable bail without just cause. He applied to the Quebec Superior Court for a review of the bail order, challenging the validity of the *Criminal Code* sections that put the onus on him to show why he should not be detained. Morales was released on order of the Quebec Superior Court, subject to a number of conditions. The court ruled that pre-trial detention is only justified where it is established that the accused will not appear for trial or would represent a danger to public safety if released. The Crown appealed that decision to the Supreme Court of Canada, which ruled that the *Criminal Code* sections that placed the onus on Morales were valid.

1. **What is "reverse onus"?**
2. **Section 11(d) of the *Charter* requires that one be presumed innocent until proven guilty according to law in a fair and public hearing. Did the reverse onus requirement unreasonably limit this right of Morales?**
3. **Why would the *Criminal Code* provide that in the situation described above the accused must show why he should not be detained?**
4. **Do you think Morales' section 9 *Charter* right not to be arbitrarily detained was violated?**

Fingerprints and Photographs

If an offence is indictable and the accused is released, he or she may be required to be fingerprinted and photographed before release, if these things were not done at the time of arrest.

The right of the accused to have fingerprint and photograph records removed from police files, if he or she is subsequently acquitted, is not stated in statute form. This has been left to the discretion of each police force. Similarly, if someone is mistakenly arrested and fingerprinted, it *is* difficult to have the file destroyed.

Protection of Society

The aforementioned discussion of the rights of the accused and the procedures available to law enforcers reveals an attempt to balance the rights of the individual against the need to protect society. The accused has rights concerning search, but where the law has recognized serious matters, such as the abuse of laws relating to drugs, alcohol, and weapons, these rights are reduced. A similar balance can be observed for both arrest and release procedures. The police may arrest a person who is believed on reasonable grounds to have committed an offence. However, the accused has the right to a show-cause hearing.

Maintaining the balance of rights between citizens and society should be a matter of concern for all Canadians. A distortion in favour of the individual could lead to increased crime; a distortion in favour of the state could lead to police rule. It is up to both the public and police to reduce the possibility of conflict. The public can do this by intelligent application of its rights. The police can do this by intelligent application of their duty to society.

Reviewing Your Reading

1. **Explain why the presumption of innocence requires that those who have been arrested be released, pending trial.**

2. **Explain in what situations, and by what means, the police can release an accused, pending trial.**

3. **Under what circumstances does the accused bear the burden of proof instead of the Crown?**

4.7 Awaiting Trial

The accused should consult a lawyer and disclose everything that pertains to the case, so that the lawyer can prepare the best defence possible. The preparations will include reading the relevant section or sections of the law that apply to the offence, interviewing witnesses, examining precedents, and studying legal texts. The accused has the right to make suggestions to the lawyer. If there is serious disagreement, the accused can change lawyers, or the lawyer can withdraw.

Legal Aid

The accused should also get an estimate of the lawyer's fees before the trial. If he or she cannot afford a lawyer, legal aid may be available, depending on whether the accused meets the requirements of the province. Once awarded legal aid, a person can choose his or her lawyer. Duty counsels, and also legal aid lawyers, are usually available at the court for consultation or to assist the accused with the legal aid application. Frequently an accused has not had an opportunity to contact a lawyer, or does not know his or her legal rights because it is the first time dealing with the legal system.

Disclosure

The *Criminal Code* makes it mandatory for the Crown prosecutor and the accused to meet prior to a trial by judge and jury. The Crown is required to disclose its evidence, so that the accused has a full understanding of the Crown's case and can prepare a defence. Disclosure promotes a fair trial and reduces the time, and therefore the cost, of conducting it. The defence may also be able to put forth evidence or arguments that prove to the Crown that it does not have a case. The defence has the right to request examination of the Crown's evidence and exhibits, whether they favour the defence's case or not. Emphasis has been placed on this procedure in recent years to reduce the time and cost of trials. In non-jury trials, the accused or the Crown may ask for such a meeting for the same purpose.

Collecting Evidence

Before a criminal trial, both the Crown and the defence are likely to examine available exhibits to obtain evidence for their cases. In so doing, they will make use of the findings of **forensic science**—the application of medicine and other sciences to legal problems. The term is perhaps used most often in connection with doing an autopsy to determine the cause of death.

Forensic scientists can find clues in samples of blood and other bodily fluids, teeth, bones, hair, fingerprints, handwriting, clothing fibres, and other items.

Recent technology has led to many advances in forensic science. For instance, fingerprinting now involves optical scanners and computers, rather than ink and paper. A computer can be used to compare fingerprints to a vast number of other fingerprints on file, reducing to a few hours a task that could take months.

Another procedure makes use of the fact that every cell of a particular human being contains a unique form of the complex chemical DNA (deoxyribonucleic acid). The uniqueness of each person's DNA makes possible the technique of DNA matching. This is a powerful tool. It allows

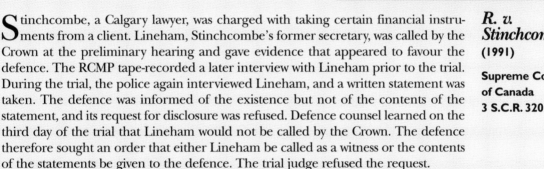

CASE

R. v. Stinchcombe
(1991)

Supreme Court of Canada
3 S.C.R. 320

Stinchcombe, a Calgary lawyer, was charged with taking certain financial instruments from a client. Lineham, Stinchcombe's former secretary, was called by the Crown at the preliminary hearing and gave evidence that appeared to favour the defence. The RCMP tape-recorded a later interview with Lineham prior to the trial. During the trial, the police again interviewed Lineham, and a written statement was taken. The defence was informed of the existence but not of the contents of the statement, and its request for disclosure was refused. Defence counsel learned on the third day of the trial that Lineham would not be called by the Crown. The defence therefore sought an order that either Lineham be called as a witness or the contents of the statements be given to the defence. The trial judge refused the request.

Stinchcombe was convicted of breach of trust and fraud. The Alberta Court of Appeal dismissed his appeal. The Supreme Court of Canada allowed his appeal and ordered a new trial. The Court ruled that the Crown has a legal duty to disclose all relevant information to the defence. "The fruits of the investigation which are in its possession are not the property of the Crown for use in securing a conviction but the property of the public to be used to ensure that justice is done . . . The Crown's discretion [to disclose] is reviewable by the trial judge, who should be guided by the general principle that information should not be withheld if there is a reasonable possibility that this will impair the right of the accused to make full answer and defence."

1. **What is disclosure?**
2. **Why must the Crown make full disclosure to the defence?**
3. **Can you think of circumstances where the Crown would not have to disclose information to the defence?**
4. **What must the defence do to obtain disclosure if the Crown is not cooperating?**

the Crown to enter into evidence a DNA match, or the defence to show that there is no match between the accused and evidence collected at the scene. Other identification techniques, such as fingerprinting and the analysis of blood and semen samples, are not positive—they merely indicate a possibility. Because of the significance of DNA matching as evidence, the *Criminal Code* was amended in 1995 to permit police to obtain samples of bodily substances by way of a warrant from a person who is reasonably believed to have been a party to certain designated *Criminal Code* offences.

Court Appearances

As indicated earlier, the first court appearance for those who are arrested and not released is a show-cause hearing. The second appearance is either to set a trial date or to ask for an **adjournment**, which puts the matter over to a later date and gives the accused time to obtain legal advice.

At the second appearance, a provincial court judge will indicate in which court the case will be tried. The three possibilities are determined by the offence:

1. Offences over which a provincial court has absolute authority. These include all summary conviction offences and indictable offences listed in section 553 of the *Criminal Code* which include theft, fraud, mischief, and keeping a bawdy-house. The accused will likely receive a remand.

2. Offences that can be tried only by a superior court of the province. These are listed in section 469 of the *Code* and include treason, piracy, murder, and conspiracy to commit any of these offences. The provincial court judge will set a date for a preliminary hearing.

3. For all other offences, the accused can elect to be tried by a provincial court judge without a jury, or tried in higher court by either a judge without a jury, or a judge and jury. If the accused chooses the lower court, the process follows that of the first possibility outlined above. If the accused chooses the higher court, the process follows that of the second possibility.

The Preliminary Hearing

The **preliminary hearing** enables the provincial court judge to decide whether there is sufficient evidence to proceed with a trial in a higher court. If there is not, the accused will be discharged, and the charges dropped. If there is sufficient evidence, the trial date is established.

At the preliminary hearing, the Crown presents some of its evidence. The Crown prosecutor has only to make a *prima facie* case; that is, present enough evidence to convince the judge that a reasonable jury could find the accused person guilty on the evidence available. It is not necessary at this stage to prove that the accused is guilty beyond a reasonable doubt.

THEY SAY I HAVE MY FATHER'S EYES...

BUT THAT WAS BACK BEFORE DNA EVIDENCE...

SO THE CHARGES WERE DROPPED.

Stillman, 17 years old, was found guilty of murdering a 14-year-old girl. He was the last person seen with the victim. Prior to his arrest, Stillman had given different stories as to when he had last seen her and to explain his unusual appearance several hours later. When the girl's body was found, it was obvious that she had been sexually assaulted. Stillman was arrested and consulted with a lawyer. The lawyer presented the police with a letter indicating that Stillman had been advised not to consent to providing any body samples, including hair and teeth impressions, which the police wanted, and not to give any statements without a lawyer being present.

As soon as counsel departed, the police obtained hair samples and proceeded to interview the accused for an hour, during which time they attempted to persuade Stillman to give a statement. Later, the accused was brought to a washroom by an officer where he used a tissue to blow his nose. The tissue, containing mucous, was seized by the police. Stillman was brought before Youth Court and released.

The hair and mucous samples were then subjected to DNA analysis and were matched to semen found in the girl's body. Stillman was rearrested. Without his consent, a dentist took an impression of his teeth. The impression was compared with a bite mark on the body of the deceased. An expert indicated that they matched. More hair samples were also taken as were a saliva sample and swabs from his mouth cavity. At trial, the judge held that Stillman's right to protection against unreasonable search and seizure was violated in respect to all the items except the tissue, but that the evidence should not be excluded under section 24(2) of the *Charter.* He based his decision on a ruling given by the Supreme Court of Canada in *R. v. Collins* (1987). In that decision the Court stated 10 factors that it had considered in determining whether the evidence should be excluded:

1. What kind of evidence was obtained? Real evidence, such as the tissue, would probably be admitted, self-incriminating or not.

2. What *Charter* right was infringed?

3. Was the infringement of the *Charter* right serious or was it merely of a technical nature?

4. Was the violation deliberate, flagrant, or was it committed in good faith?

5. Did the violation occur in circumstances of urgency or necessity?

6. Were other investigating techniques available?

7. Would this evidence have been obtained in any event?

8. Is the offence serious?

9. Is the evidence necessary to substantiate the charge?

10. Are other remedies available?

The New Brunswick Court of Appeal dismissed Stillman's appeal. At the end of 1995, his further appeal was before the Supreme Court of Canada.

R. v. Stillman
(1995)

New Brunswick Court of Appeal 97 C.C.C. (3d) 164

1. **Was there legal authority for the seizure of the swabs, samples of hairs, tissue, and teeth impressions?**
2. **In your opinion, was the violation of Stillman's rights serious enough that the evidence obtained by police should be excluded as evidence?**
3. **In your opinion, would the admission of the evidence in this case condone the police action and therefore send a message to other police officers that such action is acceptable?**
4. **Analyze each of the 10 factors that the Supreme Court had considered for excluding evidence to the seizure of (a) the hair and (b) the tissue. Indicate why you believe the seizure does or does not fulfill the criteria.**

The defence need not call evidence at the preliminary hearing but can cross-examine Crown witnesses. All evidence is recorded and may be referred to at trial to attack the credibility of a witness who changes his or her story. It is also available if a witness later refuses to testify, absconds, or dies.

The accused has the right to waive a preliminary hearing and go directly to trial. As of 1995, the Minister of Justice was conducting an ongoing study into the need for preliminary hearings. Frequently, disclosure of the evidence to the defence results in a guilty plea. It is possible that increased disclosure of evidence by the Crown before the preliminary hearing would eliminate the need for preliminary hearings.

Pretrial Motions

A number of motions may be made before a trial to alter the set procedure.

- Adjournment. A motion for adjournment (delay) may be sought because a material witness is absent. A **material witness** is one whose evidence will have a major bearing on the decision made in the case.
- Change of venue. If the accused is unlikely to receive a fair trial because of media reporting of the case, a motion may be made for a change of **venue** (the location of the trial).
- Inspection and testing. The accused also has the right to move for the inspection or testing of certain evidence or exhibits that the Crown may have.

- Quash or amend. A motion may be made to quash or amend an indictment on a technicality; it may not have specified the time, place, or date of the offence.
- Admissibility of evidence. *Charter* motions may be brought to determine whether certain evidence can be presented at the trial.
- Separate trial. A motion for a separate trial may be made where a person has been charged together with other persons, or for more than one offence.

Plea Bargaining

Before trial, the defence attorney may ask the client if he or she wishes to **plea bargain**. The lawyer may feel the evidence against the accused is very compelling and, therefore, propose that the accused plead guilty to a lesser charge in the hope of receiving a lesser sentence. A guilty plea to a lesser charge benefits the court as well, saving both time and costs, makes it unnecessary to select a jury, and frees the courts for other cases.

The proposal is brought before the judge, who examines the suggested sentence possibilities, and either accepts or rejects the proposal. In *R. v. Burlingham* (1994) the Supreme Court of Canada ruled that the Crown or police cannot enter into a plea bargain without the participation of defence counsel, unless the accused expressly waives that right. By this decision, the Court was extending and reinforcing the *Charter* right to retain and instruct counsel without delay.

Disadvantages

Plea bargaining is not formally recognized in the *Criminal Code*. In a plea bargain, the accused gives up the right to a fair public hearing in court, where he or she may receive a verdict of "not guilty." Moreover, if the plea bargain is rejected, any evidence disclosed during the negotiations can be used at trial. This may weaken the position of the accused.

Plea bargaining is often regarded as compromising justice. Negotiations are conducted in private, out of the public eye. The 1993 plea bargain that resulted in a 12-year sentence for Karla Homolka has led many to question the validity of this process. Homolka was sentenced before the public became aware of many of the gruesome facts that were revealed during the trial of her ex-husband Paul Bernardo. By court order, testimony in her case could not be reported until his trial was complete.

Advantages

Without plea bargaining, the court system would be strangled by the number of cases going through the full trial procedure. Justice is served to the extent that the Crown obtains a conviction, and the accused is penalized, though not to the maximum. Plea bargaining has also been seen as beneficial where the Crown has recognized that a victim or victim's family is suffering greatly as a result of the offence and would suffer trauma if forced to take the witness stand.

Reviewing Your Reading

1. Describe the relationship between client and lawyer.

2. a) Define "forensic science."
   b) Name some items from which forensic scientists can obtain clues about a crime.

3. a) Under what circumstances can a judge issue a warrant for the obtaining of a sample of a body fluid for DNA testing?
   b) What three body samples can be obtained under a warrant?

4. a) Distinguish between the first appearance of an accused who has been kept in custody and an accused who has been released.
   b) On what basis does the *Criminal Code* establish the court in which a case will be tried?

5. Give the purpose of a preliminary hearing and discuss what happens at this time.

6. Name five pretrial motions that an accused may make.

7. a) What is plea bargaining?
   b) What advantage may it have for (i) the accused and (ii) the Crown?

ISSUE

Should a suspect be forced to provide samples for DNA testing?

Deoxyribonucleic acid (DNA) contains the genetic code that governs life. DNA is a powerful form of genetic fingerprinting. The DNA is extracted from an individual's cells and, after a series of manipulations, an image is made that is unique to that individual. The chances of any two individuals, except identical twins, having the same DNA fingerprint is about one in ten billion. Since its discovery in 1984, DNA matching has been used over 1000 times in Canadian courts. Even very small traces of blood, bone, hair, saliva, or semen left at the scene of the crime contain DNA. Perhaps the most publicized use of DNA was to exonerate Guy Paul Morin who had been convicted of murdering nine-year-old Christine Jessop.

Police forces consider DNA the biggest crime-solving breakthrough of the century. DNA tests help them solve crimes more effectively and in many cases eliminate suspects. Indeed, police have lobbied for legislation giving them the right to take samples from violent suspects and store them in a central data bank.

In 1995, the federal government drafted a bill that would permit police officers to take blood, hair, or saliva samples from uncooperative suspects of violent crimes. It was passed unanimously and received royal assent on July 13, 1995. The bill provides a legislative framework to regulate DNA procedure. In August 1995, the Justice Minister announced plans to introduce another statute in the fall that would establish a data bank of DNA samples.

Guy Paul Morin

On One Side

Canadians who fear for their safety and advocates of victims' rights consider the legislation that allows police officers to take DNA samples from suspects of violent crimes a victory. Indeed, a 1995 public opinion survey shows that 88 percent of Canadians support the use of DNA in criminal trials. Those who support the new law believe that the rights of suspects are protected because the new law includes the following safeguards:

- police must have reasonable grounds and obtain a warrant from a provincial judge before samples are taken;
- a trained person must obtain the samples from the suspect;
- if the testing exonerates the suspect, if the accused is acquitted, or if the charges are withdrawn or stayed, the DNA sample and the results must be destroyed;
- the samples must be used for a specific offence.

Also, they feel that since the purpose of DNA evidence is to determine the guilt or innocence of the suspect, there should be no argument.

On the Other Side

The critics of the 1995 DNA law argue that it infringes upon the *Charter of Rights and Freedoms*. They feel that the individual's right to protection from unreasonable search and seizure is violated when a suspect is forced to provide samples for DNA testing against his or her will. All citizens, they insist, have the right to due process. It is the state's responsibility to assemble a compelling body of evidence before it invades the privacy of the individual. Critics contend that taking DNA samples to prove guilt or innocence is akin to tapping telephones, opening mail, or searching homes to obtain evidence that proves guilt or innocence.

Moreover, controversy surrounds the testing itself. Scientists can never say with absolute certainty that the samples are from the same DNA; they can only make a statement of probability. Even that probability can be questioned. The two principal methods—the original technique and a simplified faster system—produce different statistical data. One method might show that one person in a billion is likely to have the same genetic profile of the suspect, whereas the other might indicate only one in a thousand. Critics feel more work needs to be done to improve the reliability of testing. They fear that juries may be overwhelmed by positive scientific evidence of DNA tests and fail to consider other evidence that points to the innocence of accused persons, which could lead to the conviction of innocent people.

The Bottom Line

There is no doubt that DNA tests are a powerful tool in police investigations. However, should suspects be forced to provide samples for testing against their wishes? Or should the rights of the individual outweigh those of society? You be the judge!

1. **What is DNA? Why has it become so important an issue in the Canadian justice system?**

2. **What safeguards have been built into the new DNA law to protect individual rights? Are they sufficient?**

3. **What criticisms are made of the new DNA law?**

4. **State and explain your position on DNA testing.**

CHAPTER REVIEW

Reviewing Key Terms

For each of the following statements, indicate the key term being defined:

a) a machine that measures changes in the blood pressure, respiration, and pulse rate to indicate whether the truth is being told

b) to put a trial off to a later date

c) a lawyer available to help an accused at the time of arrest or first appearance

d) a document signed wherein the person recognizes that he or she is alleged to have committed an offence and is required to appear in court

e) a person who has significant evidence that few others can give

f) a written complaint, made under oath, stating that there is reason to believe that a person has committed a criminal offence

g) a meeting to determine if there is sufficient evidence to justify a trial

h) a meeting wherein the Crown must show reasons why the accused should be detained pending trial

Exploring Legal Concepts

1. A police officer was demoted for failing to meet quotas for laying charges. The officer was expected to lay four *Criminal Code* charges, three liquor-licence charges, and five radar-related traffic charges each month. Also, during each 48-hour work week, he was required to lay five traffic charges, issue four warnings, and conduct various duties concerning crime prevention and public relations. Should police officers have a quota system? Explain.

2. Police services in most jurisdictions do not have the right to strike as do most other groups in society. Police and their employers are forced to go to binding arbitration to solve labour disputes. In your opinion, should police have the right to strike? Why or why not?

3. The media frequently have photographs or videotapes of persons who are committing offences. Should the media have to turn over these items to the police to assist them in obtaining evidence? Why or why not?

4. Increasingly, questions arise about the necessity of a police officer having to shoot someone in the execution of his or her duty. Under what circumstances might an officer be justified in drawing his or her gun? In cases where a gun is used, who should investigate the conduct?

5. Discuss the following statement: "In order to make crime detection easier and to protect all members of society, all persons should be photographed and fingerprinted." To whom does the word "persons" appear to refer?

6. Recent changes in legislation permit the police to obtain a warrant from a judge to obtain blood samples for DNA testing. If a person admits that he or she committed sexual assault, should the court be able to order a test of the accused's blood to see if it is infected with HIV? Why or why not?

7. A police officer observes the following occurrences. Indicate for which actions the officer can make a legal arrest. A person is

a) about to jaywalk,

b) jaywalking,

c) about to rob a store,

d) robbing a store,

e) running away after robbing a store.

8. A citizen observes the following occurrences. Indicate for which actions the citizen can make a legal arrest. A person is

a) driving through an intersection without stopping at a stop sign,

b) about to go into a store and commit a robbery,

c) robbing a store,

d) running out of a store after a robbery,

e) stealing the citizen's lawnmower.

9. Do the release procedures pending trial adequately protect society from those who commit offences?

10. What are some of the dangers that face a citizen who tries to make an arrest?

11. Does the legal system truly treat accused offenders as "innocent until proven guilty"?

12. To prevent "trial by media" some people have suggested that the name of a person charged with an offence should not be published until the person is found guilty. Discuss the advantages and disadvantages of such a proposal.

Applying Legal Concepts

1. Page was a back-seat passenger in a car stopped by police for speeding. He began to act in an obnoxious and irresponsible manner. When the police noticed several open beer cans near Page, they assumed he was guilty of drinking in public and demanded identification. Page refused to cooperate with the police and demanded to be allowed to enter his home just across the street. The police refused to let him go. As Page became noisier and began to cause a disturbance, the police arrested him. A shoving and pushing match then broke out, and Page was charged with two counts of assault.

• **Is Page guilty? Explain.**

2. Van Haarlem was charged with attempted murder, robbery, and unlawful confinement. As part of Van Haarlem's release conditions, he was not to contact directly or indirectly any person who had been called as a witness at the preliminary hearing. The following day, by chance, he met an officer whom he had known for many years and who had testified at the preliminary hearing. They agreed not to talk about the case. In the course of their ensuing conversation, Van Haarlem made an incriminating remark, indicating that he would have pleaded guilty if not for the fact that an acquaintance had testified against him at the preliminary hearing.

• **Should the evidence be admitted, or was Van Haarlem's right to counsel or his right to silence infringed?**

3. *R. v. Broyles* (1991) Supreme Court of Canada 3 S.C.R. 595

   Broyles was convicted of second-degree murder. The body of the victim was found under a stairwell seven days after her death. The police arranged for a friend to visit Broyles while he was in custody. They provided the friend with a body-pack recording device. The friend encouraged Broyles to ignore his lawyer's advice that he remain silent and tried to get him to give information. The tape recording established that Broyles knew the victim was dead the day that she went missing. Broyles added to the taped conversation "but the cops don't know that I knew she was downstairs." The evidence given to the friend was admitted and Broyles was convicted. He appealed to the Supreme Court of Canada.

   - **On what basis would he appeal? Did he win his appeal?**

4. Smith, severely beaten in a fight, left the scene but returned with a shotgun and shot the victim in the face and the chest. He surrendered to police. The officer advised him that he was under arrest "for a shooting incident," told him he had the right to retain and instruct counsel, and gave the standard police warning. Smith indicated that he understood his rights, and was given a second opportunity to exercise his rights at the police station. Smith declined and made a statement in which he admitted the shooting. He said that he was drunk and provoked. After his statement was taken, the police advised Smith that the victim had died. Smith appealed his conviction on the basis that he was not informed on his arrest of the fact that the victim was dead.

   - **Did the police proceed properly? Explain.**

5. Evans was a youth of limited mental capacity. The police thought that his brother had murdered two women. They arrested Evans on a marijuana charge, hoping that he would provide evidence against his brother. After being informed of his right to counsel, Evans told the police that he did not understand. He gave a garbled version of American rights that he had witnessed on television. The police did not attempt to communicate the meaning of his right to counsel to him.

   During the interrogation, Evans became the prime suspect in the two murders, which the police did not tell him. Nor did they restate his right to counsel. Incriminating evidence was obtained from Evans after aggressive interrogation, which included lying to him about finding his fingerprints at the scene of one of the murders. He was convicted of the murders at trial. The statements given by Evans were the only significant evidence in his conviction.

   - **Did the police proceed properly? Explain.**

6. *R. v. Antinello* (1995) Alberta Court of Appeal 97 C.C.C. (3d) 126

   Antinello was in jail awaiting trial. Eleven weeks before the commencement of his trial, a fellow inmate of Antinello's contacted the police and offered to testify concerning admissions that Antinello had made. The inmate insisted that he would not testify unless he had some arrangement with the Crown concerning his own pending charges and protection for him. Lengthy negotiations ensued and a decision was made to call the witness. Defence counsel was told of the existence of this witness three days after the jury trial started. Crown counsel explained that the delay was to make arrangements for the personal security of the witness. The judge ruled that the Crown should pay for Antinello to have a private investigator to assist in his preparation of cross-examining the witness. Antinello had nine days in which to prepare for the calling of the witness.

- **Has adequate disclosure been given to the defence?**

Extending Legal Concepts

1. Now that you have completed this chapter, review the opening article and Something to Think About. Have your answers or opinions changed? Why or why not?

2. With a partner, discuss the issues related to plea bargaining. Try to reach consensus or agreement. Find another set of partners who have reached agreement, and compare your findings. Discuss, negotiate, and attempt to reach a consensus in your expanded group. Repeat the procedure with another group of four. Then, as a class, discuss the steps necessary to reach a final consensus. Place the list of key issues on the board for further discussion.

3. Working in groups, prepare a skit demonstrating a legal or illegal arrest. In your skit include an offence, an arrest, and the detention of the accused. The skit can be original, a scenario from a case discussed in this chapter, or one that has been covered in the news media. After each group's performance, have a class discussion about the elements involved in the situation.

4. With the class, brainstorm a list of survey questions that would elicit people's attitudes on the role and authority of the police in our society, citizens' rights at the time of arrest, and Canada's bail system. Prepare a final survey and ask people in your school or community to complete it. Collect the surveys and prepare a written report that summarizes the results of your data and the attitudes of those that you surveyed. Include any visuals that will help to summarize your data.

Researching an Issue

High Speed Chases

The police use of high-speed chases receives wide media attention each time an innocent person is killed in such a chase. Police have guidelines to use in high-speed chases, but each time a situation arises an officer has to make a split-second decision whether to pursue or not.

Statement

High-speed chases should not be allowed.

Point

If an offence is or has been committed, police have a legal obligation to pursue the offender.

Counterpoint

The worth of an innocent human is much greater than the need to apprehend an offender or recover stolen property such as a car.

- **With a partner, research this issue and reflect on your findings.**
- **Prepare points on this statement that could be used for a class debate.**
- **Discuss your findings with others in your class.**

TRIAL PROCEDURE

These are the key terms introduced in this chapter:

adversary system
affirmation
alibi
arraignment
automatism
autrefois acquit
autrefois convict
challenge for cause
circumstantial evidence
confession
contempt of court
credibility
direct evidence
directed verdict

dominant party
double jeopardy
duress
empanelling
entrapment
examination-in-chief
exculpatory confession
hearsay evidence
honest mistake
hung jury
inculpatory confession
necessity
oath
opinion evidence

peremptory challenge
perjury
polygraph
privileged communications
provocation
rebut (rebuttal)
self-incrimination
sequestered
similar fact evidence
stay of proceedings
subpoena
surrebuttal
verdict
voir dire

Chapter at a Glance

Learning Outcomes

At the end of this chapter, you will be able to

1. prepare a diagram of a typical courtroom;
2. describe the tasks of each person connected with the court;
3. outline the steps followed in jury selection;
4. describe the various types of evidence;
5. identify which defence(s) can be used, given the facts of a case;
6. explain the significance of the charge to the jury;
7. describe the role of the jury in reaching a verdict.

Mental Disorder Clears Killer of Peel Couple

A man who admitted gunning down two fellow tenants in an alcohol-induced mental blackout has been found not criminally responsible on account of a psychiatric disorder.

After deliberating 15 [and a] 1/2 hours, a Peel jury acquitted Sandor Brunczlik of two counts of first-degree murder in the March 19, 1992, shooting deaths of pool hall manager Frank Cavaliere, 39, and his girlfriend, Gracie Girolmini, 42.

Cavaliere's three sisters were stunned by the jury's verdict.

"This is crazy, we don't understand it," Lina Stellato said. "He killed two people and could be out by Christmas."

Another sister, Ida Lieberman, angrily demanded a new trial.

"He killed two people and he's not going to get away with it," she declared. "We came here for the truth, but the truth and the whole truth was withheld from the jury because of a stupid technicality.

At a pre-trial hearing in October, 1994, the trial judge, Mr. Justice Casey Hill, excluded Brunczlik's confession to Peel Police investigators because they didn't advise him he could dial a toll-free number to talk to a legal aid duty lawyer.

In the statement, Brunczlik openly declared he had decided the night before, during an argument with Cavaliere and Girolmini, that he was going to kill them. He frankly admitted returning to the house the next morning and shooting them.

A defence pharmacologist testified Brunczlik would have been severely intoxicated if he had drunk 500 millilitres of a Mexican sugar cane brandy as he said he did on the morning of the shootings.

Two defence psychiatrists testified he was drunk at the time of the shootings and lapsed into a psychotic state because of his personality and stresses he was undergoing. He didn't realize what he was doing when he armed himself and fired off 14 shots.

A prosecution psychiatrist rejected . . . that Brunczlik was psychotic at the time.

He had too good a recall of the events, and wasn't that drunk because he performed a lot of tasks that required coordination, Dr. Andrew Malcolm said.

From: Farrell Crook, "Mental disorder clears killer of Peel couple." *The Toronto Star*, December 9, 1995. Reprinted with permission—The Toronto Star Syndicate.

Something to Think About

- **Can intoxication be used as a defence in a murder trial?**
- **How important is the testimony of expert witnesses?**
- **How does a jury weigh contradictory expert testimony?**

5.1 INTRODUCTION

Trial procedure in Canada is known as the **adversary system** because it involves two seemingly opposing sides: the Crown, representing society, and the defence, representing the accused. The onus is on the Crown to prove beyond a reasonable doubt that the accused committed the *actus reus* elements of the offence with the required *mens rea*.

You learned in Chapter 3 that the type of offence determines the form of trial available to the accused. In this chapter, you will look at trial by judge and jury. Trials for summary conviction offences and for indictable offences for which the accused is tried in Provincial Court follow the same procedures outlined in this chapter, except that no jury is chosen and the proceedings are less formal. In such trials, the judge fulfills the functions of both judge and jury.

5.2 COURTROOM ORGANIZATION

Canadian trial procedure is adapted from English law and is essentially the same in each province. The tasks of the various people who may be involved in a trial are outlined below.

Judges and Justices

Judges and justices are frequently referred to as "the Bench," or "the Court." Provincial Court judges and justices of the peace are appointed by each province; other judges are appointed by the federal government. Justices of the peace do not have the same powers as judges. They can carry out many of the functions of a judge before a trial, such as presiding over the court of first appearance where the charge is read, and issuing certain documents required for judicial matters. They may also conduct trials for offences against municipal bylaws and provincial offences, such as offences against the *Highway Traffic Act.*

Judges control the courtroom during a preliminary hearing and trial. They can exclude the public or even the accused if exclusion is considered to be in the interest of public morals, and is in the interest of the proper administration of justice and is necessary to maintain order in the courtroom.

Television cameras and the taking of photographs are not permitted in Canadian courtrooms.

Many judges' decisions concerning the admissibility of evidence and the questioning of witnesses greatly influence the outcome of a trial. Some of these decisions become the basis for appeals. In non-jury trials, the judge decides on the question of guilt and on the sentence. Imposing penalties is probably the most difficult function.

The Crown Prosecutor

The Crown prosecutor is a lawyer hired by the Attorney General of Canada or of a province. The Crown prosecutes because crime is considered an act against society. It is the prosecutor's responsibility to see that justice is done by presenting all the available evidence, even evidence that may be prejudicial to the Crown's case. With respect to this, the prosecutor can be directed by the judge to call witnesses who are not favourable to the Crown. The prosecutor has great influence, both in advising the police regarding the charge laid and also by withdrawing a charge that has been laid.

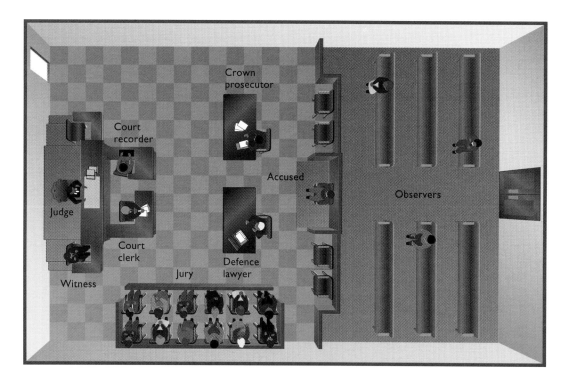

In a landmark decision in 1989, the Supreme Court of Canada ruled that Crown attorneys and attorneys general are not immune from prosecution.

The Defence Counsel

The defence represents the accused. In lower courts, the accused can represent him- or herself, but it is usually advisable to obtain counsel. Lawyers are familiar with the procedural law necessary to direct a case through the courts.

The Court Clerk

The court clerk reads the charge against the accused, swears in witnesses, tags evidence, and handles much of the paperwork and routine tasks required by the court.

The Court Recorder

The court recorder sits close to the witness box to record, word for word, the evidence given and all questions and comments made during the trial.

CASE

I n March 1981, Susan Nelles was charged with the murder of four infants at the Hospital for Sick Children in Toronto, where she was a nurse. She was placed in isolation for five days and then released on $50 000 surety given by her mother. She was discharged on all counts at the conclusion of the preliminary inquiry. Judge David Vanek, who presided over the hearing, stated, "I fear the rather astonishing fact is that there is simply no case against Susan Nelles at all."

In 1985, she sued the Ontario Attorney General's office and the two prosecutors in charge of her case for malicious prosecution. She claimed financial compensation for the pain, public humiliation, and mental anguish that she had suffered since 1981. Two lower courts ruled that she could not sue because attorneys general and Crown prosecutors are immune (completely protected) from such legal actions. The Supreme Court of Canada overruled those decisions, indicating that she could proceed with her lawsuit against the attorney general if she chose. "Granting an absolute immunity to prosecutors is akin to granting a licence to subvert individual rights," said the judgment. The Supreme Court made it clear that proof must exist that the prosecutors laid charges without reasonable and probable grounds, and displayed "malice in the form of deliberate and improper conduct." In 1991, the Ontario government agreed to pay $60 000 to Nelles for the grief and "severe mental anguish" she suffered after she was wrongly accused. Nelles received $30 000, a scholarship of $20 000 was established in her name at Queen's University School of Nursing, and an endowment fund of $10 000 was set up in memory of her father and her brother, who were doctors. Both had died during the decade-long legal battle, and friends speculated that both deaths were partly due to the stress of the case. The province also paid $255 000 in legal fees for Nelles. This was the first time in Ontario that the province paid an individual for personal suffering caused by criminal proceedings that ended in a dismissal.

Nelles v. Ontario
(1989)

Supreme Court of Canada
2 S.C.R. 170

1. **What significant precedent was established by the Supreme Court of Canada?**
2. **Judges are appointed and paid by the government. Should they be making decisions in situations like this, when their future appointment could be put in jeopardy by ruling against the government?**
3. **In your opinion, should the state be responsible for the acts of the Crown prosecutors, or should Crown prosecutors be personally liable?**

This job is an exacting one, for the court relies on the accurate recording of all evidence and may request that evidence be read back from the recording. The records are kept and a transcript can be made later, if necessary.

The Sheriff

Much of the court administration and trial preparation is carried out by the sheriff and his or her deputies. They are responsible for ensuring that the accused is present, obtaining prospective jurors, and assisting the judge. The sheriff carries out court orders such as seizing and selling property to settle claims for damages, and also serves summonses.

Other Court Officials

A probation officer may be present in Provincial Court. If requested by the judge, this person will conduct an interview with a convicted offender and convey information to the judge to help in establishing a sentence.

Various non-profit organizations such as the John Howard Society, the Elizabeth Fry Society, the Salvation Army, and Native associations may have representatives in court to help the accused. It has also become common to have services available to assist victims.

Reviewing Your Reading

1. a) **Which system of trial procedure is used in Canada?**

   b) **Discuss this system with reference to the parties involved and the onus on each.**

2. **Who appoints judges to the various levels of courts?**

3. **Why is the role of court recorder so important?**

5.3 MOTIONS AT THE BEGINNING OF THE TRIAL

Either the prosecution or the defence can make motions before the judge at the beginning of a trial. Such motions can relate to any procedure that is to be followed during the trial. One such motion is **stay of proceedings**. A stay can be either a suspension of proceedings to await further action or a total discontinuance of the proceedings. It can be ordered if there is a justifiable reason why the trial should not continue. This motion was brought before the court in the controversial case, *R. v. Askov* (1990).

5.4 JURIES AND JURY SELECTION

Although it is possible to find many faults with the jury system, the public generally finds more satisfaction in a system that provides for conflict resolution by its peers, rather than by one judge. It reflects "the conscience of the community." Due to cost, jury trials are required only for the more serious indictable offences, as outlined in section 469 of the *Criminal Code*. These offences are

- murder,
- treason,
- alarming Her Majesty,
- intimidating Parliament or a legislature,
- bribery by the holder of a judicial office,
- seditious offences,
- piracy or piratical acts,
- inciting to mutiny,
- attempting or conspiring to commit any of the above offences,
- accessory to murder or treason.

For less severe indictable offences, the accused has the right to choose either trial by judge alone or trial by judge and jury. For summary offences the accused will be tried by judge alone. The chart on p. 79 in Chapter 3 summarizes some examples of these different offences.

Advantages of Trial by Jury

There are a number of reasons why a defence lawyer might recommend trial by jury to the accused. First, in presenting the case the lawyer need sway only one of the jurors in the accused's favour, since a unanimous decision is required. Strong rhetoric may have a greater influence on a jury than on a judge who is conditioned to hearing lawyers present arguments. Second, the jury

Askov, Melo, Hussey, and Gugliotta were charged with conspiracy to commit extortion against Belmont. Belmont operated a placement agency in Montreal that supplied exotic dancers to licensed premises in Ontario. He wanted to enter the Toronto market where Melo was the supplier. Belmont informed the police that Melo had demanded a 50 percent commission from him for the privilege of operating in the Toronto area. The police assigned an undercover officer to act as Belmont's driver and bodyguard. Belmont refused to pay the commission and was pursued and threatened with a sawed-off shotgun and knife by the accused. The four men were arrested and spent almost six months in custody before being released on recognizances.

The Crown was prepared to set a date for the preliminary hearing in December 1983, but it was rescheduled to February 1984, at the request of the accused. On that date all counsel agreed to July 4, 1984, for the preliminary hearing, but due to a courtroom scheduling conflict it could not be completed until September, 10 months after the arrests. The accused were ordered to stand trial, but the earliest available trial date was October 1985, nearly two years after the arrest. When October arrived, the case still could not proceed because other cases had priority. The trial was rescheduled for September 1986.

When the trial began, nearly three years after the incident, the defence moved to stay the proceedings on the ground that the trial had been unreasonably delayed and was a violation of the accused's section 11(b) *Charter* rights. The trial judge agreed and stayed the charges. The Crown appealed this decision to the Ontario Court of Appeal, which reversed the lower court decision and ordered the trial to proceed. It found that there was no misconduct on the part of the Crown, no indication of any objection by the accused to any of the adjournments, and no evidence of any actual prejudice to the accused. The matter was appealed to the Supreme Court of Canada, which set aside the Court of Appeal judgment and stayed the proceedings. It ruled that four factors should be considered in determining whether the delay in bringing the accused to trial has been unreasonable: length of the delay, explanation for the delay, waiver of time period, and prejudice to the accused. The Court indicated: "The delay is of such an inordinate length that public confidence in the administration of justice must be shaken . . . Justice so delayed is an affront to the individual, to the community, and to the very administration of justice." The Court suggested a guideline of institutional delay of 8 to 10 months for proceedings in Provincial Court, and 6 to 8 months from the preliminary hearing until trial.

R. v. Askov

(1990)

Supreme Court of Canada
2 S.C.R. 1199

1. **What right is guaranteed by section 11(b) of the *Charter*?**
2. **What was the main cause of the delay in this situation?**
3. **Using the four criteria set by the Supreme Court of Canada, indicate how each applied to the Askov case.**
4. **Why is trial within a reasonable time so important for (a) the accused, (b) society, (c) victims, and (d) witnesses?**
5. **Should the time limits set by the Supreme Court of Canada be rigid rules? Why or why not?**

may decide a case in accordance with the social values of the time, rather than precedent. A jury may also feel empathy for the accused, especially if the charge is one to which a jury can relate.

Advantages of Trial by Judge

There are also advantages to a trial by judge alone. A jury might bring prejudices to its task. For instance, jurors may view critically an accused who is poorly dressed or they may have an abhorrence for the crime before the court, especially if it is child abuse, sexual assault, or drug trafficking. A jury may also seem not to understand the legal technicalities involved in a certain case. Finally, a jury may be convinced just as easily by the rhetoric of a good Crown counsel as the eloquence of the defence lawyer. A judge makes a decision based on the facts and the law, rather than on rhetorical skills.

Jury Selection

The **empanelling**, or selection of the 12 jurors can take many days. In some cases, the process has become very scientific. Empanelling takes place as follows. First, a list of jurors for the session of court is selected from the list of all people living in the county. This list is usually computer-generated. From this list, a selection committee headed by the sheriff randomly picks 75 to 100 names. These people are summoned to appear at the court by notice from the sheriff. The more controversial the case, the more people are called. Anyone who does not appear can have a warrant issued against him or her and can be criminally charged.

The prospective jurors assemble in the courtroom at the start of trial. A card, bearing the name of each person, is put in a barrel. After the barrel is shaken, the cards are drawn one at a time, and the person selected steps forward. A judge may exempt a person who has a personal interest in the matter to be tried, a relationship with a participant, or a personal hardship. As well, a judge may direct a juror, for reasons of personal hardship or any other reasonable cause, to stand aside. If the jury cannot be selected from the remaining prospective jurors, those who were asked to stand aside will then be called. The defence and the Crown prosecutor then have the right to accept or reject them as jurors. The judge decides which questions can be asked of prospective jurors. In selecting a jury, the Crown and defence must consider what the value system of a prospective juror might be, given the facts of the case. For example, what might be the view of an older male, a feminist, an older female, or a young bachelor toward the accused and the victim in a sexual assault case? Ethnicity, religion, age, financial status, occupation, sexual orientation, intelligence, and gender are only a few of the characteristics to be considered.

People shown in the list below are automatically excluded from jury duty. The categories vary slightly from province to province:

- anyone under 18 or over 69 years of age;
- anyone who is not a Canadian citizen;
- any member of a provincial legislature, the House of Commons, the Senate, or municipal government;
- any judge or justice of the peace, lawyer, or law student;
- any doctor, coroner, veterinarian, nurse, or dentist;
- any police officer, special constable, sheriff, prison warden, prison guard, or law-enforcement officer, or the spouse of a person having these occupations;
- anyone who is blind, or who has a mental or physical disability that would seriously impair his or her ability to discharge the duties of a juror;
- anyone convicted of an indictable offence for which he or she has not been pardoned;
- any firefighter or member of a voluntary fire brigade;
- any professor, teacher, or member of the clergy;
- any salaried official of a government;
- any editor, reporter, or printer of any public newspaper;
- anyone who has served on a jury within the preceding two or three years;
- any person required in the running of transportation or the operation of telephone and telegraph communications.

The accused, Milton Born With a Tooth, was charged with several criminal offences on the Peigan Indian Reserve near Brocket, Alberta. He elected trial by judge and jury. As required under Alberta's *Jury Act*, the sheriff issued jury summonses to 252 people residing in the Calgary area. Two hundred of the people were selected "at random" from the City of Calgary, while the remaining 52 were aboriginal persons living on the three reserves in the area to ensure a number of individuals of Native origin were on the jury panel.

The Crown filed a written challenge to the jury panel selection procedure to the Alberta Court of Queen's Bench where the challenge was upheld and a new jury panel was to be selected.

R. v. Born With a Tooth
(1993)

Alberta Court of Queen's Bench
10 Alta. L.R. (3rd) 1

1. **Why did the Crown challenge this particular jury selection procedure?**
2. **Why might the sheriff have made a specific effort to select 52 aboriginal persons as part of this jury panel?**
3. **Explain the meaning of the following statement from the court's decision: "Artificially skewing the composition of jury panels to accommodate the demands of any of the numerous distinct segments of Canadian society would compromise the integrity of the jury system."**
4. **Why did the court support the Crown's challenge? Do you agree? Why or why not?**

The Challenges

The defence is given the right to challenge the first juror. After that, the prosecutor and the defence alternate the first right of challenge. Three types of challenges can be used to eliminate prospective jurors.

Challenge of Jury List

Either side can challenge the jury list. Generally, the jury list can only be challenged successfully if it can be shown that the sheriff or selection committee was fraudulent or partial, or showed wilful misconduct in selecting the prospective jurors. For example, the selection committee may have omitted all citizens of a particular ethnic group. However, it is not necessary for there to be a person on the jury of the same ethnic origin as the accused.

Challenge for Cause

A **challenge for cause** can be made on the basis that a prospective juror does not meet the requirements of the provincial statute governing juries. For instance, a person might have been called without being on the jury list, or despite being in an exempted category. Another reason may be that the person has formed an opinion through reading or hearing about the case. Every offender has the right to trial by a judge or a judge and jury who speak either English or French, or are bilingual.

There is no limit to the number of challenges for cause that can be made, as long as the judge rules that the cause is valid. If the defence does challenge for cause, the Crown can try to prove to the court that the cause is not true. The judge will appoint the last two of the jurors who have already been selected, or two other persons, to decide whether each challenge shall be accepted.

Peremptory Challenge

A **peremptory challenge** allows either side to eliminate a prospective juror without giving a reason. The number of peremptory challenges for each side is limited as follows:

- charge of high treason or first degree murder—20 challenges,
- charge where the penalty is five years or over—12 challenges,
- charge where the penalty is under five years—4 challenges.

If a jury cannot be selected from those present because of the various challenges, the sheriff can take prospective jurors off the street if the judge so orders, or more jurors can be called from the jury list.

Jury Duties

When selected, a juror is sworn in and takes a position in the jury box. Prospective jurors who are not selected are free to go but may be required to return for later trials held during that session of the court. Selected jurors may also be required to return for later trials. However, the judge may forego this requirement and will do so if a trial is lengthy.

At the start of a trial, the judge informs the jurors of their duties during the trial. The right to take notes varies from judge to judge and jurisdiction to jurisdiction. Jurors must not discuss the case with anyone other than the other jurors, or listen to or read media reports about it. They are not allowed to disclose any information relating to the discussion the jury holds when absent from the courtroom that is not subsequently revealed in open court.

During the majority of trials, jurors are allowed to go home at the end of each day. The judge can, however, order the jury to be **sequestered** during the entire trial. They are isolated from their families, friends, homes, and work. If sequestered, the jurors may speak only to one another and to the court officer appointed to look after them. They remain together and are provided with meals and accommodation. The main purpose of sequestering is to prevent the jurors from considering any outside information in reaching a **verdict**, forming an opinion about the question of guilt, or being influenced by those interested in the case.

Thus, each juror will determine a verdict solely on the evidence presented in court. Jurors are always sequestered when they retire to reach a verdict.

A juror can be discharged during a trial if unable to continue for a valid reason. The jury cannot be reduced below 10 jurors, however, or a new trial must be ordered. For their services, jurors may be entitled to a token payment, which increases if the trial is lengthy.

Reviewing Your Reading

1. **For what reasons might motions be made at the beginning of a trial?**
2. **What are the advantages and the disadvantages to the accused of a trial by jury?**
3. **a) Describe the steps followed in jury selection.**
   b) Name six categories of people who are ineligible for jury duty, and give a reason why each category isn't eligible.
4. **In a table, summarize the jury challenges available to (a) the Crown and (b) the defence.**
5. **Give three grounds on which a prospective juror may be challenged for cause.**
6. **a) What does sequestering involve?**
   b) What is the purpose of sequestering a jury?

5.5 THE PRESENTATION OF EVIDENCE

After the judge has instructed the jury, the trial proper begins.

Arraignment of Accused

The first step is the **arraignment** of the accused—the reading of the charge. The arraignment must be on the charge contained on the indictment. Any deviation may result in an acquittal. An accused is usually arraigned on the first court appearance, but is rearraigned for trials in higher courts. The accused then enters a plea of guilty or not guilty. If the accused refuses to plead, a not-guilty plea is entered on his or her behalf.

Crown's Evidence

Section 11(d) of the *Charter* provides that all accused people are presumed to be innocent. After the arraignment, the onus is on the Crown to rebut this presumption. It presents an opening statement in which its case against the accused is summarized. It then calls evidence in the form of witness testimony and exhibits. All evidence that is relevant, reliable, and fair is admissible.

The best evidence—**direct evidence**—is usually obtained from a witness who actually saw the offence being committed. But in many instances there may have been no witnesses, or they may have left the scene of the crime without identifying themselves.

Circumstantial evidence, though not as certain as direct evidence, can still be quite useful. For instance, if a witness says she was standing outside a bank, saw a person run into the bank with a gun and a bag, heard shots, and then saw the same person run out of the bank, her evidence to the fact that a bank robbery occurred is valuable, but circumstantial in that she did not actually see the robbery committed. The accused generally cannot be convicted on circumstantial evidence alone. However, as stated in *R. v. Truscott* (1967) "if the evidence presented to the jury points conclusively to the accused as the perpetrator of the crime and excludes any reasonable hypothesis of innocence" then the accused can be convicted.

When evidence is presented, it must be proven. For example, if a glove is found at the scene of the crime, it must be proven that the glove entered as an exhibit is that glove. If the counsel is trying to claim that a specific person owned the glove, it must prove that fact. In some cases it might be easy for evidence to be proven. Fingerprints may connect a gun to its owner. Once the evidence has been presented and proven, it is up to the jury, or the judge in a non-jury trial, to decide which facts they believe.

The **examination-in-chief** is the first questioning of a witness. The Crown will have interviewed its witness when preparing and so will know what answers to expect. Therefore, during an examination-in-chief, no leading questions are permitted. A leading question indicates the answer and generally leads to a "yes" or "no" response. For example, "Did you see the accused driving a yellow car through the red light at 1:45 a.m.?" rather than "What, if anything, did you observe happening at the intersection at that time?"

After the Crown questions a witness, the defence lawyer may cross-examine. Leading questions may be used at this time. Weighing of the evidence will require the judge or jury to determine which, of one or more conflicting bits of evidence, is the most convincing. The credibility of witnesses is an important factor in this determination.

The Crown may then reexamine the witness in relation to points brought up by the defence. Recross-examination may also occur, if the judge gives permission. The purpose is to test the truth of the evidence, to give each side the chance to get more information from the other side's witness, or to obtain a different version of evidence previously given at trial or at the preliminary hearing. Questions may be asked that are not relevant to the case, but are relevant to the **credibility** of the witness (how believable the witness is). The jury must decide the question of guilt on the basis of the evidence. It helps the case of one side if it can be shown that the evidence given by the other side is not credible. When it has called all its witnesses, the Crown rests its case and is not allowed to reopen it, unless the judge feels that it would serve justice to do so.

Defence Evidence

Before it calls any evidence, the defence can make a motion for the judge to instruct the jury to return a **directed verdict** of "not guilty." The defence lawyer would make this motion if he or she believes that the elements necessary to prove that the offence was committed (*actus reus* and *mens rea*) do not exist.

If the judge agrees that the essential elements for guilt are lacking, the judge can withdraw the case from the jury and give a directed verdict of "not guilty." If the judge does not agree with the defence, the case will continue. The defence then presents its case. The defence need not prove innocence; it need only show that there is a reasonable doubt that the accused committed the offence.

The defence usually summarizes what it hopes to show and then presents evidence in the form of witnesses. The same rules apply regarding leading questions. The Crown has the opportunity to cross-examine witnesses and to **rebut** (contradict) the defence's evidence. The Crown may also give reply evidence if the defence raises a new matter that the Crown had no opportunity to deal with when presenting its examination-in-chief. The defence then has the right to present **surrebuttal** (evidence to counter the Crown's rebuttal evidence).

R. v. Biddle
(1993)

Supreme Court of Canada
I S.C.R. 761

Biddle was convicted of two counts of assault causing bodily harm and two counts of choking with intent to commit an indictable offence. On two occasions, females were attacked immediately after leaving the underground parking lot of their respective apartment buildings. They were beaten, choked, and suffered bodily harm. Biddle was arrested 2 1/2 hours after the attack on the second victim, M.S.F. He provided an alibi as to his whereabouts during the time that the attack on M.S.F. occurred.

The Crown called a witness, Guerts, in rebuttal. She testified that shortly before the time covered by the alibi, she had been followed by Biddle in his car while she was driving to the garage of her apartment building. This evidence served to undermine Biddle's credibility with respect to his whereabouts. At the time this evidence was given, the Crown did not specify its purpose and no objection was taken to its admissibility. Biddle was permitted to call surrebuttal evidence in response. Biddle appealed his conviction to the Ontario Court of Appeal, and subsequently to the Supreme Court of Canada.

In its ruling, the Supreme Court of Canada indicated that Biddle was entitled to know the full case for the Crown at the close of the Crown's case so that it is known from the outset what must be met in response. If the defence has raised some new matter that the Crown has had no opportunity to deal with, and could not reasonably have anticipated, the Crown may then bring evidence in rebuttal after the defence's case is completed. Rebuttal evidence is not permitted regarding matters that merely confirm or reinforce earlier evidence introduced in the Crown's case, which could have been brought before the defence was made. The Crown had to introduce all evidence on the key issue of identity in the examination-in-chief. The defence had not raised any new or unanticipated matter that required evidence in reply. To counter the Crown's rebuttal, the defence had to recall Biddle to the stand. The Court ordered a new trial.

1. **What was the purpose of the Crown's rebuttal evidence?**
2. **What disadvantage would there be to the defence in having to recall Biddle?**
3. **Why is it important that the defence know the full case against it before the trial begins?**
4. **Under what circumstance is rebuttal evidence admissible?**
5. **Would it make a difference whether the Crown knew during its case that the accused intended to raise an alibi?**

Witnesses

Before the trial, the Crown provides the defence with a list of witnesses. Like jurors, witnesses may be paid for their services. Witnesses can either appear voluntarily or be served with a **subpoena** to appear. A warrant can be issued for the arrest of any witness who refuses to appear, and that person can be detained for up to 30 days. During that time, if the witness is brought before a judge who believes that continued detention is justified, the witness may be detained for up to 90 days.

Furthermore, a person who fails to attend the trial or remain in attendance to give evidence may be found guilty of **contempt of court**. A fine of $100 and/or imprisonment for 90 days can be imposed.

Once the trial begins, the defence can ask that any witnesses who have not yet testified be excluded from the courtroom to prevent them from "adjusting" their testimony. An **oath** (swearing to tell the truth) on the Bible is administered when each witness is called to the stand. Alternatively, a person can make an **affirmation**—a solemn and formal declaration that he or she will tell the truth.

A witness commits the criminal offence of **perjury** if he or she knowingly gives false evidence and with intent to mislead. It is also an offence to give contradictory evidence. The maximum penalty for both offences is 14 years' imprisonment.

Anyone who can understand the nature of the oath or affirmation and the questions asked by the various parties can be called as a witness. Evidence can be declared inadmissible if the witness is found not to have the necessary mental competence. A child who does not understand the nature of an oath or affirmation can give unsworn evidence, providing the child understands the requirement to tell the truth. The judge, in the charge to the jury, should indicate the admissibility of such evidence. Apprehensive children may be permitted to give evidence from behind screens and, for certain sexual offences, on videotape, if the judge so orders.

Adverse witnesses, those hostile to a particular position, may be called by both sides. The side that calls the witness cannot provide general evidence of the witness's bad character. It can, however, contradict the witness by offering other evidence, or with the permission of the court, prove that the witness made previous statements that are inconsistent with the present testimony.

The accused does not have to take the witness stand. In many cases, it is wiser not to do so. The accused may exhibit a poor attitude or appearance on the stand, and the judge or jury may disbelieve him or her. Also, the Crown's cross-examination may lead the accused into answering questions that will lead to a conviction. The failure of the accused to testify should not be a factor in determining whether the Crown has proved its case beyond a reasonable doubt. On the other hand, a jury, or the judge in a non-jury trial, may infer guilt from the failure of the accused to take the stand. This may contribute to a decision to convict.

The key aspect in the witness's testimony is credibility. Witnesses are often tested by being asked to recall things that they said or saw to check whether their answers are consistent with earlier accounts. Each side hopes to discredit the other's witnesses. The purpose of a trial is to find the truth, and evidence is often contradictory. That does not mean that witnesses are not telling the truth. People see things differently. Beside credibility, the weight that should be given to evidence is also significant. It is up to the jury, or the judge in a non-jury trial, to decide on the credibility of a witness and the weight his or her evidence merits.

Many factors determine how much credibility and weight should be given to evidence. The interest the witness had in the outcome of the case, the opportunity the witness has had to be influenced since the offence, whether the evidence was supported by other witnesses, whether the witness gave conflicting evidence earlier or during cross-examination, and the attitude and demeanour of the witness while giving evidence are only some of the determining factors.

Rules of Evidence and Types of Evidence

The rules of evidence have developed over many years and are very complex. Most are contained in the common law, but there are also provisions in statute law, such as the *Canada Evidence Act*. If a question arises during the trial as to whether evidence is legally admissible, a *voir dire* is held. In a *voir dire*, the jury leaves the room, and the Crown and defence both present their positions on the matter. Even the accused may take the stand. On the basis of the presentations, and taking into consideration the rules of evidence, the judge rules whether all, none, or part of the evidence is admissible. The jury is then recalled, and the trial continues.

Witnesses are protected from the results that may occur due to the evidence they give by section 13 of the *Charter of Rights and Freedoms*. The law encourages them to answer all questions.

Self-Incrimination

The *Canada Evidence Act* further provides that a witness can object to a question on the grounds of **self-incrimination**. Self-incriminating evidence is evidence that would directly or indirectly help to prove the guilt of the person giving the evidence. When a witness gives evidence, he or she is protected. The evidence cannot be used in another criminal court case except for a prosecution for perjury. It can, however, be used by the police to gain further evidence so that a charge may be laid against the witness. For example, if a witness testifies that he shot the prison guard, and not the accused who is charged with the murder, the Crown cannot use the statement as a basis for charging the witness with the murder. The admission may, however, lead the police in a different direction in their investigation. If they find enough new evidence to indicate that the witness did commit the offence, they can lay a charge of murder against him.

CASE

R. v. Levogiannis
(1993)

Supreme Court of Canada
4 S.C.R. 475

Levogiannis was charged with touching a child for a sexual purpose. The Crown requested that the 12-year-old complainant be allowed to testify behind a screen, as permitted by section 486(2.1) of the *Criminal Code*.

A clinical psychologist testified that the complainant was experiencing a great deal of fear about testifying. Levogiannis challenged the constitutional validity of section 486(2.1) on the grounds that it violated his right to a fair trial guaranteed by sections 7 and 11(d) of the *Charter*.

Both the trial judge and the Court of Appeal held that section 486(2.1) did not infringe Levogiannis's rights. He appealed to the Supreme Court of Canada. The Court indicated that the main purpose of section 486(2.1) is to better get at the truth by facilitating the giving of evidence by young victims of various forms of sexual abuse. There are limits to the section. The offences for which a screen can be used are listed, and the complainant must be under the age of 18. The screen blocks the view of the accused for the complainant, but not the complainant for the accused. It can only be used when the trial judge is of the opinion that it is "necessary to obtain a full and candid account of the acts complained of from the complainant." The Court also stated that the absence of face-to-face confrontation between accused and complainant does not infringe any principle of fundamental justice. The use of the screen does not preclude the accused from effective cross-examination. Finally, a properly informed jury will not be biased by the use of such a device.

1. **What legal principle did the Supreme Court of Canada establish by this ruling?**

2. **In what way does the use of the screen assist in fulfilling the purpose of a trial?**

3. **What significance is there that there are limits to the use of section 486(2.1) of the *Charter*?**

4. **The accused's rights are still protected even though a screen is used. State these rights as indicated by the Supreme Court of Canada.**

Privileged Communication

A spouse can never be compelled to give evidence concerning communications that took place during the marriage. Communications between spouses are said to be **privileged communications**. In most situations, the Crown cannot compel an accused's spouse to give evidence *against* him or her. The spouse may, of course, give evidence for the defence. There are some exceptions to this rule—crimes of violence against the spouse, certain crimes related to sex, and some offences committed against minors. The Supreme Court of Canada ruled in *R. v. Salituro* (1991) that spouses in some situations could give testimony against their spouse.

Many other privileged communications are nullified in court. For instance, discussions between parishioners and clergy or a patient and

CASE

Kuldip was charged with failing to remain at the scene of an accident with intent to escape civil or criminal liability. He was convicted and appealed to the Summary Conviction Appeal Court, which ordered a new trial. During the second trial, the Crown sought to impeach Kuldip's credibility by cross-examining him on apparent inconsistencies in his testimony given at the first trial. He was again convicted of the offence. He appealed, based on the grounds that using his previous testimony to try and impeach his credibility violated his rights under section 13 of the *Charter*. This section states that "a witness who testifies in any proceedings has the right not to have any incriminating evidence so given used to incriminate that witness in any other proceedings." The appeal from the second conviction was dismissed by the Summary Conviction Appeal Court. His subsequent appeal to the Ontario Court of Appeal was allowed, the conviction quashed, and an acquittal entered. The Crown then appealed to the Supreme Court of Canada.

The Supreme Court of Canada ruled that Kuldip's rights were not violated. It ruled that the cross-examination at his second trial on testimony given by him at the previous trial on the same charge was clearly for the purpose of undermining his credibility. It therefore distinguished between a cross-examination for the purpose of impeaching credibility and one made to "incriminate" Kuldip. Kuldip chose to take the stand, which gave the Crown the opportunity to question his credibility. Furthermore, under the *Canada Evidence Act*, Kuldip could object to a question where the answer might tend to incriminate him. It does not, however, say that the answer will not be used in a future proceeding to challenge the accused's credibility. In a previous decision, *R. v. Dubois*, (1985) the Supreme Court of Canada had already ruled that a killer's incriminating evidence in an initial trial can't be used to incriminate him in a retrial.

R. v. Kuldip
(1990)

Supreme Court of Canada
3 S.C.R. 618

1. **What was the ruling of the Supreme Court of Canada in *R. v. Dubois*?**

2. **What distinguishing fact did the Supreme Court of Canada use to find that Kuldip's rights were not violated?**

3. **Kuldip chose to take the stand in his own defence. What risk did he take by doing this?**

4. **If Kuldip thought that a question would incriminate him, what right did he have under the *Canada Evidence Act*?**

R. v. Salituro
(1991)

Supreme Court of Canada
3 S.C.R. 654

Pasquale Salituro admitted signing his wife's name on a cheque payable to both of them. He cashed the cheque. Pasquale's defence was that he had his wife's authority to do so. Carrie Salituro denied that she gave authority. The trial judge accepted her testimony and convicted him of forgery. Without that testimony he would not have been convicted. The trial judge concluded on the basis of Pasquale's testimony that he and his wife were separated without any reasonable possibility of reconciliation at the time he forged her signature. The Court of Appeal for Ontario affirmed the conviction.

Pasquale appealed to the Supreme Court of Canada. The Court noted that there is a common-law rule that spouses cannot give evidence against each other. As well, it restated its position that complex changes to the law with uncertain ramifications should be left to the legislature. However, it stated that judges can and should make incremental changes to the common law to bring legal rules into step with a changing society when it is appropriate to do so. Judges also have to keep the common law in step with the values of the *Charter*. If a common-law rule can be changed to make it consistent with the *Charter* values without upsetting the proper balance between judicial and legislative action, then the rule should be changed. The court therefore changed the common-law rule, making a spouse a compellable witness for the prosecution if the couple is irreconcilably separated.

1. **The Supreme Court stated that the common law should be in tune with the *Charter*. What section of the *Charter* were they referring to?**

2. **The new rule is a common-law rule. Why? What jurisdictions in Canada must follow the rule?**

3. **The Supreme Court of Canada reflected on the common-law rule prohibiting a spouse from being a compellable witness for the Crown. Why do you think the rule was originally made?**

4. **What values have changed in our society that give reason for the change in the common law rule?**

5. **Give your opinion on whether or not a spouse is a competent witness at the insistence of the Crown in each of the following situations:**

   a) **The couple have a common-law relationship.**

   b) **The couple marries after the incident leading to the charge but before the trial.**

   c) **The couple is divorced, but the offence occurred during the marriage.**

a doctor can be admitted as evidence, providing the **dominant party**—the one who has received the information—presents the evidence. Even a client's admissions to his or her lawyer can be brought as evidence, but only if the client agrees.

Similar Fact Evidence

The Crown can present **similar fact evidence**, that is, cases where the accused committed a similar offence in the past, to show that it is quite possible that he or she could have committed the offence again, using the same pattern of conduct. Similar fact evidence may also be used to overcome defence claims that the commission of the offence was a mistake or accident. However, evidence to show that the accused's past conduct is discreditable is generally not admissible unless it has significant relevance to the case. The accused's case may be greatly prejudiced if the jury gives too much weight to past conduct when it may have little to do with the facts of the current case. The judge will generally hold a *voir dire* to determine whether to admit similar fact evidence.

Hearsay Evidence

What someone other than the witness said or wrote is **hearsay evidence**. Since the statement or writing was by someone other than the witness, such evidence may not be admissible. There are exceptions. The out-of-court statement may be admitted as proof only that the statement was made. Hearsay evidence is also admissible if the witness is quoting a person who was about to die, as long as the evidence would have been admitted if the person had lived. The evidence, however, must be necessary and reliable. In one case, for example, a statement given by a three-and-a-half-year-old to her mother 15 minutes after a sexual assault was found to be necessary and reliable and admitted as evidence. The trial judge would not let the girl testify at the time of trial when she was four-and-a-half years old. The Supreme Court of Canada ruled that the statement was "admissible as a spontaneous declaration made under the stress or pressure of a dramatic or startling event."

Opinion Evidence

Unless the witness is qualified as an expert, **opinion evidence** is generally not admissible. Furthermore, the expert evidence must be relevant and necessary in assisting the judge or jury to come to a decision. The evidence of an expert can have a significant bearing on a trial, for a jury may accept the evidence as being infallible. The fact that the person is an expert and is usually giving evidence on a topic unfamiliar to the jury may result in the evidence being given more weight than it deserves. For that reason, the judge will only allow the evidence if it is on a topic that is outside the "experience and knowledge of a judge or jury."

Character Evidence

The Crown may wish to introduce evidence concerning the character of the accused and previous convictions of the accused. Since such information could influence the jury, the Crown is restricted as to how it may bring forth such evidence. The Crown may not follow a path of questioning that would indicate the criminal nature of the character of the accused. The jury must decide the question of guilt from the facts of the case itself, not from prior history.

Character evidence can be admitted by the defence to support the credibility of the accused, and as the basis of an inference that the accused is unlikely to have committed the offence. Such evidence may lead to an acquittal. However, if the defence introduces evidence of good character, the Crown may bring forth evidence of previous convictions.

The *Canada Evidence Act* allows witnesses to be questioned about any of their own convictions to verify their credibility. Similarly, if the accused testifies, he or she can also be questioned as to previous convictions. The questioning must not attack the credibility of the accused, unless such cross-examination is relevant to the fact that the accused is falsifying his or her evidence.

Photographs

Photographs may be entered as evidence if they are identified as being an accurate portrait of the scene of the crime. Frequently, the photographer and the film processor will appear to outline the manner in which the photograph was taken and processed. A judge has the right not to admit photographs as evidence that are meant merely to inflame the jury.

Interception Devices and Video Surveillance

Evidence obtained through use of an interception device or video surveillance can be admitted as long as the procedures outlined in the *Criminal Code* were followed. The *Code* prohibits the interception of private conversations by electromagnetic, mechanical, acoustical, or other devices, except when one of the parties to the conversation consents to an interception, or there is an authorization issued by a court order. There is a prescribed list of offences for which the person is being investigated and for which an authorization may be obtained. They are the most serious offences in the *Code.* Court rulings have indicated that electronic surveillance should be "treated as a last-resort investigative mechanism."

A judge can authorize interceptions for a period of up to 60 days, but there can be renewals for further periods of equal length. If national security is involved, the Solicitor General of Canada can issue authorization. Teleauthorizations can also be obtained, but they are only valid for 36 hours.

Recent amendments to the *Criminal Code* allow for intercepting a private conversation without authorization if the police officer believes it is an emergency, if the interception is immediately necessary to prevent an unlawful act that would cause serious harm to any person or to property, and if one of the parties being surveilled is either performing that act or is the intended victim of the harm.

As well, a person who fears bodily harm can authorize police to intercept his or her private conversations without obtaining judicial permission. This new right is especially significant in cases of spousal abuse and stalking.

Video surveillance evidence can be entered as evidence at trial. Search warrants are not needed for surveillance in public places, but they are required in order to use video surveillance and listening devices with respect to a person or a person's property. The judge issuing the warrant must set out the terms and conditions ensuring that privacy is respected in situations in which a person has reasonable expectation of privacy.

Documentation and Affidavit

The documentation necessary to obtain judicial permission for intercepting a private communication is sealed and kept in the custody of the court, so that no one is aware of the interception. If the intercepted communication is to be an issue at trial, the accused can apply for an order to examine the contents of the documentation. The affidavit that was sworn to obtain the authorization may be edited before being viewed by the defence to protect the identity of informants.

Those being surveilled by an interception device must be informed of it. The required period for doing so is 90 days from the end of the interception, but a judge may extend that time to a maximum of three years. As well, if the communication is to be used as evidence, the accused must receive reasonable notice of this intention and either a transcript of the intercepted conversation or a statement setting out the full details of the communication.

Polygraph Evidence

A number of cases concerning the admissibility of **polygraph**, or lie-detector, tests have reached the Supreme Court of Canada. In *R. v. Phillion* (1977), the Supreme Court ruled that the results of the test would be hearsay and therefore inadmissible. Only the way in which the machine was used could be cross-examined, not the responses of the person tested because the accused does not have to take the witness stand in his or her own defence. The Court ruled in a subsequent case that even if the accused took the stand, the evidence would still not be admitted. It ruled that if the polygraph operator took the witness stand, he or she would merely be stating what the accused had said. Doubts were also expressed regarding the ability of an operator to analyze the test properly. As well, there is fear that a jury would accept the test as being infallible and convict the accused based on his or her failure of the test, rather on the credibility of the evidence presented.

Confessions

A **confession** is an acknowledgment by the accused of the truth of the charge, or of some essential part of it. A statement can be either **inculpatory**, an admission, or **exculpatory**, a denial. Upon arrest or detention, the *Charter* requires the accused to be informed without delay of the right to legal counsel. If the accused is not told of this right, and then gives a statement about committing the offence charged, the judge has the right to exclude it as evidence.

The manner in which a confession is obtained may also affect its validity as evidence. A judge may exclude a confession that he or she believes was not given voluntarily; for example, if the confession was made after police promises of leniency, or after lengthy questioning. Even if such a confession is admitted as evidence, the jury may not give it much credence and reject it in rendering its decision. The following case provides an example of how the Supreme Court of Canada has upheld the *Charter* rights of an accused.

Herbert was arrested and charged with robbery after he was accused of walking into the Klondike Inn in Whitehorse in 1987, wearing a ski mask. He threatened the clerk with a claw hammer to rob him of $180. As a result of information police received from several reliable sources, Herbert was arrested a few months later. At the police station, after consulting legal counsel, he denied that he had committed the offence and advised the police that he did not wish to make a statement.

Herbert was put in a cell and an undercover officer was placed there to try to get Herbert to talk. After some time had passed, Herbert confessed to the robbery but added, "They'll never pin anything on me."

Prior to trial, a *voir dire* was held to determine the admissibility of the undercover officer's testimony. Since his statements were the only evidence against Herbert, the judge refused to accept the confession and acquitted Herbert.

The Crown appealed the acquittal to the Yukon Court of Appeal which ordered a new trial on the basis that none of Herbert's *Charter* rights had been infringed. Herbert appealed to the Supreme Court of Canada where, in a 9–0 decision, the judges agreed that Herbert's acquittal should be restored.

R. v. Herbert
[1990]

Supreme Court of Canada
2 S.C.R. 151

1. **Outline what the Crown would argue to have the undercover officer's testimony admitted.**
2. **Outline what the defence counsel would argue to have the undercover officer's testimony ruled inadmissible.**
3. **What *Charter* rights did Herbert believe had been infringed?**
4. **Why did the trial judge and the Supreme Court acquit Herbert?**
5. **In your view, was Herbert's confession voluntary? Why or why not?**

Illegally Obtained Evidence

The admission of illegally obtained evidence has been the subject of much debate since the passing of the *Charter of Rights and Freedoms* (See section 24.)

Each case must be weighed on its own merits. The test of whether the admission of certain evidence would bring the administration of justice into disrepute relies on whether the reasonable person, fully informed of the facts, would be shocked if a judge allowed the evidence to be admitted. Therefore, the severity of the offence, the manner in which it was committed, and the manner in which the evidence was obtained, all must be considered.

Reviewing Your Reading

1. **Summarize the order in which evidence is presented and state the purpose of each stage of the examination.**
2. **What is a leading question? Why is a leading question not asked in an examination-in-chief? When would it be appropriate to ask a leading question? Why?**
3. **When would the defence ask the judge for a directed verdict?**
4. **What are the characteristics of admissible evidence?**
5. **What does it mean to "give weight" to evidence?**

6. Compare direct evidence to circumstantial evidence.

7. Briefly describe (a) a subpoena, and (b) contempt of court.

8. Who may be called as a witness?

9. a) Distinguish between credibility of witnesses and weight given to evidence.

   b) Who determines credibility?

10. Discuss the concept of privileged communication, and indicate when communication privileges are nullified by the courts.

11. Briefly describe each of the following: (a) direct evidence, (b) circumstantial evidence, (c) similar fact evidence, (d) hearsay evidence, (e) evidence of opinion.

12. Under what circumstances is a confession inadmissible in court?

13. Describe the present status of the use of each of the following in Canadian courts: (a) photographs, (b) video or tape recordings, (c) interception devices, (d) polygraph evidence.

14. What is the purpose of a *voir dire*?

5.6 DEFENCES

Various defences exist that may prove either that the accused is not guilty of the offence charged or is guilty of a lesser offence.

Alibi

The best defence possible is an acceptable **alibi**, proof that the accused could not possibly have committed the offence. For instance, the accused may be able to prove that he or she was in another place at the time of the offence. It is important that the accused disclose any alibi to the Crown at the earliest opportunity. Failing to do so may erode the accused's credibility.

Self-defence

The *Criminal Code* permits one to defend oneself, those under one's protection, one's movable property, and one's dwelling and real property.

However, only necessary and reasonable force may be used according to the circumstances. The following two sections of the *Criminal Code* apply to self-defence in cases of assault.

34.

(1) Every one who is unlawfully assaulted without having provoked the assault is justified in repelling force by force if the force he uses is not intended to cause death or grievous bodily harm and is no more than is necessary to enable him to defend himself.

(2) Every one who is unlawfully assaulted and who causes death or grievous bodily harm in repelling the assault is justified if:

(a) he causes it under reasonable apprehension of death or grievous bodily harm from the violence with which the assault was originally made or with which the assailant pursues his purposes; and

(b) he believes, on reasonable grounds, that he cannot otherwise preserve himself from death or grievous bodily harm.

35.

Every one who has without justification assaulted another but did not commence the assault with intent to cause death or grievous bodily harm, or has without justification provoked an assault on himself by another, may justify the use of force subsequent to the assault if

(a) he uses the force

   (i) under reasonable apprehension of death or grievous bodily harm from the violence of the person whom he has assaulted or provoked, and

   (ii) in the belief, on reasonable grounds, that it is necessary in order to preserve himself from death or grievous bodily harm;

> **(b)** he did not, at any time before the necessity of preserving himself from death or grievous bodily harm arose, endeavour to cause death or grievous bodily harm; and
>
> **(c)** he declined further conflict and quitted or retreated from it as far as it was feasible to do so before the necessity of preserving himself from death or grievous bodily harm arose.

In recent years, battered spouses have claimed in their defence that lethal force against their abusers was necessary to "preserve [themselves] from death or grievous bodily harm."

Legal Duty

A person under legal duty can commit certain actions that would otherwise constitute offences. For example, a police officer can drive above the speed limit when chasing a suspected criminal. The officer may also use as much force as necessary to make an arrest. The *Criminal Code* (section 43) also allows the use of reasonable force in the correction of a child either by a schoolteacher, a parent, or a person standing in the place of a parent.

Excusable Conduct

Provocation may be used as a partial defence for a charge of murder. The *Criminal Code* states that provocation can consist of blows, words, or gestures. If provocation is accepted as a defence for murder, the accused could then be found guilty of manslaughter. This defence may be an important factor when a judge is deciding upon a sentence.

To use provocation as a defence, the criminal act must happen immediately after the provoking act. If more time were allowed between the provocation and the offence, then all murderers would be able to use provocation as a defence. Secondly, the provocation must be either an unlawful act or an insult. If a person strikes someone who in turn strikes back and kills that person, then provocation has occurred, for the original striking was an unlawful act. Finally, the act

or insult must be of such a nature that an ordinary person would have been deprived of his self-control.

Excusable conduct also includes **necessity** and **duress**. The case *R. v. Dudley and Stephens* (1884), discussed in Chapter 1, was based mainly on a defence of necessity. In *R. v. Morgentaler* (1985), the Supreme Court of Canada stated that the defence would be successful only in "urgent situations of clear and imminent peril when compliance with the law is demonstrably impossible." The *Criminal Code* states that duress can be used as a defence if a person commits an offence under threat of immediate death or bodily harm from a person who is present when the offence is committed. Duress does not serve as a defence where the offence committed is of a serious nature, such as murder, sexual assault, assault causing bodily harm, or arson.

Honest mistake may also be accepted as a defence, and is similar to excusable conduct. When Lorne Nystrom, a Saskatchewan Member of Parliament (MP) was charged with theft under $1000, he based his defence on the defence of honest mistake. He said he made an honest mistake when he took a $7.79 item from a drugstore shelf, put it in his pocket, and walked out without paying. Nystrom called two MPs and one former MP to testify on his behalf. The question was one of credibility. Lorne Nystrom was acquitted.

The honest mistake defence is the one most commonly used by those caught in possession of an unpaid item. Many people make the mistake of putting something in their pocket while doing something else in a store. The onus is on the Crown to prove beyond a reasonable doubt that the person accused of shoplifting did it intentionally.

Mental Disorder

Mental disorder as a defence has caused considerable discussion among members of the legal profession in recent years. The 1991 decision of the Supreme Court of Canada in *R. v. Swain* gave Parliament six months to update the law relating to the rights of those acquitted on account of insanity. This decision led to a rewriting of the applicable *Criminal Code* sections.

The terms "mental disorder" and "unfit to stand trial" are defined by the *Criminal Code*:

2.

In this Act, "mental disorder" means a disease of the mind; "unfit to stand trial" means unable on account of mental disorder to conduct a defence at any stage of the proceedings before a verdict is rendered or to instruct counsel to do so, and, in particular, unable on account of mental disorder to

    (a) understand the nature or object of the proceedings,

    (b) understand the possible consequences of the proceedings, or

    (c) communicate with counsel.

Mental Fitness to Stand Trial

A judge has authority to order the accused remanded for up to five days for the purpose of evaluating fitness to stand trial. The remand can also include an assessment to help determine the individual's mental status at the time of the offence. With some exceptions, the evidence given during a court-ordered psychiatric assessment cannot be used as evidence in court without the consent of the accused. Obviously, the evidence can be used when determining whether the accused is fit to stand trial.

New legislation requires that Review Boards be formed in the provinces. Boards determine whether an accused is fit to stand trial. After the assessment, the accused is sent back to court. If he or she is fit, the case is heard. If the accused is unfit, the court can order treatment. The purpose of this treatment is to make the accused fit to stand trial. In this case, an inquiry will be held every two years until the accused is tried. The purpose of this inquiry is to ensure that there is still enough evidence to bring the accused to trial should he or she become fit.

Mental Fitness at the Time of the Offence

There is a presumption of sanity. The Supreme Court of Canada ruled in *R. v. Swain* (1991) that the Crown cannot introduce evidence of mental disorder until after it has proved *actus reus* and *mens rea*. The defence decides whether to introduce the defence of mental disorder, which then must be proved on the balance of probabilities.

Prior to 1991, a person could be found "not guilty on account of insanity." This decision in some cases deluded the offender into thinking that he or she had not done anything wrong, which interfered with the treatment of the disorder. Now the verdict states that "the accused committed the act or omission but is not criminally responsible on account of mental disorder." Previously, offenders found not guilty on account of insanity were often held in "strict custody" for decades, a longer period than if they had pleaded guilty and received a sentence. The Supreme Court of Canada ruled in *R. v. Swain* (1991) that such detention violated section 7, right to liberty, and section 9, right not to be arbitrarily detained, of the *Charter*. The Court so ruled because there were no criteria or standards for the detention, and no provision for a hearing of any kind into the mental condition of the accused at the completion of the trial. However, at the time of this decision, a number of detainees had committed violent offences while on release with day passes. Parliament was faced with balancing the rights of the mentally disordered offender with the rights of society to be protected against the few who are mentally disordered and dangerous.

Not Criminally Responsible

Once a person is found not criminally responsible on account of mental disorder, the court may hold a hearing to determine what should be done with the accused. Alternatively, the Review Board must determine the future of the offender. The court or Review Board, when making its decision is required to take "into consideration the need to protect the public from dangerous persons, the mental condition of the accused, the reintegration of the accused into society, and the other needs of the accused." Note that it is the mental state of the accused at the time of the hearing that is the prime consideration, not the mental state at the time of the offence. If not considered to be a significant threat, the accused may be discharged absolutely. Otherwise, the accused may be discharged subject to appropriate conditions, or be detained in custody in a hospital. Treatment may not be ordered as a condition of release.

The new legislation also provides for maximum limits on the detention of those found not criminally responsible on account of mental disorder or those found unfit to stand trial.

Intoxication

The discussion in Chapter 3 of specific intent and general intent offences is significant in relation to the defence of intoxication. Recall that a general intent offence is one "in which the only intent involved relates solely to the performance of the act in question." Thus, a person who in anger strikes someone has committed the general intent offence of assault. Compare this with the person who strikes another with the intent to kill—aggravated assault. That person has a specific intent to commit the act.

An intoxicated person who strikes another may not have been able to form the intent and, therefore, could not be found guilty of aggravated assault. However, that person could be found guilty of the offence of assault—a general intent offence for which it is only necessary to find that the person did strike someone. Similarly, a person who is charged with murder could rely on the defence of intoxication, but it would only serve to lower the conviction to manslaughter, for which specific intent does not have to be proven.

Intoxication was ruled as an acceptable defence in a case of sexual assault by the Supreme Court of Canada in *R. v. Daviault* (1994). The decision was one of the most discussed in recent years, for it appeared to give licence to people to get drunk and then sexually assault someone. The Justice Minister at first promised that a discussion paper on the issue would be released, but the public outcry demanded faster action. Thus, Bill C-72 was quickly passed through Parliament to limit the use of the defence of self-induced intoxication. The preamble to the bill described the concern that Canadian society has with the extent of violence due to drunkenness and, in particular, violence against women and children.

For specified offences, the *Criminal Code* now states that it is not a defence "that the accused, by reason of self-induced intoxication, lacked the general intent or the voluntariness required to commit the offence, where the accused departed markedly from a given standard of care." A person "departs markedly from a standard of reasonable care generally recognized in Canadian society and is thereby criminally at fault where the person, while in a state of self-induced intoxication that renders the person unaware of, or incapable of consciously controlling, their behaviour, voluntarily or involuntarily interferes or threatens to interfere with the bodily integrity of another person." The *Criminal Code* specifies that the offences to which this section applies are those that include an assault, or any other interference or threat of interference by a person with the bodily integrity of another person.

Automatism

Automatism has been described as "unconscious, involuntary behaviour—the state of a person who, though capable of action, is not conscious of what he is doing." Examples include sleepwalking, convulsions, psychological stress, or behaviour while concussed due to a blow on the head. The accused must prove that the offence was committed in a state of automatism. If proven, the accused would be acquitted.

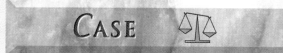

CASE

The complainant, a 65-year old woman who was partially paralyzed and confined to a wheelchair, invited Daviault to her home. Daviault brought a 1.14-litre bottle of brandy. The complainant drank part of a glass of brandy and then fell asleep in her wheelchair. When she awoke during the night to go to the bathroom, Daviault appeared, grabbed her chair, wheeled her into the bedroom, threw her on the bed, and sexually assaulted her. Daviault left the apartment and the complainant subsequently discovered that the bottle of brandy was empty. The trial judge found

R. v. Daviault
(1994)

Supreme Court of Canada
3 S.C.R. 63

as a fact that Daviault had drunk the rest of the bottle. He was a chronic alcoholic. He testified that he had spent the day at a bar where he had consumed seven or eight bottles of beer. He recalled having a glass of brandy upon his arrival at the complainant's residence but had no recollection of what occurred between then and when he awoke nude in her bed. He denied sexually assaulting her.

The defence raised the issue that evidence of extreme intoxication tantamount to a state of automatism negates the intent required for sexual assault, which is an offence of general intent. The defence called a pharmacologist to testify. He testified that Daviault's alcoholic history made him less susceptible to the effects of alcohol. He hypothesized that, if Daviault had consumed seven or eight beers during the day and then a litre of brandy in the evening, his blood-alcohol content would have been between 400 and 600 milligrams per 100 millilitres of blood. That blood-alcohol level would cause death or a coma in an ordinary person. He also testified that Daviault may have had an episode of black-out—losing contact with reality with the brain temporarily dissociated from normal functioning.

The trial judge found that Daviault had committed the offence but acquitted him because he had a reasonable doubt about whether he had possessed the minimal intent necessary to commit the offence of sexual assault. The Court of Appeal for Quebec allowed the Crown's appeal and ordered that a verdict of guilty be entered. Daviault appealed to the Supreme Court of Canada.

The Supreme Court of Canada ruled that it was necessary for the Crown to establish all elements of the crime. In most general intent offences, the necessary mental element can be inferred from the fact that the accused committed the assault. However, the intention to become drunk cannot establish the *mens rea* to commit the assault. The Court indicated that it would offend the *Charter* to minimize the mental element that is needed to commit the offence. Thus, the defence of drunkenness, even though self-induced, where the extreme intoxication is akin to automatism or insanity was accepted. A person in a state of automatism cannot perform a voluntary willed act, and someone in an extreme state of intoxication akin to automatism must also be deprived of that ability. The Court indicated that the defence would be available only in the rarest of cases. Daviault could not form the necessary intent, and a new trial was ordered.

1. **What two elements are necessary for a person to be convicted of a criminal offence?**

2. **Distinguish between general intent offences and specific intent offences.**

3. **What level of mental element is required for general intent offences?**

4. **The trial judge noted that it is for the legislature to create a new offence (change the defence of intoxication in relation to offences). What is the significance of this statement?**

5. **The trial judge also indicated that in weighing the requirements of public protection (from those committing offences while voluntarily intoxicated) against the requirement that the prosecution prove the existence of *mens rea* beyond a reasonable doubt, he preferred to give priority to the latter. State your views on this position.**

6. **Should persons who voluntarily become intoxicated to such an extent that they cannot form the intent to commit an offence be found liable for their actions? Explain.**

Automatism can also be due to a disease of the mind, referred to as insane automatism. The source of the malfunctioning is internal, possibly being the psychological or emotional makeup of the person. The accused is entitled to a verdict of "not criminally responsible on account of a mental disorder." The offender would then be subject to the procedures outlined under mental disorder.

Consent

Consent is a valid defence for the accused if the injured party consented to the action administered. Hockey and football players have often been charged with the assault of opponents during a game. Their defence has been that since the injured parties participated in the game, they consented to be subjected to the physical contact implicit in the game. However, recent court rulings indicate that a person who goes beyond the norm in contact will be found guilty of assault. The defence of consent cannot be used in the case of murder, or for offences committed against a person under 14 years of age.

CASE

Parks attacked his parents-in-law while they were sleeping, killing his mother-in-law with a kitchen knife and seriously injuring his father-in-law. The incidents occurred at the home of his parents-in-law, which was 23 kilometres from his own home. Immediately after the incidents, Parks went to the nearby police station, driving his own car. He told police that he had killed someone with his bare hands. He had apparently gone to sleep and, while sleep-walking, had driven to his in-laws home and committed the acts. He was charged with first-degree murder and attempted murder.

At his trial, Parks presented a defence of automatism. He had always slept very deeply and had a lot of trouble waking up. He had had a very stressful year at his job, had financial problems from betting on horses, and had stolen $30 000 from his employer. Through all these events, his parents-in-law had supported him, and he had excellent relations with them.

Several members of Parks' family also suffered from sleep problems. The defence called several expert witnesses including experts in sleep disorders. They testified that sleep-walking is not regarded as a disease of the mind but rather as a disorder of sleep. A sleep-walker's ability to control voluntarily even complex behaviour is severely limited or not available. Aggression while sleep-walking is quite rare and repetition of violence is unknown. Parks was acquitted of the two charges. The Crown appealed to the Court of Appeal for Ontario arguing that sleep-walking is a disease of the mind. The appeal was dismissed, and the Crown appealed to the Supreme Court of Canada. The Court ruled that sleep-walking was not an illness but a sleep disorder.

R. v. Parks
(1992)

Supreme Court of Canada
75 C.C.C. (3d) 287

1. **What is automatism? Distinguish between automatism and insane automatism. Which of the defences would Parks rely on?**

2. **What will happen to an accused who successfully argues automatism? insane automatism?**

3. **Why would the Crown want the courts to acknowledge that sleep-walking is a disease of the mind?**

CASE

R. v. Mack
(1989)

Supreme Court of Canada
67 C.R. (3d) 1

The Vancouver police had evidence that Mack was a drug dealer. Momotiuk was brought to Vancouver and placed under police "handlers," because Mack knew him. Over a six-month period beginning in October 1979, Momotiuk asked Mack, both in person and by telephone, to provide him with cocaine. Mack consistently refused. Momotiuk threatened Mack with a pistol, but Mack was adamant that he had no knowledge of drug sources.

In March, Mack met Momotiuk at a hotel. Mack was asked to go outside to a car. There a man showed him $50 000 to prove that he had money available to buy drugs. Unknown to Mack, the person in the car was an undercover police officer. Mack went back into the hotel, where Momotiuk asked him to get a sample. He gave Mack $50 for this purpose.

Mack went to a supplier whom he had known many years before and obtained a sample to get Momotiuk "off me." Momotiuk liked the sample and asked Mack to get as much as he could. Mack was arrested in the course of the delivery and charged with unlawful possession of a narcotic for the purpose of trafficking.

Mack had five previous drug convictions. He said he had used drugs to relieve back pain but had given up narcotics when he discovered relief through yoga. The defence applied for a stay of proceedings on the basis of entrapment, but the application was refused. Mack was found guilty at trial by judge alone. Mack's appeal to the British Columbia Court of Appeal was dismissed. He then appealed to the Supreme Court of Canada.

The Supreme Court found that Mack had been entrapped. In this case, the police were not interrupting an ongoing criminal enterprise, for Mack had had to be hounded into committing the offence. The Supreme Court did not agree with the trial judge that the accused had acted out of a desire for profit. It ruled that an abuse of process had occurred and stayed the proceedings.

In its decision, the Supreme Court outlined the following principles concerning entrapment. Emphasis should not be placed on the accused's state of mind. The judge should evaluate the conduct of the police objectively, to see whether there is evidence of entrapment. The onus is on the accused to prove, on the balance of probabilities, that entrapment occurred. Entrapment exists when the authorities provide a person with the opportunity to commit an offence without acting on a reasonable suspicion that the person is already engaged in criminal activity. Entrapment exists when, having such a reasonable suspicion, the authorities go beyond providing an opportunity and induce the commission of an offence.

1. **What evidence was there that Mack was a drug dealer?**

2. **What suggests that Mack was entrapped?**

3. **Why should a judge not place undue emphasis on the state of mind of the accused in determining whether entrapment has occurred?**

4. **Why is it an abuse of process to bring to trial an accused who has been entrapped by police?**

5. **What sort of police behaviour is the Court trying to discourage? Why?**

Entrapment

Entrapment is the police action of encouraging or aiding a person to commit an offence. It is not recognized as a valid defence. Rather, it is an abuse of process, so a judge who finds that entrapment has occurred should stay the proceedings.

Mistake of Fact

Ignorance of the law is generally not accepted as a defence. Ignorance of the facts, however, can be accepted as a defence under two conditions:

1. If there was a genuine mistake that did not result from the negligence of the accused in not finding out the facts.
2. If there is no provision in the law that ignorance of fact is not a defence.

Mistake of fact will likely be a successful defence, for instance, if someone receives a counterfeit bill as change while shopping in a store and is arrested for passing the money to someone else. The shopper cannot be considered negligent for not finding out that the money was counterfeit, since people do not check every bill they receive. Another example: the *Criminal Code* states that it is an offence to be "knowingly" in possession of stolen goods. If a person did not know that the goods he or she bought were stolen, then the mistake of fact could succeed as a defence. Mistake of fact will be examined more closely in Chapter 7.

Double Jeopardy

The *Charter of Rights and Freedoms* provides that "Any person charged with an offence has the right, if finally acquitted of the offence, not to be tried for it again and, if finally found guilty and punished for the offence, not to be tried or punished for it again." Trying someone twice for the same offence could invoke the defence of **double jeopardy**, which is covered by section 11 of the *Charter*. Indeed, a pretrial-motion would probably be made, with one of two pleas. In bringing a plea of *autrefois acquit*, the accused states that he or she has already been acquitted of the charge. In *autrefois convict*, the accused states that he or she has already been convicted on the charge. The

judge then investigates the matter and rules on whether the current charge is founded on the same facts as the previous charge that was tried. If so, the judge will dismiss the case.

Reviewing Your Reading

1. Describe a situation in which an alibi may successfully be used as a defence.
2. How much force may one use to defend oneself or one's property?
3. Define "legal duty" and give two examples of its use as a defence.
4. Name the three categories described as excusable conduct, and give an example of each.
5. a) Why is the defence of mental disorder used only for the most serious offences?
   b) Summarize the possible steps that occur before trial for a person with a mental disorder.
   c) Who decides on the future of a person deemed not criminally responsible?
6. a) Why would an accused invoke the defence of drunkenness if charged with an offence requiring specific intent?
   b) In what situations would the defence of drunkenness fail?
7. Name three examples of automatism.
8. Against what offences can the defence of consent not be used?
9. Under what circumstances has entrapment been accepted as a defence?
10. Describe the two conditions that must exist for mistake of fact to be used as a defence.
11. a) What is double jeopardy?
    b) Distinguish between *autrefois convict* and *autrefois acquit*.

5.7 REACHING A VERDICT

The decision as to the guilt of the accused—the **verdict**—is the culmination of the trial process.

The Summation

After all witnesses have been called, each side summarizes its case before the jury. If the defence presented evidence on its behalf, it closes first; otherwise, the Crown closes first. No new evidence can be introduced during the summation.

The Charge to the Jury

Once the summaries have been presented, the judge reviews the facts for the jury and defines and explains the law applying to the case. For example, the judge may point out that intent was necessary for the offence, or may indicate that, if the evidence does not establish beyond a reasonable doubt that an offence was committed, the jury might bring a conviction for an attempt. The judge may also indicate which evidence should be given weight, and which should not.

Once the judge has finished the charge to the jury, either side can challenge it as the judge might have erred. The jury is excluded from the courtroom while the two sides outline any reasons for challenging the charge. When the jurors return, the judge may provide a recharge. Many appeals result from the charge to the jury.

Jury Deliberation

The jury, in the custody of the sheriff, leaves the courtroom to make its decision. The decision must be unanimous. A foreperson is selected to preside over the deliberations. Unless note-taking was allowed, the jurors must rely on their memories and decide which facts they believe or disbelieve. They can return to the courtroom and ask that certain evidence or laws be reviewed if they feel it necessary.

It is the role of the jury to determine the facts of the case; the judge's role is to determine the law. The jurors should follow a two-step process in applying the facts to the law. First, they should dis-card any evidence that they do not believe. Second, they should determine the weight that they are going to give the remainder of the evidence.

The set of facts that the jury believes will determine which law applies to the case, and thus what decision the jury makes. In a murder case, for example, the jury may believe facts presented by the Crown that a hunter had intentionally killed the deceased. The hunter would then be convicted of murder. Alternatively, they may believe the facts, presented by the defence, that show the killing occurred as a result of an accident and convict the person of manslaughter.

Finally, they should apply the concept of reasonable doubt. If the jury believes the evidence of the accused, or is unable to decide whom to believe, it must acquit. If the jurors are left with a reasonable doubt they must acquit the accused, even if they don't believe him or her. They must always give the accused the benefit of any doubt.

If the jury cannot come to a decision, it presents this fact to the judge, who may review the evidence and ask the jurors to deliberate further.

When the jurors reach a verdict, the foreperson presents it to the court. Both defence and prosecution can ask the jurors to be polled individually. Each juror must stand and state "guilty" or "not guilty." Then, after being told not to disclose anything that occurred in the jury room, the jurors are discharged from their duties.

It sometimes happens that a jury still cannot come to a unanimous decision. If the judge is satisfied that further examination of the evidence would yield no verdict, he or she can dismiss the jury. Such a jury is called a **hung jury**. The accused may then be tried by a new jury. The decision of the judge to declare a hung jury cannot be appealed.

An accused who is acquitted by the jury is permitted to leave. An offender who is guilty will either be sentenced then or at a later date.

The jury usually has no influence in deciding the penalty, except when an accused is found guilty of second-degree murder. Although not required to do so, the jury may make a recommendation to the judge regarding the number of years that the offender should serve before being eligible for parole. Appeals and sentencing will be examined in detail in the next chapter.

Reviewing Your Reading

1. What determines which side presents its summation first?

2. What is the role of the judge in a trial by jury?

3. What is the purpose of the charge to the jury?

4. What happens in a trial in which there is a hung jury?

Adam®

by Brian Basset

Adam copyright 1991 *UNIVERSAL PRESS SYNDICATE*. Reprinted with permission. All rights reserved.

ISSUE

Should the effects of prolonged abuse be considered a defence for killing another human being?

In 1990, the Supreme Court of Canada first recognized battered women's syndrome as a defence when it upheld a jury's acquittal of Angelique Lyn Lavallee. Lavallee, fearing that her partner might kill her later that evening, shot him in the back of the head as he left the room. Her action followed years of enduring physical abuse from him. The Court found that it was reasonable for Lavallee to believe that she had no choice but to use lethal force to defend herself.

Violence against women by their spouses is widespread. A 1993 survey by Statistics Canada found that 29 percent of women had been physically or sexually assaulted by their partner. Many of their injuries were severe enough to require medical attention. For almost two-thirds of these women, the violence had occurred on more than one occasion. Moreover, a weapon was used against 44 percent of the abused women. It comes as no surprise, therefore, that one in three of these abused women reported that at some point during the relationship they feared for their lives.

After the 1990 Lavallee judgment, the Canadian Association of Elizabeth Fry Societies, a national support group for women prisoners, lobbied the government to review the cases of women who were convicted before the 1990 ruling. In October 1995, they had a measure of success when the federal government ordered a review to determine whether more than a dozen women imprisoned for killing their abusive partners should be freed or retried. The government had concerns that these women may have been denied a proper defence.

On One Side

In the past, the legal system has failed women in domestic violence situations. Although the majority of abused women did not report the abuse, those who did found police officers were reluctant to get involved. Abusers were reprimanded and warned not to repeat the offence. When charges were laid, many abused women subsequently dropped the charges because of fear, shame, self-blame, or "learned helplessness."

In this atmosphere of repetitive spousal violence and extensive use of weapons, it was only a matter of time before the effects of years of spousal abuse manifested itself in defensive behaviour. Those who support battered women's syndrome as a defence for killing another human being point to the victimization of these individuals as justification for their actions.

On the Other Side

Those who oppose the victimization defence argue that abuse does not give the victim licence to respond with an act of violence, unless it is in self-defence. They argue that by allowing the victim to successfully use abuse as justification for killing, the courts have created a right out of two wrongs. Moreover it is the court's role to make existing laws work, not give approval for violations of them.

Opponents of a victimization defence believe that if the abuse is serious enough to be used as a defence, it should have been treated seriously by the legal system before its long-term effects resulted in death. Toward this end, they advocate educating the abused to come forward early, having trained personnel available to hear their complaints, and increasing the power of police officers.

The Bottom Line

In the 1990s, the legal system began to recognize the seriousness of the problem of spousal abuse. Police have tightened their charging practices against abusive spouses. In some communities, charges are laid by the police rather than the abused spouse so that charges cannot be dropped. Another measure was the passage of the anti-stalking legislation in 1993. Are these measures enough to curb abuse and its effects? You be the judge!

1. What is the meaning of "battered women's syndrome"? How has it been used by the courts and the government in recent years?

2. What stereotypical thinking exists that might adversely affect consideration of a battered woman's claim to have acted in self-defence?

3. What statistics support the statement "violence against women is widespread"? Do you find any of these statistics surprising? Explain.

4. Why do you think many abused women drop the charges against their abusive partners?

5. Write a paragraph to either support or reject the defence of "battered women's syndrome."

6. Although not as common, men are also abused by their spouses. Do you think the courts would accept a defence of abuse if a man killed his spouse? Why or why not?

CHAPTER REVIEW

Reviewing Key Terms

For each of the following statements, indicate the key term being defined:

a) a prohibition against being tried for the same offence twice

b) preventing a jury from interacting with non-jurors and keeping it together until the jurors reach a decision

c) to stop a judicial process by a court, either temporarily or permanently

d) the presenting of evidence that counteracts or disproves evidence given by the opposite side

e) a jury that cannot come to a unanimous decision in a criminal case

f) a court document ordering a person to appear in court, usually as a witness

g) the process of selecting a jury

h) an action by the police that encourages a person to commit an offence

i) a trial within a trial to decide upon the admissibility of evidence

j) the act of knowingly giving false evidence in a judicial proceeding, with intent to mislead

Exploring Legal Concepts

1. Some people believe that allowing a child to testify from behind a screen is a physical prejudice against the accused. They argue that the screen gives the jury the impression that the crime is so terrible that the accused must be blocked from the view of the child. In your opinion, does the giving of testimony by a child out of view of the accused reduce the rights of the accused?

2. How far can one go in defending one's property? In your opinion, should defence of property be a valid defence for property owners who shoot at persons attempting to rob them?

3. Prepare an organizer to compare the role of the jury and the judge in a jury trial.

4. Serving on a jury is considered one of the most important contributions a person can make to society. Discuss why this is so.

5. Some critics of the court system believe that the jury process is too costly for the benefits it provides. Do you feel jury trials should be abolished? Give reasons for your opinion.

6. Give your opinion on whether televising court proceedings should be adopted by Canadian courts.

7. Jurors are usually paid a token amount after they have served a specified number of days. Should jurors be paid an amount equal to their lost wages by the state?

Applying Legal Concepts

1. Dikah and Naoufal were charged with trafficking in cocaine. All charges involved alleged sales of cocaine to a paid police agent. The RCMP hired

the agent to assist them in their investigation. He had assisted the RCMP in previous investigations in exchange for payment. In a written agreement, he acknowledged that his full fee of $10 000 would not be paid unless the RCMP's investigation was successful and the suspects were charged.

- **Is offering payment to an informant only if suspects are charged a valid law enforcement technique?**

2. On trial for murder, Worth relied on the defence of mental disorder. He had refused to be examined by a Crown psychiatrist and did not take the stand in his own defence. In his charge to the jury, the trial judge said that this was the accused's right. He also indicated that the jurors might infer from Worth's refusal to take the stand that his defence of mental disorder would not withstand scrutiny. Worth was found guilty of second-degree murder and sentenced to life imprisonment without eligibility for parole for 23 years.

- **Was Worth's right to remain silent, as guaranteed by the *Charter*, infringed?**

3. Jobidon was charged with manslaughter following a fist fight in a bar. X was winning the fight when the bar owner separated them and ordered Jobidon to leave. He waited outside, and the fight continued before a crowd. As both men stood facing each other, Jobidon struck X with his fist, hitting him on the head with great force and knocking him backward onto the hood of a car. Jobidon moved forward and in a brief flurry repeatedly struck the victim on the head. X rolled off the hood and lay limp. He was taken to hospital where he died.

- **What defence(s) might Jobidon successfully employ? Based on the facts presented, would Jobidon be found guilty? Why or why not?**

4. The Crown believed that Gruenke had enlisted the aid of her boyfriend in the planning and committing of a murder to stop the victim from sexually harassing her and to benefit from the provisions of his will. A lay counsellor went to talk to Gruenke on hearing of the victim's death. When Gruenke began speaking of her involvement in the murder, the pastor was called and the conversation continued. The lay person and the pastor were subsequently called by the Crown as witnesses. Their evidence supported the Crown's theory.

- **Is the evidence of the lay person and the pastor admissible?**

Extending Legal Concepts

1. Now that you have completed this chapter, review the opening article and Something to Think About. Have your answers or opinions changed? Why or why not? Do you think an appeal court would uphold the acquittal of the man in the article? Why or why not?

2. Is it possible to be guilty in fact, but not guilty in law? With a partner, brainstorm to make a list of situations in which this would be true.

3. Using reference materials in your resource centre, including CD-ROM and the Internet, obtain from the *Jurors' Act* of your province a list of people who are not

eligible for jury duty. For each category of persons, write a reason why they are not eligible for jury duty.

4. Research the inquisitorial system of trial. Prepare an organizer to show the ways in which it differs from the adversary system.

5. With the class, brainstorm a list of interview questions to ask a Crown prosecutor, a defence lawyer, or a person who has been a juror. Use the questions to interview one of them and report your findings to the class. Alternatively, invite the person to class and ask the questions.

6. Using reference materials in your resource centre, including CD-ROM and the Internet, find information on a famous trial. Prepare a review of the case, focusing on the evidence and issues relevant to the Crown and the defence.

7. Collect newspaper articles concerning five criminal law cases. For each case, indicate the offence committed, the evidence that the Crown and the defence could present, defences available to the accused, and the judge's decision.

Researching an Issue

Drunkenness as a Defence

When the Supreme Court of Canada allowed drunkenness to be a defence for the crime of sexual assault, many legal reviewers suggested that it was a situation of "impaired justice."

Statement

Voluntary drunkenness should not be a defence for any criminal act.

Point

If a person voluntarily gets drunk and is beyond the state of reason, he or she should be held accountable for any criminal act that he or she commits.

Counterpoint

A person who commits a criminal act while drunk and beyond the state of reason, whether voluntarily drunk or not, should not be held accountable for his or her action because he or she could not form the necessary intent to commit the offence.

- **With a partner, research this issue and reflect on your findings.**
- **Prepare points on this statement that could be used for a class debate.**
- **Discuss your findings with others in your class.**

SENTENCING, APPEALS, AND PRISON

These are the key terms introduced in this chapter:

absolute discharge
accelerated review
appellant
binding-over
bonding
capital punishment
community service order
compensation
concurrent sentence
conditional discharge
consecutive sentence
correctional services
dangerous offender
day parole
deportation
deterrence
diversion programs

escorted absence
factum
fine option program
free pardon
full parole
incarceration
indeterminate sentence
information
intermittent sentence
ordinary pardon
parole
parolee
penology
pre-sentence report
principle of totality
probation
probation order

recidivism
rehabilitation
resocialization
respondent
restitution
retribution
Royal Prerogative of Mercy
segregation
statutory release
suspended sentence
suspension
temporary absence
trial *de novo*
unescorted absence
victim impact statement
work release

Chapter at a Glance

Learning Outcomes

At the end of this chapter, you will be able to

1. assess the pressures on a judge who is passing a sentence;
2. discuss the objectives of sentencing;
3. describe the sentencing options available;
4. outline the provisions made for the victim of a criminal act;
5. distinguish between the appeal rights of the Crown and the defence;
6. describe the duties of correctional services;
7. outline the options for release available to an offender.

Alberta Jails No Place Like Home

Criminals sent to provincial prisons in Alberta these days are finding that jail no longer has many of the comforts of home.

The provincial government, over the past few months, has removed pool tables and other recreational games from its 10 adult and four young-offender centres. Colour televisions have been hauled away and replaced with black-and-white models with 30-centimetre screens.

Inmates no longer receive pay for doing chores in the institution or on work crews. Conjugal visits have become a thing of the past, and magazines that feature naked women or men or graphic sexual prose are prohibited.

What's more, there is talk of introducing chain gangs, which have recently made a comeback in the United States. And, perhaps most distressing for some inmates, justice officials are considering a ban on smoking in all provincial correctional centres.

"People are in prison because they've been convicted of offences, and that forfeits certain rights they normally would have as law-abiding citizens," Justice Minister Brian Evans said this week.

"Lack of colour TV doesn't take away any civil rights."

The move to make prisons less posh is clearly directed at appeasing Albertans who feel the scales of justice have become tilted in favour of those who commit crimes, and that the punishment being meted out by the system is inadequate.

Since they are powerless to increase the length of sentences or control parole, the governing Conservatives seem set on satisfying voters with the promise that they will make a prisoner's time behind bars as austere as possible.

"Prisons should not be a comfortable place," Premier Ralph Klein told reporters this week.

"You're in there because you did a bad thing."

Officials also hope the initiatives will serve as a disincentive to those who are considering a foray into crime.

From: Scott Feschuk, "Alberta jails no place like home," *The Globe and Mail*, July 15, 1995. Reprinted with permission of *The Globe and Mail*.

Something to Think About

- **What are conjugal visits?**
- **Do you think that taking away inmates' privileges will deter people from committing crimes?**
- **Do you agree with the move to make prison life less comfortable?**
- **Boot camps have been suggested as an appropriate sentence for some offenders. Do you agree?**

6.1 INTRODUCTION

One of the most difficult tasks for any judge is imposing the sentence. Establishing a penalty that is in the best interests of both the guilty party and society is a serious responsibility. Once a sentence has been imposed, either side may seek to appeal in a higher court. If, after appeal, the final sentence involves imprisonment, the offender is placed in a penal institution. At the end of the term or some part of it, the offender is released to return to society, which imposed the penalty for breaking its laws. The study of sentencing and prison discipline is called **penology**.

6.2 THE PROCESS AND OBJECTIVES OF SENTENCING

Views on sentencing illustrate the different value systems that people have. At one end of the spectrum are people who believe that our prisons are too soft on inmates and that many of the privileges they enjoy should be removed. At the other end are those who believe that the cost of operating our prison system is a burden on society, that prisons are of no benefit to the guilty, and that non-violent offenders should pay their debt to society in other ways. Between these two ends of the spectrum are many other views.

Sentencing may occur immediately after the accused has been found guilty. A judge may order a probation officer to prepare a **pre-sentence report**, which sets out the individual circumstances of the convicted offender. The report will include interviews with the offender and others who may be able to shed light on the person's past history and future potential. The judge will consider the report when passing sentence. Pre-sentence reports are usually not made for minor offences, or when the judge believes that sentence can be passed without further information being available.

The defence and the Crown have the right to speak on the sentencing and to call witnesses to give evidence about the offender's background. The Crown may mention any previous criminal record at this time. The convicted person may also make a statement. If there is a dispute at the time of sentencing between the evidence given by the Crown and the convicted person, the judge can listen to sworn evidence.

When passing sentence, the judge must make reference to the *Criminal Code* which specifies the penalties available. The judge must also consider that the *Charter of Rights and Freedoms* grants everyone the right not to be subjected to "cruel and unusual punishment."

Imposing Sentence

Unlike other countries, Canadian judges have considerable freedom in imposing sentences. For example, an offender found guilty of an indictable offence that carries a penalty of 14 years can receive any term up to that maximum. To determine appropriate penalties, judges often refer to previous similar cases. The more often a certain sentence recurs for a particular offence, the better defined are the limits for future sentencing. Nonetheless, judges are not required to follow sentences imposed in similar cases. Suppose, for instance, that the crime for which an accused was found guilty occurred frequently in a certain community. To deter others in that community from committing the same offence, the judge might impose a more severe penalty than usual. Studies indicate that the penalty given for the same offence varies greatly from community to community.

A judge may also consider the time spent in custody awaiting trial and/or sentencing, the circumstances of the convicted person, and the potential for rehabilitation. The victim may also be considered when sentencing. This is a social consideration that has increased in recent years. Section 7 of the *Charter of Rights and Freedoms* guarantees "security of the person" while section 15 states, "Every individual is equal before and under the law." Thus, the judge may ask for a **victim impact statement**, wherein the victim, and others affected by the offence, describe the effect the offence has had on their lives. Such a statement is especially significant for offences such as assault causing bodily harm, sexual assault, and murder, which may have lasting psychological and financial effects on the victim and/or the victim's family.

CASE

R. v. Goltz
(1991)

Supreme Court of Canada
3 S.C.R. 485

Goltz had his driver's licence withdrawn after accumulating numerous penalty points for driving infractions. He was stopped while speeding, and the officer noted that his licence was suspended. He was found guilty of driving while prohibited under the *British Columbia Motor Vehicle Act.* The minimum penalty of seven days' imprisonment was imposed, along with a $300 fine. The Provincial Court found that the imposition of a minimum sentence of imprisonment did not infringe the guarantee against cruel and unusual punishment in section 12 of the *Charter.*

Goltz appealed to the County Court, which ruled that the sentencing provision violated section 12 of the *Charter* and could not be justified under section 1. The Crown appealed to the British Columbia Court of Appeal, which agreed with the County Court findings. The Crown subsequently appealed to the Supreme Court of Canada.

The majority of the Supreme Court, in a 6–3 decision, indicated that for a punishment to be cruel and unusual it must be grossly disproportionate to the crime. The gravity of the offence, the personal characteristics of the offender, and the particular circumstances of the case must be considered. Other factors to be considered include whether the punishment is necessary to achieve a valid penal purpose, whether it is founded on recognized sentencing principles, whether there exist valid alternatives to the punishment imposed, and to some extent whether a comparison with punishments imposed for other crimes in the same jurisdiction reveals great disproportion. The Court looked upon the offence as being grave. The prohibition is aimed in large measure at safeguarding the health and lives of citizens using the highways. The Court stated that "the test is not one which is quick to invalidate sentences crafted by legislators." The Court found that Goltz knowingly and contemptuously violated the prohibition. The effects of the sentence cannot reasonably be said to outrage standards of decency or be seen as grossly disproportionate to the wrongdoing. The effect of the seven-day sentence is lighter than might first appear, since the sentence can be served on weekends.

Those dissenters in the Supreme Court of Canada decision felt that the mandatory minimum sentence of seven days' imprisonment plus a fine would in some cases be clearly disproportionate and shocking to the Canadian conscience, and hence violate the guarantee against cruel and unusual punishment. They felt that the provision could not be saved under section 1 of the *Charter* because it was not demonstrated that there was an obvious or probable need for a deterrent which has such an indiscriminate reach.

1. **Give reasons why the majority of the Supreme Court of Canada did not believe that the seven-day minimum sentence was cruel and unusual punishment.**

2. **Why is it significant that the majority stated that "the test (of whether the punishment is cruel and unusual) is not one which is quick to invalidate sentences crafted by legislators"?**

3. **In your opinion, would a minimum sentence of seven days' mandatory imprisonment plus a fine for driving while prohibited "be clearly disproportionate and shocking to the Canadian conscience, and hence violate the guarantee against cruel and unusual punishment"?**

Looking Back

Penalties have changed over the centuries. As recently as 160 years ago, 222 offences were punishable by death in England. Early punishments were often very brutal: strangulation, decapitation, drowning, torture, flogging, and mutilation. Confiscation of an offender's property was also common. In England, penalties that ridiculed the guilty were often imposed: having to wear the drunkard's cloak in public—a wooden barrel with openings for arms and legs; being forced to stand in public, locked in a pillory—a wooden frame with holes through which a person's head and hands were secured, or with fingers locked into a finger pillory; or being dunked in water on a dunking stool—a long piece of wood with a seat on it. Society's views on the objectives of sentencing have changed, and such punishments are no longer used.

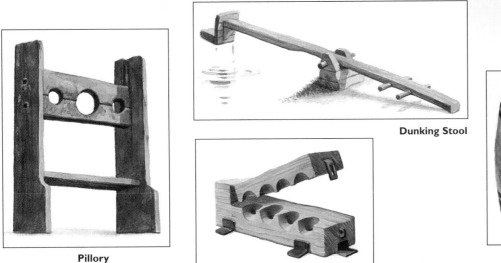

Pillory

Dunking Stool

Finger Pillory

Drunkard's Cloak

Circle Sentencing

An experimental form of sentencing called circle sentencing is being used in some jurisdictions in Canada. It is an attempt to meet the needs of the offender and the victim. You will read more about circle sentencing in Chaper 22.

Sentencing Objectives

There are four fundamental objectives behind the punishment of offenders against society: **deterrence**, **retribution**, **rehabilitation** or **resocialization**, and **segregation**. The chief purpose of each is the protection of society. However, critics of the sentencing process state there is little proof that any of these objectives are met. Studies have shown, for instance, that deterrents such as the death penalty are not effective in preventing the crime. Rehabilitation programs are frequently criticized by convicts, sociologists, and citizens, who point to the high rate of **recidivism** (return to prison because of a relapse into crime) as proof that the programs don't work. Even the ability of our prison system to segregate criminals has been questioned, for many serious offences are committed by prisoners on parole.

Deterrence

Society imposes penalties on those who commit wrongful actions to deter others in the community from committing the same offences, and to deter the same offender from repeating the offence.

If an offence is committed more frequently, the penalty may be increased as a deterrent. Arguments supporting the death penalty are based on this principle of deterrence.

The principle of deterrence is also a consideration when society begins to look on certain offences as being more serious than it did previously. Many amendments to the *Criminal Code* reflect these changes in attitude, for example, the 1985 amendments that increased the penalties for offences related to drinking and driving, and the 1995 amendments that increased the penalties for assaults.

Retribution

Sentencing as retribution is based on the principle of "an eye for an eye." In other words, an offender should be repaid in kind. Through a judge, society imposes an appropriate retributive penalty on the offender for harming society. Retribution as punishment has existed for thousands of years. Society has tended to move away from retribution as an objective of sentencing.

Rehabilitation or Resocialization

Over the years, the views of society have shifted to make rehabilitation, also called resocialization, a more important purpose of sentencing. Today, the inmates of penal institutions are provided with psychiatric and medical help, as well as religious counselling. Job training is available to make prisoners employable when they are released. Supervised parole enables offenders to prepare for a return to society. Halfway houses allow prisoners to adjust gradually to living in a community while still under the control of prison authorities. It is hoped that such assistance programs will help former inmates when they return to society, and thus reduce recidivism.

Segregation

The purpose of segregation is to remove criminals from society so that they cannot repeat their offence or commit other offences against society. For this reason, many people feel that criminals should not be given temporary releases, but should be kept in prison until they have served their full term.

Reviewing Your Reading

1. **What is the purpose of a pre-sentence report? What might such a report contain?**

2. **What factors must a judge consider when deciding upon a sentence?**

3. **What is a victim impact statement, and what is its purpose?**

4. **a) Name the four objectives of sentencing. Briefly explain each one.**

   b) Are the objectives of punishment being successfully met? Explain your answer.

5. **What is recidivism?**

THE WIZARD OF ID   Brant parker and Johnny hart

Dated 4-20-1993. By permission of Johnny Hart and Creators Syndicate, Inc.

6.3 SENTENCING AN OFFENDER

For most people the word "sentencing" means imprisonment. However, just as society's views on the objectives of sentencing have changed, so have attitudes toward appropriate sentences. Because of the high cost of maintaining the prison system, **diversion programs**—sentences that keep offenders out of the prison system—are increasing. Besides reducing the cost to taxpayers, diversion programs reduce the exposure of the accused to criminal society and allow the accused to pay his or her debt to society in a more meaningful way. All of the diversion programs and imprisonment are discussed below.

Absolute or Conditional Discharge

When an accused is convicted of an offence for which the penalty is less than 14 years, and no minimum sentence is provided in the *Criminal Code*, the court may grant either an **absolute discharge** or a **conditional discharge**. In either case, no conviction is recorded against the accused. Generally, a discharge is granted when it is the offender's first offence, or when the publicity attached to the case in itself constitutes a penalty. In *R. v. Fallofield* (1973), the British Columbia Supreme Court noted that two conditions must exist for either of these sentencing options to be used. First, the discharge must be in the best interests of the accused; second, it must not be contrary to the public interest. Furthermore, there must be no deterrence or punishment in the conditions of a discharge.

An absolute discharge is effective immediately with no conditions attached. A conditional discharge means that the conviction will not be recorded *only if* the accused follows certain conditions laid out by the judge in a **probation order** at the time of sentencing. A probation order usually requires the accused to keep the peace and to refrain from associating with known criminals and from various habits, such as drinking or frequenting certain areas. Other requirements can be added at the judge's discretion.

If the probation order is not followed, the offender could be required to return to court for sentencing on the original offence plus the offence of breach of probation. The courts have ruled that this is not double jeopardy, which is prohibited by section 11(h) of the *Charter* because the probation order was a part of the original sentence, and thus the accused has not been "finally tried and punished" for the first offence until the probation period is complete.

Suspended Sentence and Probation

A judge may give a **suspended sentence** after taking into consideration the age and character of the accused and the nature of and the circumstances surrounding the offence. A suspended sentence cannot be given when there is a minimum sentence prescribed by the *Criminal Code*. Instead, a probation order is issued. The offender would still have a conviction record and could be placed on **probation**—released instead of imprisoned—for up to three years. Probation orders can also be used in addition to fines, and in addition to sentences of less than two years.

"..The court orders an electronic monitoring device placed on your ankle—batteries not included."

A probation order requires that the accused keep the peace, be of good behaviour, appear before the court when required to do so, and do anything else the judge adds to the order. The judge could order, among other things, that the offender

- report to a probation officer;
- provide spousal support or support for any dependents;
- abstain from the consumption of alcohol;
- abstain from owning, possessing, or carrying a weapon;
- make restitution to any injured person;
- remain within the jurisdiction of the court and notify the probation officer of any change in address or employment;
- make reasonable efforts to find and maintain suitable employment.

In recent years, electronic monitoring of non-dangerous offenders has increased. The offender wears a bracelet or anklet containing a tiny transmitter that sends coded messages to a receiver. A central computer monitors all receivers, setting off a police alert the moment an offender moves out of the receiver's range. Many of the high-tech monitoring devices also include alcohol detection units. Electronic monitoring gives offenders the chance to attend school, work in the community, and live at home, while authorities still control their movements. The programs operate in British Columbia, Saskatchewan, Newfoundland, and Ontario.

Suspension of a Privilege

Many offences call for the **suspension** of a social privilege, such as a licence to drive, or a licence to serve liquor in a restaurant. A person whose driver's licence has been suspended will usually have to surrender it before leaving the courtroom. In many jurisdictions, authorities can refuse to issue or renew a licence if a fine has not been paid. This measure has been introduced to reduce the tremendous backlog of unpaid fines, as well as encourage respect for the decisions of the court.

Binding-over

Any person who fears that someone may cause him or her personal injury, or injury to his or her spouse or child, or damage to his or her property can lay an **information** before a judge or justice. The court will then order the two parties to appear and may order the defendant to keep the peace and be of good behaviour for up to 12 months. This is referred to as **binding-over**. The offender can also be required to enter into a recognizance, with or without sureties. If the person refuses to enter into the recognizance, a prison term of up to one year may be imposed. If the person fails to keep the peace, the money deposited as a recognizance may be forfeited. Recent amendments to the *Criminal Code* recognize the increased plight of victims of relationship abuse. The court is now permitted to restrict the defendant from being within a specified distance of the complainant, and/or communicating with him or her.

Restitution or Compensation

Restitution, also called **compensation**, is a relatively new penalty that requires the offender to repay the victim. The purpose is to reduce the impact of the offence on the victim and save time and money if it results in the victim not having to sue the offender.

A victim may ask for restitution at the time of sentencing. The courts are required to consider restitution in all cases involving either harm to property, or expenses arising from bodily injuries. In granting restitution, the judge may consider a victim impact statement and must take into account the offender's ability to provide restitution. If monetary compensation is ordered, payments can be made over time. Restitution can also be in the form of work. The victim can still take civil action against the offender to obtain anything to which he or she feels entitled. The penalty for ignoring a court order granting restitution is imprisonment.

Some communities have introduced a program whereby the offender and victim meet to work out the terms of restitution. Supporters of the idea believe that it has a more positive effect on the offender than a prison sentence would have. The meeting also benefits the victim, who can express feelings directly to the offender. This helps to dispel anger or fear.

McLeod had an extensive criminal record dating back 15 years. On one occasion, he was put on an electronic monitoring program, but failed to comply with the terms. He pled guilty to failing to comply and was sentenced to five months' imprisonment. After being released, but while still on probation, he was arrested for unlawfully trafficking in a drug, contrary to the *Food and Drug Act.*

The trial judge suspended the passing of sentence for two years and placed the accused on intensive supervised probation on condition that he participate for six months in the electronic monitoring program. Part of the reason for again putting him on the monitoring program was that the pre-sentence report indicated that McLeod substantially turned his life around in the 13 months between the commission of the offence and entering a guilty plea. He was very successful in school, performed volunteer work, organized the grade 12 graduation, participated in study groups, organized classes and gave instruction in the proper use of weight-training equipment, participated in weekly Bible studies at his church, and regularly attended Alcoholics Anonymous meetings. The Crown appealed the sentence to the Saskatchewan Court of Appeal on the basis that McLeod had committed a serious offence, had an extensive record, and was on probation. As well, the sentencing failed to consider general deterrence.

The Court of Appeal referred to a number of inquiries that indicated the use of incarceration has failed and should be used with restraint. The Ouimet Report noted that the object of the Canadian judicial system is to protect society from crime in a manner commanding public support while avoiding needless injury to the offender. Numerous references were made to reports indicating that higher sentences do not necessarily provide a general deterrent and reduce the crime rate. The court noted that in deciding whether a non-custodial sentence should be imposed, the court should take into account the following factors:

- whether the accused's conduct caused or threatened serious harm to another person or his property;
- whether the act was planned or the resultant harm was planned;
- the conduct of the offender during the commission of the offence;
- whether the victim's conduct facilitated the commission of the offence;
- the likelihood of reoffending;
- the possibility of the offender responding positively to probationary treatment, and
- the record of the offender.

In accepting the sentence imposed by the trial judge, the Court of Appeal noted that the following factors are significant in the use of electronic monitoring as an appropriate sanction.

- The offender's liberty is severely restricted.
- The intensive probation supervision/electronic monitoring is the middle range of sanctions, more severe than probation or community service, but less severe than imprisonment.
- There is no earned remission. The offender's liberty is restricted for the full term imposed by the intensive probation supervision order.

R. v. McLeod
(1993)

**Saskatchewan
Court of Appeal
81 C.C.C. (3d) 83**

- An illusion of liberty exists, but the sanction is partially custodial.
- The authorities recommend that a maximum of six months' electronic monitoring be assessed.

1. **What benefit for the judge was there in receiving a pre-sentence report?**
2. **What is a general deterrent? Did this case provide a general deterrent?**
3. **Should the goal in sentencing McLeod have been to set a general deterrent? Why or why not?**
4. **In what situations is a non-custodial sentence appropriate? Which of the considerations for non-custodial sentence did McLeod not fulfill?**
5. **In your opinion, does electronic monitoring help offenders reintegrate into the community? Explain.**
6. **Why do the authorities recommend a maximum of six months' electronic monitoring?**
7. **Do you agree with the sentence imposed on McLeod? Explain.**

Community Service Orders

A judge may sentence an offender to work a certain number of hours for a local organization or on a government project. This is known as a **community service order**. Community service orders may give the offender a feeling of worth for making a useful social contribution. Further, community service allows the offender to associate with people in the community, instead of with criminals in institutions. Since community service occupies much of the offender's free time, it may serve as a deterrent from committing other offences. Community service orders that will benefit the community are frequently part of a sentence for high-profile individuals. For example, a recording artist may be sentenced to perform a concert for a specific charity.

Deportation

Anyone who is not a Canadian citizen and who commits a serious offence within Canada can be subject to **deportation** to his or her country of origin, or to any other country. Usually the federal government applies to the courts for such a deportation order. Also, under the *Extradition Act,* Canadian residents who commit serious offences in other countries can be returned to those countries to stand trial or receive punishment.

Fines

For summary offences committed by individuals, the maximum fine is generally $2000 under the *Criminal Code,* but under other statutes, the maximum can be higher. To show society's concern about the number of violent offences that occur, the penalty for assault when the Crown proceeds summarily was increased in 1995 to $5000. For corporations, the maximum fine for summary offences is $25 000. No maximum fine is provided for indictable offences. If the penalty for an offence is five years or less, the offender may be fined instead of being imprisoned. Where the maximum penalty is more than five years, a fine may be imposed but only *in addition to* imprisonment. The judge establishes the amount of the fine.

An offender may ask to have at least 14 days to pay the fine. A **fine option program** is also available for both provincial and federal offences. Instead of paying a fine, an offender can earn credits for doing work. The jobs, set up by the organizers of the program, are similar to tasks performed under community service orders. The rate at which credits are earned is determined by each province. One great advantage of the program is that it allows poor offenders to perform useful services instead of going to jail because they cannot pay their fines.

Imprisonment

Imprisonment is still the most common sentence imposed. The *Criminal Code* specifies up to six months for most summary conviction offences. To recognize the concern of society with assault, amendments in 1995 increased the summary offence penalty for assault offences to 18 months. Maximum imprisonment for indictable offences can be from two years to life imprisonment, depending on the seriousness of the crime. For offences such as driving while impaired and failure to give a breath sample, a minimum penalty is stated. While a sentence of less than five years may be replaced by a fine, a sentence of over five years cannot be. Also, fines cannot be substituted if the stated penalty defines a minimum jail term.

If imprisonment is for 30 days or less, the offender is usually kept at the local detention centre. If the sentence is more than 30 days but less than two years, the offender is placed in a provincial prison. If the sentence is two years or over, the offender is sent to a federal institution.

A person convicted of two or more offences may serve the sentence either concurrently or consecutively, at the judge's discretion. A **concurrent sentence** is when a prisoner serves the penalties for two or more offences at the same time. Concurrent sentencing is used when the offences are of one kind, or were committed in one time span. A **consecutive sentence** is when a prisoner serves the penalties for each offence one after the other.

The **principle of totality** applies here. A person who is convicted of several violations of the same offence, or of committing an offence while on probation for a similar offence, should not be sentenced to an oppressively long prison term. For instance, for someone found guilty of 24 charges of passing forged cheques, a year's sentence for each violation would be severe. A more reasonable total penalty would be two years. However, penalties should not be reduced to the extent that the commission of multiple crimes becomes worthwhile.

At the discretion of the judge, a prisoner may receive an **intermittent sentence**, serving it on weekends, or even at night while maintaining a job. An intermittent sentence can be imposed only if the original sentence is less than 90 days. The court would also issue a probation order outlining the conditions of the intermittent sentence.

THE WIZARD OF ID

Brant parker and Johnny hart

Dated 11-11-1995. By permission of Johnny Hart and Creators Syndicate, Inc.

CASE

R. v. Joe
(1993)

Manitoba Court
of Appeal
87 C.C.C. (3d) 234

Mr. Joe was sent default conviction notices for 35 parking tickets, for which he owed $1665. He was informed that if arrangements to pay were not made, a warrant could be issued for his arrest. He did not respond to any of the notices, nor were any returned to the police department indicating that he had moved. Mr. Joe was informed that if the tickets were not paid, he could be incarcerated. He then contacted the police department and arrangements were made for him to enter the fine option program. If the program was not completed, an arrest warrant could be issued, and he could be incarcerated. He completed 27.25 hours of the 350 hours of community work required to pay off the amount. He became disillusioned when he discovered that others were working fewer hours for *Criminal Code* offences. Also, having found full-time employment, Mr. Joe thought that he would be able to pay off the fine and tried to make arrangements for installment payments. He was informed that such payments could not be made. Mr. Joe faced a prison term of approximately five months. He brought an application to quash the convictions and the warrant of committal. He believed that his rights under section 7 of the *Charter* were violated, for a warrant could be issued for default in payment of fines without the intervention of any judicial officer. As well, he held that incarceration was a cruel and unusual punishment for parking tickets.

Mr. Joe's application to quash the convictions and the warrant was dismissed by the court, so he appealed to the Manitoba Court of Appeal. The court agreed that his right not to be deprived of liberty except in accordance with the principles of fundamental justice were infringed. It also ruled that the automatic imposition of a fixed term of imprisonment upon the default of payment of a parking fine was cruel and unusual punishment. The court indicated that imprisonment is disproportionate to the offence of over-parking and would outrage standards of decency.

1. **What do you think the Manitoba Court of Appeal decided concerning payment of the tickets?**

2. **Are there situations in which incarceration should be a penalty for those who do not pay their fines? Explain.**

3. **Since there was a fine option program as an alternative to paying the fine, why did the court find that the penalty was cruel and unusual?**

The Imprisonment of Dangerous Offenders

A **dangerous offender** is one who has committed a serious personal injury offence—other than treason, or first- or second-degree murder—involving the use or attempted use of violence. On the basis of the evidence, such a person may be found to be a threat to the life, safety, or physical or mental well-being of others.

If the Crown asks that a person be classified as a dangerous offender, it must prove to the satisfac-

tion of the court that the person has a pattern of aggressive behaviour toward others that is unlikely to be restrained in the future. A person who is indifferent about the consequences of his or her behaviour could also be classified as a dangerous offender, as well as one whose sexual impulses will likely cause injury or pain to others. The prospects of treatment or cure are irrelevant in determining if the accused is a dangerous offender.

A hearing is held before a judge, and the evidence of at least two psychiatrists must be heard.

The accused, M., pleaded guilty to 11 counts of offences against his children, who had lived a life of physical, mental, and sexual abuse. The longest sentences were 8 years and 7 years. There were two 5-year sentences. All sentences were consecutive, so as to constitute a total of 25 years. Two sentences of 3 years, three of 2 years, and one of 1 year, were concurrent. The 8-year sentence was for many sexual assaults with respect to twin 13-year-old daughters. The 7-year sentence was for many instances of incest with the same two daughters when they were 14 years old. In all, the offences fit within the title "worst offences" for sentencing purposes. The trial judge said, "To suggest that these offences are grave is perhaps to understate them. The violence that was one of the elements of this case is shocking." The court referred to a previous case where it was stated that "a life sentence should be reserved for the worst offence committed by the worst offender and the next step down should, generally speaking, be to 20 years. Now, . . . there may be circumstances which direct a specific term of years in excess of 20." M. was 52 years old and had no previous convictions. His family lived in fear that he would come back from prison to carry out his threats and that they would require years of counselling to overcome their terror.

M. appealed his 25-year sentence to the British Columbia Court of Appeal.

**R. v. M.
(C.A.)**
(1994)

**British Columbia
Court of Appeal
28 C.R. (4th) 106**

1. **The totality principle operates in this case to curtail a single sentence at how many years?**

2. **In your opinion, would these offences fit into the category of "worst offences"?**

3. **Should the fact that M. was 52 years old and had no previous convictions have much weight in the sentencing?**

4. **What sentencing option is available to keep an offender in prison for a lengthy period in situations where the principle of totality is restrictive?**

5. **The court indicated that sentencing must be based on definable and rational objectives. In this case, general deterrence, denunciation, and protection through isolation required a long sentence. What sentence would you impose on M.?**

If deemed necessary, the offender may be confined for up to 60 days for observation. The judge may give an **indeterminate sentence**: the offender is kept in an institution until it can be shown that he or she is able to return to society and display normal behaviour. The National Parole Board must review the condition, history, and circumstances of each dangerous offender within three years of institutionalization, and not later than every two years thereafter.

Capital Punishment

The issue of **capital punishment** has been extensively debated in Parliament and in the media. In 1962, the law on capital punishment was amended to distinguish a capital murder from a non-capital murder. Capital murder included premeditated murder, murder committed during a violent crime, and the murder of a police officer or prison guard on duty. All other types of murder were non-capital, punishable by life imprisonment.

A person convicted of a capital murder was sentenced to death by hanging, but the sentence could be commuted (changed to a lesser penalty) by the federal Cabinet. After 1962, all death sentences were commuted to life imprisonment by the federal Cabinet. Because of the continual commutation of sentences, the issue of capital punishment was brought before Parliament. In 1967, capital punishment was suspended for five years, except for convicted murderers of police officers and prison guards. In 1972, it was extended for another five years. In 1976, by a six-vote margin, Parliament abolished the death penalty for *Criminal Code* offences. A further debate and vote took place in Parliament in 1984, which resulted in the continuation of no capital punishment. Capital punishment remains a contentious issue. It still exists for certain offences under the National Defence Act.

Reviewing Your Reading

1. What is a diversion program? What are the benefits of diverting people from prison?

2. a) What is probation, and what might a probation order involve?

   b) Discuss breach of probation.

3. a) Distinguish between an absolute and a conditional discharge.

   b) Distinguish between a conditional discharge and a suspended sentence.

4. Give two examples of the suspension of a social privilege.

5. What is binding-over, and what is its purpose?

6. a) When must a judge consider ordering restitution to a victim?

   b) What developments are occurring in the area of compensation?

7. Why are community service orders used?

8. a) In what situations can a fine be imposed instead of imprisonment?

   b) What is a fine option program?

9. What determines the location where an offender spends a prison term?

10. Define the following terms: consecutive sentence; concurrent sentence; intermittent sentence; indeterminate sentence.

11. Who is considered a dangerous offender?

6.4 PROVISION FOR VICTIMS OF CRIME

Until quite recently, criminal law did not consider or provide for the suffering of victims of crime. Current debates focus on whether or not criminal law should provide financial compensation for victims. A number of police forces now have a victim crisis unit that offers assistance when a crime is committed. Also, many community organizations provide assistance. Pressure from victims' groups has led to the creation of federal and provincial government programs to assist victims of crimes. A bill before Parliament in 1995 proposed providing compensation to victims of domestic violence for reasonable expenses incurred in moving away from the abuser. Such

WIZARD OF ID   BY BRANT PARKER & JOHNNY HART

Dated 9-23-1985. By permission of Johnny Hart and Creators Syndicate, Inc.

compensation could be ordered by a judge if the abuser is convicted of an offence such as assault.

The *Corrections and Conditional Release Act* gives the victim the right to know the offence for which the offender was convicted, the length of the sentence, and the penitentiary where the sentence is being served. With respect to the offender's prison absences and parole, the victim also has a right to know the eligibility dates, review dates, and the dates of any hearings. The victim also has the right to provide the National Parole Board with information to help it assess whether an offender's release might pose a risk to society. Then, if he or she requests it, the victim must be advised of the date of release, the destination of the offender, and any conditions that were attached to the release. Furthermore, any other person, who can satisfy the Chairperson of the Parole Board that he or she has been harmed "as a result of an act of the offender" may receive this information as well. This is applicable "whether or not the offender was prosecuted or convicted for that act" provided that the act was complained of to the police or Crown attorney.

Criminal Injuries Compensation Fund

The Criminal Injuries Compensation Fund has existed since 1973. Financed by the federal and provincial governments, this fund uses public money to compensate a person who is injured in some way when a crime is committed, or when he or she assists an officer making an arrest, makes a citizen's arrest, or attempts to prevent a crime. In such circumstances, the injured person often has no other redress because the criminal either has no money or has not yet been apprehended.

The injured person must file an application for compensation within one year of the event. The application is heard by a provincially appointed board, which may make either a lump sum award or payments spread over a period of time. The award is intended to cover specific, verifiable situations such as lost pay, pain and suffering from injuries, support of a child born as the result of sexual assault, medical bills and prescriptions, loss of income by dependants if the victim dies, funeral expenses, or anything else that the board feels is reasonable. No award is made for damage to or loss of personal goods such as cash, clothing, or jewellery. Nor does the board compensate for loss suffered in automo-bile accidents or for loss of property, because such items are usually insured.

If a victim takes civil action against the offender and is successful, the award granted by the Criminal Injuries Compensation Fund must be repaid in full or in part, depending on the amount awarded to the victim in the civil case.

Victim Assistance Fund

The Victim Assistance Fund has been established to set up education, counselling, and other programs for victims of crime. Part of the fund's financing is provided by convicted offenders, who must pay a surcharge on their fines. This can be up to 15 percent of the fine, or an amount not greater than $10 000, where no fine is imposed. A Statement of Principles for Victims of Crimes has been established to guide each province in establishing its program.

Reviewing Your Reading

1. **Outline the changes to legislation which have given the victim a more significant role in the criminal process.**

2. **What is the purpose of victim compensation programs?**

3. a) **Who may obtain an award from the Criminal Injuries Compensation Fund?**

   b) **Name five types of losses that are covered by the fund.**

4. **Describe the funding and functions of the Victim Assistance Fund.**

6.5 *A*PPEALS

The right to appeal a court decision, introduced in 1923, is now an integral part of Canadian criminal procedure. Appeals have often resulted in the correction of serious injustices, and the establishment of significant precedents.

The purpose of an appeal is to have the decision of the trial judge, or the judge and jury, reviewed by one or more judges of the Court of Appeal (also called the Appellate Court). Judges are usually appointed to the Court of Appeal because they have distinguished themselves in their profession.

Both the Crown and defence have 30 days to apply for an appeal, although an extension can be obtained for a valid reason. An application may also be made to have the offender released during the appeal time. Generally, such an application will be granted where the appeal has merit. The party who makes the appeal is called the **appellant** and the other party is called the **respondent**.

Appeals of Summary Convictions

Depending on the matter, there are two methods for appealing summary offences. If the accused wishes to appeal a sentence, a conviction, a verdict of "unfit to stand trial," or a verdict on whether or not he or she is "not criminally responsible on account of mental disorder," the appeal may be brought on a question of law, fact, or mixed law and fact. The Crown may also appeal on these grounds when it wishes to appeal a verdict of "not criminally responsible," "unfit to stand trial," or the dismissal of a charge. (The Crown cannot appeal a conviction.) The permission of the court is not required to bring this type of appeal. Appeals on a question of law frequently result when one party feels that evidence should or should not have been permitted.

The appeal court rehearing is based on the records of the trial court. The appellant is responsible for ensuring that a trial transcript is forwarded to the appeal court. If the trial documents are for some reason unusable, the appellate court may order a **trial *de novo*** (a new trial). In making its decision, the appeal court may dismiss the appeal, change the trial court's decision, or order a new trial.

The second type of appeal from summary offences can be brought only on either a question of law or jurisdiction, not on a question of fact or mixed law and fact. For example, an accused might appeal that the Provincial Court tried the accused's case without the jurisdiction to do so. An appeal of this sort can be brought only in the appeals division of the Supreme Court of the province and is heard by one judge of that court. The appeal is based on the trial transcript and on an agreed statement of fact.

Under either type of appeal, a summary conviction can be further appealed to the Court of Appeal of the province. Further appeals can only be on a question of law and require the leave of the appeal court.

Appeals of Indictable Offence Decisions

The appeal procedure for indictable offences is somewhat simpler. These offences are appealed to the appeal court of the province.

The accused can appeal a conviction under the following circumstances:

- on any ground of appeal that involves a question of law alone;
- on any ground of appeal that involves a question of fact or of mixed law and fact, with leave of the court;
- on any other ground that appears to the court to be sufficient, with permission of the court.

The accused may also appeal against the sentence passed by the trial court, with leave of the Court of Appeal.

In the case of indictable offences, the Crown may appeal against

- an acquittal, on the basis of law alone;
- an order that quashes an indictment or stays proceedings;
- the sentence passed at trial, with leave of the court.

The Court of Appeal may ask the trial judge to furnish the court with a report on the case. A transcript of the evidence taken at trial, the charge to the jury, if there was one, and the reasons for the decision, if any, are also given to the court. The appeal is argued on either the transcript or an agreed statement of facts. Both the appellant and the respondent prepare a ***factum***, a document that summarizes each party's position in the matter. At the appeal, the appellant presents the points of law applicable to the case, the respondent presents his or her view, and the appellant replies. Generally, new evidence, referred to as fresh evidence, is admitted only if it is relevant, credible, and expected to have affected the results of the trial. The appeal court renders its decision by majority vote, since either three or five judges generally hear the appeal. The majority then explains its decision. Any dissenting judges also give their reasons for disagreeing with the decision.

The accused, W., was convicted on three counts of indecent assault, one count of gross indecency, and one count of sexual assault against three young girls. He was the uncle of one of the girls, and the stepfather of two of them. The niece was between 2 and 4 years old when the incidents occurred, 7 years old when the offences were reported to the authorities, and 9 years old at the time of trial. One stepdaughter was between 9 and 10 years old at the time of the incidents, 11 when the incidents were reported, and 12 at the time of trial. The other stepdaughter was 10 years old at the time of the incidents, 14 at the time of reporting, and 16 at the time of trial.

The evidence of the oldest girl was, aside from W.'s denial, uncontradicted and consistent. The evidence of the two younger children was also denied by W. It revealed a number of inconsistencies and was contradicted in some respects. The incidents were all in private. The trial judge convicted W. on all five counts and sentenced him to 15 months. He indicated that "the law does not require the evidence of the particular complainant to be supported in order to convict the accused and corroboration in law is not necessary . . . I have considered the inconsistencies in the girls' evidence which I have referred to, as minor and attributable to their youth and the passage of time." W. appealed to the Ontario Court of Appeal, which set aside the conviction and entered an acquittal. The court stated, "There was really no confirmatory evidence, the evidence of the two younger children was fraught with inaccuracy and in the case of the older children [it was] perfectly clear that neither was aware or concerned that anything untoward occurred which is really the best test of the quality of the acts." The Crown appealed to the Supreme Court of Canada on the basis that the Court of Appeal was not entitled to conclude that the judge could not reasonably have decided that W. was guilty beyond a reasonable doubt.

The Supreme Court of Canada indicated that a Court of Appeal, "in determining whether the trier of fact could reasonably have reached the conclusion that the accused is guilty beyond a reasonable doubt, must re-examine, and to some extent at least, reweigh and consider the effect of the evidence." In verdicts based on findings of credibility, the test is "could a jury or judge properly instructed and acting reasonably have convicted? . . . the Court of Appeal should show great deference to findings of credibility made at trial." The Court allowed the appeal.

R. v. W.
(1992)

Supreme Court of Canada
2 S.C.R. 122

1. **In this case, what is the key issue concerning evidence given by the witnesses? Why?**
2. **Why did the Supreme Court of Canada state that a "Court of Appeal should show great deference to findings of credibility made at trial?"**
3. **Can a Court of Appeal overturn a verdict based on findings of credibility?**
4. **What was the basis for the decision of the Supreme Court of Canada in this case?**

Appeals to the Supreme Court of Canada

The Supreme Court of Canada is the highest appellate court in the land. Only appeals based on questions of law may be brought before it. The Court must grant leave to appeal in the following situations:

- when the provincial appeal court agreed with the conviction at trial, but one judge dissented;
- when the provincial appeal court overruled an acquittal;
- when the accused was tried jointly with a person whose acquittal was set aside by the appeal court, but the accused's conviction was sustained by that court;
- when the accused was found not criminally responsible on account of mental disorder, and that decision was either upheld or imposed by the appeal court.

Decisions of the Appeal Courts

The appeal courts may give an immediate decision, or reserve judgment until a later date. In such cases, written reasons are usually provided and, if significant, are recorded in case books. Under the rule of *stare decisis* (to stand by previous decisions), such decisions must be followed by lower courts. If the appellant is not successful, the case is dismissed. The appeal court may allow the trial court decision to stand even if there were errors in the trial process, as long as no substantial wrong or miscarriage of justice resulted from the errors.

The appellant may be successful if the verdict is not reasonably supported by the evidence, an error of law was made, or there has been a miscarriage of justice. If the appellant is successful, a new trial may be ordered, the judgment of the trial court changed if the original verdict was given by a judge only, or the matter may be remitted to the trial court and that court directed to impose a sentence. If the original verdict was given by a court composed of judge and a jury, the matter must be retried.

Reviewing Your Reading

1. a) Describe the two methods by which summary convictions can be appealed.

   b) For the first method, when may (i) the offender and (ii) the Crown appeal? For the second method?

2. a) Under what circumstances may an offender appeal (i) a sentence and (ii) a conviction for an indictable offence?

   b) On what basis may the Crown appeal in the case of an indictable offence?

3. Explain each of the following: *factum*; trial *de novo*.

4. a) What types of appeals may be brought before the Supreme Court of Canada?

   b) Under what circumstances may an appeal be brought before a provincial court of appeal?

6.6 *P*RISON AND PAROLE

Canadians have vastly different opinions about **parole**, which is the release from prison before a complete sentence has been served. Some suggest that offenders should be sentenced and kept in prison to the maximum the law allows. Others believe that since offenders have grown up in society, and that since society has allowed them to become as they are, society should work to rehabilitate these offenders. The issue gains focus each time paroled offender commits an offence, especially a violent one. Despite publicity given to the violation of the parole process, the success rates for conditional release are fairly high.

Canada has one of the highest incarceration rates in the world. The cost of keeping offenders in prison, and the desire to rehabilitate offenders so they can successfully return to society are significant arguments to keep the conditional release program. Public pressure is usually aimed toward making the assessment process more comprehensive and imposing stricter conditions before the release of violent offenders. To make the parole process more comprehensive, the *Corrections and Conditional Release Act*, formerly the *Parole Act*, was completely rewritten in 1992.

An offender who has been sentenced to imprisonment comes under the jurisdiction of provincial or federal **correctional services**. Each province has its own legislation and regulations regarding correctional services and is responsible for offenders in provincial prisons. As mentioned, offenders in these institutions have been sentenced to prison terms of less than two years. Correctional services are responsible for the following:

- the **incarceration** (confinement) of all offenders;
- case preparation for all parole applications submitted;
- the supervision of all offenders who are granted any type of early release;
- mandatory supervision of all persons released from institutions before the end of their sentence;
- all probation services.

Federal correctional institutions are categorized by the level of security required (maximum, medium, minimum, and community corrections centre). Offenders are assessed after sentencing to determine their level of risk and their rehabilitation needs. They are then placed in an institution based on type of offence, risk of escape, availability of programs and services to assist in rehabilitation, and the location of their families. Approximately 48 percent of those in prison are in provincial institutions, 50 percent are in maximum security, and the remaining 2 percent are in medium, minimum, and community correction facilities.

Once classified, an inmate is assigned to a case management team consisting of a supervisor, a classification officer, a parole officer and, if needed, a psychologist, a security officer, or medical staff. A plan is drafted to help the inmate with rehabilitative needs and to broaden social contacts. The management team assesses progress and regularly informs the inmate about the assessment.

A broad range of programs is offered within each institution, including life skills, dealing with substance abuse, literacy, and treatment for sex offenders and those involved in family violence. As well, offenders are encouraged to enroll in educational programs. They are paid a daily allowance, which can be used at the canteen. Ten percent of any earnings and money sent to the offenders are put into savings accounts for use upon release from prison.

The Canadian government has entered into agreements with other countries for the exchange of offenders. Thus, Canadian citizens who have been convicted of offences in other countries can be incarcerated in Canadian institutions to continue their sentences.

Did You Know

In 1995, federal correctional services were responsible for the operation of 57 federal penitentiaries for men and 5 for women. All inmates were serving sentences of two years or more.

CASE

Conway was an inmate at Collins Bay Penitentiary. Regular surveillance, by either male or female guards, consisted of scheduled "counts," four times daily and "winds," unannounced patrols conducted hourly at random times. During these surveillances, the prisoners could be subjected to body-frisk searches that avoided touching the genital area. These searches included using hand-held scanning devices. The search ordinarily lasted five seconds but could take up to fifteen.

Conway objected to the cross-gender touching that occurs during a frisk search and during the surveillance because of the possibility of female guards viewing inmates while undressed or using the toilet. In the Federal Court, Trial Division, he asserted that his rights were being violated, specifically according to sections 7, 8,

Weatherall v. Canada (Attorney General) (1993)

Supreme Court of Canada 2 S.C.R. 872

and 15 of the *Charter*. The trial judge supported his claim, ruling that the frisk searches did not violate sections 7, 8, and 15 of the *Charter*, but that winds conducted by female guards constituted an invasion of privacy of male inmates contrary to section 8. The Federal Court of Appeal set aside the judgment, holding that neither the cross-gender frisk searches nor the cross-gender winds were unconstitutional.

Conway appealed to the Supreme Court of Canada on the basis that both section 8 of the *Charter*, the right to be secure against unreasonable search or seizure, and section 7, the right to life, liberty, and security of the person, were violated. He also appealed that his equality rights under section 15 were violated, specifically to the equal protection and equal benefit of the law without discrimination according to gender. He noted that the female prisoners in other institutions were not similarly subjected to frisks by male guards.

In its decision, the Court ruled that the "counts" and the "winds" are practices necessary for the security of the institution, the public, and the prisoners. It noted that the possible inappropriate effects of the frisks are minimized by the provision of special training to ensure they are professionally executed with due regard for the dignity of the inmate. Furthermore, a substantially reduced level of privacy can be expected by inmates in that a prison cell is expected to be exposed and to require observation. The Court referred to *Hunter v. Southam Inc.* (1984) wherein the Court stated that to appreciate the reasonableness of a search under section 8, a balance had to be made between the individual's reasonable expectation of privacy, i.e., his reasonable expectation that he will be "left alone by government," and "the government's interest in intruding on the individual's privacy in order to advance its goals, notably those of law enforcement."

1. **Why was the case tried in the Federal Court of Canada?**
2. **In what ways was Conway deprived of his right to be secure against unreasonable search?**
3. **Do you think that Conway's right to be secure against unreasonable search was violated?**
4. **Was Conway's section 15—the right to equality without discrimination according to gender—violated because female prisoners were not searched by members of the opposite gender?**

Parole

The objective of **parole** is to allow an offender to return to society under supervision in preparation for an unsupervised release. The National Parole Board has jurisdiction over parole for all of Canada, with the exception of the provincial prisons in Quebec, Ontario, and British Columbia, which have their own parole boards.

At the start of an offender's incarceration, a date is automatically set for review for **full parole**. Except where a minimum sentence is stated in law or imposed by a judge, the review date for full parole will occur after one-third of the sentence has been served, or seven years, whichever is less.

At review time, a report is compiled that contains, among other things, the following information: the offender's efforts during imprisonment, a personality assessment, whether the offender has received and benefited from treatment, the offender's understanding of the nature and seriousness of the offence, the availability of a place to live, and any job possibilities upon parole. A hearing is then set. The offender and anyone over 18 years of age may attend the hearing as an observer. The board reviews the information before it, which may, as noted previously, include a submission from a victim and sometimes persons who have had harm done to them by the offender.

There are two main conditions for parole:

- the offender will not, by committing another offence, present an undue risk to society before the end of the sentence; and
- the release of the offender will contribute to the protection of society by facilitating return to the community as a law-abiding citizen.

The parole board is empowered to set a date for parole, reserve its decision until further investigation, defer parole, or deny parole. If parole is denied, the board generally must review the case every two years. If parole is granted, a parole supervisor is assigned. Parole is a conditional system. If the **parolee** (the person who has been granted parole) violates any conditions set by the board, he or she may be brought back to serve the rest of the sentence. If the conditions are respected, parole ends when the original sentence would have ended. The parole term for a convicted murderer, however, continues for life. About 75 percent of those released on full parole complete it successfully. Of those who violate parole, one-half violate the conditions while the other half commit a new offence.

Other forms of release are also considered by the parole board. **Temporary absence** includes escorted and unescorted absences, work release, and day parole.

Escorted and Unescorted Absences

All offenders are eligible for **escorted absences** from the date of admission to the penitentiary. For escorted absences, offenders are at all times accompanied by correctional services staff or citizen volunteers. Offenders generally become eligible for **unescorted absences** if they are halfway to eligibility for full parole, or after serving six months of their sentence, whichever is greater.

Temporary absences may be granted to allow offenders to visit relatives, attend a funeral, return home for religious holidays, or to obtain medical treatment. The National Parole Board must give its permission for unescorted temporary absences for those who were sentenced for committing a violent offence, a sexual offence involving children, or a drug-related offence as set out in Schedule 1 or 2 of the *Corrections and Conditional Release Act*. In all other cases, the head of the institution authorizes the absences of inmates. Over 99 percent of temporary absences are completed successfully.

Work Release

Work release allows the offender to be released to perform work for a specified period, or to perform a community service. The Correctional Service of Canada has sole authority to grant work release. The circumstances of work release depend upon the offender's particular case.

Day Parole

Under **day parole**, an offender is released during the day but must return to the institution or halfway house each night. Day parole is used to perform work or attend a learning institution. An offender is usually eligible for it six months before being eligible for full parole.

Parole for Murder

Parole for those convicted of murder differs from parole for other offenders. The *Criminal Code* provides that persons convicted of first-degree murder are not eligible for full parole for 25 years. Those convicted of second-degree murder have their parole eligibility established by the judge at the time of sentencing, but it is between 10 and 25 years. Both groups become eligible for consideration for unescorted temporary absences and day parole three years before their full parole eligibility date. As well, those sentenced to serve more than 15 years before being eligible for full parole may apply for a judicial review after 15 years. A Superior Court judge holds a hearing with a jury; a two-thirds majority of the jury may advance parole eligibility. In this way, offenders serving life sentences could be released on parole—for life—unless reincarcerated for violating the conditions of the parole. If the jury does not advance the parole date, they may set a date at which another application may be made.

Did You Know

In the early 1990s, approximately 70 percent of first-degree murderers who applied for early parole were successful in their request. A bill before Parliament is seeking to eliminate the *Criminal Code* section that allows for early parole for convicted murderers.

CASE

R. v. Swietlinski
(1994)

Supreme Court of Canada
3 S.C.R. 481

Swietlinski was convicted of first-degree murder. He had stabbed the victim many times using five different knives. He was sentenced to life imprisonment. During Swietlinski's first two years of incarceration he committed various disciplinary offences connected with smuggling, and an attempted escape. After being placed in punitive segregation for the latter offence, he underwent a complete change of heart and became a model prisoner. He was subsequently transferred to a medium and then a minimum security institution, each time becoming involved in charitable or religious groups and participating in work programs. He received several permits for escorted temporary absences. He took part in Alcoholics Anonymous activities, participated in some training sessions, and requested the assistance of a psychologist.

After serving 15 years of his sentence, Swietlinski applied under the *Criminal Code* for a reduction in the number of years of imprisonment without eligibility for parole. The jury refused to reduce the period of Swietlinski's ineligibility for parole and set his next review date at the end of his mandatory 25-year imprisonment term. Swietlinski appealed the decision to the Supreme Court of Canada, alleging that the hearing was unfair. Crown counsel, in addressing the trial jury, suggested that it unduly favoured the applicant, even to the extent of subverting the intent of Parliament in imposing the 25-year mandatory sentence. The Crown also pointed out that the murder victim had had no chance to reduce her suffering and the mandatory sentence was a bargain compared with the death penalty it had replaced. Reference was made to the quality of life in minimum security institutions. The Crown drew the jury's attention to other cases of murderers who had murdered again while on parole and made comments about the increasing violence in society and the need to do something about it. The trial judge limited discussion of the applicant's character to matters prior to or at the time of the murder.

1. **What is the purpose of the procedure that allows a person convicted of murder to apply for a parole review sooner than the stated parole eligibility?**

2. **The Supreme Court of Canada indicated that the Crown conducted itself improperly in three situations. What are they?**

3. **What should be considered by the jury when making a decision concerning parole eligibility?**

4. **What do you think should be done about Swietlinski's appeal?**

Accelerated Review

Offenders who are serving their first term in a penitentiary, and either committed a non-violent offence or a drug offence, are eligible for an **accelerated review**, provided that the judge did not set parole eligibility at one-half of the sentence. They must be released on full parole unless the parole board can find reasonable grounds to believe the offender is likely to commit an offence involving violence before the end of the sentence.

Statutory Release

By statute, prisoners are entitled to **statutory release**—to be released after serving two-thirds of their sentence if they have not already been released on parole. Offenders serving life or indeterminate sentences are not eligible for statutory release. Although statutory release is automatic for most offenders, the parole board can add conditions to the release. If the offender is likely to commit an offence causing death or serious harm to another person or to commit a serious drug offence before the end of the sentence, even statutory release can be denied.

Royal Prerogative of Mercy

The federal government has the power to grant a **Royal Prerogative of Mercy**. Applications are made to the National Parole Board, which investigates and makes recommendations to the Solicitor General. The alternatives are remission of a fine or imprisonment, a change in the penalty, a free pardon, or an ordinary pardon. A **free pardon** is granted where evidence shows that the convicted person is innocent. An **ordinary pardon** is usually granted on compassionate grounds. All alternatives release the offender from the conviction and related penalties.

The most celebrated case of pardons in Canada was that of Donald Marshall, Jr., a 17-year-old Micmac who was wrongfully convicted of the second-degree murder of an acquaintance named Sandy Seale in Sydney, Nova Scotia, in 1971. He was sentenced to life imprisonment and spent 11 years in prison before being released. Another man, Roy Ebsary, was eventually convicted of manslaughter in Seale's death and sentenced to one year in jail. A Royal Commission cleared Marshall of any responsibility in Seale's death.

Criminal Records

Over 2.5 million people in Canada have criminal records. For some people, the penalty for having a criminal record may be only embarrassment. For others, it may mean the loss of job opportunities. For instance, many jobs require **bonding**—insurance that guarantees the honesty of a person who handles money or other valuables. A person with a record usually cannot be bonded. Also, some countries refuse to admit persons with a criminal record.

If an accused is given an absolute or a conditional discharge (which are not convictions), the RCMP will automatically remove the information from their computers one year and three years, respectively, after the court decision. This applies to cases after July 24, 1992. For removal of records prior to that time, application must be made to the RCMP.

A convicted person can have a criminal record erased, though not destroyed, by applying for a pardon to the National Parole Board. If the conviction

was for an indictable offence, application for a pardon can be made five years after the completion of a sentence, and for a summary conviction, three years after the completion of a sentence. For summary convictions, the board will issue a pardon if the waiting period has been completed and the offender has been free of any other conviction since the sentence was completed. For indictable offences, the board verifies that the waiting period has been completed and there are no further convictions.

The board asks the RCMP to conduct an investigation into the offender's behaviour since the sentence was completed. If the board is convinced of the applicant's good behaviour and feels that the conviction should no longer be a blot on his or her record, it may grant a pardon. The pardon may subsequently be revoked if the application was in some way fraudulent, or if the person is no longer of good behaviour or is convicted of a summary offence. The pardon is automatically revoked if the person is later convicted of an indictable offence.

The *Human Rights Act* of each province also provides that a person with a criminal record cannot be discriminated against with respect to job opportunities.

Reviewing Your Reading

1. **List the responsibilities of correctional services.**

2. **What procedure is followed when an offender enters the prison system?**

3. a) **Who has jurisdiction over parole?**

   b) **What factors are considered in a parole review?**

4. **Define and discuss (a) unescorted temporary absences and (b) remission.**

5. a) **Who may receive an accelerated review? When must they be released?**

   b) **What is statutory release?**

6. **Discuss the alternatives available when the Royal Prerogative of Mercy is granted.**

7. a) **What are the disadvantages of having a criminal record?**

   b) **Who is eligible to have a criminal record erased?**

   c) **Describe the process for having a criminal record pardoned.**

*I*SSUE

Should all offenders receive equal treatment?

Canada has the second highest incarceration rate in the western world. The population in Canadian prisons averaged 32 340 in 1993–94. It costs an average of $43 800 a year to keep one person in jail. In other words, the Canadian prison population costs taxpayers over $3.9 million a *day*. This is a rather high price to pay considering one-third of the adult offenders in Canadian jails are there because they did not pay a fine.

In June 1995, the House of Commons approved Bill C-41 that included legislation that would make prison a last resort for offenders. The law emphasizes that judges should first consider probation for non-violent offenders. It offers a conditional sentencing scheme under which judges could suspend penalties of two years or less in return for supervised community service of up to 240 hours.

The following purposes of sentencing, spelled out in the legislation, serve as a guide for judges in making their determinations:

- to help rehabilitate offenders,
- to separate offenders from society where necessary,
- to provide restitution to victims of crimes,
- to deter offenders and others from committing offences.

On One Side

Many Canadians support this legislation and feel that prison is not the answer for all offenders. They believe that there is a difference between violent and non-violent offenders and point out that 80 percent of crimes are non-violent. Many people believe that fines alone should be imposed for a number of non-violent offences. They also think that prisons tend to make minor offenders better criminals, not better citizens, and therefore such offenders should be rehabilitated rather than imprisoned. Community service is a way not only to achieve this goal, but also a means to provide much needed help in the community.

On the Other Side

A number of Canadians oppose this type of legislation. They support a "get tough" approach to convicted offenders. They advocate the return of the death penalty, longer jail terms with no parole, no time off for good behaviour, and no rehabilitation programs. They lump violent and non-violent offenders together. Their basic philosophy—"You do the crime, you do the time"—opposes alternatives such as the conditional sentencing sanction in the new legislation. Supporters of the "get tough" approach believe that criminals respect strength, not weakness.

The Bottom Line

Community service such as public works for a municipality or doing work for a charitable organization may help to rehabilitate some non-violent offenders. Clearly, it would reduce the overcrowding of Canadian prisons and reduce the cost to taxpayers of maintaining the prison population. At the same time, some offenders may regard a community service sentence as a mere slap on the wrist, while they plan their next offence. Do the benefits outweigh the disadvantages? You be the judge!

Electronic monitoring devices are used for non-dangerous offenders.

1. a) Do you think that non-violent offenders should serve prison terms?
       Explain your answer.

    b) Is supervised community service a good substitute for prison?

2. How can prisons "make minor offenders better criminals"?

3. Apply the purposes of sentencing contained in Bill C-41 to those who
    support more community-service sentencing and those who support a
    "get tough" approach. Which purposes apply to each?

4. Do you think that most Canadians support different treatment for violent
    and non-violent offenders? Explain.

CHAPTER REVIEW

Reviewing Key Terms

For each of the following statements, indicate the key terms being defined:

a) the return to prison of repeat offenders

b) the study of the rehabilitation of offenders and the management of prisons

c) a sentence that discourages a person from committing the same offence

d) a sentence that keeps an offender in an institution until the offender can show that he or she will be able to return to society and display normal behaviour

e) the right to be released after serving two-thirds of a sentence if the offender has not already been released on parole

f) the principle that a person who is convicted of several violations of the same offence should not be sentenced to an oppressively long prison term

g) more than one penalty is served at the same time

h) to be discharged with no conditions and no conviction recorded

i) to be imprisoned

j) the act of returning that which has been unlawfully taken away from a person

Exploring Legal Concepts

1. If, on appeal, a new trial is ordered and the accused is again found guilty, should the courts be allowed to impose a more severe penalty in the second trial than that imposed in the first trial?

2. In your opinion, which of the sentencing objectives should be given the most weight? Explain.

3. In your opinion, should the correctional system be allowed to use electronic monitoring to track the location of those on probation or parole? Explain.

4. The Canadian Sentencing Commission in its report *Sentencing Reform: A Canadian Approach* concluded that the use of incarceration has failed and that it should be used with restraint. Give your opinion on this matter.

5. California has a three-strikes law, wherein a person convicted of three offences receives life imprisonment. Steven White, a two-time offender, stole a $146 video-cassette. Rather than face life in prison, he committed suicide. Another person faced life in prison for having stolen four cookies. Do you think that Canada, like California, should institute more severe penalties for repeat offenders? Why or why not?

6. Many Canadians think that we release from prison too many "walking time bombs" on parole. In your opinion, should a parole board have more freedom to extend the incarceration time for those it does not believe are ready for returning to freedom?

7. In 1995, Clifford Olson, murderer of 11 British Columbia children, had the right to request a reduction of his imprisonment time to 15 years. Should Canadian law provide for more severe penalties for those who commit multiple murders? Explain.

8. In recent years, new legislation has given many rights to victims. Critics fear that this trend is shifting the balance from fairness toward revenge. Give your opinion on this issue.

9. Many citizens are charged but found not guilty. The accused goes through great personal trauma and expense while trying to clear his or her name and, in some cases, the charges should probably have never been laid. Since the state lays the charges, should a citizen have a right to redress if found not guilty?

Applying Legal Concepts

1. For each of the following cases, impose a sentence on the offender. Outline the rationale for your decision, including which sentencing objective is most important. (The maximum sentence allowed for the offence is shown in brackets at the end of each case.)

   a) A London high school student had just finished lunch and was preparing to head to a science class. While retrieving his books from a locker, he was slammed into the wall by Laureano. The victim told Laureano "That's not necessary." Laureano replied by punching the youth in the face and stomach, causing him to momentarily black out. Laureano did not know the fellow student. The judge declared that "violence will not be tolerated in London's schools—it's time students realized this." (10 years)

   b) Welch was an 18-year-old when he and several others robbed a grocery store of $3200. Weapons and disguises were used. A small country store was similarly robbed 30 days later, and the victim was treated roughly. Welch was apprehended, and while out on bail, he and others robbed two Calgary service stations at gunpoint, departing from the crime scenes in Welch's car. Evidence at trial indicated that Welch came from a stable, supportive family, and he had done well in school and in community activities. He had hung around with friends who had a bad influence on him, and he had been somewhat out of control for four years. (life imprisonment)

   c) Travis was charged with the theft of just over $17 worth of pens, markers, and other items from the University of Western Ontario bookstore. At the time of the offence, Travis had already purchased $125 worth of goods and had $36 in his wallet. He had continued in an MBA program after completing his undergraduate work. Evidence indicated that he had been under emotional stress because of problems with his family and with his university studies. Prior to his trial, Travis apologized to the bookstore management and offered to work in the store on a voluntary basis as a penalty for his offence and as a form of compensation. (2 years)

   d) Campbell had been drinking in a bar all evening when he exchanged words with the 59-year-old victim. The words led to blows, and the two men had to be separated by bar staff. Later that evening, the victim left the premises, Campbell followed him out, and a fight started. Witnesses testified that after the victim was on the ground and defenceless, Campbell punched and kicked him in the face. The force of the blows caused the cheekbone to break away from the base of the victim's skull and he died. It was determined that both men were heavily intoxicated while fighting. Campbell pleaded guilty to the lesser charge of manslaughter. His lawyer asked for leniency in Campbell's sentencing because he had no prior convictions for violent crimes, and he had been slightly provoked by the victim. Also, he acknowledged his alcohol problem, showed genuine remorse for what happened, and had been in detention for nine months pending trial. (life imprisonment)

e) Millar was charged with first-degree murder in the killing of his father. In a frenzied state and blind with rage, Millar struck the fatal blow. For over 25 years, Millar had been dominated and humiliated horrendously by his father. The court found that Millar had been physically, sexually, and psychologically abused in ways that can only be described as cruel, insensitive, inhumane, and unthinkable. The judge noted that in more than 20 years in the practice of criminal law this case stood out as one of the most tragic. Shortly before the killing, Millar's father menaced him with a knife and castigated him in a cruel and inhuman fashion for his inadequacies. The father's rage was due to Millar's failure to respond to his father's suggestion that it would "be nice to have a glass of milk." The jury found Millar not guilty as charged but guilty of the lesser offence of manslaughter. After being released on bail pending sentencing, he faithfully attended treatment sessions. (life imprisonment)

2. Carroll, a 42-year-old amateur soccer player, head-butted an opposing player during a soccer game. The linesman gave evidence that Carroll suddenly and without warning head-butted the complainant, resulting in three broken teeth and necessitating reconstructive surgery to his palate. The trial judge disbelieved Carroll's evidence that the complainant became aggressive toward him and that the collision of heads occurred inadvertently during Carroll's attempt to wrestle the complainant to the ground. At the sentence hearing the Crown suggested that a jail term was not appropriate and invited the court to levy a substantial fine in addition to the making of a probation order. A criminal record would destroy Carroll's ability to pursue his career in the field of financial services, and he was otherwise of good character. The trial judge imposed a conditional discharge that included a fine of $1500 and probation.

   • **On what basis would Carroll appeal his sentence?**

3. When Steele was 18 years old he pleaded guilty to a charge of attempted rape and was declared to be a "criminal sexual psychopath." The judge imposed an indeterminate sentence and emphasized that Steele should receive proper psychiatric treatment. There was no psychiatric help available to treat Steele's condition in the penitentiary. Yet he responded well initially to incarceration. When various attempts at supervised parole were tried, they ended because of some infraction usually stemming from substance abuse or breach of discipline. He had little hope for release unless he could receive psychiatric treatment. Yet the institutions where he was sent to serve his sentence did not have facilities to provide treatment. When the facilities for treatment finally became available after some 20 years' imprisonment, admission was twice denied because Steele's condition had

deteriorated to the point where he would not benefit from the program.

Most reports concerning Steele recommended some form of release; those that did not noted that he had become "institutionalized" and that he had not been treated for his disorder. The Parole Board repeatedly denied parole because of his risk to society. After 37 years of imprisonment, when he was 55 years old, Steele filed a petition in the nature of *habeas corpus*, seeking release.

- **Was his continued detention cruel and unusual punishment?**

4. Schneider was convicted of impaired driving causing death and was sentenced to 15 months' imprisonment and prohibited from driving for three years. He had run a red light, resulting in the death of the driver of another vehicle. Schneider appealed his sentence, arguing that he had no prior criminal record and no alcohol abuse problem. His level of impairment at the time of the accident was low, and there was little chance of reoffending. Finally, the main issue raised by Schneider was whether all or part of the sentence should have been served under the electronic monitoring system. The Court of Appeal affirmed the 15 months' sentence, reduced the driving prohibition to 15 months from three years, but did not feel that electronic monitoring was appropriate.

- **Why did the Court of Appeal deny the request to allow part of the sentence to be served under the electronic monitoring system?**

5. *R. v. Jones* (1994) Supreme Court of Canada 89 C.C.C. (3d) 353

Jones was convicted of rape, gross indecency, and attempted rape and sentenced to five years' imprisonment. He spent two years in a sex offender program and was released on mandatory supervision. While on parole, he was charged with three counts of sexual assault with a weapon and three counts of unlawful confinement. Jones's counsel obtained a court order after the second set of offences to have him observed to see if he was fit to stand trial, to determine whether he was sane at the time of the offence, and to gain some insight into the accused for the purpose of sentencing. He was warned that whatever he told the psychiatrists could be used against him and might be included in a report to the court. He was not told that what he said on the examination could also be used for the purpose of a determination of whether he was a dangerous offender. He was told that he had the right to refuse to answer questions and had the right to consult counsel prior to answering any questions. Jones said that he understood, and he cooperated willingly. On a *voir dire* to determine admissibility of the evidence from the two psychiatrists and the psychologist, the judge rejected Jones's argument that admitting the evidence would violate his *Charter* section 7 rights to life, liberty, and security of the person.

- **Were Jones's rights violated?**

Extending Legal Concepts

1. Now that you have completed this chapter, review the opening article and Something to Think About. Have your answers or opinions changed? Why or why not?

2. With a partner, discuss this statement: "The answer to community safety is longer sentences and bigger prisons." Try to reach a consensus or agreement. Compare your findings with another set of partners. Discuss, negotiate, and attempt a larger group consensus. Compare these results with those of another group of four. Attempt to reach agreement with this larger group. As a class, discuss the steps necessary to reach a final consensus. Place the final list of key issues on the chalkboard for further discussion.

3. With a partner, brainstorm a list of advantages and disadvantages to each of the following:

   a) incarceration of offenders

   b) community service orders

   c) capital punishment

4. Using reference materials in your resource centre, including CD-ROM and the Internet, obtain current information on sentencing in your province, in Canada, and in other countries. Write a one-page summary of your findings, and create a poster to display your information.

Researching an Issue

Nonsmoking in Penitentiaries

Smoking in virtually all public buildings has become a thing of the past. Law-abiding citizens who work in these buildings are not allowed to smoke inside. Yet offenders are allowed to smoke inside correctional institutions. Some people believe that this is a privilege that should be denied. The federal government is considering banning smoking inside the buildings of federal penitentiaries.

Statement

There should be a ban on smoking inside penitentiaries and other correctional institutions.

Point

Inmates who are smokers should have to respect the rights of nonsmoking inmates.

Counterpoint

A prohibition of smoking will result in a backlash by the smoking population in these institutions.

- **With a partner, research this issue and reflect on your findings.**
- **Prepare points on this statement that could be used for a class debate.**
- **Discuss your findings with others in your class.**

THE CRIMINAL CODE

These are the key terms introduced in this chapter:

abduction

aggravated assault

aggravated sexual assault

arson

artistic merit

assault

assault causing bodily harm

break and enter

causation

colour of right

community tolerance

complainant

criminal negligence

culpable homicide

enterprise crime

enticing

euthanasia

false pretences

first-degree murder

homicide

incest

infanticide

manslaughter

mischief

molesting

murder

non-culpable homicide

procuring

prohibited weapons

restricted weapons

robbery

second-degree murder

sexual assault

soliciting

theft

theft over

theft under

Chapter at a Glance

Learning Outcomes

At the end of this chapter, you will be able to

1. distinguish between crimes of violence, property crimes, social impact crimes, and other crimes;
2. appraise Canadian laws relating to abortion, weapons, obscenity, and soliciting;
3. distinguish between procuring and soliciting, murder and manslaughter, and first- and second-degree murder;
4. describe the various categories of assault and sexual assault;
5. describe laws relating to the protection of children;
6. discuss changes that have been made to the *Criminal Code* in response to social problems.

Justice Minister Allan Rock introduced more than 150 amendments to the *Criminal Code* yesterday, but it's unclear if they'll ever get to a House of Commons vote.

Rock introduced the amendments on the final day before the Commons Christmas break.

Prime Minister Jean Chrétien has not yet indicated whether he will prorogue this session, effectively killing all government business including the Rock amendments, before MPs return in February.

Rock moved on child prostitution, stalking, proceeds of crime, computer crime, credit-card fraud, impaired driving, and joyriding.

Rock's Crime Amendments Might Never Get to a Vote

"These new measures help in the continuing effort to address the problem of violence by men against women and children," Rock told a news conference.

On youth prostitution, pimps would now face a mandatory five-year minimum sentence on conviction, and he has introduced a move to make it easier for young prostitutes to testify against their pimps.

If a stalking victim is murdered, the charge would automatically be first-degree murder, regardless of circumstances, if the victim feared for his or her safety prior to the crime.

Rock also introduced an amendment for tougher penalties against those convicted of stalking while under a restraining order.

He has called for the *Criminal Code* to be fine-tuned.

"You table legislation to start the process, but you do it to show the government is taking action," he said.

From: Tim Harper, "Rock's crime amendments might never get to a vote." *The Toronto Star*, December 15, 1995. Reprinted with permission— The Toronto Star Syndicate.

Something to Think About

- **What types of crimes are identified in this article?**
- **Why does Justice Minister Allan Rock feel that amendments to the *Criminal Code* are necessary?**
- **What penalties does the *Code* currently specify for some of these offences?**

7.1 INTRODUCTION

The Canadian *Criminal Code* is a federal statute that reflects the social values of Canadians. As society's values change, the *Code* changes. New crimes may be added, such as harassment, stalking, or crimes involving computer communication, while outdated crimes may be deleted or revised. For example possession of marijuana once carried a lengthy prison sentence, but is now treated as a summary conviction offence.

The *Criminal Code* contains the main body of criminal law and identifies hundreds of acts that are considered criminal. These offences account for approximately 80 percent of all offences committed in a given year. Because criminal law falls under federal jurisdiction, the offences are the same across Canada. Many of these, with their penalties, are listed later in this chapter in section 7.6.

You will have noted in reading earlier chapters that the descriptions of offences are extremely technical and precise. Careful wording is necessary to ensure that citizens are not arrested on a criminal charge that is in fact a noncriminal matter, and that offenders are not exonerated on technicalities. The elements required for the Crown to obtain a conviction must be specified clearly. Despite the precision of the wording, many cases are appealed on a point of law, thanks to subtleties in the interpretation of various terms.

It is impossible to examine all the offences in the *Criminal Code* in this text. We will discuss the most common crimes, and those that involve significant social issues. For clarity, these offences have been divided according to the headings found under "Chapter at a Glance," although this does not reflect the *Criminal Code* classification.

7.2 $\mathcal{V}$IOLENT CRIMES

Violent crimes are offences that violate the human body in some way. Approximately 11 percent of all *Criminal Code* offences committed are of a violent nature. We will look at the following violent crimes: homicide, assault, robbery, abduction, and sexual offences.

Homicide

Killing another human being, directly or indirectly, is **homicide**. **Culpable homicide** is murder, manslaughter, or infanticide. Culpable means deserving blame or blameworthy. Culpable homicide is committed when the injured person dies within a year and a day from the event that caused the injury. **Non-culpable homicide** is death caused by complete accident or in self-defence.

Murder

The most serious violent crime that one person can commit against another is **murder**—intentional killing. The specific intent required need not only be the intent of the killer. It may also arise from the circumstances. Section 229 of the *Criminal Code* specifies the circumstances under which a person may be found guilty of murder, even if he or she did not intend to commit murder.

Suppose Allis shoots Bakuska with intent to kill, but her shot kills Martin instead. Allis is guilty of murder, although she did not intend to kill Martin. If Domingo seeks revenge against Eisen by committing arson, and the resulting fire causes the death of Freeman, who is in the building, Domingo will be charged with murder.

Canada recognizes two classes of murder— **first-degree murder** and **second-degree murder**— as specified in section 231 of the *Criminal Code*. According to the Supreme Court of Canada, this section is "designed to impose the longest possible term of imprisonment without eligibility for parole upon those who commit the most grievous murders."

First-degree murder occurs if any one of three main categories of circumstances exists:

- The murder is planned and deliberate. This category would include cases where money or anything of value passes as consideration for causing or assisting in causing the death,

---

229.

Culpable homicide is murder

(a) where the person who causes the death of a human being

   (i) means to cause his death, or

   (ii) means to cause him bodily harm that he knows is likely to cause his death, and is reckless whether death ensues or not;

(b) where a person, meaning to cause death to a human being or meaning to cause him bodily harm that he knows is likely to cause death, and being reckless whether death ensues or not, by accident or mistake causes death to another human being, notwithstanding that he does not mean to cause death or bodily harm to that human being; or

(c) where a person, for an unlawful object, does anything that he knows or ought to know is likely to cause death, and thereby causes death to a human being, notwithstanding that he desires to effect his object without causing death or bodily harm to any human being.

---

or if there is any action that causes or assists in causing the death. "Planned" and "deliberate" are separate items. Planned means "a calculated scheme or design that has been thought out carefully, and the nature and consequences of which have been considered and weighed" . . . but it need not "be a complicated one." Deliberate means "considered" and "not impulsive."

- The victim is a law-enforcement agent, as defined by the *Criminal Code*.
- The death occurs while certain crimes particularly offensive to society are committed. These crimes include hijacking an aircraft, sexual assault, aggravated sexual assault, sexual assault with a weapon, threats or causing bodily harm to a third party, kidnapping and forcible confinement, and hostage taking.

CASE

R. v. Martineau
(1990)

Supreme Court of Canada
2 S.C.R. 632

Tremblay and Martineau set out with a pellet pistol and rifle to commit a crime. Although armed, Martineau thought that it would only be a break and enter. They entered the McLeans' house and robbed the couple. Then Tremblay shot and killed them. After Martineau heard the shot that killed the first victim, he allegedly said, "Lady, say your prayers."

Martineau asked Tremblay why he killed the couple, and Tremblay replied that the couple had seen their faces. Martineau responded that they couldn't have seen his because he was wearing a mask.

The Supreme Court of Canada held that section 213(a) [now section 230] of the *Criminal Code* was inconsistent with sections 7 and 11(d) of the *Charter*. Furthermore, the sections could not be justified by section 1 of the *Charter*.

The *Criminal Code* states, "Culpable homicide is murder where a person causes the death of a human being while committing or attempting to commit . . . breaking and entering . . . whether or not he knows that death is likely to be caused to any human being, if he means to cause bodily harm for the purpose of . . . facilitating his flight after committing or attempting to commit the offence, and the death ensues from the bodily harm."

1. The Supreme Court of Canada stated that in "a free and democratic society that values the autonomy and free will of the individual, the stigma and punishment attached to murder should be reserved for those who choose intentionally to cause death or who choose to inflict bodily harm knowing that it is likely to cause death." What is the *mens rea* of murder? Did Martineau have it?

2. The Court ruled that for a conviction for murder to be sustained, subjective foresight of death must be proven beyond a reasonable doubt. Explain what this means.

3. Chief Justice Lamer indicated that "to label and punish a person as a murderer who did not intend or foresee death unnecessarily stigmatizes and punishes those whose moral blameworthiness is not that of a murderer." What could the offender be convicted of, and what maximum penalty imposed?

Intentionally causing death is second-degree murder in all but the circumstances mentioned above. The minimum sentence for both first- and second-degree murder is life imprisonment.

Causation is a frequent issue in murder trials. For example, if a person is viciously struck and falls into a river and drowns, did the striking or the falling into the river cause the death? Causation frequently arises where the aiding or abetting of a death occurred, as shown in the case of *R. v. Kirkness* (1990) discussed in Chapter 3. In many cases where causation is an issue, expert evidence can be very significant.

Manslaughter

Manslaughter is culpable homicide but requires only general intent, unlike murder, which requires specific intent. The *actus reus* elements of **manslaughter** are directly or indirectly causing the death of a human being by means of an unlawful act. The *mens rea*, which must be proved beyond a reasonable doubt, is that a reasonable person would inevitably recognize that the unlawful act could subject a victim to the risk of bodily harm or death. Thus, for example, a person who loses control of his or her car while speeding and kills a pedestrian would be charged with manslaughter, not murder.

Criminal Code Incidents, 1993

2 736 096 *Criminal Code* Incidents

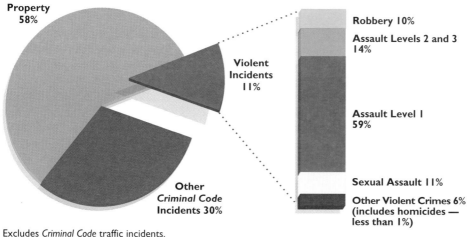

310 187 Violent Incidents

Property 58%

Violent Incidents 11%

Other *Criminal Code* Incidents 30%

Robbery 10%

Assault Levels 2 and 3 14%

Assault Level 1 59%

Sexual Assault 11%

Other Violent Crimes 6% (includes homicides — less than 1%)

Excludes *Criminal Code* traffic incidents.
Source: Statistics Canada.

A conviction for manslaughter will result from a murder charge if the accused can successfully put forth either of two defences: provocation or intoxication. For the first defence to be successful, the accused must suddenly lose self-control "in the heat of passion caused by sudden provocation" and cause another's death. Further, the provocation must be a wrongful act or insult. It must also be such that it would cause an ordinary person (not one who is drugged or drunk) to lose self-control. Finally, the killing must take place during the loss of self-control. If, after being provoked, the accused has time to plan to kill the other person, the charge will be murder, not manslaughter.

The issue of intoxication is frequently significant in murder cases, for it might influence a person's ability to foresee the consequences of his or her action. The Crown must prove both the killing and the necessary intent where drunkenness is at issue. If there is doubt as to the ability to form the necessary intent due to the ingestion of alcohol or drugs, the accused must be found guilty of manslaughter, not murder.

The defence of drunkenness will be successful if it can be proved that the accused was so intoxicated as to be incapable of forming the specific intent necessary for committing murder. The issue of drunkenness as a defence to murder was being reviewed in early 1996.

CASE

Gosset, a 16-year veteran of the Montreal police force, and his partner, Kimberley, responded to a call from a taxi-driver complaining of a customer who refused to pay his fare. The customer identified himself as Tony Bowers, but Gosset learned over the police radio that this information was false. Papers that the customer was carrying revealed that he was Tony Griffin, for whom there was an arrest warrant outstanding. Griffin was arrested and taken to the police station. The officers received a bag belonging to Griffin from the cab driver. In the bag were approximately 150 packs of cigarettes.

R. v. Gosset
(1993)

Supreme Court of Canada
83 C.C.C. (3d) 494

At the police station, Griffin attempted to flee when Gosset opened the rear door to let him out. Gosset chased him, taking his gun from its holster as he ran. The gun was held at the side of his right leg, pointing toward the ground. Gosset shouted a warning, then pointed his gun at Griffin with his index finger on the trigger. The gun went off, and Griffin was struck fatally in the head.

At trial, Gosset claimed that he pointed his gun to intimidate Griffin, who was not responding to the order to stop. The Crown's position was that Griffin had already stopped running forward and had begun running on the spot, dodging like a boxer, when he turned to face Gosset.

Gosset's gun could be fired either by "single action," where the gun is already cocked and only slight pressure on the trigger is required, or by "double action," requiring very strong pressure on the trigger to raise the hammer and fire a shot. Gosset testified that he was not aware of cocking the gun and never made a decision to do so, but he acknowledged that the gun must have been cocked at the time he pointed it at Griffin. He indicated that he never intended to shoot and that the gun discharged accidentally.

Gosset was charged with manslaughter. He was acquitted after the judge directed the jury that Gosset could only be convicted if there was proof of a "criminal state of mind." The acquittal was set aside by the Quebec Court of Appeal and a new trial ordered. Gosset's appeal to the Supreme Court of Canada was dismissed.

1. **In your opinion, did Gosset's conduct constitute a marked departure from the standard of care a reasonably prudent person would have in the same circumstances?**

2. **If there was a marked departure, there would also have to be a foreseeability of the risk of death. Did that foreseeability exist in this case?**

3. **To be found guilty, must Gosset have had a criminal state of mind?**

Infanticide

The killing of a newborn by the child's mother, who is mentally disturbed as an after-effect of having given birth is **infanticide**. The maximum punishment is imprisonment for five years. Infanticide is a charge seldom seen before the courts.

Suicide and Euthanasia

It is an offence to counsel anyone to commit suicide, or to help anyone accomplish the deed. Until 1972, it was also an offence to attempt to commit suicide.

Suicide is closely tied to **euthanasia**, or mercy killing. There are different categories of euthanasia. The first is *voluntary* euthanasia, where the patient wants to be allowed to die. *Involuntary* euthanasia occurs in cases where the patient cannot give consent, for example, after an accident when the patient is in a coma and there is no hope of recovery. In this case, the patient's family and doctors make the decision.

Euthanasia can also be either passive or active. *Passive* euthanasia occurs when a person's condition is considered hopeless and so is never treated. *Active* euthanasia occurs when drugs are given or treatment withdrawn to bring about the death of a person. If a person has a terminal disease for which there is no cure and has requested no further treatment, euthanasia would be both voluntary and active. Doctor-assisted suicide, a form of active euthanasia, is an offence according to section 241 of the *Criminal Code*, which states, "Every one who (a) counsels a person to commit suicide, or (b) aids or abets a person to commit suicide, whether suicide ensues or not, is guilty of an indictable offence and liable to imprisonment for a term not exceeding 14 years."

The issue of euthanasia is considered at the end of this chapter.

Assault

The laws on assault have changed in recent years to reflect the increase of violence in our society and the public awareness of family and sexual assaults. The *Criminal Code* classifies assault according to three levels of severity, with increasing penalties. Intent is a key element in all three. If the action is the result of carelessness or reflex, rather than intent, a charge of assault will not succeed. A threat can constitute an assault if there is an ability to carry it out at the time it is made.

The first level of **assault** consists of any of the following actions:

- applying intentional force to another person, either directly or indirectly, without that person's consent;
- attempting or threatening, by an act or a gesture, to apply force;
- accosting or impeding another person, or begging, while openly wearing or carrying a weapon or an imitation thereof.

Words unaccompanied by any gesture do not constitute an assault. Thus, to say "I am going to belt you" would not constitute an assault unless one waved a fist. It is not necessary that the victim knows that the assault is occurring. Thus, if one shoots a gun at someone and misses, an assault may have occurred. Consent is not necessarily given in a sporting activity, such as in a hockey game, just because one participates. That defence will fail if the person went beyond what is normally recognized as being acceptable in the activity.

The second level of severity is **assault causing bodily harm**. It is committed by anyone who, while committing assault, carries, uses, or threatens to use a weapon or an imitation thereof, or causes bodily harm to the **complainant**. "Bodily harm" is defined as "anything that interferes with the complainant's health or comfort and that is more than merely transient or trifling in nature."

The third level, **aggravated assault**, is the most severe. It is committed if a person wounds, maims, disfigures, or endangers the life of the victim. The *mens rea* required is only to commit bodily harm, and not necessarily to wound, maim, disfigure, or endanger the life. The defence of consent may be negated in some circumstances for this level of assault. For example, if a woman consented to a non-medical person using an instrument to perform an abortion that later led to complications, consent would probably not be a viable defence.

CASE

Godin was taking care of his girlfriend's baby. The baby was cranky and vomited his milk. Godin called an ambulance. At the hospital the baby was diagnosed as having suffered a major head trauma. X-rays revealed a fracture of the skull. Internal bleeding had caused the baby to be critically ill. There was also bruising on the top of the baby's mouth. The doctor expressed an opinion that it would take a "violent impact" to cause such an injury.

Godin told the ambulance attendants that the baby had choked on his medication. When confronted with the skull fracture, he explained that he had slipped down the stairs while carrying the child and the child had struck the door frame.

At trial, Godin testified that while administering medication to the baby, the baby choked. Godin said he panicked and slapped the baby on the back, and the baby struck his head on the table. Godin was charged with assault causing bodily harm. The trial judge noted that Godin never sincerely endeavoured to provide a totally candid account of what took place that night. The judge noted that "in the face of such strong inculpatory facts, the accused, in my view, had to offer some explanation which might reasonably be true or otherwise . . . he runs the risk of being convicted."

R. v. Godin
(1994)

Supreme Court of Canada
89 C.C.C. (3d) 574

Godin was convicted, but the Court of Appeal for New Brunswick upheld his appeal and ordered a new trial. The Crown appealed to the Supreme Court of Canada, which reinstated the trial decision.

1. **On what basis would Godin have appealed to the Court of Appeal of New Brunswick?**
2. **What weight should be given to Godin's evidence?**
3. **What kind of evidence did the doctor provide?**
4. **In your opinion, did Godin have the necessary *mens rea* to have committed the offence?**
5. **Why did the Court reinstate the trial decision?**

Sexual Assault

The offences of rape and indecent assault were rewritten in the 1980s to emphasize the violent, rather than sexual, nature of these crimes. The part of the body touched, the nature of the contact, the situation in which it occurred, the words and gestures accompanying the act, and all other circumstances surrounding the conduct, including threats, which may or may not have been accompanied by force, are relevant in considering whether the conduct of the accused had a sexual nature.

There are three levels of **sexual assault** that parallel the three types of assault described above. The first level of sexual assault is included in the definition of assault, but the assault has to occur in relation to sexual conduct. An example is **molesting**.

The second level is defined in section 272 as follows: "Every one who, in committing a sexual assault, (a) carries, uses, or threatens to use a weapon or an imitation thereof, (b) threatens to cause bodily harm to a person other than the complainant, (c) causes bodily harm to the complainant, or (d) is a party to the offence with any other person, is guilty of an indictable offence and liable to imprisonment for a term not exceeding 14 years." Note that the wording does not include the words "knowingly" or "with intent," so this is a general intent offence. Thus, drunkenness is not a defence.

The most severe level, **aggravated sexual assault**, is defined in section 273: "(1) Every one commits an aggravated sexual assault who, in committing a sexual assault, wounds, maims, disfigures, or endangers the life of the complainant. (2) Every one who commits an aggravated sexual

assault is guilty of an indictable offence and liable to imprisonment for life."

Consent is frequently an issue in sexual assault trials. Consent no longer serves as a defence in situations where the victim submits or does not resist because force has been applied, force has been threatened, fraud has been perpetrated, or authority has been exercised (see section 265(3) of the *Code*).

Consent is not a defence where the victim is under 14 years of age, unless the accused is less

Where sexual assaults by strangers occur

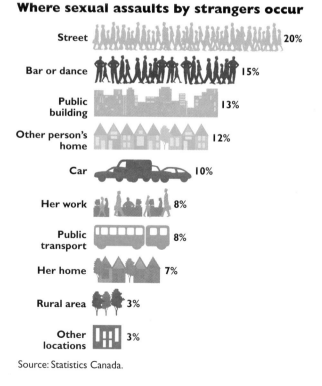

Street	20%
Bar or dance	15%
Public building	13%
Other person's home	12%
Car	10%
Her work	8%
Public transport	8%
Her home	7%
Rural area	3%
Other locations	3%

Source: Statistics Canada.

than three years older than the victim. In *R. v. M.M.L.* (1994), which involved a 16-year-old girl who had been sexually assaulted by her stepfather, the Supreme Court of Canada ruled that it is not necessary to verbally or physically resist to show lack of consent. The girl had said that she was too "scared" to resist.

Part of the *mens rea* of assault is knowledge of the fact that the victim is not consenting. It is possible that the accused could believe that the victim was consenting to contact even though he or she was not. In such a situation, the accused would not be guilty because she or he lacked *mens rea*. Although knowledge must be subjective, consideration may be given to the reasonableness of a belief that the consent was given in determining its honesty.

The Crown must persuade the jury beyond a reasonable doubt that the accused knew the complainant was not consenting; or that the accused's belief arose from the accused's self-induced intoxication, or recklessness, or wilful blindness; or that the accused did not take reasonable steps to ascertain that the complainant was consenting. The issue of intoxication as a defence is discussed in Chapter 5 in *R. v. Daviault.*

The *Criminal Code* permits one spouse to bring charges against the other for any of the three levels of sexual assault, whether or not they are living together.

The admission of evidence concerning the past behaviour, or lifestyle, of the complainant in sexual assault trials has long been an issue. It will often influence a jury as to whether consent was given or whether the accused could honestly have believed that it was. In 1983, the so-called "rape shield" law was added to the *Criminal Code.* This law was designed to shield sexual assault victims from being cross-examined about their sexual history.

CASE

Seaboyer was charged with the sexual assault of a woman with whom he had been drinking in a bar. During the preliminary inquiry, the judge refused to allow Seaboyer to cross-examine the complainant on her sexual conduct on other occasions. Seaboyer contended that he should have been permitted to cross-examine about other acts of sexual intercourse, which may have caused bruises and other aspects of the complainant's condition that the Crown had put in evidence. Such evidence might have been relevant to consent.

The matter eventually found its way to the Supreme Court of Canada. That Court struck down Canada's 1983 "rape shield" law that protected alleged sexual assault victims from being questioned about their sexual history in court as being unconstitutional. The Court said that the law infringed on an accused person's section 7 and 11(d) *Charter* rights. A law that prevents a judge and jury from getting at the truth by excluding certain relevant evidence critical to the defence "runs afoul of our fundamental conceptions of justice and what constitutes a fair trial." The Court supported the objectives of the 1983 law, but indicated that it overshot the mark and rendered inadmissible evidence that may be essential to the presentation of legitimate defences and hence to a fair trial. The Court recommended strict guidelines to ensure that only relevant information about the victim could be raised in court.

R. v. Seaboyer
(1991)

Supreme Court of Canada
7 C.R. (4th) 117

1. **Prior to 1983, what were the reasons for defence counsels' tough and often brutal cross-examination of sexual assault victims?**
2. **Why was the "rape shield" law enacted in 1983?**
3. **What rights are guaranteed by sections 7 and 11(d) of the *Charter*?**
4. **Why did Seaboyer believe that his rights had been violated?**

Before Parliament passed the "rape shield" law, victims had been needlessly exposed to brutal and humiliating cross-examination concerning previous sexual activity that usually had no bearing on the case being tried. The purpose was to highlight two misconceptions: that women with previous sexual activity would more likely have consented to sex willingly, and that such women were less likely to tell the truth in court.

In response to public reaction to the Supreme Court's ruling in *R. v. Seaboyer*, the Minister of Justice introduced a bill to partially restore the principle that the victim of sexual assault cannot have her sexual history used to discredit her on the witness stand. Under the 1992 legislation, evidence can be admitted only if a judge determines that it "is of specific instances of sexual activity, is relevant to an issue at trial, and has significant probative value that is not substantially outweighed by the danger of prejudice to the proper administration of justice." To consider whether or not to admit the evidence, a hearing is held with the jury and public excluded. Section 276(3) applies in these situations.

The *Criminal Code* also prohibits the admission of evidence of sexual reputation for the purpose of challenging or supporting the credibility of the complainant. However, in a precedent-setting decision in *R. v. O'Connor* (1995) the Supreme Court of Canada ruled that in certain circumstances an accused rapist can have access to the alleged victim's private counselling records. A two-step procedure was established by the Court to gain access. First, the defence lawyers must convince a trial judge the counselling records contain information that is relevant to mounting a complete defence. Second, if the records are deemed relevant, the judge must determine which portions, if any, to release to the defence. The Court outlined a variety of factors that the judge should consider when determining which records should be disclosed. For example, are the records potentially harmful to the complainant's dignity, privacy, or security? As of early 1996, the Minister was studying the Court's decision.

Other Sexual Offences

The law protects young people from being pressured into having sexual relationships with those who are older. The *Criminal Code* states that it is an

276.

(3) In determining whether evidence is admissible under subsection (2), the judge, provincial court judge, or justice shall take into account
- **(a)** the interests of justice, including the right of the accused to make a full answer and defence;
- **(b)** society's interest in encouraging the reporting of sexual assault offences;
- **(c)** whether there is a reasonable prospect that the evidence will assist in arriving at a just determination in the case;
- **(d)** the need to remove from the fact-finding process any discriminatory belief or bias;
- **(e)** the risk that the evidence may unduly arouse sentiments of prejudice, sympathy, or hostility in the jury;
- **(f)** the potential prejudice to the complainant's personal dignity and right of privacy;
- **(g)** the right of the complainant and of every individual to personal security and to the full protection and benefit of the law; and
- **(h)** any other factor that the judge, provincial court judge, or justice considers relevant.

offence for a person to touch, for sexual purpose, a part of the body of a person under the age of 14 years, or to invite, counsel or incite that person to touch, for sexual purpose, a part of the body of any person. It is not a defence that the victim consented unless the accused is less than three years older than the victim.

A similar offence exists if the person is in a position of trust or authority toward a person 14 years of age or more but under the age of 18 years, or with whom the young person is in a relationship of dependency. It is not a defence to the charge that the accused did not know the age of the victim unless the accused took all reasonable steps to ascertain the age of the complainant, nor that the

Dolls like these are used to assist children when describing their abuse.

victim consented. Generally, a person who is aged 12 or 13 cannot be tried for these offences.

It is an offence to

- have anal intercourse, unless engaged in private between husband and wife or two persons each of whom is 18 years of age or more.

    In *R. v. M. (C.)* (1995), the Ontario Court of Appeal ruled that this section of the *Criminal Code* violated section 15 of the *Charter* on the grounds of sexual orientation. The section arbitrarily denied gay men their choice of sexual expression with a consenting partner until they were 18, while unmarried heterosexual adolescents 14 and over could participate in consensual intercourse without criminal penalty. By early 1996, the Crown had not appealed the decision.

- commit bestiality, or compel another to commit bestiality, or to commit bestiality in the presence of a person under the age of 14, or to incite a person under 14 to commit bestiality.

- procure a person under the age of 18 years for the purpose of engaging in any sexual activity prohibited by the *Criminal Code*.

- as owner, occupier, or manager of premises, knowingly permit a person under the age of 18 years to resort to or to be in or on the premises for the purpose of engaging in any sexual activity prohibited by the *Criminal Code*.

- in the home of a person under 18, participate in adultery or sexual immorality or indulge in habitual drunkenness or any other form of vice, and thereby endanger the morals of the child or render the home an unfit place for the child to be in.

- commit an indecent act in a public place, or be nude in a public place, or be nude on private property and exposed to public view.

- commit **incest** (have sexual intercourse with a blood relative).

The protection of the victim of an assault has become a focus of the law in recent years. Victims have new rights during the trial, during sentencing, and during incarceration. The offence of criminal harassment, or stalking, was added to the *Criminal Code* in 1994. It prohibits anyone from repeatedly communicating with or following another person, any member of the other person's family, or anyone known to that person, where in all the circumstances, they reasonably fear for their safety. A related addition to the *Code* allows a judge to prohibit sex offenders from frequenting places where children gather and from being employed in positions of trust over children.

Abduction

Due to the growing number of separated families, **abductions** now occur more frequently. The *Criminal Code* makes it an offence to take an unmarried person under the age of 16 years from the possession of and against the will of his or her parent, guardian, or any other person who has lawful care or charge of the person. A guardian is defined to include foster parents, as well as the Children's Aid Society.

A separate offence is the unlawful taking, enticing, concealing, detaining, receiving, or harbouring of a person under 14 years of age by anyone other than the parent or guardian.

Disputes over custody may result in one parent enticing a child away from the custodial parent prior to the custody order, or later on. The offence of **enticing** was created to cover such situations. Its provisions also take effect when a custodial parent refuses to give access to a child according to the terms of an agreement, or a noncustodial parent detains or runs away with the child while exercising access.

One defence against enticing is that the other parent consented to the action. Another is that it was necessary to protect the child from imminent harm. Accommodating a child who prefers to live with the noncustodial parent is not a defence.

Robbery

Unlike theft, **robbery** involves the use of violence, the threat of violence, assault, or the use of offensive weapons. Generally, "to assault" means "to apply force intentionally to another person." Where the Crown is basing its case on the threat of violence, it must prove that the victim felt threatened, and that there were reasonable and probable grounds for the fear. It has been held that phrases such as "empty your till" or "this is a holdup" implied the threat of violence if the command was not obeyed. It has been held that to simulate a weapon with a part of the body—such as a fist or finger—does not mean that an offensive weapon was used, although it does indicate a threat of violence. An imitation weapon is categorized as an offensive weapon. The severe punishment for robbery—life imprisonment—clearly indicates society's revulsion for those who steal using violent means.

Reviewing Your Reading

1. **What constitutes a violent crime?**

2. **Distinguish between culpable and non-culpable homicide.**

3. **What are the *actus reus* and *mens rea* of murder? What circumstances must exist?**

4. **Distinguish between first- and second-degree murder, and describe the penalties for each.**

5. a) **What is manslaughter?**

   b) **When can a charge of murder be reduced to manslaughter?**

6. **Define infanticide and state the maximum penalty.**

7. **Distinguish among the three levels of assault.**

8. a) **Why was the offence of rape changed to sexual assault?**

   b) **Distinguish among the three levels of sexual assault.**

9. **In what situations is consent *not* a defence to sexual assault?**

10. **Under what circumstances can the past conduct of the complainant be introduced in a sexual assault trial?**

11. **Describe the elements of (a) abduction and (b) enticing.**

12. **Describe four separate offences that pertain to sexual intercourse involving persons under the age of 18.**

13. **Describe the elements of robbery.**

7.3 $\mathcal{P}$ROPERTY CRIMES

At one time, the protection of property was one of the most important functions of criminal law. Until the eighteenth century, death was a common penalty for theft; property such as livestock and horses was so important to the owners this extreme punishment was deemed necessary. The *Criminal Code* continues to provide major penalties for offences against property, which make up approximately two-thirds of all offences under the *Code*. The major property crimes are arson, theft over $5000, theft under $5000, motor-vehicle theft, break and enter, possession of stolen goods, and fraud.

Arson

Due to an increase in intentional fires and explosions, the *Criminal Code* was amended in 1990 to expand the acts that are considered to be **arson** and the penalties related to them. Arson is the cause of over 12 percent of all fires in Canada, which kill more than 50 and injure over 500 people annually. Property damage each year due to arson exceeds $150 million.

The *Code* defines arson as the intentional or reckless causing of damage by fire or explosion to property, whether or not the arsonist owns the property. If the person is aware that the property is inhabited or occupied, or is reckless in that regard, or if the fire or explosion causes bodily harm to another person, the penalty is life imprisonment. Where there is no danger to life the penalty is 14 years in prison. Since 1990, these sections in the *Code* also apply to automobiles.

To commit arson with intent to defraud, such as to collect on an insurance policy, is an offence with a maximum penalty of 10 years. It is also an offence to cause bodily harm or damage to property by not following a standard of care that a "reasonably prudent person" would and allowing a fire or explosion to occur. To possess any incendiary material or device, such as a bomb, for the purpose of committing arson is illegal. Finally, to set off a false fire alarm is a hybrid offence—the maximum penalty is two years if the Crown proceeds by indictment.

Did You Know

Over 50 percent of arson incidents are committed by people between 12 and 17 years of age.

Theft

Anyone who fraudulently and without colour of right takes or converts to his or her own use anything, whether animate or inanimate, with the intent to deprive the owner of it temporarily or absolutely, commits **theft**, according to the *Criminal Code*. **Colour of right** means that the person who takes the item believes that he or she has a right to do so and therefore has no intent to steal. If the value of the goods is below $5000, the offence is generally referred to as **theft under**; over $5000, as **theft over**. The penalties are substantially different. Theft under is a hybrid offence with a maximum penalty of two years. Theft over has a maximum penalty of 10 years.

A person can be charged with theft on the basis of the principle of recent possession. When arrested, a person who has possession of items that were recently stolen must be able to explain at trial how he or she came to possess them. If the accused provides an explanation, the onus is on the Crown to disprove it, and, if it fails to do so, the accused must be acquitted.

The *Criminal Code* also makes it an offence to obtain fraudulently and without colour of right any computer service, to intercept any function of a computer system, or to use a computer system to commit a crime.

Did You Know

One in 10 Canadian households with a motor vehicle was a victim of a motor vehicle crime in 1993. That year, losses from the 156 811 vehicles stolen and vandalized totalled $1.6 billion.

Break and Enter

The law considers **break and enter**, commonly called burglary, a serious offence. The terms "break" and "enter" are defined in sections 321 and 350 of the *Criminal Code*. In defining break, section 321 states, "In this Part, 'break' means (a) to break any part, internal or external, or (b) to open any thing that is used or intended to be used to close or to cover an internal or external opening." The definition of enter, in section 350(a), states, "a person enters as soon as any

CASE

R. v. Holmes
(1988)

Supreme Court of Canada
64 C.R. (3rd) 97

Holmes was charged with possession of housebreaking tools, under section 309(1) [now 351(1)] of the *Criminal Code*. The tools were a pair of pliers and a pair of vise-grips. The section requires a person in possession of tools that give rise to a reasonable inference that they may be used for housebreaking to prove that they are not for illegal purposes. Holmes argued that this requirement violated the presumption of innocence guaranteed by section 11(d) of the *Charter*. Before entering his plea, Holmes moved to have the indictment quashed. The trial judge granted the motion. The Crown appealed, and the Ontario Court of Appeal set aside the order. Holmes appealed to the Supreme Court of Canada.

The Supreme Court of Canada ruled that the words "reasonable inference" do not permit a finding of guilt on something less than proof beyond a reasonable doubt. Therefore, the Crown had to prove that there was possession, and that there was no doubt that the instruments were possessed for the purpose of committing a crime. The words "without lawful excuse, the proof of which lies upon him" were included in the *Code* to make available the defence of innocent purpose. Hence, the section did not impose reverse onus; it did not require the accused to prove that the tools were not for an illegal purpose.

1. **What three elements must be proved for the Crown to obtain a conviction on possession of housebreaking tools?**

2. **Review section 11(d) of the *Charter*. What does it provide? Because of section 11(d), the burden of proof is usually on the prosecution to prove all the elements of an offence beyond a reasonable doubt. What is reverse onus? How does a reverse onus limit the right protected under section 11(d)?**

3. **On what basis did the Supreme Court of Canada rule that the offence was not one of reverse onus?**

4. **What is the defence of innocent purpose?**

part of his body or any part of an instrument that he uses is within any thing that is being entered."

The offence of break and enter is described in section 348 of the *Criminal Code*, which was cited on p. 62 in Chapter 3.

When entrance without lawful excuse is gained by means other than break and enter, and the person is in the dwelling-house with the intent to commit an indictable offence, a separate offence carrying a lesser penalty has been committed: being unlawfully in a dwelling-house.

It is also an offence to possess housebreaking, vault-breaking, or safe-breaking tools if, under the circumstances, possession of the tools appears to be for the purpose of breaking in. No break-in need actually have occurred; the accused must justify the possession of the tools.

It is also an offence to mask or colour one's face with the intent to commit an indictable offence.

Possession of Stolen Goods

To possess any property or thing, knowing that all or part of it was obtained by the commission of an indictable offence, is itself an offence. Further to the offence, if one possesses an automobile whose serial number is wholly or partly removed or obliterated, it will be presumed that it was obtained by the commission of an indictable offence.

Three break-ins in Winnipeg occurred in houses whose owners had died recently. In August 1982, Barry Kowlyk, the brother of the accused, Ray Kowlyk, was arrested while committing a theft. He admitted that he had committed the three break and enters in question, and then led the police to a house that he shared with the accused. The officers found 76 items stolen during the break and enters, 14 of them in Ray's bedroom, grouped according to the break-ins. Ray Kowlyk was charged with break, enter, and theft.

When questioned by the police about his involvement in the burglaries, Ray replied: "All you got me for is possession. I'm not saying anything." He made no further comment and did not testify at his trial. His brother Barry testified that he was the sole participant in the offences. No evidence was given that Ray was seen at or near the scenes of the offences. The accused was convicted on three counts of break, enter, and theft. His appeal to the Manitoba Court of Appeal was dismissed. His appeal to the Supreme Court of Canada was also dismissed.

Kowlyk v. The Queen (1988)

Supreme Court of Canada 43 C.C.C. (3rd) 1

1. **Why should Barry Kowlyk's evidence not be given any weight in this case?**
2. a) **What is the doctrine of recent possession?**
   b) **What evidence is there that it applies to this case?**
   c) **Why did the Crown have to rely on it for a conviction?**
3. **What did the Crown have to prove to obtain a conviction?**

False Pretences

The making of false statements to obtain credit or a loan has become more prevalent today. For example, a businessperson might alter financial statements to obtain a loan to cover financial difficulties. That person may be charged for obtaining credit by **false pretences** under section 361(1) of the *Criminal Code*, which states, "A false pretence is a representation of a matter of fact either present or past, made by words or otherwise, that is known by the person who makes it to be false and that is made with a fraudulent intent to induce the person to whom it is made to act upon it."

The amount of "money" that can be spent through the use of stolen credit cards is frequently more than the amount that could be obtained by the robbery of a person. Section 342 of the *Criminal Code* describes this offence.

The *Criminal Code* also provides that a person who writes a cheque for which insufficient funds are available when the cheque is cashed is guilty of an offence. It is a defence if the person can prove that, when the cheque was issued, there was every reason to believe that the funds were available.

> **342.**
>
> Every one who
> **(a)** steals a credit card,
> **(b)** forges or falsifies a credit card,
> **(c)** has in his possession, uses, or deals in any other way with a credit card that he knows was obtained
>   **(i)** by the commission in Canada of an offence, or
>   **(ii)** by an act or omission anywhere that, if it had occurred in Canada, would have constituted an offence, or
> **(d)** uses a credit card that he knows has been revoked or cancelled . . .

Reviewing Your Reading

1. Name and explain the elements necessary for a theft conviction.
2. Give the legal meaning of the terms "break" and "enter."
3. Explain the concept of reverse onus as it applies to the possession of housebreaking instruments and the possession of stolen goods.
4. Describe three examples of fraud.

7.4 CRIMES WITH HIGH SOCIAL IMPACT

Certain crimes have high social impact and are discussed frequently by the public and the media, as well as in Parliament.

Abortion

Abortion is not a crime in Canada. Nonetheless, in 1991, Dr. Henry Morgentaler was charged in Nova Scotia with 14 counts of performing unauthorized abortions in a private clinic. The *Medical Services Act* of Nova Scotia had been passed by the province to prohibit abortions being performed

223.

(1) A child becomes a human being within the meaning of this Act when it has completely proceeded, in a living state, from the body of its mother whether or not
  (a) it has breathed,
  (b) it has an independent circulation, or
  (c) the navel string is severed.
(2) A person commits homicide when he causes injury to a child before or during its birth as a result of which the child dies after becoming a human being.

in private clinics. This was a response to the Supreme Court of Canada ruling that section 251 on abortion [now section 287] of the *Criminal Code* was unconstitutional. The trial judge dismissed the charges, as did the Nova Scotia Court of Appeal on a Crown appeal. Both courts ruled that the *Medical Services Act* was *ultra vires* [beyond the powers of] the legislature of Nova Scotia, as the law was in essence criminal law and not within the jurisdiction of the province.

CASE

R. v. Lemay and Sullivan
(1991)

Supreme Court of Canada
63 C.C.C. (3d) 97

Jewel Voth hired two midwives, Mary Sullivan and Gloria Lemay, to deliver her baby. The two women had no formal medical training but had some experience with home births and had done some background reading. Voth began a difficult labour on May 7, 1985. After several hours, the baby's head emerged but, despite repeated attempts, the midwives could not extract the baby from the birth canal. The midwives called an ambulance, and Voth was taken to a hospital emergency department where the baby was delivered within two minutes of arrival, using standard obstetrical techniques. By that time, the baby had suffocated from lack of oxygen. Attempts to revive it failed.

Sullivan and Lemay were charged with one count of criminal negligence causing death to the child and a second count of criminal negligence causing bodily harm to the mother. At trial in Vancouver's County Court in October 1986, they were convicted on the first charge but acquitted on the second charge. The two women were given suspended sentences and placed on three years' probation.

The women appealed their conviction to the British Columbia Court of Appeal where the court, in July 1988, dismissed the charge of criminal negligence causing death and substituted a conviction on the second count of criminal negligence caus-ing bodily harm, even though the Crown had not appealed the acquittal by the trial judge on that charge. The court's decision was based on the fact that an injury to the unborn child equalled an injury to the mother. In its judgment, the court stated, "As a matter of law, a child remains part of the mother when it is in the birth canal."

Sullivan and Lemay appealed their substituted conviction on the second count to the Supreme Court of Canada, while the Crown appealed the overturning of the trial conviction on the first count. The appeals were heard in late October 1990, and, in a unanimous decision released on March 21, 1991, the Court upheld the acquit-tal of the two Vancouver midwives.

1. **Criminal negligence, defined in section 219 of the *Criminal Code*, is dis-cussed on p. 200. Review this section. Based on the facts presented in the case, do you think Sullivan and Lemay were guilty of criminal negligence?**

2. **Prepare an organizer to summarize the main arguments that would be presented by the Crown and by the defence. Beside each, indicate whether you agree or disagree.**

3. **Why would the British Columbia Court of Appeal dismiss the conviction of the charge of criminal negligence causing death and substitute a con-viction for criminal negligence causing bodily harm?**

4. **What is the significance of the Supreme Court of Canada decision? Do you agree with it? Why or why not?**

LOOKING BACK

In 1988, the Supreme Court of Canada ruled that the 1969 amendments to the *Criminal Code* on abortion were unconstitutional. This law specified that it was an offence for any person, including the woman herself, to procure a mis-carriage. Even if an attempt to abort met with failure, all concerned with the abortion were liable to prosecution. A legal abortion could be obtained only if the woman obtained the permission of the therapeutic abortion committee of an accredited or approved hospital. The committee would approve the abortion only if, in its opinion, the continuation of the pregnancy would en-danger or would be likely to endanger the woman's life or health.

The Minister of Health for each province approved certain hospitals for abortion purposes, and the hospital's governing board of directors appointed a committee of at least three qualified medical practitioners whose task it was to decide whether a therapeutic abortion should be carried out.

In 1989, after the Supreme Court decision, a bill on abortion legislation was introduced into Parliament. It would have permitted abortions only when a doc-tor considered a woman's physical, mental, or psychological health to be threat-ened. The House of Commons passed the legislation, but it was subsequently defeated in the Senate. Then Justice Minister Kim Campbell announced that the government would not introduce new legislation. Thus, Canada does not have a law that prohibits abortion.

An important part of the abortion issue concerns the point when a fetus should be considered a human being. (The legal definition of a fetus is "an unborn product of conception after the embryo stage.") The *Criminal Code* defines the matter in section 223.

The Supreme Court of Canada has not ruled specifically on when a fetus becomes a human being. In one case it gave no ruling on the issue, stating that it was up to Parliament to legislate on such an important matter. A similar decision was made in *R. v. Lemay and Sullivan*.

Weapons

The *Criminal Code* defines a weapon as anything used or intended for use in causing death or injury to a person, whether designed for such a purpose or not, or anything used or intended for use in threatening or intimidating any person. It goes on to distinguish between prohibited weapons and restricted weapons. **Prohibited weapons** include gun silencers, switchblade knives, automatic firearms, rifles and shotguns that are sawed off or otherwise modified, and any other weapon that has been declared prohibited. **Restricted weapons** include firearms that can be fired with one hand; semi-automatic weapons having a barrel length from the muzzle end of the barrel, up to and including the chamber, of less than 470 mm; firearms that can be folded or telescoped; firearms that can fire bullets in rapid succession and form part of a gun collection; and any other weapon that has been declared restricted.

Firearms Acquisition Certificates (FACs) for the acquisition, registration, and carrying of restricted weapons can be obtained from the local registrar of firearms. To apply for a FAC, a person must be 18 years of age, provide a photograph, and the names of two references. Persons who may act as references are listed in the regulations. Persons aged 12–17 can obtain a FAC with parental permission; prescribed conditions of supervision may apply. All applicants for a FAC must successfully complete a course or test in the safe handling and use of firearms and the laws and social responsibilities related to them. When a person applies for a FAC, a community check can be made by the firearms officer for screening purposes.

While other laws were introduced between 1992 and 1994, the proposed legislation introduced in late 1994, and passed into law as the *Firearms Act* in June 1995, engendered the most debate. A discussion of this subject was presented in the Issue in Chapter 3.

To discourage people from keeping weapons, the government has in the past provided amnesty periods, during which weapons could be registered or turned over to the police with no questions asked. The weapons collected were given to approved museums and forensic collections, used for safety education training, or destroyed.

The use of weapons while committing a serious crime greatly concerns members of society. The *Criminal Code* provides a one-year minimum sentence, to be served consecutively to any other punishment for offences arising from the same event. If the person has a previous firearms conviction, the minimum sentence is increased to three years, and if there is more than one weapons offence, each sentence must be served consecutively. The government proposed that these minimums be raised to four years. The law was challenged on the basis that it violated section 12 of the *Charter*. The Supreme Court of Canada disagreed.

Procuring and Soliciting

Prostitution is legal in Canada. But some activities related to prostitution, such as **procuring** and communicating for the purpose of prostitution, commonly known as **soliciting**, are illegal. The *Criminal Code* provides a lengthy definition of procuring, but in general it is either attempting to obtain a person for illicit sexual intercourse, or living wholly or in part on the avails of the prostitution of another person.

Communicating for the purpose of prostitution, according to a Supreme Court of Canada decision, must be "pressing or persistent" to constitute an offence.

Procuring and soliciting can be considered "crimes without victims," although it could be argued that prostitutes are victims. Nonetheless, some Canadians believe that the government should not be interfering with the morals of its citizens by legislating on such matters. However, legislators are concerned about the peripheral issues that surround prostitution—its frequent occurrence in crime areas, its connections with the drug trade, the subjection of people to pimps, and the effect on neighbourhoods where open prostitution occurs.

Obscenity

Obscenity, described in section 163 of the *Criminal Code*, continues to be controversial. The Supreme Court of Canada generally follows the "community standards test." It has stated that "the courts must determine as best they can what the community would tolerate others being exposed to on the basis of the degree of harm that may flow from such exposure." Sex acts must be "degrading or dehumanizing" to be deemed obscene.

CASE

Butler opened the Avenue Video Boutique in Winnipeg in 1987. His shop sold and rented "hard-core" videotapes and magazines as well as sexual paraphernalia. During the first month of operation police entered the store with a search warrant and seized all the inventory. Butler was charged with selling obscene material, possessing obscene material for the purpose of distribution, possessing obscene material for the purpose of sale, and exposing obscene material to public view.

Butler reopened the store and again was charged. At trial, he was convicted of eight counts relating to eight films and fined $1000 per offence. Acquittals were entered on the remaining 242 charges. The Crown appealed the 242 acquittals and Butler cross-appealed the eight convictions. The majority of the Manitoba Court of Appeal allowed the appeal of the Crown and entered convictions for Butler with respect to all of the counts. Butler appealed to the Supreme Court of Canada.

In its decision, the Supreme Court of Canada divided pornography into three categories:

- *Explicit sex with violence*, which would almost always constitute undue **sexual exploitation**.
- *Explicit sex without violence that subjects people to degrading or dehumanizing treatment*, which may be undue if the risk of harm is substantial. Whether the exploitation is undue would depend on
    - a determination of what the community would tolerate others being exposed to on the basis of the harm that may flow from such exposure. Harm can be presumed if the material predisposes a person to act in an antisocial manner.
    - whether the materials place women (and sometimes men) in positions of subordination and therefore infringe the principle of equality.
- *Explicit sex without violence that is neither degrading nor dehumanizing*, which would be tolerated. The onus is on the state to prove that the exploitation is undue. Any doubt will be resolved in favour of freedom of expression.

The Court ruled that section 163 of the *Criminal Code* violates the guarantee to freedom of expression in section 2(b) of the *Charter*, but that it is a reasonable limit prescribed by law and is therefore constitutional. Butler's case was sent back to trial to be decided on the basis of the new rules.

R. v. Butler
(1992)

Supreme Court of Canada
70 C.C.C. (3d) 129

1. Explain the differences between the categories of pornography established by the Supreme Court of Canada.

2. Which category would always be classified as obscene?

3. For the second category, what two factors would be used to determine if the exploitation of sex was undue?

4. The Supreme Court ruled that section 163 of the *Criminal Code* violates section 2(b) of the *Charter*, but that it was a reasonable limit. Do you agree with this ruling? Why or why not?

5. In your opinion, should the criteria for determining whether material is degrading be what one thinks others should not be subjected to, or what one thinks that oneself should not be subjected to?

CASE

R. v. Langer
(1995)

Ontario Court
of Justice
40 C.R. (4th) 204

The Globe and Mail published an art critic's review. It concerned a showing of paintings and drawings dealing with sexual themes involving adults and children, which was on display at the Mercer Union art gallery in Toronto. A complaint was filed with the police about the review, and the resulting investigation led to seizure of the paintings and drawings. The artist and the director of the gallery were charged under both the obscenity provisions and the new child pornography provisions of the *Criminal Code*.

The Crown later withdrew the charges against the individuals and proceeded, instead, with a forfeiture application. A forfeiture hearing is like a criminal trial, except that the things seized are treated as if they are the accused. The *Criminal Code* specifies that a judge "shall issue a warrant authorizing seizure of the copies" of material that offends the child pornography provisions.

The main defence to the hearing was the defence of **artistic merit**. The *Criminal Code* provides that the accused shall be found not guilty "if the representation or written material that is alleged to constitute child pornography has artistic merit or an educational, scientific, or medical purpose." As well, the court ruled that, in comparing the paintings and drawings to other types of child pornography filed as exhibits, and in view of the differing opinions of experts, there did not seem to be a realistic risk of harm to children. There was thus a reasonable doubt about whether the paintings and drawings exceeded standards of **community tolerance**, that is, what a community is willing to accept.

The court also ruled that the child pornography provisions of the *Criminal Code* infringe the fundamental freedom of expression guaranteed by the *Charter*, but were justified under section 1. Finally, the court ruled that the *Criminal Code* provision, which states that a judge "shall" issue a warrant for seizure of the material, violated the protection against unreasonable search and seizure under section 8 of the *Charter* and freedom of expression under section 2(b). The violations could not be saved under section 1. In order to have the *Code* provision remain constitutional, the court read down the section by interpreting "shall" as "may."

1. **What benefit is there to having a forfeiture hearing instead of charging the artist?**

2. **Who might the Crown and defence call to discuss artistic merit?**

3. **Should people who are in the field of the art in question decide on artistic merit, or should citizens who view the display make the determination?**

4. **On what basis do you think the court ruled that the provisions of the *Code* could be clearly justified under section I of the *Charter*?**

5. **The court read down the warrant section regarding seizure of material subject to forfeiture. What change does that make in who decides what material will be subject to forfeiture?**

Section 163(8) states, "For the purposes of this Act, any publication a dominant characteristic of which is the undue exploitation of sex, or of sex and any one or more of the following subjects, namely crime, horror, cruelty, and violence, shall be deemed to be obscene." The expressions "dominant characteristic" and "undue exploitation" are the bases on which many defences are founded.

A variety of offences relate to obscenity: making, printing, circulating, mailing, or distributing obscene material; and presenting or taking part in an immoral theatrical performance. Police can obtain a warrant to seize any materials that they consider to be obscene and to lay charges. Customs officers also have the right to seize materials considered obscene and forbid their entry into Canada.

Concerns regarding the use of children in pornography resulted in amendments to the *Criminal Code*. Child pornography is defined as "photographic, film, video, or other visual representation, whether or not it was made by electronic or mechanical means, that shows a person who is or is depicted as being under the age of 18 years and is engaged in or is depicted as engaged in explicit sexual activity." Any person in possession of, producing, or distributing and selling any child pornography is guilty of an offence.

Corruption and Abandonment of Children

It is an offence for a parent or guardian of a child to procure that child for the purpose of engaging in any sexual activity prohibited by the *Criminal Code*. As well, it is an offence to be the owner, occupier, or manager of premises that children are using for sexual activity prohibited by the *Code*.

It is also an offence to abandon or expose a child under the age of 10 years, so that the child's life is or is likely to be endangered or the child's health is or is likely to be permanently harmed.

Reviewing Your Reading

1. **What significant decision regarding abortion was made in 1988 by the Supreme Court of Canada?**

2. **Prior to the Supreme Court's 1988 ruling, what was the only procedure by which a woman could obtain a legal abortion?**

3. **When does a child become a human being, according to the *Criminal Code*?**

4. **Distinguish between prohibited and restricted weapons.**

5. **Under what circumstances may a restricted weapon be carried?**

6. **List five offences pertaining to weapons, other than those that deal with prohibited and restricted weapons.**

7. **a) Distinguish between procuring and soliciting.**

   b) What elements must exist for a conviction on soliciting?

8. **Name four issues related to prostitution that are of concern to legislators.**

9. **How does the *Code* define obscenity?**

7.5 OTHER CRIMES

The following offences are significant because they occur frequently, are recent additions to the *Code*, or are of general interest.

Criminal Negligence

The definition of **criminal negligence** is found under section 219 of the *Criminal Code*.

> **219.**
>
> **(1)** Every one is criminally negligent who
>   **(a)** in doing anything, or
>   **(b)** in omitting to do anything that it is his duty to do, shows wanton or reckless disregard for the lives or safety of other persons.
> **(2)** For the purposes of this section, "duty" means a duty imposed by law.

Criminal negligence comprises three categories: criminal negligence in the operation of a motor vehicle (examined in Chapter 8); criminal negligence causing bodily harm; and criminal negligence causing death. It is not necessary that there be intent—indifference as to what the reasonable person would do under the circumstances may result in a conviction. Thus, a person who drives in a manner very different from that of the reasonable person and who is inconsiderate of the safety of others is criminally negligent.

Mischief

The offence of **mischief** can relate to a variety of circumstances involving the deliberate destruction or damaging of property. Additionally, the increased use of computers has made data valuable property. Because of the possibility that data may be deliberately destroyed, for example, by a computer virus, the definition of mischief includes harm to data. These offences are defined in sections 430(1) and 430(2) of the *Criminal Code*.

> **430.**
>
> **(1)** Every one commits mischief who wilfully
>   **(a)** destroys or damages property;
>   **(b)** renders property dangerous, useless, inoperative, or ineffective;
>   **(c)** obstructs, interrupts, or interferes with the lawful use, enjoyment, or operation of property; or
>   **(d)** obstructs, interrupts, or interferes with any person in the lawful use, enjoyment, or operation of property.
> **(2)** Everyone commits mischief who wilfully
>   **(a)** destroys or alters data;
>   **(b)** renders data meaningless, useless, or ineffective;
>   **(c)** obstructs, interrupts, or interferes with the lawful use of data; or
>   **(d)** obstructs, interrupts, or interferes with any person in the lawful use of data or denies access to data to any person who is entitled to access thereto.

Enterprise Crime

Increased profits from illegal drug trade and the use of the banking system to transfer those profits led to the creation of the offence known as **enterprise crime**. The proceeds of crime are defined as any property, benefit, or advantage that is derived directly or indirectly from the commission of an enterprise-crime offence or a designated-drug offence. An enterprise crime can be any of a long list of offences, including procuring, illegal betting, and fraudulent manipulation of stock exchange transactions. Designated-drug offences include trafficking, the importing of drugs, and the cultivation of opium or marijuana plants. The latter offences are specified in the *Narcotic Control Act*.

It is a criminal offence to use, transfer possession of, send, or deliver property to any person

To deliberately damage property is known as mischief.

or place, with the knowledge that it was obtained by the commission of an enterprise offence or a designated-drug offence. Police can obtain a warrant to freeze a bank account containing money obtained from drug transactions.

If a person is convicted of an enterprise crime or released under a discharge, the court can order any property obtained as a result of the crime to be forfeited to the Crown. Even if certain property was not obtained through the crime for which the accused was charged, the court may order the goods forfeited if it is satisfied beyond a reasonable doubt that they are the proceeds of crime. Such a circumstance would exist if an unemployed person was convicted of trafficking and had possession of a large sum of money.

Reviewing Your Reading

1. What elements must be proven to obtain a conviction on a charge of criminal negligence?

2. a) How is mischief defined in law?

   b) How does the *Criminal Code* define mischief relating to data?

3. a) Give two examples of enterprise crime offences.

   b) What action can be taken against those who profit from enterprise crime?

7.6 OFFENCES AND PENALTIES

Indictable Offence—Life Imprisonment

Accessory after fact to murder
Aircraft—endangering safety
Attempting to commit murder
Breaking and entering a dwelling-house
Conspiracy to commit murder
Criminal negligence causing death
Extortion
Hijacking
Hostage taking
Killing unborn child in act of birth
Manslaughter
Mischief (if dangerous to life)
Murder
Murder—conspiring to commit
Perjury (or 14 years)
Riot Act—hindering reading of
Robbery
Sexual assault—aggravated
Sexual intercourse with female under 14
Stopping mail with intent to rob

Indictable Offence—14 years

Administering noxious thing endangering life
Aggravated assault
Arson
Bodily harm—causing with intent
Break and enter other than dwelling-house
Bribery of judicial officers, peace officers
Buggery, bestiality
Causing bodily harm with intent
Contradictory evidence by witness
Counterfeit money—making, possession, or
    uttering
Fabricating evidence
Firearm—use of during offence
Forgery
Housebreaking instruments—possession of
Impeding attempt to save life

Incest
Lightening gold or silver coin
Parent procuring defilement (under age of 14)
Perjury (or life)
Piracy
Sexual assault, using weapon, or causing bodily harm
Suicide—counselling, aiding
Uttering forged document

Indictable Offence—10 years

Abduction of person under 14
Assault, using weapon, or causing bodily harm
Criminal negligence causing bodily harm
Dwelling-house—being unlawfully in
Escape and being at large without excuse
Face masked or coloured
Mail theft
Possession of weapon
Prison breach
Procuring
Theft, or possession of property obtained by
    crime, if over $5000

Indictable Offence—5 years

Abduction of person under 16
Animals—injuring or endangering
Arson
Bigamy
Confining or imprisoning illegally
Childbirth—failing to obtain assistance in
Explosives—illegal possession
Fire—setting by negligence
Frauds upon the government
Genocide—advocating
Gross indecency
Indignity to dead body
Infanticide
Municipal corruption
Parent procuring defilement (over age of 14)
Polygamy
Procuring feigned marriage
Sexual intercourse with female 14 or 15 years of age
Traps likely to cause bodily harm
Unlawful drilling

Indictable Offence—2 years

Abandoning child
Administering noxious things
Automobile master key—selling
Betting, pool-selling, book-making
Cheating at play
Coin device—possession of instrument
    for breaking
Coin—uttering
Common bawdy-house—keeping
Common nuisance
Corrupting children
Disobeying order of court
Disposing of body of child to conceal birth
Duelling
Eavesdropping equipment—illegal possession of
Escape—permitting or assisting
False messages
Forcible entry
Gaming-house—keeping
Gaming- or betting-house—found-in
Hatred—public incitement of
Intercepted information—illegal disclosure of
Lotteries—illegal
Misconduct of officers executing process
Municipal corruption
Procuring own miscarriage
Riot—taking part
Seduction of female between 16 and 17 years
Seduction under promise of marriage
Seduction of female passenger on vessel
Sexual intercourse with stepdaughter, or
    female employee
Spreading false news

Hybrid Offence

Abduction in contravention of custody order
Abduction where no custody order
Assaulting a peace officer
Credit card—theft; forgery
Failing to appear

False alarm of fire
Mailing obscene matter
Mischief
Necessaries—failing to provide
Obstructing, resisting an officer
Pointing a firearm
Possession of prohibited weapon
Possession of unregistered restricted weapon
Public mischief
Sexual assault
Theft, or possession of property obtained by
    crime, if under $5000
Transfer of weapon to person under 16, no permit

Summary Offence

Advertising reward and immunity
Carrying concealed weapon
Causing a disturbance
Coins—defacing
Common bawdy-house—inmate
Cruelty to animals
Found in gaming- or betting-house
Impersonating a peace officer
Indecent acts
Motor vehicle theft
Nudity
Participating in unlawful assembly
Possessing weapon at public meeting
Slugs—having or making
Soliciting
Telephone calls—indecent
Trespassing at night

Attempt

Of an offence with life imprisonment as
    maximum: 14 years
Of an offence with penalty of 14 years or less:
    one-half the term
Of an offence punishable on summary
    conviction: summary conviction

ISSUE

Should euthanasia be legalized for the terminally ill who request it?

On September 30, 1993, the Supreme Court of Canada ruled against Sue Rodriguez, ending her lengthy fight for the right to doctor-assisted suicide. Sue Rodriguez suffered from ALS (Amyotropic Lateral Sclerosis), also known as Lou Gehrig's disease. ALS is a debilitating disease that attacks the central nervous system, eventually causing death. The Rodriguez case attracted national attention and opened a debate on an issue that had long remained taboo.

The sensitive nature of the issue was underlined on October 24, 1993, when Robert Latimer killed his 12-year-old daughter, Tracy, with carbon monoxide in the cab of his truck. Tracy suffered from severe cerebral palsy and could not talk, walk, or take care of herself. At the time of her death she weighed 38 pounds. At his trial, her father maintained that he had ended his daughter's life out of compassion. Despite his defence that he killed her out of "necessity" the Saskatchewan Court of Queen's Bench found him guilty of second-degree murder and made him ineligible for parole for 10 years. It was upheld by the Saskatchewan Court of Appeal. Latimer appealed to the Supreme Court of Canada, which ordered a new trial.

About 190 000 Canadians die each year and 15 percent of them endure lengthy and painful deaths. A 1992 Gallup Poll survey showed that 77 percent of Canadians approved mercy killing where a dying person in great pain requested it. The Law Reform Commission (1983) recommended that the *Criminal Code* be changed to protect doctors who help patients die at their request, but by 1996 no action had yet been taken. As a result, many doctors are reluctant to support euthanasia or admit their role in such cases. In 1994, the Canadian Medical Association voted 93–74 in favour of a resolution that doctors should not participate "in euthanasia and physician-assisted suicide."

In 1995, a Special Senate Committee on Euthanasia and Assisted Suicide voted 4–3 against making it legal to assist suicide and 5–2 against legalizing euthanasia.

On One Side

In an age of transplants, intravenous feedings, and artificial hearts, machine-sustained life can be prolonged for months, even years. Some people believe that those who are terminally ill or suffering from severe mental and/or physical damage should be allowed to die instead of being kept alive by machines. They are concerned about the quality of those lives prolonged by medical means. In general, supporters of euthanasia believe that life should be free of pain and that human dignity should be preserved.

The organization known as Dying With Dignity wants the *Criminal Code* amended to make hastening death legal in certain situations. They want some forms of euthanasia to be clearly defined in the *Criminal Code* and legalized.

On the Other Side

Opponents of euthanasia argue that no form of it should be legalized. They believe that human life is sacred and that all forms of euthanasia are murder and should be treated as such. Moreover, they fear that if legislation is passed to make euthanasia legal, there is a risk to society that euthanasia may be extended to include those who cannot function or are considered undesirable in society. Those who cannot speak for themselves must be protected by the law and its institutions.

The Bottom Line

Individuals who are physically able to end their own lives may do so legally. Those who are physically challenged and need assistance, may not. Euthanasia raises important legal, medical, and moral questions:

- Should a person who is physically or mentally incapable of committing suicide be compelled to face an agonizing death without dignity?
- Should doctors and family members be legally permitted to decide the fate of a patient who has no hope of recovery?
- Should the courts decide whether another human being will live or die?
- Should the law regarding euthanasia remain as it now stands?

You be the judge!

Sue Rodriguez committed suicide with the assistance of a doctor in February 1994. No charges were laid against Svend Robinson, the MP from Vancouver, who admitted being with her at the time.

1. **How do the Sue Rodriguez and Robert Latimer cases relate to the issue of euthanasia? Compare the two cases and give your opinions.**

2. **Why do you think doctors are reluctant to support euthanasia?**

3. **Which side of the euthanasia debate do you support? Give your reasons.**

4. **Work in four groups, one for each of the questions posed in The Bottom Line. Brainstorm for answers to your group's question and present your conclusions to the class.**

CHAPTER REVIEW

Reviewing Legal Terms

For each of the following statements, indicate the key term being defined:

a) criminally causing the death of another human being

b) sexual intercourse between a man and a woman related to each other by blood

c) anything that serves to indicate a person has true ownership of something

d) what citizens are willing to accept

e) painlessly putting to death as an act of mercy a person suffering from an incurable and disabling disease

f) obtaining a person for prostitution

g) direct or indirect touching of a person under 14 for a sexual purpose

h) killing of an infant shortly after birth, by its mother who has become mentally disturbed from the effects of giving birth

i) material designed with skill, good taste

j) planned and deliberate killing

Exploring Legal Concepts

1. Prepare an organizer that will show the distinction between the types of homicide and categories of murder. In your organizer, include the defining characteristics of each item.

2. Give an example for each circumstance under which a person may be found guilty of murder, even if he or she did not intend to commit murder, as specified in section 229 of the *Criminal Code*.

3. Prepare an organizer to show the different categories of assault and of sexual assault. Include the defining characteristics of each category.

4. The commission of many offences increases during periods of recession and high unemployment.

   a) Identify some offences that you think follow this pattern.

   b) What action can governments take to prevent this from happening?

5. Statute law tries to keep up with changes in social values. Identify four offences discussed in this chapter that have been introduced into the *Criminal Code* during the past decade to reflect social change.

6. The *Criminal Code* specifies a number of offences that are often referred to as "crimes without victims." They include communicating for the purpose of prostitution, obscenity, and keeping a bawdy-house (brothel). Should the police control such activities, or should people be allowed to decide for themselves whether or not to engage in them?

Applying Legal Concepts

1. Johnson, a juvenile, opened a bank account with a $2 deposit. He was given an account number that had previously been assigned to a lawyer. The account had been closed for over a year. The lawyer had arranged with his firm to deposit the sum of $1500 twice a month. By mistake, the bank began putting the $1500 into Johnson's account. The boy received a statement in the mail, showing a balance of $2997.07. He went to the bank and asked that his balance be checked. It proved to be correct.

   At trial, Johnson gave evidence that he "almost flipped out." He withdrew $1500, bought a car for $1000, and left Winnipeg for British Columbia. The car broke down, and he sold it for $50. Johnson was upset with the bank for not transferring funds to him in British Columbia. He was determined to close the account when he got back to Winnipeg. On his return, he found even more money in the account. He withdrew a large amount and spent it.

   - **With what offence(s) should Johnson be charged?**

   - **What was the *actus reus*?**

   - **What was the *mens rea*?**

2. A security guard found Holzer's 15-month-old son unattended in the cab of an unheated, unlocked pickup truck in a shopping mall parking lot at 12:50 p.m. The temperature was -14°C inside the truck. The child was wearing a snowsuit and socks, but no mittens. His diaper was wet, and the wetness had spread to the snowsuit. A social worker took charge of the child and reported the incident to the police. The police found the mother, Holzer, in a bingo hall at 3:15 p.m. She had gone into the mall to pay a bill, but could not resist the temptation to play bingo, which was to end at 4:00 p.m. She had not checked on the child since leaving him at 11:00 a.m. The bingo hall was a two-minute walk from the truck.

   - **With what offence could Holzer be charged?**

   - **What would the Crown have to prove to obtain a conviction?**

   - **Based on the facts presented, would Holzer be found guilty?**

3. *R. v. Creighton* (1993) Supreme Court of Canada 3 S.C.R. 3

   Creighton, Caddedu, and Martin shared a large quantity of alcohol and cocaine at Martin's apartment over an 18-hour period. All of the parties involved were experienced cocaine users. Creighton injected cocaine into Martin's forearm with her consent. She immediately began to convulse violently and appeared to cease breathing. The other two could not resuscitate her. Caddedu wanted to call 911 but was dissuaded by Creighton who placed Martin on the bed, cleaned the apartment of any possible fingerprints, and left with Caddedu. Seven hours later, Caddedu returned and called for emergency assistance. Martin was pronounced dead. As a result of the injection, she had experienced a cardiac arrest and later asphyxiated on the contents of her stomach. The defence conceded that trafficking had taken place. The Crown argued that Creighton was guilty of manslaughter as the death was the direct consequence of an unlawful act.

   - **Is Creighton guilty of manslaughter?**

4. *R. v. Downey* (1992) Supreme Court of Canada 2 S.C.R. 10

Downey and his companion, Corrine Reynolds, were charged with living on the avails of prostitution, contrary to section 195(2) [now 212(3)] of the *Criminal Code*. Reynolds owned an escort service. Downey answered the telephone, made up the receipts, and did the banking at the agency. He had no other employment. On one occasion when Reynolds was away, Downey ran the agency for a month.

The agency received an introduction fee, but the escorts kept any money they received for sexual services which were provided in 85–90 percent of the dates. Both Reynolds and Downey were aware of the sexual activity.

Section 212(3) provides that "evidence that a person lives with or is habitually in the company of prostitutes . . . is, in the absence of evidence to the contrary, proof that the person lives on the avails of prostitution." Downey applied to have the section be of no effect because it violated his *Charter* right to be presumed innocent.

- **Were Downey's rights violated since it was presumed that his being in the company of prostitutes meant that he was living on the avails of prostitution?**

5. *R. v. Thornton* 1993 Supreme Court of Canada 82 C.C.C. (3d) 530

Thornton was well informed about HIV and its means of transmission. He knew that he was a member of a group that was highly at risk of contracting AIDS. Moreover, he knew that he had twice tested positive for HIV antibodies and that he was therefore infectious. Thornton nevertheless donated blood to the Red Cross in 1987.

Thornton was charged with committing a common nuisance, which is defined as doing an unlawful act or failing to discharge a legal duty and thereby endangering the life, safety, health, property, or comfort of the public. The *Criminal Code* provides in section 216 "that every one who undertakes to administer surgical or medical treatment to another person or to do any other lawful act that may endanger the life of another person is, except in cases of necessity, under a legal duty to have and to use reasonable knowledge, skill and care in so doing."

- **Was Thornton guilty? Why or why not?**

6. *R. v. Felawka* (1993) Supreme Court of Canada 4 S.C.R. 199

Felawka went target shooting with a friend outside Hope, British Columbia. He took a rapid transit train to return home. He wrapped his .22-calibre rifle in his jacket because he felt that it was not "proper" to carry his rifle openly. Felawka had a valid firearms acquisition certificate. Two passengers became alarmed and notified a train employee. The employee asked Felawka what he had in his jacket, and he laughingly replied that he was "going on a killing spree." When Felawka left the train and boarded a connecting bus, three plain clothes officers also boarded the bus. When one of the officers called out "City Police," Felawka appeared to reach for his rifle. The officers drew their revolvers and arrested him. There was still a clip with one live round in the rifle. Felawka was charged with carrying a weapon for a purpose dangerous to the public peace and with unlawfully carrying a concealed weapon.

- **Is Felawka guilty of the charges? Why or why not?**

7. *R. v. Plourde* (1993) New Brunswick Provincial Court 140 N.B.R. (2d) 273

Plourde was a grade eight homeroom teacher at the Thomas-Albert High School in Grand Falls, New Brunswick. Two students, Cyr and Leclerc, were pulling at each other and hitting each other on the shoulders with fists as they entered the classroom. The teacher physically intervened and ordered the two students to sit at their desks. As it was April Fools' Day, there was considerable noise in the classroom. Several students described it as a place of "utter confusion."

As Plourde tried to settle the class down, Cyr and Leclerc made disrespectful remarks and kicked a metal filing cabinet. The teacher then used force to evict Cyr from the classroom, allegedly grabbing him by the arms, lifting him from his desk, and pushing him against the chalkboard. As a result, Cyr sustained red marks on his back and on his forearm which disappeared with time and required no medical attention. Once Plourde re-entered the room, Leclerc told him he was crazy to act that way with Cyr. As Leclerc got up from his desk, Plourde allegedly slapped him on the head while grabbing his shoulders to make him sit down. Plourde was charged with assault for his actions against the two students.

- **Is he guilty? Why or why not?**

Extending Legal Concepts

1. Now that you have completed this chapter, review the opening article and Something to Think About. Do you think amendments are required to the *Criminal Code*? Why or why not?

2. With a partner, discuss this statement: "Where personal selection of literature and audio-video material is involved, a citizen should be able to choose any material that he or she wishes to view." Try to reach a consensus or agreement. Compare your findings with another pair of partners. Discuss, negotiate, and attempt a larger group consensus. Share your results with the class and discuss the steps necessary to reach agreement. List the key arguments on the chalkboard.

3. Using reference materials in your resource centre, including CD-ROM and the Internet, obtain current information on any one of the following topics, either for your province, Canada, or another country: (a) murder, (b) assault, (c) sexual assault. Write a one-page summary of your findings, and create a poster to display your information.

4. Using a copy of *Martin's Annual Criminal Code*, or *Tremeear's Criminal Code*, prepare answers to the following questions:

   a) What does each of the thumb indexes refer to?

   b) Table of Contents—How many parts are there in the *Criminal Code*? Indicate the three parts that interest you the most.

   c) What is the purpose of the *Criminal Code* Table of Concordance?

   d) Table of Cases

      i) In what order is the Table of Cases?

      ii) What is an annotation?

      iii) Why is it important to a user of the Annotated *Criminal Code* to have annotations for each section?

e) Refer to section 342.1 of the *Criminal Code*.

   i) What is the name of the section?

   ii) Why does the section number include a decimal?

   iii) How many subsections does the section have?

   iv) In your own words, describe the offence that is outlined in section 342.1

   v) What significant information is given in subsection (2)?

   vi) What is the significance of the date given at the end of the section?

   vii) What is the purpose of each of the cross-references, the synopsis, and the annotations given after the section?

5. Over a two-week period, collect newspaper articles, editorials, cartoons, and letters to the editor on the following topics. Prepare a report that summarizes the contents of your collection.

   a) violence   c) pornography   e) weapons

   b) censorship   d) euthanasia   f) abortion

6. Write a letter to your local member of Parliament outlining your position on any of the topics in question 5.

Researching an Issue

Sexual Assault and the Victim's Rights

In *R. v. Seaboyer* (1991) (see p. 187) and *R. v. O'Connor* (1995) (see p. 188), the Supreme Court of Canada made two controversial decisions regarding the rights of both an accused and a complainant in a sexual assault case. At issue here is the limitation of the rights of an accused to protect the rights of a complainant.

Statement

The protection of a complainant's confidential therapeutic records justifies limiting the rights of an accused in a sexual assault case.

Point

The Supreme Court rulings perpetuate the myth that women who report sexual assault are likely to be liars, discreditable, or easily duped. While the accused has a right to a full defence, the guidelines that permit access to confidential therapeutic records are too sweeping and vague. The threat of public exposure of confidential records will deter victims from reporting the sexual violation.

Counterpoint

Civil libertarians and defence lawyers maintain that both the *Seaboyer* and *O'Connor* rulings struck a necessary and fair balance between the accused's rights and those of the complainant. The presumption of innocence is at the heart of our system and access to therapeutic records will sometimes be necessary to avoid convicting an innocent person.

- **With a partner, research this issue and reflect on your findings.**

- **Prepare points on this statement that could be used for a class debate.**

- **Discuss your findings with others in your class.**

8

DRUG USE, DRINKING AND DRIVING

These are the key terms introduced in this chapter:

Breathalyzer

controlled drugs

demerit points

double doctoring

laundering

LeDain Commission

motor vehicle

narcotic

possession

prescription shopping

random virtue testing

restricted drugs

roadside screening test

trafficking

Chapter at a Glance

8.1   Introduction
8.2   The *Narcotic Control Act*
8.3   The *Food and Drug Act*
8.4   Driving and Drinking
        and Driving

Learning Outcomes

At the end of this chapter, you will be able to

1. describe the effects of impaired driving and the use of
    narcotics on Canadian society;
2. list the offences connected with drug use;
3. recognize the right of police in the search for and seizure
    of narcotics;
4. distinguish between restricted and controlled drugs;
5. list the offences connected with impaired driving;
6. describe the procedures for roadside testing and taking
    breath samples;
7. recognize the effect of a conviction for drinking and
    driving on an offender's future.

Unborn Baby Killed in Crash, Driver Gets 1 Year

The father of an unborn boy killed by a drinking driver cried out for a miracle before the baby was removed from his wife's womb, a Brampton court has heard.

"My husband David sobbed as if his heart had been shattered and asked aloud for a miracle that could never be," Caledon resident Cindy Sink wrote in her victim impact statement.

A judge yesterday sentenced David James Davenport, a 28-year-old Brampton auto worker, to a year in jail for impaired driving, causing bodily harm to Sink on July 6, 1994, when he entered a Mississauga intersection without looking and was struck broadside by Sink's Blazer.

Davenport had drunk at least nine cans of beer that afternoon while lounging around a swimming pool at a friend's house.

While stopped at the intersection he had been arguing with his former girlfriend, Mr. Justice Kenneth Langdon ruled.

Sink, who had been wearing a seatbelt and was severely bruised, testified she felt her baby drop and felt no further movement from him.

Davenport could not be charged with the more serious offence of impaired driving causing death because a fetus is not considered a person in Canadian law.

From: Farrell Crook, "Unborn baby killed in crash, driver gets 1 year." *The Toronto Star*, September 19, 1995. Reprinted with permission—The Toronto Star Syndicate.

Something to Think About

- **Do you agree with the penalty imposed in this case? Why or why not?**
- **Should victims have more influence over the sentence imposed for personal injury offences?**
- **Should a fetus be considered a person?**
- **Are Canada's laws on drinking and driving strict enough?**

8.1 INTRODUCTION

Impaired driving and the use of narcotics continue to be two of the most pressing issues facing Canadian society. They carry immense costs in the form of lost and wasted lives, broken families, tax spending for hospitals and legal assistance, and soaring insurance rates. Federal and provincial governments have tried to cope with the two problems by introducing stiffer penalties and other deterrents. Nevertheless, the frequency of media reports about these and related offences suggests that the campaign against them is not succeeding as well as legislators and other Canadians would like. There is still a widespread belief that neither drug users nor impaired drivers are penalized severely enough. As you read through this chapter, reflect upon your own views of the matter, and see whether becoming aware of more facts affects your attitudes in any way.

8.2 THE NARCOTIC CONTROL ACT

In the 1960s there was a great increase in the use of narcotics. Public opinion changed. People challenged the criminalization of some drugs.

These social changes led to the appointment of the Royal Commission into the Non-Medical Use of Drugs. The **LeDain Commission**, as it came to be known, carried out an exhaustive study of the drug culture in Canada at the time.

In its report, the Commission defined a drug as being "any substance that by its chemical nature alters structure or function in a living organism." Of course, not all chemicals that have these effects are classified as illegal drugs; otherwise, tea, beer, cola, and aspirin would be classed with heroin and cocaine. The criminal classification of drugs is based on the restriction(s) imposed upon their use. The relevant statutes—the *Narcotic Control Act* and the *Food and Drug Act*—are examined in this chapter.

The *Narcotic Control Act* criminalizes possession and trafficking in narcotics. Because crime falls under federal jurisdiction, the law governing narcotics is the same across Canada. A schedule in the *Act* lists over 100 drugs that are con-

sidered to be narcotics. The *Act* defines a **narcotic** as being "any substance included in the schedule or anything that contains any substance included in the schedule." Thus, the fact that marijuana is technically not a narcotic has been ruled by the courts to be of no relevance, for it falls in the list of substances defined as a narcotic by Parliament. The statute applies to all listed narcotics. However, a separate section of the *Act* prohibits the cultivation of opium and cannabis (marijuana).

Most prosecutions under the *Narcotic Control Act* are for the offences of possession, possession for the purpose of trafficking, importing, and exporting. To deter drug users and the drug trade, the offences of prescription shopping or double doctoring, enterprise crime (possession of property obtained from the drug trade), and laundering of profits from the drug trade were added to the *Act* in the late 1980s. The table shows the penalties available for these offences.

CASE

Hamon was found guilty of cultivation and possession of marijuana. He challenged the constitutionality of the relevant sections of the *Narcotic Control Act*. He argued that the provisions violated section 7 of the *Charter*. Hamon based his challenge on the following points:

a) "liberty" as used in section 7 includes the right to make fundamental personal decisions without state interference;

b) there were benefits to the non-abusive use of marijuana;

c) if the objective is to protect those around the user, a complete ban on cultivation and possession is overly broad;

d) the prohibition is not rationally connected to the achievement of its objective since the state has not prohibited alcohol or tobacco use;

e) marijuana is not a narcotic and is not similar to narcotics;

f) the prohibition is not minimal and could be achieved by less intrusive measures—regulation;

g) the intrusiveness of the prohibition is not proportionate to the seriousness of the problem.

The Quebec Court of Appeal dismissed Hamon's appeal of his conviction.

R. v. Hamon
(1993)

**Quebec Court of Appeal
85 C.C.C. (3d) 490**

1. **What does section 7 of the *Charter* guarantee?**

2. **Present a counter-argument for each of Hamon's arguments.**

Penalties for Criminal Offences under the *Narcotic Control Act*

Offence	Penalty	
Possession; prescription shopping	**Summary Offence**	
	First Offence	6 months and/or $1000 fine
	After First Offence	1 year and/or $2000 fine
	Indictable	7 years
Trafficking; possession for the purpose of trafficking; importing; exporting	Indictable	life
Cultivation of opium poppy, marijuana	Indictable	7 years
Possession of property obtained by designated drug offences		
Over $1000:	Indictable	10 years
Under $1000:	**Summary Offence or**	
	Indictable	2 years
Laundering proceeds of designated drug offences	**Summary Offence or**	
	Indictable	10 years

Possession

The *Narcotic Control Act* makes it an offence to possess a narcotic, unless legal permission has been given to do so. **Possession** is a hybrid offence, which allows the Crown to use discretion in proceeding. A person found with one marijuana cigarette will therefore not be treated the same as someone who has a much larger amount. The Crown can also discriminate between first offenders and those with numerous possession convictions.

Definition of Possession

The quantity is of no importance for a charge of possession. As long as the drug is identifiable, a charge can be laid. In addition, the *Narcotic Control Act* adopts the definition of possession given in section 4(3) of the *Criminal Code*.

In other words, a person is defined as having possession in situations other than simply having personal ownership. Having control over a drug can therefore lead to a charge. For instance, a person who gives a narcotic to a friend for safekeeping is as guilty of possession as is the friend. A person who is part of a group using a narcotic can also be found in possession. If five people are smoking marijuana at a card party, they could all be convicted of the offence of possession. The owner of the house is particularly vulnerable, even if he or she does not use the narcotic, because allowing its use in his or her home implies consent.

4.

(3)

For the purposes of this Act,

(a) a person has anything in possession when he has it in his personal possession or knowingly

  (i) has it in the actual possession or custody of another person, or

  (ii) has it in any place, whether or not that place belongs to or is occupied by him, for the use or benefit of himself or of another person; and

(b) where one of two or more persons, with the knowledge and consent of the rest, has anything in his custody or possession, it shall be deemed to be in the custody and possession of each and all of them.

Intent to Possess

Besides proving possession and that the drug in question is a narcotic, the Crown must show that there was intent to possess, that is, the accused must know that the substance is a drug. The Supreme Court of Canada ruled in *R. v. Beaver* (1957) that *mens rea* is a necessary element of the offence. Beaver had a package which he believed to contain sugar of milk. In fact, it contained a narcotic. Beaver was acquitted.

Simple Possession

The fact that simple possession of a narcotic can lead to criminal charges has been criticized. Research has not established the long-term effects of the use of most drugs. Alcohol, which is unquestionably a drug, is legal; indeed, the government in most provinces operates the stores, and all provinces profit from the stores in which it is sold. Moreover, the abuse of alcohol can lead to social problems much greater than the use of some items on the list of narcotics. Should the use of cannabis be legalized? Should the use of cocaine? Or would legalizing either of them imply that the drug is harmless, and thus increase its use and the related problems? The state is in a difficult position with regard to the legality of the use of certain drugs.

Offences Related to Trafficking

Section 4 of the *Narcotic Control Act* states that no person shall traffic in a narcotic or possess any narcotic for the purpose of trafficking.

The *Act* defines **trafficking** as meaning "to manufacture, sell, give, administer, transport, send, deliver, or distribute." Thus, merely to give drugs to another person constitutes trafficking; no profit motive is necessary. However, the LeDain Commission recommended that giving another person a quantity that could reasonably be used on a single occasion should be decriminalized. A person who transports a drug is also guilty of trafficking, but the purchaser is not.

Whether police will charge someone with simple possession or trafficking often depends on the amount of narcotic seized. Before 1986, if the accused was found guilty of possession, the onus was on that person to prove that he or she did *not* have the narcotic for the purpose of trafficking.

In 1986, the Supreme Court of Canada ruled that this "reverse onus" violated the presumption of innocence contained in section 11(d) of the *Charter of Rights and Freedoms*. Since then, the onus has been on the Crown to prove that the person possessed the narcotic for the purpose of trafficking. The Crown may be aided in proving trafficking if paraphernalia related to the drug trade, such as scales, are found. Large amounts of cash may also be used as evidence that trafficking is occurring.

Prior to the LeDain Commission, police had used questionable procedures to investigate drug offences and obtain evidence. Some of these practices, such as having police officers orchestrate drug deals to entrap drug offenders, threatened to bring the administration of justice into disrepute by allowing the police too many intrusive powers over the lives and activities of citizens. Since the LeDain Commission and after the rulings of several courts, police may no longer entrap individuals nor use physical violence to obtain evidence. Nor may police undertake **random virtue testing**, which is the practice of investigating an individual for drug offences without having reasonable and probable grounds for so doing.

Importing and Exporting

Section 5 of the *Narcotic Control Act* makes it an offence to import or export any narcotic. The accused need not bring the goods into the country; merely arranging for their importation can result in a conviction. The offence is complete when the goods enter or leave the country. The maximum penalty for this offence is life imprisonment.

Prescription Shopping or Double Doctoring

It is possible to obtain prescriptions for narcotics necessary for medical reasons. However, some people engage in **prescription shopping** or **double doctoring**, that is, they try to obtain the same prescription from a number of doctors. It is now an offence to seek or obtain a narcotic or prescription from a doctor without disclosing all other narcotics or prescriptions for narcotics received within the previous 30 days. This is a hybrid offence, with a maximum penalty of seven years' imprisonment.

CASE

R. v. Virgo
(1992)

**Ontario General
Division
(Unreported)**

Police had received a Crime Stoppers Report providing names, pager numbers, and descriptions of people said to be involved in drug trafficking. They were supposedly operating out of an apartment complex. Police investigated the report by calling the pager numbers and arranging to meet with and to purchase cocaine.

Virgo arranged to meet Officer Shaw and sold her $60 worth of cocaine. He sold her more later but did not show up at a third meeting. Another officer called, and again Virgo did not show up. He had been alerted that the calls were a set-up. He was arrested for the two sales and was also found in possession of cocaine.

Virgo argued that he purchased the drug for his own use and not to deal. The police had engaged in random virtue testing by calling the pager numbers and offering to buy drugs. The police were acting on an anonymous tip, and thus could not have a "reasonable suspicion" that those named were engaged in criminal activity. They also did nothing to confirm that the people were operating out of the apartment complex. The trial court issued a stay of proceedings.

1. **What is a stay of proceedings?**

2. **Did the police have reasonable suspicion when acting on the Crime Stoppers Report?**

3. **What is random virtue testing? Why do police find it useful? How did it occur in this case?**

4. **What *Charter* rights does random virtue testing potentially violate? In your view, is it ever a "reasonable limitation" of those rights?**

5. **The court did not condone the fact that the police attempted more than one transaction with Virgo. Why did the police attempt to do so? Why doesn't the court condone this practice?**

Enterprise Crime and Laundering

To deter people from trafficking in narcotics, a 1988 amendment to the *Narcotic Control Act* provided for enterprise crime offences. The government can seize any money, property, or money from the sale of property that was obtained by means of any offence under the *Act*. A separate offence, known as **laundering**, was also added. In law, it means to use, transfer the possession of, send, transport, transmit, alter, dispose of, or otherwise deal with any property or proceeds from certain offences. These offences include those under the *Narcotic Control Act*. The purpose of this section of the *Act* is to reduce the easy movement of property, especially cash, obtained through the drug trade.

Police Rights of Search and Seizure under the *Act*

The *Narcotic Control Act* grants police the right to search for narcotics. Other rights that are incidental to the search, such as arrest, are granted by the *Criminal Code*.

Warrantless Searches

Because society considers the control of narcotics important, under section 10 of the *Narcotic Control Act* the police are given the power to search places other than a residence without a warrant.

10.

A peace officer may, at any time, without a warrant enter and search any place other than a dwelling-house, and under the authority of a warrant . . . enter and search any dwelling-house in which the peace officer believes on reasonable grounds there is a narcotic by means of or in respect of which an offence under this Act has been committed.

This section appears to be contrary to section 8 of the *Charter*, which provides that everyone has the right to be secure against unreasonable search or seizure. Justice Dickson, in the Supreme Court of Canada decision in *Hunter v. Southam Inc.* (1984) stated "I recognize that it may not be reasonable in every instance to insist on prior authorization in order to validate governmental intrusions upon individuals' expectations of privacy. Nevertheless, where it is feasible to obtain prior authorization, I would hold that such authorization is a pre-condition for a valid search and seizure."

The Supreme Court of Canada also ruled on important issues related to the warrantless search of the perimeter of a dwelling-house and of an automobile in *R. v. Grant* (1993), described in Chapter 4, and *R. v. Zammit*, described below.

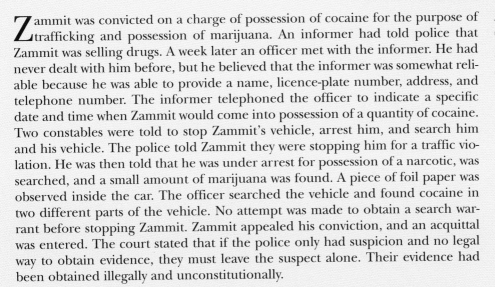

CASE

Zammit was convicted on a charge of possession of cocaine for the purpose of trafficking and possession of marijuana. An informer had told police that Zammit was selling drugs. A week later an officer met with the informer. He had never dealt with him before, but he believed that the informer was somewhat reliable because he was able to provide a name, licence-plate number, address, and telephone number. The informer telephoned the officer to indicate a specific date and time when Zammit would come into possession of a quantity of cocaine. Two constables were told to stop Zammit's vehicle, arrest him, and search him and his vehicle. The police told Zammit they were stopping him for a traffic violation. He was then told that he was under arrest for possession of a narcotic, was searched, and a small amount of marijuana was found. A piece of foil paper was observed inside the car. The officer searched the vehicle and found cocaine in two different parts of the vehicle. No attempt was made to obtain a search warrant before stopping Zammit. Zammit appealed his conviction, and an acquittal was entered. The court stated that if the police only had suspicion and no legal way to obtain evidence, they must leave the suspect alone. Their evidence had been obtained illegally and unconstitutionally.

R. v. Zammit
(1993)

Ontario Court of Appeal
21 C.R. (4th) 86

1. According to section 10 of the *Narcotic Control Act*, what do the police need to carry out a search of Zammit's vehicle?
2. On what grounds would Zammit appeal?
3. Why should the informer's tip not be considered sufficient justification to arrest Zammit and search him?
4. If the police did not have reasonable and probable grounds to make an arrest and conduct a search, what procedure should they have followed?

Search Authorized by a Warrant

Section 10 of the *Narcotic Control Act* provides that a warrant is required for search of a dwelling-house. There are exceptions as indicated in the statement from *Hunter v. Southam Inc.* (1984) quoted earlier. The courts expect that a warrant will be obtained if possible, given the circumstances.

In general, the procedure for obtaining a search warrant under the *Narcotic Control Act* is the same as under the *Criminal Code*. The police must convince the court that they have reasonable grounds to believe that drugs are present. The warrant is issued to a specific officer. The *Narcotic Control Act* specifically states that, in order to conduct the search, an officer may break open any door, window, lock, fastener, floor, wall, ceiling, compartment, plumbing fixture, box, container, or any other thing.

Once inside, the officer may search any person found there, if there are reasonable grounds to believe that the person is in possession of a narcotic. The officer may seize any narcotics, or any items that the officer reasonably suspects contains or conceals a narcotic. Objects that may have been used in the commission of the offence may also be seized.

No provision in the *Narcotic Control Act* gives police the power to stop and search a person for drugs in a public place. The *Criminal Code* authorizes this type of search. Again, there must be reasonable grounds for believing that the person is in possession of a drug.

Reviewing Your Reading

1. a) How did the LeDain Commission define a drug?

    b) How does the *Narcotic Control Act* define a narcotic drug?

2. Describe two situations in which someone may be charged with possession, while not having physical possession.

3. Is intent necessary for possession? Explain.

4. How does the *Narcotic Control Act* define trafficking?

5. What two points must the Crown prove to obtain a conviction for trafficking?

6. Who can be charged with the offence of importing and exporting narcotics?

7. What is prescription shopping?

8. Describe a situation in which a warrantless search would be legal. Explain why.

8.3 THE *FOOD AND DRUG ACT*

The *Food and Drug Act* is in force to ensure that food, medicines, cosmetics, and medical devices are safe for Canadian consumers. The *Act* covers two categories: controlled drugs and restricted drugs. The penalties for offences under the *Food and Drug Act* are shown in the table below.

Penalties for Criminal Offences under the Food and Drug Act

The search and seizure provisions related to controlled and restricted drugs are the same as those under the *Narcotic Control Act*. In addition, the amendments relating to enterprise crime and laundering apply to the *Food and Drug Act* just as they do to the *Narcotic Control Act*.

Penalties for Criminal Offences under the *Food and Drug Act*

Offence	Penalty	
Prescription shopping; possession of restricted drug	Summary Offence	
	First Offence	6 months and/or $1000 fine
	After First Offence	1 year and/or $2000 fine
	Indictable	3 years and/or $5000 fine
Trafficking; possession for the purpose of trafficking	Summary Offence	18 months
	Indictable	10 years

CASE

An informer told Constable Gutteridge that Kevin DeBot, Greg Carpenter, and Gerry List were going to meet that day for the purpose of completing a drug transaction. The informer had given reliable information in the past. Approximately 113 g of speed (amphetamines) were involved in the drug transaction. The speed was being brought to the area by a supplier, named by the informer who had been in conversation with Carpenter.

Gutteridge also testified that he had received confidential information in the past that DeBot was involved in trafficking in speed and narcotic drugs. DeBot had a prior conviction for possession. Carpenter was a known trafficker with a lengthy record of convictions for narcotics offences. His home was under surveillance when Debot's automobile was seen leaving the residence. Police radioed to have another officer stop DeBot and search his vehicle. Approximately 28 g of speed were found in DeBot's pocket. DeBot admitted that he had two plastic syringes concealed in his socks.

At the conclusion of a lengthy *voir dire*, the judge held that the search of the respondent contravened section 8 of the *Charter*. He held that the stopping of the car was arbitrary, and that there were no reasonable grounds for searching DeBot. DeBot was acquitted. The Crown appealed. The Ontario Court of Appeal ordered a new trial.

R. v. DeBot
(1986)

Ontario Court of Appeal
30 C.C.C. (3d) 207

1. **What evidence was found as a result of the search?**
2. **Refer to section 24(2) of the *Charter*. In order to exclude the evidence what must be proved? Who would have the burden of proof?**
3. **Does section 8 of the *Charter* protect individuals from *all* police searches?**
4. **What would make a search "reasonable"?**
5. **Under what circumstance would information from an informer constitute "reasonable grounds" to search?**
6. **Would the officer have grounds to believe that the informer was reliable?**
7. **Did the Court of Appeal find that the search contravened section 8 of the *Charter*? How do you know?**
8. **Was the Court of Appeal correct or incorrect? Give your reasons.**

Controlled Drugs

Drugs listed in Schedule G of the *Food and Drug Act* are **controlled drugs**. They include amphetamines and barbiturates, commonly called "uppers" and "downers." Amphetamines are used to treat depression and decrease the appetite to achieve weight reduction. Barbiturates are used as sedatives or hypnotics; sleeping pills are an example. It is not an offence to be in possession of controlled drugs, since they are regularly prescribed by doctors. But it is an offence to traffic in controlled drugs and to possess them for the purpose of trafficking. However, the definition of trafficking is slightly different from that in the *Narcotic Control Act*. In the *Food and Drug Act*, "to give" and "to administer" are not included. There is no separate offence of importing and exporting. They are included in the definition of trafficking.

Like users of prescription narcotics, users of controlled drugs commit an offence if, when seeking a prescription for such a drug, they do not inform a doctor of all controlled drugs or related prescriptions received within the previous 30 days.

Restricted Drugs

Drugs listed in Schedule H of the *Food and Drug Act* are **restricted drugs**. Some well-known examples are LSD (lysergic acid diethylamide), DMT (dimethyltryptamine), and MDA (methylene-dioxyamphetamine). Restricted drugs are not used for medical purposes. It is an offence to possess them, traffic in them, or possess them for the purpose of trafficking.

Reviewing Your Reading

1. **What is the purpose of the *Food and Drug Act*?**
2. **a) Give two examples of controlled drugs.**
   b) What offences can be committed in relation to controlled drugs?
3. **a) Give two examples of restricted drugs.**
   b) What offences can be committed in relation to restricted drugs?

8.4 *D*RIVING AND DRINKING AND DRIVING

Jurisdiction over driving and drinking and driving is divided between the federal and provincial governments. Provincial laws regulate highways, the licensing of drivers, and alcohol consumption. Such matters were assigned to the provinces by the *Constitution Act, 1867*. The *Criminal Code* covers criminal offences arising from driving and alcohol consumption. The 1985 amendments to the *Code* were intended to introduce new impaired driving offences, provide increased penalties and more penalty options, and augment police powers in obtaining evidence.

Definition of a Motor Vehicle

As you read, keep in mind that a **motor vehicle** is defined in the *Criminal Code* as "a vehicle that is drawn, propelled, or driven by any means other than by muscular power, but does not include a vehicle of a railway that operates on rails." Although it is not always made explicit, therefore, the discussion below pertains to water vessels and aircraft as well as to automobiles, trucks, motorcycles, snowmobiles, and other motorized land vehicles.

Dangerous Operation of a Motor Vehicle

It is an offence to operate a motor vehicle in a manner dangerous to the public on a street, road, highway, or other public place. The interpretation of "public place" has been given in many cases and has been found to include parking lots at shopping plazas and schools, as well as private roads regularly used by the public.

To obtain a conviction on the offence, the Crown must establish fault. In determining fault, the court must consider the standard of care that a prudent driver would have exercised. All the circumstances, including the nature, condition, and use of the public place where the offence occurred, and the amount of traffic at the time and in that place, must also be considered. It is not necessary for there to be persons present in the "public place." Also, if the offender consumed alcohol in circumstances knowing it would impair his or her ability to drive, fault is established.

Before the 1985 amendments to the *Criminal Code*, the charge of criminal negligence in the operation of a motor vehicle was brought in many cases involving bodily harm. However, because the courts' view of negligence was rather narrow, and the Crown had to prove "wanton and reckless disregard," the accused was frequently acquitted.

To overcome this problem, two new offences were added to the *Criminal Code* that specifically apply to the dangerous operation of a motor vehicle—dangerous operation of a motor vehicle causing bodily harm, and dangerous operation of a motor vehicle causing death. The Supreme Court of Canada has taken a rather liberal view of the intent required to be found guilty of these offences, as illustrated by the decision in *R. v. Hundal*.

Failure to Stop at the Scene of an Accident

It is a criminal offence for someone involved in an accident to fail to stop at the scene. The law requires an individual to give his or her name and address to the other party. If the other party has been injured or appears to require assistance, assistance must be given.

To be found guilty of failing to stop both *actus reus* and *mens rea* must be proved. The Crown must prove that the accused knew of the accident. The intent to leave can be inferred from the act of leaving. The intent to escape criminal and civil liability can also be inferred.

Occasionally, there is a justifiable excuse for leaving the scene of an accident. It may be necessary to leave to get help. However, if the accused knows there has been an accident and panics and leaves, it is not justifiable.

Impaired Driving

Impaired driving has become the principle criminal cause of death in Canada. Yet, offenders have often received sentences that seem trivial compared with the consequences of their actions. Canadians have urged legislators to increase penalties for this offence, as a deterrent.

In response to social concern, the criminal law relating to drinking and driving was changed in 1985.

In 1993, police reported 117 567 impaired driving incidents. This accounted for 59 percent of all *Criminal Code* traffic incidents. The Traffic Injury Research Foundation estimates that between 25 and 30 percent of all drivers injured in motor vehicle accidents are impaired, and almost one-half of all traffic fatalities involve someone who has been drinking.

Section 253 of the *Criminal Code* describes the offence of impaired driving:

CASE

Hundal was driving in heavy afternoon traffic on a wet, four-lane street in downtown Vancouver. His truck collided with a car, killing the driver instantly. The driver had stopped for a red light and was proceeding through the intersection after the light turned green. He had passed the crosswalk and the two west-bound lanes when his car was struck broadside by Hundal's overloaded dump truck in the east-bound passing lane. Hundal testified that he thought he could not stop when the light turned amber: he sounded his horn and proceeded through the intersection.

Several witnesses testified that Hundal's truck entered the intersection after the traffic light had turned red. Police testimony established that the light was timed to provide a significant delay between the traffic going in one direction receiving an amber light and the other traffic receiving a green light. Another witness, who had driven behind the truck for 12 intersections, testified that Hundal had gone through another intersection as the light turned red. The witness estimated the truck's speed at the time of the collision to be between 50 and 60 km/h. The trial judge found that Hundal's actions represented a gross departure from the standard of care to be expected from a prudent driver and found him guilty of dangerous driving causing death. That decision was upheld on appeal to the British Columbia Court of Appeal and by the Supreme Court of Canada.

R. v. Hundal
(1993)

**Supreme Court
of Canada
I S.C.R. 867**

1. **What standard of care should Hundal have shown while driving his vehicle?**
2. **The Supreme Court of Canada indicated that the *mens rea* for the offence of dangerous driving should be assessed objectively but in the context of all the events surrounding the incident. Explain what this means.**
3. **In your opinion, did Hundal meet the standard of care required?**
4. **What penalty would you impose in this situation?**

Criminal Code Traffic Incidents, 1993

110 576 persons charged

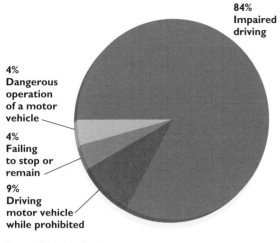

84% Impaired driving

4% Dangerous operation of a motor vehicle

4% Failing to stop or remain

9% Driving motor vehicle while prohibited

Source: Statistics Canada.

253.

Every one commits an offence who operates a motor vehicle or vessel or operates or assists in the operation of an aircraft or of railway equipment or has the care or control of a motor vehicle, vessel, aircraft or railway equipment, whether it is in motion or not,

(a) while the person's ability to operate the vehicle, vessel, aircraft or railway equipment is impaired by alcohol or a drug; or

(b) having consumed alcohol in such a quantity that the concentration in the person's blood exceeds 80 mg of alcohol in 100 mL of blood.

The section actually sets out four offences:

1. driving while ability is impaired by alcohol or drugs,
2. care or control of a motor vehicle when impaired by alcohol or drugs,
3. driving while the blood-alcohol level is over 80, and
4. care or control of a motor vehicle when the blood-alcohol level is over 80.

A person can be charged with the first two offences when the blood-alcohol level is below 80 mg in 100 mL of blood.

Certain key aspects of these offences warrant discussion. First, for a person to be charged with either of the "care or control" offences, it is not necessary for the vehicle to be in motion, or even running. *Mens rea* occurs when there is intent to assume the care or control of the vehicle after consuming alcohol, while impaired, or when the blood-alcohol level is over 80. *Actus reus* is the action of assuming care or control. Sitting in the driver's seat implies care or control, unless the driver can establish that he or she did not intend to set the car in motion. In other cases, such as when the driver is lying down in the car, the Crown must prove beyond a reasonable doubt that the accused was in care or control of the vehicle.

The answer to the legal question of whether or not a vehicle was in the "care or control" of the accused has been a central issue in many cases. A person who was standing beside his vehicle after having called a tow-truck was ruled to be in care or control, as was a person who sat in her car for 15 minutes after stopping.

The term "impaired" in section 253(a) is not defined in the *Criminal Code*. The court does not have to take notice of the blood-alcohol level that would be necessary for a person to be impaired. Rather, it is up to the court to determine, on the evidence presented, whether the ability to drive was impaired. It also does not matter how the accused was driving; all that is needed for a charge to be brought is for the ability to operate a vehicle to be impaired. Finally, the word "drug" is interpreted much more broadly than what one might think. In one case it was found to include the toluene in plastic model cement.

With regard to section 253(b), it again does not matter how the accused is driving—the only relevant factor is the blood-alcohol level. The amount of alcohol that one must drink in order to reach the "80 mg of alcohol in 100 mL of blood" limit depends on several factors, including body size, metabolism, fitness level, gender, and the time of the most recent meal.

Some drinking establishments provide devices to measure the blood-alcohol level. However, an

CASE

The accused, Raymond Anderson, was charged in Winnipeg, in May 1983, with criminal negligence causing death when he ran a red light and hit another car broadside, injuring two passengers and killing a young mother. Although Anderson told the police he was "thinking about something else" at the time of the accident, he was not speeding or driving erratically. He gave a breath sample at the police station, and his blood-alcohol level was more than twice the legal limit. Yet, the officer who administered the test and who had 34 years' experience testified that the accused had "shown very little impairment at all."

At trial, the judge found that the Crown had failed to prove the charge beyond a reasonable doubt and acquitted Anderson. The Crown appealed to the Manitoba Court of Appeal where a new trial was ordered in May 1985. Anderson appealed to the Supreme Court of Canada where, in a 7–0 decision in March 1990, his acquittal was restored.

R. v. Anderson
(1990)

Supreme Court of Canada
1 S.C.R. 265

1. **What are the *actus reus* and *mens rea* of criminal negligence?**

2. **On these facts, what evidence is there of *actus reus*? Of *mens rea*? Is that evidence adequate to establish both beyond a reasonable doubt?**

3. **What charge might have been more appropriate? What are the *actus reus* and *mens rea* of that charge? What evidence of each is there?**

4. **Refer to the *mens rea* of criminal negligence. Was there evidence of objective *mens rea*? What was it?**

5. **Refer to the trial court's decision. Must the Crown establish subjective *mens rea* or objective *mens rea*? How do you know?**

incorrect reading from such a device will not prove to be a successful defence. The police use certain approved devices to obtain a measure of the blood-alcohol level.

Tests for Impaired Driving

As Justice Finlayson indicated in *R. v. Seo* (1986), the most effective deterrent to impaired driving is the possibility of detection. The *Criminal Code* provides for various procedures to aid in detection: approved screening devices at the roadside, breath samples, and blood tests. As well, coordination tests can be given at the time of being stopped.

The use of roadside stops has been found constitutional by the Supreme Court of Canada, whether they are part of an organized program or done randomly. Drivers questioned the right of

the police to stop them when they had no reasonable and probable grounds that an offence had been or was being committed. The court recognized the intent of Parliament to reduce the problem of drinking drivers and ruled that spot checks are a reasonable limit prescribed by law.

When stopped in a roadside spot check, a driver may be asked by the police to undergo a **roadside screening test**. The officer will demand that the driver breathe into an approved testing device. The demand may be made only if the officer has reasonable grounds to suspect that the driver has consumed alcohol. It is an offence to refuse the demand. Approved roadside screening devices are described in the *Criminal Code of Canada*. The screening device does not measure the amount of alcohol in the blood, but merely indicates PASS, WARN, or FAIL. If the person fails, no offence has been committed—the results can only be used to show that the officer had grounds to demand a breath sample.

Several legal principles related to roadside testing have been established. It must be the officer who demanded the test who decides upon the adequacy of the sample. Moreover, the courts have ruled that it is not necessary for the testing officer to show the results of a roadside test to the person tested.

The Breathalyzer

The police may require a person to take a Breathalyzer test if there are reasonable and probable grounds to believe that the person is committing, or at any time within the preceding two hours has committed, an impaired driving offence. Again, it is an offence to refuse. A **Breathalyzer** is an approved instrument that analyzes a sample of a person's breath to measure the concentration of alcohol in the person's blood. The demand to take a Breathalyzer may be

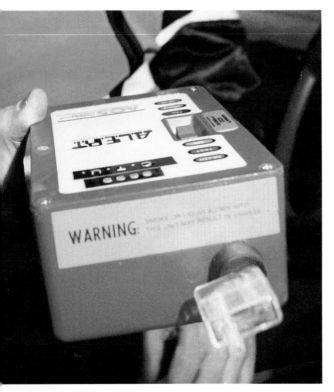

A Breathalyzer is used to obtain a breath sample.

made after an approved screening device test has been administered, but the roadside test is not necessary. There is no approved wording for the demand; it merely must be made clear that a breath sample is being demanded, not requested. The demand must be made "forthwith or as soon as practicable." Each case is weighed on its own merits to determine whether this requirement has been met. A number of cases have indicated that the officer must be certain the person has the ability to understand his or her rights. A person would probably be acquitted if he or she refused to take a test and was found to have a concussion, or to be so drunk as to be incapable of understanding the demand.

The breath sample is usually given at the police station, although some forces have portable Breathalyzer units. Whenever the driver is required to accompany the officer, detention, or arrest, exists. Under the *Charter of Rights and Freedoms*, the person must be advised of his or her right to legal counsel without delay and to obtain free advice from a legal-aid lawyer. This is not an absolute right. A person is given only a reasonable time to obtain counsel. The *Charter* also guarantees the right to discuss with counsel in private.

The breath sample must be taken by a qualified technician, using an approved device. Two samples must be taken, with an interval of at least 15 minutes between them.

If the person is incapable of giving a breath sample because of a physical condition, or it is not possible to obtain one, the officer may demand a blood sample. Blood samples may be taken only by or under the direction of a qualified medical practitioner. The practitioner can refuse, if taking a sample would endanger the life or health of the accused. The Vautainer XF947 is the only approved device for taking blood samples. The sample must be taken within two hours of the alleged offence. Two blood samples are actually taken, one of which is made available to the accused for testing. If the accused is not able to give permission for a blood sample, a warrant must be obtained. In *R. v. Colarusso*, however, the Supreme Court of Canada admitted blood samples that were obtained under questionable circumstances.

R. v. Bernshaw (1995)

Supreme Court of Canada I S.C.R. 234

B ernshaw was pulled over by a police officer who noticed his car travelling over the speed limit and drifting across the road with the brake lights flickering. Officer Mashford could smell alcohol coming from Bernshaw, whose eyes were red and glassy. He admitted to drinking when asked. Mashford made a demand for a breath sample under section 254(2) of the *Criminal Code*. It provides that a police officer may demand that a driver provide a sample of breath "forthwith." Bernshaw provided a sample but failed. Mashford did not ask Bernshaw when the last drink was consumed nor did he wait the required 15 minutes to administer the roadside test. Mashford arrested Bernshaw, gave him the standard breath sample demand and took him to the police station. There, two breath samples indicated that Bernshaw was well over the limit of 80 mg.

At trial, Bernshaw argued that the results of the breath analysis should not be admitted on the grounds that the officer did not have the reasonable and probable grounds required to make the demand. He indicated that the officer knew or ought to have known that the fail result recorded on the screening device might have been inaccurate due to the presence of mouth alcohol. The trial judge nonetheless admitted the test results and Bernshaw was convicted. His summary conviction appeal was dismissed, but the Court of Appeal for British Columbia substituted a verdict of acquittal. The Crown appealed the acquittal to the Supreme Court of Canada.

The Crown's position was that the Criminal Code section provided that the demand be made "forthwith." The Supreme Court of Canada agreed, indicating that it was not necessary to wait the 15 minutes before demanding a roadside test. The Supreme Court of Canada recommended that police develop a standard practice. If the officer honestly believes that the motorist has engaged in drinking activity within the last 15 minutes that could affect the reliability of the test, the officer should read a prepared statement to the motorist, advising that person of the reason for the delay. The Supreme Court of Canada, in its decision, indicated that the 15-minute postponement would only be necessary to accommodate drinkers with indigestion or, more frequently, those who see fit to take a drink shortly before driving their car. The Court indicated that if a driver took a drink in those circumstances, the driver should be prepared to accept the consequences.

1. **What protection is there to the driver if he or she does fail the roadside test?**
2. **What does the Supreme Court's decision indicate about the Court's attitude toward drinking and driving?**
3. **Why should police develop and follow a standard procedure?**

An officer may require a driver to perform a sobriety test, such as walking a straight line. In such cases, the driver has been detained. Legislation in British Columbia and Ontario has given the police the right to conduct such tests. The British Columbia and Ontario Supreme Courts have therefore ruled that the demand to perform such tests constitutes a reasonable limit on the right to retain and instruct counsel and to be informed of that right prior to performing a sobriety test. The Supreme Courts in Alberta, Nova Scotia, and Prince Edward Island have

**R. v.
Colarusso**

(1994)

**Supreme Court
of Canada
87 C.C.C. (3d) 192**

Colarusso was driving without his lights on. He rear-ended a pickup truck, sending it into a ditch where it flipped over. The occupants of the truck were seriously injured. An off-duty police officer saw Colarusso stop briefly before he continued southbound in the northbound land. He then collided head-on with another car. An occupant of that car was killed. Colarusso was injured.

Colarusso was arrested at the scene by police officers who observed signs of impairment. He was charged with a number of offences, including criminal negligence causing death, and advised of his *Charter* rights. A demand was made for a sample of his breath. Before that could occur, Colarusso was driven by the police to hospital for treatment of injuries. No Breathalyzer test was given, nor did the police make a demand for a blood sample.

At the hospital, Colarusso consented to blood and urine samples being taken for medical purposes. The urine sample was supplied by Colarusso in the presence of a police officer. The samples were sent to the hospital lab to be used in tests. The coroner investigated the scene of the second accident, and then went to the hospital to investigate the car occupant's death. He needed samples of Colarusso's blood and urine. The coroner gave the samples to the police, requesting that they be taken to the centre of forensic sciences and stored properly.

The Crown called the forensic toxicologist who had analyzed Colarusso's samples at the request of the coroner. The toxicologist testified that at the time of the accidents Colarusso's blood-alcohol level was between 144 and 165. Colarusso argued that the evidence of the toxicologist should be excluded because the blood and urine had been seized in violation of his rights under section 8 of the *Charter*. He was convicted at trial, and his appeals to the Ontario Court of Appeal and Supreme Court of Canada were dismissed.

1. **What is a forensic scientist?**

2. **What is a coroner?**

3. **a) Who obtained the blood and urine samples and for what purpose?**

   b) How did the police get access to the samples?

   c) Did the way the police gained access to the samples tend to bring the administration of justice into disrepute?

4. **Should the Crown be able to use the samples obtained by the coroner as part of their case? Why or why not?**

5. **Why did the Supreme Court of Canada find that the evidence could be admitted?**

ruled that as there is no legislation giving the right to an officer to demand the test, the driver must be informed of his or her right to counsel before being required to do the tests.

Penalties

The penalties for impaired driving offences are outlined in the chart below. Note that a second offence does not necessarily mean a second charge on the same offence, but simply two motor vehicle offences related to drinking. In *R. v. Kumar* (1993), decided by the Supreme Court of British Columbia, it was ruled that the penalty for a second offence can be varied if it is found to be cruel and unusual punishment, and therefore contravenes section 12 of the *Charter of Rights and Freedoms*.

In some provinces, a judge may discharge an offender whom he or she feels would benefit from treatment for alcohol or drug addiction. This may be done in cases of impaired operation of a motor vehicle and operating a motor vehicle with a blood-alcohol level over 80. Releasing the offender must not be contrary to the public interest, and the offender must go for treatment.

The chart shows that certain offences carry a prohibition from driving. The *Criminal Code* sets out a separate offence of operating a motor vehicle while being disqualified from doing so. To avoid impinging on provincial jurisdiction, the *Criminal Code* indicates that such disqualification occurs only in the case of impaired driving, driving with a blood-alcohol level of over 80, and refusing to provide a breath sample. It also applies to offences in which a conditional discharge was given, and where one of the conditions was to refrain from driving.

Penalties for Driving Offences under the *Criminal Code*

Offence	Penalty	
Dangerous driving	Hybrid	5 years
Dangerous driving causing bodily harm	Indictable	10 years
Dangerous driving causing death	Indictable	14 years
Driving while impaired; driving with over 80 mg of alcohol per 100 mL of blood; refusal to provide a breath sample on an approved screening device, or refusal to provide a blood sample	**Hybrid — minimums**	
	First Offence	fine of not less than $300
		3-month prohibition from driving
	Second Offence	14-day imprisonment
		6-month prohibition from driving
	Third Offence	3-month imprisonment
		1-year prohibition from driving
	Hybrid — maximums	
	Summary Offence	$200 fine
		6-month imprisonment
		3-year prohibition from driving
	Indictable Offence	unlimited fine
		5-year imprisonment
		3-year prohibition from driving
Impaired driving causing bodily harm		10-year imprisonment
		10-year prohibition
Impaired driving causing death		14-year imprisonment
		14-year prohibition from driving

CASE

R. v. Hufsky
(1988)

Supreme Court
of Canada
40 C.C.C. (3rd) 398

In January 1983, at about 12:30 a.m., Hufsky was stopped in a random spot check. Officers were checking licences, proof of insurance, mechanical fitness of vehicles, and driver sobriety. No guidelines were used to determine which vehicles should be checked, and there had been nothing unusual about Hufsky's driving when he was stopped.

Detecting the odour of alcohol on Hufsky's breath and noticing slightly slurred speech, the officer made a formal breath-test demand that was refused. Hufsky was then charged with refusing to provide a breath sample without reasonable excuse. He was informed of his rights under section 10(b) of the *Charter* and released on an appearance notice.

At trial in Provincial Court, the accused argued that random spot checks infringed his rights under sections 8 and 9 of the *Charter* to be secure against unreasonable search and seizure and not to be arbitrarily detained. However, the judge convicted Hufsky and fined him $100. His appeals to the County Court (now District Court) and the Ontario Court of Appeal were dismissed. Hufsky requested leave to appeal to the Supreme Court of Canada. In a 7–0 decision, the appeal was dismissed, and the conviction upheld.

1. **What rights of an accused are protected under sections 8 and 9 of the *Charter*? Why did Hufsky contend that his rights under these sections had been infringed?**

2. **Everyone is presumed to be innocent. Yet, certain statutes give police the right to randomly stop cars. Do these statutes limit section 8 or 9 rights of the *Charter*?**

3. **Do you agree or disagree with the decision in this case?**

Provincial Offences Related to Impaired Driving

Each province has legislation related to drinking and driving. For example, some provincial laws allow vehicles to be stopped at random. When a police officer stops someone under the authority of a provincial statute, the smell of alcohol or drugs, or evidence discovered during a safety check, may lead to further investigation under the *Narcotic Control Act* or the *Criminal Code*. The officer must have grounds for searching the automobile for the offence in question; a "fishing expedition" cannot be undertaken in hopes of finding illegal items.

Provincial laws allow the licences of persons convicted of federal impaired driving offences to be suspended for additional periods. A convicted offender therefore may be subject not only to a

fine or imprisonment and a federal driving prohibition, but also to a provincial suspension.

The provinces also have legislation permitting the licence of a person whose blood alcohol is above a specified limit to be suspended for a short period, such as 12 or 24 hours. This is obviously to protect the public from the driver. In Ontario, a driver's licence can be taken away for 12 hours if an approved screening device shows a reading of over 50 mg of alcohol in 100 mL of blood. It can be suspended for 24 hours in British Columbia. Anyone who drives during this period can, of course, be charged with the additional offence of driving without a licence. The licence must be handed over on the spot and can be retrieved from the local police station after the time limit expires. The driver's vehicle may be towed away at the owner's expense. It is up to the police officer to decide whether a passenger will be permitted to drive the

vehicle. This type of suspension has the advantage of carrying no penalty other than a notation on the person's provincial driving record.

Other Ramifications for the Drinking Driver

Impaired driving has ramifications other than those described above. A conviction will result in **demerit points**, which could lead to licence suspension. It may also lead to an increase in the offender's automobile insurance rate. An insurer can even refuse to pay any claim on behalf of a person who is at fault in an accident that occurred because of impaired driving or while the person's licence was suspended.

Reviewing Your Reading

1. What circumstances are considered in establishing fault for the dangerous operation of a motor vehicle?

2. What is a public place, in relation to the operation of a vehicle?

3. Identify the offences that supplemented the law on negligence in the operation of a motor vehicle. Why were they added?

4. What must a driver do at the scene of an accident in which he or she is involved?

5. What does "care or control" mean with respect to a motor vehicle?

6. Discuss in detail the two offences that relate to impaired driving.

7. a) Distinguish between a roadside test and a Breathalyzer test.

   b) When can each be demanded?

   c) Where do each usually occur?

   d) What procedures must the police follow when administering each?

8. When can blood samples be taken as evidence of impaired driving?

9. What consequences other than a fine or imprisonment does a conviction for impaired driving carry?

ISSUE

Should people who use illegal drugs be punished?

Marijuana, cocaine, and heroin are just three of the illegal drugs listed in the *Narcotic Control Act* that are regularly used by Canadians. Indeed, the Canadian Centre on Substance Abuse reports that one million Canadians—4.2 percent of the population—are regular marijuana users.

Marijuana and hashish, drugs from the plant *Cannabis sativa* produce a state of relaxation, accelerated heart rate, a heightened state of the senses, and a perceived slowing of time. Experts report that marijuana is 50 percent more cancer-causing than ordinary cigarettes. Regular use can affect the immune system and damage the brain, heart, and reproductive system. An American report on marijuana use released in July 1995 by the National Institute on Drug Abuse says the drug can cause physical addiction in teens and adults and long-term health problems in children exposed prenatally.

Heroin, a substance derived from opium, produces a "rush"—a feeling of excitement—immediately after it is taken. The euphoria that the user experiences produces a state of profound indifference that serves as a temporary escape from personal problems. As the body develops a tolerance for the drug, increasing amounts are needed to achieve the same effect. Nausea, diarrhea, and pain are symptoms experienced after the drug's effect wears off.

Cocaine, a stimulant extracted from the South American coca bush, can lead to severe physiological and psychological problems. Regular cocaine use can damage nasal passages, cause impotence, and create paranoia or depression. Large doses can cause violent behaviour, convulsions, and even death.

In addition to physiological and psychological changes in the body, drug use leads to social problems as well. Yet people continue to use and abuse these drugs, despite the fact that they are illegal.

On One Side

Many people advocate a firm stand in dealing with drug abuse. They believe that higher fines and longer jail sentences for drug users and traffickers would reduce drug use.

They applaud the fact that between 1983 and 1991 the number of cocaine-related convictions

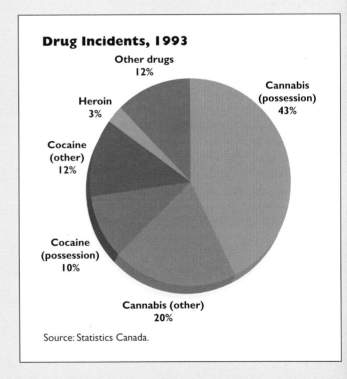

Drug Incidents, 1993

- Other drugs 12%
- Cannabis (possession) 43%
- Heroin 3%
- Cocaine (other) 12%
- Cocaine (possession) 10%
- Cannabis (other) 20%

Source: Statistics Canada.

in the courts increased by 500 percent (60 convictions per 100 000 Canadians).

To these people, the $100 million a year it costs Canadian taxpayers to enforce Canada's drug laws is money well spent.

On the Other Side

Many Canadians feel that stiffer penalties will not rehabilitate or reform drug users. These people believe that those who use illegal drugs should be given treatment rather than be punished.

Whether the addiction is psychological or physical, it is regarded as a disease that needs to be cured.

To these people, the millions of taxpayers' dollars spent to apprehend and punish drug offenders would be better spent treating drug addicts to cure and rehabilitate them.

The Bottom Line

As long as some drugs are identified as being illegal, the *Narcotic Control Act* is necessary to control their trafficking. However, should this statute also apply to drug users? Or should drug users be considered victims who require treatment? You be the judge!

1. **Why do people use illegal drugs? What are some problems associated with these drugs?**

2. **Working in groups, half the class should brainstorm for arguments to support stiffer penalties for illegal drugs. The other half should list points to support rehabilitation of users. Each group can present its conclusions to the class.**

3. **As a class, discuss the idea that all drugs should be decriminalized with no penalties for their use. Identify the advantages and disadvantages for society.**

Chapter Review

Reviewing Key Terms

For each of the following statements, indicate the key term being defined:

a) manufacturing or giving illegal drugs to another person

b) transferring money obtained from the commission of *Narcotic Control Act* offences

c) trying to obtain the same narcotic prescription from different doctors

d) drugs listed in Schedule G of the *Food and Drug Act*

e) Royal Commission that studied the non-medical use of drugs

f) drugs listed in Schedule H of the *Food and Drug Act*

g) without grounds, trying to find out if someone is a drug dealer by encouraging them to sell drugs

h) test carried out to determine if a Breathalyzer should be demanded

Exploring Legal Concepts

1. One of the arguments given in support of legalizing the possession of marijuana in amounts sufficient for one's use is that less damage is caused by use of marijuana than from the use of alcohol. In your opinion, is that argument valid in supporting the legalization of marijuana?

2. How does the *Narcotic Control Act* allow the police, when laying a charge, to distinguish between a person found in possession of one marijuana cigarette and someone who possesses 30 of them?

3. a) What is random virtue testing? Why do the police use it in drug-related cases.

   b) In what way does random virtue testing violate rights protected in the *Charter*?

   c) In your view, does the use of random virtue testing tend to bring the administration of justice into disrepute? Why or why not?

4. a) Why have laws on drinking and driving become more strict?

   b) What do you think would be the best way to reduce the number of drinking and driving offences?

5. What is the important governmental objective in criminalizing drug use? Is this objective important enough to justify allowing the police fewer restrictions in searching for illegal drugs?

Applying Legal Concepts

1. *R. v. Rousseau* (1991) Quebec Court of Appeal 70 C.C.C. (3d) 445

   Rousseau, a physician, was charged with a number of offences of trafficking in narcotics. He sold prescriptions for narcotics to persons he believed to be drug addicts. He did not actually provide the narcotics. The trial judge therefore acquitted Rousseau on the basis that his acts did not fall within the definition of "traffic" in the *Narcotic Control Act*. The Crown appealed to the Quebec Court of Appeal.

- **How is "trafficking" defined in the *Narcotic Control Act*?**

- **Did Rousseau's acts fall within the definition of trafficking? Explain.**

2. *R. v. Silveira* (1995) Supreme Court of Canada 2 S.C.R. 296

An undercover drug operation had indicated that a cache of cocaine for trafficking purposes was located in Silveira's house. Silveira was arrested near his home. En route to the police station, the police car was stopped by Officer Clifford, who told Silveira that police were at his house, although he did not know if this was true. Silveira then admitted that there was cocaine there but that he did not want his family involved.

When he arrived at the police station, Silveira was denied the use of a telephone. The request was delayed to protect the safety of the officers at Silveira's house. Clifford then proceeded to obtain a search warrant.

To prevent the destruction or the removal of the evidence between the time of the arrest and the arrival of the search warrant, officers went to Silveira's house, knocked, identified themselves, and entered without an invitation with guns drawn. Silveira's family was in the house. The police checked the premises for weapons, holstered their weapons, confined the occupants to the house and advised them to continue with their activities. Although they looked around the house to ensure their own safety, the police did not begin to search for evidence until the arrival of the search warrant 75 minutes later. The justice of the peace issuing the warrant was not informed of the occupation of the house by the police.

Cocaine and cash were discovered on the search and seized, but no weapons were found. Some of the cash was marked money used by undercover officers to purchase cocaine on earlier occasions.

- **What rights of Silveira may have been violated?**

- **What three things should the court consider in determining whether or not to exclude the evidence found by the police under section 24(2) of the *Charter*?**

- **The Supreme Court of Canada ruled that the evidence could be admitted. Why did it do so?**

3. *R. v. Weir* (1993) Nova Scotia Court of Appeal 79 C.C.C. (3d) 538

Weir was given a demand to provide a breath sample after being stopped while driving a van. He refused to attempt to give a breath sample because he said he had suffered a fractured skull when he was 11 years old. The injury still gave him discomfort. He offered to give a blood sample. The local hospital was only a short distance from the police station. He was charged with refusal to provide a breath sample under section 254(5) of the *Criminal Code*, which says "Every one commits an offence who, without reasonable excuse, fails or refuses to comply with a demand made to him by a peace officer under this section." Weir did not bring any medical evidence at trial to indicate that there was a reason for not providing a breath sample.

- **Is Weir guilty? Explain**

4. *R. v. St. Pierre* (1995) Supreme Court of Canada 1 S.C.R. 1

St. Pierre was charged with having the care or control of a motor vehicle while her blood-alcohol level was over 80. She was stopped because a police officer saw her driving erratically. She failed a roadside screening test and was taken to the police station for Breathalyzer tests. She had to wait about an hour for her testing session. She went to the washroom three times during that period.

Both of her breath samples produced a reading of 180. St. Pierre showed the officer two empty 50 mL vodka bottles and told him she was an alcoholic and had consumed the contents of the bottles while in the washroom, to calm herself. The officer testified that the bottles contained no residue and did not smell of vodka. The *Criminal Code* provides that the results of the tests are evidence of driving with a blood-alcohol level over 80, unless there is evidence to the contrary.

St. Pierre was acquitted by the trial judge. The summary conviction appeal court upheld the acquittal, but the Ontario Court of Appeal allowed the Crown's appeal. St. Pierre appealed to the Supreme Court of Canada.

- **Was there a way to determine what St. Pierre's blood-alcohol level was at the time of driving? Explain.**

- **Along with driving with a blood-alcohol level of over 80, what other charge could have been laid?**

- **Based on the facts, what do you think was the ruling of the Supreme Court of Canada?**

5. *R. v. Pontes* (1995) Supreme Court of Canada 100 C.C.C. (3d) 353

Pontes was charged with driving a motor vehicle in Vancouver at a time when he was prohibited from driving pursuant to the *Motor Vehicle Act*. The *Motor Vehicle Act* provides that a person convicted of certain serious provincial and *Criminal Code* motor vehicle offences be "automatically and without notice" prohibited from driving a motor vehicle from the date of sentencing. The *Act* also provides that a person who drives a motor vehicle while prohibited is liable to a first conviction with a fine of not less than $300 and to imprisonment of not less than seven days. The *Offence Act of British Columbia* provides that "no person is liable to imprisonment with respect to an absolute liability offence."

Pontes argued at trial that the *Motor Vehicle Act* created an absolute liability offence for which imprisonment was a punishment, and that the offence therefore violated section 7 of the *Charter of Rights and Freedoms*.

- **What is an absolute liability offence? How does it differ from a strict liability offence? How does it differ from a crime?**

- **What right in section 7 of the *Charter* is limited by a jail term? How does section 7 provide that the right can be limited?**

- **Since the prohibition to drive under the *Motor Vehicle Act* is automatic and without notice, what defence could Pontes not raise?**

- **Since Pontes could not raise the above defence, what kind of offence must driving while prohibited be?**

- **Is Pontes correct in his defence? Would it make a difference if the only penalty for the offence was a fine?**

Extending Legal Concepts

1. Now that you have completed this chapter, review the opening article and Something to Think About. Have your answers or opinions changed? Why or why not?

2. Using reference materials in your resource centre, including CD-ROM and the Internet, obtain current information on either "drug use and drug laws" or "drinking and driving laws" in Canada and another country. Prepare a one-page report comparing your findings about the two countries. Create a poster or use graphics software to illustrate your information.

3. With the class, brainstorm a list of survey questions to research attitudes on "drug use and laws," and "drinking and driving incidents and laws." Prepare a survey form and distribute it to the people in your school and/or community. Collect the forms and analyze the data. Prepare a written report with visuals to summarize the results of your survey.

4. From a newspaper, collect five examples of legal cases involving drug offences or drinking and driving offences. Prepare a summary of each case, showing the offence committed, the facts in favour of the Crown and the defence, respectively, the maximum penalty for the offence, and if possible, the sentence. Attach the newspaper articles to your summary.

5. Using one of the newspaper articles that you collected in question 4 as a springboard, prepare a five-minute speech outlining your views on the topic of "drug use and drug laws" or "drinking and driving laws."

Researching an Issue

Drinking and Driving Penalties
Provinces treat drivers who fail Breathalyzer tests in different ways. Manitoba has the toughest law: if it is determined that the driver has more then 80 mg of alcohol in 100 mL of blood in his or her system, the driver's licence is suspended for 90 days (or until the criminal trial) and the vehicle is impounded.

Statement
Penalties for driving while impaired by alcohol or drugs should include mandatory licence suspension.

Point
To reduce the carnage on our highways and to protect innocent persons, licence suspension should be mandatory for any driver who fails a Breathalyzer test.

Counterpoint
Every person has the right to be presumed innocent until proven guilty. Mandatory suspension of a person's driver's licence after he or she fails a Breathalyzer test is a denial of this right.

- **With a partner, research this issue and reflect on your findings.**
- **Prepare points on this statement that could be used for a class debate.**
- **Discuss your findings with others in your class.**

Chapter
9

THE YOUNG OFFENDER

These are the key terms introduced in this chapter:

alternative measures program

custody

disposition

diversion

foster home

group home

in camera

open custody

pre-disposition report

secure custody

young offender

Chapter at a Glance

Learning Outcomes

At the end of this chapter, you will be able to

1. understand why the *Young Offenders Act* was needed;
2. outline its four basic principles;
3. explain the special rights and protection the *Act* gives young offenders;
4. explain the purpose of alternative measures and when they might be used;
5. compare trial procedures in Youth Court with those in adult courts;
6. outline the range of dispositions available for young offenders;
7. discuss the reasons for recent amendments to the *Young Offenders Act*;
8. judge the effectiveness of the *Act* in its present form.

Youth Sentenced to 7 Years for Role in Drive-by Shooting

A 17-year-old youth, Cory Robert Cyr, has been handed a seven-year jail term for the drive-by shooting of a British engineer, Nicholas Battersby. Cyr pleaded guilty to manslaughter, theft, and weapons charges in the March, 1994, slaying of Battersby, a 27-year-old engineer at Northern Telecom who had recently moved to Canada. Cyr was sentenced to five years in prison for manslaughter and also received two years for dangerous use of a weapon. Sixteen months already spent in custody were deducted from the total sentences.

Battersby died after being shot through the heart with a .22 calibre rifle fired from a stolen Jeep. He was shot in front of one of Ottawa's downtown rock clubs as he was walking home.

The shooting sparked demands for the toughening of the *Young Offenders Act*.

Cyr had tried to fight the prosecution's bid to move his trial to adult court. But it was upheld by the Ontario Court of Appeal, which called Battersby's death a "senseless, irrational killing."

Brian Raymond, the 17-year-old who drove the Jeep in the shooting, has already been sentenced in adult court to 4 1/2 years in jail.

A preliminary hearing into the second-degree murder charge against the youth who allegedly fired the shot that killed Battersby will begin shortly. The youth, 16, cannot be named as he is fighting the transfer to adult court at the Ontario Court of Appeal.

From: Mark Bourrie, "Youth gets 7 years for role in drive-by shooting." *The Toronto Star*, August 15, 1995. Reprinted with permission—The Toronto Star Syndicate.

Something to Think About

- **Why could the names of the two 17-year-old offenders be published?**
- **Why did the Crown want all three of these offenders tried in adult court? Do you agree? Explain.**

9.1 INTRODUCTION

Young offenders are defined as young people between the ages of 12 and 17 inclusive, who commit criminal offences. They are dealt with under the *Young Offenders Act* and have the same rights as adults under the *Charter*. Young offenders undergo many of the same procedures as adults in the criminal justice system. However, the range of sentences tends to be less severe. The *Young Offenders Act* outlines the procedures for dealing with young offenders and provides them with additional rights upon arrest.

The intent of the *Act* is to hold youths responsible for their crimes and to protect society from their behaviour. At the same time it recognizes and safeguards their legal rights. Since its passage, the *Act* has come under considerable attack from many critics who believe that the law is too lenient.

Is the *Young Offenders Act* too lenient, or is it misunderstood by the general public? Does the media tend to sensationalize violent crimes and thus present a biased picture of crime committed by the young? Does Canada need tougher laws to deal with teenage offenders? The background information in this chapter will enable you to answer these and other questions about youth crimes and the related laws in Canada.

Looking Back

Since the beginning of legal history, special rules have existed for handling youths who break the law. Under English common law, children between 7 and 13 years of age were often not charged for criminal offences. It was believed that they did not understand their actions or the consequences of such actions. However, if it could be proved that a child had the ability to form criminal intent, then the young person would be charged. Children 14 years of age or older were held responsible for their crimes, were tried in adult court, and faced the same penalties as adults: hanging, whipping, or imprisonment. In the dark, filthy, overcrowded prisons of the time, petty criminals and children mingled with hardened criminals and the insane.

By the latter part of the nineteenth century, society realized that children differ from adults and should be treated differently. In 1892, Canada amended its *Criminal Code* to guarantee that children were tried privately and separately from adults. Special laws, child welfare agencies, and a separate justice system were developed for young people. These efforts resulted in the passage of the federal *Juvenile Delinquents Act* in 1908. Juvenile offenders were not convicted of an offence but were considered "delinquent." The *Act*'s primary objectives were rehabilitation, child welfare, and assistance to help the youth reform, rather than punishment.

As time passed, the legal rights of young people seemed to be ignored under the *Juvenile Delinquents Act*. Youths were seldom represented by lawyers in Juvenile Court, and judges, police, and probation officers had too much power to do whatever they believed was in a youth's "best interests." Further, the lack of formal guidelines for sentencing juveniles resulted in a wide variety of sentences, some harsh and unfair, others lenient. Youths could be charged with delinquency for a violation of any federal or provincial statute (including excessive truancy from school) or municipal bylaw, as well as sexual immorality or similar vice. The definition of delinquency was so broad that youths often did not realize that they had committed an offence. Youths sent to training schools by the courts were sentenced to indefinite periods of time. Release occurred when staff at the correction institution felt that the juvenile delinquent had been rehabilitated adequately—a subjective determination that varied from case to case. Clearly reform was needed.

In the early 1960s, the federal government began to take steps to replace the *Juvenile Delinquents Act*. On July 7, 1982, the *Young Offenders Act* was given Royal Assent by the Governor General, but it did not become law until its proclamation date, April 2, 1984. The delay was to allow the provinces to make the necessary changes to their programs and services.

9.2 AGES OF CRIMINAL RESPONSIBILITY

The introduction of the *Young Offenders Act* in 1984 radically changed Canada's system of criminal justice for young people. Part of the reason for passing the *Young Offenders Act* involved society's changing views regarding the position of young people in society. Also, a more uniform and national plan was needed for dealing with youth who were found guilty of committing crimes.

Declaration of Principle

The guiding philosophy of the *Young Offenders Act* is outlined in a Declaration of Principle in section 3. It attempts to balance the need to make young offenders responsible for their crimes while recognizing their vulnerability and special needs. The following are the four basic principles:

- Young people charged with offences should be held responsible and accountable for their actions in a manner appropriate to their age and maturity.
- Society has a right to protection from the illegal behaviour of young people.
- Young people have special needs because of their age and should not suffer the same consequences as adults.

- Young people have the same rights as adults under the law, but they require additional legal rights.

The *Young Offenders Act* is criminal law. It relates only to young people between the ages of 12 and 17 inclusive, who are charged with offences under the *Criminal Code* and other federal laws, such as the *Narcotic Control Act* and the *Food and Drug Act*. These statutes define the offences, and the *Young Offenders Act* outlines how the youths are to be dealt with once they are charged with an offence. Violations of provincial statutes, such as drinking under age and traffic violations, or municipal bylaws, are tried under provincial or municipal legislation.

The *Young Offenders Act* raised the minimum age for charging a youth with a crime from age 7 under the *Juvenile Delinquents Act* to 12 years of age. This change reflected a belief that children younger than the age of 12 are too young to form criminal intent and, therefore, are too young to be dealt with in the criminal justice system. That is, a youth can intend an action but not understand that it is legally wrong. Children under 12 who get into trouble may be dealt with under provincial laws, such as child-welfare legislation.

Raising the age of criminal responsibility has led to complaints. The police are no longer able to charge children under 12 years of age, even if they have committed serious crimes. Critics of the age provisions are concerned that child-welfare

Anthony Jenkins/*The Globe and Mail*, Toronto

legislation does not provide suitable penalties for such offences. Many feel that the age should be reduced to at least 10 years, or even back to age 7.

The *Young Offenders Act* also raised the maximum age for charging a youth with a crime from 16 years under the *Juvenile Delinquents Act* to the accused's eighteenth birthday. The legislation recognized that the period of adolescence from 12 to 17 years inclusive is a distinct stage of life, a time of transition from childhood to adulthood. Anyone aged 18 and over is considered an adult and is subject to adult trial procedures and penalties.

The raising of the maximum age to the accused's eighteenth birthday also generated much debate and criticism during passage of the *Young Offenders Act*. Although there was support for having a common maximum age across Canada, there was considerable disagreement as to what that age should be. Because 16 was the maximum age for juvenile delinquency in most provinces, many believed that this was the appropriate age to select. As well, many people believed that younger people were becoming more involved in criminal activities such as shoplifting and break and enter, and that 16 years of age was therefore an appropriate maximum.

The reasons for finally adopting the accused's eighteenth birthday as the common maximum age were as follows:

- Under civil law in most provinces, 18 is the age at which young people can vote, marry without parental consent, and sign contracts. Thus, young people will be treated uniformly under criminal and civil law.
- It allows young offenders to benefit from the resources of the juvenile justice system, with its emphasis on individual needs and rehabilitation, for a little longer into their formative years.
- It keeps 16- and 17-year-old offenders out of adult correctional institutions, where they would come in contact with more experienced offenders and be exposed to the grim realities of prison life.
- Failure to establish a uniform age across Canada would violate section 15 of the *Charter*, which guarantees equality rights for all.

CASE

R. v. E.A.A.
(1987)

Ontario Court of Appeal
22 O.A.C. 83

The accused, E.A.A., was charged with the sexual assault of a four-year-old girl whom he was babysitting. The alleged assault occurred sometime between 9:00 p.m. July 25 and 1:00 a.m. July 26, but the Crown could not prove the specific time. The accused turned 18 at midnight on July 26.

At trial in Youth Court, the judge ruled that he had no jurisdiction to proceed with the case, as the age of the accused at the time of the offence was unknown. The Crown applied for and obtained a court order requiring the judge to try the case. The accused appealed the order. In a 3–0 decision, the Ontario Court of Appeal dismissed his appeal.

1. **Why was it so important to determine exactly when the offence had occurred?**

2. **The defence argued that, since the exact time of the offence was unknown, no court had jurisdiction to try E.A.A., so the charge should be dropped. Do you agree? Explain.**

3. **Why did the Court of Appeal support the order to have E.A.A.'s trial heard in Youth Court?**

Reviewing Your Reading

1. **When did the _Young Offenders Act_ become law?**

2. **List the four basic principles of the _Young Offenders Act_.**

3. **Under the _Young Offenders Act_, with what types of offences can a youth be charged?**

4. **Why was the minimum age for charging a youth with a crime raised from 7 to 12 years of age?**

5. **Why do many critics feel that this age should be lowered? What minimum age do they recommend?**

6. **What is the maximum age of criminal responsibility in Canada under the _Young Offenders Act_? List three reasons why this age was selected.**

9.3 $\mathcal{R}$IGHTS OF YOUNG OFFENDERS

The police have various alternatives other than to arrest if a suspect is a young offender. If the crime is a shoplifting offence, for example, the police may simply talk to the young offenders before taking them home or calling their parents or guardians. These facts are noted so that charges may be laid if the offenders get into trouble again. Although retail stores are eager to see all shoplifters taken to court, regardless of their age, because of the increased costs caused by shoplifting, the decision to lay charges rests with the police. They consider several factors, including the youth's cooperation with store security and the police, the youth's attitude on being caught, and the value of the items stolen.

Alternative Measures Programs

For non-violent or first-time offenders who are unlikely to reoffend, a trial in Youth Court can often be avoided. **Alternative measures programs**, which are outside the formal criminal justice system, are outlined in section 4 of the _Young Offenders Act_. Since the _Act_ allows each province to set up its own programs, they may vary somewhat across Canada. Alternative measures were

included because, under the _Juvenile Delinquents Act_, many young people had been brought to juvenile court for minor offences. These programs allow young offenders to learn from their mistakes before having to appear before a judge and getting a criminal record.

Alternative measures programs are essentially **diversion** programs. One category of alternative measures involves apologizing to the victim, returning stolen goods, or working for the victim as compensation. Others include community service work, counselling programs, and special school programs. All these diversion programs increase the involvement of parents and the community and focus on rehabilitation. Some parts of Canada have Youth Court committees composed of students from senior law classes who make recommendations on appropriate alternative measures. Such programs are also less expensive to administer than the Youth Court system.

Young offenders must be told of their right to obtain legal counsel before they participate in an alternative measures program. Otherwise, they might admit to doing something they did not do, just to avoid trial. They must also accept responsibility by admitting to some involvement with the offence. This does not mean that they are pleading guilty. In fact, acceptance of responsibility for certain actions cannot be used as evidence against a young offender in any later court appearance.

Offenders who freely agree to participate in a diversion program and complete all the requirements may have the charges against them stayed; no criminal conviction is recorded. Youths who fail to complete the program, however, can be tried in Youth Court.

Diversion is discretionary and can be refused by a youth. A youth who has a valid defence for what happened should choose a trial in Youth Court rather than the alternative measures program which implies some acceptance of responsibility for the offence.

Arrest and Detention

For serious offences, the police have no choice but to arrest a youth as they would an adult. From the moment the police decide to arrest the young person, certain legal rights and safeguards come into effect. First, the legal rights available under the *Charter*—the right to know the reason for the arrest, the automatic right to obtain free advice from a legal aid counsel, the right to be released from custody unless certain procedures occur, and the right to a fair trial—apply to young people.

Did You Know

Due to the high cost of defending young offenders, in future, it is possible that only those alleged young offenders who genuinely cannot afford a lawyer may be entitled to free legal aid.

Section 56 of the *Young Offenders Act* provides additional protection to that found in the *Charter* to ensure that young people are not questioned improperly by the police or others in authority.

The arresting officer or person in authority, including school principals, must tell the youths of their rights in language that they can understand. They must be told that they have no obligation to make a statement, and that any statements made may be used as evidence against them in court. Also, youths must be told that they may consult a lawyer and that a parent or another adult, as an alternative to counsel, may be present during any questioning. This option is not an alternative to a person's section 10(b) *Charter* right to counsel unless that right is clearly waived. Thus, youths who do not want to take advantage of these rights must sign a statement to that effect. The rights are all very important. Young people may have no idea of their legal position, or may be so nervous that they say things they don't mean. Young persons are often intimidated or frightened by adults, especially the police. The additional safeguards of the *Young Offenders Act* are essential.

Canadian courts, including the Supreme Court of Canada, have issued several judgments that indicate the extreme importance of the additional section 56 rights provided for alleged young offenders. In situations where the police have failed to follow all of these requirements strictly, courts have refused to allow confessions by youths as admissible evidence.

56.

(2) No oral or written statement given by a young person to a peace officer or other person who is, in law, a person of authority is admissible against the young person unless

(a) the statement was voluntary;

(b) the person to whom the statement was given has, before the statement was made, clearly explained to the young person, in language appropriate to his age and understanding, that

   (i) the young person is under no obligation to give a statement,

   (ii) any statement given by him may be used in evidence in proceedings against him,

   (iii) the young person has the right to consult another person in accordance with paragraph (c), and

   (iv) any statement made by the young person is required to be made in the presence of the person consulted, unless the young person desires otherwise;

(c) the young person has, before the statement was made, been given a reasonable opportunity to consult with counsel or a parent, or in the absence of a parent, an adult relative, or in the absence of a parent or adult relative, any other appropriate adult chosen by the young person; and

(d) where the young person consults with any person pursuant to paragraph (c), the young person has been given a reasonable opportunity to make the statement in the presence of that person.

Three young offenders, L.R.I., E.T., and A., and a young adult were charged with the first-degree murder of a taxicab driver in late 1988. In adult court, a conviction for this offence could result in life imprisonment. However, the Crown's attempt to transfer the case to adult court was unsuccessful. At trial in Youth Court, the Crown's case depended largely on statements that E.T. had made to the police hours after the killing when they arrested him at the home of his great-aunt where he lived. His great-aunt was 62 years old and had a very limited education.

When they arrived at the police station, E.T. and his great-aunt were taken to an interview room and questioned for about four-and-one-half hours. During this time, the police officer completed a Statement to Person in Authority form as required under section 56 of the *Young Offenders Act*. In completing the form, the officer confirmed that E.T. had been given an opportunity "to speak to a lawyer or parent or adult relative" and that his choice was to speak to the officer in front of his great-aunt. After completing the statement, E.T. provided the police with a knife and the cab driver's keys. He then talked to his lawyer for about half an hour.

The next morning after talking to his lawyer again, the offender told the police that he wanted to add some things to his first statement; this included the youths' plans regarding the cab driver's death. Prior to taking the second statement, the police officer again filled out the required form, and E.T. indicated that he did not wish to speak to anyone other than the officer or have anyone present.

At trial, the judge excluded E.T.'s first statement but admitted the second statement. L.R.I. was convicted of manslaughter while E.T., A., and the adult were all convicted of second-degree murder. E.T. appealed his conviction to the British Columbia Court of Appeal, seeking to have his second statement excluded, but the court dismissed his appeal. A further appeal to the Supreme Court of Canada was granted, and an acquittal was entered in a 7–0 judgment because the Court ruled that the second statement should also have been excluded.

R. v. I. (L.R.) and T. (E.)
(1993)

Supreme Court of Canada
109 D.L.R. (4th) 140

1. All statements made by an accused person to a person in authority must be "voluntary" to be admissible in court. What does "voluntary" mean? Why might it be difficult to determine if a young person's statement is in fact "voluntary"?

2. Explain why a young person is entitled to have an adult present when giving a statement to the police.

3. Is it likely that E.T. and his great-aunt understood and appreciated his act of confession? Explain.

4. Why did the trial judge exclude the first statement as evidence? Do you agree? Why or why not?

5. Why did the trial judge admit the second statement as evidence? Do you agree? Why or why not?

6. Why did the Supreme Court of Canada exclude the admissibility of the second statement and enter an acquittal against E. T.'s second-degree murder conviction? Do you agree? Explain.

Detention and Bail

The *Criminal Code* grants young offenders the same right to bail as adult offenders. Terms often include a curfew or a prohibition of contact with victims and association with certain peers. For many offences, youths who have been arrested are generally released into the custody of their parents. If there is risk of re-offence or concern about nonappearance for trial, youths may be released into foster homes or placed under "house arrest" programs in some provinces prior to trial or sentencing. Youths may be required to sign a recognizance or undertaking to the court. The youths must also be kept separate from adult offenders as much as possible.

Young offenders can be fingerprinted and photographed only when they are charged with indictable offences. To protect a youth's rights, the *Young Offenders Act* requires the police to destroy the photos and fingerprints if the young person is acquitted, if the charge is dismissed, or if the proceedings are discontinued.

Notice to Parents

Parents must be notified of the detention and all procedures involving their child as soon as possible. They are encouraged to be present during all steps of the legal process and are given the opportunity to provide input prior to sentencing, if the child is found guilty. Because their role is so important, a judge can order parents to attend a hearing. Parents who do not appear may be found in contempt of court, and the judge can issue a warrant for their arrest if necessary.

Reviewing Your Reading

1. What options are available to the police in the case of a youth who has committed a minor offence?
2. List three factors the police may consider before laying charges for a shoplifting offence.
3. What are alternative measures programs?
4. What two conditions must be met before a young offender can participate in such a program?
5. What rights are available to young offenders who are arrested?
6. What must be considered before a young offender's statement can be admitted as evidence at trial?
7. When may a young offender be fingerprinted and photographed?

9.4 TRIAL PROCEDURES

Depending on the province, trials under the *Young Offenders Act* may be conducted in Family Court or Youth Court. However, the proceedings may be held at different times from adult trials. Thus, the same judge might hear adult criminal cases some of the time and young-offender cases at other times. Ontario has established a two-tier Youth Court system in which 12- to 15-year-olds are tried in Family Court, while 16- and 17-year-olds are tried in Provincial Court.

Trial proceedings are just as formal as in adult trials and follow the same rules of evidence. The same form of defence counsel, including legal aid, is available to youths as to adults. Some differences do exist. Young offenders do not have the right to decide in which court they will be tried. All trials occur in Youth Court, unless the case is transferred to adult court. No preliminary hearing is held, and all trials are conducted by a judge alone, regardless of the offence. The intent of the justice system is to deal with young offenders as rapidly as possible and allow them to return home quickly.

Privacy of Hearings

Under the *Juvenile Delinquents Act*, trials were held **in camera** (in private). The public and the media were excluded, in the belief that it was not in the youth's best interests to have the case or the accused's name reported. The only people allowed to attend the hearing were the judge, court officials, parents, defence counsel, and the accused.

Under the *Young Offenders Act*, the public and the press may attend Youth Court hearings. Proceedings can be reported in the media; however, the young offender's identity and that of any other young person involved as a witness or victim cannot be revealed. Public access to Youth Court hearings is intended to improve monitoring of the system and to make everyone involved in the trial more accountable to society. On rare occasions, the judge may exclude the general public to protect the youth's interests.

Transfer to Adult Court

There are occasions when the transfer of a young offender's trial to adult court may be permitted. A transfer may occur only if the offender is 14 years of age or older at the time of the offence and is accused of a violent crime such as murder, manslaughter, robbery, or sexual assault. Even then, transfers to adult court are not automatic. A transfer can have very serious consequences for the accused youth, who will now be tried as an adult and be subject to a severe and lengthy sentence.

The decision to transfer the trial must be made before hearing the accused's plea or determining innocence or guilt. Section 16(2) of the *Young Offenders Act* outlines the criteria that a judge must consider:

16.

(2) In considering an application in respect to a young person, a youth court shall take into account
- **(a)** the seriousness of the alleged offence and the circumstances in which it was allegedly committed;
- **(b)** the age, maturity, character, and background of the young person and any record or summary of previous findings . . . of guilt under this Act or any other Act of Parliament or any regulation made thereunder; . . .
- **(d)** the availability of treatment or correctional resources;
- **(e)** any representations made to the court by or on behalf of the young person or by the Attorney General or his agent; and
- **(f)** any other factors that the court considers relevant.

A transfer hearing is not intended to determine the innocence or guilt of the accused. It is held to determine which court is more appropriate for trial given the circumstances. At the hearing, witnesses are often asked for their opinion as to the benefits and harms of custody under the *Young Offenders Act* or imprisonment under the *Criminal Code*. The youth's parents are also given an opportunity to present their views. In making a decision regarding a transfer, a judge must consider both the interests of society and the needs of the young person. However, since 1992 amendments to the *Young Offenders Act*, protection of the public is emphasized and given greater importance.

It is usually the Crown that applies for a transfer to adult court, in the belief that the offence requires an adult punishment. The young offender also has the right to request a transfer, but this option is seldom used. It might occur, for instance, if the youth felt that a jury might be sympathetic and therefore wanted a jury trial. If several co-accused were charged with an offence, and only one was a young offender, defence counsel might want to transfer the case to adult court so that the same judge would hear all of the cases.

The transfer process is controversial within the youth justice system. Because it is subject to a judge's discretion, some critics believe that youths charged with similar offences may be treated differently. In addition, very serious offences have been committed by 12- and 13-year-olds, but youths cannot be considered for transfer before the age of 14. There are many Canadians who feel that all young offenders who commit murder should be tried in adult court.

Reviewing Your Reading

1. **List two similarities and three differences between trial proceedings in adult and Youth Court.**

2. **What major difference exists in trials held under the *Juvenile Delinquents* Act and the *Young Offenders Act*?**

3. **What two conditions must exist before considering a transfer of a young offender's trial from Youth Court to adult court?**

4. **Why is the transfer of youths to adult court for violent crimes still controversial?**

9.5 DISPOSITIONS

A **disposition** in a Youth Court trial is similar to a sentence in an adult trial. The wide range of possible dispositions allows judges to consider each young person's special needs and circumstances, the victim's needs and concerns, and the protection of society. Even if the Crown or defence recommends a specific disposition, the judge makes the final decision.

Disposing a young offender is a difficult task. The judge must keep the community interest in mind while providing a personalized disposition that will help the offender accept responsibility for breaking the law. This involves a consideration of the three basic objectives of sentencing—deterrence, rehabilitation, and retribution—and the section 3 Declaration of Principle in the *Young Offenders Act.* Because of their ages, young offenders cannot be held as accountable as adults. However, they must accept responsibility for what they have done.

Before a final decision is made, a disposition hearing may be held during which the judge reviews a **pre-disposition report**. The more serious the offence, the more likely such a hearing will occur. The pre-disposition report, prepared by a probation officer or Youth Court worker, is similar to a pre-sentence report for an adult offender. It provides information about the young person, including the following:

- the results of an interview with the youth, the parents, and the victim;
- any intention by the offender to change his or her conduct;
- a record of school attendance and performance;
- a history of any previous criminal offences;
- the offender's attitude toward the offence;
- any important information that will provide insight into the offender's character.

Where there is concern for the youth's state of mind, a medical and psychiatric profile may be included.

The following sections briefly examine the range of available dispositions, from the most lenient to the most severe.

Absolute Discharges

An absolute discharge may be given to a first offender who has committed a minor offence, such as theft under $5000, a minor assault, or mischief, when it is in the youth's best interest and is not contrary to the public interest. An offender granted a discharge has still been found guilty of the offence, but no formal conviction is entered. No further action is taken against the young person. If the youth is later found guilty of another offence, the judge will be informed of the earlier discharge in the pre-disposition report.

Fines

A young offender may be fined up to $1000 for summary offences under provincial and municipal legislation. These include minor property damage, trespassing, or driving offences. In ordering a fine, the judge must consider the youth's ability to pay. If the youth has no way of earning money or has no savings, imposing a fine is senseless. The youth, not his or her parents, must pay the fine as a penalty for the crime. The offender may ask the court to extend the deadline to pay the fine, if necessary. If payment is not received after a reasonable length of time, the judge can place the youth in custody. Fines can also be combined with other dispositions such as probation or community service work.

Compensation

An offender may be required to pay monetary compensation to the victim, to make up for any damage to property or loss of income caused by the crime. For example, a youth who stole $50 from a friend's purse could be ordered to repay that sum. If a youth commits the crime of mischief by deliberately breaking a neighbour's window, appropriate compensation would be the cost of repairing the window.

Similarly, a young person who has stolen property while committing an offence such as break and enter will be required to return the stolen goods to the rightful owner. Once the judge determines the youth's ability to pay a fine or compensation, the judge sets an amount and may also set a schedule for the offender to follow. Compensation is often combined with probation.

Personal and Community Service

Many young offenders do not have the means to pay a fine or compensation. An offender who cannot afford to compensate the victim might do some work for the victim instead. If, for example, the offender damaged the victim's prize-winning garden, the youth could be ordered to help the victim with the gardening or lawn care for a certain period. Such a disposition requires the victim's consent. Since many victims express fear or anger after an offence, few want further contact with the offender. As a result, personal service orders are not a commonly used disposition. When used, they are usually the result of property offences.

When the victim does not want a personal service order, or when the offender has caused some harm to the community, the judge may impose a community service order. Its purpose is to have the young offender put something back into the community that has been violated. For instance, a young offender who destroys city property may have to work for a certain number of hours with the city's Parks and Recreation Department. Shovelling snow and cutting grass for senior citizens, or working for a charity, in a day-care facility, a food bank, or a literacy program are other examples of community service.

The *Young Offenders Act* states that personal or community service orders cannot exceed 240 hours in a year. The government in British Columbia has set a limit of 100 hours within three months.

Probation

When a judge feels that a young offender needs some limits imposed on his or her freedom, a probation order may be issued. This means that the youth will be placed under the supervision of a probation officer for up to two years. Section 23 of the *Young Offenders Act* outlines the conditions applying to all probation orders.

There is no limit to the number of conditions that can be included in a probation order. A basic condition is that the young offender must stay out of trouble while on probation. Other conditions depend on the offence committed and the offender's background. Usually they include reporting to a probation officer at specified times, attending school regularly, following a curfew, remaining at home with one's parents, not

using alcohol or drugs, staying away from shopping malls or particular stores, apologizing to the victims, and so on. Personal service and community service orders are also common conditions in a probation order.

23.

(1) The following conditions shall be included in a probation order . . .

   (a) that the young person bound by the probation order shall keep the peace and be of good behaviour; and

   (b) that the young person appear before the Youth Court when required by the court to do so.

Every offender must be given a copy of his or her probation order, in order to be fully aware of the conditions imposed. An offender who breaks any of the terms of probation may be returned to court for an increase in the punishment. Breach of probation is a criminal charge.

When probation is combined with custody in sentencing, the probation order takes effect after the completion of the custody term.

Did You Know

An average of 34 000 young offenders were on probation each day in 1992–93. This is a rate of 152 per 10 000 youths, up 12 percent from the 1988–89 total of 136.

Custody

The dispositions described above are being used more and more commonly by the courts, since they benefit the victim and also reduce the burden to taxpayers of placing young offenders in custody. **Custody** is the most serious disposition available for young offenders. It is used when a youth is thought to be a danger to society, when other forms of disposition have not worked and the youth must be supervised, or when the crime in question is very violent. First-time offenders convicted of serious and violent crimes usually receive a term in custody for the protection of society.

Custody can be either open or secure (closed). The judge will specify in which one the offender will serve time. While the judge indicates the level of security, provincial correctional officials select the specific facility for the offender.

Open Custody

For young offenders who need more supervision and structure in their lives than they are getting at home, **open custody** is ordered. Access to the community is still available, but it is limited and supervised. Open custody facilities do not resemble penitentiaries. Rather, they are facilities dedicated to the long-term welfare and rehabilitation of young offenders and include foster or group homes, child-care facilities, and wilderness camps, depending on the province.

One example of an open custody arrangement in some provinces is the **foster home** where a youth lives with another family. Only a few restrictions, perhaps including a curfew, are placed on the young offender. Foster parents receive some financial compensation from the provincial government for their services. They are usually people who are genuinely interested in children but have no special professional child-care training.

A secure custody facility in Burnaby, British Columbia.

A facility designed to house several young offenders and operated by a professionally trained staff is called a **group home**. It is hoped that in this type of setting the youths will learn how to behave responsibly and get along with others. These facilities also draw on community resources such as schools, drug-abuse, alcohol-counselling and anger-management programs, and practical life-skills training. Foster and group homes are not available as dispositions in British Columbia.

Young offenders may also be placed in the care of the regional Children's Aid Society or Ministry of Community and Social Services. In some provinces, such as British Columbia, Alberta, and Ontario, some of the open-custody facilities are forest or wilderness camps where the offenders can work together in groups, away from the pressures and problems of life in urban communities.

Secure Custody

When young offenders have committed previous offences or serious violent crimes and pose a threat to society, **secure custody** is ordered. Secure custody facilities are used as a last resort. The youth's freedom is restricted totally with very limited community contact. These facilities usually have bars on the windows and locks on the doors. Some secure custody facilities are located in a separate wing of an adult jail or prison or in isolated rural areas. Young offenders must be kept totally isolated from adult offenders.

Many secure-custody facilities provide offenders with recreational and educational facilities. Education upgrading and skills training are important goals in custodial facilities. Youths in secure facilities are often sent to an open facility before the end of their sentence to ease the transition back into the community.

If a young person turns 18 while in custody, correctional officials may apply to a Youth Court judge to transfer the youth to an adult facility to serve the balance of the sentence. The best interests of the young person and society are weighed when considering the transfer request.

Unlike adult offenders in prison, young offenders in custody are not eligible for parole or time off for good behaviour. However, they may be granted a temporary absence or day release for medical, humanitarian, or educational reasons.

A 17-year-old youth, M.R.W., and a co-accused, were driving through city streets when they decided they needed money for drugs and a birthday present for M.R.W.'s sister. They pulled up beside a cyclist and told the victim "give us your wallet or else." The two youths stopped the cyclist, beat him with a metal pipe, and attempted to steal his wallet. Bystanders saw the incident and apprehended M.R.W.

Evidence presented at trial indicated that M.R.W.'s parents divorced when he was very young, and he had difficulty accepting the changed situation. He had a grade 10 education and had been fired from two jobs for suspected theft. He was a daily drug user, unable to control his anger, and often uncontrollable at home. His parents, however, were prepared to support him.

At trial, he pleaded guilty to two counts of robbery and was sentenced to two months' closed custody, one year's open custody, and 18 months' probation. The Crown appealed this disposition to the Court of Appeal, but the appeal was dismissed.

R. v. M.R.W.
(1994)

Saskatchewan
Court of Appeal
128 Sask. R. 88

1. **Why do you think the Crown appealed M.R.W.'s trial disposition?**
2. **While in both secure and open custody, what conditions or controls would you place on M.R.W., and why?**
3. **Why do you think the Court of Appeal dismissed the Crown's appeal?**

The maximum period for which young offenders may be sent to an open or secure custody facility is two years for most offences. If the offence is one for which an adult might be sentenced to life imprisonment, such as murder or robbery, the maximum penalty for a young offender originally was three years. This three-year maximum penalty for murder received considerable criticism for being too lenient and, as a result, led to the recent changes discussed in section 9.6 of this chapter.

Publication of Identities

The *Young Offenders Act* provides that the media cannot publish anything that would identify young offenders or young victims. Originally, the *Act* prevented the publication of information about all young offenders, even when they escaped from custody and were at large. Now, however, police are able to publicize the names of dangerous youths who have escaped custody, breached a probation order, who are suspects in violent crimes and may be dangerous to the public, or whose speedy capture requires public assistance. Photos and descriptions of youths wanted for murder and attempted murder have been published for these reasons.

To publicize a young person's identity, the police must obtain a court order from a Youth Court judge. The order allows the publication of the youth's identity for two days. If the media publishes the youth's identity beyond this period, a charge may be laid against them.

Appeals and Reviews

The *Young Offenders Act* gives both the offender and the Crown the right to appeal a Youth Court disposition that seems inappropriate. Young offenders' rights of appeal are similar to those of adult offenders, as outlined in the *Criminal Code*. A decision to transfer a case to adult court may also be appealed by either party.

In addition, the *Young Offenders Act* provides for a court review of all dispositions. A review may be requested by the young offender, his or her family, or by provincial authorities. Application for a review may be made six months after the disposition has been imposed. Offenders in custody for longer than one year receive an automatic review

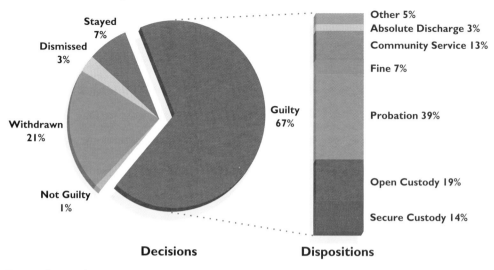

Distribution of Cases Heard in Youth Courts by Most Serious Decision and Disposition, Canada, 1993–94

Stayed 7%

Dismissed 3%

Withdrawn 21%

Not Guilty 1%

Guilty 67%

Other 5%

Absolute Discharge 3%

Community Service 13%

Fine 7%

Probation 39%

Open Custody 19%

Secure Custody 14%

Decisions   **Dispositions**

Decision figures refer to the most significant decision and Disposition figures to the most significant disposition.
Source: Statistics Canada.

of their situation at the end of the first year. This procedure is intended to allow the courts to alter a disposition to reflect a young offender's progress. The judge may retain the disposition or reduce it. It cannot be increased. The review provision makes it possible for a youth to avoid serving the complete term in custody and thereby provides an incentive for reform.

Youth Court Records

The *Young Offenders Act* contains very specific provisions for the handling of records from Youth Court hearings. If a youth is acquitted or the charge is dismissed, all records (including photographs and fingerprints) are destroyed. If, however, the youth is found guilty, the records must be kept for a certain length of time, depending on the offence. In the case of a summary offence conviction, the records are destroyed five years after the conviction. For an indictable conviction, the records are destroyed five years after the completion of the disposition—for example, an offender given a sentence of one year in open custody and one year's probation will have a Youth Court record for the next seven years.

If a youth convicted of an indictable offence commits one or more additional indictable offences within the five-year period, however, the record of the original offence(s) will be used at trial. Suppose, for example, that a 17-year-old offender is convicted of an indictable offence and given a disposition of community service and two years' probation. At the end of probation, the youth will be 19 years old. Five years later, when he or she is 24, the Youth Court record would be destroyed. However, if as a 22-year-old adult, the same person is convicted in adult court of an indictable offence, the Youth Court record could be used in sentencing.

Youth Court records are destroyed to prevent young persons from being branded as offenders for the rest of their lives. Once they have proved themselves by committing no more offences, they are given a new start. Unlike adults, youths do not need to apply to have their records destroyed; the *Young Offenders Act* makes the process automatic. Access to Youth Court records is restricted to the young offender, the defence, the Crown, the youth's parents, and the judge. Anyone else who wishes to see any of these records must apply to a Youth Court judge. Access may be granted to allow statistical and other research, bail applications, or further sentencing in Youth Court or adult court.

Elizabeth M. and four high school friends went to an outdoor party to celebrate their last day of high school. They arranged for an adult to buy beer and coolers for them because they were under the legal drinking age of 19. Because she had consumed a few beers, Elizabeth was reluctant to drive her father's car home and asked her friend, Deanna N., to drive. Deanna agreed but said she did not know how to drive a car with a stick shift. Accordingly, Elizabeth spent about 45 minutes in a parking lot teaching her friend how to drive the car.

When the group started home, Deanna got into the driver's seat, steered the car and changed gears, while Elizabeth operated the gas, clutch, and brake pedals from the passenger's seat. About 12 km down the road, Elizabeth decided that she wanted to pass the car in front; she grabbed the steering wheel and accelerated to pass. At about 110 km/h, the car fishtailed and went out of control. The lead car braked and pulled onto the shoulder of the road to avoid a collision. Deanna tried to regain control of the car. It continued out of control, left the roadway, struck a utility pole and turned over, killing Carly M. who was a passenger in the back seat.

According to expert witnesses, Elizabeth had a blood alcohol reading between 46 and 96 mg of alcohol in 100 mL of blood and was impaired to some extent. At trial, Deanna was convicted of dangerous driving, while Elizabeth was convicted of criminal negligence causing death. Because she was a first-time offender and an outstanding student who had been accepted into the Faculty of Engineering at Queen's University and would miss her year if she didn't register at once, the trial judge disposed Elizabeth to three years' probation with suspension of her driving licence and 150 hours of community service work.

The Crown appealed this disposition, asking for a term in custody and questioning the legality of the probation order. In its judgment, all three justices of the Ontario Court of Appeal believed that a custodial disposition was appropriate. A majority of the court sentenced Elizabeth M. to 90 days' open custody to be served on weekends because she had begun her engineering program at Queen's, plus two years' probation, the driving prohibition, and the community service which had already been performed. However, the court was reconvened when it was informed that while there were facilities for young male offenders near Kingston and Queen's University, there were no such facilities for young females. The nearest facilities were in Ottawa and Peterborough. As a result, the disposition was altered to allow Elizabeth to continue her education uninterrupted and then to serve the 90 days after the end of the 1993 academic year in a facility as close to her family as possible.

In his dissenting judgment, Mr. Justice Finlayson argued for a period of six months' open custody and one year's probation. He stated, "In my opinion, there has been too little attention paid in this matter to the need to demonstrate that this type of conduct will not be treated lightly, despite the fact that we are dealing with teenagers with stellar qualities. There must be a message in the disposition so that other teenagers will realize that drinking and driving will not be overlooked in the court's anxiety not to interfere unnecessarily with the young offender's schooling."

R. v. Elizabeth M.
(1992)

Ontario Court of Appeal
10 O.R. (3d) 481

1. Why did the Crown ask for a custodial term? In your answer, consider the basic objectives of sentencing. Do you agree? Why or why not?
2. Why did the Crown argue that the three-year probation was illegal?
3. Should Elizabeth's disposition have been delayed so that she could attend university? Why or why not?
4. Why did a majority of the court feel that delaying the implementation of the open custodial term did not minimize the seriousness of the offence?
5. What does Justice Finlayson's statement mean? Do you agree or disagree with this viewpoint? Explain.

Reviewing Your Reading

1. What is the purpose of a pre-disposition report? What kind of information does it contain?
2. What is the most lenient disposition that a young offender can receive, and why is it the best option?
3. What is the maximum fine under the *Young Offenders Act*, and who pays it?
4. What is the difference between a personal service order and a community service order? Give examples in your answer.
5. List four conditions that may be imposed in a young offender's probation order.
6. Using examples, distinguish between open and secure custody.
7. When may it be necessary for the media to publish specific information about a young offender?
8. When are Youth Court records destroyed for offenders found guilty of (a) indictable offences and (b) summary offences?

9.6 RECENT AMENDMENTS

Since its introduction in 1984, the *Young Offenders Act* has been criticized by the police, politicians, lawyers, judges, and other concerned citizens. Media attention and public fear about increasingly violent offenders created a climate calling for further punishment as a deterrent for young offenders.

The 1992 Amendments

In response to these criticisms, the first major amendments were made to the *Act* in 1992 and involved:

1. An increase in the maximum penalty given to youths convicted of murder from three to five years less a day—three years in secure custody, followed by two years less a day of supervision in open custody. Those youths transferred to adult court for first-degree murder charges faced life in prison, and a minimum 25-year sentence.
2. Youths transferred to adult court on murder charges could apply for parole between 5 and 10 years as determined by the courts. Adults convicted of first-degree murder could not apply for parole until they had served a minimum of 25 years. The earlier parole possibilities for young offenders was passed in the hope that judges might transfer murder cases to adult court more readily if there was the possibility of earlier release for the young offenders.
3. In transfer applications, the main factor to be considered was the protection of the public. Where society's protection came in conflict with the young person's needs, society came first.

The 1995 Amendments

Further criticisms between 1992 and 1994 led to additional amendments. In June 1994, the federal Minister of Justice introduced Bill C-37 in Parliament, *An Act to Amend the Young Offenders Act and the Criminal Code*. The government believed that these changes addressed the public's concerns over violent youth crime, while continuing to recognize that efforts still must be made to rehabilitate young offenders. By the summer of 1995, the following amendments had been passed by Parliament and the Senate, with proclamation on January 1, 1996:

Increased Penalties for Murder. The penalty for youths convicted of first-degree murder was increased from a maximum of 5 years to 10 years, and a maximum of 7 years for second-degree murder.

Eligibility for Parole. Youths transferred to adult court and convicted of murder face life imprisonment. They may apply for parole after serving 10 and 7 years for first- and second-degree murder, respectively. There is still no parole in the youth system.

Transfer to Adult Court. All 16- and 17-year-old youths accused of serious personal-injury offences (murder, manslaughter, attempted murder, aggravated assault, and aggravated sexual assault) are transferred automatically to adult court unless the youths can show they can be rehabilitated in the youth justice system.

Information Sharing. As you read earlier, sharing or releasing information about young offenders and their records has been very restricted. Yet, police officers, school officials, and social workers want to know when young offenders are released back into the community. Even some members of the general public want to know if and when they may be in grave risk from youths convicted of serious personal injury offences. The changes have improved the sharing of information about young offenders among these professionals and other selected people. However, the media still cannot release information identifying young offenders without a court order.

Retention of Records. Changes allow police to keep the records of youths convicted of a very serious offence for 10 years and 3 years for less serious summary offences, as long as the youths remain crime-free. The intention here is to ensure that regular or constant offenders do not "lose" their criminal record at age 18. The increased retention of these records will ensure that repeat and violent offenders are identified and not treated as first-time offenders if, or

when, they appear in the adult system. This change is intended for better public protection.

Victim Impact Statements. Amendments permit victims, if they wish, to make a statement about how a youth's crime has affected them before sentence is passed. Previously, this option was available only in the adult system.

Alternatives to Custody for Minor Offences. In cases where youth-system professionals have recommended custody for an offending youth, reasons have to be given as to why community-based alternatives are not appropriate. Youth Court judges also have to give reasons why they sentenced an offender to custody rather than use other alternatives.

These harsher punishments and other amendments to the *Young Offenders Act* reflect the government's response to the public outcry for a visible response to crime and violence by young offenders in society. These amendments were the first of a two-phase program to review and reform the *Young Offenders Act*. In the second phase, that began in the fall of 1995, the Minister of Justice referred the *Young Offenders Act* to a government justice committee for a comprehensive review regarding future amendments. It is probable that the *Young Offenders Act* will continue to be an issue of controversy for years to come.

Reviewing Your Reading

1. In the 1992 amendments to the *Young Offenders Act*, what happened to the maximum sentence for youths convicted of murder?

2. How was society better protected in the 1992 amendments than in the original *Act*?

3. In the 1995 amendments to the *Young Offenders Act*, what happened to the maximum sentence for youths convicted of murder?

4. What changes occurred in the 1995 amendments concerning the transfer to adult court of 16- and 17-year-old youths charged with the most serious offences? Do you agree? Explain.

5. What change in the *Act* occurred in 1995 concerning the use of victim impact statements in Youth Court?

ISSUE

Should violent teens be expelled from school to protect teachers and other students?

In 1994, the federal government published a report called "Weapons' Use in Canadian Schools." The report indicated that violence in schools has increased significantly and that more students carry weapons—clubs, knives, machetes, and handguns—to school. Some students use these weapons to impress or intimidate; others carry them for protection. Large urban centres like Toronto, Vancouver, and Montreal, along with Guelph, Ontario, had the highest reported use of weapons in schools.

Provincial and local studies also verify an increase in violence. The Ontario Teachers' Federation reports that major incidents of violence in schools increased 150 percent between 1987 and 1990. The British Columbia Teachers' Federation reports widespread violence against teachers and students. A 1991 survey of the Alberta Teachers' Association membership found that 8 percent had been physically assaulted and 57 percent had been verbally abused. In May 1993, a Calgary public system report indicated that 1 in 5 high school students admitted taking a weapon to school because they felt unsafe.

Even though statistics released in August 1995 indicate a reduction in the Canadian crime rate, it seems Canadian society is becoming more violent. Generally, people are more insecure about their personal safety. The number of young Canadians between the ages of 12 and 17 charged with violent crimes increased 251 percent between the years 1980–83 and 1990–93. In 1992, this age group represented 25 percent of all people charged with criminal offences in Canada. This increase in violence in society is reflected in the schools.

In many classrooms and hallways, there is a general air of disrespect and misbehaviour, which sometimes leads to violent incidents. Educators, concerned about the increasing level of violence, are divided about policy and procedures for dealing with the problem.

On One Side

Educators who support a get-tough policy believe that it is the permissive attitude of allowing students to discover and develop their own morals that generated the violence problem in the first place. They advocate teaching and enforcing what's right and wrong, even if it involves calling police.

Some school boards have adopted a "zero tolerance" policy on violence. Students who bring weapons to school or are involved in violent incidents are expelled from school for *life*. Supporters of this policy feel that rigidly enforced discipline will effectively deter the chronic trouble-makers. It will also create a safer environment for students who previously carried weapons because they feared for their safety.

On the Other Side

Critics of a get-tough approach see students as confused and alienated young people, rather than violent thugs. They argue that counselling

students about their problems and helping them develop a sense of self-esteem and self-worth will achieve better results than rigid discipline. They support anger- and stress-management programs that involve peer mediation. Such programs help students in conflict with one another to reach a solution or agreement. Teaching these life skills will benefit students in school and also later in the workplace.

Advocates of student service programs feel they are more effective in the long run than stern penalties, such as expulsion.

The Bottom Line

If violence continues to escalate, Canadian schools could soon resemble some schools in the United States where armed guards patrol the hallways. Before Canadian schools reach this extreme, measures must be taken to curb school violence. The question remains: What measures? Should violent teens be expelled or sentenced to fines and community service? Or should schools be implementing more counselling and treatment programs to deal with troubled teens? You be the judge!

1. What evidence is there to indicate that violence in Canadian schools is increasing?

2. What is meant by the statement, "This increase in violence in society is reflected in the schools"? Do you agree with this statement?

3. Do you think that the policy of "zero tolerance" works?

4. How is "self-esteem" related to violence in the schools?

5. What programs do you think would be most effective to reduce school violence and why?

CHAPTER REVIEW

Reviewing Key Terms

For each of the following statements, indicate the key term being defined:

a) a person between the ages of 12 and 17, inclusive, found guilty of a federal offence

b) the sentence a judge hands down in Youth Court

c) a place of detention for a young offender with 24-hour supervision, locked doors, and bars on the windows

d) a place of detention for a young offender in a special home or a wilderness camp

e) phrase meaning "in private"; refers to matters heard in a courtroom from which spectators have been excluded

f) a family home where a young offender may be placed for rehabilitation

g) a home operated by a non-profit agency and run by a professional staff where young offenders are placed for rehabilitation

h) the practice of keeping an offender out of the prison system by imposing a sentence or disposition not involving incarceration

i) a report prepared by a youth probation officer at a judge's request before sentencing a young offender

Exploring Legal Concepts

1. The *Young Offenders Act* raised the age of criminal responsibility from 7 to 12 years. Critics of the *Act* say the minimum age limit should be lowered to 10 years of age. At the present time 10- or 11-year-olds can commit murder and literally get away with it. What do you think should be the minimum age, and why? Discuss this issue with your peers.

2. Critics believe that the maximum age for young offenders should be lowered to 16 years of age. What do you think should be the maximum age, and why? Discuss this issue with your peers.

3. Why does section 56 of the *Young Offenders Act* offer additional protection and rights to youths who are arrested? Is this protection necessary? Why or why not?

4. Does the extra protection in section 56 of the *Young Offenders Act* violate the section 15 equality rights provision of the *Charter of Rights and Freedoms* by discriminating on the basis of age? Why or why not?

5. In what court are trials under the *Young Offenders Act* held in your province?

6. In your opinion, should all trials of all young offenders charged with murder or manslaughter be transferred automatically from Youth Court to adult court? Defend your position in a discussion with a partner.

7. On the whole, do you feel that the *Young Offenders Act* is effective in balancing the interests and protection of society with the rights of young offenders? Explain.

Applying Legal Concepts

1. Manny is 16 years old and has been charged with robbery for the third time. He lives with his father, who is on social assistance. Neither of them can afford to pay for a lawyer for Manny's court appearance next week.

   • **Is there anything Manny can do, or must he pay his own legal costs?**

2. Angie, who is 13 years old, stole $12 worth of cosmetics from a major department store. She was caught by the store's security officer and turned over to the police. This is Angie's first offence.

   • **If you were the police officer, what would you do, and why?**

3. *R. v. J.M.G.* [1986] Ontario Court of Appeal 33 D.L.R. (4th) 277
   The accused was a 14-year-old grade seven student in Thunder Bay. One of the boy's teachers informed the principal that the boy had placed something, believed to be drugs, in his sock. The principal called a police officer and another principal whom he knew, and asked them for advice on how to handle the situation. He then called J.M.G. to his office and told him that he had reason to suspect that he was in possession of drugs. In the presence of the vice-principal, the principal asked the youth to remove his shoes and socks. There was some delay, during which the accused swallowed a rolled cigarette that he had removed from his pants cuff. The principal then took some tinfoil, which contained three butts about 1.5 cm in length, from J.M.G.'s right sock. He finally called the police, who arrested the youth on a charge of possession of a narcotic and advised him of his legal rights.

   The accused was convicted under the *Young Offenders Act* for possession of marijuana and was fined $25 in Youth Court. J.M.G. appealed the decision to District Court, where his conviction and disposition were set aside. An appeal by the Crown to the Ontario Court of Appeal was allowed, and the conviction was restored. Leave to appeal this decision to the Supreme Court of Canada was denied in late January 1987.

   • **Why do you think J.M.G. appealed this decision?**

   • **What two *Charter* rights did the accused feel had been violated?**

   • **Based on the provisions of the *Young Offenders Act*, what advice should the other principal have given the principal of J.M.G.'s school?**

   • **What alternatives does a person in authority have in a situation involving a minor offence such as this one?**

   • **Based on the information given, why did the Court of Appeal rule that the youth's rights were not infringed?**

   • **The Court of Appeal ruled that a school principal may search a student without violation of the student's *Charter* rights. Explain the meaning of the following statement, made by a lawyer when she learned of the judgment in this case: "This decision is an attempt to leave the *Charter of Rights and Freedoms* on the doormat of the schoolhouse."**

4. *R. v. G.A.W.* (1993) Nova Scotia Court of Appeal 125 N.S.R. (2d) 312

The 17-year-old youth, G.A.W., pleaded guilty to four counts of break, enter, and theft; six counts of theft; and one count of prowling at night. The latter seven counts were summary convictions. All offences involved private homes, cars, and yachts and occurred over a three-day period, but they were separate and distinct actions.

Evidence presented at trial indicated that G.A.W. had not previously been convicted of any criminal offence, although he had been dealt with by the alternative measures program. He was enrolled in grade 10. He had some attendance problems at school and personal problems at home.

The Youth Court judge sentenced G.A.W. to consecutive sentences totalling 10 months' open custody plus two years' probation. The youth appealed this sentence to the Court of Appeal, but his appeal was dismissed.

- **What is a consecutive sentence?**

- **Explain the rationale behind the Youth Court judge's consecutive disposition of 10 months' open custody.**

- **Why did G.A.W. appeal the trial disposition?**

- **Why did the Court of Appeal dismiss the appeal?**

5. *R. v. C.J.K.* (1994) Manitoba Court of Appeal 88 C.C.C. (3d) 82

After consuming alcohol on New Year's Eve, the offender, C.J.K., began to assault his girlfriend for no apparent reason. He stabbed her and then stabbed himself in the abdomen. The police and an ambulance were called. While he was being treated for his injuries, the accused stated, "Save her, not me." His girlfriend died as a result of the injuries.

At the time of the incident, C.J.K. was just two months short of his 17th birthday. He had no previous record. He was described as open, friendly, and cooperative. He was a bright student and a good worker. However, he became a totally different person under the influence of alcohol.

C.J.K. was charged with the second-degree murder of his girlfriend. The Crown applied to transfer the trial to adult court. The Youth Court judge hearing the application described the killing as brutal, shocking, and without reason. The application pointed out that amendments to the *Young Offenders Act* in 1992 were clearly intended to make protection of the public a greater concern. The judge believed that the youth could only receive the necessary psychotherapy in the penitentiary, although no evidence was called as to the availability of resources at the youth centre. The judge granted the Crown's application.

The young offender appealed the transfer order to the Manitoba Court of Appeal where his appeal was allowed and the order set aside.

- **How did the 1992 amendments to the *Young Offenders Act* affect the issue of transfer applications?**

- **What were the two main factors favouring transfer to adult court?**

- Do you think that a life sentence was required to protect the public from this young offender? Explain.

- Based on the facts presented, why did the Court of Appeal set aside the transfer order so that C.J.K. would be tried in Youth Court? Do you agree? Why or why not?

Extending Legal Concepts

1. Now that you have completed this chapter, review the opening article and Something to Think About. Have your answers or opinions changed? Why or why not?

2. A 16-year-old teen was charged with the first-degree murder of a man who sexually assaulted her. While trying to escape her attacker, she hit him on the head with a baseball bat, killing him. She requested a hearing to consider the transfer of her trial to adult court. Why would she want her trial transferred when the Crown has not asked for a transfer application? Is this a wise move? Why or why not?

3. Young offenders are not eligible for parole, unlike adult offenders who have been incarcerated.

   a) Why do you think this provision exists, and do you agree with it? Explain.

   b) Does the absence of parole opportunities for young offenders violate the section 15 equality rights of the *Charter?* Why or why not?

4. Build an organizer to compare the old *Juvenile Delinquents Act* with the *Young Offenders Act.* Consider using the following headings: philosophy behind the legislation; ages of criminal responsibility; type of "wrongs" or offences covered; trial procedures; and sentencing options. Consult your resource centre for additional information.

5. Write a letter to the editor of the local newspaper stating your opinion on the effectiveness of the *Young Offenders Act.* Support your position with cases and statistics. Prepare your letter in draft form, have it edited by a peer in your class, and then revise it. Show the letter to your teacher before sending it to the newspaper.

6. Some provinces, like Manitoba and Ontario, are considering the establishment of military style "boot camps" for young offenders. Youths would face a 16-hour day of military-style drills, physical exercise, and equipment inspections. With a partner, discuss both the advantages and disadvantages of this proposal; then, compare your results with other pairs of students. Attempt to reach a class consensus on the issue.

7. Using reference materials in your resource centre, including CD-ROM and the Internet, obtain current information on the following:

   a) recent amendments to the *Young Offenders Act*

   b) recent newsworthy cases in Canada and the United States

   c) public attitudes toward youth crime

   d) alternative measures programs available in your province

   e) youth violence in schools

   f) other related items of interest

Researching an Issue

Parental Responsibility

In recent years, many Canadians have strongly urged the federal government to amend the *Young Offenders Act* to make parents share the responsibility for their children's behaviour. One town of about 6000 people in Oregon has passed a parental responsibility bylaw requiring parents of delinquent children to take parenting classes, to share in community service sentences, and to acknowledge their responsibility for their children's actions. Other American cities are considering similar legislation.

Statement

Delinquents are made, not born, and parents must share the responsibility for the actions of their children.

Point

Parents should be held responsible for their children's actions because their actions, or lack of action, have influenced their children's criminal behaviour.

Counterpoint

Other people and factors also influence children. Parents cannot, and should not, be held responsible for everything their children do.

- **With a partner, research this issue and reflect on your findings.**
- **Prepare points on this statement that could be used for a class debate.**
- **Discuss your findings with others in your class.**

UNIT
3

TORT LAW

Introduction

Maintaining accurate records of what is said during court trials and other formal legal proceedings is essential to the effective operation of our judicial system. In many instances, it is the court reporter's responsibility to prepare such records.

In Focus: COURT REPORTER

A court reporter participates in trials and attends hearings such as examinations for discovery, coroners' inquests, and arbitration hearings of administrative boards. She or he takes down all testimony and prepares official transcripts of the proceedings. It is a demanding and exacting job. Proficient court reporters can earn in excess of $60 000 per year.

Education and Other Qualifications

If it is your ambition to be a court reporter, you must first complete your high school education. It is advisable that you take courses in English—language and technical writing, Canadian law, and word processing. Courses in business education and the biological sciences are also desirable.

Formal training for a court reporter typically lasts two years. The main components of the training include mastering shorthand at the level of 200 words-per-minute, and learning computer-related skills. Academic subjects such as English, law, and medical terminology are also studied in more detail. Trainees must pass a practicum, where they work on the job with actual court reporters, who evaluate their skills.

Responsibilities

As a court reporter, you will participate in many types of formal hearings. You will be responsible for making verbatim records of what is said by all parties. Afterwards, you will prepare legal transcripts reporting the testimony that was given. These documents must conform to set formats.

Work Environment

Your schedule will vary considerably. On any given day you may have to travel to several different locations and be part of many kinds of proceedings. You must be punctual and have planned carefully so that you can meet all of your appointments.

At each hearing, you must be able to give your complete attention to the task at hand and remain fully focused. Also, you must provide for enough time in your working day to prepare final documents. In short, you must be able to meet a continuing series of deadlines according to an ever-changing schedule.

Do You Fit the Job?

You must have excellent listening skills to be a court reporter. You must value accuracy and attention to detail. You must also be a capable organizer, a self-starter, and be able to work independently. Above all, your personal integrity must be beyond reproach.

$\mathcal{P}$ROFILE: Minori Arai

Minori Arai began her career as a court reporter in 1990, when she joined a private company as an associate. In 1994, due to changes introduced by the provincial government, she became a part-time employee of the British Columbia Ministry of the Attorney General. She now divides her time between her role as an associate and her work as a public servant.

Ms. Arai started her training as a court reporter after working for a year as a receptionist. She was initially attracted to court reporting because it appeared to offer more flexible hours. Also, a friend who was a court reporter told her about the job and spoke highly of it. Ms. Arai spent the next four years enrolled as a part-time student in a court reporter training program, while continuing to work part-time as a receptionist.

As a court reporter, Ms. Arai spends a good deal of her time in court or in other formal hearings such as pre-trial and arbitration hearings. But she devotes most of her time to editing her transcripts and transforming them into formal legal records.

Ms. Arai enjoys her profession very much. In addition to its flexible working hours, her job presents her with a variety of experiences. Her work schedule changes weekly and she has considerable autonomy in her day-to-day activities. Ms. Arai has met and worked with many interesting people, and she appreciates the direct role she has had in hearings and court proceedings that have commanded the public's interest.

Ms. Arai believes that the keys to success in court reporting are the abilities to remain focused and to pay attention to detail. As well, students who are interested in becoming court reporters should have a strong work ethic and be able to complete tasks on their own.

Questions and Activities

1. Why is it important that accurate transcripts of trials and other legal proceedings be kept?

2. Obtain and examine the syllabus for a court reporter training program in your province. Ask yourself whether this type of work would appeal to you, and why.

3. As part of a class field trip to the local law courts, arrange to have a court reporter speak to your class. Examine examples of court transcripts prepared by court reporters.

4. Compare the training and duties of court reporters and court recorders.

CIVIL PROCEDURE AND COMPENSATION

These are the key terms introduced in this chapter:

alternative dispute resolution
arbitration
balance of probabilities
claim
compensation
contingency fee system
counterclaim
damages
default judgment
defendant
Examination for Discovery
examination of the debtor
exemplary damages
garnishment

general damages
guardian ad litem
injunction
litigants
litigation
litigation guardian
mediation
minor
negotiation
next friend
no-fault insurance
nominal damages
non-pecuniary losses
out-of-court settlement

pecuniary losses
plaintiff
pleadings
pre-trial conference
punitive damages
special damages
Statement of Claim
statement of defence
summons
third-party liability insurance
tort
Writ of Summons

Chapter at a Glance

Learning Outcomes

At the end of this chapter, you will be able to

1. distinguish between a crime and a tort;
2. identify the purposes of tort law;
3. describe the courts that try civil actions and the types of cases tried in each;
4. outline the rights of minors in civil actions;
5. summarize the procedures in bringing a civil action;
6. recognize the benefits of an out-of-court settlement;
7. identify the types of damages: general, nominal, punitive, and special;
8. describe the three remedies available for enforcing a judgment;
9. explain the importance of insuring against civil liability;
10. describe the methods of alternative dispute resolution.

Prisoner Awarded $18 750 after Being Hurt in Jail Sport Accident

axpayers will have to pay a convicted robber $18 750 because he was hurt playing racquetball [suffering a hip fracture], while in a federal prison in British Columbia, a judge has ruled.

In his decision, Federal Court Justice Marshall Rothstein awarded the money to Allan Roe Coulter, 37, who is serving a nine-year sentence for armed robbery at Matsqui Institution.

Coulter was first jailed in June 1987 after being convicted of armed robbery. He was released in 1992, but convicted of armed robbery again in 1993.

The judge found the prison 75 percent responsible for injuries Coulter suffered when he slipped on water on the floor of a racquetball court at the prison [during a game with two other prisoners].

The water came from a hole in the roof that prison officials knew of, but had not repaired.

The judge said the government is responsible for damage caused by its negligence, regardless of who is hurt.

The leaky racquetball court roof had not been repaired because of a dispute with the contractor who installed it. But Rothstein said the jail had a duty to prevent the leak.

From: Bob Cox, "Prisoner awarded $18 750 after being hurt in jail sport accident." *The Canadian Press,* as reported in the *Kingston Whig Standard,* February 10, 1994. Reprinted with the permission of *The Canadian Press.*

Something to Think About

- As a prisoner, why should Allan Coulter be able to sue the government for his injuries?
- Should ordinary laws pertaining to torts and damages be available to incarcerated prisoners?
- The prison was found to be 75 percent responsible for Coulter's injuries. Why was Coulter found liable for the remaining 25 percent?
- Do you think the federal government has any right of action against the contractor who had not repaired the leaky roof? Why or why not?

10.1 INTRODUCTION

Civil law, also known as private law, relates to disputes between individuals or between individuals and businesses, organizations, or governments. They do not affect society directly and are a matter of personal concern only between the parties involved. While the main purpose of *criminal* law is to punish the offenders and to protect society from people who pose a threat to its stability, the main purpose of *civil* law is to compensate victims.

Tort law, the subject of this unit, is a division of civil law. The word **tort** means "a wrong." It is derived from the Latin word *tortus,* meaning

"crooked" or "twisted." Torts fall into three categories—unintentional, intentional, and strict liability. These will be discussed in Chapters 11 and 12.

A civil suit results from injury. A personal injury could be caused by a stray puck at a hockey game, a collision with a careless driver, or a fall on a wet floor. Economic loss also constitutes injury. A civil suit can result from intentional or negligent damage to property.

The victim of a tort, or civil wrong, may bring a civil action against the wrongdoer for damages, or some other civil remedy.

10.2 CRIMES VERSUS TORTS

Tort law involves many aspects of life, including real property, possessions, animals, sports, purchasing consumer goods, and personal freedom and reputation. Knowledge about the basic principles of tort law is useful for every Canadian. Modern tort law is largely the product of case law decisions made by judges over hundreds of years.

Tort law is not codified. This means that, like criminal law, tort law changes as society changes. For example, we used to drive in motor vehicles without wearing seat belts and ride on motorcycles and bicycles without wearing helmets. However, studies have clearly indicated that the use of seat belts and helmets will reduce injuries, and provincial governments have made wearing them compulsory. Failure to do so may also reduce, or even eliminate, compensation to those injured.

As you know, Canada's justice system involves both criminal and civil law. Some forms of conduct may involve both a crime and a tort. For instance, Heidi, while under the influence of alcohol, attempts to drive home. She runs a red light, hits Tyler's car, and seriously injures him.

Did You Know

The Ontario Trauma Registry reports that 33 people died from cycling injuries in 1993, up from 25 in 1992 and 28 in 1991. About half of the cyclists died from head injuries.

Society, represented by the Crown, may begin criminal action against Heidi on the grounds of impaired or dangerous driving. If convicted, her punishment is outlined in the *Criminal Code*. At the same time, Tyler can begin a civil action to sue Heidi for **compensation** or **damages**. Tort law entitles Tyler to receive compensation (usually money) for the injuries he sustained and other losses suffered. It is Tyler's personal responsibility to bring this action. A civil court will award him what it sees as suitable damages for his injuries. Each action, criminal and civil, proceeds independently of the other. Each is tried in a different court with a different judge, and there is no set order in which the cases must be tried.

People who can prove that they have suffered injury or loss through another person's fault deserve some remedy. Although compensation is the most important purpose of tort law from the victim's viewpoint, some tort actions also contain elements of punishment and deterrence. An

interesting tort case will be followed closely by the media. The resulting publicity may affect the future behaviour of both the party against whom the suit has been brought and others. For instance, an action against a soft drink company by a customer who finds a dead wasp at the bottom of a bottle might have a negative effect on the company's sales and public image. The company itself will probably try to avoid another similar lawsuit. Most likely, the negative publicity from this case will cause other manufacturers to review, and improve if necessary, their production facilities and quality-control inspections. Likewise, a large monetary judgment against someone like Heidi in the motor vehicle scenario may have a deterrent effect on other negligent drivers.

Reviewing Your Reading

1. **Define "tort" and give three original examples of torts.**

2. **Why is tort law constantly changing?**

3. **Using an original example, explain how an offence can be both a crime and a tort.**

4. **What is the primary purpose of tort law?**

5. **Name the secondary purposes of tort law.**

10.3 CIVIL COURTS

In Chapter 3, you learned about Canada's criminal courts. This section examines Canada's civil courts.

Small Claims Court

Depending on the province, claims for small debts are presented either to Small Claims Court or the Provincial Court, Small Claims Division. In Ontario, Small Claims Court is a branch of the Ontario Court, General Division. The dollar limit for such claims varies from province to province and presently ranges from $1000 to $10 000. For example, the limits for British Columbia, Ontario, and New Brunswick are $10 000, $6000, and $1000, respectively.

Often called "The People's Court," Small Claims Court provides a simple and inexpensive way for people to settle disputes concerning money or property. Cases are tried informally by a judge without a jury. Both parties are given the chance to tell their stories and are usually not represented by lawyers. In fact, Quebec has barred lawyers from its Small Claims Courts.

All provinces issue free, easy-to-read booklets with step-by-step procedures for filing a claim. Also, court staff are willing to answer questions and explain how to fill out the proper forms.

Typical small claims include landlord and tenant conflicts, consumer complaints, unpaid bills, the recovery of personal property from another party, unpaid wages, consumer debts, and claims for minor car accidents. Many businesses use this court to collect unpaid accounts from customers.

Provincial Supreme Court

All civil cases above the small claims limit go directly to the Supreme Court of the province, or to the Court of Queen's Bench. Disputes that reach this top level of court require the presence of lawyers as the cases may be very complex and may require several years of preparation. Examples include serious motor vehicle accidents, medical malpractice or injury, breach of contract, divorce, division of property, and so on. Cases here may be tried by a judge alone or by judge and jury. Unlike a criminal trial jury, a civil trial jury has only six members in most provinces, and they can reach a decision by majority vote. In recent years, jury trials in civil cases have become rare because of the cost and complexity of the cases.

Procedures for hearing civil disputes in Small Claims Court and provincial superior courts are discussed in section 10.4.

Court of Appeal

All provinces have provincial Courts of Appeal that hear appeals from their lower courts. Appeals are heard by a panel of three or more judges, depending on the case, and their decisions may be either unanimous judgments or majority/minority judgments. As you have seen, a 2–1 judgment is not uncommon from this level of court. The court will release its decision and provide explanations for the majority vote. Dissenting judges will also provide their reasons for disagreeing with the majority vote.

Federal Court of Canada

The Federal Court of Canada's trial division deals with civil cases involving the federal government and its employees, disputes over federal income tax, patents, copyrights and trademarks, and maritime legal disputes. The appeals division hears appeals from the court's trial division and from federal boards, agencies, and commissions.

Supreme Court of Canada

The Supreme Court, the highest court in Canada, is a court of appeal that hears only those cases from the Federal Court of Canada and provincial Courts of Appeal that it believes are of national importance or in which an important issue or question of law must be decided or interpreted.

All other persons wanting to appeal their lower court judgments to the Supreme Court of Canada must seek "leave to appeal" or permission from the court itself. There is an automatic right of appeal where there is a split decision from a provincial Court of Appeal.

Like the provincial Courts of Appeal, the Supreme Court of Canada may issue unanimous or split decisions.

Reviewing Your Reading

1. **What kind of dollar limits exist for cases tried in Small Claims Court?**

2. **List four examples of cases that could be tried in your province's Small Claims Court.**

3. **Why are juries seldom used in civil suits?**

4. **What types of appeals will the Supreme Court of Canada hear?**

10.4 $\mathcal{T}$RIAL PROCEDURES

A civil lawsuit involves two parties: the **plaintiff**, who is suing, and the **defendant**, who is being sued. The cause of action may be a tort, a contract or consumer dispute, or a family matter such as divorce, custody, or division of property. If more than one person has suffered the harm, all injured parties should sue together as plaintiffs in one action. This is called a class action suit. If more than one person is responsible for causing the loss, they all should be sued as defendants. The process of suing is called **litigation**, and the parties in the action are the **litigants**.

Civil procedure is similar to criminal procedure discussed in Chapter 5. The litigants must prepare and present the facts of the case. The court's role is to determine the law that applies to the situation. The burden of proof is on the plaintiff to prove his or her case. However, unlike criminal cases, the plaintiff is not required to prove that the defendant was at fault beyond a reasonable doubt. Instead, the plaintiff must prove the case on the **balance of probabilities**. This means that if you are the plaintiff, you must prove that the events took place in the way you are claiming. The defendant will then try to show that his or her version is the one that really happened. The judge will determine which side is more credible or believable.

Minors and Civil Actions

A **minor** is a person under the age of majority, 18 or 19 years of age, depending on the province. A minor can neither bring a civil suit in his or her own name, nor have one brought against him or her. A minor who wishes to sue must be represented by an adult, known as a "**next friend**," who will ensure that the minor's action is responsible and valid. This person will file a statement of consent to act as the next friend at the court office. Usually, the child's parent will act in this capacity, but any willing adult can do so. Another minor cannot fill this position.

Similarly, a minor being sued in a civil action must be represented by an adult. The court will appoint an adult, usually a parent or other competent adult, as the minor's representative, or *guardian ad litem* (**litigation guardian**).

Civil Procedure in Small Claims Court

We will now examine civil procedure through a more detailed scenario. Assume that Bjorn Svendsen runs a red light and hits Penny Chow's car. As in the earlier scenario involving Tyler and Heidi, the Crown may lay criminal charges against Svendsen for the accident. Chow, too, must decide whether to take legal action against Svendsen. She must determine whether she has a cause for action, that is, a reason accepted by the courts for seeking compensation. If Chow finds she has a cause, she must then determine the proper court in which to proceed.

CASE

A bout 7 o'clock one dark, drizzly morning in January 1984, the 71-year-old plaintiff, Keating, was crossing a street in Halifax at a marked crosswalk. He was struck by a car driven by the defendant, Dorey. The plaintiff, dressed in black, was not wearing his glasses because of the mist. Dorey's car was travelling between 40 km/h and 50 km/h, which was acceptable given the weather conditions. Dorey was wearing his glasses, the windshield wipers and defogger were on, and the windshield was clear.

Keating was hospitalized with a severe fracture of the right leg. After leaving the hospital, he stayed for several months in a nursing home before returning to his residence, where he lived alone. Although the fracture healed fairly well, he did have some difficulty in walking and needed a cane.

The defendant and his 14-year-old son, who was in the passenger's seat, testified that they were proceeding on a green light when the plaintiff suddenly appeared and was struck by their car. The plaintiff claimed that the light was green in his favour at the time he was struck. No other evidence was available to help the judge determine who had the green light.

Keating brought an action for damages to the Supreme Court of Nova Scotia, Trial Division, but his action was dismissed.

Keating v. Dorey
(1987)

**Nova Scotia
Supreme Court
81 N.S.R. (2d) 217**

1. **Why did Keating bring an action against Dorey?**
2. **Since there was conflicting evidence as to who had the green light, how could the judge reach a fair decision?**
3. **Based on the information given, why do you think the plaintiff failed in his action?**

Comparison between Criminal and Civil Law

	Criminal/Public	Civil/Private
Parties involved	Crown attorney v. accused or defendant	plaintiff v. defendant
Grounds/reason	laying of criminal charge to determine innocence or guilt	resolving a dispute
Purpose of action	to punish offender	to compensate victims
Onus of proof	on Crown attorney	on the plaintiff
Burden of proof	beyond a reasonable doubt	balance of probabilities
Result of action	accused "guilty" or "not guilty"	defendant liable or not liable
Action if guilt or liability found	defendant is sentenced	plaintiff is awarded some compensation or remedy

Before a legal action is brought, the litigants should attempt to settle the dispute between themselves, which is considerably less expensive than preparing for and appearing in court. Chow should contact Svendsen by mail, explain her viewpoint in some detail, and ask for the desired compensation. Settling in this way saves the expense and delay of court proceedings. If the parties cannot resolve their dispute, it can be brought to court.

Summons or Claim

As you have seen, the court in which a civil action will be tried depends on the sum involved. Assume that Penny Chow's action will begin in Small Claims Court.

The plaintiff's first step is to file a **summons**. If the action is brought in Ontario, a **claim** is prepared and filed in the Small Claims Court office, instead. Either document must include Penny Chow's full name and address, Bjorn Svendsen's full name and address, the reasons why Chow is suing, and the amount she is claiming. If more than one defendant is involved, each one must be named and identified correctly. The summons may be typed or handwritten. After completing the appropriate document, Chow mails or hand delivers it to the court clerk, along with the required filing fee. The fee is the cost of handling the claim, and the amount depends on the amount the plaintiff is claiming. The fee the plaintiff pays is added to the claim by the court.

Chow receives a copy of the summons, and the court clerk retains a copy. Svendsen must be served with a copy as well. The document is usually served in person by a bailiff or sheriff, so that the defendant may not evade it.

At this time, Chow must choose a location to bring her action. It may be a Small Claims Court near the accident location, near Svendsen's residence, or near her residence. They may, in fact, be one and the same. In early 1995, the Supreme Court of Canada ruled that a plaintiff should sue in the jurisdiction where the tort occurred.

When Bjorn Svendsen receives the summons or claim, he has several options. If he agrees that he owes Chow the full amount of the claim, he can pay the amount plus court costs to the Small Claims Court office. He must do so within 10 to 30 days, depending on the province. The court clerk will then pay Chow, ending the dispute.

Payment into Court

If Svendsen feels that Penny Chow is entitled to some part of the claim, he can pay that amount into the Small Claims Court office. Chow will then be notified and can either accept the amount and drop the balance of her claim, or pursue the case in the hope of obtaining the full amount.

Defence

If Svendsen feels that he does not owe Penny Chow anything, he prepares a **statement of defence**, a document that clearly outlines his reasons for disagreeing with her claim. Svendsen may have a number of reasons. He might argue that the light was not red when he went through and hit Chow's car. Or he might say that the brakes on his car failed and he could not stop in time to prevent the accident. If Svendsen intends to dispute the claim, he must do so within 10 to 30 days of receiving the summons or claim. A copy of the statement of defence will be sent to the plaintiff by the court.

Counterclaim

The defendant may also make a **counterclaim**, saying that it was actually the plaintiff who was at fault for the accident. Svendsen will attempt to claim damages from Chow for his own loss. A counterclaim must relate to the problem that caused the plaintiff's claim. When a civil action involves damage to cars, the defendant will often counterclaim.

In our example, Svendsen defends against Chow's claim and makes one of his own against her, arguing that she began to move before her traffic light had turned green and that she was driving too quickly to stop. The judge will examine the counterclaim and the plaintiff's claim at the same time if the case comes to trial and decide who is at fault and who will receive what from whom.

Third Party Claim

Another option available to the defendant is to involve a third party who the defendant feels is partly or completely responsible for the dispute. If Svendsen had his brakes repaired just before the accident, and if the failure of the brakes was responsible for the accident, Svendsen might involve the repair garage as a third party to share some of the blame and the cost. Taking this action saves time and money, for the case can proceed in the presence of all three parties.

Default Judgment

If Bjorn Svendsen does not reply to the summons or claim within the required time, a **default judgment** is automatically made against him. This means that Penny Chow wins her action. She is awarded a judgment against Svendsen by default, since he has not responded to the claim. Chow is entitled to recover the amount she claimed, plus any related costs.

Civil Procedure in Higher Courts

If Chow's case were being tried in a higher court, she would file a **Statement of Claim** or a **Writ of Summons**, depending on the province. This document contains the same information as a claim, but is longer and more detailed. A plaintiff taking action in a higher court should hire a lawyer.

For actions in higher courts, there are additional procedures to help the parties settle their dispute without a trial. The litigants could send legal documents back and forth over several months or even years. The statement of claim, the statement of defence, the counterclaim, the third-party claim, and all other documents filed with the court are called **pleadings**. They are an attempt to define and narrow the disputed issues and to assist the judge in understanding the details of the dispute. Once all of the pleadings have been filed, the discovery process begins.

The **Examination for Discovery** is a "question-and-answer" session for the parties involved and their lawyers. Its purpose is to reduce surprise by providing information about each side's case, and to reach agreement on certain issues. This reduces court time, saves money, and makes settlement easier. Both parties must disclose *all* documents relevant to the lawsuit. Discovery can be verbal with either party questioning the other under oath. The questions and answers are tran-

scribed by the court reporter and are available at trial, if needed.

This is the first time that the defendant's lawyer has a chance to question the plaintiff, and vice versa. Each side is able to assess the other side's strengths and weaknesses. If the evidence given at discovery differs from the evidence given at trial, the credibility of the witness may be damaged. Either party can also ask the court to issue an order permitting inspection of physical objects in the case; in our scenario, Chow's and Svendsen's cars might be inspected. If Chow claimed for serious injuries from the accident, Svendsen could request that she undergo a medical examination.

Out-of-Court Settlement

When all of the facts and evidence have been presented by both parties at discovery, an **out-of-court settlement** may be reached. In fact, at any point thus far, either party can make a formal or informal offer to settle the dispute instead of proceeding to trial. The litigants should make every effort to negotiate an agreeable settlement.

The plaintiff must balance the proposed offer with the chance of winning the full claim at trial. Thus, Penny Chow might now prefer to settle for a large portion of her claim rather than involve herself in a lengthy, formal trial. If the offer is not accepted, the action will proceed to trial.

Pre-trial Conference

A **pre-trial conference** is the last chance for the parties to reach a settlement without a formal trial. This step, first introduced in Nova Scotia in the 1970s, is now used in most provinces. Both litigants and their lawyers appear before a judge to review the case openly, honestly, and informally. With assistance from the judge, the two parties solve as many unsettled issues as possible before the case goes to trial. Based on what has been said, the judge gives an opinion as to the possible judgment if the case were to go to trial. Many cases are settled on the basis of this opinion, without going to trial. If the case does go to trial, the trial judge will not be the same person as the judge at the pre-trial conference.

CASE

*Thomas v.
Hamilton
Board of
Education*
(1994)

Ontario Court
of Appeal
20 O.R. (3d) 598

Jeffry Thomas, an athletic 16-year-old student at Scott Park Secondary School, was one of the best and most experienced players on his school's junior football team. He also played on the Steel City Peewee League and was named the most valuable offensive player in the league. Football skills were taught as part of the regular classroom physical education program and as an extra-curricular activity in Hamilton high schools; games were coached by teachers selected by school principals. Students were eligible to play junior football if they were not older than 15 years at the beginning of the school year and if they provided a permission form signed by their parents and a medical certificate indicating that they were fit to play football. Between 1980 and 1982, Thomas played football, basketball, frequently rode his bike, jogged, and lifted weights four times a week. By the fall of 1982, he was 183 cm tall and weighed about 68 kg.

In October 1982, during a football game, Thomas tackled an opposing player, head first, and crashed head on into the punt returner's hip. Thomas was running at jogging speed or faster; the punt returner was running at full speed. All witnesses agreed that the contact between the two players was substantial, and that Thomas's body was extended but his head was not up at the point of contact. He and the other players had been taught to tackle with their shoulders, not their heads, and contact should be made with a shoulder.

Thomas suffered serious injury to his cervical spine which left him quadriplegic. Thomas and his family sued the school board and the school football coaches. The action was dismissed at trial, and Thomas and his family appealed to the Ontario Court of Appeal where, in a 3–0 judgment in late 1994, the appeal was dismissed.

1. **How much compensation do you think Thomas may require because of his injury?**

2. **Why was this action heard in the Ontario Court, General Division, rather than in Small Claims Court?**

3. **Why did the plaintiff sue the Hamilton Board of Education?**

4. **What other third parties might have also been involved in this action, and why?**

5. **List all the people who were in a position to have prevented Thomas's injuries from occurring. Examine each individual separately and determine whether you believe that a reasonable person in his or her position would have acted differently.**

6. **Based on the facts presented, why was the school board found not responsible for the plaintiff's injuries?**

The Trial

If no settlement can be reached, the parties are ready to go to court. Except in Small Claims Court, either party can elect to have a jury. However, juries for civil actions are not common.

Procedures in a civil trial are similar to those used in criminal trials. Depending on the court involved, the plaintiff, Penny Chow, or her lawyer presents her case first. Witnesses for Chow are called to the stand and are examined by Chow or her lawyer. The defendant, Bjorn Svendsen, or his lawyer, then has an opportunity to cross-examine the witnesses. When the plaintiff's case has been presented, the defendant's case is summarized and witnesses are called. They are examined by the defence and cross-examined by the plaintiff or the plaintiff's lawyer.

When all of the evidence has been presented, each party sums up his or her case. Each party attempts to point out the weaknesses in the opponent's case and to highlight the strengths in his or her own. Neither party can present new evidence at this point, but reference can be made to evidence presented earlier.

If the trial is by jury, the judge instructs the jury members on the law to be applied to the facts of the case. The jury, or, if there is no jury, the judge, must consider the evidence, as well as questions such as these: Who was at fault? Is that person totally at fault, or are both parties somewhat to blame? How should damages be determined? How much should the damages be? All of these factors must be considered in reaching a judgment.

Reviewing Your Reading

1. Explain the meaning of "balance of probabilities" as it relates to civil actions.

2. Why must a minor be represented by a "next friend" in a civil suit?

3. List four key pieces of information that must appear on a summons or claim.

4. Briefly outline the four options available to a defendant who is being sued.

5. What is a default judgment?

6. What is an Examination for Discovery? List its three purposes.

7. What are the benefits of an out-of-court settlement?

8. Why are pre-trial conferences being used more often in civil actions?

10.5 *The* JUDGMENT

After the trial, the judge delivers a judgment. In Small Claims Court, the judge usually makes an oral judgment while all the parties involved are still present. In higher courts, the judge often needs some time to review the evidence and to consider the case itself and the relevant law. The judge is then said to be "reserving judgment."

Civil Remedies

The main reason for civil actions is to allow plaintiffs to receive money, or damages, as compensation for the injury or loss they have suffered. The intent is to return the plaintiffs, as far as possible, to the same position as if the circumstances had not occurred. Although no amount of money can adequately compensate victims, a major purpose of awarding damages is to provide satisfactory future care for the injured plaintiffs. There are four categories of financial compensation, and plaintiffs may be awarded one or more of the following.

General Damages

In the case of a serious accident, plaintiffs might be subjected to pain and suffering, mental anguish, or the inability to enjoy a normal life. They might lose a skill or the ability to perform certain activities. If the injury causes temporary disability, plaintiffs may not be able to work for some time after the accident. If the injury causes permanent disability, the victims may never be able to work again. All of these injuries and losses must have a dollar value placed on them to compensate plaintiffs. Items that cannot be calculated easily and require a judge or jury's discretion are **general damages**.

As the above suggests, there are two categories of general damages. Financial losses such as loss of future earnings and the cost of future care are **pecuniary losses**. Loss of enjoyment of life, pain and suffering, and the shortening of the victim's life are **non-pecuniary losses**. It is difficult to place a dollar value on any of these forms of loss.

Pecuniary Loss. Factors that a judge must consider in determining pecuniary losses include the plaintiff's earning capacity, the percentage by which this capacity has been reduced, and the plaintiff's life expectancy. The longer the injured or disabled plaintiff is expected to live, the greater the necessary compensation. If the victim is already following or had definite plans to enter a specific profession or trade, then the average earnings for that occupation may be used. The settlement must, moreover, be fair to both the plaintiff and the defendant.

Determining adequate compensation is extremely difficult when the injured plaintiff is very young or has not yet entered the work force. For example, do you know what you intend to do after high school? Are your school marks high enough to enter college or university or a particular trade? Have you given any realistic consideration to what type of employment you intend to seek? If so, who knows about these decisions, and who could testify on your behalf at a trial to support your claims if you were an injured plaintiff?

Pecuniary losses for future care are intended to cover professional help, equipment, and facilities necessary for the injured plaintiff. If you are permanently disabled, the court must determine whether your future care should be at home or in an institution. Home care is preferable because a home provides privacy and a sense of security, with no restrictions on activities such as visits from friends. Homes can be modified with wheelchair ramps, wider halls, and special kitchens and bathrooms. However, the cost of home care tends to be higher than that of institutions.

Non-pecuniary Loss. While the calculation of pecuniary losses is difficult, determining non-pecuniary losses may be even harder. How do you place a price on pain? Is one person more tolerant of pain than another? It isn't easy, but judges and juries give pain a value for such things as whiplash, loss of an eye, severe headaches, and so on. What is the loss of enjoyment of life worth to a person permanently injured in an accident? Should an athletic, socially active youth be given more money for loss of enjoyment of life than a quiet, less-active one? Money cannot restore what has been injured or lost. However, it can provide substitutes for pleasures that are no longer possible. Non-pecuniary losses can, for instance, make it possible for an injured plaintiff who can no longer skate or ski to enjoy a winter vacation.

Courts consider that every Canadian deserves equal compensation for similar non-pecuniary losses. They tend, therefore, to cover all concerns about non-pecuniary losses with a single amount. Doing this gives some uniformity and predictability to judgments. In early 1978, the Supreme Court of Canada handed down three precedent-setting decisions that established an upper limit of $100 000 for non-pecuniary losses for the most serious type of injuries—those resulting in severe, life-long physical incapacity. The Court decisions dealt with awards in two young-adult quadriplegic cases and one case involving an infant plaintiff whose physical abilities and speech were severely handicapped, and whose mental ability had been reduced as a result of a serious car accident. The judgment set aside $100 000 as the maximum compensation that anyone can recover for pain and suffering in most cases. This maximum can be exceeded only in "exceptional circumstances," on the basis of severity of injuries, the victim's disability, and changing economic conditions. These decisions were intended to discourage a trend to greater damage awards, such as several millions of dollars commonly awarded in the United States. The Supreme Court has since allowed the $100 000 ceiling to be adjusted to compensate for the value of the dollar. The current adjusted limit is worth about $250 000. However, no limit has ever been set for such *pecuniary* losses as medical expenses, loss of future income, or the cost of future care.

One of these three cases, *Thornton et al. v. Board of School Trustees of School District No. 57 (Prince George) et al.* is discussed on the next page. Another, *Teno et al. v. Arnold et al.* will be discussed in Chapter 11.

On a school day in 1971, Gary Thornton was participating in a physical education class at Prince George High School in British Columbia. Thornton was 15 years old, and about 185 cm tall. A box horse had been placed at the lower end of a springboard, so that a spring would elevate the gymnasts high enough to do a somersault. The instructor, David Edamura, had approved this arrangement. However, the boys had never before used the equipment in this way. After organizing the class, Edamura went to one end of the gym to complete report cards. As a result, he was not able to observe the class activity directly.

After one student had landed on the floor and suffered a broken wrist while attempting a double somersault, foam rubber mats were added around the springboard. When Thornton's turn came to use the springboard, he overshot the thick landing mats and landed on his head on the thin foam mats. He was taken immediately to hospital. Thornton was found to have a fracture of the spinal cord that left him almost completely paralyzed in all four limbs, a quadriplegic. He had minimal use of his hands and some use of his arms up to his shoulders, but he would require constant care for the rest of his life. His life expectancy was 54 years. Although physically handicapped, his mental faculties were unimpaired.

Thornton's parents brought a suit on his behalf. He claimed damages on the grounds that Edamura and the school authorities were negligent. In January 1975, the British Columbia Supreme Court awarded $1.5 million. On appeal by the school board, the British Columbia Court of Appeal confirmed in 1976 that Edamura and the school board were negligent but reduced the award to $600 000. Thornton's lawyers stated that the appeal court erred in its calculations for the award for future care and appealed the decision to the Supreme Court of Canada in the spring of 1977. In January 1978, the Supreme Court made a final award of $810 000.

Thornton et al. v. Board of School Trustees of School District No. 57 (Prince George) et al.
(1978)

Supreme Court of Canada
83 D.L.R. (3d) 480

1. **Why did Thornton's parents bring this action to court on his behalf?**

2. **Why was the action brought against the Prince George School District?**

3. **Did the teacher do what was expected or required of him as a physical education teacher? Did he act as a reasonable person in his position? Why or why not?**

4. **In the case of permanent disability, a key issue for courts to consider is whether the victim's future care should be in an institutional or a modified-home environment. Part of Gary Thorton's damages was intended for the purchase of a home for him. Should he have been institutionalized for the rest of his life instead? List the arguments for and against each type of environment.**

5. **Another part of Thornton's settlement was compensation for non-pecuniary loss. The original trial judgment awarded him $200 000; however, the Supreme Court of Canada reduced this amount to $100 000. Do you think this is a fair and reasonable upper limit? Discuss.**

6. **In a chart, compare and contrast the Gary Thornton case with the Jeffry Thomas case on p. 272. Consider the standard of care employed by each teacher and the foreseeability of each incident.**

Special Damages

A plaintiff may have to be hospitalized after an accident, losing income, and/or incurring expenses for ambulance service, drugs, therapy, rehabilitation, car repairs, and so on. In another situation, a plaintiff might have to pay for the repair of a fence damaged by a neighbour. **Special damages** compensate for out-of-pocket expenses for which the plaintiff can produce a receipt or bill. Lost wages between the accident and the trial are also special damages because they can be calculated exactly.

Punitive Damages

If the accident is the result of a violent action, or the judge wants to penalize the defendant, the plaintiff may be awarded an increased amount, known as **punitive** or **exemplary damages**. The intention is deterrence—to discourage both the defendant and the public from committing similar actions. However, punitive damages are rarely awarded in cases where the defendant has already been punished by the criminal courts for the same action. They are most commonly awarded for false arrest or imprisonment, trespass to the person from assault and battery, and for vicious lies intentionally told to damage a person's reputation. These torts are discussed in Chapter 12.

Nominal Damages

A judge who wants to indicate support for a plaintiff may award **nominal damages**. Such an award suggests that, although the plaintiff has suffered little or no loss or harm, he or she has won a moral victory. If, for example, someone trespasses on another person's property but does not actually damage the property, nominal damages may be awarded to tell trespassers that they have affected the owner's right of property use. A small sum, such as one dollar, is commonly awarded for nominal damages.

Injunctions

In a small number of civil actions, the plaintiff is not as interested in monetary compensation as in another form of judgment. Suppose that Kyle Anstey and Brad Chun are members of a band that rehearses late each evening at their home.

Their neighbours, the Ollsens, feel that their right to quiet enjoyment of their property is being disturbed. The Ollsens might seek the assistance of the courts to prevent the continuation of late-night rehearsals. The courts could respond by issuing Anstey and Chun with an **injunction,** a court order restricting the rehearsals to reasonable hours.

A factory that is polluting a lake by dumping its waste into it might be subject to an injunction requiring the owners to stop this activity. In Alberta, injunctions were issued to prevent unlawful use of the Olympic symbols and trademarks during the 1988 Winter Olympic Games. The most common use of injunctions is to require striking workers to return to work. Failure to comply with an injunction might result in a charge for contempt of court, followed by a fine or jail sentence.

Did You Know

Contempt of court is a serious criminal offence for which the judge can issue a range of options from a fine to imprisonment. Causing a disturbance during a trial is a common example of contempt of court.

Costs

If the plaintiff wins the case, the judge must determine whether court costs will be allowed. Usually, the losing party is required to pay the legal fees and other expenses of the successful party. Such costs, based on a fee schedule published by the courts, vary somewhat by province. The winning party prepares a bill of costs and gives it to the losing party for payment. However, the amount the judge awards may cover only part of the costs, especially for a long trial in a higher court. The rest might have to come from the award of damages, leaving little for the plaintiff.

In response to this problem, a **contingency fee system** exists everywhere in Canada except Ontario, which has announced plans to introduce legislation in 1996.

Price, the 75-year-old plaintiff, was employed as a cook in the Arctic. He took a week off and travelled to Edmonton where he took a room for one night at the defendant Cecil Hotel. The next day when he had overstayed the noon checkout by 15 minutes, the defendant hotel bouncer, William Stoley, entered Price's room with a pass key, roughly pulled Price from his bed, slapped him, called him a bum, stomped on his foot, forcefully partially dressed him, and shoved him out of the room.

After complaining to the police, Price returned to the hotel to get his luggage and the rest of his clothes and belongings. The defendant bouncer once again shoved or kicked the plaintiff toward the hotel door and out of the hotel.

As a result of these two incidents, Price suffered bruising to his neck and toes. He was unable to work for nearly 8 months and then suffered decreasing discomfort for another 12 months. He missed 70.5 days of work owing to his injuries at a loss of $100 a day.

Price brought an action for damages to the Alberta Court of Queen's Bench, which was successful, and he was awarded $4050 in general damages, $7050 in special damages, and $1000 in punitive damages.

Price v.
Stoley
et al.
(1984)

**Alberta Court of
Queen's Bench
34 Alta. L.R. (2d) 356**

1. **Why did the plaintiff sue the hotel bouncer, William Stoley?**
2. **Were Stoley's actions toward the plaintiff reasonable? Explain.**
3. **Why did the plaintiff also sue the Cecil Hotel as a defendant?**
4. **For what kinds of things would the general and special damages have been awarded? Give specific examples in your answer.**
5. **Why was only Stoley required to pay the $1000 in punitive damages?**
6. **Was this an appropriate use of punitive damages? Why or why not?**

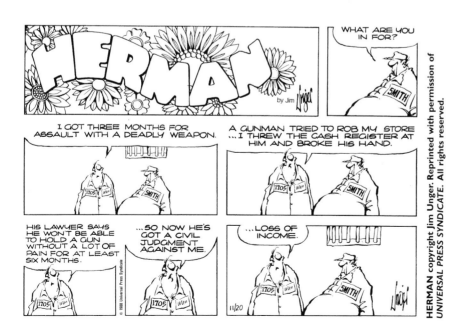

Under this scheme, client and lawyer negotiate a fee in the hope of a successful action. The client agrees in advance to pay the lawyer between 10 and 50 percent of the judgment. If the case is successful, the lawyer receives the agreed-upon percentage. If the client loses the case, the lawyer receives nothing. The contingency fee system allows those who cannot afford to pay legal fees in advance to take legal action. However, opponents of the scheme fear that it will lead to an excessive number of actions and multi-million dollar lawsuits, as has happened in the United States.

Enforcing a Judgment

In a civil case, it is up to the successful party to collect on the judgment. The court has no responsibility to ensure that the losing party pays the damages. The loser may have little money, or may be reluctant to pay. Thus, being awarded a judgment is one thing; collecting on it is quite another. The following legal remedies, however, are available to force payment.

Garnishment

The remedy of **garnishment** provides that, if a third party owes money to the losing defendant, the successful plaintiff can obtain a court order forcing the third party to pay the debt into court. In turn, the court will give the money to the plaintiff as a payment on the judgment. The third party is responsible only for the amount owed to the unsuccessful defendant, not for the total amount of the judgment.

Bank accounts, unpaid rent, and money owing on contracts may all be garnisheed. Wages, too, can be garnisheed, but only for 20 to 30 percent of a person's total wage. The percentage differs from province to province. If the defendant cannot afford to have this percentage of wages taken, an application may be made to the court to have the amount altered. In most provinces, a garnishment remains in effect for six months but can be renewed if the entire amount is not paid within that time.

Examination of a Debtor

If the defendant still refuses to pay, the plaintiff can request an **examination of the debtor**. The defendant debtor is ordered to appear in court to satisfy the judge as to the availability of resources to settle the claim. The debtor is examined under oath regarding income, assets, and any money owing from others. An agreement is usually reached as to how much, if anything, the debtor can afford to pay. Instalment payments can be arranged, if necessary.

Seizing Assets

Another alternative is for the plaintiff to apply to the courts to take legal possession of the debtor's property and sell it to settle the judgment. The bailiff or sheriff seizes the assets and notifies the defendant of the seizure. The assets are held for a certain period, to give the defendant an opportunity to settle the judgment and redeem the goods. If this is not done, the goods are sold at public auction. The court deducts all of its costs from the sale, and then pays the plaintiff the amount of the judgment, or as much as possible. Any money remaining is returned to the debtor.

Certain goods, such as clothing, furniture, utensils, and workers' tools, are exempt from seizure, up to $2000. One difficulty in seizing goods is that it is necessary to be certain that they belong to the person from whom they are seized.

Automobile Judgments

In any case involving an automobile accident, an additional remedy is available. The plaintiff can send a copy of the final court judgment to the Registrar or Superintendent of Motor Vehicles. This official has the authority to suspend the defendant driver's licence until the debt is paid or arrangements for payment have been made.

Reviewing Your Reading

1. Using examples, distinguish between
   a) general and special damages;
   b) pecuniary and non-pecuniary losses.

2. Why is it difficult to determine what damages to award a very young child or a young person between the ages of 7 and 16?

3. Using examples, distinguish between nominal and punitive damages.

4. **What is an injunction, and when might it be awarded in a civil judgment?**

5. **What is a contingency fee system? List one advantage and one disadvantage of this system.**

6. **Briefly outline three remedies available for enforcing a judgment.**

10.6 OTHER SOURCES OF COMPENSATION

The awarding of damages is the most common method of obtaining compensation in tort law. However, there are other sources of compensation, including the Workers' Compensation Fund, the Criminal Injuries Compensation Board (discussed in Chapter 6), and various types of liability insurance.

Workers' Compensation

Provincial *Workers' Compensation Acts* have established a Workers' Compensation Fund to provide employees compensation without delay. Payments to the Fund are made by employers, not employees, and are based on the type and size of business. Not all employees are covered under the *Workers' Compensation Act*, so employees should find out from their employers whether they have coverage. Injured workers engaged in a business not covered by the *Act* must seek compensation through a civil action if the employer refuses to pay damages for injuries.

An injured employee can apply to the board for an award covering medical expenses and a portion of lost wages. If the employee is fatally injured, the dependents receive the benefits. Board members decide who is entitled to receive benefits, how much will be paid, and for how long. Awards are limited to a maximum percentage of the worker's average salary before the accident. The board does not pay for pain and suffering or loss of enjoyment of life. The board's decisions may be appealed to a Board of Review, but this takes time.

It is significant that benefits are given, no matter who was at fault. Even an employee who causes an accident collects compensation, unless it was caused willfully. Nor is it necessary to prove the employer's negligence. For this gain, the worker gives up the right to sue the employer.

The workers' compensation system has definite advantages over seeking damages in court. Most cases are heard quickly, and benefits are paid immediately. There is no cost for an application to the board. A court case, on the other hand, can be long and expensive. In addition, the board's decisions can always be reopened and payments increased, if necessary. Trial judgments are final unless overturned by a Court of Appeal, and a judge awards damages on the basis of a prediction of the plaintiff's probable future earnings and possible medical problems. Court judgments can therefore be less suitable to an injured worker's situation.

However, the system also has disadvantages. Some applicants have felt that the awards are inadequate. While they have the right to appeal, some workers have lost this right because they did not know it was available.

Motor Vehicle Liability Insurance

Probably the largest percentage of civil actions today arise from disputes over motor vehicle accidents. It is likely that lawyers specializing in civil lawsuits spend more time dealing with negligence actions from such accidents than from any other type of tort. In fact, such actions often take several years from the time of the accident to the completion of the trial and the awarding of damages.

As you read earlier in this chapter, a person injured in an automobile accident can claim both special damages and general damages from the driver responsible. More recently, the courts have determined that persons who were not directly involved in the accident may also claim damages on such grounds as mental anguish and loss of companionship of a relative or a loved one. Statutes in several provinces allow such claims.

Even minor accidents in which no one has been seriously injured can result in damage claims so high that most people would be unable to pay them. For this reason, all car owners in Canada are legally required to purchase motor vehicle liability insurance. The insurance company pays any claims for damages arising from an accident, up to a certain maximum. This type of insurance is called

third-party liability insurance, because three parties are involved when a claim is made: the person who caused the accident, that person's insurance company, and the victim who claims damages. The minimum amount of insurance coverage required by law in all provinces and the Northwest Territories in 1995 was $200 000.

Insurance is compulsory and provides compensation, regardless of fault, to certain dollar limits for which the parties are insured. For more serious injury, victims may sue for amounts above the insured limits. Increases in the size of damages awarded for automobile accidents have prompted many drivers to purchase insurance coverage of $500 000 to $1 million—far higher than the required minimum.

Special arrangements exist for compensating people who suffer loss in an accident with an uninsured driver. Some drivers have no insurance, although this is illegal in Canada and carries severe fines. In some provinces, a fund run by the insurance industry handles such claims; in the other provinces, the fund is administered by the government.

Because victims of motor vehicle accidents often have to wait years for damages, a limited form of **no-fault insurance** has been instituted throughout Canada. It is designed to put money in the hands of victims immediately, whether or not they are at fault in the accident. An injured person who suffers loss beyond that covered by no-fault insurance can still bring a tort action for damages. However, if the person wins additional damages from the courts, any no-fault insurance benefits are deducted from the award.

Motor vehicle insurance regulations differ from province to province, and their details are too complex to be discussed here. You can obtain information about the specifics of your provincial regulations from a local insurance agent.

Other Liability Insurance

In recent years it has become common practice for people and businesses to minimize losses from possible civil actions by buying insurance. Any type of liability insurance policy has an upper dollar limit for insurance coverage. If a court awards damages greater than the maximum, the defendant must pay the difference. This may mean having to sell possessions and having wages garnisheed. Often, the damages can never be paid fully because the sum is too large to repay in a person's lifetime.

When all forms of damages are considered, awards in civil actions can involve millions of dollars. While such large awards occur far more often in the United States, personal injury accidents, ranging from cut fingers to paralysis for life, now cost Canadians at least $2.5 billion a year in medical treatment and future care, lost wages, and pain and suffering.

The number of medical malpractice suits and the size of the settlements is increasing in Canada as well. Most Canadian doctors pay fees to the Canadian Medical Protective Association. This organization provides medical insurance that covers legal costs and damage awards for doctors who are sued successfully for malpractice. Malpractice insurance is also available from insurance companies.

Many Canadian lawyers also purchase malpractice insurance from insurance companies to protect themselves against civil actions from dissatisfied clients.

Retail outlets, shopping centres, schools, churches, clubs, municipalities, and community organizations purchase insurance coverage to protect themselves in the event of lawsuits arising from injuries to persons on their property. Both homeowners and tenants who rent property also buy liability insurance to cover damages in case of injuries to visitors. The increasing readiness of many people to sue makes it wise for all businesses and individuals to carry liability insurance.

Did You Know

In 1994, there were 1208 legal actions brought against Canadian physicians on the basis of allegations of medical malpractice or negligence. Awards and settlements for that year totalled $62 403 000.

In August 1977, the 14-year-old plaintiff, Michael McErlean, and a friend were riding their trail bikes in an abandoned quarry owned by the defendant City of Brampton. The property was scheduled for park development, but was not yet a public park area when this accident occurred. The City of Brampton was aware that the site was used for riding trail bikes and that it held a dangerous curve. A "No Trespassing" sign was posted on the land. There was a fence around part of the quarry, but a gate in the existing fence was down.

McErlean and his friend agreed to race down a smooth gravel road in the pit. Their bikes reached speeds between 55 and 80 km/h. At a point where the road narrowed into a sharp, blind S-curve, McErlean collided head-on with a bike driven by the 13-year-old defendant, Neil Sarel, an inexperienced rider. He was weaving back and forth as he approached the curve and was on McErlean's side of the road at the moment of impact. The plaintiff suffered massive and permanent brain damage. He was left a quadriplegic, had the mental capacity of an infant, was unable to speak, and would require constant care.

McErlean brought an action for personal injuries to the Ontario High Court of Justice. In March 1985, the court found the City of Brampton to be negligent and 75 percent at fault for the accident. Sarel was found to be 15 percent at fault; McErlean, 10 percent at fault. Damages were calculated at just over $7 million, of which the City of Brampton was ordered to pay the plaintiff $6.3 million. This was the largest negligence award in Canadian legal history at that time.

The City of Brampton appealed the decision to the Ontario Court of Appeal. In September 1987, a 5–0 judgment overturned the trial judgment and set aside a finding of negligence against the city and the order to pay $6.3 million in damages. Leave to appeal this decision to the Supreme Court of Canada was denied in early 1988.

McErlean v.
Sarel et al.
(1987)

Ontario Court
of Appeal
42 D.L.R. (4th) 577

1. **Why did the trial judge find the City of Brampton largely responsible for the accident?**

2. **What might the city have done to avoid liability?**

3. **If damages were assessed at just over $7 million, why was Brampton ordered to pay McErlean only $6.3 million?**

4. **What effect do you think the original trial judgment had on liability insurance premiums in Ontario for such institutions as hospitals and schools?**

5. **The Court of Appeal judgment noted that the trial judge had placed too much emphasis on the boys' ages. It said, in part: "When a child engages in what may be classified as an 'adult activity,' he or she will not be accorded special treatment and no allowance will be made for his or her immaturity." What is your opinion of this statement?**

Reviewing Your Reading

1. What is the purpose of the Workers' Compensation Fund?

2. Identify two advantages and two disadvantages of the Workers' Compensation Fund.

3. What is third-party liability insurance? Identify the "three parties" involved.

4. What is the legal requirement for third party liability insurance in your province, and why should motorists purchase more than this limit?

5. What is no-fault insurance?

6. What is the purpose of the Canadian Medical Protective Association?

7. Name three groups, besides doctors and lawyers, who would be wise to purchase liability insurance, and explain why in each case.

10.7 ALTERNATIVE DISPUTE RESOLUTION

As you have seen in this chapter, civil litigation often takes considerable time and money. Courts all across Canada are backlogged, and it may take several years and thousands of dollars before a case comes to trial. In Ontario, a complex civil action may take three to five years for both sides to be ready for court. In Alberta and British Columbia, three to four years is common; in other parts of Canada, the time is slightly less. Moving even simple cases through the justice system becomes a complex, drawn-out procedure that often involves lengthy pleadings, the production of a large number of detailed documents, and long pre-trial conferences.

Recently, new directions in civil law have been developed to help speed cases to a quicker resolution. The pre-trial conference discussed earlier is one way to help litigants reach an out-of-court settlement. Since the spring of 1995, trials expected to last 10 days or longer in British Columbia were assigned to a single judge for both pre-trial and trial stages. It is hoped the result will be more out-of-court settlements and fewer delaying tactics on the part of the litigants' lawyers.

As Canadians become frustrated with the excessive costs and delays in their civil courts, they are beginning to move from adversarial means of resolving disputes to alternative options. Mediation, negotiation, and arbitration, or **alternative dispute resolution** (ADR), have become an alternative to litigation. Using ADR avoids the cost and risks of litigation and usually results in a win/win situation with both parties gaining some benefit.

Mediation

Mediation is probably the primary ADR used as an alternative to litigation in resolving civil disputes. A neutral third party, the mediator, involves the parties in a cooperative decision-making process to resolve and settle their dispute privately by mutual agreement. The parties involved control the decision making to reach an acceptable decision, while the mediator manages or facilitates the process.

The mediator's main role is to provide a relaxed, informal, and comfortable environment in which the parties can exchange comments openly and honestly about the facts and issues in dispute. Discussion should flow between the parties, rather than the mediator, as they attempt to develop an understanding of the unresolved issues. Once an agreement is reached, it can be included in a written contract.

Mediation leaves the parties in control of their own decision making and emphasizes cooperation as opposed to confrontation.

Did You Know
In Alberta in 1994, Social Services mediated 750 divorce cases.

Negotiation

Negotiation is an informal and voluntary dispute resolution process. No third party is involved. The two parties determine the process, communicate with each other, and reach mutually acceptable decisions. Discussions may relate to proof, witnesses and evidence, and problem solving to consider available options. As in mediation, any agreement reached can be written into a contract.

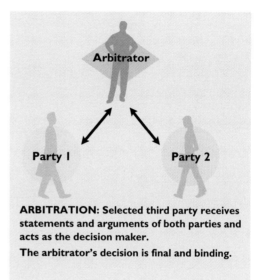

NEGOTIATION: Parties communicate with each other and make their own decisions.

Outcome is a contract that is final and binding.

MEDIATION: Selected neutral third party facilitates parties to make their own decision.

Outcome is an agreement to which the parties are committed, when written into a contract and signed becomes final and binding.

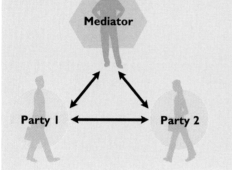

ARBITRATION: Selected third party receives statements and arguments of both parties and acts as the decision maker.

The arbitrator's decision is final and binding.

Arbitration

Arbitration is a more formal ADR in which the parties involved select a neutral third party who has specific technical knowledge. Although arbitration is more formal than mediation or negotiation procedures, it is less formal than litigation in a courtroom.

Unlike mediation and negotiation, the parties no longer have control over their decision making. The arbitrator's role is to receive statements of issues and position and hear arguments. Both parties have the chance to present evidence, and examine and cross-examine witnesses. Communication here flows mainly between the parties and the arbitrator. With his or her specific knowledge, the arbitrator will consider the two positions and make a final, binding decision or ruling on both parties. Here there is a winner and a loser, unlike in mediation.

The choice of ADR will vary according to the interests of both parties. As you have seen, there is a range of options. Mediation can be used at any time when a neutral third party can bring fresh perspectives to deadlocked negotiation. Arbitration is effective if negotiation and mediation have failed, and neither party is ready to sue in court.

Reviewing Your Reading

1. **What is ADR? What three options to litigation are suggested?**
2. **Distinguish between negotiation and mediation.**
3. **List three benefits of mediation.**
4. **Distinguish between mediation and arbitration.**

ISSUE

No-fault Insurance:

Does it encourage

fraud?

Automobile liability insurance offers financial protection to policy holders who may be held liable for injury or loss sustained by others, arising from the operation of their vehicles. Throughout Canada, automobile liability insurance is mandatory.

At one time, most provinces relied on the civil court system to satisfy insurance claims. Frequently, this meant costly litigation, which led to increases in insurance premiums. It also meant that people injured in motor vehicle accidents often had to wait months and even years to collect damages for their injuries from the policy holder's insurer. For those injured and unable to work, such delays could be ruinous.

As a result, some provinces implemented "no-fault" insurance systems. These plans vary from province to province, but they all allow accident victims to claim compensation from their own insurance companies for injuries sustained, regardless of fault. In addition to improving settlement of claims, no-fault insurance is intended to reduce insurance costs by avoiding costly legal battles in civil court.

In Ontario, where benefits are generous and easy to get, no-fault insurance has come under attack. In 1995, 19 people were arrested and charged with defrauding 29 Ontario insurance companies of $1.1 million. These people deliberately staged accidents, and then submitted insurance claims for phony injuries. Police suspect that law clerks, doctors, and body-shop employees may have been involved in this scheme as well. They estimate that the $1.1 million figure could rise to as much as $10 million from this one scheme alone.

On One Side

Ontario's Bill 164 requires insurance companies to pay accident benefits to victims within 14 days after a claim has been submitted. The benefit package includes 90 percent of weekly wages up to a maximum of $1000.

Insurance companies in Ontario want the laws regulating no-fault insurance changed. They feel Bill 164 makes it too tempting for unscrupulous people to defraud the system.

Insurers feel that having only 14 days to investigate the accident is not enough time to detect fraudulent claims. They would like payment to be delayed until a full investigation can be conducted. Moreover, they maintain that the present rates are too high and encourage fraud. They want weekly no-fault payments reduced to a maximum of $450.

On the Other Side

Alberta and the Maritime provinces presently operate under tort law with civil courts determining fault and awarding damages. However, this may change soon. The number of claims before their courts has risen sharply in recent years. In Alberta alone, the number jumped from 11 000 in 1991 to 13 500 in 1993. Yet, there had been a reduction in the number of car accidents for the same period. This dramatic increase in civil actions is a strain on the courts. Politicians feel that a no-fault insurance scheme might eliminate this problem.

Indeed, in 1994 Manitoba eliminated the civil court system and the right to sue. Saskatchewan followed suit early in 1995. In its first year, the Manitoba scheme showed dramatic results. There was a 35 percent reduction in the number of personal-injury claims. The elimination of claims involving "pain and suffering" helped to reduce this number.

Those who support the no-fault system argue that it is more efficient, less time consuming, and less expensive than the civil court system. They feel that the costs of fraud are less than the expenses involved in suing for damages in the courts.

The Bottom Line

Regardless of the system in place, insurance companies recover their losses by increasing their premiums. Is the no-fault system more efficient and less expensive, or does it encourage fraudulent claims that ultimately penalize honest policy holders? What do you think? You be the judge!

1. **Should automobile liability insurance be mandatory? Explain.**

2. **How is no-fault insurance being used to defraud insurance companies?**

3. **Create a two-column organizer. List your arguments for the advantages and disadvantages of no-fault insurance.**

4. **What changes to the existing laws on no-fault insurance do insurance companies want? How could these changes reduce the incidence of fraud?**

5. **In your opinion, should the no-fault insurance system be abandoned or modified? Present your conclusions to the class.**

CHAPTER REVIEW

Reviewing Key Terms

For each of the following statements, indicate the key term being defined:

a) a defendant's claim in a civil action in response to the plaintiff's related claim

b) money paid to a plaintiff for the purpose of punishing the defendant for an uncaring or violent act

c) money paid to a plaintiff for future monetary loss, pain and suffering, and loss of enjoyment of life

d) the degree of proof in a civil action; a greater likelihood

e) a decision made in the plaintiff's favour when the defendant fails to appear or file a statement of defence

f) the person who brings an action on behalf of a minor

g) a process in which money owed to or by a defendant is attached by a plaintiff to settle an unpaid judgment

h) the reconciliation of a dispute through cooperative decision making by a neutral third party

i) a lawsuit; a legal action

j) a court order directing a person to do or not to do something

Exploring Legal Concepts

1. Although the primary function of tort law is to compensate the victims of torts, some people feel that it also acts as a deterrent or a penalty. Using original examples, describe two situations in which tort law serves each of these functions.

2. The dollar limit for actions in Small Claims Court is regularly reviewed by provincial governments and increased from time to time. Give two reasons for shifting the limit upward. Find out what the limit is in your province.

3. Discuss the following statement: "The economy of the Small Claims Court means that pursuing partial compensation there might be cheaper than getting the whole amount from a higher court."

4. Explain the meaning of the following statement as it relates to civil judgments and the awarding of damages: "You can't get blood from a stone!"

5. In 1978, the Supreme Court of Canada established a ceiling of $100 000 for non-pecuniary losses such as pain and suffering, mental anguish, and loss of enjoyment of life. This ceiling was to be exceeded only in exceptional circumstances.
   a) Do you feel that this ceiling for non-pecuniary losses is appropriate?
   b) Can you suggest some circumstances in which it might be exceeded?

6. a) If you were involved in an accident today that left you disabled, what evidence would you bring to justify your claim for loss of future income?
   b) How would such evidence differ for (i) a five-year-old, (ii) a 48-year-old executive, and (iii) a homemaker?

Applying Legal Concepts

1. Ryan, the plaintiff, was a man known to have experience with horses. For this reason, the defendant, McNeill, gave his horse to Ryan for boarding and training. A year after McNeill's death, his wife and son sent for the horse, but Ryan refused to deliver it unless he received payment for the boarding and training of the animal. Ryan brought an action for the money owed him for these services, while the McNeills counterclaimed for damages.

   - **Was Ryan entitled to refuse to deliver the horse to the McNeills?**
   - **Did Ryan's action succeed? Why or why not?**

2. The British Columbia government granted a 21-year lease on some land to the District of North Saanich. The lease covered the foreshore around the upper portion of a peninsula on Vancouver Island, for a distance of some 300 m from the high-water mark to the ocean. The Murray brothers built wharves that were situated to a considerable extent on the foreshore, without first obtaining the District government's permission. The District took action against the Murrays and was awarded nominal damages.

   - **Did the Murray brothers commit any offence by building the wharves where they did?**
   - **How could this problem be corrected?**
   - **Why was the District awarded only nominal damages?**

3. *Unger et al. v. City of Ottawa et al.* (1989) Ontario High Court of Justice 68 O.R. (2d) 263

   The 17-year-old plaintiff, Steven Unger, and several of his friends celebrated the last day of June exams by holding a party at the home of one of the students. During the afternoon, most of the students, including Unger, drank several beers. At about 7:00 p.m. the group decided, as it was a hot day, to go to Britannia Beach, operated by the defendant city.

   Unger and two friends sat on the life-guard chair and chatted for a while and looked at the other students who were playing in front of the chair on the beach. A sign was posted on the chair that read, "Beach Unsupervised. Swim at Own Risk." Unger stood up and jumped feet first into the ankle-deep water. After climbing back on the chair, he announced that he was going to dive. Both friends grabbed him and said, "Don't dive. It's stupid." But Unger dove head first into the shallow water, about one-metre deep, and about three metres ahead of the chair. When his friends saw that he remained face down, arms extended, and not moving, they called an ambulance and took Unger to the hospital. As a result of the dive, Unger became a quadriplegic.

   Unger brought an action for damages for personal injuries to the Ontario High Court of Justice (now the Ontario Court, General Division). Evidence was presented that showed the plaintiff was physically fit, was a good swimmer, and could dive.

   - **Why did Unger sue the City of Ottawa?**
   - **Examine all of the parties who might have been in a position to have prevented these injuries. Did they do what they were supposed to do, and do you think their actions were reasonable? Explain.**

- **As lawyer for the defendant city, what arguments would you present to defend against Unger's claim?**

- **What types of damages would the plaintiff seek, and why?**

- **Based on the facts presented, do you think the plaintiff won his action? Why or why not?**

4. *McEvay et al. v. Tory et al.* (1990) British Columbia Court of Appeal
49 B.C.L.R. (2d) 162

David McEvay, the six-year-old plaintiff, got off a B.C. transit bus which had stopped at a bus stop and ran around the front of the bus. The boy was on his way to his Junior One class at the elementary school opposite the bus stop in Victoria. This particular morning, David had slept in and had missed catching the school bus that took him directly onto the school grounds.

David's mother went part way on the bus with him that morning. She had given David road instructions and had told him the importance of crossing at the crosswalk many times before. The boy had been instructed in road safety and had been told not to cross the road until any approaching cars had passed. His father had also pointed out to him the danger of being hit by a car. Before Mrs. McEvay got off the bus, she asked the bus driver, Norman Wills, if he would drop David off at the school.

Wills agreed and let the boy off the bus with clear instructions to cross the road back at the crosswalk behind the bus and to be careful in doing so. The boy said, "Yes." However, the boy ignored the bus driver's warning, ran around the front of the bus, and was hit by a car driven by the defendant, Samantha Tory, and owned by Margaret Walsh. The boy was thrown and severely injured. The defendant was driving at the same speed as the other traffic, about 40 km/h, and witnesses testified to this fact at the trial. The posted speed limit was 50 km/h on the road signs.

The plaintiff and his "next friend" brought an action for damages sustained in the accident to the British Columbia Supreme Court, but his action was dismissed. He then appealed this dismissal to the Court of Appeal where it was also dismissed.

- **Who did the plaintiff sue in this action, and why?**

- **Should the bus driver have been required to get out of his bus and help David across the road? Why or why not?**

- **Could the boy's actions have been expected or anticipated by Mrs. Tory? Explain.**

- **Why do you think the trial judge dismissed David's case?**

- **Why did the boy appeal this dismissal to the Court of Appeal?**

- **Why did the Court of Appeal dismiss McEvay's appeal? Do you agree? Why or why not?**

Extending Legal Concepts

1. Now that you have completed this chapter, review the opening article and Something to Think About. Have your answers or opinions changed? Why or why not?

2. As you have learned, juries in criminal trials must reach unanimous decisions, while juries in civil cases only have to reach majority decisions. Also, Courts of Appeal may also reach majority/minority judgments.

   a) Is it fair and reasonable? Why or why not?

   b) Should Canadian law be changed so that all three groups of decisions are the same, either all unanimous or all majority judgments? Discuss with a partner, and be prepared to defend your decision in class.

3. Explain the meaning of the following statement: "Critics of contingency fees say they encourage unnecessary lawsuits that clog up the courts and drive up the cost of insurance as everybody tries to sue for wrongs and injuries." Do you agree or disagree with the critics, and why?

4. With a partner, collect at least eight newspaper articles over a two-week period that discuss or describe civil actions, civil courts, damage awards, and any other issues studied in this chapter. If possible, try to find articles from successive days that describe a case currently being heard in your community.

   Underline the parts of the article that are significant and add comments of your own about the sections that you have underlined. Your comments might include your opinion of proposed changes in the law or your personal feelings about a certain court decision or judgment.

   Sort the articles so that each appears on a separate page with an appropriate heading on each page. Indicate at the bottom of the page, the source of each article and the date on which it was published.

   When the assignment is complete, compile a table of contents, indicating the sections contained in your report and the page numbers you assigned them.

Researching an Issue

Mandatory Bicycle Helmets

Debates concerning the need for compulsory laws for bicycle helmets are increasing across Canada with the growing number of injuries and escalating medical costs. Ontario was the first province to enact mandatory bicycle helmet laws.

Statement

All Canadian provinces and the territories should require the mandatory wearing of bicycle helmets for all bicycle riders, regardless of age.

Point

Wearing helmets saves lives, which is reason enough to require all riders by law to wear helmets.

Counterpoint

The *Charter of Rights and Freedoms* allows freedom of choice and expression, and individuals should be allowed to make their own decisions without government interference.

- **With a partner, research this issue and reflect on your findings.**
- **Prepare points on this statement that could be used for a class debate.**
- **Discuss your findings with others in your class.**

NEGLIGENCE AND UNINTENTIONAL TORTS

These are the key terms introduced in this chapter:

allurement	informed consent	reasonable person
causation	invitee	*res ipsa loquitur*
contributory negligence	licensee	standard of care
duty of care	material risk	trespasser
foreseeable	negligence	vicarious liability
gross negligence	occupier	voluntary assumption of risk

Chapter at a Glance

Learning Outcomes

At the end of this chapter, you will be able to

1. identify the elements necessary for a negligence action;
2. explain the relationship between standard of care and the reasonable person and foreseeability;
3. outline the main defences for negligence;
4. describe tort liability of minors and parental responsibility;
5. identify the liabilities that may apply to the driver and owner of a motor vehicle as a result of a motor vehicle accident;
6. explain the principle of vicarious liability and its effect on motor vehicle owners and employers;
7. discuss the duty of care owed by professionals to their clients or patients;
8. state the significance of informed consent in medical treatment;
9. discuss the duty of care owed by occupiers of land to persons entering their property.

Burn Victim Fights for Life

The families of three boys burned at a SaskPower transformer site Sunday want to know if the accident was preventable, says a family spokesman.

But right now their biggest concern is the well-being of the boys, one of whom lies in a Regina hospital critically injured, Adele White said Monday night.

Jeremy Taypotat, 6, his cousin, Jeffrey Taypotat, 8, and neighbourhood friend, Chad Berger, 9, were burned after they slipped by a gate at a SaskPower transformer site, just east of the IMAX theatre, at about 7:30 p.m. Sunday.

The accident occurred near a 72 000-volt transformer after the boys slipped through a fence gate that was secured with a chain and padlock.

Vern Fowke, vice-president of corporate communications for SaskPower, said the public utility and police are still investigating, but it appears Jeremy Taypotat touched some wires after climbing a ladder on the transformer. The electricity was conducted through him, then burned the other boys.

As for how the boys entered the site, Fowke said the chain securing the gate wasn't padlocked as tightly as it normally is.

White said the boys have told their families the gap between the gate and fence was big enough for them to run through.

"This is what we believe," she said. "Children don't climb over barbed-wire fences . . ."

Fowke said the Crown corporation is currently reviewing safety procedures.

More chain and a second padlock have already been added to the fence the boys slipped through, he said. Fences around other switching stations will also be checked.

From: Kevin Blevins and Barb Pacholik, "Burn victim fights for life." *The Leader-Post*, March 24, 1992. Reprinted with permission of *The Leader Post*.

Something to Think About

- **What responsibility did SaskPower owe to others for safety at their transformer site?**
- **Were the boys in any way responsible for this accident? Why or why not?**
- **Was this accident preventable? Explain.**

11.1 INTRODUCTION

As you learned in Chapter 10, tort law deals with any injury or loss that one person causes another, and with providing compensation for victims. This chapter will examine the most common form of tort law before the courts today—the unintentional or unplanned tort of negligence.

Social changes, such as greater mobility and increased social interaction, have led to a large increase in negligence actions. Common examples include automobile accidents, medical malpractice, injuries suffered from defective products and by visitors to dangerous or unsafe premises, and injuries that occur while students are in school or are involved in school-related functions. Most daily activities must now conform to the guidelines established by the laws of negligence. This is the focus of this chapter.

11.2 THE ELEMENTS OF NEGLIGENCE

The concept of **negligence** is very simple. Anyone who creates an unreasonable risk and carelessly injures another person or a person's property should compensate the victim for that injury. A careless person will not be liable for negligence unless someone has actually been injured by his or her conduct. For instance, if Liam O'Reilly does not clear his slippery sidewalk after a winter storm, he will not be liable for negligence unless somebody actually falls and is injured. If someone does slip and fall, however, Liam would be held liable in any legal action that might occur.

The following elements must be established for a plaintiff in a negligence action to be successful.

Duty of Care

The first step in a negligence action is to establish that the defendant owed the plaintiff a **duty of care**. You have a duty of care to everyone with whom you come in contact on a daily basis to see that your actions do not cause harm to them or their property. This principle is central to the study of the laws governing negligence. Liam owed pedestrians a duty of care to keep his sidewalk clear of ice and safe for anyone walking by his home.

Duty of care between two parties was initiated in the 1930s by a landmark decision from the British House of Lords. In the historic Scottish case of *Donoghue v. Stevenson*, it was established that a manufacturer owes a duty of care to the buyer of a product and to most other persons who might be harmed as a result of that manufacturer's negligence. This duty of care gave rise to manufacturer's liability and marked the beginning of negligence law.

Even today, many lawyers claim this decision is the common law's best-known and most important precedent. Since the manufacturer has allowed harmful or defective products to be sold, it is only reasonable to hold it directly responsible for the safety of consumers. The manufacturer should be able to anticipate or foresee that its

CASE

Donoghue v. Stevenson
[1932]

**House of Lords
A.C. 562**

The plaintiff, May Donoghue, and a friend were in a shop in Paisley, Scotland. Donoghue's friend bought her a bottle of ginger beer and ice cream. The bottle was made of dark, opaque glass, obscuring the contents of the bottle. Donoghue drank one mouthful, then poured more ginger beer from the bottle into her glass, and discovered a decomposed snail at the bottom of the bottle. Donoghue became violently ill from the contaminated drink and ended up in hospital.

Donoghue brought an action against David Stevenson, the manufacturer of the drink. She claimed that Stevenson was negligent for not having a proper system of cleaning and inspecting bottles. Stevenson argued that no contact existed between him and Donoghue, because her friend had bought the drink for her. As a result, Stevenson claimed, Donoghue could not sue him or his firm. Nor could she sue the shopkeeper, because he had received the sealed bottle directly from the manufacturer and simply sold it to her friend.

Donoghue lost her case at trial, but appealed the decision. The British House of Lords reversed the trial judgment.

1. **Donoghue based her action on the manufacturer's negligence. How might she claim he was negligent?**

2. **Why did the manufacturer argue that he did not owe Donoghue any duty of care? Do you agree? Why or why not?**

3. **What responsibility does a manufacturer have to potential customers for the goods it produces?**

4. **Why was this decision such a landmark judgment?**

products will be used by people other than the actual purchasers. Thus, a general duty of care is owed to anyone who might come in contact with the product.

To avoid liability, the manufacturer must convince the court that reasonable precautions were taken during all production and inspection procedures to prevent defective goods from reaching the marketplace and causing harm. This decision has made it possible for today's consumers to succeed in tort actions against manufacturers of goods that are dangerous or hazardous or that could cause other kinds of harm. Anyone involved in producing consumer goods may be held liable for negligence if consumers are injured by their faulty products in the normal use of the product.

For example, because of a manufacturer's duty of care to consumers, a soft drink manufacturer would probably be held liable for injuries to customers injured from the company's bottles exploding on a store shelf. However, that duty of care does not extend to someone who uses that drink bottle to pound nails into a cupboard and has the bottle shatter and cause injury.

Standard of Care

Once a duty of care has been established between defendant and plaintiff, the court must determine the **standard of care**, that is, the degree of care society expects of the defendant. Normally, this is what is expected from all adults who are not physically or mentally challenged. However, the standard of care expected of someone who has expertise in a particular area would be greater than that expected from an average person. If the negligence involved an engineering accident, for example, the engineer would be held to have a higher standard of care than the worker who was simply following the engineer's blueprints.

A child cannot be expected to be as responsible or as careful as an adult; children and negligence will be discussed in greater depth later in this chapter.

Foreseeability

If the type of injury or loss suffered by the plaintiff could have reasonably been anticipated or expected to result from the defendant's action, then it was **foreseeable**. Defendants are not liable for their actions if the results are not reasonably foreseeable. In our example, Liam O'Reilly should definitely have foreseen that somebody might slip and fall and be injured because of the snow and ice on the sidewalk.

However, if the pedestrian who slipped on Liam's sidewalk broke a glass jar containing a toxic liquid that flowed into the nearby sewer and caused an explosion and neighbouring property damage, would that be considered foreseeable? Probably not, as this is not a normal consequence that could have been anticipated by Liam or anyone else as a result of not properly clearing a slippery sidewalk.

The Reasonable Person

Related to the concept of foreseeability is the principle of the **reasonable person**, a mythical person, whose conduct is the standard against which the actions of a negligent person are compared or measured. Such a person is careful, thoughtful, of normal intelligence, and considerate of other people in all dealings. The reasonable person is never expected to be perfect. Standards will change from place to place and over time. What is reasonable for a person in downtown Vancouver, for example, may not necessarily be reasonable for a person in Yellowknife in the Northwest Territories. Nor does the reasonable person standard of 50 years ago remain reasonable in today's busy and interactive society!

A person or company whose conduct falls below the reasonable standard of care expected is liable for the results of the negligence. This is the case even if the person was acting within the law. For example, a person who is driving too fast in a blinding snowstorm is not acting as a reasonable person, even if he or she is driving within the speed limit. Because the driver is in breach of the expected standard of care, he or she may be found liable if involved in an accident with any vehicle or pedestrian.

Foreseeability is a difficult standard to apply. The courts have tended to follow the principle that defendants should not be held responsible, even when they are the actual cause of injury, when the harmful results are not foreseeable. Tort liability is determined, to a large extent, by asking the question: "Would a reasonable person

CASE

**Plumb v.
Cowichan
School District
No. 65**
(1993)

**British Columbia
Court of Appeal
83 B.C.L.R. (2d) 161**

During a school lunch break, four grade nine students were playing catch with a hardball in front of their school. This game was a regular activity at the school. The boys threw the ball from one to the other while their friend, James Plumb, watched. Plumb had forgotten his glove that day and was lying with a friend on the grass nearby, not paying particular attention to the game of catch. The teacher on supervisory duty did not see the game as any hazard or risk. In fact, the principal and teacher had never heard of any serious injury occurring from this type of play.

One of the boys threw the ball wide, and the intended catcher missed it. The ball bounced on the grass and struck the plaintiff in the right eye, causing serious injury to his face and eye. At the time of the accident, none of the boys was acting in a foolish manner, and Plumb believed that he was a safe distance from the game.

The plaintiff, with his mother as a *guardian ad litem*, brought an action in negligence against the defendant school board, the supervising teacher, and the boy who threw the ball. At trial, the action was dismissed, and the plaintiff appealed to the Court of Appeal where his action was also dismissed.

1. **Was the student who threw the ball negligent? Why or why not?**

2. **In the trial judgment, the judge distinguished between "an activity which was potentially dangerous in which a *possibility* of harm was foreseeable and an inherently dangerous activity in which a *probability* of harm was foreseeable." What is the difference between these descriptions, and which one applied to this case?**

3. **Did the teacher on duty exercise a reasonable duty of care in allowing the students to play catch? Explain.**

4. **Was the plaintiff in any way responsible for his own accident?**

5. **Why did the Court of Appeal dismiss Plumb's appeal?**

in similar circumstances have foreseen the injury to the victim as a result of his or her action?" If the answer is "yes," fault and liability exist; if the answer is "no," there is no liability.

The nature of the standard of care principle gives courts considerable flexibility in interpreting what the parties should have done, given the circumstances, and what reasonable persons would have done in a similar situation. This flexibility allows courts to respond to social change and helps establish the rights of individuals in ordinary situations. In 1993, in what may have been the first case of its kind in Canada, an Ontario judge ruled that parents have a civil-law duty to protect their children from any type of harm, including sexual abuse.

Causation

Once the court has determined that the defendant has breached the required standard of care, the plaintiff must be able to prove that the defendant's negligent conduct was a cause of the plaintiff's injury or loss. There may be additional causes for the loss, but there must be a direct connection between the defendant's negligent act and the plaintiff's cause of action. This relationship is called **causation**; without it, no liability for negligence exists.

Consider Liam O'Reilly. Because there is a connection between the pedestrian's injury and O'Reilly's failure to clear the walk, he could be held liable. Once it has been established that the

The 20-year-old female plaintiff, L.A.J., brought an action against her mother and her father for negligence, and against her mother for breach of duty of care as a parent.

J. (L.A.) v. J. (H.)
(1993)

Ontario Court, General Division
16 C.C.L.T. (2d) 254

Evidence presented in court indicated that the father, H.J., started sexually molesting the plaintiff when she reached the age of 12. She was told that such activity was natural, and H.J. gave the girl money and gifts to obtain her cooperation and silence. When the mother caught her husband having sexual intercourse with their daughter, she accepted her husband's promise that it would never happen again because she feared losing him and his financial support.

Over the next six years, the abuse continued. At one point, the mother and daughter left home for a shelter for abused women. However, when the Children's Aid Society inquired about possible sexual abuse, the mother denied any problem.

At trial on the criminal charges, the defendant father assumed responsibility for his actions and characterized his wife as an unwitting victim of his misconduct. He was sentenced to a four-year prison sentence for the sexual assaults.

In a separate civil action, the plaintiff daughter was awarded $90 700 in general damages jointly from her mother and father, and an additional $45 000 in punitive damages against the mother alone.

1. **What duty of care did the mother owe to her daughter?**
2. **What choices were available to the mother when she discovered that the sexual abuse was occurring?**
3. **Why was the mother ordered to pay an additional $45 000 in punitive damages to her daughter? Do you agree with this?**
4. **Why was the father not ordered to pay punitive damages as the abuser?**
5. **What is the significance of this judgment concerning a parent's duty of care toward his or her children? Do you agree?**

defendant's action was a cause of the plaintiff's injury, the court must decide how direct a connection there was between the action and the injury. In our example, the connection is very direct. There is no doubt that O'Reilly's actions caused the injury to the pedestrian.

Now suppose that, as the pedestrian slips on the ice, Erika Richter is driving by and is startled to see the pedestrian falling toward her car. To avoid an accident, Richter swerves and loses control of her car on the slippery road. She hits a telephone pole, knocking out service to the subdivision and damaging her car. Because the telephone lines are out of order as a result of the accident, Penny Mitchell is unable to call an ambulance for her husband, who is having a heart attack. Since she cannot drive and is unable to get an ambulance, Mitchell's husband dies. Is O'Reilly responsible for this man's death, or for the damage to Richter's car?

To answer this question, the court must examine the connection between O'Reilly's actions and the various losses. Even if his negligence ultimately caused the damage to Richter's car and the death of Mitchell's husband, O'Reilly would not be held liable if the court decides that these losses are too far removed or remote to be recoverable in damages. Thus, causation depends on the facts of each case, judged on its own merits.

Bain v. Calgary Board of Education et al.
(1993)

Alberta Court of Queen's Bench
14 Alta. L.R. (3d) 319

The plaintiff, Kevin Bain, was a 19-year-old, grade 11 student at a vocational school for the learning disabled. Due in part to the efforts of the defendant teacher, Douglas Streibel, whom Bain admired as a father figure, Bain had good prospects of securing an apprentice position at a cabinet-making shop and becoming a journeyman cabinet maker after graduation. Because of Bain's special needs, his mother and teachers always monitored his activities closely, especially at the beginning of any new venture. For example, Bain's use of power tools was strictly supervised and controlled in his carpentry classes.

The defendant teacher took Bain and four other students on a school-sponsored forestry products tour in British Columbia. The school sent the parents a very detailed agenda and information package on the field trip, and Mrs. Bain signed her son's consent form. Instead of watching a movie about the area listed on the field trip agenda, the boys wanted to climb to the top of a nearby mountain. Initially, the teacher refused because he could not supervise the hike, and he was advised that it was a difficult hike. However, after continued pressure from the students, the teacher consented, "to save the trip from going sour," and dropped the boys off at the foot of this extremely steep mountain at 6:00 p.m., promising to return in three hours. The boys were dressed in shorts and sneakers, had not eaten supper, took nothing in the way of food, water, watches, or a flashlight, and the teacher was unaware of whether any of the boys had hiking experience.

There were no hiking trails so the students took the most direct, but very difficult and dangerous, route to the top. Part way up, two of the students recognized the danger, left the hike, and made their way back to safety. As the three remaining students attempted to climb a steep rock face, Bain fell off the cliff, head first onto a protruding rock and continued to roll down until he was stopped by a fallen tree. The other students carried and dragged the plaintiff down the mountain and sought help at a nearby house.

Bain was in a coma for several months and remained in hospital for almost one year. He sustained brain injury and could not read, and had poor speech, limited memory, and a functionally useless right arm. He required assistance with the basic tasks necessary for independent living and was unemployable.

Bain and his mother brought an action for negligence against the teacher and the school board and Kevin was awarded just over $3 million.

1. **Identify causation in this action.**

2. **What duty of care did the teacher owe to Bain and the other students?**

3. **Was the risk of harm to the students reasonably foreseeable? Explain.**

4. **List three things that a reasonable teacher could have done to avoid the accident.**

5. **How significant is the argument that it was an important part of the students' education "to turn them loose on the mountain"?**

Actual Loss

Finally, the plaintiff must be able to prove that he or she suffered some actual injury or loss as a result of the defendant's negligence. If nobody had been injured as a result of O'Reilly's actions, no loss would have been suffered by anyone, and no legal action would be successful against him.

The Burden of Proof

As you learned in Chapter 10, the burden of proof in a tort action rests with the plaintiff, who must prove all of the negligence elements on the balance of probabilities. If the evidence is evenly balanced between the plaintiff and the defendant at the end of the trial, the plaintiff will not succeed.

Sometimes, it may be difficult for a plaintiff to prove his or her case. Consider a train accident in which passengers are injured or killed. It is almost impossible for passengers to prove that the engineer did not exercise a proper duty of care or act as a reasonable person. Only the engineer may know the reason for the accident, although in some cases even he or she may not be able to explain the cause. Think, too, of the number of airplane tragedies for which there is no official explanation. Finally, consider a situation in which consumers become seriously ill as a result of consuming food or a beverage from a bottle. Did the manufacturer's conduct contribute to the illness, or was something deliberately added to the product after it had left the manufacturer's production line?

Passengers have the right to expect a safe trip, and consumers have the right to expect safe food and beverages. In all of these situations, therefore, the fact that an injury or loss occurred suggests possible negligence on the defendant's part. Travellers and consumers alike need only establish that the defendant's action caused the harm. The burden of proof then shifts to each defendant to prove that there was no negligence.

The legal principle here, *res ipsa loquitur* (the facts speak for themselves), first appeared in an old British case, *Byrne v. Boadle*, in 1863. In this case, the plaintiff was walking past the defendant's store when he was injured by a barrel of flour that fell from the defendant's upstairs window. The injured party sued the shopkeeper for his injuries, but he and his witnesses could not explain how the accident happened. The court ruled in the plaintiff's favour, since he was injured by the defendant's barrel of flour through no fault of his. It was reasonable to assume that the accident was probably caused by the defendant's or an employee's negligence. The barrel could not have fallen from the window without someone's negligence. The burden shifted to the defendant to disprove negligence. *Res ipsa loquitur* is applicable only where the facts of the accident are unknown.

Reviewing Your Reading

1. **What is negligence, and why is it the most common form of tort law?**
2. **List the key elements that a plaintiff must prove to succeed in a negligence action.**
3. **Why was the *Donoghue v. Stevenson* case judgment so important for today's consumers?**
4. **Explain the difference between a duty of care and a standard of care in a negligence action.**
5. **What is the connection between foreseeability and a reasonable person?**
6. **Why is proof of causation so important in a negligence action?**
7. **In a tort action, on whom does the burden of proof normally rest, and why?**
8. **What is the principle of *res ipsa loquitur*, and how does it shift the burden of proof in a negligence action?**

11.3 DEFENCES TO NEGLIGENCE

Various defences are available to persons being sued for negligence. The best defences are that negligence did not exist, or that the defendant did not owe the plaintiff any duty of care. But even a plaintiff who is able to prove that negligence exists may not be able to recover as much as expected. If the plaintiff has also been negligent in the incident or has assumed a risk voluntarily, then damages may be reduced or not awarded at all.

Contributory Negligence

At one time, under common law, a plaintiff found to be in any way at fault for an accident was denied the right to claim damages from the defendant. Society's attitude was that the law should not protect people who should have looked after their own safety better. However, such treatment seemed harsh for plaintiffs who were only slightly at fault for their loss or injury.

Today, if both the plaintiff and the defendant are negligent to some degree, damages are apportioned between them, according to the principle of **contributory negligence**. The court must determine which party was more negligent, or whether both parties were equally at fault. In making this decision, the judge must consider all the essential elements of negligence discussed earlier in this chapter. The burden is on the defendant to prove the plaintiff's contributory negligence. All provinces have a *Contributory Negligence Act* or a *Negligence Act* that determines fault in negligence actions. Fault is considered to lie mainly with the person who has the last clear chance to avoid the accident, even if that person did not cause the danger.

For instance, a motor vehicle accident results in damages of $80 000. The court finds the defendant 75 percent at fault for driving well above the speed limit through a red light. The plaintiff, however, is found 25 percent at fault for driving through the intersection on an amber light. As a result of this finding of contributory negligence, the plaintiff will receive $60 000 from the defendant. The plaintiff is liable for the remaining $20 000 and will not receive it.

Voluntary Assumption of Risk

For the defence of **voluntary assumption of risk** to succeed, the defendant must prove that the plaintiff clearly knew of the possible risk of his or her actions and made a choice to assume that risk. For example, a fan struck and injured by a baseball at a game will probably not succeed in an action against the player who hit the ball, because the fan should be aware of the possible risks of the game. On the other hand, if an angry player threw the bat or ball into the stands and injured a fan, the fan might well succeed in a legal action. In this case, injury does not arise from an ordinary risk of the game. Generally, possibility of risk is stated on the ticket. The ticket holder enters into a contract to attend the event and assumes this risk. If risk is not stated on the ticket, there is an implication that the person voluntarily assumes the risk merely by observing the activity.

Voluntary assumption of risk is also used as a defence in negligence actions brought by passengers injured while driving with impaired drivers. The burden of proof is on the defendant. The court assumes that a plaintiff who gets into a car knowing that the driver is drunk voluntarily assumes a risk if an injury occurs. The plaintiff will therefore receive reduced damages.

Inevitable Accident

Injury or loss may result from a situation that is unavoidable, no matter what precautions the reasonable person would have taken under the circumstances. If lightning strikes a moving car, causing the driver to lose control and to collide with oncoming traffic, the driver would not likely be held liable, since he or she could not foresee such an occurrence and could not prevent it anyway. This is an inevitable accident.

The plaintiff, Margaret Temple, was a catcher participating in a game in a mixed softball league with its own unique rules. The rules, drawn up with the intent to avoid injuries, stated that "sliding is allowed." Another rule stated that "runners blocked or interfered with in trying to reach a base or home plate will automatically be awarded the base they were trying to reach." During the game the defendant, Thomas Hallem, in an attempt to reach home plate by sliding, collided with the plaintiff who tagged him out. Temple was knocked backward about 1.5 m and was injured, but not seriously.

She brought a claim for damages against Hallem for her personal injuries and was awarded $8000 at trial. The defendant appealed to the Court of Appeal where, in a unanimous decision, the appeal was allowed and the trial judge's decision was overturned. Leave to appeal to the Supreme Court of Canada was refused without reasons in February 1990.

Temple v. Hallem
(1989)

**Manitoba Court of Appeal
58 D.L.R. (4th) 541**

1. **Why did the plaintiff claim the defendant was negligent?**
2. **Why did the trial judge award damages to the plaintiff?**
3. **What defence would be argued by Hallem?**
4. **Were Hallem's actions a deliberate violation of the league's rules? Explain.**
5. **Why did the Court of Appeal find the defendant not liable?**

Reviewing Your Reading

1. **What is the best defence in a negligence action?**
2. **Define contributory negligence, using an original example.**
3. **What is voluntary assumption of risk?**
4. **List the two factors that the defendant must prove for the defence of voluntary assumption of risk.**
5. **Give two examples of situations involving an inevitable accident.**

11.4 CHILDREN AND NEGLIGENCE

You learned in Chapter 9 that, because of the *Young Offenders Act*, children under the age of 12 cannot be charged with a criminal offence. If a child under 12 injures someone or damages another person's property, can the victim sue the child for compensation? In fact, the law makes it possible for the child, or the child's parents or guardians, to be held liable in certain circumstances. However, there is no legislation that clearly outlines the tort liability of children. Legal principles in this area have developed through common-law tradition. Each case is judged on its own facts, and the court must decide liability on the merits of each case and the child's background.

A child under the age of six or seven is seldom held liable for negligence. Children below this age not only don't usually realize what they have done, but they also can't understand the consequences of their actions. In any incident involving an older child, the courts will consider what a child of similar age, experience, and intelligence might have done. Children must provide the duty of care expected from reasonable children of a similar age. In general, a lower standard of care is expected from children than from adults.

CASE

Floyd et al. v. Bowers et al.
(1979)

Ontario Court of Appeal
106 D.L.R. (3d) 702

Stephen Bowers and Michael Floyd, both 13 years old, were playing at the Bowers' summer cottage at Wasaga Beach. When an argument developed between them, Bowers fetched a pump-action pellet gun and began firing at the plaintiff. One shot hit the plaintiff in the right eye. At the time of the accident, Bowers' parents were visiting neighbours who lived nearby.

Mr. Bowers had bought the gun a year earlier, and he and his son used it together for target practice. Stephen had been given no instruction on the proper handling of the gun, and his father had no knowledge of guns. Although the Bowers had laid down the rule that Stephen could use the gun only under proper supervision, the gun and ammunition were not locked up, and Stephen knew where they were. The Bowers knew that Stephen was an aggressive youth, inclined to tease and sometimes bully other children.

The shooting was especially unfortunate, since Michael Floyd had had poor vision in the left eye before losing the right eye. He could just distinguish between light and dark and would be unable to drive a car. His reading would be limited, and his athletic and social activities reduced. At the time of the accident, Michael was in grade nine, where he showed interest and ability in working with mechanical devices. Job evaluation experts testified that he might find employment as a machine operator, in automotive work, or in drafting. Retail sales was another possibility. However, there was no doubt that his earning capacity would be reduced by at least 25 percent as a result of the shooting. He was expected to work for about 44 years before reaching retirement age of 65, earning from $200 to $300 a week.

Floyd took action against Bowers in the Supreme Court of Ontario, Trial Division, and succeeded in his action. He was awarded $50 000 in pecuniary damages for loss of earning capacity, $30 000 in non-pecuniary damages for loss of sight in one eye, and $1973.99 in special damages. This total was rounded off to $80 000.

The Bowers appealed this decision for damages holding them responsible for their son's action, while the Floyds cross-appealed the amount of damages. The Ontario Court of Appeal dismissed the Bowers' appeal and allowed the Floyds' cross-appeal for damages, even if an average victim would not have been so affected. In a 3–0 judgment, the court ruled that Michael Floyd's employment prospects had been reduced by 50 percent, not 25 percent, and that the loss of the eye was more serious than originally assumed. The court increased the award from $80 000 to $150 000: $100 000 in pecuniary damages and $50 000 in non-pecuniary damages.

1. **Why were Stephen's parents found to be at fault for this accident even though they were not present?**

2. **Why did the Court of Appeal double the amount of Michael Floyd's pecuniary damages? Do you agree with this judgment?**

3. **What kinds of problems and frustrations would Floyd experience that caused the Court of Appeal judges to increase his non-pecuniary damages?**

4. **What does the Court of Appeal decision state about parental responsibility for the storage of weapons?**

Parental Liability

Parents are not automatically liable for their children's torts simply because they are parents. However, parents have a duty of care toward persons with whom they and their children come in contact to prevent the children from causing harm or loss to those persons. The standard of care required of parents is that of "a reasonably prudent parent in the particular community." Parents living in large cities or on busy streets must exercise a different standard of care from parents in a small town or rural area. The main responsibility for children's safety lies with their parents. If the parents do not meet this standard, they have breached their duty of care and may be held liable for damages.

Parents are liable for accidents caused by their child driving the family car, snowmobile, or powerboat, or engaging in some other dangerous activity. This is known as the principle of **vicarious liability**, the responsibility in law of one person for another person's actions. When children participate in adult activities such as these, the courts expect from them a standard of care similar to that of a reasonable adult. The potential danger from the activity makes it unfair to society to apply a lower standard of care.

Parents may also be found liable if it can be shown that they were negligent in the supervising of their child, or if they had instructed the child to commit a wrong. The liability of a child who continually plays with matches will be transferred to the parents, for example, since they should have taken the matches away and cautioned their child about the dangers. Also, parents with guns in their homes must exert an extraordinary duty of care in locking up the weapons and instructing their children in the proper and safe use of the guns under supervision. The *Floyd v. Bowers* case on p. 300 is still a classic judgment in Canada regarding parental duty of care for guns in the home.

Parents can protect themselves and their children against possible liability by purchasing insurance. Most homeowners' policies contain provisions protecting parents and children against legal actions arising from their negligent acts.

The *Floyd v. Bowers* case on p. 300

Reviewing Your Reading

1. **Distinguish between the tort liability for children under six or seven and older children.**

2. **List two situations in which parents may be held liable for their children's torts.**

3. **When is a higher than reasonable standard of care required of children?**

4. **What standard of care is required of parents for their children?**

5. **How can parents protect themselves and their children against possible tort liability?**

11.5 *Motor Vehicle Negligence*

Motor vehicle accidents are one of the leading causes of both criminal and civil cases. Each province has a *Highway Traffic Act* or *Motor Vehicle Act* that outlines the regulations to be observed by drivers. The regulations cover everything from speed limits to mandatory seat belt laws. Motor vehicle accidents generally result from breaches of the duty of care set out in the regulations. Provincial traffic legislation is given very serious consideration by the courts in determining liability. The violation of any section of an *Act* usually suggests driver negligence.

You have seen that the burden of proof usually rests on the plaintiff in a negligence action. However, this burden has been shifted by statute to the defendant in some motor vehicle cases. Once a plaintiff proves that he or she was struck by another vehicle, the burden of proof shifts to the defendant to prove to the court that any loss or injury did not result from the defendant's negligence.

If there is evidence that both drivers are responsible for an accident to some extent, liability will be split between them unless one party can prove otherwise. Thus, motor vehicle accidents often involve contributory negligence.

Liability for Passengers

The driver of a motor vehicle is liable for the safety of passengers. However, a passenger who accepts a ride with an intoxicated driver, or with a driver who engages in dangerous activities such as excessive speeding, is presumed to have accepted the risk by voluntarily riding in the vehicle. Drivers often use voluntary assumption of risk as a defence in negligence actions brought by passengers injured under such circumstances. The burden is on the defendant to prove that the plaintiff knew about and appreciated the risk involved and willingly assumed it. If the defendant can prove this, the plaintiff will receive reduced damages.

If, however, the plaintiff is unaware of any danger, there is no voluntary assumption of risk. Suppose, for instance, that Melanie accepts a ride from Calvin, without knowing that his car has faulty brakes. If Calvin has an accident as a result of the faulty brakes and Melanie is injured, he cannot argue voluntary assumption of risk as a defence, since Melanie did not know about the problem.

The motorcyclist who fails to wear the required safety helmet will be held contributorily negligent in any accident.

Vicarious Liability

Holding a blameless person responsible for the misconduct of another is the principle of vicarious liability in tort law. Applications of this principle were mentioned earlier in section 11.4 on children and negligence. Vicarious liability with regard to motor vehicle negligence is based on the assumption that owners of vehicles have a duty of care to society to lend their vehicles only to individuals who are competent to drive them safely. It is clearly intended to encourage owners to be careful when lending their vehicles.

Provincial statutes place liability on both the driver of a vehicle and the owner. The owner is liable for the negligence of any driver when the vehicle is being used with the owner's permission. Even if the owner was not driving or was not present when an accident occurred, both parties are held responsible for any negligence. However, if the owner can prove that the vehicle was stolen and that the person driving it did not have permission to use the vehicle, the owner may avoid liability.

The concept of vicarious liability also extends into the workplace as employers are personally liable for torts committed by their employees during working hours. Although this may not seem reasonable or fair, there are two main reasons for this principle. First, employers usually

CASE

The plaintiff, Virginia Jones, had spent St. Patrick's Day in 1987 drinking with four friends at one of their homes and later at a bar. Upon leaving the bar, the group of five decided to travel to another friend's home and decided that, as Wayne Klopp, one of the defendants, was the most sober among them, he should drive. The vehicle was a small, deteriorating, 1973 pickup that he had never driven before, and his experience with manual transmissions was occasional.

The plaintiff and two others sat in the open box of the truck for the ride, while the defendant driver and Harley Green, the owner of the truck, sat in the cab. The route Klopp took was familiar to him, but he noted that the truck seemed to "shimmy" as it drove, it "cornered strangely," and it "was rocking and the wheels lifted." He testified that he drove more slowly as a result, but he did not recall the actual speed at which he was driving. As the truck rounded a corner travelling nearly 65 km/h in a 50-km zone, the rear of the truck slipped, and Klopp reacted either by freezing at the wheel or oversteering. The truck overturned, throwing the plaintiff from the box and rendering her a paraplegic.

At trial in the Alberta Court of Queen's Bench in 1993, the plaintiff's action was dismissed. The trial judge found that, under the circumstances, the defendant driver's actions did not constitute gross negligence. Jones appealed this decision to the Alberta Court of Appeal where her appeal was allowed. In a 3–0 judgment, the court found both Klopp and Green at fault and sent the case back to the trial judge for assessment of damages.

Jones v. Green et al.
(1994)

Alberta Court of Appeal
26 Alta. L.R. (3d) 268

1. **Why did the trial judge dismiss the plaintiff's claim?**
2. **Did Klopp exercise the standard of care required from a prudent driver? Explain.**
3. **Why did the Court of Appeal find Klopp partly liable for this accident?**
4. **Why was Harley Green also held liable for this accident?**
5. **With which court decision do you agree, and why?**

Galaske v. O'Donnell et al.
(1994)

Supreme Court of Canada
89 B.C.L.R. (2d) 273

In August 1985, the eight-year-old plaintiff, Karl Galaske, and his father, Peter, were riding as passengers in a pickup owned and driven by one of the defendants, Erich Stauffer, a close family friend. Karl sat in the middle between his father and Erich Stauffer.

Although the truck was fitted with seat belts, none of the occupants was wearing one. Stauffer testified that he would have insisted that Karl wear his seat belt if the boy had been in the truck alone with him. However, he didn't do this because he did not want to take the "fathership" away from his friend, Peter Galaske, whom he felt was responsible for his son's conduct. Stauffer was aware of the importance of seat belts as a safety factor, having been warned and ticketed on three occasions for failing to wear his belt. British Columbia's *Motor Vehicle Act* states that a driver *shall not* drive unless children under age 16 wear their seat belts.

While driving by a dangerous intersection, Stauffer's truck was hit by another vehicle, driven by the defendant Columcille O'Donnell. The Galaskes were thrown from the truck. The father was killed and Karl was rendered a paraplegic.

The plaintiff and his *guardian ad litem* brought a negligence action for damages for personal injuries against the defendants O'Donnell and Stauffer to the Supreme Court of British Columbia. Although the trial judge found that the Galaskes would not have suffered any serious injuries if they had been wearing their seat belts, he ruled that it was reasonable to expect Karl's father to ensure that his son wore his seat belt. Finding that the accident was caused solely by O'Donnell's negligence, the judge held that Stauffer was not negligent. A 1992 decision from the B.C. Court of Appeal agreed with the conclusions of the trial judge.

The plaintiff appealed this decision to the Supreme Court of Canada where a 5–2 decision, released in April 1994, ruled that Stauffer shared some liability. The case was referred back to the trial judge to determine the degree of contributory negligence of Stauffer and Karl and Peter Galaske.

1. **Why did the trial judge and the Court of Appeal rule that Stauffer had no liability for this accident?**

2. **Do you agree with this decision? Why or why not?**

3. **Did a duty of care exist between Erich Stauffer and Karl Galaske? Explain.**

4. **Did the presence of Peter Galaske relieve Erich Stauffer of any responsibility? Explain.**

5. **Why did a majority of the Supreme Court of Canada find Stauffer contributorily negligent?**

6. **Why do you think two judges wrote a dissenting judgment?**

have significant amounts of liability insurance to compensate victims for injury or loss, while employees have limited resources or insurance available. Second, society believes that the person who hires the employees and makes the profit should also be liable for the actions of their employees. Thus, although employees remain personally liable for their torts, their employers may also be sued because of vicarious liability.

Seat Belts and Negligence

When worn properly, seat belts reduce the severity of injuries from motor vehicle accidents. They can even prevent a person from being thrown from a vehicle and killed. It is true that belts sometimes injure the ribs and abdomen, or trap people in burning or submerged cars. However, most studies conclude that the benefits far outweigh the disadvantages and that wearing seat belts gives more protection to the public. All provinces and the territories now have seat belt laws that require both drivers and passengers, with few exceptions, to wear seat belts while a car is being driven. In fact, highway traffic statutes require that drivers have a specific duty of care to ensure that passengers in their vehicles, especially passengers under 16 years of age, wear seat belts.

Drivers or passengers who fail to wear seat belts are not acting as reasonable persons as it is foreseeable that injury may result from the failure to wear them. There is an increasing body of case law in which judges have ruled that contributory negligence exists when a person fails to "buckle up." Generally, damages are being reduced by 15 to 40 percent for those failing to wear a seat belt, even when an accident is totally the other driver's fault. A few judgments have reduced damages by up to 75 percent for a plaintiff's failure to wear a seat belt.

Reviewing Your Reading

1. How can someone who is driving a car within the legal speed limit possibly be found negligent?

2. Discuss with a partner the burden of proof that exists in motor vehicle cases.

3. Define "vicarious liability," and describe its connection to tort law.

4. List two reasons why the law holds employers responsible for their employees' actions at work.

5. What trends have appeared in judges' rulings regarding car occupants who fail to wear seat belts?

11.6 PROFESSIONAL NEGLIGENCE

Tort law has changed in recent years related to our dealings with professionals, what we can expect of them, and what we can do if they provide an unacceptable level of service. Professionals include doctors, dentists, engineers, architects, accountants, and lawyers, among others. These experts in their fields have specialized knowledge and skills on which their patients and clients depend.

As mentioned earlier, professionals must exercise a standard of care that the profession requires of its members. This does not mean that these professionals are perfect and never make mistakes. It does mean, however, that a professional's actions will be compared with the standards of members of the profession who have the same rank, qualifications, and skills. The more specialized and qualified the person, the higher the standard of care the law and society expects. For example, a heart surgeon will be held to a higher standard of care than a family doctor in dealings with patients.

To protect themselves against possible legal actions for negligence, most professionals purchase liability insurance. Although actions have occurred against many types of professionals, the largest body of case law and precedent has developed around the area of medical negligence.

Medical Negligence

Cases involving medical negligence focus on the doctor's duty of care to the patient and on whether an adequate standard of care has been met. Surgery of any type involves a risk, and things can go wrong. Even surgery that has been performed with the greatest duty of care may result in new problems. For example, the patient may not respond as expected and may be worse,

⚖️

CASE

Reibl v. Hughes
(1980)

Supreme Court
of Canada
114 D.L.R. (3d) 1

In 1970, the plaintiff, Edward Reibl, then 44 years of age, was told by his doctor, Robert Hughes, that the cause of his high blood pressure and headaches was a partially plugged artery in his neck. The artery allowed only 10 to 15 percent of the blood to get through to the brain. The doctor indicated that this problem posed a 10 percent risk of causing a stroke each year it remained untreated, and advised his patient to have surgery. However, Hughes had failed to tell Reibl that the surgery carried a 4 percent risk of death and a 10 percent risk of stroke either during the operation or soon after surgery.

Reibl accepted the doctor's advice and consented to having the operation done right away, although he had the impression that there was no rush. The surgery could have been delayed until after Reibl's retirement pension income was assured, 18 months later. Although the doctor performed the operation with proper care and competence, Reibl suffered a massive stroke soon afterward and was left with a paralyzed right arm and a lame leg. Because of his paralysis, Reibl could no longer continue in his job and was ineligible for certain disability benefits from his employer.

Reibl took legal action in the Supreme Court of Ontario in 1977. The trial judge found the defendant surgeon liable, awarding Reibl damages of $225 000. Hughes appealed this decision to the Ontario Court of Appeal, where a 2–1 decision ordered a new trial. This decision was appealed to the Supreme Court of Canada where, in a unanimous decision, the trial judgment was restored.

1. **Why did the courts find the defendant doctor at fault?**
2. **Did the patient give informed consent? Explain.**
3. **What do you think a reasonable person in Reibl's position would have decided if all of the risks had been fully explained?**
4. **What is the significance of the Supreme Court of Canada decision?**
5. **The Supreme Court judgment stated: "Even if a certain risk is only a mere possibility that ordinarily need not be disclosed, if its occurrence carries serious consequences it should be regarded as a material risk and the patient informed of it." Do you agree or disagree with this statement?**

rather than better, after surgery. A doctor who agrees to provide any medical service has a duty of care and must meet a reasonable standard of care and skill. Negligence occurs if the doctor fails to meet this standard. If loss or injury results, the doctor will likely be held responsible. If, however, the patient cannot prove negligence, no damages for injuries will be awarded, even if the harm is serious and permanent.

A doctor must also inform patients of any risks related to the proposed treatment of which the doctor is aware or ought to be aware. Notice the wording "ought to be aware." It places a very high duty of care on doctors to be familiar with all aspects of a treatment. Patients who are to undergo treatment have the right to know the truth about their medical condition, what choices are available to them, and the possible risks involved in order to make intelligent decisions about whether or not to accept or reject a medical procedure.

Since the 1980 landmark Supreme Court of Canada judgment in the case of *Reibl v. Hughes*, a doctor must fully disclose any significant or **material risks** involved in the proposed treatment.

Doctors must inform patients of known side effects, length of recovery time, recovery rates, and what life will be like after surgery. The patient has to be sufficiently informed about all risks to make a reasoned decision about whether or not to submit to the treatment. In legal terms, the patient must give **informed consent** to the doctor for the proposed treatment.

If the patient is not provided with sufficient facts to give informed consent, the doctor may be liable for negligence and even assault and battery. Negligence may exist if the doctor did not fully inform the patient about the risks involved. Battery may exist if the doctor treated the patient without any consent at all, or treatment went beyond that to which consent was given. Medical assault and battery will be examined in Chapter 12. Both torts, however, are breaches of a doctor's duty of care to a patient. In determining whether a tort has been committed, the courts must answer this question: Would a reasonable patient, after receiving full disclosure of the risks, have decided against the treatment? If the answer to the question is "yes," then the physician has been negligent.

Reviewing Your Reading

1. **Identify five types of professionals, and give an example of negligence for each.**
2. **What duties do doctors owe their patients?**
3. **Define "informed consent." What does it involve?**
4. **Distinguish between medical negligence and medical assault and battery.**

11.7 OCCUPIERS' LIABILITY

Occupiers' liability is an area of negligence law that covers the responsibility of occupiers toward persons who come onto the property and might be injured. An **occupier** is any person who has supervision and control over the property on which an injury occurs and includes both property owners and persons renting a house, an apartment, or other dwelling. Courts have determined that an occupier, as a reasonable person, should foresee that some harm may come to persons entering his or her premises. Occupiers owe a certain duty of care to others to prevent them from suffering that harm. Thus, occupiers are responsible for keeping their sidewalks and steps reasonably free of snow and ice. Store owners are responsible for keeping their floors reasonably dry and free of obstructions that could cause customers to slip or fall and injure themselves. Also, clear glass panels and doors should be clearly identified.

To establish the standard of care and the occupier's liability if injury occurs, the common law establishes three categories of persons who may enter another's land: invitees, licensees, and trespassers.

General Invitees

The highest standard of care is owed to an **invitee**, any person on the premises for a purpose other than a social visit. Invitees include students attending school, store customers, theatre patrons, persons making deliveries, and service personnel coming to make repairs. An occupier has a duty to use reasonable care to protect invitees from unusual dangers that the occupier knows about or ought to know about; in other words, known and unknown dangers. Notice the significance of the wording "ought to know" and the high duty of care on occupiers to be fully aware of the condition of their property at all times.

This high standard of care is placed on invitees in the belief that an occupier and an invitee will likely do business, so that each may obtain some material benefit from their meeting. For instance, a retail store obtains money from a customer, who in turn receives goods or services from the store. Likewise, a student receives benefit from attendance at school and so must be given the highest standard of care.

Commercial and Social Host Invitees

Under common law, the relationship between restaurant and bar owners and their customers is that of inviters/invitees. Owners of such premises have a duty of care to protect their patrons and others from harm when patrons who have been drinking leave the premises.

Courts have recognized that people who drink do not consider the duty of care for their own safety, let alone anyone else's safety. Bar and tavern

CASE

**Hague v.
Billings**
(1993)

**Ontario Court
of Appeal
15 C.C.L.T. (2d) 264**

Three young men, including the defendant, Kevin Billings, set out in Billings' car in the late morning for a bout of heavy drinking and marijuana smoking while driving in the Haliburton area. By late afternoon, they had consumed about 50 bottles of beer and a bottle of rye. About 7:15 p.m., they arrived rowdy, loud, and severely intoxicated at the Oasis Tavern in Bancroft, Ontario. The tavern staff served them one beer each but refused to serve or sell them more because of obvious signs of intoxication. As the men were leaving, the tavern owner tried unsuccessfully to persuade Billings to let one of his friends drive.

About 9:00 p.m., they arrived at the Ship and Shore Tavern in Lakefield, south of Bancroft. The place was crowded and the staff did not notice how drunk the men were. Over 90 minutes they were served four more beers each. They left about 10:30 p.m., heading south toward Peterborough. Billings' driving was so erratic that his two friends insisted he stop the car and let them out. Minutes later, Billings drove his car across the centre line of the highway into a head-on collision with a vehicle in which Jacqueline Hague and her 14-year-old twin daughters, Melissa and Jennifer, were travelling. Mrs. Hague was killed and her daughters were injured. Melissa was confined to a wheelchair for life as a paraplegic.

Breathalyzer tests taken after the accident showed blood-alcohol readings for Billings of .288, over three times the legal limit. He was convicted of criminal negligence causing death and sentenced to 30 months in prison. In a companion civil action, the Hague family brought action against Billings, the tavern, and the hotel for negligence. Billings admitted liability, and damages of $1.89 million were agreed upon to be shared equally between Billings and the Ship and Shore Hotel. The Oasis Tavern was not held liable.

The hotel appealed the finding of liability, believing that Billings was much more responsible for the accident. In a 3–0 decision, the Ontario Court of Appeal reduced the hotel's liability from 50 to 15 percent, fixing the remaining 85 percent liability on Billings.

1. **Using the concepts of foreseeability, causation, and a reasonable person, explain why Kevin Billings was found to be primarily liable.**

2. **Using the concepts of duty of care and foreseeability, explain why the Ship and Shore Hotel was found to be somewhat liable.**

3. **Although the Oasis Tavern was not held liable, the trial judge criticized the staff for not exercising a proper duty of care and for not taking "affirmative action to prevent intoxicated persons from driving on a highway." What positive steps could, or should, the Oasis staff have taken regarding Billings?**

4. **In his trial judgment, Mr. Justice Grainger bluntly stated: "If tavern owners are allowed to sell intoxicating beverages, they must accept as a price of doing business a duty to attempt to keep the highways free of drunk drivers." Defend or refute this position with appropriate arguments.**

5. **Calculate the actual dollar liability owed by the defendants to the Hague family. What problem might occur for Kevin Billings in the payment of his share of fault?**

6. **Do you agree with the Court of Appeal's judgment? Why or why not?**

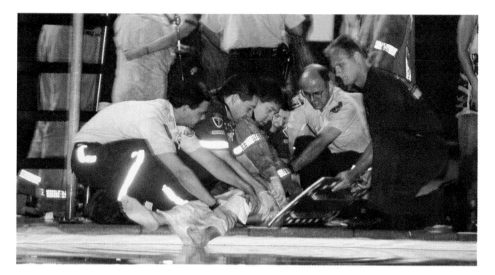

Rescue workers place Justin Boggs on a stretcher. Boggs, a 19-year-old, dove into a public outdoor pool at 3:30 a.m., hitting his head on the bottom. He and his friends gained access by climbing a 2.5-m fence around the pool.

employees must be aware of how intoxicated their patrons are and take positive steps to prevent such customers from driving. This may involve refusing to bring any more drinks, calling a taxi for the customer, or even calling the police, if necessary. These principles are illustrated in the *Hague v. Billings* case and were extended even further by a 1995, 7–0 judgment from the Supreme Court of Canada in *Stewart v. Hattie.* (See p. 317.) Restaurant and bar owners now have a clear and specific duty of care and must take positive steps to prevent intoxicated customers from driving, or they will be held liable for injuries to third parties who are hurt by drunken customers.

Licensees

A **licensee** is a person who enters property with the implied permission of the occupier; an example is a friend invited for dinner. A licensee is a guest at the occupier's premises and is usually there for a social, not a business, reason. The occupier is required to warn the licensee of any known concealed or unusual dangers. No liability exists for hazards unknown to the occupier. This is a lesser standard of care than that required for invitees, since no economic benefit is expected to be exchanged between the parties.

At times, however, it is difficult to determine whether a person is an invitee or a licensee.

Which of the two is a business associate who has been invited to dinner? Since an economic benefit will be derived if a successful business transaction is settled during dinner, it might be argued that the dinner guest is an invitee. On the other hand, the guest is coming to dinner at the occupier's invitation, and the meal is a social occasion. Recent court decisions have classed social guests as licensees, without any concern given to the reason for the dinner invitation.

Trespassers

A **trespasser** is a person who enters another person's property without permission or without a legal right to be there and would include anyone from a burglar to a wandering child. Guests who overstay their welcome may also be trespassers. Occupiers cannot set traps or cause deliberate harm to trespassers. This includes protection against an occupier firing a gun in the general direction where a trespasser is thought to be.

In fact, once occupiers are aware of a trespasser on the premises, they must exercise a reasonable standard of care and warn of unusual dangers of which they are aware. Even for trespassers, occupiers owe a duty of common humanity to act with at least a minimal degree of respect for the safety of all others who come onto the property.

**Galts v. Ultra
Care Inc. et al.**
(1995)

**Manitoba Court
of Appeal
100 Man. R. (2d) 19**

The plaintiff, Catherine Galts, was a customer at the skin care salon operated by the defendants, Ultra Care Inc. in Winnipeg. She had gone to the defendant's premises for a facial and brow wax. A trained aesthetician employed by the defendants gave the plaintiff a facial in one of the treatment rooms. As the plaintiff was short, just under five feet tall, she asked the defendant's employee to "give her a hand up" onto the cosmetic chair in the facial room.

When they moved to the brow waxing room, the defendant's employee left the room briefly during which time the plaintiff tried to lift herself onto the chair in the second room. The chair collapsed, resulting in Galts falling to the floor and injuring her tailbone. She suffered constant pain and tenderness in this area which made it difficult to do housework or participate in sports.

She brought an action for personal damages for these injuries to the Manitoba Court of Queen's Bench and was awarded about $15 000 in general damages. The defendant appealed the finding of liability and the award of damages, while the plaintiff cross-appealed the award of general damages to the Manitoba Court of Appeal. The Court of Appeal allowed the appeal and dismissed the plaintiff's claim in a 3–0 judgment.

1. **Under the three common-law categories of persons on another person's property, which one would the plaintiff be, and why?**
2. **Under Manitoba's *Occupiers' Liability Act*, what duty of care did the defendant owe to the plaintiff in this action?**
3. **Was an adequate standard of care provided by the defendant and its employees? Explain.**
4. **On the balance of probabilities and the facts provided, with which judgment do you agree, and why?**

Trespassing Children

Trespassing children are recognized as having special rights because of their age. If trespassing children are lured or attracted onto property because of some item of attraction, such as a swimming pool, they are often considered as licensees in such situations. What is considered an **allurement** varies from case to case. However, an occupier must be able to show that all reasonable precautions have been taken to prevent any accident which could reasonably have been foreseen as arising from a possible allurement.

Legislators have accepted many items as being naturally attractive to children. As a result, there are laws requiring the owners of such allurements to take specific precautions to protect children.

For instance, municipalities must erect fences of a certain height around swimming pools and construction sites, and other dangerous premises must be marked and barricaded.

Occupiers' Liability Act

You have read that the courts sometimes have difficulty determining whether a plaintiff is an invitee or licensee. The common-law distinction between these two categories was abolished in England in 1957 in an *Occupiers' Liability Act*, simply referring to both groups as visitors to the property.

In 1973, Alberta was the first Canadian province to introduce legislation patterned on the

British statute. Similar legislation has since been passed in British Columbia (1974), Ontario (1980), Manitoba (1983), and Prince Edward Island (1984). In Ontario, the *Trespass to Property Act* accompanied the *Occupiers' Liability Act* in 1980. The other provinces and the territories retain the three common-law categories, although most are reviewing this issue.

These *Occupiers' Liability Acts* eliminated the difference between invitees and licensees, and extended the higher duty of care owed to invitees to licensees as well. Thus, occupiers have a duty of care to ensure that all visitors with a right to be on the property will be reasonably safe. Also, occupiers do not owe a duty of care to trespassers, who are considered to assume their own risks. The intent of this provision is to give occupiers less responsibility to anyone who comes onto their property without their permission.

The statutes also require every visitor to act in a reasonable manner when warned of a particular danger or hazard, or contributory negligence might exist if the visitor is injured. For example, if you ignore the "Caution: Wet Floor" signs in your local shopping centre and don't act in a reasonable manner when crossing the floor, you may not be able to recover damages for any injury you suffer if you fall.

Reviewing Your Reading

1. Who are occupiers, and why are they responsible for persons entering their premises?

2. Name the three common-law categories of persons who enter another's property, and outline the duty of care occupiers owe to persons in each category.

3. Give one original example of an allurement.

4. What are occupiers required to do to prevent children from being injured by allurements?

5. How does some provincial legislation on occupiers' liability amend the common law?

6. In this legislation, what duty of care do occupiers owe to persons entering their property?

Contaminated Blood: Who has the duty of care?

The body's immune system is unable to resist serious infection when it is attacked by Acquired Immune Deficiency Syndrome (AIDS). The disease is characterized by severe weight loss, fatigue, and, frequent neurological complications. AIDS was first identified in North America in 1983, and it has spread at an alarming rate. Contracting the disease means eventual death.

The disease is caused by a virus called Human Immunodeficiency Virus (HIV). This virus is spread by intimate sexual contact, sharing of blood-contaminated needles, by infected mothers to babies in the uterus or perhaps through their milk, and by transfusions of contaminated blood. People cannot be infected by casual contact.

AIDS has raised many issues—both ethical and legal. In the early 1980s, the Laboratory Centre for Disease Control in Ottawa was ill-prepared for the onslaught of AIDS. The facility was understaffed and operated on a budget of $20 000. Yet, the staff of two was expected to test thousands of blood samples which would have cost hundreds of thousands of dollars.

The work of the lab was vital to physicians and hospitals across the country. However, requests for additional funding and staff went unheeded by Health and Welfare Canada despite warnings that the virus had been detected in the spouses of hemophiliacs.

In Canada, the AIDS question came under intense scrutiny between 1993 and 1996 with a blood inquiry headed by Mr. Justice Horace Krever. The mandate of the Krever inquiry was to find out how and why about 1400 Canadians, the majority of them hemophiliacs, were infected with the virus causing AIDS between 1978 and 1987. During the same time, an estimated 12 000 people were also infected with the hepatitis C virus through contaminated blood and blood products. The inquiry raised a number of issues, but the most important was: who had the duty of care to the recipients of the blood?

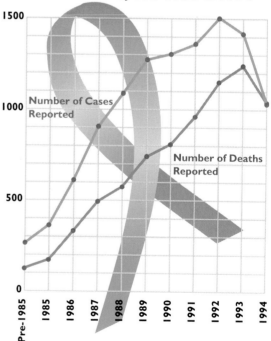

AIDS Cases Reported and Number of Deaths in Canada, Pre–1985 to 1994

On One Side

In 1985, Dr. Albert Prince of the New York Blood Center reported to Armour Pharmaceuticals, a U.S. firm, that its heating treatment process was not killing the deadly AIDS virus. Armour ordered Dr. Prince to keep silent about his findings. Later, in the Krever inquiry, Armour admitted that further studies were warranted, but that such research could not be completed in time to meet existing and forthcoming contracts.

In 1986, the Canadian Red Cross contracted with Armour to purchase 12 million units of Factorate, a blood product. The Factorate was administered to hemophiliacs who require blood replacement therapy.

In May 1987, Dr. Prince published his results in a medical journal. Armour continued to sell its blood and blood products to the Canadian market until December 1987.

On the Other Side

In October 1986, Factorate was no longer sold in the United Kingdom after it was linked to several AIDS infections. Canadian regulators were aware of this development, yet Factorate continued to be used until December 1987.

Dr. John Furesz, the former director of Ottawa's bureau of biologics, testified at the inquiry that he felt there was insufficient hard data to warrant a recall of the product, and he directed the Canadian Red Cross to continue distributing Factorate.

In British Columbia, in November 1987, six hemophiliacs—five of them children—were infected with HIV. They had received Factorate. Other cases were suspected in Ontario, the only other province where Factorate was distributed. Armour voluntarily withdrew their products from Canada the following month.

The Bottom Line

Subsequent lawsuits against the Canadian Red Cross by those infected claimed the defendant owed a duty of care to the plaintiffs to warn them of the risk of HIV transmission by blood products.

The Red Cross launched third-party claims against doctors on the grounds that it was their duty as primary caregivers to advise patients as to the risks associated with transfusions.

Who had the duty of care to the recipients of tainted blood products? You be the judge!

1. a) **What cause(s) of action do you believe the infected claimants might pursue against the Red Cross in this situation?**
   b) **Specify the evidence you would use to support your choice(s).**
   c) **What defences might the Red Cross use against the claimants' charges?**

2. a) **What cause(s) of action do you believe the Red Cross might pursue against Armour Pharmaceuticals in this situation?**
   b) **Defend your choice(s).**
   c) **Does Armour Pharmaceuticals have any arguments that would counter the Red Cross claim?**

3. **Do you think that punitive damages should be sought in this case? What reasons do you have for your position?**

4. **Should the federal or provincial governments intercede on behalf of the infected claimants? If so, to what extent? What reasons do you have for your position?**

CHAPTER REVIEW

Reviewing Key Terms

For each of the following statements, indicate the key term being defined.

a) a person's failure to exercise reasonable care that results in injury to another

b) a legal obligation to exercise caution when certain types of conduct carry the risk of harm to others

c) one who enters another's premises for business purposes with the potential of economic benefit

d) an object that attracts, like a swimming pool

e) holding a blameless person responsible for another's actions

f) the standard used in determining whether a person's conduct in a certain situation is negligent

g) an agreement that a patient gives to a medical procedure after the risks are disclosed

h) the degree of caution expected of a reasonable person when carrying out an action that involves risk of harm to others

i) the fact of being the cause of something that happened

j) the legal principle that a plaintiff may not recover damages for an injury from an action to which he or she consents

Exploring Legal Concepts

1. Given the tort law standard of the reasonable person, what standard would people of low or very low intelligence be expected to meet?

2. What is the "burden of proof" in a criminal prosecution? What is it in a civil action? Explain how an individual could be found not guilty of a criminal offence, but still be held liable in a civil action.

3. A person who attends a sporting event voluntarily assumes certain risks, but not all risks. Use your favourite sport as an example to identify general guidelines as to which risks are assumed and which are not.

4. Outline the major issues that a patient must prove for a charge of medical negligence to succeed in a court of law.

5. How are the concepts of foreseeability and the reasonable person related?

6. What is the law regarding the liability of drivers for their passengers in your province or territory?

7. The courts have increased the standard of care required of commercial establishments such as hotels, bars, restaurants, and resorts. Commercial hosts can be held responsible for injuries suffered by people who leave their establishments intoxicated. Is this fair and reasonable? Discuss.

Applying Legal Concepts

1. During the course of an operation, the surgeon inserted a number of tubes into the plaintiff's body. In the next few days, these tubes were changed by various doctors and nurses. On one occasion, part of a tube was stuck into the plaintiff's bladder, causing considerable pain and an infection. The plaintiff brought an action against the surgeon, arguing the principle of *res ipsa loquitur.*

- **Can this principle be applied here? Explain your answer.**

2. The 13-year-old plaintiff, John Mont, had been driving snowmobiles for about three years. One day, he drove his machine onto a highway without looking for approaching vehicles. He collided with a car driven by the 18-year-old defendant, James Reid. Mont was thrown into the air and came down on his face on the pavement. He suffered head injuries and retained no memory of the accident. Reid was driving at about 50 km/h when he noticed the snowmobile, which he thought at first was motionless, coming toward him. He sounded his horn and swerved to try to avoid a collision.

- **Did the plaintiff succeed in his action?**

- **Was the defendant guilty of contributory negligence? Why or why not?**

3. When an elderly gentleman dropped his change purse while inserting his bus fare into the coin box, Ruth Weinburg, an 84-year-old woman, rose from her seat to assist him. Weinberg returned to her seat, but before she could sit down the bus began to move. Weinburg fell and suffered a fractured wrist. At the time of the accident, the elderly man had not taken his seat either but was not injured. Weinburg brought a successful action against the bus company and its driver.

- **Did the bus driver act as a reasonable person?**

- **Was there contributory negligence on Weinberg's part? Explain.**

4. *Teno et al. v. Arnold et al.* (1978) Supreme Court of Canada 83 D.L.R. (3d) 609
On July 1, 1969, Diane Teno, then four and a half years old, and her six-year-old brother Paul heard the bells of an ice cream truck. The children asked their mother for money to buy ice cream. Yvonne Teno was talking long distance to her husband at the time. Both children had received instructions from their parents about crossing the street safely, and Diane had been told never to cross the street without her brother Paul. When Mrs. Teno gave the children the money, she again warned them "to watch out for cars."

Stuart Galloway, 19, had been driving the ice cream truck for about six weeks. His training had involved reading a manual and being instructed by a supervisor for part of the day. When Galloway saw the children starting to cross the street to his truck, he spotted a moving car on his side of the street that the Teno children had not noticed. He shouted at them to wait until the road was clear. The children then crossed the street to the truck, and Galloway sold Diane her ice cream. He was reaching into the freezer to get Paul's order when Diane ran across the street. She was struck by an oncoming car driven by 18-year-old Brian Arnold and owned by Arnold's father. Arnold's car was travelling at about 30 km/h as he approached the ice cream truck. Although he realized that the truck was stopped and he saw the "Watch Out for Children" sign on the back of it, Arnold did not sound his horn or apply his brakes.

Diane became totally disabled and unable to support herself for life. She was left with no reasonable possibility of support through marriage and required full-time assistance to perform the ordinary tasks required in living. Despite the serious injuries, Diane's life expectancy was nearly 67 years.

Through her parents, Diane Teno sued Brian Arnold and his father, Thomas J. Lipton Ltd., J.B. Jackson Ltd. (a subsidiary of Lipton which operated the ice cream business), and Stuart Galloway for general damages of $1.75 million. After the evidence was heard in the Trial Division of the Supreme Court of Ontario, the plaintiff was awarded the following damages in September 1984: $200 000 for pain and suffering and loss of enjoyment of life, and $750 000 for the cost of future care and loss of future income.

Stuart Galloway and J.B. Jackson Ltd. were found to be two-thirds responsible for the accident, while Brian Arnold and his father were held liable for the remaining one-third. Thomas J. Lipton Ltd. was not found to be in any way at fault.

The defendants appealed this judgment to the Ontario Court of Appeal. Their appeal against liability was dismissed, but a claim against Mrs. Teno was allowed. The three judges apportioned the fault at 25 percent each for Mrs. Teno, Brian and Wallace Arnold, Stuart Galloway, and J.B. Jackson Ltd. The Court of Appeal agreed with the award of $200 000 but reduced the $750 000 to $675 000, for total general damages of $875 000.

The Tenos appealed the Ontario Court of Appeal decision that held Mrs. Teno 25 percent responsible for the accident. The appeal was allowed, and the Court of Appeal decision was overturned. The Supreme Court of Canada ruled that Mrs. Teno could not be blamed for the accident, but all other defendants were held liable. As well, the Supreme Court of Canada reduced the $200 000 to $100 000 and the $675 000 to about $440 000 for a judgment of $540 000.

- **Why were Brian Arnold and his father found to be one-third at fault?**

- **Why was J. B. Jackson Ltd. also held one-third at fault?**

- **Why was Stuart Galloway held partly responsible for this accident?**

- **Why was Thomas J. Lipton Ltd. found to be no way at fault?**

- **Should Diane Teno have been held partly responsible for her own accident? Why or why not?**

- **Why did the Ontario Court of Appeal find Mrs. Teno partly at fault for her daughter's accident?**

- **Why did the Supreme Court of Canada reverse this decision? Do you agree? Why or why not?**

- **Explain the meaning of the following statement, made by Mr. Justice Thomas Zuber of the Court of Appeal, as it relates to liability in this case: "A pied piper cannot plead his inability to take care of his followers when it is he who played the flute."**

5. *Stewart v. Pettie* (1995) Supreme Court of Canada 25 Alta. L.R. (3d) 297

The plaintiff, Gillian Stewart, and her husband attended the Stage West Dinner Theatre with Gillian's brother, Stuart Pettie, and his wife. The theatre was owned by Mayfield Investments Ltd. and operated as the Mayfield Inn. A hostess seated the two couples at one of the tables that the plaintiff's employer had reserved for a staff Christmas party. The same server attended their table all evening, and she kept a running tab of all alcohol consumed. Of the two couples, only the husbands were drinking, and Pettie drank between five and seven double rum-and-cokes over a five-hour period. The wives only drank non-alcoholic beverages. Despite the amount he drank, Stuart Pettie showed no visible signs of intoxication by the end of the evening; however, he was intoxicated. When the four left, their server made no attempt to dissuade either man from driving.

In the parking lot, the four discussed whether Stuart Pettie was fit to drive, given the number of drinks he had consumed. Nobody had any concerns about letting him drive. On that particular December night, a frost made the roads unusually slippery. Despite the fact that Pettie was driving slower than the speed limit and was driving safely and cautiously, the car spun out of control on an icy road and struck a wall. Although three of the four persons in the vehicle suffered no serious injuries, Gillian Stewart, who was not wearing a seat belt, was thrown from the car, struck her head and broke her spine, and was rendered a quadriplegic. (Alberta did not have mandatory seat belt laws at the time of this accident.)

The Stewarts took action against Stuart Pettie, the City of Edmonton, and Mayfield Investments. The action against the City was settled prior to trial as was the action with the defendant Pettie; damages were settled at about $4.3 million. Pettie was also convicted of impaired driving in a separate criminal trial. The civil trial judge dismissed the action against Mayfield and assessed the plaintiff's contributory negligence for failing to wear her seat belt at 25 percent.

An appeal to the Alberta Court of Appeal was allowed, and the judges ruled that Mayfield breached two duties of care and was 10 percent contributorily negligent. The defendant theatre appealed this judgment to the Supreme Court of Canada where, in a 7–0 judgment, the Court of Appeal's judgment was overturned, relieving Mayfield of any liability.

- **Why did the trial judge dismiss the plaintiff's claim against Mayfield Investments?**

- **Why did the Court of Appeal find Mayfield negligent? List the two duties of care breached by Mayfield and its employees.**

- **If the server at the dinner theatre had intervened and suggested that Pettie not drive, do you think this would have had any influence on the plaintiff's decision to let her brother drive? Why or why not?**

- **Why should the plaintiff be found 25 percent at fault for not wearing her seat belt when it was not required by law in Alberta at the time?**

- **Why did the Supreme Court of Canada relieve Mayfield of any liability for this accident? List at least three reasons for its decision.**

Extending Legal Concepts

1. Now that you have completed this chapter, review the opening article and Something to Think About. Have your answers or opinions changed? Why or why not?

2. Distinguish between a moral obligation not to injure and a legal duty not to injure. Why is this distinction important?

3. Many people believe that Canadian law should automatically hold parents responsible for damages or injuries caused by their children. With a partner, discuss both sides of this issue.

4. Negligence law has expanded to the point where soon social hosts may be held liable for injuries caused to or by drunken guests. It is a logical extension of the liability of commercial hosts that social hosts who allow guests to drink where it is foreseeable that person or a third party could suffer injury or loss are likely to be held liable.

    Working with a partner, brainstorm what a host of a party might do to reduce possible liability from any guests at that party who might leave in an intoxicated state and cause harm or injury to others.

5. Using reference materials in your resource centre, including CD-ROM and the Internet, obtain current information on any of the following:

    a) recent negligence cases

    b) trends in liability for not wearing one's seat belt

    c) children and negligence torts

    d) any other topics pertinent to this chapter

    Write a one- to two-page summary of your findings and, if possible or appropriate, create a poster to display your information.

Researching an Issue

Medical Negligence
Debates concerning the increase of medical negligence or malpractice cases appear regularly in the media. Malpractice insurance for all types of professionals, such as lawyers, doctors, dentists, and accountants, is a growth area within the insurance industry.

Statement
All doctors found liable for medical negligence should automatically have their licences to practise medicine suspended for a minimum of two years.

Point
Automatic suspension will act as a deterrent and cause these professionals to exercise a greater duty of care toward their patients.

Counterpoint
Automatic suspension is much too harsh. Situations should be judged individually and the doctor disciplined by members of the profession.

- **With a partner, research this issue and reflect on your findings.**
- **Prepare points on this statement that could be used for a class debate.**
- **Discuss your findings with others in your class.**

Chapter 12

INTENTIONAL TORTS

These are the key terms introduced in this chapter:

absolute privilege	intent	public nuisance
assault	libel	qualified privilege
battery	malice	slander
defamation	motive	strict liability
fair comment	prescription	trespass
false imprisonment	private nuisance	truth

Chapter at a Glance

Learning Outcomes

At the end of this chapter, you will be able to

1. explain the effect of intent and motive on intentional torts;
2. distinguish between assault and battery;
3. identify the two conditions for false imprisonment;
4. describe the tort of trespass to land;
5. outline the main defences to trespass;
6. distinguish between trespass and nuisance;
7. distinguish between slander and libel as forms of defamation of character;
8. outline the main defences to defamation of character;
9. explain the concept of strict liability.

Record Libel Award Upheld

The largest libel award in Canadian history—more than $1.6 million against the Church of Scientology and Toronto lawyer Morris Manning—has been upheld by the Supreme Court of Canada.

The unanimous judgment means former Crown Attorney Casey Hill, now an Ontario Court judge, can collect more than $1.45 million from the church and $150 000 from Manning.

In making its decision, the court rejected an invitation from Manning, the church, and a coalition of media and writers to refashion Canada's libel laws along American lines. Their goal was to make it more difficult for public officials to sue.

The case dates back to the summer of 1984. While wearing his barrister's robes outside Osgoode Hall, Manning told reporters his client, the church, was bringing a contempt of court action against Hill.

Manning falsely alleged Hill misled a judge and breached a court order sealing more than 200 documents seized in a police raid on Scientology's Toronto headquarters. Hill had been advising police.

They wanted Hill charged with contempt of court, and either imprisoned or fined. Although the church knew within 10 days of the Manning news conference that some of its allegations were untrue, it continued to defend them as justified.

A shocked Hill had watched the scene on TV. The contempt charges were later dismissed but, with his reputation questioned, he determined he had no alternative but to sue for libel.

In 1992, he won the largest jury award in history. Later in upholding that decision, the Ontario Court of Appeal said he had been a victim of "character assassination."

The church and Manning appealed to the high court.

From: David Vienneau. "Record libel award upheld." *The Toronto Star*, July 21, 1995. Reprinted with permission—The Toronto Star Syndicate.

Something to Think About

- **Do you know what libel is?**
- **Why did Casey Hill feel that his reputation had been damaged?**
- **What effect might the size of this judgment have on future criticism of public officials?**

12.1 INTRODUCTION

When a person deliberately causes harm or loss to another person by assault and battery or false imprisonment, it is an intentional tort. Trespassing, causing a nuisance, and defaming (damaging a person's reputation by libel or slander) are also intentional torts in many cases.

Intentional torts are the oldest wrongs recognized by the courts. Such actions deprive individuals of their right to use their property, their bodies, or their goods as they wish because of interference from others. These causes of action have remained essentially unchanged over the years. While tort law is not uniform from province to province, the basic principles are similar.

Many tort actions, however, do not result in legal action. A certain amount of interference with individuals' rights occurs on a daily basis and is considered acceptable in a busy, interactive society. Brushing against bodies on a crowded bus or subway or taking a shortcut across someone's property are examples of torts usually accepted as a normal part of life, unless they are done in a hostile manner and cause serious harm. As people come into more regular daily contact with one another because of our busy way of life, what we are prepared to accept changes.

12.2 INTENT VERSUS MOTIVE

If one person hits another, did an intentional tort occur? The answer depends upon a number of factors. The essential element of an intentional tort is **intent**—a person's desire, plan, or hope about the consequences of an action. If your friend, Renu, throws a snowball at you and it hits you in the face causing the loss of your eye, an intentional tort has occurred. As a reasonable person, Renu should have realized in throwing the snowball that it could or would hit you. She should have realized as well the possible danger of throwing the snowball at you. As a result, she would be responsible for the loss of your eye. Even if Renu argued that she didn't intend to injure you, the consequences of her action were foreseeable. What Renu did was voluntary. She was in control of her actions. Thus, the tort would be considered intentional.

Suppose that, when Renu threw the snowball at you, it hit a passer-by. The fact that she intended to strike another person unlawfully is the key. It doesn't matter that the wrong person was hit instead of you. Renu would still be responsible for the passer-by's injuries.

Furthermore, persons committing torts must be aware of the consequences of their actions. As you read in the last chapter, children may be held responsible for their torts if they are old enough to form intent and understand that harm might result from their actions. Unlike the *Young Offenders Act* under which children under the age of 12 cannot be charged with crimes, children below 12 years of age may be held responsible for torts they commit.

Motive

The reason something was done, or **motive**, is generally not an essential element in a tort action, as long as the action was done intentionally. Providing it wasn't malicious, Renu's motive or reason for throwing the snowball is irrelevant. It doesn't matter whether she threw the snowball at you to get your attention or to tease you. She is still responsible for the loss of your eye. Motive only becomes an important factor in a tort action when self-defence is involved. This will be discussed in more detail later.

Mistake

A defendant who has committed an honest mistake of fact cannot use the defence of mistake to avoid being liable for an intentional tort. If two hunters tracking wolves shoot and kill a dog that closely resembles a wolf, they are liable for the loss. Although they were acting in good faith and really believed the animal they shot was a wolf, the defence of mistake will not be accepted in court. They intended to shoot the animal.

To use another example, a person who trespasses on another person's property, honestly believing that he or she is allowed to enter the premises, cannot plead mistake to avoid liability if the property is damaged.

Reviewing Your Reading

1. **What is an intentional tort? List three examples in your answer.**

2. **Why do many potential tort actions not result in legal action?**

3. **Why might a young child not be held responsible for an intentional tort?**

4. **Why is motive not an important factor in an intentional tort?**

5. **Is mistake a defence against an intentional tort? Explain.**

12.3 TRESPASS TO PERSONS AND LAND

In Chapter 7, you learned that different forms of assault are criminal offences tried in criminal courts. A person who has been assaulted may also bring a civil action against the offender for damages. Several forms of trespass to the person are defined in tort law. The main forms of intentional interference with another person are the torts of assault and battery and false imprisonment. Trespass to land is also an intentional tort. Both trespass to persons and to land are discussed later.

Assault and Battery

Assault as an intentional tort occurs when the victim has reason to believe or fear that bodily harm may occur. Any threat of apparent or immediate danger or violence is an assault. The essential element is the fear in the victim's mind. Assault does not involve actual physical contact and can occur without battery. It often occurs before actual contact. Thus, if someone swings a fist at another person and misses, an assault has occurred. The victim may be awarded damages for the fear and dread he or she endured as a result of that action. Pointing an unloaded gun at another person is assault if the victim believes the gun is loaded or feels fear or danger. Threatening words, such as "I'm going to knock your head off," is assault if the threatened person has a reasonable belief that the other person intends to carry out the threat.

Battery is the follow-through of assault and is the most common form of trespass to another person. **Battery** is the unlawful touching of a person without that person's consent. The actual physical contact can be injurious, offensive, or harmful. It may exist even if no injury results. Kissing or hugging is just as much a battery as hitting another person with a snowball or a fist, if the actual touching is done without consent and is offensive or upsetting to the recipient.

However, not every application of force by one person on another is a battery. Touching someone lightly to get his or her attention is accepted by most people as a normal way of life.

Assault and battery are usually tried together, since assault often occurs before or with battery. In fact, the distinction between these two torts is disappearing. Most cases based on assault include battery. The damages awarded in such actions compensate the victim for harm or loss. A defendant will be held liable for all consequences of a battery, even if they are not foreseeable or intended. If an assault was extremely vicious or committed without reason, the court may award punitive damages as well.

Did You Know
Tort action for assault alone is rarely initiated in Canada.

Medical Assault and Battery

A doctor cannot touch or treat a patient without voluntary and informed consent. If the doctor treats the patient without consent, the doctor has committed battery. The patient may take legal action against the doctor. The patient, not the

CASE

After several hours of drinking beer with friends in a pub, the plaintiff, Randy Briggs, was accosted by the defendant, Rick Laviolette, while walking home. Laviolette accused the plaintiff of breaking the windows in a car near the pub. He said that he was making a citizen's arrest. Laviolette hit the plaintiff, knocked him down, kicked him, and then dragged Briggs by the scruff of his neck and deposited him at the pub entrance, telling Briggs to stay there until the police arrived. Laviolette genuinely believed that the plaintiff was the person who had vandalized the car. An eye-witness had reported the vandalism to a waitress in the pub who then pointed the defendant in the direction in which Briggs was heading. Briggs was wearing clothing similar to the description given by the witness.

When the police arrived, Briggs had a bleeding nose and swollen lips. The police could not obtain a statement from him because of his intoxication and emotional state. However, they never charged the plaintiff with any offence as he consistently denied having damaged anyone's car. The plaintiff took a week off work because he was embarrassed by his black eyes and the condition of his face.

Briggs brought an action for personal damages against the defendant. He was awarded general damages of $3000 plus punitive damages of $1000 plus costs.

Briggs v. Laviolette (1994)

British Columbia Supreme Court 21 C.C.L.T. (2d) 105

1. **On what basis did Briggs base his claim against the defendant?**

2. **Were there reasonable and probable grounds for Laviolette to make a legal citizen's arrest here? Why or why not?**

3. **What degree of force can be used in making an arrest, and did that exist here?**

4. **Did the defendant's actions justify an award of punitive damages? Why or why not?**

doctor, must decide whether and where to undergo treatment and by whom it should be given. Battery also occurs when a treatment goes beyond what the patient has consented to have done.

An exception to this principle occurs when a doctor provides emergency treatment for an unconscious patient. In such a situation, treatment is limited to only what is necessary to protect the patient's life.

If no emergency exists, the doctor must wait for the patient to regain consciousness to obtain the necessary consent. As you learned in the last chapter, the patient must be able to give informed consent. Canadian hospitals usually obtain the signatures of all surgery patients on consent forms in advance, to protect themselves against possible liability.

False Imprisonment

Another example of intentional interference with the person is **false imprisonment**. This tort occurs when a person is confined or restrained without consent in a specific area. The word "false" means "wrongful" or "unauthorized"; "imprisonment" refers to a particular area which is not necessarily a prison. "Wrongful confinement" might be a better term to use for this tort. The restraint may be imposed by physical strength, barriers, or legal authority. Imprisonment must be total, not just a partial restriction. A plaintiff must attempt every reasonable means of escape before bringing an action for false imprisonment.

A common example of false imprisonment occurs when store detectives mistakenly detain an

CASE

Malette v.
Shulman
(1990)

Ontario Court
of Appeal
72 O.R. (2d) 417

In June 1979, Georgette Malette was rushed to the Kirkland and District Hospital in Kirkland Lake, Ontario, after being seriously injured in a car accident that killed her husband. She was treated for severe head and facial injuries and extensive bleeding by Dr. David Shulman, the physician on duty.

Because of the plaintiff's serious injuries and blood loss, the defendant doctor ordered the nurse to administer intravenous glucose treatments and a blood volume expander. This was standard medical procedure in cases of this serious nature. However, the nurse found a card, neither dated nor witnessed, bearing the heading "NO BLOOD TRANSFUSION!" in the plaintiff's purse. It indicated that Mrs. Malette was a Jehovah's Witness and would accept no blood or blood products to be given to her in the case of emergency because of her religious beliefs. Members of this faith believe it is a sin to receive a blood transfusion.

Although the nurse told Dr. Shulman about this card, he firmly believed that transfusions were necessary to save Malette's life. Shortly after the transfusions began, the plaintiff's daughter and a church elder arrived and informed the doctor once again about the patient's wishes. The daughter even signed a form, specifically preventing her mother from having further transfusions and releasing the hospital from any legal liability as a result. However, the transfusions continued as the doctor felt it was his professional responsibility to save his patient's life.

Mrs. Malette's condition eventually stabilized, and she was taken by air ambulance to a Toronto hospital, where she made a good recovery. She was discharged from hospital in mid-August 1979. In June 1980, Malette brought an action for battery and negligence against the doctor, the hospital, and the nurses attending her.

At trial in the High Court of Justice, the action was dismissed against all defendants except for the doctor. The plaintiff was awarded $20 000 in damages for the battery to her person in late 1987. The defendant doctor appealed this decision to the Ontario Court of Appeal where a 3–0 judgment dismissed the doctor's appeal and affirmed the trial judgment.

1. **Why did Dr. Shulman ignore Mrs. Malette's wishes outlined on the card in her purse? What would you have done, and why?**

2. **Based on your understanding of negligence, why did the trial judge reject the plaintiff's claim of negligence?**

3. **Why did the trial judge accept the plaintiff's claim of battery?**

4. **Would the judgment have been any different if no Jehovah's Witness card had been found in the plaintiff's purse? Why or why not?**

5. **Did the doctor's legal situation change after he had spoken to Mrs. Mallette's daughter?**

6. **Why did the Court of Appeal dismiss the doctor's appeal?**

innocent person whom they suspect of shoplifting. Actual physical restraint is not necessary for false imprisonment to exist. If suspects, when stopped by store security, have a genuine fear that an embarrassing scene will occur if they try to leave, then false imprisonment exists. In fact, it is enough for a store employee to shout, "Grab that thief!" for false imprisonment to exist.

You saw in Chapter 4 that, if the police arrest a person without a warrant or without reasonable and probable grounds for believing that a crime has been committed, the arrested person may sue for false arrest. Like "assault" and "battery," the terms "false arrest" and "false imprisonment" are often used together to mean the same thing. However, false arrest only constitutes false imprisonment if the individual is confined by someone in authority.

Infliction of Mental Suffering

A person may also commit verbal assault by using words that cause shock or mental suffering to another person. The courts have recognized that a person should not be harmed by another person's practical jokes or upsetting actions. If such an incident results in mental suffering or nervous shock that is evidenced by physical illness, loss of sleep and weight, or loss of hair, the victim may be awarded compensation.

The first such action was the classic 1897 English case *Wilkinson v. Downton*. The defendant, Downton, told Mrs. Wilkinson that her husband had been hurt in an accident and had two broken legs. He said that he had been sent by Mr. Wilkinson to get his wife to come and bring him home. In fact, nothing had happened to Mr. Wilkinson. The entire incident was a practical joke on Downton's part. However, Mrs. Wilkinson suffered mental and emotional shock and was quite ill for several weeks. She was awarded damages because the defendant's intentional action caused her actual and serious harm.

Not every practical joke or upsetting incident will result in damages. Nor is compensation generally awarded to anyone but immediate family members or close relatives. However, this principle was

CASE

A police officer for the City of Saint John stopped the plaintiff, Gary Cormier, in the early morning hours while he and his girlfriend were walking along Main Street. The officer believed Cormier was wanted for questioning. When the plaintiff said he would not cooperate unless arrested and handcuffed, the police did that, putting the plaintiff in the rear seat of the police cruiser.

On checking further at headquarters, the police learned that there was nothing outstanding on Cormier nor was he wanted for questioning, and he was released after 10 or 15 minutes in detention.

The plaintiff sued the City of Saint John in Small Claims Court for damages for false arrest, but his action was dismissed. Cormier appealed this decision to the New Brunswick Court of Appeal where his appeal was allowed, and he was awarded $2000 damages plus costs.

Cormier v. City of Saint John (1994)

New Brunswick Court of Appeal 153 N.B.R. (2d) 293

1. **Why did the plaintiff sue the City of Saint John and on what basis?**
2. **Why did the trial judge dismiss Cormier's claim?**
3. **Did the police have reasonable and probable grounds to arrest Cormier? Why or why not?**
4. **Did the plaintiff contribute to his own misfortune? Explain.**
5. **Do you agree with the Court of Appeal's decision? Why or why not?**

Hanson v. Wayne's Cafe Ltd.
(1990)

Saskatchewan Court of Queen's Bench 84 Sask. R. 220

In October 1987, the plaintiff Shelley Hanson was a waitress at the China Inn Restaurant in Saskatoon. The restaurant was operated by the defendant company. Suspecting that she was pregnant, Hanson placed a urine sample in a styrofoam cup and put a top on it to take for analysis. She then put the cup in a paper bag and hid it under her coat as she left the restaurant because she was embarrassed by the personal nature of its contents.

The restaurant owner, Wayne Mak, thought she was sneaking something out under her coat and demanded to see what it was. Being somewhat embarrassed, the plaintiff refused. When the proprietor touched her arm and asked her to sit down while he called the police, Hanson ran out the back door of the restaurant and fell in the parking area, scraping her knee. She did not return to her job.

The plaintiff then brought an action for damages for assault and false imprisonment against the proprietor and the defendant company, but her action on both counts was dismissed.

1. **Why did the plaintiff claim that she had been assaulted?**
2. **Was the alleged assault a valid claim? Why or why not?**
3. **Was her claim for false imprisonment valid? Why or why not?**
4. **Was the plaintiff in any way to blame for what happened? Explain.**
5. **Do you agree with the court's decision? Why or why not?**

---

altered by a landmark judgment from the Ontario Court of Appeal in *Bechard v. Haliburton Estate* (1992). In that case, the Court of Appeal upheld an award of $50 000 for nervous shock and mental suffering to a plaintiff, Dolores Bechard, who saw a motorcyclist killed after a collision with the car in which she was a passenger. Mrs. Bechard and her husband were driving along when Chris Haliburton ran a stop sign on his motorcycle and hit their car. Haliburton flew off the motorcycle and landed on the road. As he was lying there injured, he was run over and killed by another car, driven by Ben Damsgard. As a result of this shocking accident, Mrs. Bechard suffered insomnia, regular bad dreams, extreme nervousness, and stress.

The court ruled that Haliburton's lack of a proper duty of care and his negligence in causing the accident resulted in the creation of causation between his accident and Mrs. Bechard's suffering. Furthermore, Damsgard owed a duty of care to drive like a reasonably prudent person and so avoid running over Haliburton. This judgment marked the first time in Canadian legal history that damages for nervous shock were awarded to a bystander who was not related to the traffic accident victim.

Trespass to Property

Trespass is the action of entering and crossing another person's land without consent or legal authority and is one of the oldest torts. As in battery, no specific damage needs to occur for trespass to exist. Simply entering a person's property without permission or legal reason is a form of trespass, whether or not trespass was intended. Remaining on that property when you are asked to leave is also trespass. So is propelling an object onto another's property, or bringing an object onto another's property and not removing it. Suppose, for instance, that Kyle pushes Antonio

In late 1988, the plaintiff, Allan Mather of Sudbury, wrote to 30 bulk mailers including the defendant Columbia House asking that they remove his name from their mailing lists. While most of the other mailers stopped, Columbia House continued to send promotional materials for its record club to the plaintiff. Mather wrote to the company a few more times without effect.

In the fall of 1989, the plaintiff wrote again, warning that he would bill the company $10 an item for future unwanted mail. Several months later, he billed the company for two mailings and warned them that he would charge $100 for any future mailings. The company refused to pay the bills as it was contrary to its policy, but they agreed to remove Mather's name from its mailing list.

However, the mailings continued and, in August 1991, the plaintiff sent a bill to the defendant for almost $470. When the company refused to pay, the plaintiff sued in the Ontario Court, General Division, Small Claims Court and was awarded $480 in damages, plus costs.

**Mather v.
Columbia
House**
(1992)

**Ontario Court,
General Division
(Small Claims
Court)
Reported in**
Lawyers Weekly

1. **Why did the plaintiff take action against the defendant company?**

2. **Why did the trial judge find that the unwanted mailings from Columbia House were a form of trespass? Do you agree?**

3. **What do you think of the court's decision?**

4. **In Ontario, no appeal of this judgment is possible under Small Claims Court legislation because the amount claimed by the plaintiff is less than $500. If this were not the law, would you recommend that the defendant appeal this decision? Why or why not?**

against his will onto Robbie's property. It is Kyle, rather than Antonio, who is trespassing. Cutting down a tree, letting it fall onto a neighbour's property, and not removing it is also trespass. As long as the tree remains on the property, there is a continuing trespass.

The ownership of land permits its use above and below the surface of the earth. Therefore, if a person tunnels through to a neighbour's property to obtain access to oil under the neighbour's land, the neighbour will succeed in an action for trespass. Stringing wires or lines over another person's land is also a trespass.

However, statutes permit the use of all space at certain distances above land. This provides for the right of aircraft to fly on regulated flight paths above private property. The right of occupiers to use property is also recognized by the landlord and tenant statutes of most provinces.

For example, a landlord wishing to enter a tenant's rented property must notify the tenant in advance. Finally, most provinces have passed legislation allowing the police to lay charges against trespassers. As a result, suing for the tort of trespass is no longer very common.

Did You Know

If you open someone else's mail, you could be sued for trespass to goods.

Reviewing Your Reading

1. **What is the difference between assault and battery?**

2. **When might punitive damages be awarded for assault and battery?**

3. **When does medical assault and battery occur?**

4. **How do the torts of medical negligence and medical battery differ?**

5. **What two conditions must exist for an action for false imprisonment to succeed?**

6. **When might a victim sue for nervous shock and mental suffering?**

7. **What is the significance of the judgment in the *Bechard v. Haliburton Estate* case?**

8. **What similarity is there between trespass to land and the tort of battery?**

9. **Why is propelling an object onto another's property considered trespass?**

12.4 DEFENCES TO TRESPASS

Persons who commit intentional torts may not be liable if they have a legal defence for the actions. Once the plaintiff has established that the defendant has committed a trespass, the defendant has a number of defences that might explain or justify his or her actions. The most common defences against trespass to another person or land are consent, self-defence, defence of a third party or property, and legal authority. A defendant may use more than one defence in the same lawsuit.

Consent

Consent is the defence most often used in cases involving trespass to the person, especially battery, and must be established by the defendant. A defendant who can show that the plaintiff consented to the action is excused from liability for any injury that results. For example, say that a group of teenagers is engaged in a friendly neighbourhood game of football. During the game, one of the players is injured during a tackle; his arm is broken. The victim will not succeed in any lawsuit he brings for damages since he willingly consented to play, and no anger was displayed during the game. Also, he consented while being aware of the possible risks of the game.

Recently, many court cases involving contact sports have attempted to resolve the extent to which consent applies. Courts assume that players who participate in certain contact sports have consented to whatever bodily contact is permitted by the rules of the sport. Thus, a football player expects to get tackled, a boxer punched, a hockey player checked, and so on. Body checking is considered a normal or reasonable part of a hockey game. However, a player who deliberately slashes another player's face with his hockey stick is using excessive force and is committing an intentional tort. The injured player could succeed in a tort action, and a criminal charge could also be laid against the aggressive player as seen in the case of *R. v. Leclerc*.

Self-defence

Self-defence is often raised as a defence against battery. It is valid as long as the force used is not excessive and is reasonable and necessary in the circumstances to prevent personal injury. What is reasonable and necessary depends on the facts of

Former Leaf Bill Berg is helped off the ice after breaking his leg in a fight with Chicago's Igor Ulanov.

T he accused, Steven Leclerc, was charged with aggravated assault after cross-checking another player, James Conboy, in a "no bodily contact" semi-final industrial-league playoff game between the Calabogie and Joe's Lake teams in Lanark, Ontario, to determine the finalist team for the league championship.

Fourteen minutes into the third period, Conboy beat Leclerc to the puck, but in a check described by various witnesses as deliberate and vicious or accidental and intended to push Conboy off the puck and to prevent more serious contact so close to the boards, Leclerc cross-checked Conboy across the back of the neck or upper neck. The latter crashed headfirst into the boards and dislocated his fourth and fifth cervical vertebrae and became permanently paralyzed from the neck down. The referee immediately called a five-minute match penalty against Leclerc and halted the game to assist Conboy.

Leclerc was later charged with aggravated assault but was acquitted at trial. The Crown appealed this acquittal to the Ontario Court of Appeal where, in a 3–0 judgment, the appeal was dismissed.

R. v. Leclerc
(1991)

Ontario Court of Appeal
4 O.R. (3d) 788

1. **Why did both courts acquit the accused?**

2. **Since this was a "no bodily contact" game, should this assault even have occurred? Why or why not?**

3. **Discuss the meaning of the following statement from the Court of Appeal judgment as it relates to this case: "A player, by participating in a sport such as hockey, impliedly consents to some bodily contact necessarily incidental to the game, but not to overly violent attacks, all of which should be determined according to objective criteria." Was this accident simply a part of the game or a violent attack?**

4. **What objective criteria would you suggest be considered for implied consent in a hockey game? List at least four such factors.**

5. **Do you think James Conboy should have pursued a civil action against Steven Leclerc? Why or why not?**

each case. The defendant must convince the court that a genuine fear of being injured by the plaintiff existed, and that the plaintiff was struck in self-protection from the threat. The burden of proof rests with the defendant to prove that his or her actions were necessary and that excessive force was not used. Self-defence may even be used as a successful defence when you strike the first blow if you honestly believe, and can later convince the court, that it was the only way to protect yourself.

Provocation is not a defence for an intentional tort. If Janelle hits Kevin for provoking or annoy-ing her to the point where she loses her temper, she has no legal defence, and she may be held liable for any injury she caused to Kevin. Provocation may result in a reduction of the amount of damages that the defendant might pay. However, the victim will still be compensated for the actual loss or injury to some extent.

Defence of a Third Party

A person can come to the aid of a third party if it is reasonable to assume that the third party is in some degree of immediate danger. Again, any

Gambriell v. Caparelli
(1974)

Ontario County Court

54 D.L.R. (3d) 661

One July day, Fred Caparelli, the 21-year-old son of the defendant, was getting a hose to wash his car when the 50-year-old plaintiff, Gambriell, accidentally backed his car into the rear of Caparelli's vehicle. A small dent in the bumper of Caparelli's car resulted. An argument developed between the two, and Caparelli threatened to call the police. When Gambriell started to get back in his car, Caparelli grabbed him. Gambriell then hit Caparelli in the face. Fighting broke out, with blows being exchanged between them.

Attracted by the shouting, Mrs. Caparelli, the 57-year-old defendant, saw her son fighting with their neighbour. Her son was on the ground, and Gambriell had his hands on Caparelli's neck. Thinking that her son was being choked, the defendant ran into her garden and got a metal three-pronged garden cultivator tool with a 1.5 m wooden handle. After yelling at the plaintiff to stop, she struck him three times on the shoulder and then on the head with the tool. As soon as Gambriell saw blood flowing from his head, he released the defendant's son. He was taken to the hospital, where he received nine stitches for lacerations.

Gambriell claimed damages in County Court. The action was dismissed, because the court found Mrs. Caparelli's actions reasonable under the circumstances.

1. **On what grounds did the plaintiff base his action?**
2. **What defence did the defendant plead?**
3. **Was the use of force by Mrs. Caparelli justified in this case? Explain your reasoning.**
4. **In the decision, the judge observed, "Gambriell was the author of his own misfortune and . . . even had I found for the plaintiff, I would not have awarded damages in excess of $1." Explain the meaning of this statement.**

force used in the defence of that person must be reasonable. This defence occurs most often when a parent comes to the assistance of a child or close relative, or one spouse defends the other. The courts have accepted that, when a person honestly believes that a third party is in imminent danger, the use of reasonable force to assist that person is acceptable, even if the belief turns out to be mistaken.

Defence of Property

Property owners may use reasonable force to expel intruders from their property. The owner must first ask the trespasser to leave. If the request is ignored, then a reasonable amount of force may be used to expel the intruder. However, if the trespasser made a forcible entry onto the property, no request to leave is necessary before force can be used. Again, the amount of force used must be reasonable.

Legal Authority

In limited situations, certain individuals, such as law enforcement officers, have the legal authority to commit actions that would otherwise be intentional torts. For example, the police can detain individuals in the course of a valid arrest. Many civil actions against officers have been decided in their favour because they were carrying out a legal duty to arrest persons whom they suspected of having committed a criminal offence. Store detectives likewise have the legal authority to arrest shoplifters.

Police officers with a search warrant can use legal authority as a defence if someone claims that the officers have trespassed on their property. Prior to entry, except in an emergency, the officers should identify themselves, show the search warrant, and request entry to the premises. This is in the best interests of all concerned. An unexpected arrival on a person's property could lead to serious misunderstanding and possible injury. The personal safety of both the homeowner and the police is at stake.

The courts have also recognized the occasional use of reasonable physical force as a disciplinary measure. Examples are seen in teacher-student and parent-child relationships, where teachers and parents have legal authority over their charges. Both may take reasonable measures to control and discipline children in their care. Only if the force used is excessive, or not for the purpose of correcting behaviour, is an intentional tort committed.

Necessity

A final defence against trespass is that of necessity. A defendant is excused from liability for trespass to land if the action is strictly necessary and there is a reasonable excuse for it. The necessity to use another's property may arise unexpectedly, as when a sudden storm forces boaters to seek safety on nearby land. Although the boaters are trespassing by being on the land without permission, their defence of necessity would likely succeed. However, if they caused damage while on the property, they could be held liable for any losses.

A person trespassing on another's property to reclaim goods that rightfully belong to him or her could also argue that the action was necessary.

Reviewing Your Reading

1. **Name the four most common defences against trespass.**
2. **When is consent not a valid defence in a contact sport?**
3. **When is self-defence a valid defence against battery?**
4. **When may defence of a third party be pleaded?**
5. **Who may use the defence of legal authority, and in what situations?**
6. **Explain necessity as a defence against trespass to land.**

12.5 Nuisance

The tort of nuisance is closely related to the tort of trespass. Nuisance involves one person's unreasonable use of land, which interferes with the enjoyment and use of adjoining land by other persons or a community. While trespass is always an intentional tort, a nuisance may be intentional or unintentional. Trespass laws protect the possession and use of property, while nuisance laws protect the quality of that possession and use. For example, if a farmer enters her neighbour's property without permission and without reason, she is guilty of trespass to land. If the same farmer sprays her fruit trees and the spray drifts onto a neighbour's property, causing him to fall ill, the neighbour can claim damages for nuisance.

Nuisance has gained prominence in recent years because society has become increasingly concerned about environmental pollution. Growing awareness of environmental problems has resulted in increased government concerns and regulations. Local zoning bylaws attempt to keep land for industrial and residential use some distance apart, in the best interests of both groups. Despite these laws, a citizen still has the right to take civil action. Every occupier is entitled to make reasonable use of his or her property. It is a matter for the courts to determine what is reasonable and to balance that right against the rights of other occupiers. Courts should only become involved when an excessive use of property causes inconvenience beyond what is reasonable for occupiers in the vicinity.

The courts have recognized two basic forms of nuisance—private and public.

Schneider v. Royal Wayne Motel Ltd. et al.
(1995)

Alberta Provincial Court 164 A.R. 68

The plaintiffs, Kurt and Gertrud Schneider and Oscar and Rebecca Quashnick, owned houses adjacent to the defendant Highland Golf and Country Club of Calgary. The golf course was located on land owned by the other defendant, the Royal Wayne Motel Ltd. When the Quashnicks purchased their home in 1959, they were not aware that a golf course was being built across the street from them. When the Schneiders purchased their home in 1986, they were not aware of the golf course across the road, although they should have been aware. The Schneiders' home was the closer of the two homes to the golf course.

Since the 1980s, the plaintiffs' properties had been a frequent landing spot for golf balls, creating a hazard to their safety, damage to their properties, and a substantial interference with the use and enjoyment of their properties. The owners wore hard hats when mowing their lawns, windows were broken, cars were dented, and so on. From 1987 to 1990, for example, over 1000 golf balls were retrieved from the Schneiders' property. This situation improved considerably between 1991 and 1994 because of improvements made and reasonable steps taken by the golf course to reduce the problem; only about 200 balls landed during these years.

The plaintiffs sued the defendants for damages in nuisance, and the court awarded the Quashnicks $1000 in general damages and the Schneiders $3000 in damages.

1. **Does this action involve a public or private nuisance, and why?**
2. **The golf course argued that voluntary assumption of risk existed here for the plaintiffs. Explain why.**
3. **Does the fact that the Schneiders moved to the nuisance since the golf course was there first have any significance in this case? Why or why not?**
4. **Do you agree with the court's decision? Why or why not?**

Private Nuisance

Private nuisance laws recognize everyone's right to the normal use and enjoyment of their property, free from harmful or unreasonable interference. Compensation will not be awarded for occasional minor annoyances; the harm must be serious and continue for some time. One golf ball hit into a person's yard from a neighbouring country club is an annoyance; golf balls hit regularly into the same yard are a nuisance.

The neighbourhood in which the nuisance occurs must be considered by the courts. What is acceptable in an industrial area will not be accepted in a residential or tourist area. Zoning bylaws often define the permitted standards. However, even a defendant conducting business within the bylaws may be held liable for nuisance, if it is excessive.

Another factor to consider in the case of business activities is the benefits each brings to the community. Canada's many pulp and paper mills, for example, produce necessary goods and employ numerous people. The resulting pollution and unpleasant odours, however, constitute nuisances. Courts must balance the reasonable use of land by one person or business with the nuisance it creates and the decrease in enjoyment for neighbours or the entire community. How will a court injunction forcing a company to stop its operation affect the community? Should the court award damages for the nuisance, but allow the defendant's activity to continue because of its value to the community? The benefit of a given business to the community may result in a more lenient judgment. However, the fact that a particular activity is valuable does not necessarily allow the business to create a continuing nuisance.

Nuisances need not be tied to environmental concerns. Picketers who unlawfully carry protest signs outside the entrance to a hospital or a factory are a nuisance as they interfere with the free movement of other people in and out of these buildings.

Public Nuisance

Public nuisance refers to a small group of actions that interfere with the rights of the general public. Examples include blocking off public waters, highways, or roads and polluting of public waters with insecticide or oil spills. As long as a significant number of people are affected, it is unnecessary to prove that every member of the public has been harmed.

Actions for public nuisance are usually brought by a government official, often the provincial attorney general, on behalf of the public. The intent is to prevent defendants from being sued separately by each person and to reduce actions for petty or minor losses. A private citizen who can show special injury above and beyond that suffered by the general public may also sue, however. The usual award in a successful action for public nuisance is either the issuing of an injunction or the payment of damages.

Defences to Nuisance

Two main defences to the tort of nuisance exist: legal authority and prescription.

Legal Authority

By law, certain industries are given the legal right to emit a reasonable amount of smoke, noise, and effluent without being liable. Similar regulations apply to aircraft and vehicles requiring sirens. In passing such legislation, the government attempts to balance the right of society to enjoy land against the need of industry to generate pollution in the course of providing products and services. However, if a business exceeds the level considered reasonable in law, a nuisance action may be brought against it.

Various federal and provincial statutes have been passed to prosecute people and businesses for criminal violation of pollution standards.

Prescription

A person may acquire the right to continue using another's property by **prescription**. This occurs if the land has been used openly, continuously, and in the same manner without dispute for at least 20 years. It is assumed that if neighbours have accepted the nuisance for 20 years without complaining or taking legal action, they have given in to its presence and have accepted it. Suppose, for instance, that the eaves on the Fournier home discharge rainwater onto the neighbouring Schultz property every time there is a heavy rain. If the Schultz family does not make any complaints to the Fourniers about this problem for a period of 20 years, the Fourniers are legally able to assume that no nuisance is being created. They have acquired the right by prescription to allow this situation to continue without fear of legal liability.

Reviewing Your Reading

1. What is a nuisance?
2. In what two ways do trespass and nuisance differ?
3. Discuss the factors that a judge must consider in reaching a decision in a private nuisance action.

4. **Who usually acts as the plaintiff in a public nuisance action, and why?**

5. **Discuss the two main defences to the tort of nuisance.**

12.6 DEFAMATION OF CHARACTER

British common law developed the tradition that all persons are entitled to their good name and reputation. The tort of **defamation** occurs when an unjustified or untrue attack is made intentionally or unintentionally on a person's reputation. Whether verbal, written, or published, the attack must lower the person's reputation, cause people to avoid him or her, or expose the person to hatred, contempt, or ridicule. A damaged reputation may result in difficulty in finding or keeping jobs, or strained friendships. Thus, a person whose reputation has been damaged through defamation can sue for compensation. In such an action, the plaintiff must establish that the defendant's statements have seriously injured his or her reputation; otherwise, only nominal damages may be awarded.

Protection of a person's reputation, however, may conflict with another person's right. Freedom of thought, belief, opinion, and expression, including freedom of the press and other media of communication are guaranteed in section 2(b) of the *Charter of Rights and Freedoms*. Across Canada, the laws governing defamation attempt to balance these sometimes conflicting rights. This balance is vital to the survival of Canada's democratic system of government. People should be free to seek and

CASE

Skomar v. Rachinski
(1990)

Saskatchewan Court of Queen's Bench 88 Sask. R. 177

The parties in this action had been neighbours in Saskatoon since the early 1980s and had been good friends until 1987 when Skomar built a garage to which Rachinski took great exception. From that time on, a "state of cold war" affected their relationship, and the defendant complained continually about the plaintiff's barking dog, about his fence, his driveway, and the garage. There was ample evidence to indicate that bad feelings and a very poor relationship existed between these two neighbours. Because of his difficulties with the defendant, the plaintiff suffered from tension headaches and was taking medication to relieve his stress.

One summer day, Skomar, his wife, and his sister-in-law approached the defendant and his wife to ask why they could not be good neighbours as they had previously been. In response, Rachinski accused his neighbour of being crazy and a thief and of stealing the railway ties in his yard from Canadian National. The plaintiff responded to the effect that there was no use trying to talk to the defendant and went back home, but this outburst further strained the neighbours' relationship.

The plaintiff brought an action against the defendant for general and punitive damages and was awarded $2500 in general damages but no punitive damages.

1. **Why did the plaintiff sue the defendant?**

2. **Were the defendant's remarks to the plaintiff defamatory, or were they simply verbal abuse in the heat of anger? Explain.**

3. **What are punitive damages, and why would the plaintiff claim them?**

4. **Do you agree with the court's decision? Why or why not?**

share information and all kinds of ideas without fear of censorship or legal action. Yet, people should not make groundless or unproven statements about others without being subject to defamation of character laws. This need for a balance was seen in the opening article in this chapter.

For a statement to be defamatory, it must be false, be heard or read by a third party, and bring the person defamed into ridicule, hatred, or contempt. The more malicious or vicious the remarks, the more serious the tort. Defamation can take two forms—slander and libel.

Slander

Slander is oral defamation. It occurs when words, sounds, physical gestures, or facial expressions are used that tend to lower a person's reputation in the minds of others. Slander may be unintentional. If, for example, Lori is making negative comments to Katie about Katie herself, and Heather enters the room and overhears the conversation, then slander may have occurred. Even though Lori did not intend anyone but Katie to hear the criticism, she took the risk of having her defamatory remarks overheard.

Libel

Defamation in permanent visual or audible form is **libel**, such as in radio or television broadcasts, publications, cartoons, photographs, tape recordings, films, or videotapes. Like slander, libel does not have to be intentional. If a person writes defamatory statements about another in a private diary, the remarks are not libel. However, if someone else reads them, libel may exist.

To take another example, newspapers publish the names and addresses of persons arrested for criminal offences, so that innocent persons with the same names are not defamed. If a publication is sued for libel, the reporter, the editor, the publisher, and the owner are all liable for defamation. Often, however, it is the publisher or owner that pays damages. The award may be reduced if the defendant makes an apology or prints a correction in another issue of the newspaper.

Libel is a much more serious tort than slander because more people are likely to be damaged by libel. For this reason libel is also a criminal offence. Nevertheless, most libel actions tend to be brought in civil, rather than in criminal, courts. If libel is tried as a criminal action, the accused may be sent to prison. If it is tried as a civil action, the victim may be awarded damages. Some provinces have eliminated the distinction between slander and libel and provide that all defamations are actionable without proof of damage.

Defences to Defamation

The most common defences to defamation of character are the truth, absolute and qualified privilege, and fair comment. These defences have arisen to help ensure a balance between the protection of a person's reputation and the guarantees of freedom of speech and expression.

Truth

The best defence against defamation is to prove that the statements made about a person are the **truth**. The law protects persons from false statements only. An action for damages will not succeed if the defendant can show that the statements about the plaintiff are true in every respect. This is a complete defence, even if the remarks have harmed the plaintiff's reputation. However, the truth is not an adequate defence if a person repeats statements that are believed to be true but are actually false. Repeating remarks that harm a person's character is just as serious as making the remarks in the first place. As a result, great responsibility is placed on editors and publishers of newspapers and magazines to ensure that their reporters' stories are completely accurate.

Did You Know

A couple in Alberta sued the CBC claiming stress and injury to their reputation. The CBC had broadcast pictures of their home, identifying it as the residence of a man with the same last name, who had been accused of assaulting his wife while drunk. The couple had informed the CBC of the error prior to the broadcast.

Vander Zalm
v. Times
Publishers
et al.
(1979)

British Columbia
Court of Appeal
96 D.L.R. (3d) 172

William Vander Zalm, the plaintiff and the British Columbia Minister of Human Resources at the time of this action, took legal action against the *Victoria Times* and freelance cartoonist Bob Bierman for an alleged defamation in the cartoon shown here that appeared in the newspaper's editorial page.

An actual photograph of the minister appeared with the cartoon and an article in which he suggested that Indian youths hanging around downtown Vancouver should return to their reserves because they had better opportunities there.

The plaintiff claimed that the cartoon depicted him as a "monster" and made him fear for his safety and that of his family. He contended that the cartoon was an uncalled-for, malicious, personal attack. The defence argued that political cartoons rely on gross exaggeration and symbolism and should never be taken literally. The cartoonist argued that he had intended to portray the plaintiff as cruel and thoughtless in his ministerial performance. The flies in the cartoon represented the Indians who were being controlled by Vander Zalm with little regard for their feelings. The cartoon was not intended as an attack on Vander Zalm the person.

Vander Zalm sued for damages in the British Columbia Supreme Court and was awarded $3500 for the loss of his reputation. The defendants appealed to the Court of Appeal where, in a 5–0 judgment, the trial judgment was overturned.

Bob Bierman/Victoria Times

1. **For what form of defamation was the plaintiff claiming damages?**

2. **What defence was pleaded by the defendants?**

3. **In the Court of Appeal judgment, the following statement appeared: "We have become accustomed to witty cartoons, and this one was coarse. But a cartoon can be in bad taste and not be defamatory; mere insult or vulgar abuse have been held not to constitute defamation." Explain the meaning of this statement.**

4. **With which decision do you agree, and why?**

Absolute Privilege

Members of Parliament, members of the provincial legislatures, and all persons participating in courts, coroners' inquests, judicial hearings, and boards of review like the Workers' Compensation Board or a police disciplinary hearing are given **absolute privilege**. Under its protection, statements may be made openly, honestly, and freely, without the fear of tort liability. To be privileged, the statements must be made within the confines of where the proceedings take place. The principle of absolute privilege is based on the belief that society's interests are best served by open debate, even at the cost of someone's reputation.

If, however, a defamatory statement is repeated outside the protected locations, civil action may be taken by the person defamed. For example, if a Member of Parliament makes a defamatory statement to reporters on the front steps of the Parliament Buildings in Ottawa that is later found to be untrue, the member could be sued for slander. If the same statement had been made within the House of Commons, however, absolute privilege would have protected the member.

Qualified Privilege

People who, by the nature of their work, are required to express their opinions are protected by **qualified privilege**. Its purpose is to encourage free speech on matters of public importance. Qualified privilege will succeed as a defence if the defendant can prove that the statements were made in good faith and without **malice**. If malice is involved as a motive, qualified privilege is not a valid defence.

The law believes that there are certain times when open and honest communication is more important than protecting a person's reputation. For instance, employers and teachers are often asked to write letters of reference for former employees and students. Also, credit reporting agencies are required to provide information on a person's credit rating and ability to meet loan payments. Qualified privilege enables such people, acting in good faith, to provide honest and meaningful references without fear of legal action, even if the statements turn out to be untrue and defamatory. This defence is also extended to those who speak at public inquiries and meetings on relatively serious matters, when the remarks are made to a restricted audience.

Although government members have absolute privilege while in their government settings, media reports of government debate are given qualified privilege only. The media must therefore be careful and prudent in their reporting of events. Newspapers, for instance, have the role of informing the public about matters of concern. However, newspapers must be fair and accurate in their reporting and not use their privilege to ruin a person's reputation intentionally.

Unlike elected federal and provincial politicians who are granted absolute privilege in Parliament and provincial legislatures, government officials who take part in local or municipal council meetings are only granted qualified privilege.

Fair Comment

Media critics who review plays, theatre performances, sports events, and concerts provide information to the general public. **Fair comment**, the right to criticize openly and honestly, is an accepted part of our society. Critics should be able to comment on matters of general interest to the public without concern for legal action. However, if the comments are not fair and can be proved to be malicious, then the defendant can be held liable. It is fair comment for a critic to claim that a particular star has just given the worst performance of her life in her new film. It is not fair comment to make negative and malicious comments about the star's private life and to attack her personally, since this has no bearing on her performance.

Reviewing Your Reading

1. **What is defamation of character, and what are its two forms?**
2. **Which of the two forms of defamation is considered the more serious?**
3. **What is the best defence to the tort of defamation, and why?**
4. **Distinguish between absolute and qualified privilege.**
5. **When can fair comment be used as a defence?**

12.7 STRICT LIABILITY

All of the torts studied so far have fallen into one of two categories: intentional and unintentional. Thus, all these actions have involved an element of either intent or negligence. Another group of lawful actions is considered so dangerous that it is assumed to carry a very high risk of harm. The principle of strict liability applies to these situations. **Strict liability** recognizes fault on a person's part, even though the person did not act negligently or intend to cause harm. This may seem severe or unfair, but laws are designed to benefit and protect society, sometimes at the expense of individuals.

Suppose a company stores explosives on its property for blasting during road construction. When a hunter's stray bullet accidentally punctures the storage shed, the resulting explosion destroys a neighbouring summer cottage. Although the accident was not the company's fault in any way, the company was aware of the risk of storing explosives on its land and now must face the consequences. The hunter may also be liable for the damage.

The principle of strict liability was first recognized in a British case, *Rylands v. Fletcher* (1868): occupiers are strictly liable for any dangerous substance that is brought onto their premises and subsequently escapes. Since then, it has been applied to cases involving fires caused by gasoline drums stored indoors, deaths caused by chemicals escaping from factories, and damage caused by the escape of sewage from drainpipes.

Dangerous Animals

For legal purposes, animals are classified as wild or domestic. Wild animals are those not normally kept as pets, such as lions, tigers, bears, monkeys, and some snakes. Strict liability may apply to the owner of a wild animal for any harm it causes, even if the owner believes the animal to be harmless. Harm includes the

CASE

Rylands v. Fletcher
[1868]

English House of Lords
L.R. 3 H.L. 330

Fletcher, the plaintiff, operated a coal mine adjoining the defendant's property. Rylands owned a mill and constructed a reservoir on his property to supply water to the mill. Competent engineers were hired to complete the construction. Unknown to both parties, underneath their land were old, unused mining passages and shafts. One day, the weight of the water in the reservoir caused an overflow that broke through the shafts and flooded Fletcher's mine, causing considerable damage.

Fletcher took legal action for damages, and the court found Rylands liable. The judgment stated: "We think that the true rule of law is that the person who, for his own purposes, brings on his lands and collects there and keeps there anything likely to do mischief if it escapes, must keep it at his peril, and, if he does not do so, is . . . answerable for all the damage which is the natural consequence of its escape. He can excuse himself by showing that the escape was an Act of God, but that is not the case here. The person . . . whose mine is flooded by the water from his neighbour's reservoir . . . is damnified without fault of his own."

Rylands appealed this decision to the House of Lords, but his appeal was dismissed.

1. **Did the plaintiff have a cause for action? Why or why not?**
2. **Was the defendant negligent in this situation? Explain.**
3. **Why was Rylands held responsible for the damage to Fletcher's property?**

While visiting his grandparents' home in Atikokan, Ontario, with his family, the infant plaintiff, six-year-old Robby Strom, and his siblings went to play across the street on a church lot. While he was playing, Robby saw a golden retriever, owned by the defendant Kim White, who lived next door to the church.

The dog was on a leash that reached the church property. When Robby approached and hugged the dog, the animal growled. Because of this, Robby went to leave but was attacked and bitten by the dog. As a result of the vicious attack, the boy suffered three cuts to his face, which had to be sutured, and other cuts and abrasions. The facial cuts left permanent and obvious scarring, and Robby experienced shock, nightmares, and a fear of dogs that eventually began to subside.

The infant plaintiff and his parents sued for damages under Ontario's *Dog Owners' Liability Act* and were awarded $22 000 in general damages for the infant's physical injuries and mental suffering.

Strom et al. v. White et al.
(1994)

**Ontario Court,
General Division
21 O.R. (3d) 205**

1. Since the defendant did not enter a Statement of Defence against the plaintiff's Statement of Claim, a default judgment was issued by the court. What does this mean, and what does this imply about the claim?

2. The Ontario legislation contains the principle of strict liability for dog owners and their dogs. What does this mean?

3. From the facts, was Robby negligent or in any way at fault for his own accident? Why or why not?

4. Considering the general damages for non-pecuniary loss awarded to Gary Thornton in Chapter 10, how do you regard the damages awarded to Robby Strom? Give reasons for your answer.

animal's frightening or physically attacking a person. Since these types of animals are uncommon house pets, legal actions here usually involve animals in circuses, zoos, and animal parks.

Domestic animals include both pets and farm animals. A domestic animal is considered wild only after its owner knows from its actions that the animal is dangerous. It is commonly said that every dog is entitled to its first bite, but this is not always true. An owner can be held liable even for the first bite, if the animal has previously shown a bad temper.

All provinces and the territories have passed laws regulating the liability of dog owners, but these statutes vary greatly. British Columbia,

Alberta, Manitoba, Ontario, and Newfoundland now have legislation making dog owners strictly liable for harm arising from a dog bite or attack.

Reviewing Your Reading

1. What is strict liability?

2. List two examples of situations involving strict liability.

3. With examples, name the two legal classifications of animals.

4. How does strict liability apply to animal owners?

In recent years, the media have been filled with reports about violence in our society—violent crimes, violence against women and children, violence in schools, and violence among juveniles. It seems that violent acts are becoming part of our culture.

Another part of our culture is sports. Playing sports and watching and reading about sports and its participants is a major pastime for many Canadians. Violence has increased in sports, especially in those team sports that involve body contact, such as hockey and football. Violence has even emerged in baseball. Players and fans alike have been guilty of outbursts of violence. For many years, violence in sport was considered part of the sport; the sport itself determined the level of violence. Fans expected it and players and coaches tried not to disappoint them. However, violence in sports has escalated to the point where players deliberately provoke fights to excite the crowd. Sometimes these outbreaks of violence between teams spark fights among their respective supporters in the audience. Now violence in sports is under attack.

On One Side

Fans and players maintain that a certain amount of violence is a natural part of the game. The risk of injury in sports like hockey is as much a part of the game as winning and losing. They maintain that those who criticize this aspect of hockey do not really understand the game. If violence were eliminated, fan support would decrease and the game would suffer.

According to Bill Hay of the Chicago Blackhawks, "Hockey is a tough sport and you've got to be tough to play . . . there's nothing wrong with a good clean fight now and then. No one ever gets hurt." Players feel that they must bodycheck from time to time to avoid actions like highsticking and retaliation from opposing players.

Supporters of the status quo feel that there are enough rules and penalties in hockey to punish those who use excessive violence and that there is no need for criminal or civil action.

In sports, should a player who intentionally injures another player be subject to criminal and civil action?

In 1987, Brad Hornung, a 17-year-old star for the Regina Pats, was disabled for life after a cross-check sent him into the boards and snapped his neck.

On the Other Side

Concerned individuals and groups are seeking solutions to violence which they see as a dangerous and widespread epidemic—and this includes violence in sports.

Those who oppose violence in sports are concerned about the impression this behaviour has on youngsters. At an early age children who play hockey are taught how to bodycheck to get control of the puck; phrases like "taking him out" and "playing the man" are commonplace. Players are expected to stand up to others who fight, never back down, and always support team members who are involved in a fight. There is a fear that this learned violence will become part of their daily lives.

Fans who oppose violence in sports like hockey believe it is destroying the game. Players are more intent on the violence than they are on the skills required to play the game well. Indeed, a major focus of team acquisition is on players who can fight and intimidate opponents.

Some Canadians are even pressing for criminal prosecution and civil action against intentional violence by players. They point out that if the type of violence that occurs during play were to occur outside the sport, the perpetrators would be charged with assault and battery and sued for damages. They maintain that larger fines and indefinite suspensions by the clubs and the laying of criminal charges and civil suits in the courts would rid sports of unnecessarily violent behaviour.

The Bottom Line

Efforts are now being made to understand the nature of all forms of violence in order to deal more effectively with it. Violence in sports is no exception. Sports clubs are being pressured to make and enforce tougher rules and penalties for violence in sports. Failure to do so may lead to government intervention to deal with the problem. While some Canadians approve of violence in sports and consider it part of the game, others feel it detracts from the game and should be treated the same as any violent behaviour in our society. What do you think? You be the judge!

1. **How does violence in sports relate to tort law?**

2. **What has been the traditional attitude toward violence in sports? Is it changing?**

3. **Ask members of the class who participate in body-contact sports to give their opinion about violence in sports. Is it a necessary part of the game?**

4. **Is violence in sports a reflection of violence in society? How should it be dealt with?**

5. **Should injured players be encouraged to press charges and sue for damages?**

CHAPTER REVIEW

Reviewing Key Terms

For each of the following statements, indicate the key term being defined:

a) intentional physical contact harmful or offensive to another person

b) oral statements that defame or injure another's reputation

c) using land in a way that interferes with someone else's enjoyment and use of neighbouring land

d) a tort causing the victim to reasonably fear that bodily harm may occur

e) to enter another's property without consent

f) defamation in printed or more permanent form

g) a defence against defamation reserved for statements made in legislative debate and court hearings

h) the best defence against defamation of character

i) acquisition of a personal right to use a road, water, or air by reason of continuous usage

j) imposed in tort law when a lawful activity exposes others to serious risks even though no fault is involved on the wrongdoer's part

Exploring Legal Concepts

1. Someone who punches another person in the face may be liable for both the tort of battery and the crime of assault or assault causing bodily harm. What factors determine whether one or both charges will proceed to trial?

2. Using an original example, show how the courts distinguish between a trivial touching of one person by another and an actionable touching.

3. Give two reasons why "false imprisonment" is a misleading term. What might be more appropriate?

4. The following statement is taken from the decision in *Allan v. New Mount Sinai Hospital et al.* (1980) 28 O.R. (2d) 356 : "It is an important individual right to have control over one's body, even where medical treatment is involved. It is the patient, not the doctor, who decides whether surgery will be performed, where it will be done, when it will be done, and by whom it will be done." Give your opinion of this statement, and be prepared to defend it in class.

5. Whether a nuisance exists and there has been unreasonable interference with the use and enjoyment of land is often left to the courts to determine. As judge, what factors would you consider in reaching a decision on this issue?

6. Should a person be held liable for harm or injury to another person when neither fault nor negligence exists on the part of the first person? Why or why not?

Applying Legal Concepts

1. The headmaster of a boarding school refused to let a mother take her son home for holidays until the boy's tuition had been paid. After 17 days, the boy was finally sent home. He was unaware that he had been detained.

   - **Can the boy take action for false imprisonment when he realizes what happened?**

2. When the plaintiff, Martha Otto, left a Canadian Tire store, she was stopped by a security officer, Betty Myers. The officer claimed that she thought she saw the plaintiff open a package of wall hooks and take one. Otto denied this and agreed to accompany Myers to the security room. After a search of Otto's pockets and finding only a package of seeds, Myers then claimed that she saw the plaintiff take the seeds. Mrs. Otto explained that she had purchased them elsewhere for a friend. Otto was ultimately acquitted on the criminal charge of theft, and she brought a civil action for damages.

   - **On what grounds did she base her action, and would she succeed?**

3. A ship owned by Lake Erie Transport Company remained at dock for safety during a storm. The action of the waves resulted in the ship's crashing repeatedly against the wharf and causing damage.

   - **Was the ship trespassing? Was Lake Erie Transport held responsible for the damage to the dock?**

4. The top of the Saulniers' fence leaned several centimetres over the Manns' property. The fence had been erect when constructed, but changed position from the weight of the snow over many winters.

   - **Explain whether the sagging fence is a trespass or a nuisance.**

5. *Brushett v. Cowan* (1990) Newfoundland Supreme Court, Appeal Division
   3 C.C.L.T. (2d) 195

   The plaintiff, registered nursing assistant Sheila Brushett, consulted the defendant Dr. Cowan, an orthopaedic surgeon, in connection with a leg injury. When her condition did not respond to treatment as hoped, and as a noticeable lump appeared on her right thigh, the doctor advised a muscle biopsy, to which Ms. Brushett consented.

   The signed hospital consent form also contained a statement that the patient consented to "such further or alternative measures as may be found necessary during the course of the operation." As the muscle biopsy progressed, Dr. Cowan became suspicious of possible malignancy in the bone tissue, and he biopsied a portion of the bone also. The plaintiff was released from hospital later that same day without crutches.

   Two days later after a further visit to Dr. Cowan, arrangements were made to provide Ms. Brushett with crutches. She claimed that no instructions were given to her to avoid placing any weight on the leg; nor, she said, was she informed that bone tissue had been taken during the operation. However, the doctor claimed otherwise. Several days later, while not using her crutches, Brushett fell and broke her leg at the point where the bone biopsy had occurred.

She brought an action to the Newfoundland Supreme Court, Trial Division, for injury, alleging both battery and negligence in the provision of post operative care. The trial judge found the defendant doctor liable for both torts but found the plaintiff 20 percent contributorily negligent for her injuries.

- **Why did the plaintiff claim that battery and negligence had occurred?**

- **Why was Brushett found 20 percent at fault for her accident? Do you agree with this decision? Why or why not?**

6. *Joyce v. Yorkton Gun Club Inc.* (1990) Saskatchewan Court of Queen's Bench 84 Sask. R. 289

The plaintiffs, Colin and Louise Joyce, lived on a farm across the road from the Yorkton Gun Club. Mr. Joyce had lived all his life on the farm site in question and had built a new house there in 1982 when he married. He and his wife loved to sit on the outside deck of their home to dine, to visit with friends, and to enjoy the atmosphere and scenery of rural Yorkton.

Across the road from the plaintiffs, separated by a stand of trees and 297 m, was the defendant club that had operated for the past 16 years. The firing range was open for use from 10:00 a.m. until 10:00 p.m., seven days a week, and the sound of gunfire, which the Joyces found to be objectionable and intrusive, "shattered the peaceful atmosphere" of their farm. They were most upset by the noise, especially in the summer months.

The plaintiffs brought an action for an injunction against the defendant club to the Court of Queen's Bench.

- **Why did the plaintiffs bring an action against the defendant club?**

- **Why did they seek an injunction, rather than damages, from their court action?**

- **What arguments would the defendant gun club present?**

- **Although the judge granted the plaintiffs $1000 damages for the continued inconvenience and an injunction, the latter was suspended for six months. What do you think were the reasons for this suspension?**

7. *Allen v. Bailey et al.* (1995) Ontario Court, General Division 24 C.C.L.T. (2d) 212

The deceased husband of the plaintiff, Amie Allen, took his own life when his torrid affair with the defendant, Kate Bailey, was discovered. The deceased was a well-known physician in a small Ontario community. The defendant knew that the plaintiff was an avid reader of *The Globe and Mail* and, therefore, wrote an obituary notice that was published and included the initials "T.D.S., W.W." and ended with a Latin quotation attributed to the famous Irish writer, Jonathan Swift. The initials meant "tall distinguished surgeon" and "well worth it," and the English interpretation of the Latin quotation was: "for rage and resentment can no longer eat into the heart."

The plaintiff widow alleged that the obituary notice as a whole, whether in its natural meaning or by innuendo, was defamatory of her, suggesting that her personality and attitude to her husband had embittered his life and provoked his death, and that it was published out of malice toward her.

The defendant applied for a court order dismissing the plaintiff's action, since the words complained of were incapable of bearing a defamatory meaning and contained nothing that would implicate the plaintiff in any meaning they might bear.

The defendant's application was allowed and granted.

- **What form of defamation did the plaintiff argue?**

- **Would a reasonable person reading the doctor's obituary likely know what "T.D.S." and "W.W." meant? Explain.**

- **Do you agree with the court's decision? Why or why not?**

Extending Legal Concepts

1. Now that you have completed this chapter, review the opening article and Something to Think About. Have your answers or opinions changed? Why or why not?

2. The *Young Offenders Act* states that a child under the age of 12 cannot be charged with a criminal offence. Should there be similar statute law to regulate a child's liability in torts? If so, what should that minimum age be, and why? If not, why not?

3. Participants in sporting events are often required to sign liability release forms, or waivers, before being permitted to play. How do these forms differ from the normal common-law rule that a participant consents to all ordinary risks of the sport? In a group, collect as many of these waivers as possible, and prepare a bulletin board display for the class and an oral report on the similarities and differences among the forms.

4. Working with a partner, collect editorial cartoons or film, theatre, or book reviews from five editions of a daily or weekly local newspaper. Analyze what you have collected and determine if it is fair comment, libel, or questionable between the other two options. Prepare a bulletin board display of the material you have gathered and be prepared to defend your choices before the class.

5. In 1994, Rochelle Pittman was awarded $515 000 in general damages to compensate her for her pain and suffering, loss of past and future income, and the cost of her future care in her suit against the Canadian Red Cross, the Toronto General Hospital, and her family doctor, Stanley Bain. Pittman's husband died of AIDS, contracted when he received a transfusion of tainted blood in late 1984. The defendants never informed Pittman that he may have been exposed to the disease, and he, in turn, passed it on to his wife. Consider all the information that you have studied in the last two chapters on negligence and the function and role of medical practitioners. Discuss the implications of this case in small groups. The complete case can be found in 19 C.C.L.T. (2d) 1 and in a detailed report in *Lawyers Weekly*, March 25, 1994.

6. Using reference materials in your resource centre, including CD-ROM and the Internet, obtain current information on any of the following:

a) recent nuisance actions and their resolution

b) medical assault and battery actions

c) defamation of character actions

d) actions taken by famous people against the supermarket tabloids

e) other tort issues related to this chapter

Write a one- or two-page summary of your findings and, if possible or appropriate, create a poster to display your information.

Researching an Issue

Parental Discipline

Debate concerning parents' rights to discipline their children appears regularly in the media as the issue of child abuse is given a focus and profile. The *Criminal Code* gives parents, guardians, and teachers the right to use "force by way of correction . . . if the force does not exceed what is reasonable under the circumstance." This legal authority was examined earlier in this chapter.

In May 1995, David Peterson, a resident of Warrenville, Illinois, was acquitted of spanking his five-year-old daughter, Rachel, in a parking lot in London, Ontario. To discipline his daughter after she had pushed her two-year-old brother from the car and then slammed the door on his fingers when he tried to get back in the car, Peterson pulled her pants down and spanked her on the trunk of his car. This incident was reported to the police by a witness. A detailed description of the case appears in the May 8, 1995, edition of *Maclean's* magazine.

Statement

Parents should not be allowed to spank their children under any circumstances to discipline them as this is a form of assault and child abuse.

Point

Spanking is cruel and abusive punishment. There are other ways to discipline a child.

Counterpoint

Parents have always spanked their children to discipline them, and it is a valid form of discipline if the force used is not excessive.

• **With a partner, research this issue and reflect on your findings.**

• **Prepare points on this statement that could be used for a class debate.**

• **Discuss your findings with others in your class.**

UNIT
4

FAMILY LAW

Introduction

Family law, which deals with marriage, separation, divorce, and custody and support of children, is an area of specialization for many lawyers. A family-law practice requires a staff that is sensitive, compassionate, and understanding to deal with clients who are often feeling rejected, depressed, or angry. A key member of any law office staff is the legal secretary.

In Focus: LEGAL SECRETARY

Legal secretaries, sometimes referred to as administrative assistants, are employed in law offices and in the legal departments of business firms, real estate companies, banks, mortgage and insurance establishments, and land title offices. They play a very important role in the day-to-day operation of the office and are able to command a salary which ranges from $23 000 to $44 000 per year.

Education and Other Qualifications

If you choose a career as a legal secretary, it will be helpful for you to have studied Accounting, Computer Studies, Keyboarding, and Law at high school. Although a post-secondary education is not always necessary if you have good word-processing and communication skills, you will find your chances of becoming a legal secretary are improved greatly if you complete a legal secretarial course offered by community colleges and some private business colleges.

Responsibilities

As a legal secretary, you will be responsible for preparing and proofreading legal documents and correspondence, scheduling appointments, organizing conferences, maintaining legal records, and sometimes searching land titles. You may also be expected to take minutes or notes at meetings and supervise other office workers.

Work Environment

Your work will be in an office working for one or more lawyers. You will use a computer or word processor and other office equipment, such as copying and fax machines. You will usually work a regular seven- or eight-hour day, although it may sometimes be necessary for you to work overtime in order to complete an important task.

Do You Fit the Job?

You must have good communication skills as you will be expected to listen to and speak with clients in person or on the telephone. You may also be expected to compose some correspondence. Excellent word-processing and proofreading skills are also essential. Some of your tasks will be routine and repetitive, but you will be expected to be flexible, adaptable, and well organized with the ability to work as a team member.

$\mathcal{P}$ROFILE: Samantha Morgan

Samantha Morgan has worked as a legal secretary for a law firm in British Columbia for seven years. Upon graduation from high school she had planned to study at university but chose instead to attend business college as she felt some urgency to acquire marketable skills.

At business college, Ms. Morgan learned word processing and other computer-related skills. She learned how to operate a dictating and transcribing machine, and gained a general understanding of Canada's legal system.

When Ms. Morgan was first hired as a legal secretary, her main duties were related to conveyancing: doing title searches, assisting with real estate transfers, preparing mortgage documents, and so on. After a year with the firm she moved into the litigation field. She also works on wills and separation agreements. She sometimes organizes social functions, sits in on employment interviews for other legal secretary positions, and performs a variety of administrative tasks.

Ms. Morgan enjoys her present position because of the variety of tasks she performs, and because she is interested in people and the ways in which the law touches their lives.

When asked to identify the keys to success in her occupation, Ms. Morgan said that probably the most important thing is being well organized and being able to handle many tasks at the same time. A legal secretary has to be flexible. There is no set routine. Having an easy-going personality is an asset as the work can sometimes be quite stressful. Being able to get along with others and having good communications skills are also essential. Important also, is having the ability to work as part of a team of people who have very different roles, training, and responsibilities.

Questions and Activities

1. Interview a family lawyer and prepare an outline describing a typical day.

2. Most law firms use computer software programs to assist them in completing legal tasks. Survey at least three law firms and prepare a report describing the software they are currently using and what software they are considering purchasing and why.

3. Three jobs related to family law are: Marriage and Family Counsellor, Notary Public, and Public Trustee. Select one related position and write a profile using the following headings: Education, Responsibilities, Work Environment, Skills, and Attributes.

4. Prepare a letter and résumé applying for a summer position in a family-law practice.

EXPLORING MARRIAGE AND DIVORCE

These are the key terms introduced in this chapter:

adultery
affinity
annulment
banns of marriage
bars to divorce
bigamy
capacity
collusion
common-law marriage
condonation
connivance
consanguinity
consent
consummation

co-respondent
cruelty
decree of nullity
divorce
divorce judgment
duress
essential requirements
formal requirements
impotence
marriage
marriage breakdown
matrimonial home
mediation
mistake

monogamy
petition for divorce
petitioner
presumption of death certificate
reconciliation
respondent
separation
separation agreement
solemnization of marriage
spouses
sterility
void

Chapter at a Glance

Learning Outcomes

At the end of this chapter, you will be able to

1. outline the main areas of concern within family law;
2. distinguish between the essential and formal requirements of marriage;
3. explain the effect of a missing requirement on the validity of the marriage;
4. distinguish between an annulment and a separation, and describe the effect of each on a marriage;
5. identify the parties involved in a divorce action;
6. describe the changes in Canada's divorce laws over the years;
7. outline the grounds for divorce as given in the *Divorce Act, 1985*;
8. describe reconciliation and mediation in the divorce procedure.

Man Wins Love of His Life and Freedom from Family

It didn't matter that he didn't have his parents' blessing—or that he could barely afford a wedding ring.

Walton Sue wanted to marry the girl of his dreams, and he did.

In a simple ceremony at old city hall at 2 p.m. yesterday, Sue and Maria DeSousa wed in front of a few members of the bride's family and a couple of close friends—and a horde of reporters.

Sue, who was left partially paralyzed and brain damaged after he was struck by a car 15 years ago, has been battling with his family for their approval to marry DeSousa, his girlfriend of three years.

DeSousa has cerebral palsy and uses a wheelchair.

Charles Yeow, who is married to Sue's older sister, Angela, said the family was not opposed to the wedding, but wanted their concerns about Sue's care and finances addressed first.

"His parents wanted reassurances that Walton will be looked after because he is handicapped and she is (in a wheelchair), and that his (money) will not be unwisely spent," he said. "We were thinking about a prenuptial agreement."

Sue, who was hit by a car when he was 16, was awarded $2000 a month in an insurance settlement. His father has partial control over the money.

Yeow said the family believes his money will be spent faster now that he is married.

"And what if they divorce?" said Yeow. "We are just concerned . . . I don't think he's thought of the implications of getting married."

From: Kris Rushowy, "Man wins love of his life and freedom from family." *The Toronto Star*, June 27, 1995. Reprinted with permission—The Toronto Star Syndicate.

Something to Think About

- **Do you think Sue and DeSousa meet the requirements for marriage?**
- **Do you have any concerns about this marriage? Explain.**

13.1 INTRODUCTION

Family law is the area of the law that deals with the relationships among the members of a family: between a husband and a wife, or **spouses**, between parents and children, and sometimes other parties as well, such as grandparents and step-parents.

Traditionally, a family is formed in our society through marriage. A dictionary defines **marriage** as "the voluntary union between one man and one woman, to the exclusion of all others, joined in a special kind of social and legal dependence for the purpose of founding and maintaining a family."

When two people marry, they enter into a legally binding contract provided certain requirements are met. If they divorce, they terminate that contract. Like all contracts, marriage conveys both rights and responsibilities:

- Marriage is a partnership in which each party is expected to make an equal contribution.
- Each spouse has the right to live in the **matrimonial home**, the home in which the couple lives during their marriage.
- In the case of divorce, both have a right to a portion of their home and other assets. The support obligations of one spouse for the other may also have to be considered. Property division and support are discussed in Chapter 14. If there are children, then care, custody, visiting rights, and child support must be determined, as you will see in Chapter 15.
- The surviving spouse has legal rights with regard to the deceased spouse's property. The preparation of a will is examined in Chapter 16.

13.2 THE CHANGING FAMILY STRUCTURE

Human beings are social creatures, and the family has been the basis of our social structure since the earliest times. However, according to a 1995 Statistics Canada report, *Family Over the Life Course*, the nature of the family has changed so drastically in the past two decades that it is no longer possible to talk about a typical family.

Marriage and the Twenty-first Century

The traditional Canadian family of the 1950s and the early 1960s, consisting of a breadwinning husband, a homecaring wife, and at least two children, is becoming a minority group in the current Canadian family structure.

Marriage is still a popular institution, and most Canadians will marry at least once during their lifetime. People are marrying later in life and sometimes postpone having children for various reasons. Families are smaller, with often only one or two children, and some couples remain childless, either by choice or for medical reasons.

Today, increasing numbers of Canadian families consist of

- single-parent families in which the parent having custody of the children is the main caregiver;
- blended families, the result of divorce and remarriage;
- childless marriages;
- common-law relationships with or without children;
- same-sex partner relationships.

The family structure may also differ because of social or ethnic factors. With the aging of the Canadian population, three generations of a family living under the same roof may increase dramatically in the next century. In the 1950s, a majority of immigrants to Canada came from European countries. Today, one out of every two immigrants comes from Asia, Africa, the Caribbean, or Central America, and these new Canadians bring their family customs, traditions, and values with them.

As we approach the twenty-first century, family law is rapidly changing in response to changing family relationships. In fact, during the past

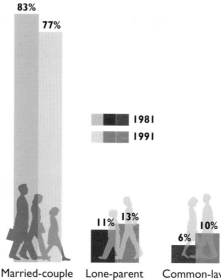

Distribution of families, by structure, 1981 and 1991

83%
77%

1981
1991

Married-couple families 11% 13%
Lone-parent families
Common-law families 6% 10%

Source: Statistics Canada.

25 years, probably no other area of law has undergone such major changes.

Primary Sources of Family Law

The primary sources of family law in Canada are found in federal, provincial, and territorial statutes. In Canada, the *Constitution Act, 1867*, divides the power of making marriage laws between the federal and the provincial governments. Section 91 gives the federal government jurisdiction over marriage and divorce and lists the **essential requirements** for a valid marriage. The purpose is to give national recognition to standard procedures for marriage and divorce. If these were provincial concerns, there would be no guarantee that procedures in one province would be valid in another. Section 92 gives the provincial governments jurisdiction over the **solemnization of marriage**, which deals with the **formal requirements** of the marriage ceremony. In turn, the provinces have delegated the responsibility for issuing marriage licences to the municipal governments. For this reason, some aspects of marriage law differ somewhat from province to province. The essential and formal requirements for marriage are outlined in the next two sections, although some overlap does exist between the two types of requirements.

LOOKING BACK

Until the mid 1700s, people under British law were often united in **common-law marriages** rather than through formal ceremonies. The requirements for such unions were a private agreement and an exchange of promises between a man and a woman. The couple then began to live together as husband and wife. Once **consummation**, or sexual intercourse, had occurred, the marriage was valid. However, the Church of England did not approve of such marriages. After considerable debate, the British Parliament passed the first *Marriage Act* in 1753. This legislation stated that common-law marriages were no longer valid and outlined certain requirements necessary for a valid marriage. Its effect was to recognize only those unions that met the requirements.

Common-law relationships still exist and occur when a man and woman choose to live together without undergoing a formal marriage ceremony. However, the term is misleading since such a relationship does not confer the same rights or responsibilities of a legal marriage upon the couple, no matter how long they live together. Recently, as increasing numbers of couples have chosen this living arrangement, the law has started to recognize the common-law relationship and to provide some legal protection for the parties. The rights of common-law spouses to property division and support upon separation are discussed in greater detail in Chapter 14.

Reviewing Your Reading

1. **What type of issues does family law address?**

2. **Which level of government has jurisdiction over (a) marriage and divorce, and (b) solemnization of marriage?**

3. **What is a common-law relationship? When is a common-law couple considered legally married?**

4. **Describe different types of family units in Canada today.**

13.3 ESSENTIAL REQUIREMENTS OF MARRIAGE

Although the federal government has jurisdiction over the essential requirements for marriage—a person's **capacity** or ability to marry—there is little actual statute law in this area. Instead, the essential requirements are determined by common-law principles. Because of this, each province has clarified any omissions in its own *Marriage Act*. If any essential requirement is lacking at the time of the marriage, the marriage contract cannot be legally recognized.

Mental Capacity

No person who lacks mental capacity by reason of illness, drugs, or alcohol can legally marry. At the time of the marriage, both parties must have the mental capacity or ability to understand not only the nature of the ceremony but also the duties and responsibilities created by the marriage. If mental capacity exists at the time of the marriage, but ceases to exist afterward, the marriage remains valid.

Re McGill
(1979)

Alberta Court of Queen's Bench
21 A.R. 449

An elderly woman, Norah McGill, had been a victim of multiple sclerosis since 1939. Over the years her condition had deteriorated, and she was confined to bed or a wheelchair most of the time. McGill developed a close friendship with David Peal, an 80-year-old man with whom she lived and who had cared for her for five years. When the couple announced that they wished to marry, McGill's two married sisters obtained an injunction to stop the marriage. They also applied to the court for an order confining their sister to a hospital or nursing home.

Medical evidence was presented suggesting that Miss McGill was not able to conduct her own affairs or to make a decision as to her marital status. Evidence was also given that she required nursing care 24 hours a day, either in an institution or at home. This evidence was strongly supported by the two sisters. McGill's personal physician for 66 years gave opposing evidence that the marriage to Peal was important for her psychological welfare, and that Peal could care for her properly. The doctor further stated that, in his opinion, McGill understood and appreciated the nature of marriage. His evidence was supported by testimony from David Peal.

McGill applied to the Alberta Court of Queen's Bench to have the injunction removed and the application for her confinement dismissed. She succeeded in her action.

1. **On what did McGill's sisters base their actions?**
2. **Use a dictionary to find the meaning of an injunction. Why did the sisters obtain one from the courts?**
3. **Which side's medical evidence do you think the court considered more convincing? Why?**
4. **Why did McGill succeed in her action?**

No Prior Marriages

In Canadian law, **monogamy** is the only accepted form of marriage; that is, a person can be married to only one spouse at a time. It is illegal for a person to enter into a second marriage while still married. A person who does so commits the crime of **bigamy**, which makes the second marriage illegal and **void**. A person convicted of bigamy can be sentenced to a maximum punishment of five years in prison, although very few charges have been laid in recent years. Before a person can remarry legally, the earlier marriage must be ended by annulment, divorce, or the death of a spouse.

If a spouse disappears and is absent for a certain period of time, usually seven years, and no one knows his or her whereabouts, the surviving spouse can apply to the courts for a **presumption of death certificate**. Once presumption of death has been declared, the surviving spouse is free to marry again. In some situations, this seven-year limit can be reduced by the courts. This might occur after a plane crash, for example, where many victims' bodies cannot be found. It is presumed that any person missing from the airplane has been killed. A victim's spouse is therefore usually free to remarry without waiting for seven years. Another option for a spouse whose partner has disappeared without a trace is to obtain a divorce in order to marry legally.

It is a difficult situation when a missing spouse, legally presumed dead, is still alive and returns home. This has occurred when people have been injured and suffered long periods of amnesia (loss of memory). The second marriage is then declared void by law. However, the courts do not consider that bigamy has occurred in these cases.

Genuine Consent

Since marriage is a contract, the parties must give their free and voluntary **consent** to it. If either party is forced or tricked into getting married, the marriage may be declared void. During a religious ceremony before a member of the clergy of any religion, or a civil ceremony before a judge or a marriage commissioner, each party, and all those present, are asked whether any reason exists to prevent the marriage. Usually, nothing is said. If either spouse then says after the ceremony that consent was not freely given, the evidence must be very strong for the marriage to be annulled. Lack of consent may result from either a mistake or duress.

Mistake
Mistake is generally one of two types: (i) mistake as to the identity of one of the parties; and (ii) mistake as to the nature of the ceremony. The first of these is quite unusual. However, it might occur when the face of one party is covered for some reason, or when one identical twin takes the place of the other at the ceremony. Mistake as to the nature of the ceremony might occur when one of the parties does not speak the language used in the ceremony and genuinely believes that the ceremony is something other than that of marriage, for example, an engagement ceremony.

Being mistaken or deceived concerning other matters involving the other party, such as wealth, religion, age, health, or personal habits, is not a valid reason for declaring a marriage void.

Duress
Duress occurs when one person marries another out of fear for his or her life, health, or freedom. It does not require the use of physical force. The most common example of duress related to marriage occurs when a pregnant girl's parents threaten to take legal action against the girl's partner if he does not marry their daughter. In any situation involving duress, the courts will annul the marriage if asked to do so by the party forced into the marriage.

Minimum Age

Another essential requirement for a valid marriage is that each party must be old enough to marry. In Canada, the federal government has not established any minimum age for marriage. This has resulted in the adoption of the minimum ages under English common law: 14 years for males, 12 years for females.

All of the provinces and territories have legislation requiring a higher minimum age, and parental consent for a child under a certain age, for marriage. Courts have not upheld legal age as an essential requirement. Age will be further discussed in the next section.

Sexual Capacity

The final essential requirement for a valid marriage is that the parties must be of the opposite sex and be physically able to have sexual intercourse to consummate the marriage. If either party lacks sexual capacity, for instance, if the man is impotent, the marriage may be dissolved.

The **impotence** may arise from a physical problem or a psychological fear of sexual intercourse. It is the inability of one or both spouses to engage in normal sexual intercourse with each other. This lack of capacity must exist at the time of the marriage. If it develops afterward, it does not affect the validity of the marriage. Do not confuse impotence with **sterility**, the inability to have children. A sterile person can consummate the marriage.

At the present time in Canada, same-sex marriages are not legally recognized as they do not meet the accepted definition of marriage.

Did You Know
In 1989, Denmark became the first country in the world to recognize and legalize same-sex marriages, or registered partnerships as they are called. Norway enacted a similar law in 1993 and Sweden in 1994.

Close Relationships

A marriage between two people who are too closely related either by **affinity** (marriage) or **consanguinity** (blood) is not valid. These restrictions were first codified by King Henry VIII in England in the sixteenth century and were based on the Old Testament. They still exist, with minor changes.

Former restricted degrees based on affinity were abolished in the early 1990s. It is now possible, for example, for a woman to marry her divorced husband's brother or nephew, or for a man to marry his divorced wife's sister or niece.

Degrees of Affinity and Consanguinity

A man may marry his	A woman may marry her
Grandfather's wife	Grandmother's husband
Wife's grandmother	Husband's grandfather
Wife's aunt	Husband's uncle
Stepmother	Stepfather
Wife's mother	Husband's father
Wife's daughter	Husband's son
Son's wife	Daughter's husband
Grandson's wife	Granddaughter's husband
Wife's granddaughter	Husband's grandson
Niece	Nephew
Nephew's wife	Niece's husband

CASE

Layland v. Ontario
(Minister of Consumer & Commercial Relations)
(1993)

Ontario Court, General Division
14 O.R. (3d) 658

The two male applicants, Todd Layland and Pierre Beaulne, met in June 1991 at Gay Pride Day in Toronto after corresponding for several months. Shortly after, they moved in together in Ottawa and wanted to marry each other. In early 1992, they applied for a marriage licence at the Ottawa city hall. There is nothing on the application that queries the sex of the applicants, nor are there any words that prohibit same-sex marriages. As well, no federal or provincial statute law prohibits marriages of same-sex persons. However, courts have traditionally recognized the common-law definition of marriage as "the union between one man and one woman." The city clerk turned down their application.

As a result, the applicants applied to the Ontario Court for a review of the clerk's refusal to issue a marriage licence to them. They argued that the limitation that prevents persons of the same sex from marrying violated their equality rights under section 15 of the *Charter of Rights and Freedoms*.

In a landmark 2–1 judgment, a panel of judges dismissed the men's application. Leave to appeal to the Ontario Court of Appeal was granted, but the appeal had not been heard by the fall of 1995.

1. **Why did the city clerk refuse to issue a marriage licence to the applicants?**

2. **Explain in what way the applicants thought that their equality rights were violated.**

3. **The following statement appeared in the court's majority judgment: "The law does not prohibit marriage by homosexuals, provided it takes place between persons of the opposite sex. The fact that many homosexuals do not choose to marry because they do not want unions with persons of the opposite sex is the result of their own preferences, not a requirement of the law ... The applicants were, in effect, seeking to use section 15 of the *Charter* to bring about a change in the definition of marriage." Do you agree or disagree with this statement, and why?**

4. **In her dissenting judgment, Justice Susan Greer stated: "The common law does not remain static. Its very essence is that it is able to meet the expanding needs of society." State your opinion of this comment.**

Reviewing Your Reading

1. a) **List the six essential requirements for a valid marriage.**

   b) **What effect does the lack of one or more of the essential requirements have on a marriage?**

2. **What specific mental capacity must an individual have to marry?**

3. **Define (a) monogamy and (b) bigamy. What effect does bigamy have on a second marriage?**

4. **What is genuine consent? In what two situations might consent to a marriage not be genuine?**

5. **Under what two circumstances might a mistake affect the validity of a marriage?**

6. **Under common law, what are the minimum ages of marriage?**

7. **Distinguish between affinity and consanguinity.**

8. **Distinguish between impotence and sterility. Which affects the validity of a marriage?**

13.4 FORMAL REQUIREMENTS OF MARRIAGE

Provincial and territorial governments have jurisdiction over the procedures for the solemnization of marriage. Formal procedural requirements are outlined in the *Marriage Act* of each province. If spouses fulfill the essential requirements, marry in good faith, and live together, the courts may consider them legally married even if a formal requirement is lacking. Suppose, for instance, that a couple was married in good faith by a person they believed to be properly licensed to marry them, but later discovered that the person was not authorized to perform marriages. The couple would be considered legally married despite the lack of this formal requirement. This problem does not occur very often.

Marriage Licence or Banns

Provincial statutes require that any couple planning to marry must either obtain a marriage licence, or alternatively (in some provinces), have the banns of marriage read in their place of worship. A marriage licence may be purchased for a fee at any city hall or township office. A couple must wait no fewer than three days and no more than three months after obtaining a licence to get married. In British Columbia, the couple must wait at least two days before marrying.

Couples who regularly attend a place of worship may prefer to have their **banns of marriage** announced instead, or as well. The reading of the banns is an alternative in Ontario, Manitoba, and Saskatchewan. In the announcement, the member of the clergy asks the congregation whether anyone is aware of any reason why the couple cannot legally marry. The banns are read at two or three successive weekly services, depending on the province. A couple must wait at least five days after the last banns are read before getting married. Banns may not be announced when either party to the intended marriage has been previously married. In this situation, it is necessary to purchase a marriage licence.

№ 43151
Marriage Licence

GROOM'S GIVEN NAMES

GROOM'S SURNAME

BRIDE'S GIVEN NAMES

BRIDE'S SURNAME

TELEPHONE NO.

DATE ISSUED

ISSUER'S COMPLETE NAME

FILE NUMBER (if Applicable)

REG 3014 (94/06) DVS 34

№ 43151

Marriage Licence

AS _____

and _____

have determined to enter into the state of matrimony and are desirous of having their marriage solemnized in Alberta, I do hereby grant to them this marriage licence by virtue of which any person authorized to solemnize marriages within the Province of Alberta is entitled to solemnize their marriage at any time within three months from the date of issue hereof.

But every person is strictly enjoined to forbear solemnizing their marriage if he has knowledge that any deception was used in obtaining this licence or that there is any lawful impediment by reason of which they ought not to be joined in wedlock.

Given under my hand at Edmonton in the Province of Alberta.

Director of Vital Statistics for the Province of Alberta

Issued on this _____ day of _____ 19 _____

by _____ An issuer for marriage
Print Complete Name

licences for the Province of Alberta, at _____

Signature of Issuer or Deputy

M -
Marriage Licence Issuer Account Number

Alberta
MUNICIPAL AFFAIRS
Registries

REG 3014 (94/06) DVS 34

IMPORTANT INFORMATION SEE REVERSE SIDE

IMPORTANT INFORMATION FOR BRIDE AND GROOM

MARRIAGE LICENCE
This licence does not represent a Legal Marriage. This licence must be given to a clergy or marriage commissioner who is authorized by Vital Statistics to perform legal marriages.

WITNESSES
You will require two witnesses who must be at least 18 years of age.

REQUIRED BRIDE AND GROOM INFORMATION
The Bride and Groom are EACH required to provide the following information prior to the solemnization of their marriage to the officiant.

— FULL NAME OF FATHER
— BIRTHPLACE OF FATHER
— MAIDEN AND GIVEN NAMES OF MOTHER
— BIRTHPLACE OF MOTHER

MARRIAGE CERTIFICATES
A legal (official) Marriage Certificate is available in framing or wallet size. To apply for a certificate complete the Application for Certificate form (supplied to you by the Marriage Licence Issuer) and submit it to Vital Statistics along with your cheque or money order payable to "THE PROVINCIAL TREASURER".

VITAL STATISTICS OFFICE
Box 2023
Edmonton, Alberta
T5J 4W7

PHONE: 427-2683

Marriage Ceremony

A marriage ceremony must be performed by someone with legal authority to conduct marriages. This is usually a minister, priest, rabbi, or a person authorized to perform a religious ceremony, or a judge, justice of the peace, or a marriage commissioner for a civil ceremony. The marriage must take place before at least two witnesses who sign (witness) the Certificate of Registration of Marriage. The couple may marry wherever they wish and may have the ceremony conducted as they wish. They may even write their own ceremony, or portions of it, with the permission of the person officiating at the ceremony. However, the statutes require both parties to make a solemn declaration during the ceremony that they know of no legal reason why they cannot marry. Each must state that he or she takes the other to be his or her lawful wedded spouse, and the person conducting the ceremony must then pronounce them husband and wife.

CASE

Shun Liang Lin, a Chinese resident, met Teresa Tang, a Canadian resident in China, and they agreed to marry in Canada. However, it was a condition of Lin's entry into Canada that he marry Tang within 90 days. About two weeks after arriving in Canada, the couple went through a traditional, non-religious Chinese wedding ceremony, presided over by the eldest member of the family, 76-year-old Pak Lun Lau. The couple did not apply for, or obtain, a marriage licence.

In the traditional Chinese wedding ceremony the focus is upon honouring one's family members. The basis of the ceremony is to have the bride and groom surrounded by family, while the eldest family member performs the ceremony. Mr. Lau was neither a member of the clergy or a marriage commissioner authorized to perform marriages.

After the ceremony, the couple lived together intermittently for two months, and it was unclear whether their marriage had been consummated. Lin brought an application to the Alberta Court of Queen's Bench for an order declaring the marriage to be valid and directing the Director of Vital Statistics to issue a marriage licence. However, Lin's application did not succeed.

Re Lin
(1992)

Alberta Court of Queen's Bench
44 R.F.L. (3d) 60

1. **Why was it so important for Lin to have this marriage declared valid?**
2. **Were the essential and formal requirements of this marriage met?**
3. **Does Lin's ignorance of Alberta marriage law affect this case? Why or why not?**
4. **Why did Lin's application not succeed?**

Minimum Age

Although the minimum marriage ages under common law stand in all provinces except Ontario, most provinces and territories have passed legislation modifying the common-law tradition of 14 years of age for males and 12 years of age for females. These ages were based on the fact that, generally speaking, females are more mature at 12 than males and these were the ages at which males and females reached puberty.

In all provinces and territories except Ontario, marriage under the age of 16 is permitted by court order only, and only when the young woman is pregnant or has a child. In Ontario, no person under 16 may legally marry. The following table shows the marriage ages across Canada.

As the table indicates, a person below the legal minimum age may marry if written consent is obtained from one or both parents. If parental consent is unreasonably withheld, the young person may apply for a court order dispensing with parental consent. The court's function is to review the parents' objections and to decide whether or not they are reasonable. However, case law in this area is limited.

Minimum Ages for Marriage across Canada

Province	Without Parental Consent	With Parental Consent
Alberta	18	16
British Columbia	19	16
Manitoba	18	16
New Brunswick	19	16
Newfoundland	19	16
Nova Scotia	19	16
Ontario	18	16
Prince Edward Island	18	16
Quebec	18	14 Male 12 Female
Saskatchewan	18	16
Yukon Territory	19	16

CASE

Re Al-Smadi
(1994)

Manitoba Court of Queen's Bench
90 Man. R. (2d) 204

In 1993, a 14-year-old girl, Emman Al-Smadi and her father, representing her because of her age, applied to the court for permission for the girl to marry a 27-year-old Jordanian student, Ra'a Ahmed Said; both were practising Muslims. At the time of the application, Said was a doctoral student in electrical engineering at the University of Manitoba, hoping to obtain his degree in 1994.

Evidence was presented to show that it is a belief of the Islamic faith that a girl, having reached puberty, may marry if she wishes, with her father's consent. Emman assumed a major role in cooking, cleaning, and caring for her younger sister as her parents were divorced, and custody of the two girls had been awarded to her father. She also confirmed her consent to the proposed marriage and stated that she was doing so freely and of her own choosing. As well, her father consented to the proposed marriage. The Director of Child and Family Services opposed the application as it was not in the best interest of the child to marry under the age of 16 simply because of parental, cultural, or religious consent.

The Manitoba Court of Queen's Bench dismissed the application. However, several months later, a second application, on the same grounds as the first, was brought to court with the additional ground that the now 15-year-old girl was pregnant with Said's child. This time the court consented to the marriage.

1. **Why was it necessary to make application to the court for this couple to marry?**

2. **What sorts of concerns might the judge have had in considering this application?**

3. **In the initial trial judgment, the judge stated: "In Canada, the rights of all people are recognized and carefully protected. Nevertheless, certain basic values now exist that are the product of hundreds of years of development . . . to protect all citizens. From time to time they may conflict with specific religious, moral, or cultural practices and beliefs . . . and any such conflict must be resolved in favour of the general public interest." Do you agree or disagree with this statement? Explain.**

Blood Tests

In some provinces, including Alberta, and Prince Edward Island, blood tests are an additional formal requirement of marriage. Their purpose is to create an awareness of spousal blood types for emergencies and to test for syphilis. No province in Canada yet requires an AIDS test for a marriage licence. However, if the disease becomes more widespread than it is at present, it is possible that an AIDS test could become a requirement. This demonstrates, once again, the evolutionary nature of the law.

Name Change upon Marriage

It is not a legal requirement for the bride to adopt the groom's surname when they marry. It is simply a custom or tradition, not a legal requirement. A woman may assume her spouse's name, keep her own birth name, or combine her name and her husband's into a surname with or without a hyphen. Whichever choice she makes becomes her legal name. The latter two options are becoming very common. Many women feel that keeping their own surnames is an important indication of their identity as equal partners in marriage. Men also have similar options when they marry, but more women change their names than men. Procedures for doing this are outlined in provincial and territorial *Change of Name Acts*.

A child born to a married couple is usually given the husband's surname, or the hyphenated names of both parents. An unmarried woman can choose between giving her child her own surname or the father's name if he grants permission or paternity is proven. However, since court challenges in the 1980s under the equality rights section, section 15, of the *Charter of Rights and Freedoms*, a married woman in most provinces may now legally give her child her own surname, if both parents consent. In the event of a dispute, a child will be given both names, hyphenated, in alphabetical order.

Non Sequitur

Reviewing Your Reading

1. a) List the formal requirements for a valid marriage.

   b) How does the lack of a formal requirement affect the validity of a marriage?

2. a) What is the purpose of having the banns of marriage read?

   b) When may banns not be read?

3. Describe the requirements for a valid marriage ceremony.

4. When is parental consent needed for a couple to marry?

5. List as many reasons as possible why a woman might want to keep her own surname after marriage.

13.5 ANNULMENT AND SEPARATION

Marriage is a legally binding contract between a man and a woman. If the spouses wish it to end, marriage must be dissolved by the courts through a legal procedure: an annulment or a divorce. The death of either spouse also terminates a marriage. A separation does not end a marriage.

Annulment

An **annulment** is a court order that states that a marriage that seems valid is legally void and never existed from the start. It differs from a divorce in that a divorce dissolves an existing marriage.

The grounds for obtaining an annulment arise from the requirements for a legal marriage. The cause for the annulment must have existed at the start of the marriage, and the parties should never have married in the first place. For example, one of the essential requirements for entering a marriage contract might not have been met; genuine consent might not have been given; or there might have been a major defect in the marriage ceremony. For any of these reasons, the marriage would be declared void, and a judge would issue a **decree of nullity**, a court order annulling the marriage and allowing the parties to go their separate ways. Annulments are commonly obtained by spouses who, for religious or personal reasons, do not want a divorce. This occurs especially in the Roman Catholic, Jewish, and Islamic faiths.

An annulment may also be granted when one spouse is unable to consummate the marriage. If, however, a spouse refuses to have sexual relations, though physically capable of doing so, an annulment will not be granted.

CASE

A.S. v A.S.
(1988)

Ontario Unified Family Court
15 R.F.L. (3d) 443

The female applicant in this action was 16 years old when she was pressured into marriage by her mother and stepfather with whom she lived. The parents received $500 for arranging this marriage to enable the respondent, a visitor to Canada, to remain here. However, when the girl expressed unwillingness to marry, more pressure was brought to bear on her by her parents. No physical force was used to persuade her to enter into the marriage, and none was threatened. The marriage was not consummated, and the applicant did not live with her husband after the marriage ceremony.

The female applicant sought annulment of her marriage in Hamilton's Unified Family Court, and her application was granted.

1. On what grounds did the applicant seek an annulment?

2. Did the applicant willingly agree to the marriage? Explain.

3. Why was the annulment granted?

Finally, there have been several cases before the courts in which the marriage occurred only to allow one of the parties to remain legally in Canada; neither party really intended the marriage to last. When this occurs, the courts will usually consider the marriage is valid and cannot be annulled because of non-consummation.

Separation

Separation is an intermediate step between marriage and divorce. It occurs when a couple decides to no longer live together as husband and wife; they "live separate and apart." Sometimes the parties go no further than this; they live out their lives separately, without getting divorced. This most often occurs when one or both spouses belong to a faith that does not recognize divorce.

The statutory phrase "living separate and apart" means that the spouses have separated physically, and the most common evidence of this is that the spouses have stopped living together and do not intend to live together again. However, if either spouse can prove that, while living under the same roof, the couple slept separately, shared little or no communication, had no common activities, and lived independent lives, Canadian courts will consider that a valid separation exists. Unless they obtain a divorce, the couple is still legally married.

Separation Agreement

Although no legal document is necessary for a separation, many couples enter into a written **separation agreement**. This document outlines the position of each spouse on such issues as the ownership and division of property and debts, support for either spouse and any children, and child custody.

Like most legal contracts, a separation agreement is usually written, signed, and witnessed. Each spouse should approach a lawyer independently and have the lawyers prepare a separation agreement. It is important for each spouse to have his or her own lawyer for independent legal advice so that each spouse's best interests are fairly and objectively represented.

The spouses determine the contents of the agreement, although the lawyers will probably give them advice. The contract must be prepared carefully, or the couple may insert terms or conditions that prove unacceptable in the future. It is essential to include provisions that will allow sections of the document to be changed, if the situation of either party changes.

The courts need not be involved in the preparation of a separation agreement. Once the lawyers have prepared the document with the approval of the spouses, it becomes as enforceable as any other private contract. It is generally felt that spouses should be allowed to determine their own affairs without interference from the legal system. However, a court may change or disregard any provision that is not in the best interests of the children. Even if the spouses have agreed on custody, access, and support, the conditions may be altered if a judge believes that some other arrangement is best for the children's welfare. These issues are discussed in greater detail in Chapters 14 and 15.

Since a separation agreement is a legally binding contract, either party to it can be sued by the other party under the law of contracts for a breach of any term. For instance, if one spouse agrees to pay a certain amount of support each month to the other, but does not do so, the spouse who suffered the loss may ask the courts to enforce payment.

A separation agreement does not give either party the right to remarry or to have sexual relations with another person. To remarry without divorce is bigamy; to engage in sexual intercourse with another person outside the marriage is **adultery**.

Reviewing Your Reading

1. **Name the three ways that a marriage may be terminated.**
2. **Define (a) annulment and (b) decree of nullity.**
3. **Under what circumstances may an annulment be obtained?**
4. **Why might some couples prefer to obtain an annulment rather than a divorce?**
5. **When does separation legally occur?**
6. **List three areas of concern that are usually included in a separation agreement.**
7. **Under what circumstances may the courts alter the conditions of a separation agreement?**

13.6 DIVORCE

Divorce is the legal procedure that ends a valid marriage. The procedures followed in a divorce case are similar to the civil procedures described in Chapter 10. Marriages today are breaking up sooner, and 25 percent of them now end within 15 years. The process begins with a document called a **petition for divorce**, outlining the reasons for the divorce and other essential information. The two parties involved in the action are the **petitioner**, the spouse seeking the divorce, and the **respondent**, the spouse being sued for divorce. If the divorce is based on the respondent's adultery, the person with whom the respondent may have committed adultery is the **co-respondent**. Divorce actions are heard in the superior courts of each province.

If the petitioner has proved the grounds on which the divorce action is based, the judge will grant a **divorce judgment** at the end of the trial. A divorce is final 31 days after judgment is pronounced. A Certificate of Divorce will be issued on application, for a fee. This is the final step in the divorce. The purpose of the waiting period is to give the spouses one last opportunity to get back together. If this occurs, the couple must apply to the courts to have the divorce judgment set aside. Another reason for the delay is to let either party appeal the judgment. If either spouse does so, the divorce is not final until the appeal has been heard. If both parties agree, and if there is a very good reason, the 31-day waiting period may be reduced. This may happen, for instance, if the woman is pregnant and wishes to remarry as soon as possible. However, the judge must be convinced of a special need before reducing the waiting period. After the divorce has been finalized, either party can remarry legally.

LOOKING BACK

You have seen that the *Constitution Act, 1867,* gives the federal government jurisdiction over divorce. However, before 1968, there was no federal law concerning divorce. Thus, divorce law varied somewhat from province to province, although most of Canada followed England's divorce laws. Adultery was almost the only ground for divorce, but this was a great hardship for most people who simply wished to divorce because they were unhappy in their marriages.

As a result of changes in social attitude toward divorce and the need for additional grounds for divorce, the federal government passed the *Divorce Act, 1968.* This statute established a national divorce law for the first time in Canada. The *Act* outlined several specific fault grounds for divorce and different waiting periods for separated couples; it also recognized a three-year separation or marriage breakdown as a new ground for divorce.

The legislation outlined procedures for trying to save the marriage if possible. Both lawyers and judges were specifically required by the *Act* to discuss the possibility of **reconciliation** between the spouses. The courts had the authority to adjourn divorce proceedings where there seemed to be a possibility that the couple might get back together. Judges might even recommend marriage counselling if they felt that it would assist the couple.

If a couple separated and then got back together, the *Divorce Act* provided that a reconciliation of 90 days or less did not affect the three years of separation required for divorce. However, if reconciliation occurred more than once, or for more than 90 days, the couple had to begin a new three-year period of separation, in order to proceed with the divorce. This provision, too, was meant to encourage reconciliation.

The *Divorce Act, 1985*

In an attempt to simplify the law, reduce the numerous grounds for divorce, and respond to social change and pressure for reform, Parliament passed the *Divorce Act, 1985,* which came into effect on June 1, 1986. The first objective of the new statute, like the previous one, was aimed at preserving the family unit through reconciliation. If reconciliation failed, its second objective was to allow the marriage to end with as few destructive consequences as possible for spouses and children.

Under current divorce law, the only valid reason for divorce is **marriage breakdown**. This is the origin of the term no-fault divorce, which allows that neither party is totally at fault or to blame for the divorce—the marriage has simply broken down.

Section 8 of the *Divorce Act, 1985,* states:

8.

(1) A court of competent jurisdiction may, on application by either or both spouses, grant a divorce to the spouse or spouses on the ground that there has been a breakdown of their marriage.

(2) Breakdown of a marriage is established only *if*

  (a) the spouses have lived separate and apart for at least one year immediately preceding the determination of the divorce proceeding and were living separate and apart at the commencement of the proceeding; *or*

  (b) the spouse against whom the divorce proceeding is brought has, since the celebration of the marriage,

    (i) committed adultery, *or*

    (ii) treated the other spouse with physical or mental cruelty of such a kind as to render intolerable the continued cohabitation of the spouses.

Separation

Most couples now use separation for at least one year as evidence of a marriage breakdown and the grounds for divorce. The one year provides a balance between rushing into a divorce and imposing unnecessary hardship on spouses who, knowing their marriage was beyond reconciliation, had to wait three years under the former *Divorce Act.* It does not matter which spouse left or why. Either spouse can begin divorce proceedings immediately upon separation, but the divorce judgment will be pronounced only at the end of the one-year separation.

Adultery and Cruelty

Adultery and **cruelty** have been grounds for divorce for many years. It is the responsibility of the petitioner to prove that adultery actually occurred. The courts usually acknowledge that adultery took place on the basis of reasonable probability. If the respondent and the co-respondent spend a weekend alone in a hotel room, for example, the judge may assume that grounds for adultery exist, unless the respondent can prove otherwise. Parties can also admit adultery by way of an interrogatory, a legal statement, or an affidavit admitting to the adultery.

Cruelty is of two types, physical and mental, and represents very serious and weighty conduct that makes living together no longer possible. Physical cruelty is relatively easy to prove because evidence usually exists in the form of medical reports and photographs that may have been taken of the injured spouse. Witnesses may also testify about the spouse's physical condition.

Mental cruelty, however, is more difficult to determine. What forms of conduct may be considered so severe, heartless, or insensitive that make living together intolerable or impossible? The day-to-day arguments that arise in most marriages do not usually constitute mental cruelty. Over the years, the courts have ruled that mental cruelty includes constant criticism, serious alcoholism, psychiatric disorders, and refusal to have sexual relations that damages the petitioner's health. The definition of mental cruelty is very subjective and may differ from spouse to spouse and from judge to judge.

If one spouse has committed adultery or treated the other spouse with cruelty, the offended spouse can sue for divorce immediately. However, the offending spouse must wait for a one-year separation period.

Turner v.
Turner
(1990)

Newfoundland
Supreme Court,
Trial Division
85 Nfld. & P.E.I.R. 43

Mr. and Mrs. Turner married in 1980 and separated in 1989. The couple had no children. In her divorce petition, Mrs. Turner stated that her husband wanted just the two of them to spend time together alone and had tried to separate her from her family and friends since the beginning of the marriage. This caused her to suffer from migraine headaches, which stopped when the couple separated.

The female petitioner also stated that, as a result of her husband's refusal to adapt to a more social lifestyle or to attempt to resolve this problem, serious differences had arisen between them. On one occasion over a major disagreement, Mr. Turner had hit his wife, but it was an isolated occurrence.

Mrs. Turner petitioned for divorce in the Newfoundland Supreme Court, but her petition was dismissed.

1. **On what ground do you believe Mrs. Turner based her petition?**

2. **For that ground to succeed, what must be proved?**

3. **Why did the court dismiss her petition?**

4. **What would Mrs. Turner now have to do to obtain a divorce?**

Uncontested Divorces

The immediate effect of the *Divorce Act, 1985*, was a sharp increase in the number of divorces granted by Canadian courts. However, the cause was not a drastic jump in the divorce rate. Rather, the increase occurred because couples who had been separated for some time could file for divorce immediately, since the waiting period had been reduced from three years to one year. Another cause was that many applicants had been waiting for the new law to take effect, because it simplified divorce procedures. Consequently, there was a backlog of cases.

Marriages and Divorces in Canada, 1930–1992

Year	Marriages	Divorces
1930	73 341	875
1940	125 797	2 416
1950	125 083	5 386
1960	130 338	6 980
1970	188 428	29 775
1980	191 069	62 019
1990	187 737	78 463
1991	172 251	77 020
1992	164 573	79 034

Source: Statistics Canada.

If no issues, such as property division, support, or custody, are disputed by the spouses, the *Divorce Act, 1985* makes it possible to obtain a divorce without appearing in court. This is known as an undefended or uncontested divorce. In this procedure, the petitioner can present the evidence to the court. A judge reads all of this documentation, along with the petition for divorce. If the judge is satisfied with the evidence, the divorce will be granted. Nearly 90 percent of divorces today are uncontested.

Bars to Divorce

Once proof of marriage breakdown is established, a divorce is generally granted. However, the courts have the power to deny a divorce application if there is some doubt over the grounds. The **bars to divorce**, or reasons for refusing to grant a divorce, are often referred to as the "three Cs"—collusion, condonation, and connivance.

Collusion occurs when spouses agree to attempt to deceive the court. For instance, a couple might lie about the length of their separation or about a non-existent adulterous affair to hasten their divorce. A court will also dismiss a divorce application if it is proven that the marriage was entered into for immigration reasons.

Condonation exists when one spouse knows that the other has committed some wrong, but has indicated that the wronging spouse is forgiven. If, for instance, one spouse commits adultery and the other spouse forgives him or her, then the wronged spouse cannot later use adultery as grounds for divorce. The most common form of condonation occurs when a couple continues living together after one spouse has committed adultery with the knowledge of the other spouse.

Connivance consists of one spouse's encouraging or permitting the other to commit an action that would normally be grounds for divorce. A wife's encouraging her husband to spend a weekend with another woman can be looked upon as connivance. The wife cannot later use her husband's behaviour in that situation as grounds for divorce.

Where either connivance or condonation exists, a divorce may still be granted if the judge feels that termination of the marriage is in the best interests of the couple and the public and, more importantly, that adequate provision has been made for any children of the marriage.

Divorce Mediation

The *Divorce Act, 1985,* established reconciliation as an important objective and included a section that encourages divorce **mediation** to resolve issues that cause conflict between the spouses. Divorce mediation is designed for couples who have decided to get divorced, but want to do so in as civilized a manner as possible. For mediation to succeed, some level of reasonable and positive communication between the spouses is necessary.

The husband and wife meet with a mediator, a neutral third party, usually without their lawyers. Mediators are trained in social work, psychology, and family counselling. Their expertise allows them to help the couple negotiate mutually satisfactory terms of property settlement, support, and custody of and access to children. The purpose of mediation is to protect the rights of all parties equally before the divorce dispute reaches the courts. A bitter court battle should be a last resort in family dispute resolution.

The mediator will help the couple identify the issues to be resolved, offer reasonable alternatives, point out possible problems, and work out an agreement that will become a legally binding part of the divorce. The couple may meet several times with the mediator. Successful mediation requires the cooperation of both spouses.

The main advantage of mediation is that it reduces or eliminates the hostility that so often arises between spouses. The participants, rather than their lawyers, control the process. Effective mediators may help couples see what is at stake in a non-confrontational environment. In many divorces, the main battle develops over child custody and visiting rights. Protection of the children's rights is another important function of mediation.

Finally, the process reduces lawyers' fees since mediation is cheaper than litigation. Successful mediation saves time and money. For example, in Saskatchewan, mediators approach couples as they enter the court system and refer them to an information session on mediation. Those interested can turn to the Department of Justice's mediators where the couple pays from zero to $80 an hour, depending on family income. However, lawyers are still needed after mediation to examine and ratify the legal aspects of the agreement and to present it in court.

Reviewing Your Reading

1. a) **What are the two main parties called in a divorce action?**
    b) **When a third party is involved, what is that party called?**
2. a) **What is the only valid ground for divorce under the *Divorce Act, 1985*?**
    b) **List the three ways this can be proven.**
3. **Why is mental cruelty often difficult to prove?**
4. a) **Define "uncontested divorce," and describe how one is conducted.**
    b) **How common are uncontested divorces?**
5. **Using original examples, distinguish among collusion, connivance, and condonation as bars to divorce.**
6. a) **What is divorce mediation?**
    b) **Name three advantages of mediation.**

Should a homosexual partner be recognized as a legal spouse?

*L*egal rights for gays and lesbians have been a contentious issue in recent years. In 1994, the Quebec Human Rights Commission called for legislation to allow same-sex couples to benefit with full equality with heterosexual couples. In Alberta there was opposition to including sexual orientation in the *Human Rights Code* because it could lead to spousal benefits and adoption rights for homosexual couples.

In June 1994, Ontario MPPs voted 68 to 59 against the New Democratic Party's controversial legislation known as the same-sex spouse bill. The intent of this bill was to extend spousal rights to homosexual couples by redefining the word "spouse" to include a partner of either sex. With its passage, pensions, drug-plan coverage, and other employment benefits would have been extended to a "spouse" of the same sex. In other words, gays and lesbians would have had the same rights as heterosexual married and common-law couples. This proposed legislation was applauded by gay activists and human-rights advocates and denounced by the leaders of the Liberal and Conservative parties and a coalition of church groups. Those who opposed giving homosexuals the legal status of spouse were triumphant. But the issue did not go away.

Less than a year later, on May 9, 1995, a decision by an Ontario family court judge extended homosexual rights. Mr. Justice James Paul Nevins ruled that a section of the *Child and Family Services Act* that prevented homosexuals from adopting their partners' children violated the *Charter of Rights and Freedoms.* This decision opened one door for same-sex couples—the right to adopt children.

Yet in the same month on the twenty-third, in *Nesbit and Egan v. the Attorney General of Canada,* the Supreme Court of Canada denied a gay couple's claim for spousal benefits by a 5–4 vote. It was a two-pronged judgment. The Court unanimously agreed that the equality section of the *Charter of Rights and Freedoms* outlaws discrimination on the basis of sexual orientation; yet the Court said the federal government had reasonable grounds for this discrimination.

More recently, in October 1995, the Nova Scotia government changed its definition of spouse to extend benefits received by heterosexual employees to partners of gay civil servants.

Pierre Beaulne and Todd Layland's application for a marriage licence was refused in early 1992.

On One Side

In the written reasons for his decision, Mr. Justice Nevins noted that "the characteristic of any relationship that transforms it into 'spouse-like' is the sharing of a committed sexual relationship, and it is this sexual commitment element of a relationship which . . . distinguishes it from a close relationship between good friends, or relatives, or roommates. It is the presence of a sexual commitment that is one of the essential ingredients of a spousal relationship."

He also indicated that there is no evidence that homosexual couples cannot provide the type of family environment that society encourages, to the same extent as "traditional" families, parented by heterosexual couples. Nor is there evidence that families in which both parents are of the same sex are any more unstable or dysfunctional than families with heterosexual parents.

On the Other Side

The Supreme Court decision gave legislative preference to the traditional family. In his reasoning, Mr. Justice Gerard La Forest argued "marriage is by nature heterosexual. It would be possible to legally define marriage to include homosexual couples, but this would not change the biological and social realities that underlay the traditional marriage." Given that "heterosexual couples have the unique ability to procreate, it is not unreasonable for Parliament to give special encouragement to this fundamental relationship."

This reasoning is consistent with Christian principles rooted in our society that the purpose of marriage is procreation and that marriages are established by nature, or God. In church doctrine, conjugal relations between homosexuals is a sin; homosexuals should remain celibate.

The Bottom Line

These decisions were about two different same-sex issues—adoption and social benefits—but they were both based on the sexual commitment in a relationship: one recognized an evolution of social values; the other clung to traditional ones. Which one is right? You be the judge!

1. **Why do you think legal rights for gays and lesbians have become an issue only in recent years?**

2. **In two columns, list the legal decisions that illustrate the successes and failures to achieving same-sex rights and benefits.**

3. **Compare the opinions of Mr. Justice Nevins and Mr. Justice La Forest on the subject of same-sex rights and benefits. Which do you most agree with, and why?**

4. **Some believe that legal recognition of same-sex rights and benefits is inevitable and just a matter of time. Do you think this is true?**

Chapter Review

Reviewing Key Terms

For each of the following statements, indicate the legal term being defined:

a) declaration that a marriage never existed

b) legal dissolution of a marriage

c) spouse who begins a divorce action

d) concept of being married to only one spouse at a time

e) partial dissolution of a marriage in which the spouses no longer live together

f) validation of a marriage by sexual intercourse between spouses

g) state of being married to two persons at the same time

h) inability to consummate the marriage and a ground for annulment

i) agreement in which two persons live together as husband and wife without being legally married

j) only valid ground for a divorce in Canada

Exploring Legal Concepts

1. Why is marriage a legally binding contract?

2. Is family pressure a form of duress that might prevent a person from giving genuine consent to marry? Explain.

3. Who should determine the age at which a person should be able to marry—the person, parents, statute law, the courts, or another party? Explain your reasoning.

4. What, if any, practical benefits are gained by recognizing legal marriages between partners of the same sex?

5. Where can you purchase a marriage licence in your community, and what is the current cost?

6. a) Are blood tests a formal requirement of marriage in your province?

   b) Do you think they should be? Why or why not?

7. In this chapter, you have read about the increasing number of women who are keeping their own surnames. What is your opinion of this social trend?

8. What options are available in your province to a married woman concerning (a) her name and (b) her baby's name?

9. In your opinion, does the *Divorce Act, 1985,* make it too easy to obtain a divorce? Explain.

10. Many people believe that the state has no business trying to persuade a couple to attempt reconciliation if they want to divorce. What is your opinion on this matter?

11. Why do you think more and more couples are choosing to live in common-law relationships rather than to marry?

Applying Legal Concepts

1. Henri Lucien was 77 years old when his wife died. Shortly afterward, two qualified physicians certified that Lucien was a mentally challenged person under the provincial *Mental Health Act*. Later that year, Lucien and Francine Dubois were married, but the person performing the ceremony was unaware of the doctors' certificate.

   • **Was the marriage valid? Why or why not?**

2. Ed Craighead came to Nova Scotia from Scotland. After living in the community for three years, he married Elsie Mawhinney, who had lived in Nova Scotia all her life. She did not know that Craighead had a wife back in Scotland from whom he was not yet divorced.

   • **What offence has Craighead committed? Was Mawhinney guilty of any offence? Which marriage was valid, and why?**

3. Sam Bukowski and Bill Stahoviak rented a small plane to fly to northern British Columbia for a hunting trip. The plane crashed in a sudden storm. Bukowski's body was found by searchers the next day, but even after two separate searches, Stahoviak's body was never located.

   • **When will Stahoviak's widow be able to remarry?**

4. Jenny Yeung and Rob Stewart had been dating for one year and planned to marry. During their engagement Stewart assumed, from comments made by Yeung, that she came from a wealthy family and that her mother was chief executive officer (CEO) of a large national corporation. A week after the marriage, Stewart realized that none of this was true.

   • **Was their marriage invalid? Why or why not?**

5. Joel and Marian Kruger were married for four years but had lived separate lives since the eighth month of their marriage. They had separate bedrooms and shared no social activities. They communicated by notes, although they had very brief conversations occasionally. Marian Kruger petitioned for divorce.

   • **On what grounds did she do so? Was her petition granted?**

6. *Khan v. Mansour* (1989) Ontario Unified Family Court 22 R.F.L. (3d) 370

   In January 1989, Sophia Khan, aged 23, entered into a marriage ceremony with the respondent Mansour. After the ceremony, the wife returned to her parents' home, and her husband returned to his own residence. This was not unusual as members of the Islamic faith usually allow the husband four months following the ceremony to set up a home under the families' supervision. Then, the couple would begin living together as a married couple. However, at the end of the four months, Mansour told his wife that he had no intention of living with her as he had no feelings for her. Khan applied for an annulment of the marriage.

   • **On what ground did the petitioner base her application?**

   • **What conditions must exist for this ground to succeed?**

   • **Based on the facts presented, do you think Khan's application for an annulment would succeed? Why or why not?**

7. *Harris v. Harris* (1989) Newfoundland Supreme Court, Trial Division
74 Nfld. & P.E.I.R. 130

The parties in this action were married to one another twice: the first time in 1963 and the second time in 1974. At the time of the first marriage, the female petitioner was only 16 years old and lacked parental consent to marry. The couple used a consent form allegedly signed by the petitioner's mother, but it was actually signed by the respondent's father. This consent form also used an incorrect first name for the petitioner; she was described as "Mary Saint" instead of her correct name, "Frances Saint." This incorrect name was used during the ceremony and on the marriage certificate. The couple continued to live in the community where the petitioner's parents lived, and she was known there as Mrs. Harris.

Eleven years later, in 1974, the couple went through a second marriage simply because the petitioner wished to be married in her own church, but they did not obtain the required marriage licence. Between the first and second marriages, the couple had five children.

In 1989, the wife petitioned for divorce from her husband on the grounds of separation for at least one year, but at issue was the validity of their marriages.

- **What concerns existed to question the validity of each marriage?**

- **Were these concerns a lack of essential or formal requirements? Explain.**

- **Should the nonfulfillment of these requirements make the marriages invalid? Why or why not?**

- **Did the couple intentionally try to conceal their identities or the fact that they were marrying? Explain.**

- **Based on the facts presented, do you think the court would grant the petitioner her divorce? Why or why not?**

8. *Bailey v. Bailey* (1994) Saskatchewan Court of Queen's Bench 119 Sask. R. 71

The parties in this action, Gail Christine Bailey and Ted Harold Bailey, had been married for several years and lived in the same house. However, as time passed, although their meals were prepared together, they ate in separate rooms. They travelled together to social events, but they did not have sexual relations.

In late 1993, Mr. Bailey moved out, and the parties lived in separate accommodations for about three months. In February 1994, Mrs. Bailey sought a divorce.

- **Who is the petitioner, and who is the respondent in this action?**

- **On what ground was the divorce petition based?**

- **Was this ground valid? Explain.**

- **Based on the facts presented, do you think the court would grant the petitioner a divorce? Why or why not?**

Extending Legal Concepts

1. Now that you have completed this chapter, review the opening article and Something to Think About. Have your answers or opinions changed? Why or why not?

2. With a partner, discuss the financial, social, and emotional issues of getting married. Make a list of the positive and negative factors involved. Try to reach consensus or agreement on the issues.

3. Using the information you and your partner compiled in Question 2, list those items that both of you strongly believe should be included in a marriage contract. Include only those items that might be enforceable in a court of law or with a mediator if problems arose later in the marriage.

   Also, make a list of other items that you might like to include but that would not be enforceable if disputed.

4. Although there are several advantages to mediation in divorce proceedings, are there any disadvantages? Brainstorm with a partner.

5. Using reference materials in your resource centre, including CD-ROM and the Internet, obtain current information on the number of marriages, divorces, and common-law relationships in Canada and in your province. Write a one-page summary of your findings, and create a poster to display your information.

Researching an Issue

Violence Against Women—What Can Be Done to Stop It?

According to the 1993 Violence Against Women Survey, violence against women by their mates is widespread. There is a growing awareness that violence is learned, not innate behaviour. Our culture emphasizes that boys and men should be competitive, strong, and unemotional; to be different results in negative stereotypes, name-calling, ridicule, and ostracism.

Professional counsellors believe that men are socialized in a way that does not allow them to express their anger, fear, and insecurity. These feelings build up and often explode; the targets of their rage are often their wives or girlfriends.

Statement

Society should direct government spending to address this situation.

Point

Government spending should be directed toward programs in schools and in the community on anger and stress management to help men deal with their feelings in more positive and constructive ways.

Counterpoint

More attention should be paid to victims of violence. More government funding should be available to women's shelters and programs designed to enable abused women and their children to live apart from their abusers.

- **With a partner, research this issue and reflect on your findings.**
- **Prepare points on this statement that could be used for a class debate.**
- **Discuss your findings with others in your class.**

Chapter

14

PROPERTY DIVISION AND SUPPORT

These are the key terms introduced in this chapter:

business assets

cohabitation agreement

domestic contract

equalization payment

family asset

marriage contract

matrimonial home

matrimonial property

net family property

non-family assets

self-sufficiency

separate property system

separation agreement

spousal support

unconscionable judgment

Chapter at a Glance

Learning Outcomes

At the end of this chapter, you will be able to

1. explain why reform was necessary in the laws regarding property sharing on marriage breakdown;
2. understand why marriage is considered to be an equal partnership between spouses;
3. outline your provincial property-sharing legislation on marriage breakdown;
4. discuss the factors that might result in an unequal division of assets, or their value;
5. discuss the key principles to consider in determining spousal support;
6. describe the procedures for enforcing support orders;
7. compare the rights of married couples with those of common-law partners concerning property division and support;
8. explain the importance of domestic contracts and the main types available.

The Divorced Dad as Cash Cow

Whitecourt chiropractor Ziegfried Zierath says he would cheerfully pay a reasonable amount to help his ex-wife Donna Hurd raise their three daughters, aged 15, 13, and 8. Last year [1993], however, Ms. Hurd convinced a judge to triple his child support payments to $2700 per month. The outraged ex-husband charges that the court appears determined to treat him as the villain and his wife as the victim of their marital split.

After a stormy marriage, Dr. Zierath and Ms. Hurd had divorced in 1986. The couple was then about $150 000 in debt. He agreed to assume that debt, and they settled on joint custody and $900 a month in child support.

In 1988, Dr. Zierath remarried, to a woman with two children of her own. They have since had another baby.

In late 1992, Ms. Hurd applied to have her child support increased.

On the basis of a budget supplied by Ms. Hurd, Mr. Justice Cote [of Edmonton Court of Queen's Bench] calculated the cost of raising the three daughters at $2036 per month. Dr. Zierath's share was $1680, since he and his wife earn over $100 000 annually compared to Ms. Hurd's $23 500. In order to provide her with $1680 after taxes, Dr. Zierath must pay Ms. Hurd $2700 monthly.

From: Les Sillars, "The divorced dad as cash cow." *Western Report*, February 7, 1994. Reprinted with permission of *Western Report*.

Something to Think About

- **Should the income of Dr. Zierath's current wife be a factor in his support payments?**
- **Should the children in his new family come first?**
- **What do you think of the court's decision? Explain.**

14.1 INTRODUCTION

As you read in Chapter 13, the *Constitution Act, 1867*, gives the federal government jurisdiction over marriage and divorce, thereby ensuring that there is a single divorce law for all Canadians. However, the provincial and territorial governments have jurisdiction over property and civil rights. It is these provincial laws that regulate

- property division,
- support,
- wills and inheritance,
- child custody and access when spouses separate.

To recognize that marriage is an equal partnership, provincial and territorial laws regarding property division changed significantly during the late 1970s and early 1980s. When a marriage breaks down today, there is legislation to regulate the fair and equal division of property, or its value, between married couples. Similar legislation does not exist for common-law partners, no matter how long they have lived together. However, some legislation exists to provide certain limited rights for common-law partners.

During a marriage, both spouses have financial obligations to support each other and any children of the marriage. When the spouses separate, these obligations do not disappear. Support is based on the need of one spouse and the other spouse's ability to pay. Provincial legislation also deals with support during separation. When couples divorce, the federal *Divorce Act* regulates support obligations.

Some couples may want to specify their rights, responsibilities, and obligations to each other, or they may want to opt out of provincial legislation that would dictate the division of property upon marriage breakdown. To accommodate these couples, provincial legislation now recognizes domestic contracts made by both married and unmarried couples.

14.2 THE NEED FOR REFORM

The *Married Woman's Property Act*, passed by the British Parliament in 1882, granted wives the right to own and control property as though they were single. In Canada, provinces that followed the common law used this statute as the basis for similar legislation. However, the **separate property system** often resulted in hardship for women if a marriage ended.

Until the early 1970s, the husband was generally the breadwinner (the spouse who worked for wages), while the wife tended the household and the children. In the event of marriage breakdown, the most common attitude was "What I paid for is mine and what you paid for is yours." Since many wives earned little, if any money, they could buy few goods. As a result, the husband, who had paid for the property, took most of it. The courts were not prepared to grant the wife an interest in property that was registered in her husband's name, or to recognize her contribution in the form of household management and homecare duties.

Even if both spouses worked, the husband usually earned much more than his wife. Often, his wages were used for the mortgage payments on their home, while her wages paid the household expenses. On the marriage breakdown, the husband was considered to be the sole owner if the home was registered in his name only, as was often the case. Although the wife's wages paid for the family's expenses, which had allowed her husband to pay for their home, her financial contribution was not recognized. At best, she might be permitted to keep the property, such as the car, for which she had paid.

Clearly, the separate property system presented problems. The problems with the existing law and its unfairness to women became the focus of public attention in the landmark case of *Murdoch v. Murdoch*.

CASE

Murdoch v. Murdoch
(1973)

Supreme Court of Canada
13 R.F.L. 185

Irene Murdoch and her husband were married in 1943 and worked together for hire on various ranches, receiving about $100 a month. In 1947, Murdoch and his father-in-law, Nash, purchased a guest ranch for $6000. When they sold it four years later, they divided the profit equally between them. In 1952, Mr. Murdoch purchased additional property from money borrowed, in part, from his mother-in-law. The loan was repaid. Over the years Murdoch bought and then sold bigger and better ranch properties, always in his name. At all times, the Murdochs lived on and operated one or more of these. In none of the purchases did Mrs. Murdoch make a direct financial contribution.

At the same time, Mr. Murdoch was employed by a cattle stock association. While her husband was away for up to five months of the year working for the association, Mrs. Murdoch performed or supervised many of the necessary chores, including driving trucks and tractors; haying; mowing; vaccinating, branding, and dehorning cattle; and working with horses. In effect, while her husband was absent, she ran their properties.

Marital problems arose and in 1968 Mrs. Murdoch left her husband after 25 years of marriage. She brought actions for separation, support, and custody of their son, as well as a one-half interest in all lands and assets owned by her husband, on the basis that they were equal partners. Mrs. Murdoch claimed that payments from her bank account were contributions to the partnership agreement. Mr. Murdoch contended that the money he received from time to time usually came from his in-laws and was always repaid. As well, all land, livestock, and equipment were held in his name, and income tax returns were filed in his name only. No formal partnership declaration existed between them.

The trial court granted Mrs. Murdoch a separation and support of $200 a month. Custody of the son was given to the father, and her claim for the one-half interest was dismissed. Mrs. Murdoch appealed to the Appellate Division of the Supreme Court of Alberta, and her action was again dismissed. She then brought a further appeal to the Supreme Court of Canada. In a 4–1 decision, the Supreme Court ruled that Mrs. Murdoch was not entitled to any interest in her husband's land and assets because there was no evidence of either a direct financial contribution on her part or a partnership agreement between them. All of the work she had done was merely the work "that would be done by any farm wife."

1. **Give three reasons why all three courts dismissed Mrs. Murdoch's claim to a one-half interest in the land and assets.**

2. **Was the work done by her typical of that done by any ranch wife? Discuss.**

3. **Why did the courts feel that there was no evidence of any partnership agreement between the Murdochs?**

4. **What is your opinion of this decision?**

5. **Should marriage be considered a partnership that recognizes contributions in the form of household management and homecare duties? Why or why not?**

The reaction of both legal observers and concerned Canadians to the Murdoch judgment was overwhelmingly negative. As a result, over the next decade all provinces and territories passed new legislation to establish more equitable property-sharing rights and support obligations between spouses upon separation or divorce. The result was that property sharing on marriage breakdown no longer depended on who purchased the property or held title to it.

Reviewing Your Reading

1. **Which level of government has jurisdiction over property division on marriage breakdown?**

2. **What is the separate property system, and why did it often result in hardship for women on marriage breakdown?**

3. **Why did *Murdoch v. Murdoch* inspire much of the family law reform legislation of the late 1970s?**

14.3 PROPERTY DIVISION

The names of the statutes passed dealing with the division of property between spouses on marriage breakdown differ. For instance, British Columbia passed the *Family Relations Act*, Alberta and Saskatchewan the *Matrimonial Property Act*, and Ontario the *Family Law Act*. The basic intent of the statutes is similar. Each recognizes marriage as a partnership to which the spouses contribute equally. All forms of contribution are considered equally significant.

This text cannot provide a detailed analysis of each statute. Since the Ontario legislation is the most detailed and comprehensive, it will be the focus of the next section. Significant differences in the legislation of other provinces will follow. All of the legislation addresses the following legal issues:

- What property is subject to division?
- What is the value of that property?
- How will the property division occur?

Ontario's Legislation

In 1978, the Ontario government passed the first major piece of property-sharing legislation, recognizing marriage as an equal partnership. This law eventually led to passage of Ontario's *Family Law Act* in 1986.

Ontario spouses are now entitled to share the value of everything acquired during the marriage, with a few exceptions that will be discussed later. However, it is important to note that common-law and same-sex partners are *not* included in the definition of a spouse, no matter how long they have lived together.

The *Family Law Act* does not divide specific property. Instead, it attempts to give each spouse an equal share of the value of the property acquired during the marriage. The law therefore requires the spouses to calculate the total net value of all of their assets at the date of separation. Almost everything of value to the couple is included, such as furniture, appliances, bank accounts, pensions, stocks and bonds, and business interests. Gifts, property acquired by inheritance, damages for personal injuries in a car accident, and proceeds from life insurance policies can be excluded from this calculation. Spouses can opt out of an equal division of property sharing by drawing up a marriage contract that exempts certain assets from division. The **matrimonial home**, however, cannot be included in such a contract. It is the most important asset for the majority of couples and forms the centre of the family's life during the marriage.

After the couple's property values are totalled, the spouse with the greater **net family property** must then give the other spouse an **equalization payment** in cash, property, or investment shares, to make up one-half the difference between the two figures. For example, when Thorne and Macy married, his assets were worth $30 000 and her assets were worth $20 000. When they separated, Thorne's assets were worth $110 000, while Macy's were worth $160 000. The example above shows how to calculate the equalization payment.

Thus, Macy would have to make a payment of $30 000 to Thorne to make the division of their property equal. This can be paid by a lump sum payment or through a transfer of property, if cash is not available. If the equalization payment

Calculations for Division of Property

Spouse	Value of Assets at Marriage	Value of Assets at Separation	Net Family Property
Thorne	$30 000	$110 000	$ 80 000
Macy	20 000	160 000	140 000

Equalization Payment = ($140 000 − $80 000) ÷ 2 = $30 000

is a large amount, it may be paid over 10 years instead of in a lump sum.

However, complications may arise in the valuation of pension plans or the value and future worth of a spouse with a professional degree, such as a doctor, dentist, or lawyer, and where one spouse has business interests, but these considerations are beyond the scope of this chapter. The new provisions reflect the intent of the legislation—to make both spouses equally self-sufficient and thereby reflect the partnership aspect of marriage.

Significant Legislative Differences

The other provinces have retained the separate property system as long as a couple remains married. The most significant difference between the various provincial statutes involves the assets that may be divided upon separation. In provinces other than Ontario, these assets are known as **matrimonial property** or marital property. For example, legislation in Alberta, Saskatchewan, Manitoba, and Quebec states that all property acquired by the spouses during marriage is to be divided equally. The intent here is the same as that of Ontario's *Family Law Act*. The Maritime provinces and Yukon Territory, on the other hand, distinguish between family or matrimonial assets, and nonfamily or business or commercial assets, associated with one spouse only.

A **family asset** is the matrimonial home and property owned by one or both spouses that is "ordinarily used or enjoyed by the spouses or one or more of their children for family purposes." Examples include the family cottage, furniture and paintings in the home and cottage, the family car or cars, and money in a joint bank account normally used for family purposes such as paying bills. The intent of the legislation is that these family assets would, in most cases, be divided equally between the spouses.

CASE

D eborah and Michael Elliott were married in 1978 and separated in 1990. When they married, they both wanted children and jointly decided that Deborah would leave her job with Bell Canada and look after the children until the youngest child was in school on a full-time basis.

In August 1981, she left her managerial position on an extended maternity leave and did not return to work until late 1989; she was earning $27 000 a year in 1981. Their first son was born in September 1981, and their second son was born in March 1983.

In 1983 when Mr. Elliott lost his job, his wife helped him obtain employment with Bell Canada where he remained for three years before leaving for another job. When Mrs. Elliott applied for full-time work with Bell after the separation, only part-time employment was available. It was anticipated that she would re-establish herself with the company in the future.

At the time of divorce proceedings in 1992, Mrs. Elliott was earning $25 000 a year, while her husband was earning $55 000. The trial judge also considered Mrs. Elliott's net family property of $99 091 and Mr. Elliott's of $76 566.34, and ordered an equalization payment to be made.

As well, the judge ruled that Mrs. Elliott should be compensated for her future economic loss. An expert witness testified that the present value of the wife's income loss from the trial to her projected retirement date in the year 2020 was about $350 000. However, the court awarded her a lump sum payment of $105 000 to compensate her for the economic loss suffered when she withdrew from the work force for eight years to look after the children.

Mr. Elliott appealed this judgment, on both the issue of the size of the payment and its form of a lump sum. Mrs. Elliott cross-appealed, arguing that the lump sum should be substantially increased. The Court of Appeal, in a 3–0 judgment, substituted an award of $1000 a month for an indefinite period of time.

Leave to appeal to the Supreme Court of Canada was dismissed in June 1994.

Elliott v. Elliott (1993)

Ontario Court of Appeal
48 R.F.L. (3d) 237

1. **What was the amount of the equalization payment made to Mr. Elliott?**
2. **What practical advantages would there be for Mrs. Elliott in receiving a lump sum payment?**
3. **Why do you think the Court of Appeal substituted monthly payments instead?**
4. **With which decision do you agree, and why?**

Nonfamily assets, or **business assets** in some provinces, include stocks and bonds, pension funds, registered retirement savings plans (RRSPs), and most business interests. These assets are not divided equally because they are not family property. Instead, they belong to the spouse who purchased them and are *not* divided equally between the spouses, unless the other spouse can prove that he or she had made a direct financial contribution to the purchase of those assets. Such a situation might arise, for example, when one spouse works to put the other through university or gives up a career opportunity to stay in the home and raise children, thereby contributing to the future success, earnings, and investments of that spouse.

British Columbia's *Family Relations Act* states that each spouse is entitled to a one-half interest in all family assets upon the breakdown of a marriage. However, "family assets" are more widely defined than in the Maritime provinces, and include such items as pension plans and RRSPs. In addition, property owned by either spouse before the marriage that is later used for a family purpose is considered a family asset. For example, a cottage and a boat owned by the wife prior to marriage and used frequently by the whole family would be a family asset. Furthermore, one spouse's interest in a business might be considered a family asset if the other spouse made some contribution to it.

Thus, three fundamental principles of law have developed for the division of marital property in all provinces:

1. The property of the marriage is to be divided equally between the spouses, unless it might be unfair and inequitable to do so.

2. Legal recognition is given to the spouse who assumes the main responsibility for child care and home management, giving the other spouse the opportunity to acquire property that might not be a family asset.

3. Legal recognition is given to the contribution of each spouse, whether in the form of money or work, toward the acquisition of property other than family assets; that is, nonfamily or business assets in those provinces that still recognize the distinction.

Exemption from the Equal Division Rule

Although the intent of all provinces' statutes is to distribute property equally, there are situations in which this might clearly be unfair. Following are several factors that may help judges determine whether the spouses should share equally in the division of all assets or their value.

- *Length of the marriage.* It may be unfair to divide family assets, or their value, equally if the couple had not been married very long, and one spouse had brought much more property into the marriage than the other.
- *Length of time that the couple has been separated.* If this period is several years, and both spouses have since purchased furnishings for their separate accommodations, it would not be fair to divide these assets equally, since each spouse bought them for personal use after they separated.
- *The date when a given asset was acquired.* An expensive asset purchased by one spouse just before separation may not be divided equally. Depending on the circumstances, it is likely that the purchaser may get it.
- *Gifts and inheritances.* An asset that was a gift or an inheritance to one spouse may also be specifically excluded from equal division. It is seen as unfair to require a spouse to share a valuable family heirloom given as a present by a close relative, or left as an inheritance in a will.

The courts will consider other relevant circumstances when determining one spouse's contribution to any property that might be considered a marriage asset. However, it is important to remember that, although the legislation gives courts discretion to make an unequal division of property, this may not happen. Judges do not have to use this discretion, but it is available to be used when appropriate.

Most provincial statutes have removed judicial discretion in property division, unless a strict application of the law of equal division would lead to an **unconscionable judgment**. The term unconscionable means "grossly or shockingly unfair" and is likely to be applied only in extreme cases; for example, when the marriage was very brief, or when one spouse has intentionally and recklessly depleted or squandered his or her assets prior to the separation.

The Matrimonial Home

Each provincial statute gives special consideration to the matrimonial home, which can be a house, a mobile home, a condominium, or any dwelling owned by one or both spouses. If, for example, Thorne and Macy spend part of the year in their Vancouver condominium and the rest at their chalet in Whistler, then both dwellings may be considered matrimonial homes. Places that are used only a few times each year for recreational purposes probably are not matrimonial homes.

Yolanta Cohen and her husband, Zvi Cohen, were married in 1975 while living in Israel and immigrated to Canada in 1982. The Cohens had two children, born in 1983 and 1986, respectively.

In late 1983, the couple purchased a home, registered in the wife's name alone. It was financed by a large mortgage, some money from the wife's mother, and from the couple's joint savings brought from Israel. When trouble arose in the marriage in 1986, the husband moved from Richmond, British Columbia, to Ottawa to get away from the marital problems.

In early 1987, Mrs. Cohen sold the matrimonial home and purchased another house for $105 000 by arranging two mortgages and using the net proceeds from the sale of the first home. Later that year, the couple negotiated a separation agreement, but no provision was made regarding the matrimonial home or other family assets.

In early 1989, Mr. Cohen declared bankruptcy, but the only asset he declared was his car, which was repossessed. He did not list any interest in the matrimonial home as an asset in the bankruptcy. In 1990, an 18-month reconciliation occurred, but the couple finally separated in 1991. Mrs. Cohen continued to look after the children and to operate a day-care business in the home.

In divorce proceedings in 1993, the trial judge awarded permanent custody of the children to the mother with reasonable access to their father and ordered him to pay interim support of $150 per month per child. The judge also ruled that the house purchased during the first separation was a family asset, and Mr. Cohen was entitled to a one-half interest with his wife in that property. Mrs. Cohen appealed this judgment to the Court of Appeal where a unanimous judgment ruled that she was entitled to a 75/25 split in her favour.

Cohen v. Cohen (1995)

British Columbia Court of Appeal 11 R.F.L. (4th) 1

1. **Why did Mrs. Cohen feel that her husband was not entitled to a one-half interest in the home?**

2. **Why did the trial judge award Mr. Cohen a one-half interest in the home?**

3. **Why did the Court of Appeal award Mrs. Cohen a 75 percent interest in the home?**

4. **With which decision do you agree, and why?**

Each spouse has an equal right to live in the matrimonial home and to share equally in the proceeds if they agree to sell it. Because the right to possession of the home does not depend on ownership, the spouse who is the legal owner cannot force the other spouse to leave. However, if one spouse unreasonably withholds consent, or cannot be located, or is mentally incompetent, the court has the power to order the sale of the home without consent.

On separation, the courts may grant one spouse total and exclusive possession of the matrimonial home and its contents for a certain period. This spouse must convince the courts first, that shared use of the home is a practical impossibility; and second, that his or her claim should be preferred over the other. In other words, remaining in the home is extremely important to him or her. In such a situation, the courts consider the financial position of both spouses, the availability of other accommodation, and the best interests of the children. This option is most often used when one spouse has custody of the children and wants to remain in the matrimonial home until they have grown up and finished school.

In some circumstances, a ski chalet may be a matrimonial home.

After the period of exclusive occupancy ends, the spouses must arrange the division of the value of the matrimonial home. This division may involve selling the property and dividing the sale proceeds; alternatively, one spouse may buy out the other's interest. If there is no end date on the exclusive occupancy order, it will be up to the parties to either agree to, or for the court to order, the end of the period of exclusive occupancy and the asset to be divided.

Reviewing Your Reading

1. How is property now divided in Ontario's *Family Law Act?*

2. List the three principles all provinces and territories follow in the division of marital property.

3. In what situations might an equal division of assets be unjust?

4. What can be considered a matrimonial home, and what rights does each spouse have concerning that home or homes?

5. What is exclusive possession of the matrimonial home? How is it different from ownership?

6. If one spouse wants exclusive possession of the home for a certain period, what two factors must be presented to the court for consideration?

14.4 SUPPORT OBLIGATIONS

Separation is all too often accompanied by financial problems. This is particularly true if one spouse has been dependent on the other during the marriage. Dependent children also often require support, especially if they live with the dependent spouse. **Spousal support**, money paid by one spouse to another after marriage breakdown, is examined below. Child support is discussed in Chapter 15. Spousal support is very often short-term, until **self-sufficiency** is established, that is the dependent spouse is able to become self-supporting. Child support may continue for years.

Both the federal *Divorce Act, 1985,* and provincial legislation contain provisions for the support of spouses and children. In the case of divorce, the federal law applies; in the event of separation, provincial and territorial legislation applies. Although support rights and obligations differ somewhat from province to province, the basic principles are similar. The chart on p. 383 lists the names of the appropriate provincial support legislation.

The 1985 *Divorce Act*

As you learned in Chapter 13, the federal government introduced the new *Divorce Act* in 1985. It outlines four objectives that spousal support orders should consider:

1. any economic advantages or disadvantages arising from the marriage breakdown;
2. financial consequences arising from the care of children over and above the obligation of child-support orders;
3. economic hardship of the spouses arising from the marriage breakdown;
4. promotion of the economic self-sufficiency of each spouse, as much as possible, within a reasonable period of time.

Once the marriage ends, each spouse has an obligation, if necessary, to seek additional education, employment, or retraining as quickly as possible to become self-supporting. Today, both spouses are likely to be employed, particularly if they are younger people. If they earn similar

Provincial Support Legislation

Province	Name of Act
Alberta	*Domestic Relations Act*
British Columbia	*Family Relations Act*
Manitoba	*Family Maintenance Act*
New Brunswick	*Family Services Act*
Newfoundland	*Family Law Act*
Northwest Territories	*Domestic Relations Act*
Nova Scotia	*Family Maintenance Act*
Ontario	*Family Law Act*
Prince Edward Island	*Family Law Reform Act*
Quebec	*Civil Code of Quebec*
Saskatchewan	*Family Maintenance Act*
Yukon Territory	*Family Property and Support Act*

salaries, and if each spouse receives a fair share of all assets upon separation, then it is possible that neither will need support.

Self-Sufficiency

After 1985 the court focused to a great extent on the objective of economic self-sufficiency. It was believed that individuals could quickly gain the necessary skills they had lost or set aside during the marriage to raise a family and become self-sufficient within a reasonable time period, usually two or three years. Also, the courts believed that support agreements reached between spouses with the help of separate and independent legal counsel should be honoured. These principles were affirmed in the 1987 landmark judgment from the Supreme Court of Canada in *Pelech v. Pelech*.

If either spouse is unable to meet his or her needs for any reason, then the other spouse has a duty to provide support, according to his or her ability to pay. Thus, the need of one spouse and the ability of the other spouse to pay are key elements for the court to consider in granting support.

The most common situation in which support is required occurs when one spouse was the homemaker, while the other spouse was the sole wage earner. An older spouse who has been out of the work force for many years while raising a family may find it especially difficult, even impossible, to gain self-sufficiency. For example, a woman who has been married for 30 years may be able to find part-time employment at a retail outlet; however, that employment is highly unlikely to allow her to become self-sufficient. In such a situation, the courts generally do not place a time limit on a support award. Court orders are often left open, or made reviewable after a certain period of time.

However, if the homemaking spouse is young and has been out of the work force for just a short period, support will be given for a limited time only, to enable him or her to upgrade employment opportunities or acquire new job skills. Once the spouse receiving support reaches this goal, there is no further need for support. A spouse cannot just sit at home, refuse to work, and expect to receive support. If the spouse needing support does not try to become self-sufficient, the other spouse may reduce or stop support payments upon application to the courts.

In another landmark judgment in *Moge v. Moge* (1992), the Supreme Court of Canada rejected the goal of self-sufficiency as the primary objective to consider. Instead, all four factors must be considered when spousal support is claimed or an order is sought to be varied. The self-sufficiency objective is only one of the listed objectives, but nothing in any legislation indicates that it should be given priority.

Factors in Determining Support

In determining whether to grant support, and the amount, the federal *Divorce Act* and all provincial laws list a number of factors that a judge must consider in reaching a decision, including

- the assets and financial status of each spouse, including present and future earning ability;
- the ability that each spouse has to be self-supporting;
- the ability of each spouse to provide support to the other spouse, if necessary;
- the age, and physical and mental health of each spouse;
- the length of time the spouses lived together;

Did You Know

Working wives spend an average of 5.3 hours a day on housework, shopping, and child care—about two hours more a day than their working husbands.

- the length of time it might take the spouse in need of support to acquire or upgrade job skills;
- the length of time one spouse spent at home raising the family instead of contributing financially by working outside the home.

Note that the conduct of the spouses is not included. The obligation to provide support for a spouse exists without regard to the other spouse's conduct. The *Divorce Act, 1985,* eliminated conduct entirely from consideration as an issue of support. Only if a spouse's conduct is so shocking or unconscionable as to cause public concern would it become a factor to consider under some provincial law. Few cases exist in which this has occurred.

A judge may order support to be paid either in the form of periodic payments or one lump sum. Periodic payments might be weekly, monthly, yearly, or for a specific period, as the judge feels appropriate. Support orders may be reviewed by the courts at the request of either party, if circumstances change. This may arise from a change in salary, remarriage, unemployment, or poor health. A change in circumstances does not mean that maintenance will be varied or ended.

Judges recognize that one spouse cannot normally be expected to support two families equally. Studies suggest that money-related issues present problems in remarriages as often as child-related problems. Financial arrangements made years ago may reoccur when a step-parent joins an existing family. When a second marriage results in a blended family, the first family generally has some priority over obligations to the second family. Where the paying parent remarries and establishes a new second family, he or she may not be able to use this fact as a reason for lowering child support to the first family. As a result, if there is not sufficient income to support both families equally, most judges will attempt to be fair to both families.

Looking Back

Before the 1968 *Divorce Act* and the provincial family law reform of the late 1970s, only wives could claim support in most provinces. This principle was based on the belief that marriage lasted "till death do us part" and that the husband provided for the family. Only fathers were required to contribute to the support of their children. By the late 1970s, therefore, the law not only failed to reflect the true state of society, but also discriminated against husbands.

The old law also provided that if a husband committed adultery, his wife was entitled to support for life because the termination of the marriage was his fault. It did not matter if the wife remarried or became financially independent. If the wife committed adultery she was not entitled to any support even in cases of real need, since she was held responsible for the end of the marriage. In either case, the law was unreasonable and punitive, because it was based on the finding of marital fault or who was to blame for the marriage breakdown, not on financial need.

By the late 1960s, women were entering the labour force in greater numbers, and marriage was seen less and less as a union for life.

The 1968 *Divorce Act* abolished fault as a basis for determining support and replaced it with the need of one spouse and the ability to pay by the other spouse. The *Act* also made it possible for husbands to claim support from their wives. Thus, reasons for granting spousal support now reflected the changing roles played by the spouses within the marriage and the fact that many marriages no longer existed for life.

The courts have the jurisdiction to increase or decrease support and even to stop payments. Some recent support orders have indicated that the amount payable is to be increased annually, to keep pace with inflation. The existence of a cost of living adjustment (COLA) clause may eliminate the need for regular applications to the court to increase support payments; however, a COLA clause usually increases support by 1 or 2 percent, yet children's needs may increase by up to 50 percent. For example, the cost of raising a 5-year-old is much less than the cost of raising a 15-year-old.

Enforcement of Support Orders

A support order, like any court judgment, may be enforced by various means. For many years, up to 75 percent of spouses, mostly men, defaulted on their court-ordered support payments. The result often was financial hardship, with families having to depend on social assistance programs. Furthermore, the victims of default (usually mothers and children) had to return to court for a remedy, which took both time and money but did not guarantee success. It is important to note that a judgment does not equal collection.

CASE

John and Shirley Mae Pelech were married in 1954 and had two children. The husband had a general contracting business; his wife worked in the business as a receptionist and bookkeeper until the mid-1960s. The couple was divorced in 1969. She was 37 years old and he was 44. Custody was awarded to the husband because of the wife's psychological problems.

When the divorce decree was granted, Shirley Mae Pelech agreed to a lump sum payment of $28 760, to be paid over a 13-month period, instead of continued support payments over a longer period. She accepted it in full satisfaction of all future support claims. This freely negotiated agreement was prepared by independent legal counsel for both parties, and all agreed that it was a fair settlement.

Following the divorce, Mr. Pelech prospered. His net worth in 1969, $128 000, had increased to about $1.8 million by 1984. Meanwhile, his former wife suffered severe psychological and physical problems, depleted the assets she had obtained when the divorce was granted, and was receiving welfare of $430 a month because she was often unable to work. Her prospects for finding employment were bleak.

In December 1982, Shirley Mae Pelech brought an action under the *Divorce Act* to change the maintenance award made in 1970. Her application was granted by the Supreme Court of British Columbia, which ordered John to pay her $2000 a month. John Pelech appealed to the British Columbia Court of Appeal, which reversed the decision. Shirley Mae was granted leave to appeal to the Supreme Court of Canada. Her appeal was dismissed in a unanimous decision in June 1987.

Pelech v. Pelech
(1987)

Supreme Court of Canada
7 R.F.L. (3d) 225

1. **Why do you think Mr. Pelech was ordered to pay a sum to his former wife?**
2. **Why do you think the Court of Appeal reversed this decision?**
3. **The Supreme Court of Canada judgment stated, in part: "While I realize that Mrs. Pelech's present hardship is great, to burden the respondent (Mr. Pelech) with her care 15 years after their marriage has ended for no other reason than that they were once married seems to me to create a fiction of marital responsibility at the expense of individual responsibility. I believe that the courts must recognize the right of an individual to end a relationship as well as to begin one . . ." What is your opinion of this statement?**

CASE

Moge v. Moge
(1992)

**Supreme Court
of Canada
43 R.F.L. (3d) 345**

Andrzej Moge and his wife, Zofia, were married in Poland in the mid-1950s and moved to Manitoba in 1960. Throughout the marriage, he worked full time as a welder and learned to speak fluent English. Mrs. Moge stayed at home during the day to raise their three children and care for their home. She worked at regular part-time jobs in the evening, cleaning offices. She had a grade 7 education and spoke little English.

When the couple separated in 1973, she was awarded custody of the children and $150 a month for spousal and child support. In 1980, Mr. Moge petitioned for divorce; Mrs. Moge did not contest the action. During this time, she was unable to find the time to improve her education or find a job that would pay her enough money to raise her and her children above the poverty line. Although she was able to provide the children with the basic necessities, she was unable to acquire much of any value. Meanwhile, her former husband bought a home and car, accumulated savings, and invested his money. He remarried in 1984.

In 1987, after losing her job when her employer closed down, Mrs. Moge sought an increase in support for herself and the one child still living with her; the court awarded her $400. Between 1987 and 1989, Mrs. Moge secured some part-time work with the province of Manitoba. Her gross pay was about $800 a month, while Mr. Moge earned about $2200 a month.

In 1989, Mr. Moge brought an application to terminate support payments as he believed that his former wife had had enough time to become financially self-sufficient. In granting Mr. Moge's application, the trial court judge stated: "She cannot expect that Mr. Moge will support her forever. He has contributed to her support since 1973."

Mrs. Moge appealed this decision to the Manitoba Court of Appeal where, in 1990, a 2–1 judgment ruled that Mr. Moge must continue indefinitely paying his former wife $150 a month since she remained economically disadvantaged as a result of her role as caregiver in a traditional marriage. This decision was appealed to the Supreme Court of Canada, and, in a landmark 6–0 judgment in December 1992, the court ruled that Andrzej Moge must continue his support payments indefinitely, even though he and his former wife had separated nearly 20 years earlier.

1. **Why did Mr. Moge bring a court action against his wife in 1989 to terminate her support payments?**

2. **Why did both the Court of Appeal and the Supreme Court of Canada rule in Mrs. Moge's favour?**

3. **Should Mrs. Moge be entitled to ongoing support from her husband for an indefinite period of time, or should spousal support be terminated? Discuss with reasons to support your position.**

Provincial Enforcement

To relieve the burden on taxpayers, as well as to reduce child poverty, several provinces and the federal government passed legislation in the 1980s to make it easier to collect payments from defaulting parents. Manitoba and Quebec were the first provinces to address this serious social problem by establishing an enforcement system for defaults on spousal and child support. Support enforcement statutes are now in effect in most provinces. Examples include Alberta's *Maintenance Enforcement Act*, British Columbia's *Family Orders Enforcement Act*, and Ontario's *Support and Custody Orders Enforcement Act*. As well, the provinces have arranged agreements among themselves and with other countries that assist in locating defaulting spouses.

Wage Deduction

In 1992, Ontario's *Family Support Plan* became Canada's first automatic wage deduction program, by which court-ordered support payments are deducted regularly from a parent's pay cheque or other income sources. Prior to this plan, about $14 million a month was collected in Ontario from about 40 percent of non-custodial parents making court-ordered payments. In 1994, just over $30 million was collected from 70 percent of non-custodial parents. Quebec intended to introduce a similar system by the end of 1995, and other provinces are looking at the Ontario model.

Federal Enforcement

Although support enforcement is primarily a provincial concern, in 1988 Parliament passed the *Family Orders and Agreements Enforcement Assistance Act*, which allows the federal government to assist in the enforcement process. Data banks in federal computers and records listing Canada Pension Plan payments and social insurance benefits can now be searched to find the address of a missing spouse and the name and address of his or her employer. The new statute also permits federal payments to the defaulting spouse, such as unemployment insurance cheques, income tax refunds, Canada Pension Plan payments, and interest from Canada Savings Bonds, to be garnisheed. Collection of unpaid child-support payments will be discussed in Chapter 15.

Reviewing Your Reading

1. **What are the two key factors that courts consider in determining support orders?**

2. **List the four objectives that spousal support orders should consider.**

3. **What was the major difference between the Supreme Court of Canada's landmark judgments in *Pelech v. Pelech* and *Moge v. Moge*?**

4. **Are spousal support orders permanent? Why or why not?**

5. **How are the courts determining support orders for blended families?**

6. **What are governments doing to assist in the enforcement of unpaid support orders?**

14.5 COMMON-LAW RELATIONSHIPS

You read in Chapter 13 that common-law relationships still exist. Many people believe that if you live with a partner for a certain length of time, you have a common-law marriage and have the same rights as married couples. However, this is *not* true!

Today's laws recognize common-law relationships to some extent, since increasing numbers of couples are choosing this form of living arrangement. In all provinces except Alberta, if a couple lives together without the benefit of a formal, legal marriage, they may have some automatic rights under the law because of the length of time they have lived together in a serious relationship. These are examined in the following sections.

Property

When married couples separate, they have an automatic right to property division and claims between them, as you have seen. This principle does not apply to common-law couples. No matter

Did You Know

As of June 1995, defaulting parents in Ontario (mostly fathers) owed $850.3 million in child support.

how long couples live together, the only property they are entitled to when their relationships end is their own property. In a common-law relationship, property belongs to the person who paid for it. The partners may have some property rights against each other for contributions of work and household maintenance. For instance, if a woman's contribution helped her common-law partner to build a successful and prosperous business, she may be entitled to a share or an interest in the business. However, she will have to prove her claim in court to obtain a portion of the asset's value. To prove this claim, the following questions must be considered by the courts:

- How many years have the partners lived together?
- What agreements, if any, did the couple have about each person's contributions and obligations?
- Is there proof that a valid contribution was made?

The 1980 landmark judgment from the Supreme Court of Canada in *Pettkus v. Becker* provides an example of such an action and was the first major recognition of the rights of common-law partners by Canadian courts.

CASE

Pettkus v. Becker
(1980)

Supreme Court of Canada
19 R.F.L. (2d) 165

Rosa Becker and Lothar Pettkus met in Montreal in 1955 shortly after both of them had arrived from Europe. She was 29 and he was 24. After a few dates, he moved in with her. She paid all of the bills for rent, food, clothing, and other living expenses from her salary, while he saved his entire salary in his own bank account. Becker expressed a desire to be married, but Pettkus said he might consider marriage after they knew each other better. By 1960, Pettkus had saved a large sum of money. He used some of it to buy a farm at Franklin Centre, near Montreal. The property was in his name only.

Becker moved to the farm with Pettkus and participated fully in a very successful bee-keeping operation over the next 14 years. In the early 1970s, Pettkus bought two pieces of property in Hawkesbury, Ontario, with funds from the Franklin Centre operation. He transferred the bees to the new property and built a house for himself and Becker there. The couple never married, but they lived together for 19 years. In 1974, Becker moved out permanently, claiming she was constantly being mistreated. She then filed for a one-half interest in the land and business, which by then was worth about $300 000.

In the original action in 1977, the trial court judge awarded her 40 beehives, minus the bees, and $1500 cash. In his decision, this judge claimed that "Rosa's contribution to the household expenses during the first few years of the relationship was in the nature of risk capital invested in the hope of seducing a young man into marriage."

Becker appealed this decision to the Ontario Court of Appeal, where three judges overturned the trial decision. In the appellate court decision, Madame Justice Bertha Wilson stated that Becker's contribution to the bee-keeping operation and her relationship with Pettkus had been greatly underrated by the trial judge and that her contribution to the success of the business and acquisition of property was very significant. Thus, Becker was awarded a one-half interest in all lands owned by Pettkus, and in the bee-keeping business.

Pettkus was then granted leave to appeal this decision to the Supreme Court of Canada. A landmark judgment in December 1980 awarded Becker a one-half interest in the assets accumulated by Pettkus during the 19 years of their relationship, and all court costs.

Addendum: In November 1986, Rosa Becker committed suicide by shooting herself in the forehead with a .22-calibre rifle. In a suicide note, she stated that her death was a protest against the legal system; she still had not received any of her $150 000 court award, because Pettkus refused to recognize the decision. He had married and placed his property in his wife's name, thereby avoiding paying the settlement.

Thus, six years after her 1980 landmark judgment, she had received very little, if anything. One payment of $68 000 was claimed by her lawyer for his fees. In May 1989, Becker's estate received $13 000 from Pettkus, which was paid to two of Becker's friends whom she had named as beneficiaries.

1. **Do couples in a common-law relationship have an automatic right to a division of property upon separating?**

2. **Why did the Supreme Court of Canada rule that Becker was entitled to a one-half interest in Pettkus's assets?**

3. **Do you agree with the decision of the trial court judge or the Supreme Court? Explain.**

4. **In the Supreme Court decision, Justice Brian Dickson stated: "Pettkus had the benefit of 19 years of unpaid labour while Miss Becker had received little or nothing in return ... This was not an economic partnership or a mere business relationship, or a casual encounter. These two people lived as 'man and wife' for almost 20 years. Their lives and their economic well-being were fully integrated." Do you agree or disagree with this decision? Explain.**

5. **Explain the meaning of the following statement: "Becker's suicide was the final, desperate act in a life that had become a bitter symbol of the shortcomings and limits of the law."**

Support

Most provinces now recognize the right of common-law partners to support. Thus, partners who have lived together for a certain period of time have the same right to support as married couples. The period is one year in Manitoba, Nova Scotia, and Newfoundland, two years in British Columbia, and three years in Ontario. In Alberta, common-law spouses have no automatic right to support, no matter how long they have lived together, but application can be made to court to justify a support claim. Quebec and the Northwest Territories do not recognize the right of common-law partners to support.

A couple who has lived in a common-law relationship for less than the required period and has a child also has a right to spousal and child support. There are no corresponding rights in statute law yet for same-sex couples.

Inheritance

A surviving common-law spouse, unlike a married survivor, has no automatic claim to the estate of the deceased. The deceased must leave a will specifically leaving everything to the survivor. However, any assets that common-law spouses jointly own— real estate, furnishings, vehicles, bank accounts— belong to the survivor, since he or she already owns them. In British Columbia, the *Estate Administration Act* allows the surviving common-law spouse to apply to be the administrator of the estate.

Pensions

Both the *Canada Pension Plan* and the *Workers' Compensation Act* in all provinces give some recognition to common-law relationships. They provide for the payment of benefits to the surviving partner when the other dies in a work-related accident.

Other statutes, such as the *Unemployment Insurance Act,* also recognize common-law partners' rights to benefits. The length of time living together to qualify for benefits varies.

Reviewing Your Reading

1. **Compare the rights of married and common-law spouses with respect to the following: property, support, and inheritance.**

2. **Why was the *Pettkus v. Becker* case such a landmark judgment?**

3. **What provisions does your provincial law contain for division of property between common-law couples?**

14.6 *D*OMESTIC CONTRACTS

One result of changing social attitudes toward personal relationships has been that many couples, whether married or living together, want to outline their rights, responsibilities, and obligations in a legally binding contract. Before the new provincial property-sharing legislation discussed earlier in this chapter, courts seldom recognized such contracts, especially those between common-law partners or those that outlined a couple's plans in case of separation. Legal authorities felt that recognizing such contracts would threaten the stability of marriage and the family. But, just as a will determines how your assets will be distributed when you die, a domestic contract may determine how your assets will be divided if, or when, your relationship with another person breaks down. Domestic contracts have clearly grown more common in the last decade in an increasing number of marriages.

Today, these contracts may be recognized by the courts, if they are prepared by couples who have each obtained independent legal advice. Lawyers must explain what a person is giving up in terms of the agreement before it is signed. Domestic contracts are becoming more common and popular as they allow couples to discover their partner's views on such things as how property will be divided if they were to separate, career plans, having and caring for children, and so on.

Contracts help couples make practical plans for potential future problems, and they provide an excellent opportunity for the prevention and resolution of disputes.

Types of Domestic Contracts

Under provincial and territorial law, a **domestic contract** is a general term referring to any of three types of contracts made between the partners in a relationship. A **marriage contract** or a **cohabitation agreement** is written before or during the relationship. A **separation agreement** is written just before or shortly after the couple separates and was discussed in Chapter 13. The contents of each type of contract depend on a couple's particular needs. However, to be legally binding, the contract must be written, signed by the two parties, and witnessed by at least one person who is not related to either spouse. Any changes to the contract must also be made in writing.

A marriage contract and a cohabitation agreement are quite similar. The main difference is that the former is between a husband and wife, while the latter is between common-law or same-sex partners who are living together and who want to make their wishes clearly known to family and friends. A cohabitation agreement may be a very valuable document for couples not legally married who want to provide a process for dividing their property on separation or death. As mentioned in this chapter, the equal-property-sharing legislation applies only to legally married couples.

Provincial legislation provides that, under most circumstances, married spouses are entitled to an equal share of the marital property when they separate. However, one spouse or both may own property that is not to be shared in the event of separation. In such situations, the couple can include their own property division in their marriage contract. Suppose, for example, Macy owned a piece of property prior to her marriage to Thorne. She may want to draw up a contract with a clause stipulating that Thorne has no right to any share of the property. In the absence of such a contract, the value of the property may be divided between the spouses if they separate, regardless of who had owned it before the marriage. Spouses who are also business partners are entering into domestic contracts to keep their business out of any marital dispute.

Independent legal advice should be obtained before agreeing to the terms of a domestic contract.

The main concerns covered in a marriage contract or a cohabitation agreement are the ownership and division of property, support obligations, and the education and upbringing of any children. Of course, a couple may include any item, as long as they both agree. For instance, the couple may wish to specify that the earnings of one may be used for mortgage or rental payments and utility expenses, while the salary of the other may be spent on household expenses such as food, clothing, entertainment, and miscellaneous items. Domestic duties, can be included but will not be enforced by the courts because they are very difficult to monitor.

Both married and common-law spouses may include terms dealing with the moral training and custody of and access to the children in the event of separation. However, the courts will not recognize these terms if they feel that the parents' decisions are not in the best interests of the children. In addition, domestic contracts cannot limit a spouse's right to live in the matrimonial home.

Terminating Domestic Contracts

Married or common-law spouses may terminate and destroy their contract by mutual agreement. Alternatively, the contract may include a term for its automatic termination, such as the day when the last child reaches the age of majority.

Some contracts include provision for review or revision at the end of a certain number of years. This allows the spouses to adjust their contract to reflect changes in their circumstances as children are born, career changes are made, and property is bought and sold.

Reviewing Your Reading

1. **In your province, how are assets divided upon marriage breakdown?**
2. **Why have the courts only recently recognized the validity of domestic contracts?**
3. **Name the three main types of domestic contracts. Why is no standard form available for such contracts?**
4. **Would you recommend that a common-law couple draw up a cohabitation agreement? Why or why not?**
5. **Name three important areas of concern that are likely to be included in a domestic contract.**
6. **List two advantages and two disadvantages of domestic contracts.**

ISSUE

Should governments institute and support day-care programs for all Canadian children?

Free day-care for all Canadian children has emerged as an important issue in recent years. According to Statistics Canada, between 1981 and 1991 there was a 17 percent increase in the number of women working outside the home who have preschool children. This dramatic increase was the result of more single parent families and of dual-income earners trying to keep up with the escalating cost of living.

Women continue to be the primary care-givers in most families. As more mothers enter the work force, the need for child-care services increases. In 1991, there were 3.1 million children with mothers in the work force, but only 333 082 licensed day-care spaces available. This means that 88 percent of working mothers had to make arrangements with babysitters, nannies, and family members for their children.

In 1986, the Report of the Task Force on Child Care estimated that the gradual adoption of universal day-care would cost $11.3 billion by the year 2001. Other estimates are even higher. The benefits are described in a 1993 government report "Child Care in Canada," which states that quality day-care can "contribute to the social and intellectual development of children." This is especially true for children who live in poverty.

On One Side

Advocates of government-funded day-care believe that access to high quality day-care is the right of all children regardless of their parents'

social and economic position. They feel that it is ironic and tragic that governments provide free education and health services to all Canadians, but deny infants, toddlers, and young children their rights. Advocates take the position that society has a responsibility to ensure that all young children have a healthy and stimulating environment. Studies show that those who do not are more likely to have problems later in their lives. Since these children are the adults of the future, their problems will be society's problems.

On the Other Side

Critics of government-funded day-care believe that those who choose to have children also have the responsibility of raising them without outside help. Taxpayers are already overburdened and should not have to assume responsibilities that rightfully belong to parents. They feel people have to learn to be responsible for their own decisions. Parents cannot expect the government to support their children from the cradle to the grave. Indeed, critics point out that the federal government already allows working parents to deduct a portion (between $2000 and $8000) of their child-care expenses from their income tax.

The Bottom Line

In the past 60 years, women have increasingly entered the labour market. As this phenomenon continues, the pressure on working parents with young children to find suitable day-care also

increases. While some employers now provide flexible work hours and part-time work to help meet the needs of the changing family, only 4 percent of employers provide day-care centres for their employees. Working parents continue to pressure the government to pass laws to provide universal day-care for all children. The debate continues over who should pay for this expensive service. Should parents be responsible for these expenses? Or is this a responsibility that should be shared by all Canadians? You be the judge!

1. **Why has the issue of universal day-care become an important issue in recent years?**

2. **Support the statement that "high quality day-care is a right of all children."**

3. **Do you think that governments and society have "a responsibility to ensure that all young children have a healthy and stimulating environment"?**

4. **What would be the advantages and disadvantages of employers providing day-care services to their employees?**

5. **In a paragraph explain your position on universal day-care. Debate it in class.**

CHAPTER REVIEW

Reviewing Key Terms

For each of the following statements, indicate the key term being defined:

a) a domestic contract between a man and a woman who are living together but are not married

b) the residence in which a married couple lives

c) a domestic contract between a man and a woman who are married and living together

d) property owned by one spouse and used primarily in the course of business carried on by that spouse

e) property owned or enjoyed by both spouses and/or their children

f) a grossly or shockingly unfair judicial decision

g) another name for a business asset in some provinces

h) the basic value of a spouse's assets, less any debts, at the date of separation

Exploring Legal Concepts

1. If the Murdoch case appeared before the Supreme Court of Canada today, what decision do you think the Court would reach, and why? Would you agree with the decision? Why or why not?

2. Should a doctor's, engineer's, or any other person's professional licence be considered an asset whose value is to be divided between the spouses when they separate? If so, why, and how should it be divided? If not, why not?

3. When a former spouse remarries, for how long should that spouse continue to pay support to his or her first spouse and family? Should a person's first or second family receive economic priority?

4. What is the name of your provincial support legislation?

5. Why might someone who is planning to marry sign a domestic contract that might not be in his or her best interests?

6. Marriage contracts take some control away from the government and give individuals more control over their personal relationships. What are the advantages and disadvantages of this?

7. As Canada approaches the twenty-first century, why are more and more couples living in common-law relationships rather than entering into legal marriages?

8. Should provincial laws be changed to give common-law partners the same automatic rights to property division as married spouses? Defend your position.

Applying Legal Concepts

1. When Martha and Rod married in Toronto, Martha's assets were valued at $80 000 and Rod's assets were valued at $20 000. When they separated eight years later, Martha's assets were valued at $160 000 and Rod's assets were valued at $180 000.

   • **Calculate the equalization payment that Martha would have to make to Rod.**

2. Winnifred Lacey was 67 and Horace Turner was 75 when they married. The newly married couple lived in Lacey's furnished home, which she had purchased during her working days. The marriage lasted 19 months before Turner petitioned for divorce on the grounds of mental cruelty.

   • **How will the court treat the division of the value of the matrimonial home, and why?**

3. Regan and Kerri Drexler were married for seven years. Long before the marriage, Regan won a sum of money in a provincial lottery and purchased $35 000 worth of Canada Savings Bonds in his name. The Drexlers accumulated a home worth $250 000, property worth $75 000, a sailboat worth $28 000, and some works of art worth $50 000. All of these assets were registered in Regan's name. Because of some disastrous business investments, Regan needed cash quickly and sold the art, the boat, and the property. Because of this and other marital problems, the Drexlers separated. Kerri later petitioned for divorce.

   • **Did the court divide the value of the matrimonial home equally between them? Why or why not? In your province, does Kerri have a claim to any of Regan's $35 000 worth of Canada Savings Bonds? Explain.**

4. A year ago, Luisa Perreira, 28, came to Canada from Costa Rica, even though her husband, Ramon, had told her that their marriage was finished and that he would not support her. Luisa obtained a series of jobs that paid her a minimum wage only. Finding it difficult to support herself, she registered in courses to learn English and obtain the skills needed for a better job.

   • **Is Luisa entitled to any spousal support from Ramon? If so, for how long? If not, why not?**

5. After the Dennises married, Carol Lynn was the main breadwinner, earning $40 000 a year as nurse and hospital director. Her husband, Larry, had a grade 11 education and worked only occasionally, playing trombone in a band. For 13 years, Larry stayed at home looking after their three children, aged 7, 9, and 10, and cooked and cleaned. When the couple separated, Mr. Dennis claimed monthly support payments from his wife to allow him to become self-supporting.

   • **Did he succeed in his action? Explain.**

Extending Legal Concepts

1. Now that you have completed this chapter, review the opening article and Something to Think About. Have your answers or opinions changed? Why or why not?

2. Compare and contrast the changes in granting support pre-1968, from 1968 to 1985, and from 1985 to the present.

3. Assume that you and the person that you have been living with for five years decide to marry in a civil ceremony. Would you prepare a marriage contract, or would you depend on your province's division of property legislation to settle any disputes if the two of you decide to separate or divorce? Prepare arguments for and against each of these two positions.

4. Explain the meaning of the following statement: "Just because an applicant is a spouse does not create an automatic right to support."

5. Using reference materials in your resource centre, including CD-ROM and the Internet, obtain current information on either recent division of property judgments or trends/concerns in spousal support. You might look at issues or concerns in your province compared with those in other provinces. Prepare a one-page report on your findings, and create a poster to display the information.

Researching an Issue

Equitable Property Division

Governments now recognize marriage as an equal partnership and property, or its value, is divided equally on marriage breakdown. These topics have been a focus of media attention over the years. Is an equal division always equitable?

Statement

The intent of all provincial and territorial legislation is to divide property, or its value, equally.

Point

Property acquired by two spouses during their marriage should, without exceptions, be divided equally when the marriage breaks down.

Counterpoint

There are some occasions in which one of the spouses has not made equal contribution to the marriage and does not warrant an equal division of property.

- **With a partner, research this issue and reflect on your findings.**
- **Prepare points on this statement that could be used for a class debate.**
- **Discuss your findings with others in your class.**

Chapter 15

CHILDREN AND FAMILY LAW

These are the key terms introduced in this chapter:

abduction	custody	siblings
access	extradition	sole custody
adoption	joint custody	specified access
best interests of the child	joint legal custody	supervised access
birth parent	joint physical custody	supervision order
child abuse	placement	temporary wardship order
Crown wardship order	reasonable access	tender years doctrine

Chapter at a Glance

Learning Outcomes

At the end of this chapter, you will be able to

1. distinguish between custody and access;
2. describe the main factors considered in determining sole or joint custody;
3. identify the three types of access orders and the use of each;
4. explain why custody and access orders are never permanent;
5. describe the factors considered in determining parents' obligations for child support;
6. discuss some of the current problems in the area of child support and the proposed solutions to remedy them;
7. define child abuse and its most common forms, and outline the reporting procedures for offences in your province;
8. outline the legal options for removing abused children from their homes;
9. explain the adoption procedures in your province.

Argentine Mom Vows to Fight for Custody

The mother of Daniela Wilner says she will accompany the five-year-old on a flight to Canada tomorrow, but intends to fight for full custody of her daughter in Canadian courts.

Gabriela Osswald says she will obey an Argentine supreme court order to bring Daniela to Canada, but will fight to reverse a Guelph court decision that gives her ex-husband Eduardo Wilner full custody of their daughter.

"I'm taking Daniela to Canada to start a custody fight so I can return with Daniela to Argentina," said Osswald.

Osswald and Wilner, both from Argentina, had been studying together at the University of Guelph and took Daniela on a Christmas trip to visit relatives after separating in 1993. During the visit, Osswald informed her husband of her intention to remain in Argentina with their daughter.

Now teaching at the University of Guelph, Wilner filed a restitution order as soon as his wife's return ticket to Canada had expired. Two months later, he was granted full custody of the girl in a Guelph court.

Now working as a receptionist, Osswald fought the court order in several Argentine courts, each ruling in favour of Daniela's return to Canada.

From: Ruth Dunley, "Argentine mom vows to fight for custody." *The Toronto Star*, June 28, 1995. Reprinted with permission—The Toronto Star Syndicate.

Something to Think About

- **Was Gabriela Osswald guilty of child abduction by remaining in Argentina with Daniela?**
- **Would sharing custody of Daniela between parents living in two different countries be practical?**
- **Which parent do you think should be awarded custody of Daniela, and why?**

15.1 INTRODUCTION

Under today's legislation, Canadian children have their own rights and freedoms. Along with these rights and freedoms, they have acquired corresponding responsibilities and duties and they can both sue and be sued. Except for federal law dealing with young offenders, and some protection for children against child abuse in the *Criminal Code*, most other laws concerning children fall under provincial jurisdiction. The courts determine custody of and access to the children if the parents separate or divorce.

Courts also are involved in determining the parents' joint obligations to support their children's basic needs. Courts can remove children from a home if they are being improperly cared for or abused. In some cases, the courts arrange adoptions. Children can also be brought before the courts in both civil matters and criminal matters. In all cases, the courts act in the best interests of the child. This chapter will discuss the role of the courts in regulating the relationship between children and their families.

Looking Back

The attitude of the law toward child-parent relationships has changed considerably during the last 100 years. For many years, English common law regarded children as property belonging to the father. This was a carry-over from Roman law, where a father had the power of life and death over his children. While some provision was made for the care and protection of orphans, there was little legislation to protect children living with their families. There was no law, as there is today, to punish parents who beat their children. In England, during the 1800s, children of poor families worked long hours under the worst conditions in factories and mines for very little pay. Serious illness and death were common because of the poor working conditions.

Though conditions in Canada were never as bad as in England, there was greater protection for animals than for children. Legislation regarding cruelty to animals was first passed around 1825, whereas the first legislation in Canada to protect children was passed by the Ontario government in 1893.

The end of the nineteenth century saw a period of major social reform, including compulsory education for children and the gradual disappearance of inhumane working conditions. In Ontario, the *Act for the Prevention of Cruelty to and Better Protection of Children* (1893) resulted in the establishment of Children's Aid Societies. It gave the courts the right to have organizations take care of neglected children. This marked the first time in Canada that the state became actively involved in the protection of children if it became necessary. Manitoba passed similar legislation in 1898, and the other provinces followed these examples in the early twentieth century.

15.2 Custody

Every year in Canada married couples separate or divorce. In those cases where children are involved, a judge may have to make a decision about **custody** (which parent the children of the marriage will live with) and **access** (what rights of visitation will be given to the other parent). In determining custody and access, courts must determine what is in the **best interests of the child**. This concept requires the courts to consider the emotional, intellectual, physical, and moral well-being of the child. Custody is the part of family law that affects children most directly. Like the rest of family law, it has changed considerably in recent years. In Canada, single-parent households represent between 20 and 25 percent of all Canadian families with children. Four out of five of these families are headed by women. In fact, the single-parent family is now the fastest growing lifestyle in North America.

Because male and female roles are changing, the courts can no longer rely on tradition to assist them in determining custody. As mothers enter the work force, and fathers assume some of the home-management responsibilities, the courts have realized that the traditional reason for giving the mother custody has disappeared. Today, both parents may have an equal right to the custody of their child or children, whether the parents are married or not.

Did You Know

The number of single-parent families headed by women has jumped from 272 000 in 1969 to 786 400 in 1991, and 60 percent of them are low-income families.

Proof that society's attitude on this subject has changed is seen in the increasing number of fathers awarded custody of their children. Although mothers still obtain sole custody in about 75 percent of all divorce actions, one in eight fathers, or about 13 percent, now receive **sole custody**. Joint custody represents most of the balance. About 1 percent of custody is awarded to some other person who has a relationship with a particular child, such as a grandparent. Judges prefer to give custody to a parent or relative unless there is a good reason to do otherwise.

Factors Determining Custody

Alberta's *Domestic Relations Act*, British Columbia's *Family Relations Act*, and Ontario's *Children's Law Reform Act*, for example, govern custody and access applications processed under provincial law. Other provincial statutes contain the same basic principles. The *Divorce Act* governs such applications under federal law. The main factors involved in determining custody are examined below.

Stability of Home Environment

The stability of a child's home environment is probably the most important factor to consider. Children form attachments. The sudden change of moving from one home to another is very stressful for many children, especially when they are also experiencing the emotional stress of the separation or divorce.

Courts do not like to shift children back and forth between contesting parents. The parent who assumes responsibility for the children at separation is usually awarded final custody. The children are settled into that home. Courts are reluctant to disturb children who are settled and doing well. It is not in their best interests. The parent with interim or temporary custody therefore has an advantage when the court rules on final custody.

Tender Years Doctrine

The **tender years doctrine** is a reminder that in the first part of the twentieth century the mother was almost certain to get legal custody of very young children, unless she was found to be a totally unfit parent. It was generally believed that mothers were more suited and capable than fathers to care for children in their "tender years." The tender years doctrine generally applied to children up to about the age of six or seven.

This principle was based on a society in which women stayed at home to care for the children and men went out to work. In recent years this has changed, and the doctrine has diminished greatly in its importance.

Mothers are no longer necessarily the primary caregiver. Today, both parties are equally entitled to custody of their children, and their parenting abilities are assessed carefully by the court.

Did You Know

In 1994, 52 percent of women aged 15 to 65 had jobs, up from 42 percent in 1976. Men's employment rate dropped from 73 to 65 percent over the same period.

Separation of Siblings

Siblings (brothers and sisters and stepbrothers and stepsisters) are not separated unless there is a good reason. Divorce for most children is a major crisis and keeping siblings together is believed to maintain some sense of security and family. Children are usually good companions for each other in this time of need. However, it is sometimes better to separate siblings, for example, if they are not getting along well with each other. In cases like this, the mother often gets custody of the girls, or the younger children, while fathers get custody of the boys, or the older children.

Children's Preferences

In deciding custody, the courts may seriously take the children's wishes and preferences into account. Young children usually cannot make a reasonable decision, since they may be manipulated by one of the parents. For instance, one parent lets the children stay up later than the other parent or is less strict or lets the children watch more television. Then it is reasonable to assume that young children will want to live with the less-strict parent. If a child is old enough to express his or her opinion, that opinion should be given careful consideration. The wishes of children between the ages of 8 and 13 years may be considered, but not

Vivian and Earl Jones were married in late 1976 and began farming near Rabbit Creek, Saskatchewan. They separated in 1993 when Mrs. Jones left the matrimonial home. The two children of the marriage were a 15-year-old boy, Brian, who lived with his father, and a 9-year-old girl, Selina, who lived with her mother in a different town. After the separation, Brian refused to see his mother, but Selina and her father maintained regular contact. The two children loved each other, got along well, and enjoyed each other's company. Selina had been diagnosed with attention deficit hyperactivity disorder and was receiving treatment; she was doing well but required considerable professional help and support.

Although Mr. and Mrs. Jones had been engaged primarily in farming while they were married, Mr. Jones had been employed at a second job that kept him away from home on a regular basis. This meant that his wife had had a more active parenting role than he. Both parties had suffered from substance abuse during the marriage but had since rehabilitated themselves.

In her divorce petition, Mrs. Jones sought custody of their daughter only, while Mr. Jones also sought custody of Selina to join him and Brian. However, the court ruled in favour of the mother, awarding her custody with generous access to the father.

Jones v. Jones
(1994)

Saskatchewan Court of Queen's Bench 4 R.F.L. (4th) 293

1. **Outline the mother's arguments for custody of Selina.**
2. **Outline the father's arguments for custody.**
3. **What is somewhat unusual about the court's decision?**
4. **Do you agree or disagree with this decision? Explain.**

isolated from other factors. The wishes of children over 14 years of age are very seriously considered. The older the child, the more weight is usually given to that child's preferences. In fact, custody disputes seldom occur over older children because any court order made contrary to a teen's wishes is likely to be ignored.

Parental Conduct

Courts generally do not consider a parent's past conduct when considering custody unless that conduct is relevant to that person's ability to act as a parent. In recent years, the sexual conduct of parents has been an issue in some court cases as judges have struggled with the extent to which a parent's sexuality should be considered in deciding custody. A parent's sexual orientation cannot be totally ignored. Yet, the quality of that person's parenting and the children's response to the parent's sexuality must also be considered. Homosexuality on a parent's part is only one of many factors to be considered. A homosexual parent may have more difficulty than a heterosexual parent in obtaining custody. Nonetheless, both gay and lesbian parents have been granted custody of their children in contested cases. The main question that the courts consider is not whether a parent is homosexual, but rather how that parent handles his or her sexuality. As well, the parent's love for his or her children, interest in their welfare, and involvement in the children's academic and recreational activities must be considered. In other words, it is the best interests of the children that will determine custody, not the parent's sexuality or sexual preference.

Religion

More and more spouses are using a child's religious upbringing as a weapon in a custody dispute. Traditionally, the courts have recognized the custodial parent's right to determine a child's religion. However, this tradition is changing as judges look closely at the noncustodial parent's relationship with his or her children. Can a Jewish father who takes his children to temple on Friday nights prevent his former wife, a Roman Catholic, from taking the children to church regularly every Sunday?

Disputes over a child's religious upbringing, especially in cases of interfaith marriages, are making custody negotiations more difficult. The most common problems occur when one spouse converts to another faith for the sake of the marriage. Although religious upbringing is a serious and honest concern in many cases, often the issue is used by the custodial parent to interfere with access rights of the other parent. Adapting to two religions can be confusing to children, but they can cope if each parent does not mock or ridicule the other parent's religion. The children's best interests, again, are still the major consideration when courts resolve parental disputes over such issues as religious freedom.

CASE

Re B. and B.
(1980)

Ontario Provincial Court, Family Division
28 O.R. 136

Mr. and Mrs. B. were married in 1962 and adopted three children, two boys and a girl. The couple separated in May 1977, shortly after Mr. B. returned from a lengthy overseas posting with the Armed Forces. All three children lived with their father after the separation, while the mother had generous access. Mrs. B. often moved back into the house to look after the children when Mr. B. was away on duty.

The daughter, Lynn, became increasingly unhappy living with her father and wanted to be in her mother's custody. In March 1979, Mrs. B. took Lynn with her. This action gave rise to court proceedings in which each parent sought sole custody of the 10-year-old child. At the time of the trial, both boys, aged 13 and 15, still lived with the father. Evidence presented at trial showed that while Mr. B. was overseas, Mrs. B. developed a lesbian relationship with a woman, with whom she was living at the time of this action. Although Mr. B. admitted that Mrs. B. was a skilled and qualified parent, he expressed concern about his daughter's being raised in such a home environment and the possibility that she might copy her mother's lifestyle.

Evidence from the Family Court clinic indicated that Lynn had a good relationship with both her parents, but felt closer to her mother and somewhat distant from her father. The clinic also provided a thorough overview of the literature on homosexual parenting which suggested that the degree of risk to Lynn would depend on how her mother handled the issue and that there was no solid basis for the father's concern.

The court awarded custody of Lynn to her mother, with reasonable access by her father.

1. **Why did the court separate the siblings in this custody action?**
2. **To what extent do you think the judge took Lynn's preferences into account?**
3. **What would be the advantages and disadvantages of awarding custody of Lynn to (a) her father, and (b) her mother?**
4. **Does Mrs. B.'s lesbian relationship represent any risk to Lynn? Discuss.**

Joseph and Juanita Ysebaert were married in 1982 and separated in 1989. Their only child, Brian, was born in 1987; he was mentally and physically challenged. Both parents were receiving social assistance because of unemployment, and the mother was also entitled to a partial disability pension from the Workers' Compensation Board due to a shoulder injury.

After the separation, the father received interim custody of their son, and the mother was granted generous access. Brian attended a community learning program and was doing well. He and his father lived in a one-bedroom apartment, and Mr. Ysebaert, in addition to welfare, received a monthly allowance relating to Brian's disabilities.

The father prepared Brian's meals every day and sent him to school on the bus, always meeting his son after school; in short, he was very capable of handling the daily needs of his son. Although he was a diligent and caring parent, his education was limited, and he had poor reading and writing skills. Mr. Ysebaert's sister helped him read Brian's report cards and messages from his teacher.

Mrs. Ysebaert, on the other hand, was better equipped to assist Brian in matters of personal hygiene, manners, and academic advancement. Also, she was better at ensuring his medical treatment was appropriate.

Both parents claimed sole custody of Brian, but the court awarded joint custody.

1. **Outline the father's arguments for sole custody of Brian.**
2. **Outline the mother's arguments for sole custody.**
3. **Why did the court award joint custody instead?**
4. **Do you agree or disagree with this decision? Explain.**

Ysebaert v. Ysebaert
(1993)

Ontario Court,
General Division
47 R.F.L. (3d) 69

It is easy to see from the preceding discussion that determining custody is not an easy decision for a judge to reach. Moreover, a custody decision is never final because children's needs change. A decision that was in the best interests of a five-year-old may not be in the best interests of the child when he or she is 16. Conditions change, and a custody order can always be brought back to court for further review. This may occur several years after the original custody order, but the courts are concerned about the best interests of the children at all times.

Joint Custody

Not as common as sole custody, **joint custody** is a court-approved custody plan in which both parents have a shared responsibility in, and control of, their children's upbringing and the major

decisions that affect their children after the parents have separated or divorced. The *Divorce Act* stresses that it is in the children's best interests if they can maintain contact with both parents, and several provincial statutes have had a joint-custody provision for years. With dual-career families, fathers are becoming more involved in parenting and asking for joint custody.

There are different forms of joint custody. In **joint physical custody**, the children will spend equal, or nearly equal, amounts of time with each parent; both parents make the major decisions. Each week or month is split in half, so that the children alternate between the permanent homes of each parent. Obviously, this form of joint custody may present major problems for the children, who might have to attend two different schools and have different groups of friends. For this reason, this form of custody is seldom used. If both parents live in the same neighbourhood, joint physical custody poses less of a problem. Critics say children need one place to call home rather than two part-time places.

In the more common form of joint custody, **joint legal custody**, the children remain with one of the parents while the other parent has generous access rights. However, both parents have an equal voice in all major decisions concerning the children. (If the parents cannot agree, the primary custodial parent usually has ultimate decision-making power.) This situation is probably much better and less stressful for the children, but it does require cooperative parents who will put the children's welfare ahead of their own personal disagreements. They must be willing to work together with some degree of mutual respect and have a high degree of communication, cooperation, and trust. The parents must be able to agree upon matters affecting the health, welfare, education, and religious upbringing of their children, and for many couples this cooperation is a problem.

The key advantage of joint custody is that the children have the continued involvement of both parents. It gives the noncustodial parent a significant role in the children's lives and gives the children a sense of being truly cared for and not abandoned by one of their parents. Studies also indicate that divorced fathers who have frequent contact with their children are much less likely to avoid their support obligations. The disadvantage of joint custody occurs when parents are too emotionally upset about the divorce and tend to belittle each other in front of the children.

In Canada, the courts generally will not impose joint custody against the wishes of one of the parents as it is not in the child's best interests to be caught between parents who are hostile toward one another.

Reviewing Your Reading

1. What is the most important factor in determining custody, and why?

2. Why does the parent with interim custody have an advantage when final custody is determined?

3. What is the tender years doctrine, and why has it become less important today in determining custody?

4. When might a judge consider a child's preferences in a custody case?

5. To what extent is a parent's sexual orientation considered in determining custody?

6. How might religion be used as a weapon by parents in a custody dispute?

7. Why are custody decisions never permanent?

8. What is joint custody, and why is it becoming more common?

9. Briefly outline the two common forms of joint custody. Which is more common, and why?

10. List two advantages and one disadvantage of joint custody.

15.3 Access

When one parent has been granted custody of the children, the courts usually award access, or visiting rights, to the other parent. (Under the *Divorce Act*, a nonparent, such as a grandparent, may now apply for an access order.) Access to a child by the noncustodial parent is something that is usually in the child's best interests. However, if a judge feels that a child might be harmed emotionally, physically, or morally, access might be very strictly controlled or denied. These situations are rare. An example is a parent whose smoking severely affects a child's asthma.

Often the courts will suggest that the parents themselves work out reasonable terms of access, if the spouses have parted on good terms. If, however, the separation or divorce has resulted in a courtroom battle, the court may outline specific conditions for access. There are three common types of access orders. In **reasonable access** the time spent with the noncustodial parent is quite flexible and on a regular basis. In **specified access**, time spent with the noncustodial parent is defined, such as certain weekends and holidays. Time is also specified in **supervised access**, however, it must be spent in the presence of a supervisor. Access includes the right for the noncustodial parent to make inquiries and receive information on the welfare, education, and health of the child. However, there are no laws requiring the noncustodial parent to visit the child.

Parental Mobility

Access orders, like custody orders, are open for review if conditions change. An example of a changing condition would be if the custodial parent moves from one province to another because of remarriage or a career opportunity. Once a custody order is made, it has generally been permissible, until recently, to take the children out of the province. For example, let us say that Luisa has custody of her two children with generous access being granted to her former husband, Antonio. Luisa has just been promoted to Vice-President and is now required to move from Halifax to Vancouver. Antonio's right to access will be greatly reduced because of the cost of travel and the distance between the two cities. If Antonio asked the courts to review either the custody or the access order, they probably would not alter it for him. Luisa's move was reasonable and necessary for her, and this is the key issue.

Canadian courts have, in the past, taken the approach that the custodial parent has the right to move the children for reasonable purposes, even if this interferes with the other parent's access rights. Courts will look closely at the reasons for the move. If the reason is a valid economic opportunity for the custodial parent, and not simply an attempt to thwart or deny access to the noncustodial parent, the court may allow the move. What is good for the custodial parent should generally be presumed also to be good for

CASE

I rene and James Kam Chen Young were married in 1974 and separated in 1987; at the time, they had three daughters, aged 6, 11, and 13. In 1985, Mr. Young converted to the Jehovah's Witness faith, and this became a source of conflict between the parents. The mother and the two older children objected to the father's insistence on sharing his religion with them.

In 1988, Mrs. Young began divorce proceedings in which she was granted sole custody of the daughters, with specified access to the father. Under the court order, the father could not discuss his religion with the children or involve them in religious activities without their mother's consent. Furthermore, he could not prevent the children from having any necessary blood transfusions.

Arguing that this order infringed upon his freedom of religion, Mr. Young appealed this decision to the British Columbia Court of Appeal in 1990. In a 2–1 judgment, the court held that the father should not be restricted from discussing his religion with his children on the ground that it was in their best interest for them to know their father fully, including his religious beliefs. Exceptions to this rule could be made only if it could be shown that the children were being harmed.

Mrs. Young appealed this decision to the Supreme Court of Canada where, in a 4–3 judgment, the Court upheld the Court of Appeal's decision, reinforcing "the best interests of the children" principle.

Young v. Young
(1993)

Supreme Court of Canada
49 R.F.L. (3d) 117

1. **What does the trial judgment suggest about the custodial parent's right to make decisions regarding the couple's children?**

2. **Should an access parent have the right to share his or her everyday lifestyle with the children, including religious beliefs, regardless of whether the custodial parent approves? Discuss.**

3. **What principle does this majority judgment seem to establish about an access parent's right to share his or her lifestyle with the children?**

CASE

Harrison v. Harrison
(1994)

British Columbia
Supreme Court
2 B.C.L.R. (3d) 293

When James and Tamara Harrison separated in June 1992, a court order gave them joint custody and guardianship of their three children, aged 5, 7, and 9. The children's primary residence was to be with the mother if she relocated their home to any one of about 10 municipalities in the Greater Vancouver area. This was done to allow frequent and convenient access by the father.

The Harrisons eventually came to live within a few blocks of each other in White Rock, British Columbia, and the father continued a very close relationship with his children. He had them twice a week during the week, generally on the weekends, and for a lengthy period of time each summer.

However, Mrs. Harrison wanted to move to the Sardis-Chilliwack area of British Columbia to be with her new partner. She claimed that the cost of living would be less and she also hoped to find a job there.

Mr. Harrison applied for a court order restraining the mother from moving the children's residence; the mother applied to vary the original order to include Sardis in the list of permitted residential areas. In reviewing the facts, the court allowed the father's application and dismissed the mother's application.

1. **What type or form of joint custody did the Harrisons have?**
2. **Should a court be able to restrain the movement of children with a custodial parent? Why or why not?**
3. **List at least two reasons why the court dismissed the mother's application.**

the children. This implies that the right of the custodial parent to create a happy home for the children may be greater than the right of access for the noncustodial parent.

However, some judges have started to issue orders forbidding one spouse from moving children some distance away from the other spouse. Courts can even require a parent to surrender his or her passport to the court to ensure that the parent does not leave Canada with the child. Maintaining consistency and stability in children's lives is in their best interests. Keeping them in the same school and being near their friends is now being looked at more seriously by the courts. Such decisions also recognize that the parent needing access has very fundamental rights.

In Luisa's case, she might be given a choice: if she stays in Halifax, the children will remain in her custody. If she moves, she will be given the same visiting rights that Antonio had under the original agreement. Noncustodial parents are demanding closer ties with their children and greater involve-

ment in their upbringing, since children separated from a parent with whom they have a strong attachment may feel rejected or abandoned.

Mobility of Custodial Parents

As the issue of the mobility of custodial parents is appearing in the courts much more regularly, some couples are adding a clause in their agreements, preventing the custodial parent from leaving a certain location with the children without the other parent's consent. The *Divorce Act* says that the court may require the custodial parent to give 30 days' notice, or other period as the court specifies, before changing the child's residence.

When problems arise and legal access is denied, the noncustodial parent's only option is to go back to court and charge the former spouse with a breach of access provisions. The judge can impose a jail sentence or a fine for contempt of court, but these measures are seldom used. A jail sentence for the custodial parent leaves the children on their own, while a fine takes money out of a household that usually has little to spare. On application, the judge may award increased or make-up access as remedies for access denial.

Parental Conflict Resolution

Often spouses will reach their own custody agreement and include it in a separation agreement. This may also occur if a divorce takes place without an earlier separation. The courts will seldom change this decision unless they feel that it is not in the best interests of the children.

However, access to children is often the area of the most bitter family disputes. Most children suffer severely when their parents engage in a bitter court battle over custody and access. This is costly in terms of money and emotional wear and tear of all of the parties involved.

Family Courts and provincial Superior Courts often have mediators, counsellors, social workers, and psychiatrists available to assist couples in resolving conflict over custody when the parents cannot reach a decision on their own. The use of a mediator to help resolve custody and access conflicts is becoming more common in Canadian courts. This trained, neutral third party will meet with the parents to try and work out a solution without having a court resolve the dispute. Other people, such as the children, grandparents, and new partners of the separating spouses, may also be consulted. If parents cannot reach an acceptable agreement with the mediator's help, custody will be determined in a court of law.

Child Abduction

Directly related to the growing number of child custody disputes being heard in Canadian courts is an increase in child **abduction**—kidnapping one's own child. This occurs when a parent decides to take a child not legally in his or her custody. The usual reasons for child abduction are that a parent expects to lose the court custody decision or has already lost it and wants custody despite the court's decision. A large number of child abductions are committed by fathers who have been denied access.

A parent who illegally removes a child under the age of 14 from the care of the custodial parent

commits a criminal offence. Child abduction is an indictable offence under the *Criminal Code*, for which the offender is liable to imprisonment for a maximum of 10 years, even if that person is a parent. However, the police and child welfare workers have been reluctant to press charges and thus become involved in family matters. But, as child abduction increases, the courts feel they must become more involved.

Many parents who abduct their children remove them to another province. As a result, all provinces have passed legislation to enforce custody orders from other provinces. As well, federal information banks may be searched under the *Family Orders and Agreements Enforcement Assistance Act*, discussed in Chapter 14. Provincial data banks, such as motor vehicle registration, must be searched first. The court, and not the parent, receives any information available from the federal data banks. To ensure confidentiality, information released is limited to the address of the missing person and the name and address of an employer. It is hoped that such a procedure will assist in locating a missing child taken by a parent contrary to a custody or access arrangement.

The problem becomes more difficult if the parent and child have left Canada. **Extradition**, or getting the other country to send the parent and child back, is possible only if child abduction is an offence in both countries. In 1980, the *Convention on the Civil Aspects of International Child Abduction* was signed at The Hague in the Netherlands by delegates from 29 governments. It established a procedure for the prompt return of children abducted in violation of custody rights. Canada ratified the *Convention*, and it came into force in late 1983 in all provinces and the Yukon Territory, and on April 1, 1988, in the Northwest Territories. Among other countries that have ratified the *Convention* are Australia, France, Luxembourg, Portugal, Switzerland, the United Kingdom, and the United States.

Reviewing Your Reading

1. **When might one parent be denied access to his or her child?**

2. **Identify the three common types of access orders, and describe how they differ.**

3. **Are custody and access orders permanent? Why or why not?**

4. **Why is the mobility of custodial parents becoming a more frequent and difficult issue in the courts?**

5. **What penalties can a court impose on a custodial parent who denies child access to the other parent?**

6. **What resources are now available to the courts to help resolve difficult custody disputes?**

7. **What assistance is available to custodial parents in locating their abducted children?**

15.4 CHILD SUPPORT

As you learned in Chapter 14, support is primarily based on two key factors: need and the ability to pay. Both parents have a joint financial obligation to support their children's basic needs, and both must contribute according to their respective abilities to pay.

The financial support of children is a prime obligation of the parents. If necessary, the parents' standard of living should diminish before that of the children. For example, when Thorne and Macy separate, the income available for their one household must now provide for two households. If, before the separation, Thorne earned $25 000 and Macy earned $35 000 yearly, the courts have ruled that their children are still entitled to enjoy the lifestyle they had in a $60 000 household had their parents not separated. But the financial circumstances of the parents will determine how practical this objective is.

In late 1994 in *Willick v. Willick*, the Supreme Court ruled that children's needs are not frozen as of the date of their parents' marriage breakdown. Thus, if a parent's capacity to pay support improves greatly after the divorce, child support may be increased, and if the supporting parent's income drops greatly, a decrease in support may also occur.

The Level of Child Support

Determining the appropriate level of child support involves the following three steps:

1. Determine what amount of money is necessary to support the children's needs.

2. Divide this amount in proportion to the parents' incomes.

3. Order the noncustodial parent to pay his or her portion to the custodial parent.

In reality, usually it is the parent who does not have custody who pays all, or most, of the child support to the custodial parent. On the other hand, if Thorne and Macy had been granted joint custody of their children, Macy, as the parent with the higher income, would probably have to pay more child support than Thorne with his lower income.

Under provincial legislation, the obligation to support unmarried children still at home continues until they reach the age of majority, either 18 or 19, depending on the province. In addition, some provinces may order continued support as long as the children are enrolled in a full-time educational program. For example, child support may be granted to an adult child for post-secondary education; however, this usually only lasts for the first undergraduate diploma or degree, or until the child attains the age of 21, whichever is first. If a child between 16 and the provincial age of majority leaves home and withdraws from parental control, this obligation ends.

However, if the parents of the child are, or were, married, the definition of child under section 2(1) of the federal *Divorce Act, 1985*, may apply. It allows a court to make an order beyond the provincial age of majority. This section states:

2.

(1) In this Act "child of the marriage" means a child of two spouses or two former spouses who, at the material time,

(a) is under the age of 16 years, or

(b) is 16 years of age or over and under their charge but unable by reason of illness, disability, or other cause to withdraw from their charge or to obtain the necessaries of life.

M r. and Mrs. Keen married in 1962 and separated in 1989. They had two sons, Troy and Earl, born in 1968 and 1969, respectively. One of the issues in this action was whether Troy and Earl were "children of the marriage" under the *Divorce Act, 1985*, and, if so, to determine if they were entitled to support while attending university.

Troy left the matrimonial home in the fall of 1988 and had not returned; he was due to graduate from university in December 1990. His father paid toward his support and helped him with his car expenses while at university.

Earl lived with his mother and graduated from high school in June 1988. During the next year, he worked to save money to attend university. He then spent about eight months taking upgrading courses during the summer and about 23 months working and travelling. Between January and June 1990, Earl lived with his father but moved back with his mother as his father was pressuring him to contribute more toward the household expenses.

Earl's action for support succeeded, and his father was ordered to pay $175 a month so long as Earl continued in full-time attendance at university.

Keen v. Keen
(1990)

**Saskatchewan
Court of
Queen's Bench
30 R.F.L. (3d) 172**

1. **Was Troy a "child of the marriage" within the meaning of the *Divorce Act*?**
2. **Was Earl a "child of the marriage"?**
3. **Do you think a child who graduates from high school and works and travels for a year should regain status as a child of the marriage if he or she returns home and enrolls in university or college? Why or why not?**

The difference between the definitions in the provincial and federal legislation should be considered in bringing a support application to court. Finally, the *Criminal Code* also requires parents to provide the basic necessities of life, such as food, clothing, and shelter, to their children up to the age of 16.

Support for Parents

Most provincial laws also require children over the age of majority to provide support for their parents who have provided and cared for them, to the extent that a child is capable of doing so and to the extent of the parents' need.

For example, in Ontario, a 60-year-old widow, Veronica Goodwin, brought a successful action against her adult children and won $1000 a month support. The mother is a live-in compan-ion-caregiver to a 94-year-old woman and earns $150 a week. This amount, plus her pension, gives her a monthly income of nearly $900.

Bringing her action under Ontario's *Family Law Act*, Goodwin relied on a section that requires an adult child to help a financially needy parent. At trial, the adult children argued that they had not been raised in a warm, nurturing home and that their mother had been a poor parent during their upbringing.

The children appealed the court's decision to the Ontario Court of Appeal, which upheld the lower court's ruling.

Income Tax and Support

A major issue at the time of publication concerns the fact that a spouse receiving child-support payments from a former spouse must report these

CASE

Baker v. Baker
(1994)

Alberta Court of
Queen's Bench
147 A.R. 227

The 20-year-old petitioner, Heather Baker, lived with her mother in Edmonton because she could not find employment due to the depressed state of the economy. The daughter had made efforts to find full-time work with no success and was now attending high school one day a week to complete her diploma requirements.

Baker's petition sought support from her father, James Richard Baker, as a "child of the marriage" within the meaning of the federal *Divorce Act*.

The court held that the petitioner was a "child of the marriage" and ordered her father to make regular support payments to her.

1. As a young adult, why did the petitioner feel that she was entitled to support from her father?

2. Should the inability to obtain employment in a depressed economy be a legitimate "other cause" under section 2, entitling the petitioner to parental support? Why or why not?

3. In determining whether a young adult requires support, should the court differentiate between children who cannot provide for themselves because they are in school and children who cannot provide for themselves because of the economic situation? Discuss.

4. If the petitioner's application had not succeeded, what alternative was available to her?

payments as income and be liable for the taxes on that income. Meanwhile, the paying spouse is able to deduct these payments from his or her taxable income. The impact of this requirement to report child-support payments as income is felt much more by women than men, and many groups have questioned the fairness of this law.

This income tax rule became law over 50 years ago when most women were not employed. At that time, most support payers were men who were in a higher tax bracket than their former wives. The intent was to provide men with a reason and incentive to pay their court-ordered support.

This high-profile issue became front-page news in 1994 when Suzanne Thibaudeau of Trois-Rivières, Quebec, successfully challenged this law in the Federal Court of Appeal on the basis that a section of the *Income Tax Act* discriminated against sole custodial parents and infringed the *Charter's* section 15 equality rights. (See *Thibaudeau v. Canada* in Chapter 2.)

Suzanne Thibaudeau

On May 25, 1995, the Supreme Court ruled 5–2 that the system was constitutional. On March 6, 1996, the government announced a new child-support structure. Starting May 1997, those receiving child-support payments will not have to pay income tax on them and those paying the support will not be able to deduct it.

Future Directions

In the early 1990s, the provincial, territorial, and the federal justice ministers announced the creation of the Child Support Guidelines Project. The committee's purpose was to study the existing child-support guidelines, to evaluate the effectiveness of these guidelines based on economic research, and to make recommendations to improve problem areas. The main goal was to increase child support for children who most needed it, as low child-support payments mean a burden on taxpayers.

All governments involved want a fair formula and guidelines to cover the cost of raising children and to remove the discretion that judges now have to set support awards based on personal, subjective motives. Currently, support awards can vary widely from province to province, and even among judges of the same court. Judges need guidelines that are realistic and reflect the cost of raising a child today.

The committee also plans to develop a national strategy to enforce child-support collection. As of early 1996, the committee's report had not been released.

Reviewing Your Reading

1. **List the three steps to be followed in determining appropriate child support.**

2. **Which parent usually pays most of the child support, and why?**

3. **What is the difference between making a child-support application under provincial versus federal legislation?**

4. **When are adult children obligated to support their parents?**

5. **Why is it necessary to establish a national strategy to enforce child-support collection?**

15.5 CHILDREN IN NEED OF PROTECTION

Our society has promoted the doctrine that parents have a right to raise their children according to their own values and beliefs and that all people should have the right to minimal government intervention in their lives. Only recently have social values and concerns changed to recognize that some parents' methods of raising children may be unacceptable. What is "unacceptable" is not easy to decide. Punishment acceptable to one parent, such as spanking, is considered physical abuse by another. The values of individuals within society vary widely, and the methods of child raising vary with these values. Sometimes the result is that some children do not receive what society deems as proper care and supervision. The legal system must then step in to protect the child from his or her family.

Child abuse is any form of physical harm, emotional deprivation, neglect, or sexual maltreatment that might result in injury or psychological harm to a child. Abuse is not confined to any one group of people; it occurs in families from all educational, economic, religious, and ethnic backgrounds. Although statistics indicate that child abuse is mainly a male offence, there is an increasing number of cases involving mothers who are single parents and who are receiving little or no help from their former partners.

Society's increasing awareness of child abuse is being reflected in specific legislation. Canadian children are protected from physical and sexual abuse by specific offences in the *Criminal Code*, including sexual interference with and exploitation of children, and invitations for sexual touching. These offences were discussed in Chapter 7. Children who are emotionally abused or neglected are protected by civil law in the form of child protection legislation, discussed later in this section. Government departments exist in each province to provide services for abused and neglected children. Agencies such as the Children's Aid Society, and the provincial Departments of Child Welfare and Ministries of Community and Social Services have been established to take custody of children in need of protection. The common

Child Protection Statutes

Province	Name of Act
Alberta	Child Welfare Act
British Columbia	Family and Child Services Act
Manitoba	Child and Family Services Act
New Brunswick	Family Services Act
Newfoundland	Child Welfare Act
Northwest Territories	Child Welfare Act
Nova Scotia	Child and Family Services Act
Ontario	Child and Family Services Act
Prince Edward Island	Child and Family Services Act
Quebec	Youth Protection Act
Saskatchewan	Child and Family Services Act
Yukon Territory	Children's Act

goals of all groups are to protect the children and to help families solve the problems that led to the abuse.

All provinces and territories have legislation to protect neglected children. For example, Ontario's *Child and Family Services Act*, passed in 1985, requires cases where children are in need of protection to be reported to the local or area Children's Aid Society or Child and Family Services, the police, or the Crown attorney. Under British Columbia's *Family and Child Services Act*, cases are reported to the Superintendent of Child Welfare. These *Acts*, and similar provincial statutes, have two main goals:

1. The need to recognize the "best interests" of the child as the most important concern of the law and the courts.
2. The need to protect the child and to support the family as the basic unit of society.

The chart lists the names of the provincial and territorial statutes.

All provincial and territorial statutes contain the same basic criteria to define a child who is substantially at risk for abuse and in need of protection. These criteria include children who have

- suffered physical harm or risk of harm;
- been sexually molested or exploited or are at risk of either;
- been deprived of necessary medical attention;

- suffered emotional harm, demonstrated by severe anxiety, depression, withdrawal, or aggressive behaviour;
- been abandoned.

According to family-law experts, the above features are most clearly and precisely outlined in the Alberta and Ontario statutes.

Reporting Child Abuse

Legislation requires every person who has information about the actual or suspected abandonment, desertion, or need for protection of a child, or infliction of emotional or physical abuse on a child, to report that information. Persons working closely with children have a special awareness of those who may be in an abusive situation. Such persons as doctors, nurses, teachers, social workers, clergy, day-care employees, and peace officers must immediately report any actual or suspected abuse to the authorities. Failure to do so may result in a fine of up to $1000, depending on the province.

To encourage people to report suspected cases of neglect and abuse, most provincial legislation treats any information reported as confidential. Furthermore, the person supplying the information is protected from legal action, unless the report was made without reasonable grounds or with malicious intent.

Symptoms of Domestic Violence

Pre-school children (birth–5 years)	School-age children (6–12 years)	Adolescents (13–16 years)
• physical complaints	• truancy	• truancy
• sleep disturbances	• antisocial behaviour	• poor academic performance
• bedwetting	• aggression	• exaggerated need to control others
• excessive separation anxieties	• sibling difficulties	• dating violence
• whining, clinging anxiety	• anxious, depressed, withdrawn	• promiscuity
• failure to thrive	• somatic complaints	• adherence to rigid sex roles

Source: Ministry of the Attorney General of Ontario.

Extreme cases of abuse are easy to identify, but they represent only a small percentage of the total picture. Even cases of severe abuse may not be readily identifiable. The injuries may be covered by clothing, or the child will have carefully rehearsed explanations for bruises and cuts. A child's behaviour may indicate abuse; such signs as withdrawal, extreme lack of self-confidence, demanding of attention or food, being too eager to please, and overtiredness may be evidence that bears watching. Emotional abuse is usually the most difficult to identify and to prove.

Central Abuse Registry

Most provinces have established a central registry that keeps a record of all reported child abuse within the province. These registries have made it harder for parents to cover up acts of abuse; for example, by taking the child to a different doctor on each occasion to avoid detection. If medical personnel suspect a possible case of child abuse, they have quick access to information files about suspected abusing parents. A person whose name is entered into the registry must be notified of this fact. Furthermore, that person has the right to request removal of his or her name if it can be proved that no abuse has occurred. Access to registry information is restricted; it is not available to the general public.

Removal of Children

Welfare and social workers and peace officers can obtain search warrants to enter a home and remove children where there is a strong suspicion that they are in need of protection. If there is a very strong reason to have children removed immediately without taking the time to obtain a warrant, it can and will be done to protect the children. Children who are taken from their parents are brought before a Family Court judge, usually within seven days in most provinces. Parents must be notified of this hearing.

The court must give paramount consideration to the best interests of the children at such a hearing and must consider the following factors, taken from British Columbia's *Family Relations Act*:

> **24.**
>
> **(1)** In assessing these interests, a court shall consider these factors:
>   **(a)** the health and emotional well being of the child including any special needs for care and treatment;
>   **(b)** where appropriate, the views of the child;
>   **(c)** the love, affection, and similar ties that exist between the child and other persons;
>   **(d)** education and training for the child; and
>   **(e)** the capacity of each person to whom guardianship, custody, or access rights and duties may be granted to exercise these rights and duties adequately; and give emphasis to each factor according to the child's needs and circumstances.

In addition, other provinces consider the religious faith, if any, in which the children are being raised, the children's cultural background, and the importance for the children's development of a positive relationship with a parent and a secure place as family members. A decision is then made concerning the children's welfare, after a report is made of the home and family. The most common actions are examined below.

Supervision Order

A **supervision order** allows the children to remain in the custody of their parents, under the supervision of the Children's Aid Society or child protection agency. This might occur where it is felt necessary to have some professional care and attention given to the children, yet still keep them at home.

Temporary Wardship Order

A **temporary wardship order** allows the legal custody and guardianship of the children to be transferred to a child protection agency on a temporary basis. In most provinces the period is 12 months; in Ontario it may be up to 24 months in some cases. Children are usually placed in a foster or group home during this time, and parents are allowed some visiting rights.

Such an order might be required when it is necessary for a child to be given medical care contrary to the parents' religious beliefs. Also, a child born drug-addicted because of the mother's addiction during pregnancy is born abused and is a child in need of protection. Since there is a risk that the child might not receive adequate care and treatment at home, an order will be issued for support services. A temporary wardship order suggests that a positive child/parent relationship will be restored within time. Like custody and access decisions, parents may usually request a review of supervision or temporary wardship orders.

Crown Wardship Order

With a **Crown wardship order** or permanent custody order, the natural parents lose all rights of control over their children. An example of such a situation would be parents who leave very young children alone exposing them to possible danger. The Crown or the province becomes the legal guardian. The children become wards of the state and can be placed with foster parents or given up for adoption. In such circumstances, the consent of the child's natural parents is not required. Once adoption occurs, the natural parents have no right to visit their children. Several statutes, including those in Yukon Territory, British Columbia, and Ontario, clearly prohibit or severely limit access rights of the natural parents to their children who have become permanent wards.

Damages for Child Abuse

Recently, sexually or physically abused children have been bringing an increasing number of civil actions against abusing parents, step-parents, relatives, or siblings for damages in the torts of assault and battery and infliction of mental harm and suffering. These torts were discussed in greater detail in Chapter 12.

Although most lawsuits for damages involve female victims suing male offenders, often for incest committed by a father, some actions have involved claims by male victims against either male or female offenders. In 1994, a British Columbia man was awarded $350 000 for childhood sexual assaults committed by his uncle. In the case of *A.D.Y. v. M.Y.Y. and D.E.Y.*, another man received $260 000 in an action against his parents who had subjected him to frequent and numerous verbal and physical abuses as a child.

Most civil actions must commence within a limited time period, and, until recently, this has prevented abused children from taking action many years after the alleged abuse. However, in 1992, the Supreme Court of Canada ruled that the time period only begins when as an adult, the victim understands and appreciates the harm to his or her emotional and psychological well-being caused by the childhood abuse or incest. Often, this does not occur until the victim obtains counselling and treatment as an adult.

A child victim may also sue a parent for breach of care in failing to protect the child. (See *J. (L.A.) v. J. (H.)* in Chapter 11.)

Reviewing Your Reading

1. **What are the more common forms of child abuse? What legal protection is available against such abuse?**

2. **What are the two main goals of child protection legislation?**

3. **Who is responsible for reporting suspected child-abuse cases? What is done to encourage people to report such cases?**

4. **What is the central child-abuse registry? What is its purpose? If a name has been incorrectly placed in the registry, what can be done about it?**

5. **Distinguish among a supervision order, a temporary wardship order, and a Crown wardship order as actions to assist children in need of protection.**

6. **Briefly describe some recent trends in legal actions for child abuse.**

15.6 ADOPTION

Adoption is the creation of a legal relationship between a child and new parents who were not previously related by blood. Adoption provides a safe home environment for the child that the birth parents could not provide for financial or emotional reasons. A **birth parent** is an adopted child's biological mother or father, and a person whose consent to that adoption was given or dispensed with. At the same time, all rights between the child and the biological parents are terminated. The first Canadian legislation providing for adoption was enacted in New Brunswick in 1873. Most provinces passed adoption laws in the early part of the twentieth century. Each province's adoption laws, which are similar in intent and outline, are part of a comprehensive plan for child care. In Alberta and Ontario, for example, adoption procedures are found in the *Child Welfare Act* and the *Child and Family Services Act*, respectively.

Until the early 1970s, there were a large number of babies available in Canada for adoption. Since then, there has been a marked decline in the number of available babies because of the greater acceptance of single parenthood, the prevalence of common-law unions providing a partner to share parenting responsibilities, more awareness of birth control, and the legality of abortions.

Did You Know

According to Statistics Canada, 51 percent of young unmarried women who placed their babies for adoption felt that they were too young to parent.

Today, there is an acute shortage of the type of babies wanted for adoption in Canada. In several provinces, the wait to adopt an infant may be an average of six years; in Canada's largest provinces, the wait may be 8 to 12 years. As a result, older children, children from other countries, and mentally and physically challenged children are being adopted by couples who want to build their families. A 1993 federal report, *Adoption in Canada*, stated that there were three international adoptions for every two domestic adoptions in Canada in the early 1990s. The adoption of older children raises the question, Should ties with natural parents be maintained if the children are old enough to remember them? When one spouse with custody of the children remarries and the new spouse wants to adopt the children, should access to the natural noncustodial parent continue? These are just some of the important questions facing the parties involved in adoption procedures today.

Eligibility

Generally a person to be adopted must be under the provincial age of majority, 18 or 19, and unmarried. Adopting parents must be at or over the age of majority and have a stable and secure relationship. In most provinces, the adopting parents must be married, although there is a growing movement to allow single people to adopt. The increased number of single-parent families in Canada is reflected in an increasing number of single-parent adoptions. When such an adoption occurs, the single person must adopt a child of the same sex.

In late 1994, British Columbia changed its adoption rules to give single people the right to apply to adopt a child. This policy change was made to give single persons and married couples equality rights under the law. Formerly, only married couples could apply to adopt a healthy child under two years of age. This change in policy means that gays and lesbians may now apply to adopt infants.

Reprinted by permission of the Southam Syndicate.

In mid-1995, an Ontario Court judge ruled that the definition of "spouse" in adoption provisions of the *Child and Family Services Act* was unconstitutional and violated the *Charter of Rights and Freedoms*; he ordered that same-sex couples be included in the definition. The ruling, which allowed a lesbian the right to adopt her partner's child, was based on a number of available studies that concluded that children raised by lesbian or gay parents are no different from those children raised by heterosexual parents.

Placement

The process of selecting adoptive parents, placing the child in their custody, and monitoring the situation for a period of time is known as **placement**. Before placing a child with adoptive parents, a social worker from the Children's Aid Society or a related government agency, such as the Department of Social Services, conducts a number of interviews with each parent and visits their home. This home study acquaints the worker with the couple and their home environment, attitudes, expectations, and lifestyles. Personal references and the possible existence of a criminal record are also checked. This gathering of information is necessary for making a placement that is in the

child's best interests. It is also necessary for the child to live with the adoptive parents for a certain length of time, usually 6 to 12 months depending on the province, before the adoption is final. If approval is given for final adoption, an adoption order is made in Family Court.

Parental Consent

In most cases, a child's natural or biological parent(s) must give consent for adoption to occur. The parent must be completely informed of all the implications of this action. Adoption severs the link between that parent and the child and is final. The consent must be honest, informed, and freely given. Any adoption that occurs as a result of uninformed consent is not legally binding. In certain situations where consent is being unreasonably withheld or when biological parents cannot be located, the courts can issue an order dispensing with consent.

In many provinces, legislation has been passed requiring a child to be a certain age before parental consent to adopt can be given. In Alberta, British Columbia, and Manitoba, the child must be 10 days old, in Ontario and Newfoundland 7 days old, and in Prince Edward Island 14 days old. This period gives the baby's mother time after the child's birth to deliberate properly and at length about this serious decision. Consent is also required from the father if he has admitted paternity of the child. The sooner an infant is placed in a secure, loving environment, the better.

Withdrawal of Consent

A parent who has given consent may have a change of heart. For this reason, a period of 21 days to one month during which consent may be withdrawn generally applies. During the waiting period, the child is usually placed in a foster home to avoid the emotional situation of having to take the child from the adoptive parents should the birth mother change her mind. However, only about 6 percent of women who give consent later change their minds.

If there is a good reason, courts may allow a parent to withdraw consent any time up to the final adoption hearing. However, this is seldom

A baby son, Jordan, was born to Cecilia Sawan, a status Indian, in Alberta on December 3, 1991, following a brief relationship with a non-Native. She was a single, 18-year-old woman at the time. In early February 1992, the mother decided to give up her son for adoption by James and Faye Tearoe, a Victoria, British Columbia, couple and signed the required consent forms.

Within 10 days, Ms. Sawan changed her mind. She mailed a written revocation to the Alberta Ministry of Family and Social Services as required by Alberta law. However, the revocation was never received. With the support of the Woodland Cree Band Council at Cadotte Lake, Alberta, Sawan began legal proceedings to regain custody of her son. Sawan and the Woodland Crees believed that the child should be raised in a Native culture.

Meanwhile, the Tearoes applied in British Columbia to adopt the child, now named David, and to dispense with Ms. Sawan's consent. At the time of this application, the baby boy had been in his mother's care for a total of 22 days, while he had been in the Tearoes' care continuously for 16 months. The Tearoes, who had married in 1978, adopted their first child, a daughter named Heidi, in 1984.

At trial in the British Columbia Supreme Court, the judge ruled in favour of Ms. Sawan, believing that it was in the child's best interests to be raised in a Native culture with his birth mother and that the bond between Ms. Sawan and her son had not been irretrievably broken. The Tearoes appealed this trial decision to the British Columbia Court of Appeal where, in a 3–0 judgment, the court allowed the appeal and ruled in favour of the Tearoes.

Leave to appeal to the Supreme Court of Canada was dismissed in February 1994.

Sawan v. Tearoe

(1993)

British Columbia Court of Appeal 84 B.C.L.R. (2d) 223

1. **What is your opinion of the trial judge's decision? Support your answer with reasons.**

2. **Do you believe that a bond had been established between Ms. Sawan and her son in the time the child was with her? Why or why not?**

3. **Prepare a chart to list the arguments for and against the Tearoes retaining custody of David.**

4. **In the Court of Appeal's judgment, Madame Justice Patricia Proudfoot wrote: "To remove David from the Tearoe home would destroy the family bonds that have been established between the child and the adoptive parents . . . Therefore, it is not in the best interests of this child to revoke Ms. Sawan's consent to adoption." Discuss.**

done. In a 7–0 landmark judgment in 1994 in the case of *Metropolitan Toronto Children's Aid Society v. C.M.*, the Supreme Court of Canada ruled that the best interests of the child take precedence over any rights of the child's biological parents.

The birth mother sought the return of her child, nearly eight years old, because she had made great strides toward becoming a better mother. The foster parents who sought to adopt the girl had cared for her for six years.

The Adoption Hearing

Once the probation period has ended, and all consents have been obtained, a private hearing is held to grant an adoption order. If the child is over the age of 7 in Ontario or the age of 12 in British Columbia, he or she must also give consent to the proposed adoption. In granting the order, the court must be completely satisfied that the parents applying for the order are suitable parents for the child. At this point, the child becomes the legal child of the adoptive parents and assumes all the rights of a natural child. All ties with the child's natural parent(s) are terminated. Even the child's birth certificate is changed to identify the adopting parents as being the biological parents of the child.

Private Adoptions

In addition to adoptions handled by the Children's Aid Society and government agencies in some provinces, private or direct placement adoptions can also be arranged by an individual or agency licensed by the appropriate government ministry. Licences are renewed on a regular basis as long as the licensee meets the required standards.

Private adoptions can occur when a pregnant woman seeks a licensed individual or agency to help her find a family for her baby, or when a prospective adoptive parent asks a licensee to help make arrangements with a woman planning to give up her child. Home studies are also required, and the licensee must arrange for a government-approved social worker to conduct the home visit. In recent years, private adoptions have overtaken those occurring through social agencies and Children's Aid Societies.

Two major differences exist between agency adoptions and private adoptions. In an agency adoption, several sets of approved parents are usually available with whom to place the child; in a private adoption, only one set of parents is usually proposed. However, the birth parent selects the child's adoptive parents after reviewing case profiles of approved parents. Agency adoptions are handled without cost, while private adoptions can cost anywhere from $3500 to $6000 for fees and services rendered. In spite of this cost, private adoptions may be more appealing to some couples because the waiting period for an infant is much shorter, usually within three years.

In 1988, Alberta passed new private adoption laws for licensing and regulating private adoption agencies. Different rules apply to adoptions, depending on whether they are agency arranged, direct from birth to adoptive parents, or public adoptions arranged by social services.

Adoption Disclosure

In most provinces, only the Attorney General or an authorized person may inspect birth records, unless a court order states otherwise. Canadian courts have ruled that an adult adoptee's natural curiosity to find out more information about his or her biological parents is not a valid reason for unsealing these records. The confidentiality of adoption records is intended to best protect the adoptive parents, the biological or natural parents, and the adoptee.

However, since July 1987 and amendments to Ontario's *Child and Family Services Act*, procedures now exist for adult adoptees in Ontario to find their natural parents or, at least, obtain more information about them than ever before. Adopted children under 18 may request this procedure with their adoptive parents' consent. At the request of an adoptee who is 18 years of age or over, the Ministry of Community and Social Services will make a "discreet search" for a natural parent or birth relative. Nonidentifying information, such as the birth family's ethnic background, medical history, type of occupation, and level of education, will be released on request, and similar information about the adoptive family's background will be provided to a birth parent. The first place one should go is the Children's Aid Society or the licensed individual or agency that arranged the adoption.

Information that reveals the identity of an

Did You Know

Private infant adoptions increased rapidly from 22 percent of all infant adoptions in Canada in 1981 to 59 percent in 1990.

A courtroom may be the setting for an adoption hearing.

adult adoptee or birth relative will be shared only if both parties have entered their names voluntarily in the Adoption Disclosure Register and consented to disclosure. Consent of the adoptive parents is not required. Because the issues surrounding adoption are so complex, emotional, and often sensitive, professional counselling is provided before the possible reunion takes place. There is no fee for this service. Once you have registered, you are not required to proceed; you can stop the process at any point. The interest in these procedures is so high that thousands of adopted people face a possible five-to-eight-year wait because of the enormous backlog in the ministry conducting the searches.

Reviewing Your Reading

1. List three reasons why there is a shortage of infants available for adoption in Canada today.
2. How has the eligibility to adopt changed in recent years?
3. Briefly describe what happens in the placement process for an adoption.
4. Why is parental consent so important before an adoption is finalized?
5. List the major differences between agency adoptions and private adoptions.
6. What is the Ontario Adoption Disclosure Register? Briefly describe how it operates. Is such a service available in your province?

Children and poverty: What should be done to remedy this situation?

*A*ll children have the right to be financially supported. Every province has legislation that deals with the support of children. In addition, the *Criminal Code* obliges parents to provide necessities. Yet some Canadian children still live in poverty.

Single parents have the highest rates of poverty: 45 percent live in poverty and most of these single parents are women. The poverty rate of children with single mothers in 1989 was 57.4 percent compared with 9.7 percent in two-parent families. Why are these single female parents living in poverty when the courts specify the child-support amount at the time custody decisions are made? The answer is that many former spouses fail to make their support payments.

On One Side

Enforcing child-support payments is a provincial responsibility and in 1994, the Justice Department provided $5.1 million to provinces for enforcement mechanisms, including garnisheeing of wages and removal of privileges. Although most provinces have support enforcement statutes, the problem persists. In 1994, in Ontario alone, more than half of all child-support agreements were in default of child-support payments despite a law called the *Family Support Plan*, which authorizes wage deductions from delinquent parents. Unfortunately, many defaulting parents are self-employed or on welfare. Either situation makes it impossible to implement the wage deduction principle.

In 1994, defaulting parents in Manitoba and Nova Scotia owed nearly $9 million each. In an attempt to catch defaulting parents, the Manitoba government, in early 1995, promised to suspend driving privileges, seize pension funds, and report delinquent parents, mostly men, to the Credit Bureau. The government also planned to raise the jail sentence from 30 to 90 days for a parent willfully avoiding child support payments. Alberta and New Brunswick also have refused to issue drivers' licences to defaulting parents until payment is made.

In August 1995, the Ontario premier proposed using the *Income Tax Act* to collect outstanding child support payments from deadbeat parents. However, this proposed plan would involve the cooperation of the federal government.

At the federal level, the Justice Minister announced plans to introduce a national child-support package in the fall of 1995 that would assist the provinces in collecting court-ordered support payments. Delinquent parents may be denied licences and privileges such as fishing licences, pilot permits, and even passports. Clearly, the federal government feels there must be a crackdown on parents who willfully neglect their legal and economic commitments to their children.

On the Other Side

Governments are taking alternative action in an effort to curb poverty. New Brunswick and British Columbia are spending $70 million on an experimental program called the Self-Sufficiency Project. It is designed to help single parents living on welfare to get back to work.

In British Columbia, a person who works a 40-hour week for the minimum wage would earn about $1000 a month and may be supporting a family on this wage. However, a single parent with two children living on welfare would receive $1300 a month. In addition to social assistance, there are medical and dental benefits available for those on welfare, whereas working people have to pay for these benefits. The obvious question is, Why work?

The Self-Sufficiency Project is designed to overcome this barrier. Those who find a full-time job receive half the difference between their wages and a benchmark amount of $37 000 in British Columbia and $30 600 in New Brunswick. The average annual income that a person receives in this program is $24 000 (the wage plus government supplement). This is to encourage people to work. Of those who found work in the first year of the program, 88 percent were still working after one year.

Despite these government initiatives, the number of poor children continues to grow. Between 1990 and 1995, the number of children using food banks doubled. The Canadian Institute of Child Health recommends that Canada follow the lead of some European countries that provide a guaranteed yearly income for children to insure their healthy development. The Caledon Institute of Social Policy wants the government to create a child benefit program for needy children and their families. This proposal would cost taxpayers an additional $2 billion.

The Bottom Line

In a 1994 study, the *Canadian Medical Association Journal* reported that children in families with incomes below the poverty line are more likely to resort to violence than children in higher income families. They also have higher rates of illiteracy, unemployment, and crime.

Obviously, Canadians and their governments have some difficult choices to make to try and reduce child poverty in Canada. It is a serious and complex problem that affects all Canadians. Should spouses who default on child-support payments be penalized more severely? Or should Canadians be expected to accept the financial burden to end child poverty in Canada? You be the judge!

1. **What problems are associated with child poverty? How are these connected to each other?**

2. **Which type of parent is more likely to live in poverty, and why?**

3. **Some governments are imposing penalties on parents who fail to make child-support payments. Do you think these penalties violate their basic rights?**

4. **What is the purpose(s) of the Self-Sufficiency Project? Do you think all governments should adopt such a program?**

5. **In groups, brainstorm ways to end child poverty in Canada. Present your conclusions to the class.**

6. **Why does child poverty affect all Canadians?**

CHAPTER REVIEW

Reviewing Key Terms

For each of the following statements, indicate the key term being defined:

a) the care and control of a child

b) to have leave to see children who are in the care of someone else

c) time spent with the noncustodial parent in the presence of another person

d) the act by which a person legally takes as his or her own the child of another person

e) the surrender by one state or country to another, on request, of persons accused or convicted of committing a crime in the state seeking the surrender

f) a person who has the same biological mother or father as another person

g) the key factor in determining in which person's home to place a child in a custody hearing

h) a court order making the state or society the legal guardian of a child in need of protection

i) the process of selecting adoptive parents with whom to place a child

Exploring Legal Concepts

1. Instead of following the tender years doctrine slavishly, the courts are now considering each parent's parenting abilities. Do you agree or disagree with this direction in awarding custody? Defend your position.

2. Should a child whose parents are involved in a custody dispute be represented by his or her own lawyer? Why or why not?

3. With a partner, assume that the two of you are children of a blended family; prepare arguments

  a) why your natural father should continue to make the same level of support payments to you as before, in spite of the fact that he has remarried and formed a new family with children;

  b) why your natural father should be able to reduce the level of support payments to you now that he has remarried and assumed responsibility for a new family with children.

  Look at your respective arguments and objectively determine which set of reasons is better for all concerned.

4. Should children be placed with adoptive parents who are of the same race, cultural background, and religion as the child? Discuss, stating your reasons.

Applying Legal Concepts

1. The Solomons separated, and a custody dispute arose over their eight-year-old son, Arnold. The mother lived in an apartment and earned a minimum wage working as a server at night in a licensed restaurant. The father had some drinking problems but was working steadily and was willing to pay a neighbour to prepare lunch for Arnold.

- **Which parent should be awarded custody of Arnold, and why?**

2. Bill Danko, the custodial parent, applied to terminate his former wife's access to their seven-year-old daughter, Cheryl. The mother, Judy Danko, loved Cheryl very much and took every opportunity to be with her daughter. The little girl was sickly and had asthma and numerous allergies. Judy was a smoker who did not refrain from smoking when exercising her access, although she knew of her daughter's allergies.

- **Based on the facts presented, do you think the courts found in favour of Bill Danko? Why or why not? Support your explanation with legal reasoning.**

3. James Worby entered into a relationship with a woman, whom he married and with whom he had two children. He was a homosexual, and this was known to his wife prior to their marriage. After the birth of the children, Worby moved out of the matrimonial home and moved into another home with his male partner. An attempt at reconciliation with his wife failed. Worby asked the court to clarify his right of access to his children, aged four and six. Mrs. Worby expressed concern about this issue.

- **As the judge, what type of access would you allow, and what conditions, if any, would you impose?**

4. *White v. White* (1994) New Brunswick Court of Queen's Bench 7 R.F.L. (4th) 414
Paul and Constance White were married in 1980 and separated in 1992. They had three children: a son born in 1981 and twin boys born in 1983. After their separation, the parents agreed that the father would have interim custody of the boys and that the mother would have reasonable access.

However, access problems developed, and behaviour and discipline problems occurred at home and at school. There was obvious and considerable animosity between the parents. In 1993, with the father's approval, the oldest son and one of the twins went to live with their mother. Since the separation, Mrs. White had been residing with another man whom she intended to marry.

In divorce proceedings, Mr. White proposed that custody of the son in his care be granted to him and that Mrs. White be granted custody of the other two sons. She, in turn, sought custody of all three children.

- **Which factor in determining custody is the most important here?**

- **What other factors might also be considered?**

- **In determining custody of the boys, what is in the best interests of the children, and why?**

- **What access, if any, would you award the other parent? Explain.**

5. *MacGuyver v. Richards* (1995) Ontario Court of Appeal 123 D.L.R. (4th) 562
Lee MacGuyver and Mary Richards met in 1983 while attending Memorial University in Newfoundland and relocated to North Bay, Ontario. After living together for several years, they separated shortly before the birth of their daughter, Vanessa, in late 1989. During her pregnancy, Richards went home to live with her mother but returned to North Bay when her child was seven

months old. The couple lived together for six months but separated permanently thereafter. The relationship broke down because of MacGuyver's drug and alcohol problems and his abusive behaviour toward Richards.

In June 1991, a judge of the Ontario Court, Provincial Division, awarded sole custody of the child to Richards. MacGuyver, who had entered a treatment program for his addictions, was given alternate weekend access. In 1993, Richards made plans to marry a master corporal in the military who had been transferred to Washington for four years. After the wedding, she planned to move there with her daughter.

MacGuyver applied to the court to vary the custody order to provide for joint custody and to prohibit either parent from removing the child from North Bay without the other parent's consent. The trial judge ordered that the mother retain sole custody but that the child continue to reside in North Bay.

Mary Richards successfully appealed to the Ontario Court, General Division, which confirmed her sole custody and removed the requirement that the child remain in North Bay. MacGuyver appealed this decision to the Ontario Court of Appeal, but his appeal was dismissed.

- **Considering MacGuyver's request for joint custody of their child, prepare arguments for and against this position.**

- **Why did the trial judge order sole custody for the mother but require the child to continue to reside in North Bay?**

- **Why did the Court of Appeal confirm sole custody but remove the residency requirement?**

- **Explain the meaning of the following statement from the Court of Appeal judgment: "The trial judge put the mother in the position of having to choose between her child and her marriage." Do you agree with this statement? Why or why not?**

- **What is the possible impact of this judgment on families in custody and access disputes?**

Extending Legal Concepts

1. Now that you have completed this chapter, review the opening article and Something to Think About. Have your answers or opinions changed? Why or why not?

2. a) Imagine that you are the custodial parent of two children, aged six and nine. Think of a valid reason, not mentioned in this chapter, why you would move out of the province with your children, thereby making access difficult for your former spouse. Support your right to mobility before the court that is hearing your application for a custody and access change.

   b) Now take the role of the noncustodial parent in this scenario, and present your side of the issue to the judge.

   c) Have the class determine a fair resolution to this conflict, keeping in mind "the best interests of the children."

3. A baby born out of wedlock was offered for adoption by the birth mother. A year after the baby was adopted the biological father demanded his child, claiming his consent had not been given for the adoption. The adoptive parents claim the child is theirs since they have provided a secure and loving environment.

Work in groups of three. One student will be the judge. The other two students are to prepare arguments, each taking one side in the dispute. In a forum, each student must present his or her arguments to the judge, who must then decide the case. In handing down the decision, the judge must explain his or her legal reasoning.

4. In small groups, create an advertising campaign on the issue of child abuse that could be used in your school. This activity could include posters, school announcements, and video presentations.

5. Using reference materials in your resource centre, including CD-ROM and the Internet, obtain current information and prepare a report on any of the following:

   a) federal government initiatives to obtain better support payments from defaulting parents

   b) current initiatives on this issue in your province or territory

   c) the federal government's treatment on the issue of taxing support payments to the custodial spouse

   d) recent trends in the prevention of child abuse

   e) the status of same-sex partner child adoptions and related legislation in your province or territory

   f) the Baby Jessica adoption case: *Schmidts v. DeBoers* (1993)

   g) the Kimberly Mays adoption case: *Twiggs v. Mays* (1993)

Researching an Issue

Teen Welfare

In some provinces, 16- and 17-year-olds are eligible for social assistance to enable them to leave an abusive home. This has not been a popular policy with the public, which has an unfounded distrust of teens. As a result, provincial governments are examining their teen-welfare policies.

Alberta welfare rules now make it almost impossible for 16- and 17-year-olds to qualify for social assistance. In 1995, the Ontario government was threatening to cut off 16- and 17-year-olds altogether.

Statement

Teens of this age are simply too old and often too hardened to live as wards of Children's Aid Societies. These teens need a rescue plan.

Point

Whether they live at home or away from home, 16- and 17-years-olds should remain the financial responsibility of their parents and not the state.

Counterpoint

For some 16- and 17-year-olds, the alternative to being on welfare is being on the street.

- **With a partner, research this issue and reflect on your findings.**
- **Prepare points on this statement that could be used for a class debate.**
- **Discuss your findings with others in your class.**

WILLS: PLANNING FOR THE FUTURE

These are the key terms introduced in this chapter:

administrator

administratrix

beneficiaries

codicil

collateral relatives

distribution clauses

execution

executor

executrix

guardian

heirs

holograph will

intestate

letters probate

lineal descendants

probate

revoke

testator

testatrix

will

Chapter at a Glance

Learning Outcomes

At the end of this chapter, you will be able to

1. state the requirements for making a valid will;
2. explain who can make a will;
3. identify the types of wills and what is required for each;
4. explain how to change and how to revoke a will;
5. outline the duties of an executor/executrix;
6. describe the procedures involved in probating a will;
7. describe what happens when a person dies without a will;
8. explain the grounds for contesting a will.

Top Court Okays Will

Sandra Vout will get the bulk of her 81-year-old bachelor friend's $320 000 estate after all.

The Supreme Court of Canada ruled yesterday that Clarence Hay's will leaving most of his worldly possessions to a 27-year-old woman he had known for only a few years before his death was valid.

The family of the eccentric Eastern Ontario farmer, all but cut off in the will he prepared three years before his murder, had contested the document, arguing "suspicious circumstances" rendered it invalid.

But the country's top court unanimously agreed with a judge who, in 1990, decided Vout had not exerted "undue influence" on Hay to change his will.

His original will, drafted in 1968, left everything to his brother and sister and their children.

But three years before his death, Hay wrote a new will.

Vout, a denture therapist, and her mother were frequent visitors to the Hay farm, helping him bale hay, clean barns and stalls, shovel manure, and water and feed his horses.

In challenging the will, the family claimed his signature was really that of Vout: He went to a lawyer recommended by her, she stayed with him while the will was prepared, and coached him when he hesitated.

"He may well have been somewhat captivated by her; they may have been simply friends and she was a person whom he wished to benefit in his will."

From: Stephen Bindman, "Top court okays will." *The Toronto Star,* June 23, 1995. Reprinted with permission—The Toronto Star Syndicate.

Something to Think About

- **If Clarence Hay was under duress, would the will be valid?**
- **If the Supreme Court had overturned the 1990 judgment, would the will drafted in 1968 be valid?**
- **What do you think about the Court's decision? Explain.**

16.1 INTRODUCTION

A **will** is an important legal document outlining how a person wishes his or her property to be divided and distributed after death. Most people do not like to prepare wills because it reminds them of their mortality. However, most adults who have anything of value should have a will. Unless you have a will, you may cause your family and close friends considerable distress and expense in deciding what happens to your estate following your death.

A properly prepared will outlines how you want your personal and financial affairs handled at the time of your death. Thus, a will often prevents family arguments from occurring, because you have clearly outlined who will receive what after your death. A will is prepared for the survivors; it is a way to plan for the future.

The maker of a will is called a **testator** if a man, a **testatrix** if a woman. The maker has the opportunity to appoint a particular person to carry out the terms of the will and the distribution of the property according to the maker's wishes. Although the appointed person may be a man (**executor**), woman (**executrix**), or a financial institution, the words "executor" and the pronoun "he" will be used throughout this section to simplify matters. The person or persons receiving some benefit from the terms of the will are the **heirs** or **beneficiaries**.

Laws exist that outline the procedures to be followed when a person dies without having made a will or when both spouses die at the same time. These laws will be examined later in this chapter.

16.2 *R*EQUIREMENTS FOR PREPARING A WILL

Wills and the inheritance of property fall under provincial jurisdiction in the *Constitution Act, 1867*. Certain legal requirements, similar in all of the provinces and territories, are necessary for a valid will. They are outlined in the *Succession Law Reform Act* in Ontario and in the *Wills Act* in other provinces and the territories. As a result, there are some differences in the general descriptions that follow, and you will need to check your province's legislation for specific details.

As in a valid marriage, you must have the legal capacity to make a will. This means you must have reached the age of majority (18 or 19 depending on the province or territory), be mentally competent and free of duress or any kind of pressure, and have prepared the will voluntarily.

In addition to the essential legal requirements, there are certain formal requirements that make it easier for the courts to accept, understand, and distribute the property in a will. These additional details are discussed below.

Correct Form

The will must be handwritten, printed, or typed. Other than this writing requirement, there is no special form that a will must follow in most provinces. A computer program is often used now to prepare the will. However, a will scratched with a knife on a tractor fender by a man trapped under the tractor, which said simply, "all to my wife," was ruled valid in Saskatchewan in 1948. It is also possible to purchase a printed form in an office supplies store, fill in the appropriate blanks, and sign the completed form. However, because such forms combine printed words and your own handwriting, they must also be witnessed.

The "tractor will" of Cecil George Harris.

THE WIZARD OF ID by Brant parker and Johnny hart

I THINK I'LL MAKE OUT MY WILL

WOULD YOU LIKE A 3X5 CARD?

NO....THAT'S WHAT YOU'RE GETTING

I'D LIKE TO MAKE OUT A WILL

I WANT MY KIN PROVIDED FOR

WITH NO FIGHTIN' AMONGST 'EM!

VERY WELL, ...LET'S GET STARTED

FIRST I'LL EXPLAIN TRUST FUNDS

THEN TAX BENEFITS ON STOCKS AND ANNUITIES

AND FINALLY YOUR PERSONAL PROPERTY

SEEMS LIKE A LOTTA RIG-A-MA-ROLE FOR A MULE AND A PLOW

Many people who prepare their own wills may, because of a lack of knowledge or experience, make serious errors in the wording or the intended meaning of a word or phrase. What is clear to you may not be as clear to your executor or to the courts. Since the language of a will must be clear and precise and the rules of interpretation of wills is very strict, many people have a lawyer prepare a will to ensure it is legally valid. Using a lawyer's services avoids problems after your death in case someone challenges or contests the will. If a will contains provisions that seem rather peculiar—for example, leaving all your money to your dog instead of your family—it will be especially important later to have a lawyer who can declare your mental capacity at the time the will was prepared. A lawyer's fee for preparing a will is based on the amount of time it takes to prepare the document and how complicated its terms are, but simple wills can be prepared for a reasonable fee.

As well, the will should be dated and should state that it is your last will and testament, and that all previous wills are destroyed or **revoked** (cancelled).

Holograph Wills

One of the major changes made by the *Succession Law Reform Act* in Ontario was the recognition of holograph wills. Holograph wills are not recog-

nized in all provinces. A **holograph will**, one completely written and signed by you, is accepted by the courts. It need not be written in any special form using legal language, and it does not require witnesses' signatures in some provinces. The will written by the Saskatchewan farmer on his tractor fender is a good example of a holograph will.

Execution

The final step in making a will is the **execution**. This is the signing of a will by you, the maker, and two witnesses of legal age. The witnesses must see you sign the will; all three of you must be present at the same time. Then the two witnesses must sign, in the presence of each other and you. It is not necessary for the witnesses to know what is in the will; they are simply indicating that they have witnessed your signing the will and that your signature is genuine. Neither a witness to a will nor his or her spouse may receive anything from the estate as a beneficiary. In Ontario, however, a witness or that person's spouse may receive a gift from the will if the court is satisfied that there was no undue influence or pressure involved in the making of the will. The executor, who is entitled to a fee for his services, may be a witness, however.

CASE

Re McDermid Estate
(1994)

Saskatchewan
Court of
Queen's Bench
122 Sask. R. 232

John and Stella McDermid of Erwood, Saskatchewan, obtained commercial will forms and filled in the blanks by hand in 1980. The wills were almost identical, except for the designated beneficiary. Each spouse left all property to the other spouse and appointed the other as executor/executrix of the estate.

When the wills were executed, the husband unintentionally signed his wife's will and had it witnessed, while the wife also mistakenly signed her husband's will and had it witnessed. After this was done, the wills were put away.

When John McDermid died in 1994, his will was taken to a lawyer's office for processing and the mistake was discovered.

An application on behalf of McDermid's estate was brought to the Court of Queen's Bench to determine the validity of the will. The court granted that application.

1. **What was the problem with the validity of McDermid's will?**

2. **In resolving this problem, what needed to be determined?**

3. **Why did the court rule that the will was valid?**

Reviewing Your Reading

1. **What is the purpose of a will?**

2. **Identify each of the following people connected with wills:**

   a) **testator/testatrix**

   b) **executor/executrix**

   c) **heir/beneficiary**

3. **To make a will, you must have legal capacity. What are the three requirements of legal capacity?**

4. **Why is it a good idea to have a lawyer prepare your will?**

5. **What is a holograph will?**

6. **What is meant by executing a will?**

16.3 OTHER PROVISIONS IN A WILL

As mentioned earlier, a will is for the survivors; it is a plan for the future. Its purpose is not to benefit you but to ensure that your property will be divided according to your plan. Thus, you should include certain other provisions in your will to help make the process of distribution easier to accomplish.

Executors

You should appoint one or more executors or executrixes to supervise the distribution of your estate and carry out the provisions of the will after your death. By personally choosing the executor, you guarantee that the person responsible for the distribution of your estate is someone whom you trust.

The executor's duties may be quite complex and time-consuming, depending on the details in the will. As a result, you should carefully consider naming an executor who has the time and ability to handle the responsibility. Many testators appoint an executor younger than themselves in the hope that this person will outlive them and so be able to execute the will. This also explains why many testators appoint more than one executor; appointing co-executors or alternate executors is a common practice.

An executor is someone trustworthy who knows you and your family, often a close friend or a relative. Many people name a spouse or a child as executor. A lawyer or a trust company, or any combination of these, can also fulfill the function, especially for large, complex estates. Often a trust company and a friend or relative are appointed as co-executors. The main advantage of using financial institutions as executors is that they have the financial, legal, accounting, and investment expertise to handle estate distribution. By law, a friend or relative acting as an executor will receive a reasonable fee for the time and effort used in providing services; lawyers and financial institutions usually charge a fee based on a certain percentage of the estate's value.

The executor's duties include, among other things, collecting the deceased's property, paying all outstanding debts and taxes against the estate, and then distributing the remainder (sometimes called the "residue") of the estate according to the terms of the will.

Make certain that your executors know what is in your will so they will know how much work is involved. A person is under no obligation to accept the responsibility of being an executor. Therefore, it makes good sense for you to seek a person's permission before appointing him or her as your executor. Even if two people agree to be co-executors, they have the right to change their minds before your death.

Did You Know

In his will, a Toronto millionaire promised almost $500 000 to the woman who gave birth to the most children during the 10 years following his death in 1926. The prize was divided among four women who had each given birth nine times during the decade.

Guardians

If the testator/testatrix has any children under the age of majority, some plans must be made to appoint a **guardian** for the children in the event of the maker's death. Usually the guardian is a close relative and only assumes responsibility for the children in the event of both parents' death. It is important to discuss concerns about the general upbringing and education of the children with the guardian in advance, so that he or she will follow your wishes. Your will can even name anyone you do *not* want appointed as guardian. However, a will is not binding in the appointment of a guardian. The court must approve the appointment. If it does not think the guardian named in the will is suitable, the court will make an appointment itself.

Distribution Clauses

The **distribution clauses** in the will that outline how the property is to be distributed are the most significant clauses. If you want to leave specific items of value to certain beneficiaries, both the items and beneficiaries must be listed in enough detail for the executor to know who receives what. Sometimes, the beneficiary's name and address is given to provide necessary detail.

A beneficiary accepts a gift, subject to claims against the property. For example, a car not fully paid for and given to a daughter must be paid for by the daughter, unless the will states that the estate is to complete the payments. A beneficiary can refuse to accept a gift, but this seldom happens. If the beneficiary dies before the maker of the will, the item or its value is added to the residue or remainder of the estate.

Changing a Will

Since a will does not come into effect until your death, you can change it as often as you want. To alter a will, it is only necessary to cross out existing words and insert new ones. These changes must be signed or initialled in the margin near the alterations by you and two witnesses. These witnesses need not be the same as those who witnessed the original will. However, if a change is not initialled by you and the witnesses, the change is invalid and has no legal effect.

If you prepared a holograph will, it is not necessary for changes to be witnessed, since there were no witnesses to the original document. But the changes must be made in your own handwriting and signed.

For more extensive changes to a will, a codicil is attached to the original will. A **codicil** is a separate page or pages describing in detail exactly what

CASE

Hope v. Raeder Estate (1994)

British Columbia Court of Appeal
2 B.C.L.R. (3d) 58

The plaintiff, Stefanie Hope, was born in Germany in 1944. She became an orphan shortly after her birth and was taken in by Mr. and Mrs. Kurt Raeder Senior who treated her as if she were their own child. However, the Raeders never formally adopted the plaintiff.

In 1950, the Raeders had a natural child of their own, a son Kurt, named after his father. The Raeders, their son, and Stefanie emigrated to Canada in 1951, and Stefanie lived with the family until she married.

Mrs. Raeder died in 1991, and Mr. Raeder died in 1992. In Mr. Raeder's will, made in 1980, he established a $200 000 trust fund for Stefanie in which she was to receive up to a maximum income of $750 per month for her lifetime.

The plaintiff brought an action to the British Columbia Supreme Court to be considered a "child" of the family under the *Wills Variation Act*, but the trial judge ruled against the plaintiff. Her appeal to the Court of Appeal was also dismissed.

1. **Why do you think the plaintiff wanted to be considered a "child" of the family?**
2. **Why did both courts rule against the plaintiff?**
3. **What do you think of the courts' decisions, and why?**

changes are to be made. It too must be signed and witnessed, like any other changes. As well, a notation should be made in the original will that a codicil exists. This is done to prevent anyone from destroying the codicil so that the original will would then stand as originally written. A codicil might be added to a will after a marriage or a divorce, the birth of children, the changing of an executor, or significant changes in the maker's estate.

Revoking a Will

However, if there are any changes to be made in a will, it is best to destroy the old will and prepare a new one. An old will is destroyed or revoked by burning or shredding it. Also, a new will automatically revokes all previous wills, if it states so, even if the earlier ones are not physically destroyed.

The courts may also have to rule on whether a will is the last one made by the testator. If your will cannot be found when you die, it is presumed that it was revoked unless evidence to the contrary is produced. The courts must be satisfied that an executor who claims that there was no will really has conducted a complete and thorough search to find it. Delays in distributing the estate could otherwise result until this matter is resolved. In British Columbia, for example, this could be determined through the provincial wills registry.

The courts can also revoke a will if they find that you lacked legal capacity. In short, a will may be revoked if one of the essential requirements is lacking. In Alberta, divorce does not revoke a will, but remarriage does.

Did You Know

Clive Wishart of Tabusintac, New Brunswick, included a death sentence in his will. Fearing that his four horses would be abused, Wishart asked that they be shot after his death. A judge spared the animals after a public outcry.

The deceased, Peter Krushel, was an elderly man in frail health. He had immigrated to Canada from Ukraine in 1928 and settled in Sudbury where he worked as a barber. Krushel never married and had no children.

For over 40 years, he and Ed Jones had been good friends; they often hunted and socialized together. During the last three years of Krushel's life, Jones visited his friend daily to tend to his needs, such as shopping, paying bills, housekeeping, and taking him for doctor and hospital visits.

Several days prior to his death, Krushel repeatedly expressed a wish that Jones would ultimately own his house. On one occasion, he wrote on a piece of paper: "I want to leave my house and my money to Ed Jones" and signed it. Concerned that Krushel was contemplating suicide, Jones tore up the paper in Krushel's presence. There was no further discussion about the "will" over the next few days on Jones's daily visits. Several days later, Krushel killed himself.

The torn-up "will pieces" were discovered in a garbage bag in the deceased's home, and Jones applied to have the validity of this "will" determined. He succeeded in his application.

Re Krushel Estate (1990)

Ontario Court, General Division
1 O.R. (3d) 552

1. **Were these torn-up pieces of paper a valid holograph will? Why or why not?**

2. **Was Krushel's will revoked when Jones tore it up? Explain.**

3. **Why did the court rule in Jones's favour as to the validity of this "will"?**

Reviewing Your Reading

1. **Why do many people appoint co-executors for their wills?**

2. **Why might you appoint a financial institution as an executor?**

3. **When should the maker of a will appoint a guardian?**

4. **What are the distribution clauses in a will?**

5. **List the two main ways to change a will. Why should they be avoided?**

6. **How can a will be revoked? What effect does a new will have on previous wills?**

16.4 DUTIES OF AN EXECUTOR

As you read earlier, the executor is a trustworthy person or firm that can be relied on to carry out the duties listed here.

Probating a Will

When you have made your will, you should leave a copy of it with your lawyer or place it in a safe place in your home so that it can be found easily. You should not keep it in a safety deposit box at a financial institution because the institution usually seals these boxes on your death. However, they will allow access to search for a will and will turn over the original to the executor. When you die, the executor's first function is to search all places possible to locate your will. Once it has been located, the executor submits the will to the courts to have it probated to prove its legal correctness.

To **probate** a will to determine its originality and validity, the executor must file certain documents with the court to prove that the will is, in fact, your last will and testament. Thus, a probated will is recognized by the courts as the deceased's last will and testament.

Once the courts have these documents of proof, they will issue **letters probate** to the executor, which indicates to others that the executor has legal control over the estate. When all of the deceased's property becomes the executor's sole responsibility, it is essential for him to maintain it in a reasonable manner. He must act in the beneficiaries' best interests, in the same way that a reasonable person would conduct his own personal and business affairs. If the executor is found negligent by the courts in carrying out his duties, he may be held personally liable for any losses resulting from his negligence. He would be required to make good any loss out of his own funds. The will may protect the executor from losses made "in good faith."

Funeral Expenses

The executor must also make final arrangements for the deceased. Usually, he will take into consideration the deceased's preferences contained in the will or those of the next-of-kin. Arrangements made in the deceased's will cannot be changed by the surviving spouse or the deceased's partner. They can be changed by the executor. The deceased's body belongs to the executor now. Reasonable funeral expenses are one of the first items to be paid from the estate. They are paid before any property is divided and bequests distributed.

Administration Expenses

The executor is entitled to a fee for probating the will and settling the estate. This fee can be agreed upon by the executor and beneficiaries. If there is no agreement, the fee can be determined by the court.

Income Tax

Within six months of a person's death, the executor must file the deceased's last income tax return. If the executor does not prepare his own income tax return, he should not attempt to prepare the deceased's return. A lawyer or accountant should be involved in this process. Revenue Canada has information available to assist in this task. Any provincial estate or death taxes must be paid as well.

Asset Inventory

Determining what assets the deceased owned at the time of death and the value of these assets may occupy a considerable amount of the executor's time. This procedure involves locating bank accounts, insurance policies, safety-deposit boxes and contents, real estate, and anything else of value. With your will, you should include details of where these assets are located. In preparing this inventory, items that have been specifically willed to certain people may be excluded.

Creditors' Inventory

As well as preparing an inventory of what the deceased owned of value, the executor must prepare a list of people to whom the deceased owed money. All creditors have the right to be paid from the deceased's estate before it is distributed to the heirs.

To allow all possible creditors, both known and unknown, to make their claims, the executor will place an advertisement in a newspaper in the area in which the deceased lived. This advertisement will usually appear three times in consecutive weeks. It is intended to let the creditors know of the deceased's death, so that they can notify the executor of their claims on the deceased's estate. If the creditors do not come forward within a certain amount of time, their claims against the executor are invalid but in certain circumstances may still proceed against the estate.

Distribution to Beneficiaries

The executor can, before making the distribution, sell any assets. When distributing the residue of the estate, the executor should obtain a release from the beneficiaries indicating that they have received the property willed to them. The executor then prepares the necessary documents for final approval by the court and the beneficiaries that his duties have been fulfilled.

Relief for Testator's Dependants

If the testator failed to provide for his dependants in the will, they have the right to appeal to the courts to challenge the will. The courts do not have to change the will, but they usually do so and award dependants any amount up to the amount that they would have received by law if no will had been made.

Dependants include a spouse, children, parents, or siblings of the deceased, if they were being supported by the deceased. In addition, most provinces now recognize the rights of a common-law spouse to inherit from an estate, depending on the length of time the couple lived together.

Jean Louise Barnes, the testatrix, made a will in 1976, leaving bequests to her grandchildren among others. These bequests were to be distributed when her eldest living grandchild reached the age of 25. After the will was made, a boy, Jason, was born and began to live with Thomas Barnes, the testatrix's son, but Jason was not adopted by Thomas Barnes until after the testatrix's death.

The applicant in this action, Helen Wilson, was the testatrix's daughter and executrix of her mother's will. She stated that, a few months before her death, her mother was concerned that Thomas might adopt Jason and that Jean Barnes had allegedly told Thomas that he could not afford to support another child.

The executrix brought this application to determine whether Jason was entitled to share in the grandchildren's inheritance. The court held that Jason Barnes, as a grandchild of Jean Louise Barnes, was a beneficiary under the will.

Barnes Estate v. Wilson
(1992)

Newfoundland Supreme Court
91 D.L.R. (4th) 22

1. What is the dictionary definition of a "grandchild"?

2. If Jean Barnes believed that her son might adopt Jason and if she did not intend Jason to be a beneficiary, what could she have done?

3. Why did the court rule in favour of Jason Barnes?

NOTICE TO CREDITORS AND OTHERS

All claims against the Estate of Kateryna (Katerina) Kaminsky, late of the City of Halifax, who died on August 22, 1996, must be filed with the estate trustee Verna Catherina Garbowsky before December 15, 1996, after which date the assets of the Estate will be distributed having regard only to the claims then filed.

DATED: October 10, 1996

SIGNED BY:

Verna (Catherina) Garbowsky
Personal Representative
by her Solicitors
OWENS, WRIGHT
1787 Barrington Street
Halifax, Nova Scotia
B3H 4V7
(902) 555-1177

The rights of all children of a common-law relationship are also recognized, since all provinces have abolished the concept of illegitimacy.

From British Columbia to Ontario, plus Nova Scotia, the statutes state that an adopted child becomes the child of the adopting parents and vice versa, as if the child had been born to those parents. Thus, all rights to inheritance are the same as those for any natural children. The adoptees' rights in the provinces of Quebec, New Brunswick, Prince Edward Island, and Newfoundland are not as clear, and claims must be resolved in the courts.

Reviewing Your Reading

1. What is meant by "probating a will"?

2. What items must be paid from a deceased's estate before the estate is distributed to the beneficiaries?

3. What is the purpose of a Notice to Creditors?

ISSUE

Organ Donation: How can the number of donors be increased?

Organ donation is an opportunity to give someone a healthy productive life. For patients with end-stage organ failure, it means life itself. Most organized religions find organ donation and transplantation acceptable. Some religions regard donation as a moral obligation.

In Canada, organ donation is voluntary. All provinces have organ donor programs. Although organ donor cards are legal documents in Canada, health professionals will not recover organs or tissue without the consent of surviving family members. This is called the "opting-in" system. For this reason it is important that those wishing to donate their organs make their wishes known to their family members. However, this should not be done in a will, since organs need to be taken quickly after death.

Some European countries, specifically Austria, Belgium, and France, use a "presumed consent" for organ donation. In these countries, it is presumed that everyone consents to donate their organs, unless they specify otherwise. This is known as the "opting-out" system.

The number of organ donors in Canada has decreased since 1990. Indeed, in North America there is a critical shortage of donated organs. In Ontario alone in 1994, of 1451 people requiring an organ, only 610 received an organ transplant. In the same year, 138 Canadians died waiting for an organ transplant.

In public opinion polls, most Canadians have indicated they are willing to donate their relative's organs. Indeed, a 1994 survey showed that 90 percent of people in Ontario were willing to donate organs of loved ones. Yet, only 38 percent of people in Ontario had actually signed a donor card. The most common reason cited for not completing a donor card was that the individual had never thought about it.

On One Side

Some people have suggested that strategies and incentives be employed to increase the number of organs donated for transplant. One suggestion is to offer financial compensation to the donor's families. Such payment might be used to offset funeral expenses.

A second suggestion is to amend legislation to require hospital staff to request donations from the family on the death of a patient. A third is to implement legislation that would change the current voluntary system to one of presumed consent.

Medical attendants transporting a donated organ.

Putting the onus on the individual to "opt-out" would gain donors from that pool of individuals who had never thought about it.

A fourth incentive suggested is the implementation of a "preferred status" system. This would guarantee that people who are on record as voluntary donors are given preferential treatment on a waiting list should they themselves ever need an organ transplant.

On the Other Side

Those who oppose such incentives feel that organ donation should be an individual decision. It should not be legislated by governments, nor should it be motivated by profit. Such decisions are intensely personal.

Others suggest that implementing a "preferred status" system makes this an egoistic decision rather than an altruistic one. In other words, the donor is looking out for his or her own interests, instead of the health of someone else.

Many people who oppose incentives believe that efforts should be directed toward educating the public instead. People should be made aware of how the program works, such as procedures for identifying donors and matching them with patients. Another important part of that education is dispelling myths, such as the belief that hospital staff will make less of an effort to prolong life if the patient is a known donor.

The Bottom Line

About 100 of every million people will one day need a transplant, while only 25 of every million can ever become a donor. This makes it even more important to find a way to increase the number of available donors. How do you think this can be accomplished? You be the judge!

1. **Do you think that the government should make organ donation compulsory?**

2. **Which suggestion do you most agree with to increase organ donations? Which suggestion do you least agree with? Explain.**

3. **Why do you think organ donations are not recognized in an ordinary will?**

4. **Why do so few people sign donor cards? Do you have one?**

5. **Do you think there could be an ethical or moral dilemma associated with organ donation that might bring a legal challenge to this issue?**

16.5 DEATH WITHOUT A WILL

If you die without having prepared a will you are said to have died **intestate**, and the court will appoint an **administrator** or **administratrix** to be responsible for the distribution of the estate. This person has duties similar to those of an executor. It is usual for one of the next-of-kin to apply to the courts to do this. If no one applies, the courts will appoint a Public Trustee, a government official, to handle the distribution of the estate. Various trust companies specialize in this type of business.

Each province has its own statute concerning inheritance, such as the *Devolution of Estates Act* in New Brunswick, Alberta's *Intestate Succession Act*, and Ontario's *Succession Law Reform Act*. Check your province's statute for specific details.

Distribution of the Property

The only people entitled to inherit property if a person dies intestate are the decedent's blood relatives and legal spouse. Relatives are generally divided into two categories: lineal and collateral.

Lineal descendants are those in a direct line of descent. Priority is given to the deceased's spouse, then children, then grandchildren, and so on. Adopted children share equally with natural children. If a person dies leaving a spouse and no children, the entire estate passes to the spouse.

Collateral relatives are those not in a direct line of descent. Priority is given to the intestate's parents first, brothers and sisters and grandparents second, nephews and nieces third, and so on to any surviving next-of-kin.

The details of each province's legislation follow the same general principles. The closer the relationship of the relative to the deceased, the greater the portion of the estate that person receives. If a man dies leaving a widow, the majority of the estate will go to her and to any children the deceased may have. If there are no lineal relatives, then the estate will go to the collateral relatives. Finally, if there are no relatives, the estate passes to the Crown in the province where the intestate lived. In Alberta, the University of Alberta has been granted the right to such estates.

Survivorship Acts

Difficulties arise when spouses die at the same time; for example, in the same car accident or fire. If they left their property to each other by will, as is most common, it must be determined how this property will be divided. To simplify this problem, most provinces have *Survivorship Acts*. In Ontario, this legislation is the *Succession Law Reform Act*. These *Acts* provide that, where two or more persons die at the same time or in a situation in which there is some doubt, it is presumed that the deaths occurred in the order of seniority. Thus, the younger is assumed to have survived the elder.

Most wills contain a provision that specifies subsequent beneficiaries in the event the spouse should predecease or die within 30 days following the decedent. If both died at the same time, the problem would then be resolved by the will.

Similarly, the *Insurance Act* of the various provinces provides that where a person whose life is insured and the beneficiary under the policy die at the same time, the insurance money is payable as if the beneficiary had predeceased the person whose life is insured. Generally, this would mean that the policy would be paid into the insured's estate to be distributed by will or by law.

Reviewing Your Reading

1. **When is an administrator appointed? What are the administrator's responsibilities?**

2. **Distinguish between lineal and collateral relatives.**

3. **What happens to a deceased's property if that person dies without making a will and has no relatives?**

4. **Why is it important to determine the order of death of spouses who died together?**

CHAPTER REVIEW

Reviewing Key Terms

For each of the following statements, indicate the key term being defined:

a) a person making or preparing a will

b) the condition or state of dying without a valid will

c) an addition or change made to a will by its maker

d) a person appointed in a will to carry out the provisions of the will

e) a person entitled to benefit from a will

f) to destroy or void an existing will

g) a process to prove the originality and validity of a will

h) a will written entirely in the maker's own hand

i) the spouse and children of the deceased

j) a court order giving an executor the authority to carry out the provisions of a person's will

Exploring Legal Concepts

1. In what way is the preparation of a will similar to the preparation of a contract?

2. Why is it advisable to have a lawyer assist you in the preparation of a will?

3. Are holograph wills recognized in your province?

4. When a will is witnessed, why don't the witnesses have to know what is in the will?

5. Why should a witness to a will not be a beneficiary?

6. Why should the maker of a will review it on a regular basis?

7. You may legally alter a will by crossing out existing words, inserting new ones, initialling or signing beside the alterations, and having them witnessed. Why is it wise *not* to do this? What should you do instead?

8. When a person dies without having prepared a will, what problems or concerns might arise? Brainstorm a list of issues with a partner.

9. If a husband and wife die together in a motor vehicle accident, how is the distribution of their estate handled or determined?

Applying Legal Concepts

1. Elvira Tomas died, and in her will she bequeathed the residue of her estate in two equal parts to branches of a charitable organization situated in Winnipeg and Montreal, respectively. Prior to Tomas's death, the Winnipeg branch had ceased its operation. The court was asked to determine whether

there was an intestacy of the gift to the Winnipeg branch, and, if not, who was entitled to the gift.

- **Based on the facts presented, what decision do you think the court reached? Support your opinion with legal reasoning.**

2. Ms. VanderRee died of liver disease. In her will, she left her money to the Liver Foundation of Canada Inc. Before she died, VanderRee had had some discussions with the Canadian Liver Foundation about founding a branch of the organization in the area in which she lived and contributing to it. When she died no such organization existed.

- **Since the terms of the woman's will were ambiguous or unclear, was the Canadian Liver Foundation entitled to this bequest? Why or why not?**

3. The testatrix, Fomich, aged 90, had begun to deteriorate both physically and mentally after her husband died in 1988. Her lawyers were sufficiently concerned about her health that they were reluctant to prepare a will for her. A will was finally prepared in which Fomich left three parcels of land to Lichota, the sole beneficiary. However, Fomich only owned half of this property.

- **Based on the facts presented, what do you think the court determined about the validity of this will? Support your opinion with legal reasoning.**

4. Mrs. Kartsonas and her brother-in-law went to a lawyer's office with instructions to draw up her husband's will, since he was critically ill in hospital. The will was then taken to Mr. Kartsonas for signing. He was in a very weak condition and could only sign the will with his wife's assistance. He died the next day. Medical evidence indicated that the deceased was unable to recognize his physician, was not capable of making any kind of sounds, and did not respond to any verbal communication during the last few days of his life.

- **Would this will be probated? Why or why not?**

5. *Kury Estate v. Kury* [1991] Alberta Court of Queen's Bench 1 W.W.R. 89
   The widow testatrix, Anna Kury, executed a will in her lawyer's office directing that her estate be sold and the net proceeds divided in equal shares among Joseph Kury Jr. and his three married sisters.

   When Anna died, an envelope, containing the following handwritten document dated two months after her will had been executed, was found among her effects.

   The Alberta Court of Queen's Bench was asked for advice and directions on whether the one-quarter property interest was an outright bequest to Joseph Kury Jr. or willed to him in trust for his infant son, Karl Kury.

- **What is the legal term for Anna Kury's handwritten document?**

- **What was the intent of Kury's will regarding her son as beneficiary?**

- **Why did the trial judge state: "A careful examination of the third paragraph of the letter contained in the envelope suggests these are explanatory words of why she did something rather than an expression of an intention to change what she had done"?**

- **Did Anna Kury's handwritten document change the intent of her bequest from her son to her grandson, Karl? Explain.**

Vega. Oct. 28 ᵗʰ 83

Anna Kury
Box 68
Vega Alberta.

THIS is Exhibit "A" to the Affidavit of
PAUL (otherwise PAULA) SATTLER sworn
before me this 10 day of May A.D. 1988.
A COMMISSIONER FOR OATHS in and for the
Province of Alberta GERALD AMBROSE

Dear Loise, Faye, Paula,

I left my Will at Mrs Callum's office in
Barrhead.
Beside that I have a few wishes. If
possible I would like to rest beside
Andy.
2nd: I will my personal Stuff to
Loise Kury and Fay Fisher to dispose
of it, the way you like.
May old blue internation ½ ton Truck 1957
I sell to Bill Fisher, so did I one
Allis Chalmas Tracktor and one Cutewiter to Joe
Kury jun. The Rest you get, Joe is on
account of Karls. So you are equal with
your Sister's. I hope you can see that;

Thanks verry much to all, wat you
did for me, and the good times we
had together   love Anna   —

Extending Legal Concepts

1. Now that you have completed this chapter, review the opening article and Something to Think About. Have your answers or opinions changed? Why or why not?

2. With a partner, interview 10 adults of varying ages whom you know. Ask the following questions:

   a) Which is your age group: 20–30, 30–40, 40–50, over 50?

   b) Have you prepared a will?

   c) If so, how recently? If not, why not?

   d) If you have a will, when did you last look at it or review it?

   e) Do you know what happens to your estate if you die without a will?

   Summarize your findings in a report to the class. Then, as a class, determine what percentage of adults surveyed have prepared wills. Also, determine what age groups were the most likely to have wills.

3. Look at the Births and Deaths section of your local or area newspaper for a minimum two-week period of time and record the following information:
   - the number of births
   - the gender of the babies born
   - the number of deaths
   - the ages and gender of the deceased

   Then, prepare a brief report on your findings to obtain answers to the following issues:

   a) a comparison of the number of births and deaths

   b) a comparison of the gender of those born and deceased

   c) a comparison of the ages and gender of the deceased

   d) conclusions for analysis of this data

   Draw a graph to present your findings in an interesting and informative format; report to the class on your conclusions.

4. Using reference materials in your resource centre, including CD-ROM and the Internet, obtain current information on any of the following items: unusual bequests in wills, imprecise wills taken to court for resolution, trends in "living wills," and so on. Write a one- or two-page report on your findings, and, if possible, create a poster to display your information.

Researching an Issue

Living Wills

A living will is a written document that specifies a person's wishes regarding medical treatment desired if that person is unable to communicate those wishes to others. Debates concerning the issue of "living wills" and the right to die with dignity to preserve a quality of life are becoming increasingly common in this age of modern medical technology.

Statement

A living will expresses a person's wishes just as a will does. Therefore, it should be considered a legally binding document.

Point

I should have the legal right to prepare a "living will" informing my physician that I do not want to be kept alive by medical technology in the event of a serious illness or accident that renders me incapable of taking care of myself.

Counterpoint

A living will is potentially dangerous because it could be used to end a person's life prematurely.

- **With a partner, research this issue and reflect on your findings.**
- **Prepare points on this statement that could be used for a class debate.**
- **Discuss your findings with others in your class.**

CONTRACT LAW

Introduction

Among court personnel, the deputy sheriff is normally a low profile person, although the duties of the deputy sheriff are vital for the courts to function properly. The deputy sheriff's work is both demanding and varied.

In Focus: DEPUTY SHERIFF

Deputy sheriffs may be employed by provincial justice departments, or they may be self-employed. The preparatory work for a trial is carried out by several people, including the deputy sheriffs, who have a prominent role at this time. During a trial, deputy sheriffs provide security in the courtroom. And afterwards, they are responsible for seeing that the decisions of the court are fulfilled.

The entry-level salary for deputy sheriffs is approximately $37 000 per year, while experienced deputy sheriffs can earn as much as $50 000 per year.

Education and Other Qualifications

If it is your ambition to become a deputy sheriff, you must complete your high school education. Recommended subjects to study include English, law, modern languages, word processing, and physical education. In some jurisdictions, college level studies in the area of law may be a requirement. Work experience related to law enforcement would certainly be an asset.

Responsibilities

As a deputy sheriff, you will serve summonses, statements of claim, divorce petitions and other court documents. You will also be responsible for obtaining prospective jurors. Once a trial begins, you will have to ensure the safety of persons in the courtroom, and assist the judge as and when you are needed. You will also escort prisoners to and from the courts and correctional institutions and jury members and some witnesses to and from the courtroom. Following a trial, you may serve orders to pay maintenance, or carry out writs of execution by seizing and selling property, as well as distributing the proceeds according to the directions of the court.

Work Environment

Your work hours will be irregular and in some situations you may face risk of injury. For example, upon being served with an unwelcome court order, the recipient may want to direct his or her anger or frustration at the messenger, that is, you, the deputy sheriff. You will also perform many routine tasks. Here, you must follow exact procedures and meet strict standards of performance.

Do You Fit the Job?

As a deputy sheriff, you must be practical, sociable, enterprising, and trustworthy. You must also be able to cope with persons who are experiencing great stress, and know how to prevent potentially bad situations from becoming worse.

$\mathscr{P}$ROFILE: **William Siemens**

William Siemens is the sheriff at the Judicial Centre in Regina, Saskatchewan. He has been a sheriff with the Saskatchewan Department of Justice for the past 18 years. Prior to this, he served 26 years as an officer in the Royal Canadian Mounted Police (RCMP), which has prepared him well for his current profession.

Sheriff Siemens's interest in becoming a sheriff began after acquaintances persuaded him that he would be suited for the job. He was also attracted to the work of a sheriff because he had enjoyed his time with the RCMP. Thus, he was familiar with the law and the working operations of Saskatchewan's justice system. His first task as sheriff was to assist with empanelling a jury.

Presently, Sheriff Siemens spends much of his time supervising the work of deputy sheriffs: 10 who are assigned to the holding unit (provincial jail) for prisoners awaiting trial; 7 who provide security in the Regina Courthouse; and 4 who serve and execute court orders. An important part of his job is the hiring and training of the deputy sheriff staff. Sheriff Siemens also supervises the maintenance and functioning of all recording equipment in the courtrooms.

Sheriff Siemens says the most enjoyable part of his job is his association with people: co-workers, members of the bar, and the general public. His work is never boring—tasks change daily, and new laws and improved technology pose a constant challenge for him to adopt different ways to do his job.

For those students who are interested in a career as a deputy sheriff, Sheriff Siemens suggests that they be outgoing and interested in human nature. They should also have self-control and be able to remain calm in awkward situations. Furthermore, they must be able to maintain strict confidentiality with respect to people's private lives.

Questions and Activities

1. Arrange for a deputy sheriff to visit your class. Ask him or her the following questions: What are the most interesting and/or demanding aspects of your job? In a typical work week, what kinds of tasks do you perform most often? What hours do you keep? What situations, if any, have posed the greatest risk to your safety? How did you deal with these situations? What are the most important requirements for being a deputy sheriff?

2. Following the deputy sheriff's visit, assess your own potential to be a deputy sheriff. Ask a classmate, whom you trust, to appraise your suitability for the job. Compare his or her observations with your own.

Chapter 7

FORMING A CONTRACT

These are the key terms introduced in this chapter:

age of majority	legal object	repudiation
capacity	"meeting of the minds"	revocation
consent	necessaries	simple contract
consideration	non-necessaries	station-in-life
contract	offer and acceptance	under seal [contract]
counter-offer	offeree	valid contract
express contract	offeror	void contract
future consideration	past consideration	voidable contract
implied contract	present consideration	
lapse	ratification	

Chapter at a Glance

Learning Outcomes

At the end of this chapter, you will be able to

1. distinguish between an agreement and a contract;
2. identify the five essential elements of a contract;
3. distinguish between simple contracts and contracts under seal, and between express and implied contracts;
4. describe the legal requirements of a valid offer and acceptance or a "meeting of the minds";
5. distinguish between the lapse and revocation of an offer;
6. identify the types of consideration and the legality of each;
7. explain the position of minors, intoxicated, and developmentally challenged persons for contracts for necessaries and non-necessaries;
8. distinguish between the repudiation and ratification of contracts as they relate to the persons in point 7 above, and especially to minors;
9. distinguish among valid, void, and voidable contracts.

A multimillion-dollar lawsuit . . . may hinge on just what fax number is printed on a National Hockey League club's letterhead. Free-agent goaltender Mike Vernon is suing the Detroit Red Wings in hopes of forcing the NHL team to stick to a two-year, $5.45 million contract offer that he and his lawyers say he accepted on June 30.

The offer in question was made June 19 during the Stanley Cup final (won by the New Jersey Devils). Written on the Red Wings' letterhead, the offer . . . calls for a $250 000 signing bonus and a $2.6 million salary in both 1995–96 and 1996–97. The offer also includes a list of playoff performance bonuses.

Wings' Fax Number May Be Key to Suit

In a statement of claim, Vernon's agent, Larry Kelly of Ottawa, contends he faxed the acceptance of the deal to the Red Wings' fax number listed on the letterhead the morning of June 30, and has a confirmation slip saying the transmission was received . . . When they arrived the same afternoon to sign the contract with the team's senior vice-president, Jim Devellano, they were told that the team had never received the fax. Devellano said he was withdrawing the offer.

Four days later, Devellano submitted a second offer for less money, a two-year deal for $4 million. A deadline of August 8 was placed on this offer, which was accepted by letter and fax on August 4. Kelly said he was informed by Devellano that this offer, too, had been withdrawn.

In his acceptance of the second offer, Kelly informed Devellano that he and Vernon still planned to seek compensation for the larger, first offer . . . Wings' spokeswoman Kathy Best told The Canadian Press that the team would not comment.

From: David Shoalts "Wings' fax number may be key to suit." *The Globe and Mail*, August 10, 1995. Reprinted with permission of *The Globe and Mail*.

Something to Think About

- **When, or how quickly, should an offer be accepted?**
- **When should an acceptance by fax be legally binding?**
- **How would you resolve this contract dispute, and why?**

17.1 INTRODUCTION

The law of contracts is the basis of business. As consumers we enter into many contracts in our lives, often without realizing it. Every time you buy goods or a service, go to a movie or a rock concert, ride on a bus or subway, or are hired for a job a contract is made. Because contracts are so important, the courts have established specific rules to determine exactly when a legal contract has been formed. The law of contracts is mainly judge-made common law that has developed over time. In short, contract law has developed as courts have reached decisions in cases over the years.

Agreements that are legal contracts impose both rights and responsibilities on each party. However, not all agreements are recognized by the courts as legally binding and enforceable, even though the two parties have agreed to the duties imposed. If someone offers to take you to dinner and a movie and you accept, you could not take that person to court if he or she backs out of the invitation. Although a promise was made, the agreement is not enforceable in court; it is simply a social or moral obligation.

Thus, a **contract** can be defined as an agreement or a promise that the law will enforce. All contracts involve agreements, but not all agreements become contracts. Five essential elements must exist to ensure that a contract is valid: offer and acceptance or a "meeting of the minds," consideration, capacity, genuine consent, and legal purpose.

Suppose you decide to buy a pair of in-line skates in a local sports store. When you select the in-line skates and the sales clerk accepts your money, an **offer and acceptance** has taken place. Although there is no written agreement, a contract was made between you and the clerk.

Besides the offer and acceptance, some other essentials were present in your purchase. **Consideration**, something of value, was exchanged between you and the clerk. You gave money to the clerk, and the clerk gave you your in-line skates. As well, each of you had the legal **capacity** or ability to enter into the contract. You were old enough to make the purchase, and you were aware of what you were doing.

Finally, both you and the clerk entered into this contractual agreement in good faith; **consent** was freely given by both of you. No pressure or trickery was involved to force you to make your purchase, nor did you force the clerk to sell the blades to you. Finally, the contract had a **legal object** or purpose—there was nothing illegal about the transaction. An agreement in which all of these elements are present is a **valid contract** and can be enforced by the courts. A contract that lacks one or more of the essential elements is **void** and cannot be enforced by either party in the courts.

In this unit, we will look closely at these five essential elements, the procedures for completing and discharging a contract, and the rights of consumers and sellers.

17.2 Types of Contracts

All contracts fall into two main types: simple contracts and contracts under seal.

Simple Contracts

Most contracts used in day-to-day transactions are considered **simple contracts**. They can be verbal, written, or implied by conduct or performance. A verbal contract, although valid, may be difficult to enforce. Without witnesses, it may be difficult to prove the terms of the agreement or that a contract exists at all. Therefore, most contracts should be in writing. Simple contracts need not be formal, as long as the basic terms, the date, and the signatures of the parties involved are present.

All contracts are express or implied. An **express contract** is one in which all terms and conditions are defined clearly; these are both verbal and written contracts. In **implied contracts** nothing is stated or written precisely. These are agreements suggested by a person's actions.

Waving your hand to stop a taxi cab for a ride suggests that you will pay the cab driver when you arrive at your destination. Ordering a meal in a restaurant suggests that you will pay for that meal once it is served and you have eaten it. These are examples of implied contracts.

You enter into a contractual agreement when purchasing a product.

Contracts under Seal

Certain contracts must be in writing, signed, witnessed, and **under seal**. The use of seals dates back to the days when people pressed their family rings in sealing wax on a contract. Today the seal is usually a red dot or just the word "seal." The presence of the seal indicates to the courts that both parties gave serious thought to entering the contract, that both were aware of their rights and responsibilities in the contract, and that both fully intended to complete their legal obligations. In some provinces, contracts, such as deeds to property and mortgages, must be affixed with a seal to be legally binding.

Some special rules apply to contracts under seal and these will be dealt with in the appropriate sections in this unit.

Any later changes made to a written contract should also be made in writing and initialled by the parties. The courts can ignore verbal agreements or changes made after a contract is written if they contradict or alter the original document. In cases of dispute, the parties would have to satisfy the courts that any verbal agreement was a genuine agreement to change the terms of the original contract.

Reviewing Your Reading

1. **Explain what makes an agreement a legally enforceable contract.**

2. **List the five essential elements of a contract.**

3. **What forms can a simple contract take?**

4. **Distinguish between an express contract and an implied contract, using original examples.**

5. **What is the significance of a seal on a contract?**

17.3 THE ELEMENTS OF OFFERS

The first essential element for a legally binding contract is a valid offer and acceptance. One party, the **offeror**, must make a clear, precise offer and the other party, the **offeree**, must accept the offer. "I'll have one eight-slice pizza with green peppers, pepperoni, double cheese, and tomato, please" is a definite offer you make in a restaurant. When that specific pizza is brought to your

table, the offer has been accepted and payment is required. There is a **"meeting of the minds"** in which both parties clearly understand their rights and responsibilities in the agreement that is developing between them. The basic rules concerning valid offers and acceptances are examined further.

Serious Intent

An offer must be definite and seriously intended. For example, if Jamie says to Karen, "I'll sell you my blue 18-speed mountain bike for $375," and Karen replies, "That's a deal; I'll take it for $375," there is a definite offer and acceptance. This element must exist before a contract is legally binding.

If Jamie says, "I'll sell you my blue 18-speed mountain bike for $375," and Karen says, "It looks like a good bike and a good deal and I'd like to have it," there has been a valid offer only. Karen's remarks are not a valid acceptance, and no contract has been made.

Offers made as a joke or in anger are not serious offers. A frustrated driver of an automobile that won't start during a winter storm does not make a serious offer in shouting, "I'll sell this useless piece of junk for one dollar!" A neighbour who responds, "I'll take it for one dollar!" would not win a legal action if the owner refused to sell the car. The owner's offer was not seriously intended.

The offeror's words or conduct must indicate that he or she is willing to carry out the promise when the offer is accepted. The words must be a clear and legal offer, and not just an inquiry or vague expression of some possible intention. "I think I might sell my old roller blades for $60" is merely a vague statement of possible intent, not a definite offer.

Definite Terms

The terms of an offer must be stated clearly and precisely. For the sale of goods, the quantity, price, size, colour, terms of sale, and delivery date are all important and should be included. To avoid confusion, it is important that Jamie state precisely the features of his bike: blue, 18-speed mountain, and $375, especially if he has more than one bike.

Some terms can be implied or assumed. Many goods have a standard day-to-day price, and it is not necessary to quote it. Consumers do not generally ask for an exact price before entering every agreement they make; for example, in buying a daily newspaper or riding the bus or subway. Similarly, patients do not ask dentists their fees before seeking dental assistance. It is often best, however, to request an estimate before proceeding with the actual treatment since fees for the same work can often vary.

Invitations to Buy and Misleading Advertising

Are advertisements in newspapers and magazines clear and definite offers? When a retail store displays merchandise in customer catalogues or on store shelves, is the store making a definite offer to sell goods to customers? When you go into a supermarket, select goods from the shelves, and present the goods and your money at the cash register, has a contract been formed?

None of the above examples involves the formation of a contract. Courts have ruled that these examples are merely invitations to do business; that is, invitations by sellers for customers to make an offer to buy the items advertised. A retailer does not expect everyone who sees its advertisement to buy the particular item; it is simply providing information for consumers to consider making offers to buy. The basic rule is that customers make a definite offer to purchase by selecting the advertised item or by selecting goods from the store's stock. The store's cashier then has the right to accept or reject that offer. In most cases, the cashier accepts the customer's money and hands over the merchandise. Once both of these actions have occurred, a contract has been formed and completed.

Advertisers are able to describe their products and services with some degree of enthusiasm and creativity, as long as the advertisements do not mislead prospective consumers. The federal *Competition Act* is the main law regulating Canadian advertising. Any misleading statements made about a product or service could result in criminal prosecution.

Sometimes misleading claims are made in statements by sales clerks, signs in stores, and advertisements on radio, on television, and in print. For example a store might advertise a "great sale price" for a new computer system with

Gordon Pickett, the plaintiff, and Brenda Love, the defendant, entered into a romantic relationship in June 1981. Each had a key to the other's apartment. Their relationship continued until December 31, although the defendant's feelings toward the plaintiff had started to cool in October. Love told Pickett that she just wanted to be a friend. (She had become interested in one of his friends.) However, the plaintiff persisted in his advances. He gave the defendant presents, including a new watch and the offer of a plane ticket to New Orleans.

Later, he offered to renovate Love's bathroom. She indicated that she would like this, but that she could not afford to pay him for the work. In February after the renovations were completed, a conversation took place between the parties in which Pickett claimed that Love had agreed to pay him what she could each month until the bill was paid, although the plaintiff was not certain what that amount was. Love indicated to Pickett that their relationship was over and that he was to return the key.

After discovering that Love was seeing his friend, Pickett placed a claim on the defendant's property for $759. The court was not certain as to what had been agreed between the parties, but the judge believed that the plaintiff had done the work in a bid for the defendant's continued affection. Pickett's claim was dismissed.

Pickett v. Love
(1982)

Saskatchewan
Court of
Queen's Bench
20 Sask. R. 115

1. **Was there a legally binding contract between the parties? Why or why not?**
2. **Did the defendant have an obligation to pay the plaintiff for the renovations made to her property? Give reasons.**
3. **Why did the plaintiff's action not succeed?**
4. **If Love had not shunned Pickett's affections, do you think he would have presented her with a bill or taken her to court? Explain.**

a detailed warranty. If the small print on the warranty requires that the computer be sent to Japan for servicing at the buyer's expense, then the advertisement could be considered to be misleading. It would also be a misleading statement, prohibited by the federal *Competition Act*, if a store were to advertise a VCR as being on sale for $399, reduced from the original price of $600, if the store regularly sells the VCR for $500.

Also, most provinces have passed legislation like British Columbia's *Trade Practices Act*, Alberta's *Unfair Trade Practices Act*, Ontario's *Business Practices Act*, and the four Atlantic provinces' *Direct Sellers Act*. These *Acts* outline a number of unfair or deceptive consumer selling practices and provide consumers, who have

purchased goods or services as a result of these practices, with remedies to compensate them for any problems. For example, an auto mechanic claims that certain repairs need to be made on a car when they are not necessary, or a seller claims that a compact disc player is a deluxe or "top-of-the-line" model when the seller knows that this is not true.

Generally speaking, advertisements are not normally considered to be promises that are legally binding on the advertisers. However, some advertisements that are worded very precisely and have a seriously intended offer are considered to be offers by the courts. The following landmark judgment was the first to illustrate this point.

CASE

Carlill v. Carbolic Smoke Ball Co.

[1893]

English Court of Appeal
1 Q.B. 256

The defendant company made and sold a medical preparation called "The Carbolic Smoke Ball." The company advertised its product in various English newspapers stating that a "£100 reward will be paid by the Carbolic Smoke Ball Company to any person who contracts the increasing epidemic influenza, colds, or any disease caused by taking cold, after having used the ball three times daily for two weeks according to the printed instructions supplied with each ball. £1000 is deposited with the Alliance Bank, Regent Street, showing our sincerity in the matter."

Mrs. Carlill, the plaintiff, read the advertisement, bought one of the balls at a chemist's store, and used it as directed three times a day from November 20, 1891, to January 17, 1892. Then she caught influenza. When the company refused to pay Mrs. Carlill the £100, she sued the company and succeeded. The defendant company appealed the trial judgment, but the appeal was dismissed.

1. **Must an offer be made to one specific person, or is it valid and legal to make an offer to an indefinite number of people? Explain.**

2. **What argument do you think the defendant company used in its attempt to avoid paying the plaintiff?**

3. **Was it necessary for Mrs. Carlill to communicate to the company her intention to purchase the smoke ball and use it as directed? Why or why not?**

4. **Why did the court rule that the advertisement was a valid offer?**

Communication of an Offer

An offer must be communicated by the offeror to the offeree before acceptance occurs. This can be done in person or by mail, courier service, fax machines, and so on. It is important to know exactly when the offeree is aware of the offer because it is not valid until it is received. Identical offers that cross in the mail do not constitute a contract, as neither party has accepted the other party's offer.

Suppose Tom writes to Erin offering to sell her his painting *From the North Shore, Lake Superior* by Group of Seven artist Lawren Harris for $75 000. At the same time, Erin writes to Tom offering to buy that same painting for the same price. It would seem that a contract has been made as Erin's letter could be considered the "acceptance" of Tom's "offer." However, perhaps Tom changes his mind after sending his offer to Erin, or one of the letters is lost in the mail and never arrives at the intended address. In this example two separate offers exist. The fact that they contain the same features is immaterial. A contract requires a specific reply to a specific offer, and if one is not given, then the courts assume that no contract was formed.

An offer may be communicated to a specific person, or to people in general, as in an offer of a reward.

Suppose you find a wandering dog, look at its name and address tag, and return Molly to her owner. That evening, you notice the reward notice in the newspaper. You might wish to contact Molly's owner and ask for the reward. However, you are not legally entitled to the reward, because the offer of the reward was not communicated to

From the North Shore, Lake Superior (1926) by Lawren Harris
National Gallery of Canada, Ottawa

you (through the newspaper ad) until after you returned the dog. You returned the dog without intending to create a contract, since you did not know about the reward.

If you had read the notice first, and then found Molly and returned her to her owner, you would have been entitled to the reward. In this case, the offer would have been communicated to you prior to returning the dog. By returning Molly, you would have been accepting the offer, and thus forming and executing a contract.

Termination of an Offer

Until an offer is accepted, no legal rights or obligations arise. Offerors can protect themselves when making an offer by including a deadline for acceptance. If the offer is not accepted by that date, then it is automatically terminated or ended. An offer may be terminated by the lapse or revocation of the offer.

Lapse of an Offer. If no deadline is mentioned, an offer remains open for a reasonable length of time. How long is this? There is no single answer to this question, since it depends on the nature of

"Are you the guy who advertised he'd found a wallet?"

the contract. An offer for the sale of stocks or bonds is open for a much shorter time than an offer for the sale of a house, because the price of stocks and bonds changes daily, even hourly. When no time limit has been specified, an offer **lapses**, or ends, when the offeree fails to accept the offer within a reasonable amount of time.

A verbal offer ends when the parties leave one another, unless the offeree is given some extra time to reach a decision about the acceptance. Assume that one day at school Kevin offers to sell Kyle his used skis at a specific price. Once the two friends leave one another, the offer ends if Kyle has not accepted it. But if Kevin has given Kyle seven days to make up his mind, the offer does not end until the seven days have passed, or Kyle has clearly accepted or rejected the offer.

An offer also lapses if one of the parties dies, becomes bankrupt, or is declared incapable before the contract has been accepted by the other party. However, if any of these events occurs after acceptance, the contract is valid and must be carried out provided that the other elements of a contract exist.

Revocation of an Offer. An offeror may also terminate an offer by revoking or withdrawing it before the offeree accepts, even if the offeror has promised to hold the offer open for a certain period of time. If, on the fourth day of the seven that Kyle was given to make up his mind, Kevin tells Kyle that he doesn't want to sell his skis, Kevin has revoked the offer. This withdrawal of the offer before acceptance of it is **revocation**. It does not matter that the seven days have not yet gone by. Kevin has the legal right to change his mind any time before Kyle has accepted the offer. However, Kevin must clearly communicate his revocation to Kyle before Kyle accepts the offer.

An exception to the right of revocation occurs when the parties have a specific, separate contract stating that the offer cannot be withdrawn by the offeror for a specific period of time. If Kyle gives Kevin a deposit on the purchase of the skis to show his sincerity in considering the offer, then Kevin cannot withdraw his offer until the end of the seven days. The purchaser of a house can make a deposit to keep the house available to him or her alone. This is called placing an option. If the purchase is made, the deposit is applied to the purchase price of the house. If the offeree decides not to purchase, the deposit may or may not be returned, depending on the original terms of the agreement.

Reviewing Your Reading

1. In a contract, who is the offeror and who is the offeree?
2. Explain the term "meeting of the minds" as it relates to the laws of offer and acceptance.
3. List four things wrong with the following offer: "I offer to sell you one of my watercolour paintings at a fair price on generous terms with a quick delivery."
4. What laws exist to protect consumers against false or misleading advertising?
5. Why must an offer be communicated before the offer may be accepted?
6. If Louise returns a lost watch to its owner, is she legally entitled to the reward being offered if Louise did not see the reward notice until after she returned the watch? Explain.
7. For what period of time does an offer remain open?
8. Distinguish between the lapse and revocation of an offer.

17.4 $\mathcal{T}$HE ELEMENTS OF ACCEPTANCE

Acceptances, whether in words or by conduct, must be made according to certain rules that have been established by the courts over the years. Many offers are accepted by performance. You leave your television set to be repaired, the service person agrees to fix it, and you agree to pay the charges. Most offers made over a store counter are accepted without any words spoken between the parties. To be valid, the acceptance of an offer must be unconditional, within the specified time limit (if one is given), and in the manner specified by the offeror.

If the offeree does not accept the offer in the manner offered, the "acceptance" is really a **counter-offer**, which the offeror can then accept or reject. A counter-offer occurs when the offeree is in general agreement with the offer but wants to change one or more terms of the original offer and proposes a contract on different terms. This counter-offer brings the original offer to an end. The counter-offer then becomes the new offer. (If the counter-offer is rejected, the offeree cannot try to retroactively accept the original offer.) The parties may bargain until one of them finally accepts the last proposal from the other party without any further changes. For example, Katya offers to sell her car to Dino for $4000. Dino is interested in the offer and replies, "I'd really like to have the car; I'll give you $3500 for it." Although Dino's statement may sound like a valid acceptance, it is not. Rather, it is a counter-offer. Dino's remarks bring the original offer to an end. Now Katya has the choice of accepting or rejecting the counter-offer. Of course, Katya can also make a counter-offer of her own, which may even be the amount of the original offer.

Communication of Acceptance

The manner of acceptance of an offer determines whether or not the contract is binding. No contract exists until acceptance is communicated to the offeror. It is assumed that acceptance will be communicated using the same method used for making the offer, or by a method specified in the offer. For example, it is more common to accept a written offer in writing than to accept it verbally. Contracts sent and accepted by mail are a common part of everyday business; hence, specific rules have been established to determine a valid acceptance.

An offer made and accepted by mail becomes binding when the properly stamped and addressed letter of acceptance is dropped into the mailbox. Proof of mailing date is indicated by the postmark. For further protection, the offer can be sent by special delivery or a courier service. When offerors mail an offer, they usually expect the acceptance to be mailed.

If the letter of acceptance is lost or delayed in the mail, the parties are still bound to the contract if the offeree has proof that the letter was mailed in time. Lost or delayed acceptance letters may present problems. The offeror could, for example, make an offer to another person, not realizing that the offeree's acceptance has been delayed in the mail. By not specifying that acceptance is not complete until the letter is received, the offeror assumes the risk of loss by Canada Post. In reality, sometimes this lack of proof may make it impossible for the offeree to establish the existence of a contract. How can you prove in court that you definitely mailed a valid and properly addressed acceptance?

If an offer is made by mail with no specific method of acceptance indicated, a reasonable method of acceptance must be used. "Reasonable" has been interpreted to mean a method as fast as, or faster than, the offeror's method. Thus, a reasonable means of accepting a mailed offer is by mail, telephone, or fax machine. As evidence "in writing" for contract disputes, signed faxed documents appear to be as legal as originally signed documents. Courts seem to recognize the importance of fax machines as a communication tool in today's business world.

The ever-increasing use of electronic communication from computer to computer through e-mail may be the next area of contract law that governments and the courts have to address. Where an offer requires an acceptance to be in writing, does an e-mail acceptance meet this requirement? Presently, there are no Canadian precedents or case law to answer this question.

When acceptance is made in the same manner as the offer, for example, by mail, the contract is formed as soon as the acceptance is mailed unless otherwise specified. When acceptance is made in some other reasonable manner, the contract is not formed until the acceptance reaches the offeror.

For example, D'Amico sends Bannerman an offer in the mail, requesting acceptance by mail. Bannerman accepts by fax machine because it is faster. However, this is not a valid acceptance, since Bannerman did not follow instructions. If D'Amico had not indicated how to communicate acceptance, then the contract would have been formed when D'Amico received the fax message.

Finally, if D'Amico dies before Bannerman communicates acceptance, the offer lapses. D'Amico is no longer able to fulfill any contractual agreement. If the acceptance arrives at any time before D'Amico's death, however, the contract is binding on D'Amico's estate and must be honoured.

CASE

Rolling v. Willann Investments. Ltd.
(1989)

Ontario Court of Appeal
70 O.R. (2d) 578

As a result of a real estate transaction between William and Vera Rolling and Willann Investments Ltd., the Rollings gave Willann "the first right to meet any offer to purchase that the Rollings might receive" for certain property owned by them in Collingwood, Ontario. The agreement further stated that "Willann shall have 72 hours from the date such offer is delivered to it by Rolling within which to exercise this option by submitting . . . an offer on identical terms to those contained in the first-mentioned offer. Failing which this option shall terminate and Rollings may accept the first offer."

Some years later, Rollings received an offer from a third party, Sam Spodek, to purchase the property and, as required, the Rollings sent a copy and a covering letter to Willann by fax machine at 2:12 p.m. on May 19. Over 100 hours later, on May 23, Willann submitted an identical offer.

The Rollings brought these two offers to court to determine which of Spodek or Willann had a binding agreement of purchase and sale; the court ruled in favour of Willann. Spodek appealed that ruling to the Ontario Court of Appeal where the appeal was allowed, and judgment was issued in Spodek's favour.

1. **Was it necessary for Rolling to deliver the signed original offer to Willann? Why or why not?**
2. **From the facts provided, when would Willann probably have received delivery of the offer?**
3. **Within what time, or by when, should Willann have accepted the offer?**
4. **Why did the Ontario Court of Appeal rule in favour of the third party, Spodek?**

Silence and Inaction

Remaining silent will not result in a legal acceptance. Stating "If you don't notify me within five days, I'll assume you've accepted my offer" has no legal value. Acceptance of an offer must be actively communicated to the offeror.

One exception to this rule exists with the operation of book and record clubs. Members will be automatically sent the current month's book or record offering unless they return a form before a specified due date. Here, silence, or not returning the form, is considered a valid acceptance because of the pre-existing agreement between the clubs and their members.

Consumer Protection

A problem with legal acceptance arose from the past practice of credit card companies issuing unsolicited cards to consumers. Use of these cards amounted to acceptance by performance. There was no protection for the intended recipient if the cards were stolen and used by a third party. The original addressee was held liable. Consumers also received unsolicited goods by mail. Most provinces have now passed consumer protection legislation governing such items. In Ontario, unsolicited goods can be treated as gifts. In British Columbia, people can use unsolicited credit cards and not be held liable for the expenditures. Consequently, most companies now send credit cards only on request.

Where such provincial laws protecting the consumer do not exist, people who receive unsolicited goods are liable for them only if the goods are used. If consumers do not want to accept the goods, they can mark "Refuse to accept; return to sender" across the package and return to the sender without any liability. Consumers may also keep the goods and simply not use them. There is no obligation to return them.

This same protection applies to members of book and record clubs who have fulfilled their minimum contractual requirements and sent a cancellation. Any goods subsequently received need not be accepted or returned.

Reviewing Your Reading

1. **What is a counter-offer, and what effect does it have on the original offer?**

2. a) **When is acceptance by mail legally binding?**

   b) **What happens if the acceptance letter is mailed but never received by the offeror?**

3. **If the offer does not specify the method of acceptance, what options are available to the offeree?**

4. **What is the current legal status of offers and acceptances sent by fax machines?**

5. **Explain the meaning of this statement: "Remaining silent is not a valid acceptance."**

17.5 *T*HE ELEMENTS OF CONSIDERATION

After a valid offer and acceptance have occurred, the next essential element for a contract is consideration, something of value, exchanged between the parties; for example, the payment of money or the performance of a specific service. In most contracts, consideration for one party is the purchase of a particular item or a service; for the other party it is the money paid.

Present and Future Consideration

The two most common legal forms of consideration are present consideration and future consideration. **Present consideration** occurs at the time the contract is formed and usually consists of the exchange of money for goods and/or services. **Future consideration**, as the term suggests, occurs when one or both of the parties promises to do something in the future. Buying goods on credit is an example, because the seller will not receive payment or consideration until a later date. Another example of future consideration occurs in sports; a team may trade a player this season for future consideration, that is, for a player to be selected from the other team next year. Both present and future consideration are valid forms of consideration.

Past Consideration

A promise by one person to pay another for gratuitous or free services that have already been performed is **past consideration** and is not legally binding. Suppose Penny is painting her house, and Kate comes by to help her as a friend. Appreciating her assistance, Penny tells Kate after they have finished that she will give her $50 the following week, when she gets paid. If Penny does not do this, Kate cannot take legal action since she had not been promised any money to help paint the house before she offered her assistance. This is past consideration and not legally binding because the job was completed before the promise was made.

However, many promises of past consideration are carried out. This is generally because the person paying appreciates or is grateful for the services performed. But there is no legal obligation to make such a payment.

Contracts under Seal

Courts assume that if the parties have taken the time and trouble to prepare a contract under seal, they are both gaining benefit in some manner. There is serious intent on the part of the two parties to be bound by their contract; they really mean business. Thus, the courts assume that consideration exists in these types of contracts, without having to prove its existence. The seal satisfies the requirement for consideration.

Adequacy of Consideration

The courts are not concerned with the amount of consideration exchanged, as long as something is given by one party to the other. The courts will not bargain for anyone. If someone freely sells something for much less than it is worth, the contract is still binding since both parties received something of value and benefit. Parties are free to make good or bad bargains, unless evidence suggests that one of the parties was pressured or the consideration is grossly inadequate.

Love, affection, respect, and honour are not regarded by the courts as valuable legal consideration. An aunt's promise of a car to her niece on reaching the age of majority is not an enforceable contract. This is a gift, and promises for gifts are generally not enforceable.

Charitable Donations

Are charitable donations and pledges legally enforceable? Such promises are often regarded as gifts, so they are not normally enforceable because there is no consideration received by the persons making the donations or pledges. They are receiving nothing in return for the donations or pledges.

However, if the promise to donate is made in a contract under seal, it is assumed that some form of consideration is present and that there is serious intent behind the pledge. For these reasons, courts will enforce such contracts. They will also usually enforce a donation or pledge to a charity if the community will benefit from the money.

Finally, courts will look on a promise to donate as a binding contract if the recipient has spent some money in anticipation of the donation. An example occurs when the construction of a building or a major landscaping job has been started on the basis of pledges made. A person making a pledge or donation is usually aware of what the money will be used for, and this awareness is legally seen as being adequate consideration for that person.

Partial Payments

A problem arises when creditors, unable to collect money from debtors, ask those persons to pay part of the debt and to forget the rest. Many creditors are willing to accept part payment rather than risk getting nothing. Can the creditors later demand the balance of the payment? The law differs across Canada on this point.

Assume that Lafratta owes Marello $800 and Marello says, "Give me $750 now and forget the remaining $50." In the western provinces, the Northwest Territories, the Yukon Territory, and Ontario, Marello would not have any legal claim to the $50 once she receives and accepts the lesser amount of $750 in full payment of the debt.

CASE

The defendants, Eddie Cogan and Cogan Corporation, had been purchasing and renewing season tickets at field level behind first base for the Toronto Blue Jays baseball team's home games since 1976. When Cogan first did this, he informed the plaintiff companies, Fobasco Ltd. and Sher-Hay Holdings Ltd., who were eager to have the use of some of the tickets for their own enjoyment and for promotional use with their clients. The owners of these two companies were long-time business associates and old friends of Cogan.

For the first 10 years, the defendant purchased eight tickets and allowed the plaintiffs to use six of them; the plaintiffs always reimbursed Cogan. By 1986, however, Cogan's relationship with the plaintiffs had changed with minimal social contact and business dealings. The defendant then decided to keep the tickets for his own use and informed the plaintiffs of this fact.

The plaintiffs brought an action to the Ontario High Court of Justice (now the Ontario Court, General Division) for a declaration that they were the legitimate owners of six of the tickets, but their action was dismissed.

Fobasco Ltd. v. Cogan
(1990)

Ontario High Court of Justice
72 O.R. (2d) 254

1. **What arguments would the plaintiffs present for the existence of a valid contract between them and the defendant?**

2. **What arguments would the defendant present for the non-existence of a valid contract?**

3. **How could the plaintiffs demonstrate to the court that this agreement was intended to be a binding contract?**

4. **Why did the court dismiss the plaintiffs' action for lack of consideration?**

This is believed to be valid consideration. From Quebec to Newfoundland, however, Marello would have the right to claim the $50 balance, because she did not receive any consideration for that amount of money. She would not have a claim if she had received the $750 two weeks before it was due, since courts in the eastern provinces would regard early payment as valuable consideration.

Marello and Lafratta might also come to a mutual agreement to change the original terms, and the new terms would be binding, or they could compromise. Lafratta may believe that he owes a lesser amount than is being demanded by Marello. To avoid the time and cost of a court case, a binding agreement based on their compromise could be made to settle for some amount between $750 and $800.

Reviewing Your Reading

1. **What is consideration in a contract?**

2. **With examples, distinguish between past, present, and future consideration, and discuss the legality of each type.**

3. **Does a contract under seal require consideration? Why or why not?**

4. **Why are the courts not concerned that both parties obtain equal value for consideration?**

5. **When are charitable donations legally enforceable?**

17.6 THE ELEMENTS OF CAPACITY

With a valid offer, and acceptance and consideration exchanged between the parties, the next essential element is that of capacity. Although the law allows sane and sober adults to make their own contracts, laws have been established to protect certain groups of people from being exploited when making contracts because of their age, inexperience, or mental ability. Contracts entered into by minors, the developmentally challenged, or the intoxicated may not be binding in court under certain circumstances. These groups are seen as lacking the ability or the capacity to make wise decisions.

Minors and Contracts

A minor is any person under the **age of majority**, the age at which a person has full rights and responsibilities in legal matters, including the signing of contracts. At one time, persons under 21 years of age were considered minors in most provinces. Each province determines its own "age of majority" and all provinces have reduced this age to 18 or 19 years. However, each provincial legislature can also restrict the rights and responsibilities that attach to that age. In Ontario and Saskatchewan, for example, the "age of majority" is 18, but in either province, you must be 19 to legally purchase and consume alcohol. In Nova Scotia you must be 19 to purchase alcohol and cigarettes.

When determining laws for minors and their contracts, courts over the years have developed a set of rules in determining if a minor's contract is valid and enforceable. They are outlined below.

Valid Contracts

There are many occasions when minors buy goods and pay for them, thus forming valid binding contracts. Some minors live on their own and must support themselves with social assistance from municipal governments. They may need to rent accommodation and to make purchases on credit. The law recognizes these legitimate needs by making certain contracts binding on minors.

Minors are obligated to fulfill contracts for **necessaries**, those items that everyone needs on a daily basis: food, clothing, shelter, education, and medical services. If minors could break these contracts at will, businesses would not enter into any contracts with minors. This might be harmful or damaging to minors in times of need, especially those minors between the ages of 16 and 18.

A necessary must also be needed for or suitable to a minor's social position or **station-in-life**. This is determined by looking at the minor's personal, family, and financial background. A necessity for one person may not be a necessity for another. Consider a tuxedo and a formal dress for the mayor's son and daughter to attend important civic functions and formal banquets with their parents versus the clothes required by other teens for going places with their parents. However, even on contracts for necessaries, a minor might not be obligated to pay the contract price if the courts were to find that the terms of the contract were not in the minor's best interests. Only a reasonable price must be paid. For example, if Becky, a minor, purchases a winter coat that she needs for $400 but finds an identical coat for $250 at another reputable clothing store, she may be obligated to pay only $250, the reasonable price, to the store from which she purchased the coat.

Apprenticeship and employment contracts are also considered necessary for minors, if they are beneficial and do not take advantage of the minors. If the court feels that the minor was so overwhelmed by the bargaining power of the other party, the contract will be judged unenforceable. This inequality of bargaining power must be examined carefully by the courts.

Void Contracts

Contracts that are not in a minor's best interests are void or said to have never existed. If a person has taken unfair advantage of a minor to have the youth enter into a contract, courts will rule that this prejudicial contract has no legal effect. The John Tonelli case is one of the rare examples that illustrates this concept.

Voidable Contracts

Contract law has always given special protection to minors, but some protection is also needed for persons dealing with minors. The basic desire to protect minors has resulted in the general rule

CASE

John Tonelli was a young hockey player of star potential. In 1973, at the age of 16 he and his father signed a two-year contract with the plaintiff hockey club. A year later, the plaintiff required Tonelli to sign a new player's contract for a three-year term with a fourth year at the club's option. If he did not sign the contract, he would not be allowed to play in the next game. As a result, he eventually signed the contract.

The contract provided that if Tonelli obtained a contract with a professional hockey club, he would pay the Marlboros 20 percent of his gross earnings for each year of his first three years with that club. In return, Tonelli would receive a minimal salary, coaching, and the opportunity to play hockey in the Junior "A" league. The contract could be terminated at the discretion of the Marlboro hockey club.

When Tonelli turned 18 in March of 1975, he repudiated, or cancelled, this contract and signed a contract to play with a World Hockey Association team, the Houston Aeros. His new contract would pay him about $320 000 over three years. The Marlboros brought action against Tonelli and his agent, Gus Badali, for damages for breach of contract. In the original trial in the Supreme Court of Ontario, the Marlboros lost their action. This decision was appealed by the plaintiff team to the Ontario Court of Appeal. In a 2–1 decision, the Ontario Court of Appeal upheld the trial judgment.

Toronto Marlboro Major Junior "A" Hockey Club et al. v. Tonelli et al. (1979)

Ontario Court of Appeal
23 O.R. (2d) 193

1. **Under what circumstances will a minor's contracts be enforced by a court? Are these the circumstances in this case? Explain.**

2. **In contract law, a minor's contract for services is enforceable only if the contract is for the minor's benefit. The Toronto Marlboros contended that their contract with Tonelli met this requirement. What did they consider to be the benefits that Tonelli received? Why would Tonelli consider that the contract was not for his benefit?**

3. **What legal principle do you believe was used by the trial judge and two of the appeal court judges to rule in Tonelli's favour? What argument may have been raised by the dissenting appeal court judge that would cause him to rule against Tonelli and in favour of the Marlboros?**

4. **Do you agree with the majority or the minority judgment? Explain.**

that a minor's contracts, in many cases, are voidable at the minor's option. A **voidable contract** is one in which one of the parties has the right to make the contract either binding or not binding. In the case of a minor, for example, a voidable contract may be enforced by the minor, but it cannot be enforced against the minor if he or she does not want it to be enforced.

It is in the area of uncompleted contracts for **non-necessaries** that voidable contracts for minors sometimes arise. That is, the minor can decide whether he or she wants to be bound by

the promises made in the contract. Most minors do complete such contracts, since they entered into them in good faith.

Let us say that Fiona purchased a CD player from a local retailer, made a down payment on her purchase, and then took it home. If she decided after the weekend that she really did not want the CD player, Fiona is not bound to complete the payments on her contract. However, she does not have the right to keep her purchase. She must return it to the retailer and cancel the contract. The retailer has the right to keep Fiona's down payment, since she obtained some benefit from the use of the CD player.

If there is any damage to the CD player that Fiona did not deliberately cause, the cost is not recoverable by the retailer; also, the cost of "wear and tear" is not recoverable. However, any deliberate damage to the CD player caused by Fiona may be recovered.

On the other hand, if the retailer had learned over the weekend that Fiona was a minor, he could not cancel the contract without Fiona's permission. An adult who enters a contract with a minor is bound by it if the minor wishes to fulfill its terms.

Repudiation and Ratification

Partly completed contracts for non-necessaries have a special status when minors reach the age of majority, since they may become liable for obligations that could not be enforced while they were minors. For legal purposes, these contracts are examined from two points of view—repudiation and ratification.

Some contracts continue to be binding on the minor unless **repudiation** occurs, that is, the minor rejects or disowns them. For all contracts involving the acquisition of an interest in property of a permanent nature (partnership agreements, the purchase of shares in a company, rights to land), repudiation must take place within a reasonable time after the minor reaches majority. If this is not done, the minor is bound by the terms of the contract.

For all contracts other than those involving property of a permanent nature, a minor is not bound unless **ratification** takes place, that is the minor confirms and makes valid those contracts after reaching the age of majority. This category contains the more common types of contracts made by minors. In some provinces, ratification must be done in writing. If Miyako, a minor, bought a home computer on credit and subsequently did not ratify the contract at majority, she could return the computer and terminate the contract.

It is not necessarily to a minor's benefit to terminate all voidable contracts. Payments made on the contract are refunded only if the minor has received no benefit from the contract. In the earlier example, Fiona did not get a refund of her down payment on the CD player because she received a benefit from the use of it.

CASE

City of Edmonton Library Board v. Morrill
(1989)

Alberta Court of Queen's Bench 58 D.L.R. (4th) 354

The defendant, Elizabeth Morrill, agreed to "be responsible for any fines, loss, or damage occasioned by the use of the Library Card" issued to her 14-year-old son, Clinton, by the Edmonton Public Library Board. Because of Clinton's age, the library would not issue a card to him unless an adult accepted responsibility for the card's use.

The card was lost or stolen and used by an unidentified and unauthorized person to borrow 30 items worth $240.95 that were not returned by the due date of November 6. On November 18, the defendant's son informed the library about his missing card.

The plaintiff library board brought a successful action against the boy's mother for the replacement value of the books.

1. **Briefly outline what you believe to be the plaintiff's argument for this action.**
2. **Briefly outline what you believe to be the defendant's arguments as to why she should not be held liable.**
3. **The defendant also argued that the library card is similar to a credit card, and liability should be limited to $50. Do you agree? Explain.**
4. **Why did the plaintiff library board win its action?**

A minor is bound in a situation where both parties have fulfilled their obligations and completed a contract. If Fiona had finished paying for her CD player, her contract with the retailer would have been fully completed. The goods would have been received and consideration made. It does not matter in this event whether the goods are necessaries or non-necessaries.

Misrepresentation of Age

The fact that a minor lies about his or her age does not change either the minor's or retailer's legal rights or the minor's protection under the law. As a result, retailers deal with minors at their own risk. However, a retailer who can prove that the minor intentionally lied about his or her age can lay criminal charges for fraud.

Because of the great protection given to minors, most retailers will only sell goods to minors for cash. Retailers know that a contract is voidable at the minor's option. To protect themselves further, many retailers require that an adult co-sign any contract involving a minor.

Parental Liability

Parents are generally not liable for any part of a minor's contract if it was solely between the minor and the retailer. Parents are liable only if they co-sign the contract. Then they are responsible for full payment if their child does not pay.

In some situations parents are held liable for a child's contracts. If a minor uses his or her parents' credit card and the parents pay the account, it is implied or assumed that the parents will continue to do so in the future. If the parents wish to cancel this arrangement, they must notify the retailer involved. The parents are also responsible if they expressly tell a retailer that their child may purchase items for which they will pay.

Developmentally Challenged and Impaired Persons

The law treats developmentally challenged and impaired persons in much the same way as minors in their capacity to make contracts. A person who has been certified developmentally challenged and has been institutionalized is not bound by contracts relating to property, since his or her estate is administered by a trustee. Impairment may be due to illness, alcohol, drugs, or hypnosis. Like a minor, a developmentally challenged or impaired person is liable to pay only a reasonable price for necessaries.

A contract for non-necessaries is voidable if the developmentally challenged or impaired person can prove that at the time of making the contract he or she was incapable of understanding what was happening, and that the other party knew of this condition. Even then, in the case of an impaired person, the contract must be voided within a reasonable time after recovery and the goods must be returned. If an impaired person, after recovery, continues to benefit from a contract, that person is bound by the contract.

Reviewing Your Reading

1. What three groups of people are protected by the law from being taken advantage of when they enter into contracts?

2. What types of contracts are binding on minors?

3. Distinguish between void and voidable contracts made by minors.

4. When can minors (a) ratify, and (b) repudiate contracts that they have made?

5. If you were a retailer, what would you do to reduce the risk when entering into contracts with minors? Why would you do so?

6. When are parents liable for their children's contracts?

7. What two points must be established before impaired and developmentally challenged persons can avoid liability for signed contracts?

Should commercial surrogacy contracts be allowed?

*I*n the late 1970s, the term surrogate mother was first used in connection with in vitro fertilization (IVF). In vitro fertilization is a reproductive technique for the conception of a human embryo outside the mother's body. The ovum, or egg, is removed from the mother (or one is provided) and placed in a Petri dish. The father's sperm is added to the ovum. If fertilization occurs, the fertilized ovum is then transferred to the mother's body. However, if the mother is incapable of carrying a developing fetus, the fertilized ovum can be implanted in a surrogate mother who has agreed to bear the child for the couple. Agreements between the couple and the surrogate mother usually involve the signing of a contract and payment of a fee.

The subject of commercial surrogate parenting has raised ethical as well as legal questions. Should the practice be illegal? Should it be strictly regulated? For example, should fees be limited or prohibited altogether?

In April 1989, the federal government announced that a royal commission would be set up to examine questions related to scientific developments in reproductive technology and their effects on society. One of the issues targeted for consideration was commercial contracts for surrogate motherhood.

On One Side

Those who oppose commercial surrogacy tend to regard it as formalized baby selling. They point out that some women could become professional surrogates, who repeatedly rent out their wombs or provide eggs for fertilization. Most of these women are from lower-income groups and are probably being exploited.

Suzanne Scorsone, the Director of Communication and Catholic Family Life for the Archdiocese of Toronto, refers to the practice of surrogacy as high-tech concubinage. According to Scorsone, based on about 40 weeks of work at a standard fee of $10 000, a surrogate mother is paid $1.49 an hour. The doctors and lawyers, on the other hand, earn about $1000 an hour.

On the Other Side

Those who support commercial surrogacy applaud the practice. In response to charges that surrogacy is formalized baby selling, they point out that the husband of the couple receiving the child is always the child's biological father and the mother could be the biological mother. They also stress the benefits of this technology that provides a childless couple the gift of a child.

Supporters also maintain that a formal contract between the surrogate mother and the couple is better than putting stress on a friend or a relative to provide the service. Not only does having a contract protect the couple from lawsuits over child custody after the child is born, it also eliminates the potential for conflict and interference that might arise otherwise.

The Bottom Line

In November 1993, the Royal Commission on the New Reproductive Technologies filed a massive report that contained many strongly worded recommendations. Nineteen months later, in

Mary Beth Whitehead, a surrogate mother, later fought for custody in the famous Baby M. trial in the United States.

July 1995, the federal government responded to these recommendations. In the matter of commercial contracts for surrogate motherhood, the Health Minister called for a voluntary moratorium on the practice. The Royal Commission had recommended outlawing the practice. Should people be allowed to enter contractual agreements for the reproduction of babies? You be the judge!

1. Which side of the issue do you support, and why?

2. What is your opinion of the recommendation of the Royal Commission?

3. Use your resource centre to find out details about the Baby M. case and answer the following questions:
   a) Who provided the sperm for Baby M.? Who provided the egg?
   b) What argument(s) did Mary Beth Whitehead use in her custody suit?
   c) What argument(s) did William and Elizabeth Stern use?
   d) What was the decision in the Baby M. case? Do you agree with the decision? Why or why not?
   e) Could the Baby M. case have happened in Canada? Explain.

CHAPTER REVIEW

Reviewing Key Terms

For each of the following statements, indicate the key term being defined:

a) something of value exchanged between the parties to a contract

b) a person to whom an offer is made

c) goods and services required to maintain a person's basic station-in-life

d) the act of approving or confirming a contract

e) a contract invalid until validated

f) the legal ability to enter or make a contract on one's own behalf

g) cancelling, destroying, or voiding a contract

h) to no longer be in effect; termination of an offer or a right

i) a contract that is suggested or understood without being specifically stated

j) a statement by the offeree rejecting the offer and creating a new offer

Exploring Legal Concepts

1. Why does an auctioneer have the right to withdraw items from an auction sale if the bidding does not go as high as expected?

2. What principles of law did the *Carlill v. Carbolic Smoke Ball Co.* case illustrate?

3. Is an advertisement with a reward offer for a lost necklace a valid offer? How does it differ from an advertisement for the sale of goods?

4. Explain the meaning of the following statement: "The use of a seal on a contract answers for the failure to satisfy all essentials of a binding contract."

5. A supplier's invoice for goods contains the following common business terms: "terms—net 30 days; 3 percent discount if paid within 15 days." If the buyer pays the invoice price less the discount within 15 days, can the supplier later sue successfully for the sum deducted for the discount? Why or why not?

6. Explain the meaning of the following statement made by an English judge, Sir George Jessel (1824–1883): "A creditor might accept anything in satisfaction of a debt . . . He might take a horse, or a canary if he chooses, and that was accord and satisfaction."

7. What is the law in your province concerning acceptance of unsolicited goods received in the mail?

8. What is the position of a minor who wishes to cancel a contract for non-necessaries that have been used but are still in good condition?

9. Explain the meaning of the following statement: "The protection afforded to a minor should be used as a shield, not a sword."

10. Under what circumstances might parents be held liable for their child's debts for (a) necessaries and (b) non-necessaries?

11. What are the laws in your province concerning early payment of a debt as it relates to the laws of consideration?

Applying Legal Concepts

1. Cranston offers to sell a painting to Parker for $1000. Parker is prepared to pay the price and mails a properly stamped and addressed envelope with his acceptance by return mail. Cranston does not receive Parker's letter of acceptance.

   - **Is there a binding contract between them? If not, why not? If so, what must be proved and by whom?**

2. While sitting in the lobby of the Playa Tambor resort hotel, Andrea hears cries for help coming from the direction of the swimming pool. Andrea jumps in the pool and rescues an elderly man. The grateful gentleman asks Andrea to return later that afternoon for a $100 reward for saving his life. However, instead of paying her the reward, he simply thanks her once again.

   - **What can Andrea do about this, and why?**

3. While Marg McKim is attempting to make some minor adjustments to her snowmobile, her neighbour, Anton Lewicki, offers to assist her. Lewicki owns and operates the local snowmobile agency. He makes the necessary adjustments to McKim's snowmobile. There is no discussion of money between them.

   - **Can Lewicki later sue McKim for the cost of his services?**

   - **If McKim had offered to pay Lewicki at the end of the month, would this be legally enforceable? Explain.**

4. Kirk, 17 years of age, leaves home to live in Winnipeg. He secures room and board there at a reasonable price and, for some time, pays his landlord regularly. Then for several weeks, he fails to pay his weekly rent because he has been laid off his part-time job and cannot find employment. His mother sends him money, and he pays his back rent. Later, he falls behind again, and the landlord demands money directly from Kirk's mother, knowing that she helped Kirk out the last time. She claims she has no responsibility in this matter.

   - **How would you decide this case, and why? What would have to happen in this case to alter your answer?**

5. Bates, 53 years of age, is subject to periods of mental illness during which he must receive medical help. During one of his periods of lucidity, he enters into a contract to purchase a new television set and a VCR.

   - **Can Bates later repudiate the contract during an attack of depression, citing his problems as grounds for repudiation?**

6. *City Parking Services v. Murray et al.* (1992) Newfoundland Supreme Court, Trial Division 99 Nfld. & P.E.I.R. 11

   The plaintiff company held a lease on property on Duckworth Street in St. John's, Newfoundland, on which it operated a parking lot. There was no attendant at the site, nor was there an automated system regulating admission to the lot or collecting a fee. There were two large, prominent signs that stated parking a car without a permit constituted acceptance of a binding contract including a $45 parking fee for use of space only. This allowed persons to park their vehicles for up to 24 hours.

Defendants Paul Murray, Joan Norman, and Gerard Dunphy all parked on the plaintiff's lot without a permit, and each was given a "demand letter" under their respective windshield wipers. These letters contained a "Notice of $45 charge" and a demand for payment of that fee.

When these notices were not paid because the price was too high according to the defendants, the plaintiff lot owner sued the vehicle owners in contract and in trespass.

- **What argument did the plaintiff present to suggest that a contract had been formed?**

- **Why did the court conclude that no contract existed among the parties?**

- **Why, though, did the court order the vehicle owners to pay the plaintiff $25 each for intentional trespass?**

- **Do you agree or disagree with the court's decision, and why?**

Extending Legal Concepts

1. Now that you have completed this chapter, review the opening article and Something to Think About. Have your answers or opinions changed? Why or why not?

2. For the next week, make a list of *everything* that you do that involves making a contract. Include implied and express contracts, as well as verbal and written agreements you make with friends, family, your employer, and anyone else. Prepare a chart to summarize this information under the following headings:

   - parties to the contract
   - purpose of the contract
   - what is exchanged
   - type of contract—verbal or written, implied or express

   Give an oral report to the class. After all of the reports have been presented, what conclusions can you draw as a class about the effect of contract law on your lives?

3. In groups, visit a major department store, a local retail store popular with teens, or a financial institution (bank, trust company, or credit union) in your community, and obtain answers to the following questions:

   a) Do you grant credit or make loans to minors? If so, what is your official policy? If not, why not?

   b) Is an adult co-signer required? Why or why not?

   c) Is there any other important information related to this issue that you can provide?

   If possible, also obtain a copy of the credit or loan application form. With this information, prepare a group oral report of your findings and present it to the class. Compare the application forms from each group and note the similarities and differences. Prepare a bulletin board display of these forms for class information.

4. Explain the meaning of the following statement: "If they do things right, the parties to a contract create their own legal rights and duties." Do you agree or disagree, and why?

5. Using reference materials in your resource centre, including CD-ROM and the Internet, obtain current information on any of the following:

a) federal government action against firms for misleading advertising

b) contract disputes with professional athletes or entertainment personalities

c) commercial contracts for surrogate motherhood

d) anything else relating to contract issues studied in this chapter

Write a one- or two-page summary of your findings, and, if possible or appropriate, create a poster to display your information.

Researching an Issue

Legal Age of Majority

Debates concerning adulthood and the legal age when one can engage in "adult" activities are never ending. As you learned in this chapter, at one time in Canada, persons under 21 years of age were considered minors.

Today, the legal "age of majority" is 18 or 19, depending on the province in which you live. You must be 18 to vote in federal elections, and across Canada the legal smoking age is 19. But in some provinces, you must be 19 years of age to legally purchase and consume alcohol. In many provinces, you may get your learner's permit to drive at the age of 16, and you require parental consent at ages 16 and 17 to marry. This can be very confusing and often seems unfair.

Statement

The age of majority should be the common-law age of 21 for all things that involve the issue of law in any way.

Point

This return to common-law and traditional values is a good idea as it will provide equality and uniformity.

Counterpoint

This is unreasonable. Young people mature earlier today than in the past and responsibilities should be considered accordingly.

- **With a partner, research this issue. Find out why 21 was first or originally selected. Reflect on your findings.**

- **Prepare points on this statement that could be used for a class debate.**

- **Discuss your findings with others in your class.**

COMPLETING AND DISCHARGING THE CONTRACT

These are the key terms introduced in this chapter:

absolute sale	express warranty	mitigation of loss
barter	fraud	*non est factum*
breach of condition	fraudulent misrepresentation	performance
breach of contract	full disclosure	public policy
breach of warranty	guarantee	rescission
caveat emptor	implied condition	restraint of trade
clerical mistake	implied warranty	right of lien
common mistake	innocent misrepresentation	specific performance
cooling-off period	itinerant seller	substantial performance
discharge	legal tender	title
disclaimer clause	liquidated damages	undue influence
duress	material fact	unilateral mistake
exemption clause	merchantable quality	
express condition	misrepresentation	

Chapter at a Glance

Learning Outcomes

At the end of this chapter, you will be able to

1. list four situations that may prevent genuine consent;
2. distinguish between innocent and fraudulent misrepresentation;
3. identify the different types of mistakes recognized in contract law;
4. explain the effect that misrepresentation and mistakes have on the validity of contracts;
5. distinguish between undue influence and duress;
6. explain why contracts against public policy are illegal;
7. describe the ways in which contracts are discharged;
8. explain the difference between express and implied conditions and warranties;
9. outline the basic protection provided to consumers by provincial *Sale of Goods Acts*;
10. explain why consumer protection laws are needed.

Suzy Shier Fined $300 000

Something to Think About

- **Why is the federal government concerned about misleading advertising?**
- **What is double tagging? Do any stores in your community use it?**
- **Was the $300 000 fine appropriate? Why or why not?**

18.1 INTRODUCTION

In Chapter 17, three of the five essential elements for a legally binding contract—offer and acceptance, consideration, and capacity—were discussed. For a valid contract, there must also be genuine consent and legal purpose. Both parties must enter a contract freely, and the contract must have a legal object or purpose. With these two additional elements present, a valid contract now exists. A contract signed under pressure, or to perform an illegal act such as murder, is not legal and, therefore, is void and unenforceable.

Once a contract exists, each party has rights and responsibilities that must be carried out. When they are carried out as planned, the contract is discharged successfully by one of several methods. When they are not carried out properly, there is a breach of contract, and the party breaching the contract can be sued.

In addition to the above, a very specific area of contract law, the sale of goods, will be examined in this chapter. Governments have recognized the need to protect consumers and to restore the equality of bargaining power that once existed between buyers and sellers. The provincial *Sale of Goods Acts* and other federal and provincial consumer protection legislation help provide some of this balance.

18.2 THE ELEMENTS OF CONSENT

When two parties enter into a contract, it is assumed that each is aware of what the contract is about, and each wants to complete the agreement freely and willingly. Four situations, however, may prevent genuine consent from occurring: misrepresentation, mistakes, undue influence, and duress.

Misrepresentation

Persons entering a contract must be prepared to accept the consequences of their actions. Generally, the principle of *caveat emptor*—let the buyer beware—applies. Buyers have a responsibility, whenever possible, to check the claims about a product before buying it. If either party enters the contract willingly and later finds that it is a bad deal, the contract cannot be voided on that fact alone, if consideration exists for both parties. A seller does not have to disclose facts to the buyer that would be to the seller's disadvantage and might affect the buyer's decision. For example, say Lisa DeLuca owns a service station and motel unit on a main highway. She learns that a major multi-lane highway will soon be built north of her operation, jeopardizing her business. DeLuca decides to put her property up for sale. She is not legally required to inform any prospective buyers of the future highway construction. Giving such information would be to her disadvantage, and any prospective buyers can discover the same information through research.

Although the law permits DeLuca to remain silent, it does not allow her to misrepresent facts. **Misrepresentation** is a false statement by one person concerning a very important or **material fact** that is so important that it causes the other person to enter a contract. It is more than a small detail or an opinion. Thus, if a prospective buyer hears about the proposed highway and asks DeLuca about it, she is not legally permitted to state falsely that she has it personally from the mayor that the proposed highway will never be built. Such statements give rise to the most frequent claim for voiding a contract because of lack of genuine consent. There are two types of misrepresentation—innocent and fraudulent.

Innocent Misrepresentation

When a false statement of a material fact is made by a person who believes that it is true, **innocent misrepresentation** exists. A seller may be repeating facts provided by usually reliable sources, such as a manufacturer. The seller may also have made a genuine error in the quoting of facts. All that it is necessary to prove in such a situation is that the statements are not true.

For example, a beautician may sell a hair-colouring product believing the manufacturer's claim that it will last through seven or eight washings when, in fact, the colour washes out after the second time. A genuine error might occur when a travel agent misreads a travel brochure and informs two clients that their total costs for a cruise are $3500 when, in fact, this cost does not include the airfare to get to the cruise ship at its port and only includes certain meals.

In spite of the seller's innocence, the buyer is entitled to rescind or void the contract if the misrepresentation is material to the contract. **Rescission** of the contract is the basic remedy for innocent misrepresentation. The result of rescission is to return both parties to their original positions before the contract was formed. The buyer returns the goods, while the retailer refunds the money. Thus, when innocent misrepresentation exists, the contract is voidable at the option of the party who suffered from the false statement.

Fraudulent Misrepresentation

If a seller makes a false statement about a material fact, in the full knowledge that the statement is false, then **fraudulent misrepresentation** exists. Obviously, this is a more serious offence than innocent misrepresentation, since the seller is intentionally lying to cheat the buyer. In short, it is **fraud**, and the party charging fraud must have suffered some loss from entering into the agreement. If fraud exists, not only is the buyer able to rescind the contract, but damages may also be awarded by the court.

Fact must not be confused with opinion. Courts have ruled that a party who expresses views as to the value of property, now or in the future, is not guilty of misrepresentation. This prevents people who may have made a bad or foolish deal from being able to void the contract by claiming misrepresentation. The courts will, though, protect innocent parties from fraud.

The plaintiffs, Jean and Carole Aucoin, offered to purchase the defendant's house which was situated in the country and serviced by a well. After the agreement to purchase and sale had been executed, Aucoin made inquiries of the defendant vendor concerning the quality of the drinking water. He had heard rumours that there had been some water problems. The defendant vendor, Robert Young, acknowledged there had been problems and that the Department of Health had stated that minerals in the water were a danger for young children, but Young said that the problems had been corrected. Following advice from the Department of Health, Young had purchased a water softener and filter for his home. The putrid odour in the water subsided, and the taste improved greatly.

A few months later, the Aucoins completed the transaction. After moving into the house, they discovered that the water was unfit for drinking or washing clothes. The water would be normal for a few days at a time. Then the problem would begin again; sludge rather than water would spurt out. The Aucoins who had a 3-year-old child and a 10-month old baby were forced to go elsewhere for water. Eventually they had to drill a new well to solve the problem.

They brought an action for damages to the New Brunswick Court of Queen's Bench where they were awarded $5000 in damages, the difference between the purchase price of the property and its actual value, plus another $3500 in additional damages.

On appeal by Young, this decision was reversed by the Court of Appeal as the appellate court believed that Young honestly believed that his purchases of water softening and purifying equipment had corrected the problem. Leave to appeal to the Supreme Court of Canada was refused in 1988.

Aucoin v. Young
(1988)

**New Brunswick
Court of Appeal
87 N.B.R. (2d) 170**

1. **On what grounds did the Aucoins base their action?**
2. **To what extent should the principle of *caveat emptor* apply?**
3. **Why were the Aucoins awarded $3500 in additional damages at trial?**
4. **How does the "balance of probabilities" in civil actions affect these two differing judgments?**
5. **With which judgment do you agree, and why?**

Mistake

Once a contract has been formed, the law states that it should be carried out whenever possible. It is assumed that each party has read and understood the contract. Remember the legal rule, "Ignorance of the law is no excuse." The few exceptions are described below.

Common Mistake

If both parties make the same mistake regarding the subject matter of a contract, it may be declared void. A **common mistake** occurs when each party is thinking about the same thing and intends to fulfill the contract, but the subject matter of the contract is different from what they believed it to be. Suppose Matt is negotiating with Kim to purchase her 1995 Toyota Camry LE Sport model car, which he stores in his garage. Unknown to both of them, a fire has destroyed the garage and the car. Common mistake exists. The contract would be void as there was no car to sell when the contract was made, but Matt and Kim were unaware of this.

Unilateral Mistake

A contract may also be void if one party has made a mistake and the other party knew of the mistake but made no attempt to correct it. Suppose you bought a saw in a store and indicated to the clerk that you wanted to cut masonite with it. If the clerk knew that the saw was not made to cut masonite but said nothing and sold you the saw, you could later void the contract. A **unilateral mistake** like this makes a contract void and unenforceable.

Although consumers should be aware of what they buy, the courts have recognized that there are circumstances in which unilateral mistakes sometimes occur. The two most common types of unilateral mistake are a clerical mistake and *non est factum*.

Assume farmers Seguin and Kirilenko have been discussing the sale of a used tractor for some time. At the last discussion, Kirilenko offers to sell the vehicle for $15 000 and agrees to confirm this offer in writing. In preparing the letter, Kirilenko does not notice that he has written the offer quoting the price as $1500. Failing to proofread his letter, Kirilenko never realizes his mistake. When Seguin receives the offer by mail, the error is obvious to him. Seguin cannot hold Kirilenko to selling the tractor at the price of $1500 because of this **clerical mistake**. The agreement is void and unenforceable.

Generally, the courts assume that people have read the contents of any legal document they have signed and that their signature is binding on the contract. The principle of ***non est factum***, which means "It is not my deed," is an exception to this general rule. This type of mistake was common in earlier centuries, when few people were literate. A person would be presented with a document for signing and told that it was a will, when in reality it was a guarantee on a loan. The signer could plead *non est factum*, that he was not responsible, because he couldn't read the document to make certain that it was, in fact, what he had been told it was. It would be obvious to the courts that the document

CASE

Jenkins v. Strickland
(1990)

Newfoundland Supreme Court, Trial Division
83 Nfld. & P.E.I.R. 30

Muriel Strickland, the defendant in this action, entered into an agreement with her husband William to buy a home from Herbert and Loretta Jenkins, the plaintiffs. The purchase was in Mrs. Strickland's name for only tax purposes. Both the real estate agent and Strickland's husband explained the agreement of purchase and sale to her, and she was aware that she was signing an agreement to purchase a home. In spite of her grade five education, Mrs. Strickland was functionally illiterate and could only write her name and address.

Although the financing for the purchase had been arranged, the Stricklands changed their minds as they realized that meeting the monthly payments would be very difficult to manage. Mrs. Strickland believed that all her husband had to do to terminate the deal was to inform the mortgage brokers of their decision.

The Jenkins learned about the Stricklands' decision not to complete the purchase only after Mrs. Strickland failed to show up for the final home inspection. At that time, the Jenkins brought an action against the defendant for damages and were awarded about $4800.

1. **On what basis did the plaintiffs base their action?**
2. **What defence would Mrs. Strickland plead?**
3. **Should Mrs. Strickland's illiteracy excuse her from completing this contract? Why or why not?**
4. **Why did the plaintiffs' action succeed?**

In December 1981, 80-year-old Hubert Wendell Kielly, a retired farmer, made a will in which he left a nine-acre [3.6-ha] field to his niece, Muriel Jane Knox, and the balance of his estate to Jennie Maude Kielly, the wife of a deceased cousin.

In December 1984, Mr. Kielly told his niece that he couldn't spend another winter at home alone, but he did not want to go into a nursing home. His niece, who did not have room for her uncle in the family's mobile home, offered to build a new home with a separate area for him, but she needed collateral to borrow money for the new home.

Rather than go to his bank to arrange financing for his niece's loan, in early May 1985, Kielly executed a conveyance (deed) in favour of her for all his real estate, which consisted of his house and lot and the land already left to her in the will. A lawyer was present for the execution of the deed, and she spent about 30 minutes with Kielly discussing each page of the document. When it was suggested that he sign the deed on a Sunday, he refused saying that documents signed on a Sunday were not legal. Three weeks later, Kielly died at the age of 84.

The estate of the deceased as plaintiff applied to the Supreme Court, Trial Division, to have the deed set aside on the basis of undue influence and *non est factum*, but the action was dismissed.

Kielly Estate v. Knox
(1989)

Prince Edward Island Supreme Court, Trial Division
76 Nfld. & P.E.I.R. 96

1. **Did the defendant exercise undue influence over her uncle? Explain.**
2. **For a plea of *non est factum* to succeed, what must be proved? Did that apply here? Explain.**
3. **Why was the plaintiff estate's action dismissed?**

had no connection with the will that the signer was to have signed. *Non est factum* is less common today, since most people know how to read and write. Although a person might be illiterate, the defence of *non est factum* may not succeed if evidence exists that the party pleading the defence was aware of what he or she was doing in signing a contract.

Did You Know

Almost 40 percent of Canadians, aged 16–69, have difficulty reading everyday material or doing numerical tasks.

Undue Influence

The improper use of mental or emotional pressure to induce a person to enter into a contract involuntarily is called **undue influence**. A contract formed as the result of undue influence is voidable at the option of the victim.

Undue influence usually occurs when one party is so dominated by another that the decision to form a contract is not done willingly. Typical examples of such dominant relationships include husband and wife, parent and child, doctor and patient, lawyer and client, religious leader and follower, or invalid and home-care nurse. Anyone in urgent need can be influenced by the person who can provide it. Such influence can force the person in need to give up future benefits for present needs.

Generally, a person who claims that a contract was entered into because of undue influence must first prove that such influence was possible. The victim must take prompt action to void the contract, otherwise the right to void the agreement may be lost with the passage of time. Once this has been done, the burden of proof shifts to the dominant party, who must then prove that he or she did not take advantage of the dominant position and no undue influence was used.

The husband-and-wife relationship presents a special legal situation. When a wife tries to void a contract that she either entered into with her husband or entered into for his benefit (such as guaranteeing his debts), she must prove that undue influence from her husband existed. The fact that she did not have independent advice, as from a lawyer other than her husband's, can be accepted by the courts as evidence that undue influence was exerted over her. For this reason, some lending agencies require a wife who is guaranteeing her husband's loan to sign a statement indicating that she has consulted her own lawyer about her guarantee.

The concept of undue influence was developed by the courts to provide remedies for situations not covered by fraud or duress. As a result, the concept of undue influence is more flexible and wider ranging than the other two concepts.

Duress

Related to undue influence, **duress** consists of actual or threatened violence to force a person to enter into a contract. The pressure applied may be any of the following: physical punishment, imprisonment or forced detention, threatening blackmail, criminal prosecution, or libel or slander to ruin a person's reputation. Threats against a person's spouse, children, or parents are duress as well.

Obviously, someone who has been forced to consent to a contract cannot be said to have willingly agreed to anything. The person should therefore be able to avoid any responsibilities under such a contract. Like the victim of undue influence, the victim of duress should act promptly to void the contract.

Reviewing Your Reading

1. **What four conditions may prevent genuine consent from occurring in a contract?**

2. **Using original examples, distinguish between innocent and fraudulent misrepresentation.**

3. **What remedies are available to a person who has suffered from (a) innocent**

misrepresentation and (b) intentional misrepresentation or fraud?

4. **Distinguish between a common and a unilateral mistake.**

5. **What types of unilateral mistakes are recognized by the courts?**

6. **What is undue influence? List four examples of special relationships in which undue influence might arise.**

7. **What is duress? How does it differ from undue influence?**

18.3 ILLEGAL CONTRACTS

The last essential element in a legally binding contract is legal object or purpose. An illegal contract amounts to a crime under Canadian law, or is unlawful under federal or provincial civil law. A contract may be illegal and void and still not involve criminal activity. Such contracts are against **public policy**; that is, they are not in the best interests of the general public and are void. The general good of society is considered more important than the private good of the parties. Bribing a public official or attempting to bribe a witness at a trial are examples of contracts against public policy. A government official using his or her influence to assist a friend's business in obtaining a government contract may affect the legality of the contract as it is also against public policy. Agreements that offend the public good are simply not enforceable.

Restraint of Trade

One reason business contracts are challenged on grounds of public policy is that they are in **restraint of trade**. Because the courts consider competition a necessary part of Canada's economic system, they limit agreements to restrain or restrict trade to a reasonable period of time. Such contracts may be void if the time limit is excessive, or if the restriction itself is not reasonable.

For example, Victor Paslowski is the owner of the only pharmacy in a small community of 3000 people. He enters into a contract to sell his business to Chung Sing Chen. Chen will purchase the business only if Paslowski promises not to operate another pharmacy within a radius of 100 km of the existing store for 20 years. Although it is fair and reasonable for Chen to want to prevent Paslowski from starting a competing business too soon, are these conditions reasonable?

If this contract is challenged in court, the following questions must be considered:

1. Is this contract a restraint of trade?
2. Is the restraint against public policy and, therefore, void?
3. Is the restraint reasonable for the parties involved?
4. Is the restraint reasonable for the public interest?

In this example, the contract might be considered an unreasonable restraint of trade and, therefore, void. The distance involved is too great. It is unlikely that potential customers would travel further than 50 km. Also, the 20-year time limitation is unreasonable. Only a few years should be necessary to establish a successful business with the existing customers.

The reasonableness of a restraint depends on the size of the community or area serviced by the business, the types of business and the available competition, how necessary that type of business is to the community, and the time involved in the restriction. Courts will only support restraints of trade that give a person buying a business a reasonable amount of time to establish a reputation. After a reasonable length of time, the original seller should be able to start a similar business if he or she wishes to do so.

Although courts are reluctant to restrict a person's ability to earn a living by moving from one business to another similar business, they have also accepted reasonable restraints on employees who have access to confidential information or trade secrets. A promise by such an employee not to work for a competitor for a certain period of time after leaving the place of present employment is likely to be binding.

CASE

Frederic and Brenda Toews, the defendants, sold a restaurant in Altona, Manitoba, to the plaintiff, Robert Miller, promising not to open another restaurant or food catering business within 10 miles [16 km] of Altona for five years. However, three years later, in June 1990, the Toews bought a fast-food outlet in Altona.

The plaintiff immediately sought an injunction in court, but his application was dismissed as the trial judge said that Miller would not suffer "irreparable harm" if the injunction was denied. Miller appealed this decision to the Manitoba Court of Appeal where, in a 3–0 judgment, the injunction was granted.

Miller v. Toews
[1991]

Manitoba Court of Appeal
2 W.W.R. 604

1. **Why did Miller build a restraint of trade clause into the contract that he and the Toews signed?**
2. **In your opinion, was this an unreasonable restraint of trade and against public policy? Explain.**
3. **What is the purpose of an injunction, and why did Miller want one issued against the Toews?**
4. **Why do you think the defendants breached the contract they signed?**
5. **Why did the Court of Appeal grant an injunction to Miller?**

Restraint of Competition

The federal *Competition Act*, which regulates Canadian advertising, also regulates any contracts between business firms that restrict competition with agreements contrary to the public interest. The *Act* protects the public against agreements that involve an industry fixing prices, that eliminate or reduce the number of competitors in a particular community or industry, or that reduce product output to restrict competition. The formation of mergers between companies that would reduce competition and be against the public interest might also be prohibited by the *Act*.

Bets and Wagers

Gaming and betting are legal in Canada, but they are strictly controlled by statute law. Gaming means the operation of a gambling business. To run gambling games legally, a licence must be obtained from provincial authorities. Licences are issued to genuine social clubs that are allowed to keep a small sum from the games, returning the rest as winnings to customers. Valid charitable or religious organizations are also permitted to hold gaming operations, such as bingo, if proper approval has been obtained. Under the *Criminal Code*, it is illegal to operate a common gaming house (an unlicensed gambling business). Police can enter such a house and take into custody both the operation and any people found there.

Betting, or making a wager, on the outcome of an event is not illegal according to statute law, for example, the *Gaming Act* in British Columbia and Ontario. It is legal for two co-workers to bet on the outcome of a football game; however, the courts will not assist the winner in collecting on the bet. Contracts made between people for bets are not considered important enough to warrant attention by the courts. Betting on horses at a racetrack through an authorized system is supervised and approved by federal and provincial authorities. The amounts to be paid back as winnings are specifically outlined.

Slot machines are legal in some parts of Canada where provincial governments have authorized such gambling activity. Slot machines are automatic machines that discharge a token or merchandise. The operation of the machine by

the player is a matter of chance or uncertainty.

Pinball machines and video games are legal, as long as the payoff for winning is no more than a free game. Municipal bylaws preventing video game parlours near schools reflect public concern and are considered within the law of public policy.

Reviewing Your Reading

1. Distinguish between "illegal" and "void" as these terms relate to contract law.

2. Give an example of a contract that might be against public policy.

3. List the four questions that must be considered if a contract is challenged in a court as a restraint of trade.

4. Why are courts reluctant to enforce restraint of employment contracts? When would such a contract be enforceable?

5. What is the purpose of the federal *Competition Act*?

6. Will the court assist a winner of a bet in collecting it? Explain.

18.4 DISCHARGING THE CONTRACT

Once the parties have agreed to a contract and the essential requirements have been met, an enforceable contract exists. However, all contracts must come to an end. In most cases, this happens when both parties fulfill their obligations outlined in the contract. The contract is then completed or **discharged**. Contracts are discharged by performance, mutual agreement, impossibility of performance, and by breach of contract.

Performance

The most common way for a contract to be discharged is by **performance**. This occurs when the parties involved have completed their obligations under the contract. Ursula's Plumbing Co. contracts to renovate a bathroom for a customer for a fee. After the bathroom has been renovated and the customer provides payment, both parties have performed their part of the contract.

If one party offers to perform and the other party refuses to accept, the first party is excused from any further attempt to perform his or her part of the contract and may take legal action for breach of contract.

When money is being exchanged, certain rules apply. First, it must be **legal tender** in Canada, which includes Bank of Canada notes; Canadian quarters and dimes up to $10; nickel coins up to $5; and pennies up to 25 cents. The money must be tendered at the creditor's place of business on the specified date, unless other methods are agreed upon. Creditors are not legally required to make unreasonable change, nor to accept payment in anything but legal tender. Cheques are not legal tender.

For example, sales clerks cannot be expected to make change from a $100 bill for the purchase of an item worth $1. If the customer tries to impose such a burden on the clerk, the clerk has the right to refuse to accept this form of payment because the customer is not fulfilling his or her part of the agreement. Without this principle, a customer could make payment in any form, regardless of the inconvenience it would cause the clerk.

Clearly, many of these requirements are no longer followed in today's business world. People accept pennies for amounts larger than 25 cents. They accept payment via the mail. They give change readily when more than the legal amount is tendered. Cheques, travellers' cheques, money orders, unused postage stamps, and U.S. currency are commonly used and accepted in Canada. However, such tender does not legally have to be accepted.

If an offer to perform by giving legal tender is refused by a creditor, the debtor is still liable for payment. However, the debtor is no longer obliged to seek out the creditor to try to perform his or her part of the contract. It is now up to the creditor to ask for performance.

Mutual Agreement

The parties to a contract may agree to cancel it, releasing each other from contractual obligations. Businesses often terminate contracts by replacing all earlier contracts with new ones. Some contracts may provide for termination under certain circumstances. For example, a rock concert may be cancelled if not enough tickets are sold by a certain time. A fire and theft insurance policy may be void if a house is left unattended or vacant for a specified period of time.

Impossibility of Performance

Under English common law, a party to a contract was once responsible for meeting all obligations. This was true even if circumstances arose that made it impossible to fulfill or meet those obligations. It was generally felt that any circumstances that might prevent completion of the contract could or should have been anticipated and covered by specific terms in the contract. For example, a farmer's contract for the sale of wheat might include some term covering the destruction of the crop by an early frost or flooding of the fields. To protect against such unforeseen risks, insurance policies are now sometimes purchased.

Today, the courts interpret that some contracts have implied terms that were obviously in the minds of both parties making a contract. A contract requiring a dancer to perform is impossible to discharge if the dance theatre is destroyed by fire, or if the dancer breaks her leg in a skiing accident.

A similar situation exists when a law makes certain transactions impossible to perform. Say that a contract has been drawn up between two parties for the building of an apartment complex. However, before construction begins, it turns out that the building cannot be built because it is discovered that the property is an aboriginal burial ground, which is protected by law. The contract is impossible to perform because of the existence of the law. As you have seen, legality of object is one of the requirements of an enforceable contract.

Reviewing Your Reading

1. **List four main means by which a contract may be discharged. Which is the most common method?**

2. **What is legal tender in Canada?**

3. **What are other accepted forms of payment that are not legal tender?**

4. **How can a contract be terminated by mutual agreement?**

5. **Give a new example of a contract that becomes impossible to perform.**

18.5 BREACH OF CONTRACT

A **breach of contract** exists when one party fails to fulfill his or her contractual obligations. If that person refuses to perform any major part of the contract, the injured party is released from all obligations. Breach is the opposite of performance of a contract.

If the breach concerns a fundamental term of the contract, a **breach of condition** exists. When this occurs the injured party can rescind the contract and sue for damages or, in certain circumstances, specific performance of the contract, which will be discussed later. If Angela orders flowers to be delivered to the church for her wedding, delivery of the flowers after the service is a breach of condition. The flowers, the subject matter of the contract, are of no use after the ceremony. Selling a truck with a defective steering system is another example of a fundamental breach of condition.

If the breach is of a minor nature, a **breach of warranty** exists. Such a breach does not allow the injured party to rescind the contract, because it is not serious enough. If Asher orders a specific make and colour of car with a racing stripe painted on both sides, and the car delivered to him conforms in every respect except for the racing stripes, there is a breach of warranty. The omission is a minor one. Asher can ask the dealer to paint the missing racing stripes on the car, he can deduct the cost of the stripes from the bill when he pays for the car, or he can sue for damages to obtain money to have someone else do it.

The amount of damages to which an injured party is entitled depends upon the extent of the financial loss, which would likely be greater in the case of a breach of a condition than a breach of a warranty. As you learned in Chapter 10, a legal action can be time consuming and expensive. Here is an opportunity to use alternative dispute resolution procedures in attempting to work out a solution between the parties.

Substantial Performance

As you have seen, the law protects the person who bears the inconvenience suffered. Through the rule of **substantial performance**, the courts also protect the party who has fulfilled most of his or her part of a contract. In the example with Asher, the dealer, too, is protected. Let us say that Asher really didn't like the car. The rule of substantial performance prevents him from using the missing racing stripes as an excuse to get out of the contract. The dealer fulfilled almost all of the dealership's terms of the contract, and so must Asher.

Remedies for Breach of Contract

Once the parties have entered into a legally binding contract, both are bound to the agreement. However, if a breach of contract occurs, the following remedies are available to the injured party.

Damages

Awards of damages are made only to compensate the injured party; they are not intended as punishment. The purpose of awarding damages is to place the injured party in the same position as if the contract had been completed. Specific types of damages that might be awarded were discussed in detail in Chapter 10.

Mitigation of Loss. The party who has suffered a loss as the result of a breach of contract must

Thelma Battaglia and Chris Wilson booked the well-known Sooter Studios Ltd. to photograph their wedding. The $399 contract included 102 photos taken at two different locations, albums, and thank-you cards. The couple paid a deposit of $280 with the balance to be paid on completion.

On the day of the wedding, the photographer arrived late, and then only after Chris Wilson telephoned him. He was inappropriately dressed, took photos at one location only, and was indifferent about the composition of the pictures. In fact, the bride's brother-in-law suggested many of the poses. When the Wilsons finally received their photos, of the 47 (instead of 102), only 10 were clear pictures. The others were double-exposed over shots of another wedding.

The plaintiffs brought a court action in early 1988 for breach of contract, mental distress, and the cost of re-assembling the wedding and posing for new photos. Since some of the guests had come from as far away as Brazil, Australia, and Toronto, this cost was estimated at about $7000 for airfare and accommodation. However, the trial judge disagreed and awarded the plaintiffs $1000 plus their deposit. Determined to have their wedding re-photographed properly, the Wilsons appealed to the British Columbia Court of Appeal where, in a 3–0 decision in late December 1988, their appeal was dismissed.

Wilson et al. v. Sooter Studios Ltd.
(1988)

British Columbia Court of Appeal
55 D.L.R. (4th) 303

1. **Did Wilson's action involve a complete breach of contract, a breach of condition, or a breach of warranty? Explain your choice.**

2. **Why do you think the Wilsons sought the remedy they did? Do you agree? Why or why not?**

3. **Why did the trial judge award only $1000 to the plaintiffs?**

4. **Explain the meaning of the following statement from the Court of Appeal's decision: "On legal principles, one cannot justify an award based on the cost of reconstituting the wedding as a proper measure of damages. These were not expenses incurred by the Wilsons, nor was a photographer to necessarily assume that a majority of the wedding guests were from out of town. Whatever he contracted for, he never contemplated that the cost of a breach would be to fly back six adults from Toronto."**

5. **Do you agree with the courts' decisions? Why or why not?**

attempt to mitigate (reduce) possible losses from the breach. This is called **mitigation of loss**. The reason for this is to reduce the burden on the party breaking the contract. If Boitano refuses to accept delivery from Kozak of a truckload of fresh fruit and vegetables that he had ordered for $500, Kozak must try to find another buyer and sell the produce at a reasonable price. She must do so as quickly as possible, to reduce spoilage. If Kozak, the injured party, still suffers a loss due to storage costs, transportation to the new buyer's store, or loss due to a decreased price for the produce, she can then sue Boitano for damages. If Kozak is able to sell the produce for only $300, she can sue Boitano for $200—the difference between the original contract price and the price for which she was able to sell the fruit and vegetables to minimize her loss. Any reasonable expenses involved in this resale should also be included in a suit for damages.

What if Kozak refuses to try to find another buyer for her produce, insisting that Boitano must take it? Meanwhile, the fruit and vegetables spoil and cannot be sold. Is Boitano liable for the entire $500 loss to Kozak? After all, he broke the contract between them.

The courts say that, in such circumstances, Kozak did not try in any way to mitigate her losses from the breach. Thus, she did not try to reduce the burden on Boitano. Kozak's refusal to help herself and Boitano would not be regarded sympathetically by the courts. It is unlikely that she would receive the full $500 for damages. It is to her benefit to go elsewhere to sell her produce for whatever she can get, then to collect the difference in damages from Boitano. By doing this, she loses nothing on the original contract price.

Liquidated Damages. To avoid disputes in court, many contracts provide for **liquidated damages**, a sum of money agreed on in advance, in case of breach of contract. For instance, a contract to construct a building can include a term stating that the contractor will pay a specified sum of money for each day that construction continues beyond the completion date. The amount indicated must not be so high as to penalize the contractor. It is only a reasonable sum of money that acts as compensation in the event that the work is not completed on time; for example, $100 a day for delay in completing a building contract on time, or $50 a day for delay in removing equipment from the plaintiff's land after completion of the contract.

Specific Performance

There are many times when damages are not an adequate remedy for a breach of contract. If the National Gallery of Canada contracts to buy the painting, *A September Gale, Georgian Bay,* by Group of Seven artist Arthur Lismer for $150 000, and the seller decides not to sell the painting, the National Gallery might ask the courts to order **specific performance** of the contract. Payment of damages is not an adequate remedy for the Gallery in this situation. Because the painting is unique, the Gallery wants it and nothing else.

In ordering specific performance, the courts would order the seller to sell the painting to the National Gallery for $150 000, as originally agreed. Land, homes, antiques, and one-of-a-kind items

A September Gale, Georgian Bay (1921) by Arthur Lismer / National Gallery of Canada, Ottawa

are examples of items found in contracts for which specific performance would likely be awarded if requested by the injured party. Since no two parcels of land are the same, specific performance is commonly available as a remedy for contracts for the sale of land. However, in most other cases, monetary damages are adequate compensation.

Specific performance is not an available remedy if the courts would have to continually supervise the carrying out of the order and determine whether or not it is satisfactory. For this reason, a contract for a personal service, such as painting a family portrait, cannot be specifically enforced. An employee is not required to work for any particular employer, and an employer is not required to keep a particular employee. In such cases, either money damages or an injunction are issued.

Injunctions

As you learned in Chapter 10, an injunction is a court order that requires a defendant to do, or refrain from doing, something. The difference between specific performance and an injunction is that the former remedy requires the defendant to do, or complete, a positive act, while the latter remedy usually requires the defendant to refrain from doing something.

For example, in the earlier restraint of trade example, if Paslowski set up another pharmacy within 20 km from Chen's in the next year, Chen

CASE

The plaintiffs, James and Rita Coffin, purchased a Mustang convertible from the defendant dealer in September 1989. Mr. Coffin had always wanted to own a Mustang, and the 1989 model was the 25th year of production of this car. After telephoning several dealerships, the plaintiff found the car he wanted at the defendant dealer's business in Halifax. Although Coffin wanted a new car, this particular car was a demonstrator that had been driven only by the company owner, Eric MacLellan. Coffin was also assured by MacLellan that the car would come with the manufacturer's extended new car warranty.

Three months later, the plaintiffs still had not received their warranty card from the defendant. A local car dealer suggested to the plaintiffs that he believed that the Mustang was a leased vehicle, not a demonstrator, and that the defendant probably had failed to obtain the necessary warranty extension as promised. In June 1990, upon learning this, the plaintiffs instructed their lawyer to return the vehicle and get their money back; this offer was quickly rejected by the defendant.

The plaintiffs then sued the dealer for rescission of the contract, and the case came to trial in early 1993. During this time, the plaintiffs continued to drive the Mustang which, they claimed, was in excellent condition, putting about 65 000 km on it. At trial, the Nova Scotia Supreme Court declined to grant rescission of the contract and instead awarded the plaintiffs nominal damages of $1.

Coffin v. MacLellan Lincoln Mercury Sales Ltd. et al.
(1993)

Nova Scotia Supreme Court
123 N.S.R. (2d) 171

1. **Was the plaintiff induced to enter this contract by a misrepresentation made by the defendant dealership and its personnel? Explain.**
2. **If there was a misrepresentation, was it innocent or fraudulent? Why?**
3. **Did this case involve a breach of condition or a breach of warranty? Give reasons for your answer.**
4. **In what way does mitigation of loss apply to this action?**
5. **Why did the court not grant rescission of the contract?**
6. **Why were the plaintiffs awarded nominal damages only?**

would probably seek a court injunction to prevent this from happening. Courts will only issue injunctions when it is fair and reasonable to do so.

Rescission

If the breach is for a major condition of the contract, the injured plaintiff can seek to have the contract rescinded. If successful, the action would restore the parties to their original positions.

Limitation of Actions

An injured party who has the right to take legal action against another over a breach of contract should take court action as soon as possible. The possibilities of lost or forgotten evidence, and of witnesses moving or dying, are valid reasons for beginning legal action within a certain period.

The *Statute of Limitations* or the *Limitations Act* of all provinces, and the limitations sections of various federal and provincial statutes, contain the law regulating time limits. The law varies slightly from province to province, but it is fairly uniform as it applies to both simple contracts and specialty contracts. If action is not taken within the specified time, the claim is barred; that is, the courts will not assist in enforcing it. For example, for contracts under seal actions must begin within 6 years in Alberta, Saskatchewan, and Manitoba. For most other provinces, the time period is 20 years.

Reviewing Your Reading

1. **What is a breach of contract?**
2. **Distinguish between a breach of condition and a breach of warranty. What is the effect of each on a contract?**
3. **List four remedies for breach of contract.**
4. **Why should an injured party take quick steps to mitigate loss as a result of a breach of contract?**
5. **What are liquidated damages, and why do many contracts provide for them in advance?**
6. **Distinguish between specific performance and an injunction as remedies for breach of contract.**
7. **What is the purpose of a *Statute of Limitations*?**

18.6 *The Sale of Goods*

Until the late nineteenth century, no legislation regulating the sale of goods existed. Yet many disputes settled in British courts arose between parties over the sale of goods. As a result, the British Parliament passed the *Sale of Goods Act, 1893*. Since that time, each common law province and territory in Canada has passed a similar *Act*. Quebec laws in this area are contained in the *Code Civil*. Laws covering the sale of goods are a direct response to the need for precise, clear rules that regulate the exchange of goods for money.

The sale of goods is a very specific area of contract law. It deals with contracts in which the seller transfers the ownership of goods, in the present or in the future, to the buyer for money consideration. In an **absolute sale**, ownership passes to the buyer when the contract is fulfilled. The *Sale of Goods Acts* do not cover conditional sales or exchanges of goods for goods, or services for services. Such **barter** transactions do not involve the exchange of money and are thus excluded, by definition, from these *Acts*.

"Goods" for purposes of the *Act* refers only to personal property, such as furniture, clothing, appliances, and other movable possessions of a personal nature. Such items as stocks, bonds, and cheques are not covered. The *Acts* do not apply to the sale of services, such as television repairs or carpentry work.

A sale of goods contract must contain the five essential elements of contracts to be valid. Also, it must be in writing if it is for goods over a certain value; this value ranges among the provinces and territories from $30 to $50.

Title, Delivery, and Payment

The time when ownership of, or **title** to, the goods passes to the buyer is important, because the owner must accept the burden of loss if the goods are lost, stolen, damaged, or destroyed. Most contracts specify the time when ownership changes. If no agreement is made, the provincial *Sale of Goods Acts* outline the applicable provisions.

It is the seller's responsibility to deliver the goods to the buyer at the location specified in the contract. Delivery involves the transfer of ownership of the goods from the seller to the buyer. Usually, the buyer takes delivery of the goods at the seller's place of business, unless there is an agreement that states otherwise.

The *Sale of Goods Acts* provide for payment at the time of delivery, although most contracts specify when and how payment is to be made. If no price is agreed upon, a reasonable price is due. Payment at a later date than agreed upon does not permit the seller to reclaim the goods.

However, the seller can charge interest and even take legal action against the buyer for a late payment. If a deposit has been made and the buyer has breached the contract, the seller must attempt to mitigate or reduce any loss from the breach of contract.

Express Conditions and Warranties

As you saw earlier, the distinction between a condition and a warranty is significant when breach of a sales contract occurs. If it is difficult to determine whether the breach is a condition or a warranty, the final decision will be made by the courts.

An **express condition** is essential to the contract and is clearly outlined in it. For example, if Miyoshi draws up a contract for Lingaard, a carpenter, to build a cherry-wood cabinet for her and he then builds a walnut cabinet, Miyoshi can refuse to accept it. Breaking an express condition makes a contract void.

Express warranties are specific promises made by the manufacturer or retailer concerning performance, quality, and condition of an item. These warranties, commonly known as **guarantees**, are usually in the form of a manufacturer's certificate that the buyer receives along with the purchase. Limited warranties last for a certain period, for instance, six months or one year. Car warranties commonly cover the cost of parts and repairs for a certain number of kilometres or a certain number of years, whichever comes first.

Where a contract in writing contains express warranties, any verbal promises given by the seller are ineffective and not binding. One exception to this rule occurs when a consumer makes a purchase because he or she has relied totally on the advice and information provided by the seller. In such cases, the contract may be rescinded under provincial consumer protection legislation.

Warranties and conditions that are not written into the contract but stated clearly in displays and advertisements are also binding on the seller. If the warranty promises are made by the manufacturer, not the seller, then the consumer must return faulty or defective merchandise to the manufacturer, because the contract exists between the buyer and the manufacturer.

Implied Conditions and Warranties

Promises in law that are made by implication by a seller are called **implied conditions** and **implied warranties**. These obligations have been codified in the different provincial *Sales of Goods Acts*, and include the following promises:

- that the seller has title to the goods and the right to sell them;
- that the articles or goods are of merchantable quality and suitable for the required purpose;
- that the goods supplied correspond to the samples or descriptions provided.

These implied conditions and warranties are present in every sale of goods, even if the seller does not specifically mention them. Each is examined further.

Title

It is implied that a seller of goods has title to them and therefore has the right to sell them. If the goods rightfully belong to someone else—perhaps they were stolen—the true owner can demand their return, even from a buyer who purchased them in good faith. The buyer would then have to sue or take legal action against the seller for breach of condition to obtain compensation for losing the goods.

If a seller has clear (good) title to the goods, they legally belong to the buyer after the contract of sale is fulfilled. The buyer can use the goods in any way, or even resell them. Nobody has the right to interfere with the buyer's use and enjoyment of the purchase. It is further implied that the seller does not give the right to anyone else to use the goods.

Quality and Suitability

Although the buyer should carefully check the goods before purchase, there is an implied condition in some cases that the goods will be of good quality and fit for use. If the buyer either directly or by implication makes known to the seller the purpose for which goods are to be used and is depending on the seller's knowledge and judgment, it is an implied condition that the goods will be fit and suitable for the buyer's purpose. Often the buyer knows little about the product and must depend on the seller's honesty. For example, telling the seller that you want to buy a compressed air hammer to nail wood to a concrete wall and finding out it is only suitable for nailing wood to wood is a breach of an implied condition.

CASE

Harasymko v. Campbell
(1993)

Manitoba Court of Queen's Bench
82 Man. R. (2d) 283

The plaintiff, Jerry Harasymko, purchased a used 1982 mower conditioner from the defendant, Clive Campbell, in May 1992, for $6250. Prior to the purchase of the machine, the plaintiff specifically asked the defendant if there was anything wrong with it. Other than informing Harasymko that the motor had been rebuilt for $900, Campbell replied, "No, it's in good working condition."

When the plaintiff attempted to cut his hay crop in early July, he found the machine was not working properly. He removed the motor and took it to two repair shops where he received conflicting opinions on its capabilities. The mower still did not function properly after he had purchased and installed a new motor. After a new hydraulic pump and gear box were installed, the machine finally worked properly. Because of the delays in correcting the problem, Harasymko had to rent a mower to cut his 1992 crops.

The plaintiff brought an action for damages to the Court of Queen's Bench where he was awarded about $1300, plus costs.

1. Did the defendant misrepresent the condition of the mower prior to its sale? If so, what type of misrepresentation occurred? If not, why not?

2. Under the *Sale of Goods Act*, was there a breach of any implied conditions? Explain.

3. Although the plaintiff claimed about $4000 in damages for his repair and replacement costs, the court awarded him only $1300 because of his "exaggerated claim." Explain the meaning of this judgment. Do you agree? Why or why not?

A buyer may be able to obtain a refund if a product is not of **merchantable quality**. Goods of merchantable quality are fit to be used for their normal purpose and so are usually salable. A lawn mower must be able to cut grass. A refrigerator must be able to keep goods chilled for a reasonable time without spoiling.

Not all goods of merchantable quality are salable. Electrical goods sold in Canada must have the approval of the Canadian Standards Association and must display the CSA seal. If Tascha goes to the United States to purchase a home computer and brings it back to Canada, paying duty and applicable taxes on her purchase, the lack of CSA approval technically goes against provincial regulations. Thus, although this particular home computer without the CSA seal is not salable in Canada, it is still of merchantable quality if it does the job for which it was purchased.

Sale by Sample or Description

If goods have been bought by description or sample, or both, there is an implied condition that the goods must correspond to the description or sample. The seller must clearly tell the buyer that the goods are only samples. Sample goods must be of merchantable quality, having no defects that would be noticeable on reasonable examination. In any sale by sample or description, the buyer, if he or she desires, must be allowed to compare the purchased goods with the sample seen earlier.

A sale by sample, for example, might involve buying certain qualities of a particular cut of lumber, based on examination of the one piece of that lumber kept on display in the retail outlet. A sale by description might involve the purchase of a sofa, ordered to match a model on display in the furniture store, but covered with a fabric design that was picked from manufacturer's samples.

If the goods delivered do not correspond to the samples or to the description in the catalogue or the advertisement, the buyer has the right to return them and to rescind the contract as quickly as possible. If the buyer does not examine the goods first to see that they match the description or sample and accepts them, he or she does so at risk. If the buyer discovers later that the goods are not exactly what was ordered, it is too late to do anything. Goods must be examined within a reasonable amount of time after delivery to ensure that they correspond exactly to the order.

If the buyer makes a purchase without asking for the seller's advice or buys a particular product for its brand name, the seller cannot be held responsible if the goods do not satisfy the buyer's expectations. However, the manufacturer can be held liable for the tort of negligence if the product is faulty and the buyer is injured through its use.

Disclaimer Clauses

To reduce the possibility of being sued for breach of implied warranties and conditions, many sellers add **disclaimer (exemption) clauses** to contracts. These statements are an attempt by sellers to exempt themselves from the liability normally imposed by the implied warranties and conditions of the sale. They are sometimes found on the back of standard printed contract forms used by sellers. A typical disclaimer clause might read: "There are no conditions, express or implied, statutory or otherwise, other than those contained in this written agreement."

Such a statement seeks to remove the protection of the implied warranties and conditions from the buyer. Even if such clauses appear on the back of the contract, they are not binding on the buyer unless there is some indication to the buyer on the front of the contract that additional terms are to be found on the back. Thus, if the

CASE

Greeven v. Blackcomb Skiing Enterprises Ltd.
(1995)

British Columbia Supreme Court 22 C.C.L.T. (2d) 265

The plaintiff, Judith Greeven, was an English tourist and a first-time visitor at the Blackcomb Mountain ski resort in British Columbia. She had had some limited skiing experience in Europe and the United States but had never previously visited the Whistler Blackcomb area.

Ms. Greeven purchased a ticket entitling her to ski the hills for six days, but she did not see the notices posted in front of the ticket wicket or in the ski area. She put the string with the ticket around her neck as required but did not read the ticket and was unaware of any writing on it. The back of the ticket, in quite small but clearly legible print, set out conditions excluding liability for personal injury resulting from "any cause whatsoever" including negligence on the part of the defendant and its employees.

While skiing, the plaintiff was surprised by a dangerous drop-off on the hill and was seriously injured. She brought an action for damages against the defendant, and the defendant applied to the court for an order dismissing the plaintiff's action. However, the defendant's application was dismissed.

1. **Why would the plaintiff sue the defendant ski-run operators?**

2. **What argument would the defendant present to have the plaintiff's claim dismissed?**

3. **The law states that, in an action like this, the burden of proof rests with the ski resort to demonstrate that reasonable steps had been taken to draw the broad exclusions of liability terms to their patrons' attention. Why did the court find that this had not been adequately done by the defendant?**

4. **Why was the defendant's application dismissed?**

The plaintiff Borek commissioned the defendant Hooper to paint, for a $4000 fee, a very large abstract painting to hang in a specific space in her home. It was a predominantly white painting with a splash of colour across it to hang on a white wall. When Hooper delivered the painting, Borek was thrilled with it and paid him the agreed-upon price.

About three years later, the surface of the painting began to crack, and its white areas began to yellow. Believing that this was not the painting for which she had contracted, she brought an action to Small Claims Court where she was awarded $2000 in damages (50 percent of the purchase price) plus costs for a breach under the *Sale of Goods Act*. Expert witnesses testified that the yellowing resulted from the defendant's choice of materials and that the cracks were caused by the artists' materials and techniques.

The defendant appealed this judgment to the Ontario Court, General Division where a new trial was ordered limited to the assessment of damages only.

Borek v. Hooper
(1994)

Ontario Court, General Division
18 O.R. (3d) 470

1. **What implied condition under the *Sale of Goods Act* would the plaintiff claim was breached, and why?**
2. **Why did the higher court rule that the *Sale of Goods Act* did not apply to this painting?**
3. **Should the defendant be held liable? Why or why not?**

buyer is aware of such a clause, the terms are effective; the seller is not liable for breaches of the terms. However, if the seller makes no effort to draw the buyer's attention to these key terms, then the seller may be held liable.

Remedies of the Buyer and Seller

If a breach of contract occurs over the sale of goods, remedies are available to both the buyer and the seller to settle any dispute. Some of these remedies are discussed below.

Buyer's Remedies

If the seller does not deliver the goods, or if the goods delivered do not match the samples or description in the store or the advertisements, the buyer does not need to pay for the goods. Other remedies discussed earlier include rescission of the

contract, the awarding of damages, and the ordering of specific performance.

Seller's Remedies

A seller who has not received payment for goods delivered to the buyer also has certain remedies under the *Sale of Goods Act*. These remedies vary according to who has title to the goods.

Non-delivery. Where the goods have been sold but still remain in the seller's possession, the seller has the legal right to keep the goods until payment is received. Thus, the seller has a **right of lien** over the goods. However, if the goods have been delivered to the buyer, the seller loses this right of lien.

Stoppage in Transit. If the goods are in transit, and the seller learns that the buyer is insolvent, that is, unable to pay the amount owing for the sale, the seller can order the carrier not to make delivery. The goods can be redirected to another location for sale, or returned to the seller. If the carrier delivers the goods against the seller's orders, the carrier is liable for any loss suffered by the seller. However, if the buyer has already been notified by the carrier that the goods are ready to be picked up at their destination, the carrier cannot be held responsible. Once the buyer obtains possession of the goods, this remedy naturally disappears.

Resale. Often when the goods are stopped in transit, they are resold. However, the seller must notify the buyer of the intended resale to give the buyer one last opportunity to make the required payment to obtain the goods. Perishable goods, such as fruit and vegetables, must be resold as quickly as possible before they spoil and become unsalable. Through the remedy of resale, the seller attempts to mitigate his or her losses.

Damages. Finally, the seller can sue for damages, as in any contract in which a breach occurs. If the buyer has the goods, the seller can sue for the full price. If the goods are still in the seller's possession, the damages sued for might represent the expenses involved in finding a new buyer and any price difference in the resale of the goods.

Reviewing Your Reading

1. **What types of transactions are covered by the *Sale of Goods Act*?**

2. **Why is it important to determine when title to goods passes from seller to buyer?**

3. **Distinguish between express and implied conditions and warranties, using original examples of each.**

4. **List three implied obligations that sellers have to buyers under the *Sale of Goods Act*.**

5. **Define "merchantable quality." What can a purchaser of goods do if the goods are not of merchantable quality?**

6. **If goods purchased do not match the samples or description provided, what options are open to the buyer?**

7. **What is a disclaimer clause, and when may it have no legal effect?**

8. **Briefly outline the main remedies available to the buyer of goods if the seller fails to deliver them.**

18.7 CONSUMER PROTECTION

The provincial *Sale of Goods Act* relates only to transactions between buyers and sellers. It does not extend to manufacturers of goods, nor does it help anyone who is not a buyer or consumer. Because these *Acts* have been found to be inadequate to control deceptive or unfair business practices, the federal and provincial governments have enacted significant consumer protection legislation since the late 1960s.

The laws fall into several different categories:
- laws intended to protect from hazardous or dangerous products;
- laws designed to ensure that accurate information is provided to consumers;
- laws intended to regulate activities around the actual sale of goods.

Federal and provincial legislation sometimes overlap, giving consumers a choice as to which legislation to use in seeking assistance or compensation. Furthermore, the provincial laws differ somewhat by province and cannot be covered in depth in this text. However, all provinces and the federal government provide free booklets and pamphlets about their respective laws. Refer to these for the most current information and for specific provincial statutes that help and protect consumers.

Federal Laws

The federal laws treat improper and dishonest business conduct and misleading advertising as offences against society and so provide a basis for taking criminal action against offenders through the *Competition Act*. Packaging and labelling, hazardous products, and safety of food and drugs are covered by the *Consumer Packaging and Labelling Act*, the *Hazardous Products Act*, and the *Food and Drugs Act*, respectively.

Provincial Laws

The various provincial laws deal with consumers on a more personal level. They provide a basis for seeking compensation in civil actions against offenders. Most provincial legislation covers two main concerns: selling techniques and the regulation of misleading advertising and sales practices by sellers. Laws pertaining to unfair trade practices have already been mentioned in Chapter 17. Summaries of other key provincial laws follow.

Consumer Protection Act

Most provinces have a *Consumer Protection Act*, and one of its main concerns is the **itinerant seller** or the door-to-door seller. For instance, in Alberta this matter is covered by the *Direct Sales Cancellation Act*. All itinerant sellers must be registered with the provincial Consumer Protection Bureau, the branch of each province's Consumer Affairs Ministry that deals with consumers and commercial relations. If sellers do not carry on business within the law, their registration can be suspended or cancelled.

Buying goods from a door-to-door seller is convenient and easy. On the other hand, some of these sellers use high-pressure tactics to enter a home and show reluctance to leave until the residents have signed a contract to buy goods. Laws have been set up in the realization that people may be talked into making a purchase that they really don't want or can't afford. Thus, all provinces have established a **cooling-off period** to allow buyers an opportunity to cancel a contract with a door-to-door seller without giving any reason at all. The cooling-off period covers only those contracts made at a place other than the seller's permanent place of business; usually this is the buyer's home. This period ranges from 2 days in Ontario and Manitoba, to 7 days in British Columbia, to 10 days in Newfoundland.

To cancel a contract within the cooling-off period, the buyer must notify the seller of the desire to cancel. The best way to do this is to send a letter cancelling the contract by registered mail, or to deliver the letter personally. Making a telephone call or stopping payment on any cheque written for a down payment is not sufficient. The letter does not have to be received within the number of days of each province's cooling-off period, as long as it was mailed within the allowed period.

Once the contract has been cancelled, the seller must return any money received, and the buyer must return any goods obtained under the contract. It is the seller's responsibility to pay any costs that might arise from the buyer's returning the goods.

Credit Disclosure

Credit is a convenience used increasingly in business transactions. However, goods purchased on credit cost more than if they were purchased for cash. To ensure consumers are fully aware of the cost of buying goods on credit, provincial legislation requires **full disclosure** of all credit costs. This provides consumers with a detailed statement of the cost of credit in dollars and cents and as a true annual rate of interest expressed as a percentage. It allows consumers to compare credit terms and to shop around for the best interest rates available. Consumers are not bound to contracts that do not provide full disclosure. This information is required under a province's *Consumer Protection Act*. In Alberta, it is contained in the *Credit and Loan Agreements Act*.

A number of regulations govern interest rates, most of them at the federal level. Each province also has legislation in this area. The provincial legislation gives the courts the power to look into any loan agreement to determine whether or not the interest charges were excessive. If so, the court is able to order the lender to repay the excessive interest charges to the consumer. This legislation applies to all loans, even those that have been paid in full. In making such a decision, the court will examine the costs of similar loans from other lending sources, the reputation of the lender, and the position of the two parties involved. In most provinces, the statute governing these matters is called the *Unconscionable Transactions (Relief) Act*. In British Columbia such legislation is part of the *Consumer Protection Act*.

Reviewing Your Reading

1. **List four areas of consumer concern covered by federal consumer protection laws.**

2. **List two areas of concern covered by provincial consumer protection laws.**

3. **a) Define "itinerant seller."**

   b) What is a "cooling-off" period? Find out how long this is in your province.

4. **What must a consumer do to cancel a contract during the "cooling-off" period?**

5. **a) Explain the meaning of "full disclosure."**

   b) What two types of information are required to be disclosed to the users of consumer credit?

Should governments be sued for breach of contract when they reduce or eliminate government services?

In the 1990s, government funding cuts and the elimination of government services altogether became commonplace in most provinces. The media was full of stories about the hardships that people experienced as a result of these cuts. Reports covered reduced welfare payments, reduced funding for day-care centres, elimination of funding for halfway houses, and massive government layoffs of civil servants.

Funding reductions even affected the legal system. In 1995, the Ontario government failed to provide funding to the Ontario Legal Aid Plan at the levels agreed to in a five-year deal that was signed in 1994 with the Law Society of Upper Canada. As a result, some lawyers who had performed legal-aid services were denied payment. Others, fearing the same fate, either withdrew or tried to withdraw their services. In some cases, requests to withdraw were denied because the accused would be left without representation. In other cases, the charges were stayed against the accused until the lawyers' fees could be guaranteed.

The legal-aid lawyers brought a class-action suit against the Law Society of Upper Canada for failing to requisition the money from the government. The Law Society, in turn, sued the province for full funding in November 1995.

In 1994, the Manitoba government cut funding to the University of Manitoba's Access program from $1.6 million to $630 000. The Access program is designed to encourage aboriginal, minority, and disadvantaged people to attend university by providing funding for books and tuition and a living allowance. Since Access began in the 1970s, it has helped more than 200 graduates. Its most famous alumnus is Ovide Mercredi, the Grand Chief of the Assembly of First Nations, who graduated with a law degree.

When the government reduced funding for four aboriginal students attending the university from $263 to $144 every two weeks, the students sued for breach of contract.

On One Side

People who experience government cutbacks feel victimized by their governments. They believe that they are being treated harshly and unfairly. Some believe they were targeted because they are disadvantaged and do not have the resources to dispute the cutbacks.

Many of these people feel that if governments want to change or eliminate programs and their funding, they should first be required to pass legislation regarding these proposals. This would open the issues to debate and public scrutiny, giving elected representatives an opportunity to voice the concerns of the constituents who would be affected by the cutbacks.

On the Other Side

Those who support government reductions in funding point to the democratic process. People elect governments to make decisions for them. If governments are expected to reduce deficits and control government spending, then they must have the authority to do so. They cannot be expected to pass legislation on every government decision. It would be inefficient and costly.

Part of the government's mandate is to create, change, and eliminate government programs and funding. They do not regard these programs as legally binding contracts. Indeed, if they did, governments would be reluctant to create new programs, fearing the possibility of future law-suits if changes are necessary.

The Bottom Line

In 1995, the Manitoba Court of Queen's Bench ruled that the Manitoba government was at fault when it reduced funding for the four aboriginal students. This decision set a legal precedent. Legal-aid lawyer Arne Peltz, who represented the students, commented that "the implication is, that in some circumstances, when a government offers services or programs, these can now be viewed as legally binding relations."

Do governments have the right to reduce benefits at will? Or are government programs legal contracts that must be administered? You be the judge!

Lyle Bouvier, who worked as a miner in Flin Flon, Manitoba, saw an advertisement for the Access program at his job site. He is now studying for a law degree at the University of Manitoba. Bouvier says, "Without Access, I wouldn't have gone to university, period."

1. Indicate whether or not the five essential components of a contract are present when a government program is created by answering the following with an explanation:

   a) Who made an offer and who accepted it? How?

   b) What was the consideration?

   c) Was there legal capacity?

   d) Was there genuine consent?

   e) Was there legal purpose?

2. If a contract exists when a government program is created, what type is it—express or implied? Explain.

3. Do you think people and groups should have the legal right to sue the government for breach of contract when cutbacks take place?

4. What is your opinion of the 1995 Manitoba court decision? What legal precedent might be made?

5. Should there be any restrictions upon the rights of individuals or groups to sue the federal government?

Chapter Review

Reviewing Key Terms

For each of the following statements, indicate the key term being defined:

a) the cancellation or revocation of a contract

b) an untrue statement concerning important facts, made knowing it is false and done to deceive the party to whom it was made

c) a misunderstanding that arises when both parties to a contract are in error over the same basic fact

d) threat or use of violence by one party that forces another to do something against his or her will

e) improper pressure applied by one party to another to benefit the one who pressures, as in signing a will or contract

f) marketable condition; suitable for sale

g) "let the buyer beware"

h) a court order that requires the person guilty of a breach of contract to complete the obligations under the contract

i) failure to perform a major term of a contract, entitling the injured party to treat the contract as ended

j) a clause in a contract denying that guarantees or other representations have been made

Exploring Legal Concepts

1. Suppose you are allergic to peanuts. You order a stir-fry dinner after the server assures you that it contains no peanuts. However, the server is unaware that the chef uses peanut oil in the cooking, and you become very ill. Has any misrepresentation occurred? If so, what kind? If not, why not? What remedies, if any, are available to you?

2. You write to a recording company to order the newest Beatles' CD. Instead of the new recording, you receive the Beatles' hits from the sixties. What type of mistake has occurred? Can you have the contract voided? Explain.

3. When a person applies for life insurance from an insurance company, why is he or she required to disclose all material facts? What may happen if critical information is withheld?

4. Apart from money damages, what other remedies are available for a breach of contract action? When might they be used?

5. If a buyer and seller clearly agree that the title to a purchase of specific goods is to pass one week from today, and the goods are destroyed by flood in the meantime, who sustains the loss? Why?

Applying Legal Concepts

1. Philippe found an old roll-top desk in his aunt's attic and sold it to an antique dealer for $500. Later, he learned that the desk was used by Sir John A. Macdonald in his first law practice before he became Canada's first prime minister. Philippe demanded the return of the desk, and he agreed to refund the dealer the $500.

   • **Will Philippe's claim succeed? Explain.**

2. Dawn and Katie entered into a verbal agreement in which Dawn offered to sell her used car to Katie for $8800. Katie drew up a written contract, which both parties signed, that set the price at $8000. Dawn failed to notice the change at the time she signed the contract.

   • **What advice would you give Dawn about this situation?**

3. The six-piece rock group, Orange Banana, has been booked to play at a high school spring formal on May 3. Two days before the dance, a fire destroys the gymnasium where the dance and reception are to be held.

   • **Can the band sue the school's student council to recover damages for breach of contract? Explain.**

4. Brightman owed Webber $100 for some repair work done, and Webber kept pressing Brightman for payment. Feeling very irritated about this, Brightman went to Webber's store with the $100 in 25 cent pieces. Webber refused to accept this as payment.

   • **What are the rights and obligations of the two parties?**

5. Katco Manufacturing sold plastic pipe to the Centre '99 arena to be used as part of the ice-making equipment at the hockey and skating rink. The diameter of the pipe supplied was smaller than called for in the purchase order. After installation, the pipe cracked and split in several places. The arena owners took legal action for damages.

   • **On what grounds would they base their claim? Would they succeed? Why or why not?**

6. Billingsley purchased several cases of canned lobster for his specialty food store from the defendant seafood company, a Prince Edward Island processor of frozen and canned fish products. Several customers who purchased the lobster from Billingsley returned the products as inedible. After inspection by federal food inspectors, the entire lot of canned lobster was destroyed. Billingsley claimed damages from the processor for his loss.

   • **Will he succeed in his action? Why or why not?**

7. A door-to-door seller, Kirk Wilson, called on an elderly couple and tried to persuade them to buy some aluminum siding for their home. The home had been newly painted and was in good repair. When the couple said that they didn't need any siding, Wilson told them he had a great deal for them. The couple listened to the deal and then signed the contract. A day later, they realized that they really didn't want the siding.

   • **What can the couple do, if anything, about the contract they signed?**

8. *Roussel v. Saunders* (1990) Newfoundland Supreme Court, Trial Division
85 Nfld. & P.E.I.R. 228

The plaintiff, Suzanne Roussel, agreed to purchase a house and lot from the defendant husband and wife, Frank and Donna Saunders. Mrs. Saunders told the plaintiff that their home had a septic system and that it did not contain urea formaldehyde foam insulation (UFFI), banned by the federal government as a health hazard. Saunders said that the previous owner told her and her husband that there was a septic tank, and she relied on her husband's word that the UFFI they had installed had been removed.

When the plaintiff discovered that both statements were false, she refused to make any further mortgage payments and defaulted. The bank holding the mortgage sold the house at a public sale for a price less than the amount owing on the mortgage, and Roussel was required to pay the difference. She then brought a successful action for damages against the defendants and was awarded an additional $2500 in general damages.

- **Was the statement that there was no UFFI in the home just an opinion or a misrepresentation of fact? Explain.**

- **If misrepresentation existed, what type was it?**

- **Why was the contract for the purchase of this home not rescinded?**

- **For what would the plaintiff have been awarded $2500 in general damages? Do you agree? Why or why not?**

- **Why did the trial judge feel that punitive damages were not appropriate in this action?**

9. *Wade v. Hussein et al.* (1995) Alberta Court of Queen's Bench 166 A.R. 54

The plaintiff, Brian Wade, entered into a contract with the defendants, Raymond Hussein and Hugh Keith, operating as Hair Replacement Systems Edmonton, to purchase a hairpiece. Wade made it clear to the defendants that it was essential for him to have the hairpiece for a trip he was taking to Ontario, as he was self-conscious about his baldness. The defendants were aware of his travel plans and his departure date. The contract did not contain any guaranteed delivery date or any other promises or warranties, but the defendants promised Wade that his hairpiece would be ready on time. The plaintiff relied on these promises about delivery date to enter the deal and gave the defendants a deposit of $1250.

The hair piece did not arrive in Edmonton until shortly after the plaintiff had left for Toronto. The parties held some discussions by telephone in an attempt to deliver the piece to Wade, but a dispute arose over who would pay the $250 for that delivery. As a result Wade found another suitable piece, bought it for $805, and denied any further liability to the defendants.

In an action in the Alberta Provincial Court, Small Claims Division, the Court found in Wade's favour and awarded him $2055 for the cost of a temporary hair piece and his deposit.

The defendants appealed this decision to the Alberta Court of Queen's Bench where they were held liable under Alberta's *Trade Practices Act.*

- **What should the plaintiff have done when he negotiated this contract with the defendant to have avoided all of these problems?**

- Did a breach of contract exist here? If so, what type? If not, why not?

- Who do you think should have been responsible to pay the $250 delivery cost to get the hairpiece to the plaintiff in Toronto? Why?

- Why were the defendants found liable in this action? Do you agree? Why or why not?

Extending Legal Concepts

1. Now that you have completed this chapter, review the opening article and Something to Think About. Have your answers or opinions changed? Why or why not?

2. Explain the meaning of the following statement: "Consumers must be honest and must be prepared to accept their responsibilities in the marketplace."

3. In small groups, research the following information about a piece of federal or provincial consumer protection law. Each group should investigate a different statute.

    a) the date it became law

    b) the general intent of the law

    c) description of how it benefits consumers

    Prepare a group report on your findings, collect some brochures or pamphlets for a bulletin board display, and present your findings to the class.

4. From the report done in the above project on consumer statute law, review the findings of the report on the federal *Consumer Packaging and Labelling Act.* Working in groups of three or four, select one type of product, such as breakfast cereal, jam, shampoo, toothpaste, and so on, for your group. Have each member of the group bring different brands of that type of product to school so that your group can compare the product packaging and labelling.

    Prepare a spreadsheet, table, or chart that shows the different brand names of the product and answer the following questions:

    a) Does all of the information required by law appear on the package?

    b) Is there any additional information, not required by law, that might be useful to consumers?

    c) Is the name and address of the manufacturer or distributor clearly identified?

    d) Is the print easy to read?

    e) Does the printed text provide adequate consumer information?

    f) Are the illustrations on the package label misleading?

    g) Which are the best and the poorest labels? Why?

    Write a short report explaining how consumers might use this information to make a wise and sound buying decision.

5. Using reference materials in your resource centre, including CD-ROM, the Internet, and the *Misleading Advertising Bulletin* published by the Bureau of Competition Policy, a branch of Industry Canada (formerly Consumer and Corporate Affairs Canada), obtain current information on any of the following:

    a) recent misleading advertising convictions

    b) laws in your province regarding lotteries, gambling, and bingo games

c) the various provincial cooling-off periods

d) a comparative study of new-car warranties and what is and is not covered by them

e) anything else relating to contracts and consumer issues in this chapter

Write a one- or two-page summary of your findings, and, if possible or appropriate, create a poster to display your information.

Researching an Issue

Consumer Protection Legislation

Debate continues concerning the need for consumer protection legislation at both the federal and provincial levels. Although there was very active intervention by all levels of government from the late 1960s to the early 1980s in this area, there has been little new legislation in recent years.

Statement

Most services are not protected by consumer protection legislation even though they make up 50 percent of personal consumer expenditures. Therefore, it would seem that consumer protection legislation is unnecessary.

Point

The principle of *caveat emptor* should continue to apply, and consumers should be responsible for their own decisions.

Counterpoint

There are unscrupulous sellers who are prepared to take advantage of the illiterate, the weak, and the elderly to make a sale at whatever the cost.

- **With a partner, research this issue and reflect on your findings. Look at the initial flurry of consumer protection legislation and what protection it provided. Record the name of the legislation, the year of passage, and the level of government involved. Note the time when new legislation stopped.**

- **Prepare points on this statement that could be used for a class debate.**

- **Discuss your findings with others in your class.**

PROPERTY LAW—
LANDLORD AND TENANT

These are the key terms introduced in this chapter:

acceleration clause	lease	security deposit
assignment	lessee	security of tenure
escalation clause	lessor	sublet
eviction order	offer to lease	tenancy at sufferance
fixed-term tenancy	periodic tenancy	tenancy at will
joint tenancy	quiet enjoyment	
kind	right of distress	

Chapter at a Glance

Learning Outcomes

At the end of this chapter, you will be able to

1. distinguish among the different classes of tenancies;
2. state the implications of signing an offer to lease;
3. list the essential parts of a lease;
4. describe the rights of a tenant;
5. describe the rights of a landlord;
6. state the methods of ending a tenancy;
7. distinguish between an assignment of a lease and a sublet.

Query: My landlord is insisting that I pay him double the rent I owe.

A friend and I were roommates in a one-bedroom apartment. We had signed a lease as joint tenants and we each gave the landlord $90 monthly.

My friend ran short of money. He moved out and went back home to live for a while.

He didn't make his August rent payment. But I made mine. The landlord claims my roommate's $90 rent arrears is my responsibility. How can that be when the lease makes it clear that half the rent comes from my friend?

Gary Mandino

Response: The lease does not say that. It does say you are joint tenants. The law says that makes no difference to the landlord. If one joint tenant does not pay his share, the other is responsible to come up with the full amount.

From: "Action Line", by Roger Appleton. *The Ottawa Citizen.* Reprinted with permission of *The Ottawa Citizen.*

Joint Tenants Are Responsible for Their Roommates' Rents

Something to Think About

- What law covers the relationship between Gary Mandino and the landlord?
- If Mandino pays the landlord the additional $90 rent, how can he recover it from his friend?
- What options does Mandino have before the next month's rent becomes due?

19.1 INTRODUCTION

One of the key social issues facing each level of government in Canada is the provision of satisfactory accommodation for each citizen. Public housing has become a priority spending item for the provincial governments, with financial backing from the federal government. Rent controls have been instituted to try to balance the right of landlords to receive a fair return on their investment and renters' ability to pay. This chapter will focus on the law of landlord and tenant, which is the law that applies to those who rent property.

The law covering the landlord/tenant relationship developed as common law in England, and was adopted in the nine common-law provinces and the two territories of Canada. To clarify all the case law and to try to reduce the number of disputes the courts must resolve, each of the provinces has enacted an *Act* that applies to resi-dential tenancies. Each province has also passed a *Human Rights Act*, which prohibits landlords from discriminating when renting accommodation. This *Act* will be discussed later in the chapter.

A "landlord" is a person who owns property and agrees to allow another person to use it in return for payment. In this text, the term is also to be read as including "landlady." The word "tenant" refers to a person who rents a piece of residential or commercial property. This chapter restricts its discussion to residential tenancies. The term "residential tenancy" generally does not apply to rental accommodation in hotels, or to rooms with shared facilities in private homes or boarding houses for lodgers and boarders. In some provinces, residential tenancies include mobile home owners and those who have rented a plot of land for their trailer.

19.2 LANDLORD AND TENANT LAW

An agreement between a landlord and a tenant is called a **lease**, or tenancy agreement. In the lease, the landlord is called the owner or **lessor**—and the tenant is the occupier or **lessee**. In the agreement, the landlord agrees to rent a house or apartment to a tenant for a period of time under terms and conditions agreed upon by both parties. A lease can be verbal or written. Most people prefer a written lease that clearly and in detail outlines the rights and duties of both parties. Even though there may not be a written lease, there are still rights and duties under common law and provincial statute law. The terms of many of the provincial statutes are so detailed that the need for a lease is sometimes questioned. In practice, many short-term leases are verbal. If the lease has been signed by both parties, the landlord must ensure that a copy is given to the tenant. The time limit for delivering the lease varies: from the time of signing in New Brunswick and Newfoundland to 10 days in Nova Scotia and Quebec, 20 days in Saskatchewan, and 21 days in the remaining jurisdictions, except the Northwest Territories where the time limit is 60 days.

Leases for longer than three years generally must be in writing according to the *Statute of Frauds*. They should also be under seal and registered at the land registry office. However, if partial performance has taken place in such a situation, a verbal lease is usually enforced by the courts. Partial performance can consist of a rent payment, or just leaving personal possessions at rented premises.

Classes of Tenancy

The tenant is entitled to exclusive use of the property for the length of the lease. The class of tenancy is important since it indicates the date of possession and the amount of notice, if any, that must be given to terminate the agreement. There are four tenancy classes:

Fixed-term Tenancy. A definite, or **fixed-term tenancy**, expires on a specific date, without any further notice being required of either party to the lease agreement. If the tenant does not leave

at the end of the period, the landlord can ask the courts for an **eviction order**. For example, the renting of a ski chalet for a three-month period beginning January 1 automatically terminates on March 31 without any further notice. Notice would only be required if the lease indicates that it must be given.

Periodic Tenancy. A tenancy that runs from day-to-day, week-to-week, or month-to-month is a **periodic tenancy**. Such a tenancy usually arises when a tenant stays on and makes rent payments after a fixed-term tenancy expires, or when there is no written lease. For example, a person who has a fixed-term lease for one year will have a periodic tenancy at the end of the term if the lease is not cancelled. If rent is paid monthly, the periodic tenancy is month-to-month. Either landlord or tenant may give notice of termination in periodic tenancy. The notice required can be stated in the original lease if one exists. If not, the *Landlord and Tenant Act* of the province applies.

In some provinces, the distinction between fixed-term and periodic tenancies has been abolished, and notice of termination must be given for both. In all cases, it is usual that for a weekly tenancy, four weeks' notice must be given, and for a monthly or yearly tenancy, two months' notice must be given. Notice must be given in writing.

Tenancy at Will. When a landlord permits a tenant to stay in the rented accommodation but reserves the right to ask the tenant to leave without giving notice a **tenancy at will** arises. Obviously this arrangement is not very secure for the tenant, although there are times when the tenant may benefit from such an agreement. Say the date for the tenant to vacate arrives, but the tenant's new accommodation is not ready. The landlord might then permit the tenant to remain if no new tenants are waiting to move in.

Tenancy at Sufferance. A person who occupies premises against the will or without the knowledge of the owner has a **tenancy at sufferance**. This is similar to a trespass on the premises. A tenant who stays beyond the time limit agreed on in the lease falls into this category if he or she is not paying rent or is remaining without the permission of the owner. If the owner wishes to enforce his or her right in court, the tenant at sufferance is liable for a reasonable amount of rent due.

Joint Tenancy

When more than one person signs the lease a **joint tenancy** exists. Therefore, any of the above four tenancies could also be a joint tenancy. All parties signing the contract are liable not only for their own portion of the rent, but also for the total amount if the others do not pay. That is, if one tenant leaves before the termination of the lease, that person's share of the rent must be paid by the remaining tenants. If one person signs the contract, only that person is liable—other parties using the premises are not joint tenants in law. If they all move out, only the one who signed the lease is liable for rental payments. Of course, the other "tenants" have no rights unless they are recognized by the landlord. Thus, if the person who signed the lease moves out, the others have no right to stay. Some leases even indicate the number of people entitled to occupy premises.

Reviewing Your Reading

1. **What is a tenancy agreement? Who are the parties to it?**

2. **Distinguish between a residential tenancy and a commercial tenancy.**

3. **Distinguish between a fixed-term tenancy and a periodic tenancy.**

4. **Describe a tenancy at will. Give an example of how one might occur.**

5. **Describe a tenancy at sufferance. Give an example of how one might occur.**

6. **What is a joint tenancy? What are the special implications for parties to a joint tenancy?**

Did You Know

In Ontario, any provision in a written lease that is inconsistent with the provisions of the *Landlord and Tenant Act* is void and unenforceable.

HERMAN®

"We're sharing the apartment. He gets it Mondays, Wednesdays and Fridays."

19.3 *Entering into a lease*

Before actually entering a contract, a prospective tenant may be asked to sign an **offer to lease** by a superintendent of a building, who then forwards it to the landlord to make out the actual lease. Because the offer will become binding if accepted by the landlord, tenants should be extremely careful of signing such forms and of paying a deposit unless they are certain that they will be moving into the premises. If a tenant does not subsequently sign the actual lease and rent the premises, the deposit can be lost. Also, the prospective tenant is liable for damages should the landlord be unable to rent the premises to another party for

Labelle, Gross, and Michel each entered into a standard form lease with Minto Developments. The lease contained a provision stipulating that the tenants agreed to pay a $10 penalty if their full rental payment was not received by the landlord on the due date, the first day of each month. Section 100 of the *Residential Rent Regulation Act of Ontario* provides that "No landlord or any person acting on behalf of the landlord shall, directly or indirectly, in respect of any rental unit, (a) collect or attempt to collect from a tenant or prospective tenant of the rental unit any fee, premium, commission, bonus, penalty, key deposit, or other like amount of money." Minto Developments applied to have the court rule that the section did not prevent it from collecting the $10 penalty because it was reasonable and fair under the contract.

Minto Developments Inc. v. Labelle (1992)

Ontario High Court of Justice 29 R.P.R. (2d) 122

The court ruled that to allow the penalty for late payment would be tantamount to amending the clear wording chosen by the Legislature which saw fit to prohibit any and all "penalties" for late payment and made no exception to permit reasonable penalties. It would have the effect of adding to the *Act* a new exemption permitting a charge or penalty for late payment if they are fair and reasonable, usurping the function of the Legislature.

1. **What aspect of supremacy in law-making did the court recognize by its decision?**
2. **What role did the court fulfill in making its decision?**
3. **Why do you think the Legislature put the prohibition on penalties in the Act?**

the same period. However, some offers to lease do give prospective tenants a time period, such as a week, to decide whether or not they want to sign the actual lease.

Terms of the Lease

Leases have become refined and detailed to the point where they try to provide prior solutions for all possible disagreements. If no lease is drawn up, or an existing lease fails to cover certain points, the rights and obligations implied under common law or provided by statute are applied. The *Acts* relating to renting of property of some provinces specify certain terms that must apply even if the agreement signed by the landlord and tenant varies from the provisions of the *Act*. This is looked upon as protection for an unwary tenant. The landlord and tenant must therefore look to three sources for the law as it applies to their relationship: the common law,

the statute law, and the lease. The statute law often varies from province to province.

If a term of the lease is broken, a breach of contract has occurred. The landlord or tenant is freed from obligations of the lease and may pursue legal action. However, if a breach of law occurs, the innocent party is not freed from his or her obligations, even though he or she may seek remedy through legal action. For example, legal action taken by a tenant to make a landlord provide necessary repairs does not remove the tenant's obligation of rental payments. Similarly, to terminate the lease the landlord must take legal action. The grounds for such termination must also be found in the *Act*, not only in the lease. A term which frequently causes conflict between landlord and tenant is the right to have pets on the property. Generally a no-pets clause alone is not a sufficient ground for termination of the tenancy agreement unless the statute permits it.

CASE

Penfold v. Greater Vancouver Housing Corp.
(1990)

British Columbia Supreme Court
12 R.P.R. (2d) 213

Penfold was a tenant at a low-rent housing complex. Her lease had a clause specifying that no pets were allowed on the premises. She signed the lease in 1986, aware of the clause, but promptly moved in with two cats. She said that she looked around and saw other pets, but she did not question the landlord concerning it. Nor did she tell the landlord that she had pets. The landlord did not become aware of Penfold's breach of the clause until 1989. At that time the housing corporation sought to terminate the lease due to the cats being on the premises. The landlord said that its policy had always been to enforce the no-pets clause whenever it became aware of a breach and that it advertises its premises to all potential tenants as being free of pets. Penfold sued for a declaration that the clause in the lease was unreasonable, and for an injunction to restrain the landlord from terminating her tenancy pending a trial. The court ruled in the landlord's favour.

1. **Who will suffer the greater damage if the term of the lease is not enforced?**

2. **The judge stated that the plaintiff "does not come to equity with clean hands." What evidence is there to support this statement?**

3. **Why did the court rule in favour of the landlord?**

A lease should specify at least the following:

- the period of possession of the rented accommodation;
- a statement that the lessee is granted exclusive possession;
- the specific address of the property to be possessed;
- the amount of rent to be paid.

It is very common for a person to obtain a standard form lease from a stationery shop and fill in the blanks with the relevant information. In Manitoba, New Brunswick, and Nova Scotia, an approved standard form lease must be used. Leases will usually contain clauses pertaining to rent, security deposit, repairs, quiet and privacy, utilities and taxes, and liability for injury. These are described in the following sections.

Rent

The exact amount of the rent and when it is due should be specified in the lease. Leases usually specify that payment is due at the beginning of the month, though by common law it is due at the end of the month. It is the tenant's responsibility to deliver the payment of rent to the landlord. Rent is overdue the day after it should have been paid. If it is not paid, the landlord in some provinces can sue immediately, because the tenant has breached a condition of the lease. In other provinces, the landlord cannot evict the tenant for non-payment until the landlord has obtained a court order, and this takes time. Some leases contain an **acceleration clause** to the effect that, if a payment is late, advance payments, usually for three months, are due immediately.

Payment of rent can be in money or in **kind**, as when a superintendent is given a free apartment in return for his or her services. Tenants may voluntarily give postdated cheques to their landlords for the sake of convenience, but they do so at their own risk. This practice has been abolished in some provinces to protect the tenant. Protection may be needed where, for example, a landlord has sold the property and the rent is really due to the new owner.

Escalation clauses are sometimes used in leases to allow the landlord to increase the rent to cover increased costs. Though it is reasonable that the landlord should have this right, the tenant should be certain that the lease is so worded that only a fair increase is added to the rent.

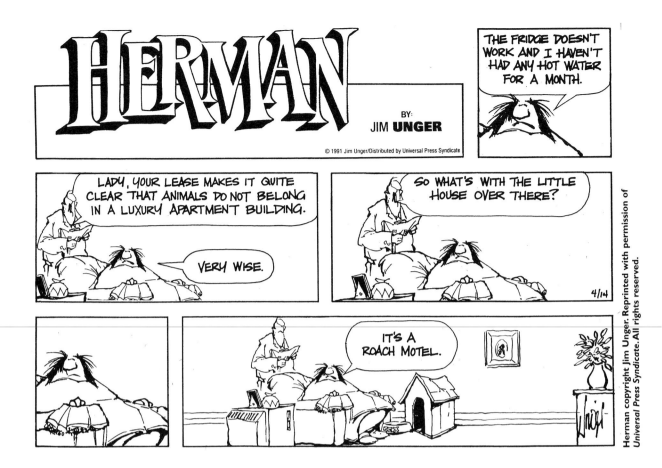

HERMAN

BY: JIM UNGER

© 1991 Jim Unger/Distributed by Universal Press Syndicate

THE FRIDGE DOESN'T WORK AND I HAVEN'T HAD ANY HOT WATER FOR A MONTH.

LADY, YOUR LEASE MAKES IT QUITE CLEAR THAT ANIMALS DO NOT BELONG IN A LUXURY APARTMENT BUILDING.

VERY WISE.

SO WHAT'S WITH THE LITTLE HOUSE OVER THERE?

IT'S A ROACH MOTEL.

Did You Know

The government of New Brunswick is the only government in Canada that keeps the interest earned on security deposits held in trust by the landlord.

If the landlord intends to increase the rent at the end of the periodic or fixed-term lease, then notice in writing must be given to the tenant. The provinces require either 90 days' or three months' notice. Manitoba, Newfoundland, Nova Scotia, Prince Edward Island, Ontario, Quebec, and Saskatchewan have rent control review. In these provinces, the law prescribes the amount of the increase that is allowed. An appeal process exists in each of these jurisdictions.

Security Deposits

The lessee is usually required to pay a **security deposit**. The requirements for, and use of, a security deposit vary from province to province,

as shown in the table on p. 506. The security deposit is held in trust by the landlord until the termination of the tenancy. Interest must be paid on the deposit; the rate varies by province. If there are unpaid rents during the tenancy, the deposit can be used to cover the amount owing in those provinces that permit it.

Some provinces, as shown in the table, allow the security deposit to be used for damage done by the tenant. When the tenancy ends, the landlord and tenant should view the premises and agree on the amount of the deposit that will be used for damages. If they cannot agree, the matter can be submitted to court. If there has been no damage by the lessee in a province that permits collection of a security deposit for damages, the fee should be returned. The settling of the amount to be withheld is probably the most common dispute between the landlord and tenant. In provinces that have abolished the collection of the security deposit for damages, the landlord must collect by suing the tenant.

Security Deposits: Amount and How They May Be Used

Province	Legislation	Amount of Deposit	Use of Deposit
Alberta	*Residential Tenancies Act*	one month's rent	as agreed
British Columbia	*Residential Tenancy Act*	one month's rent	unpaid rent, damage
Manitoba	*Residential Tenancies Act*	one-half of one month's rent	unpaid rent, damage
New Brunswick	*Residential Tenancies Act*	one month's rent	unpaid rent, damage
Newfoundland	*Residential Tenancies Act*	one-half of one month's rent	unpaid rent, damage
Northwest Territories	*Residential Tenancies Act*	one month's rent	unpaid rent, damage
Nova Scotia	*Residential Tenancies Act*	one-half of one month's rent	unpaid rent, damage
Ontario	*Landlord and Tenant Act*	one month's rent	rent for last period
Prince Edward Island	*Rental of Residential Property Act*	one month's rent	unpaid rent, damage
Quebec	*Civil Code*	one month's rent	rent for last period
Saskatchewan	*Residential Tenancies Act*	lesser of one month's rent or $125	unpaid rent, damage
Yukon Territory	*Landlord and Tenant Act*	one month's rent	rent for last period

CASE

Millan v. Hulsman et al.
(1990)

Alberta Court of Queen's Bench
9 R.P.R. (2d) 203

Millan rented his single-family dwelling to Hulsman. The rental contract was a homemade document prepared by Millan. It was for one year and covered some aspects of a landlord-tenant relationship but didn't deal with the question of responsibility for damage or insurance. After three months, Hulsman sublet the basement rooms to Tello. There was no written agreement. Millan agreed to the sublet. Evidence showed that Hulsman retained control over the premises as a whole, though he respected Tello's right to privacy.

There was a fire in the house. Tello told the fire inspector, Kilert, that he had had a metal ironing board against the side or front of the furnace. Kilert testified that Tello told him that there had been paper and other personal items on the ironing board and that he used it as a table. Tello denied having said this, but the judge accepted the evidence of Kilert where it conflicted with Tello's. Kilert testified that the paper items on the ironing board were in contact with the furnace and were ignited. Tello admitted that he knew that putting things against a furnace gives rise to a danger of fire.

Hulsman was aware that Tello kept his ironing board near the furnace, but had not seen any objects left on the ironing board. He said that he assumed the ironing board could stand heat because it was used to iron on. Millan sued for his loss of $30 730. Judgment was found in favour of Millan.

1. **What should Millan and Hulsman have done when entering into the lease in order to protect their respective interests?**

2. **What should Tello have done when entering into an agreement with Hulsman as a subtenant?**

3. **Why would the judge have accepted the evidence of Kilert over that of Tello?**

4. **What liability did Hulsman and Tello have, respectively?**

Repairs

Provincial *Acts* relating to landlords and tenants specify who will be responsible for repairs. Usually the landlord must provide and maintain the premises in a good state of repair and *fit for habitation* according to the health, safety, and housing standards in the locality where the property is situated. This includes getting rid of mice, cockroaches, and other pests. Since the dwelling is the landlord's investment, maintenance and most repairs are considered his or her responsibility. It would be unfair to have tenants make repairs that would benefit the landlord and future tenants.

The tenants, though, are responsible for ordinary cleanliness and must repair or compensate for any damage caused willfully or negligently by them, their families, or any of their guests.

Tenants have a number of ways to enforce their rights to have the property maintained in good condition. First, they are obligated to tell the landlord about any needed repairs that are the landlord's responsibility. If the landlord fails to respond, tenants should then make their complaints in writing. This provides a dated, written record of the official notification of the landlord, in case of any later disputes. If nothing is done after a reasonable amount of time, tenants can have the repairs done and deduct the cost from the next month's rent payment. However, the tenants can later be found personally liable if the repairs were not really required, or if repairs cost too much. If the landlord refuses to make the repairs or feels that they are not urgent, tenants can apply for a court order to either terminate the tenancy or request permission to make the necessary repairs. Tenants are also entitled to a reduction of their rent if they lose privileges during a period of repairs.

Quiet Enjoyment and Privacy

The right of the tenants to **quiet enjoyment** is a common-law right which is now guaranteed by statute. Quiet enjoyment means that tenants are entitled to use the property free from interference by another party. Although, by common law, the landlord has a right to enter the property of the tenants, he or she may be liable for trespass if proper procedures are not followed to gain entry.

Leases or statutes provide that the landlord cannot enter the premises unless there is an emergency, or if the tenant gives consent to the landlord at the time of entry. Written notice, given at least 24 hours in advance, is required in some provinces. Entry can then be made during daylight hours, or as otherwise agreed. Saskatchewan and New Brunswick prohibit entry on holidays and Sundays.

Leases and/or statutes may give the landlord the right to show the premises to prospective new tenants during reasonable hours, after notice of termination of the tenancy has been given by either party.

In some provinces, the law provides that the landlord cannot prohibit political canvassers from entering the building, although tradespeople can be restricted.

Finally, neither landlord nor tenants can alter the locks without the consent of the other. This is intended to prevent a landlord from evicting a tenant illegally.

Utility Services and Property Taxes

A variety of services is provided to people living in rented premises. Some of these must be provided according to local bylaws, so that the premises are habitable: water, adequate heat, electricity, garbage collection, sewers, and repairs. Other services are provided at the discretion of the landlord or the tenant: telephone, cable, and snow clearing. If services to which the tenant is entitled by law are not provided, the tenant should first notify the landlord. If there is no response, municipal inspectors should be notified. After inspecting the premises, they can issue an order for the services to be provided or necessary repairs to be carried out by the landlord. If the landlord refuses to comply, the tenant can apply to the courts for an order terminating the lease. Withholding payment of the rent, or some part of it, is not an option because that is a breach of contract.

Responsibility for payment for services should also be specified in the lease. Where the lease fails to specify responsibility, or there is no lease, the person contracting with the supplier is liable for payment. In multi-unit dwellings, the landlord might pay for water and heat, the tenant for electricity, telephone, and cable. Each tenant's rent also includes a fee to cover those services for which the landlord has paid.

CASE

Mayrand et al. v. 768565 Ontario Ltd.
(1990)

Ontario Court of Appeal
13 R.P.R. (2d) 2

Tenants in 127 units of an apartment building in Toronto sought a restraining order preventing the landlord from entering their apartments to make "repairs." The landlord wished to replace bedroom windows, living room windows, kitchen cupboards, counter tops, bathroom vanities or cabinets. Nothing had been replaced for 25 years. Some leases stated, "The Landlord may enter the rented premises and view the state of repair, and shall be entitled to make such repairs and alterations as are required and/or necessary provided that such entry shall only be made in accordance with the terms and conditions of the *Landlord and Tenant Act.*"

The landlord had sent letters to the tenants in question without inspecting each apartment. Some of the apartments had been inspected and found to be in need of repairs, so the landlord decided to do all of the apartments. The landlord stated that the matter of repairs he wished to make were "necessary to the overall management strategy of the landlord," and thus the economic factor was of very considerable importance. The plaintiff wanted the judge to adopt the definition of necessary as found in the *Oxford English Dictionary*, being "indispensable." The trial court ruled in favour of the tenants, but the defendant's appeal to the Ontario Court of Appeal was allowed.

1. **Did the landlord's proposed action in entering the apartments disturb the quiet enjoyment clause of the leases?**
2. **Who should determine whether the repairs are necessary—the landlord or the tenant?**
3. **Why would the tenants not want repairs to be done to their apartments?**
4. **In your opinion, were repairs necessary?**
5. **What could the judge award the plaintiffs as a remedy?**

The landlord is also responsible for paying the property taxes to the local government. Again, the tenant's share of the taxes is included as part of the rent. In jurisdictions not governed by rent-control legislation, some leases provide for an automatic increase in rent if the property taxes increase.

Liability for Injury

Generally, tenants are responsible for maintaining the safety of rental properties. They may be found liable for injury suffered by persons going onto the property, as outlined in Chapter 11 in the discussion of occupier's liability in the law of torts. In multi-dwelling units the landlord is liable for loss caused by injuries occurring in common-usage areas, such as hallways, stairways, and elevators.

Where the lease makes the landlord responsible for making repairs and where this obligation is imposed by statute, the landlord may be found liable if injury results because the necessary repairs were not made and the landlord knew the repairs were needed. Otherwise, the landlord is only liable to tenants for any loss suffered by tenants themselves, not their families, friends, or employees.

Where neither party is responsible for making repairs, either in the lease or by statute, an injured party can hold both the landlord and the tenant responsible.

Sparks had been a public housing tenant for over 10 years. She was a single black mother with two children and was on social assistance. She was given one month's notice by the Housing Authority to leave her residential premises. The one month's notice was specified in her lease. If Sparks had been a tenant of a private sector landlord, she would have had the benefit of the "security of tenure" provisions of the *Residential Tenancies Act of Nova Scotia.* Those provisions state that if a person has "resided in a residential premises for a period of five consecutive years or more, notice to quit may not be given except . . ." and then goes on to outline circumstances which are an exception. None of these applied in this case. The *Act* specifically stated that leases which are administered by the province or a municipality are exempt from the provisions, and the lease applies, as it did in Sparks's situation.

Dartmouth/ Halifax County Regional Housing Authority v. Sparks
(1993)

Nova Scotia Supreme Court
30 R.P.R. (2d) 146

Sparks sought a declaration that the *Act* contravened section 15(1) of the *Charter of Rights and Freedoms,* the right to equality before and under the law and the right to equal protection and equal benefit of the law without discrimination. The Housing Authority admitted that women, blacks, and social assistance recipients formed a disproportionately large percentage of tenants in public housing and on the waiting list for public housing. Sparks argued that she suffered adverse effect discrimination because of the provision in the *Residential Tenancies Act* and section 15(1) of the *Charter of Rights and Freedoms.* The Nova Scotia Supreme Court ruled that Sparks's rights had been violated.

1. **What is adverse effect discrimination?**
2. **On what grounds was Sparks arguing that her equality rights were violated?**
3. **What two groups were treated differently by the *Residential Tenancies Act*?**
4. **What obvious evidence is there that the people who qualify for public housing are a disadvantaged group?**
5. **In your opinion, did the *Residential Tenancies Act* discriminate against Sparks, and therefore violate her section 15 *Charter* rights?**
6. **If Sparks' rights were violated, could the *Act* be saved by section 1 of the *Charter,* which provided that there can be reasonable limits prescribed by law if they can be demonstrably justified?**

Landlords' and Tenants' Rights

A landlord's right to evict a tenant because of non-fulfilment of the lease varies by province. A landlord can evict a tenant or take possession of the premises only if a court order has been obtained. The landlord's right to enter the premises because of non-payment of rent cannot arise until a specified time has passed, which varies from province to province.

It is generally an offence for a landlord to harass a tenant out of the premises. A judge may refuse a landlord an order permitting eviction if the court finds that the landlord

- has not lived up to fundamental obligations;
- wants to evict a tenant because the tenant has complained to authorities about the landlord's violation of health, safety, or housing laws;

- is retaliating against a tenant who sought to exercise his or her legal rights;
- wants to evict a tenant because he or she belongs to a tenants' association or is trying to organize one; or
- wants to evict a tenant because of the presence of children (except in cases of overcrowding or premises unsuitable for children).

The landlord has to use the courts to obtain any rent owing, first by suing and then by collecting on the judgment through the use of any of the procedures outlined in Chapter 10.

At one time, the landlord had the **right of distress**, where he or she could enter the residence and seize the possessions of the tenant. This right has been abolished for residential tenancies.

Discrimination

The fact that each of us has our own value system can result in stereotyping, prejudice, and discrimination.

These were described in Chapter 2. Each province and the federal government have enacted human rights legislation to control discrimination, specifically in the areas of goods, services, facilities and accommodation offered to the public, and employment. The human rights statutes have primacy over all other provincial statutes, meaning that if there is a conflict between two statutes, the human rights legislation prevails.

A person who believes that he or she has been discriminated against can file a complaint with the federal or provincial human rights commissions.

Reviewing Your Reading

1. Why should a person be careful when signing an "Offer to Lease"?

2. What three sources must one look to in order to find the law as it applies to a landlord-tenant relationship?

3. What four clauses should be included in a lease?

4. What is a standard form lease?

5. Distinguish between an escalation clause and an acceleration clause.

6. What is a security deposit? What can it be used for in your province?

7. Summarize which repairs are the responsibility of the landlord and which are the responsibility of the tenant.

8. What services is a tenant entitled to receive? Where should the responsibility for paying them be specified?

19.4 CHANGING OR TERMINATING THE TENANCY

The tenancy of a specific person can come to an end in a number of ways. The tenant can surrender the lease and move out. A person may assign or sublet. The tenant can stay on after the lease terminates with the agreement of the landlord. Or the lease can end with proper notice having been given by either party. These options are examined below.

Surrender of the Lease

After entering into a lease, a tenant may encounter problems such as lack of finances, dropping out of school, or a change in life style. If the tenant decides to surrender the lease and leave the premises, the tenant is still liable for rent payments and the cost to the landlord of finding a new tenant. In such situations, the landlord has a responsibility to mitigate the loss. This means that the landlord must try to find a new tenant.

Assignment and Sublet

The terms assignment and sublet have different meanings. To **assign** a lease to another means that a new person will occupy the premises and pay the rent, thus becoming the new tenant until the lease terminates. The original tenant has no intent to return. To **sublet** an apartment means that the tenant either permits another person to take over the whole apartment for part of the term of the agreement, or rents part of the apartment to the other person. Under common law, the original tenant is liable for the entire lease for both an assignment and a sublet.

Wisniowski, a medical student, was a tenant in a property on College Street in Halifax. The landlord rented rooms to students only. Wisniowski paid $285 per month for room 25. He abandoned his tenancy about February 1. Cabrera, another tenant in the same premises was forced to vacate his room about February 20, due to flooding. On February 27, he moved into room 25 and stayed there for the remainder of Wisniowski's lease. He then leased the room for an additional year. On November 24, the landlord, Vinland Holdings Ltd., filed an application with the Residential Tenancies Board claiming damages against Wisniowski of $1830, being the value of the unexpired term of the lease, less the security deposit and interest of $155. The board ruled that a lease is also a contract and the damages accruing for the vacant room remain the same, whether or not the landlord has shuffled his tenants. However, since the landlord only rented to students and did not actively pursue other tenants, the board limited the damages to $997. Vinland Holdings Ltd. appealed the decision to the County Court, and Wisniowski filed a notice of objection and counter-application. That court ruled that Wisniowski's responsibility ended once Cabrera moved into the room. Vinland appealed that decision to the Nova Scotia Supreme Court Appeals Division, which ruled in favour of Wisniowski.

*Vinland
Holdings Ltd.
v. Wisniowski*
(1990)

**Nova Scotia
Supreme Court
9 R.P.R. (2d) 194**

1. **When Cabrera moved out of his room into Wisniowski's, the landlord still had an empty room. Should that influence the decision of the court?**

2. **What does it mean to mitigate damages?**

3. **What bearing did the fact that the landlord only rented to students have on the court's decision?**

4. **What amount of damages would the landlord be entitled to?**

A tenant can sublet his or her apartment for the summer months, or rent out one of the rooms in the home he or she is renting. The landlord is permitted to charge the original tenant a reasonable price for any actual subletting expenses incurred, such as drawing up a new lease for the new subtenant. The tenant in either a sublet or an assignment has the same rights and duties as the original tenant: the subtenant is liable for fulfilment of the contract even though the original tenant has the primary responsibility to the landlord. If the subtenant does not pay the landlord or causes damage, the original tenant can be liable for payment. For this reason, the original tenant is better protected if he or she is able to get the new tenant and the landlord to enter into their own agreement.

Although tenants have a right to assign or sublet their interests in the premises that they occupy, the landlord naturally has an interest in anyone who might become the new tenant. The landlord can thus require the original tenant to ask permission regarding the assignment. In the past, landlords often withheld such permission, preferring to rent an empty apartment to the prospective new tenant than to have someone take over an existing lease. Today, however, in most provinces if the tenant finds a person who will sublet the apartment or to whom the contract can be assigned, the landlord cannot unreasonably withhold permission. If the landlord does so, the tenant can apply to the courts for permission to sublet to a specific person. The only tenants who do not have the right to sublet are residents of public housing.

Tenant Staying On

A tenant may wish to stay in the premises at the end of the tenancy. If the landlord has not given the proper notice to leave, the tenant merely has to continue paying rent at the same times as previously. If the landlord continues to accept the payments, the tenant can stay. A periodic tenancy has then been established. If payment of the rent is made every month, then a month-to-month tenancy has been established. The terms of the provincial statute and the previous lease continue to apply.

In some provinces, such a tenant has **security of tenure**. This means that the landlord cannot remove the tenant simply by giving notice. The landlord must have reason. With no reason, the tenant can stay in the premises under a periodic tenancy. In Manitoba, Ontario, and Quebec, the tenant can be forced to leave only under certain circumstances. Similar rules apply in British Columbia, but the landlord can also terminate for "reasonable cause" in circumstances other than those set out in the *Act*. In Nova Scotia, special rules apply to remove a tenant who has had occupancy for five consecutive years or more.

The circumstances that allow a landlord to terminate the tenancy in any of these provinces can be divided into two broad categories:

- situations in which the tenant is at fault, such as undue damage, non-payment of rent, or disturbing others;
- situations in which the landlord wishes to change the use of the premises, such as to a condominium or to a family dwelling for his or her own family.

In the latter case, the tenant could challenge the reason given by the landlord for terminating the lease. It is usually necessary that the landlord demonstrate, in good faith, that the premises are required for the intended purpose. This requirement is to prevent landlords from making up reasons for terminating the lease because they want to get rid of the tenant. As well, statutes usually provide that the court can refuse to terminate the lease if there is evidence that the application is being made because the tenant has attempted to secure or enforce his or her legal rights.

CASE

Megan Investments Ltd. v. Funston
(1992)

Ontario High Court of Justice
25 R.P.R. (2d) 63

In 1969, Megan Investments Ltd. purchased a 77-ha farm, which contained four houses that the company rented out. Harry Zahoruk was a 50-percent owner of the company, and for many years he had carried on in the character of the landlord and performed all the duties and responsibilities attached to the position of landlord. His wife owned a 10-percent interest in the company. In 1989, Zahoruk and his wife applied for an order terminating Funston's tenancy in one of the houses so that their daughter, and possibly their son, could occupy the house.

Zahoruk attempted to raise the rent after the application, for he had never raised the rent by the annual increase allowed by the Ontario statute. He attempted to raise the rent from $475 to the maximum allowed, $595, and then because of $25 000 in improvements, to $1200. The rent was raised to $850 per month after the province suspended rent increase applications, on condition that Zahoruk make repairs. Funston searched but was unable to find suitable accommodation for his spouse and three children. Zahoruk allowed Funston more time to look and applied for possession in 1990 and again in 1991. On many occasions, Funston was late in paying his rent. In 1991, Funston delivered three months' rent at $595 because Zahoruk had not carried out the repairs.

Mrs. Zahoruk testified that her daughter was to be married, and that there was not enough room in their home for their daughter and her new husband. Her son lived in a rented apartment and could not afford the rent. The home in question, of the four on the farm, could most easily be divided into a duplex. The application was granted.

1. **Do the facts show that the Zahoruks in good faith required possession of the house?**
2. **Was there evidence that Zahoruk could have been applying for possession because Funston was trying to enforce his legal rights?**
3. **Should Zahoruk be given possession of the rented house?**

Termination by Notice

A landlord must give a tenant proper notice, even where security of tenure exists. The tenant in all provinces may terminate by giving proper notice to the landlord. The length of notice required varies greatly by province, and it also depends upon the reason for termination. Refer to the applicable provincial *Act* for details.

Reviewing Your Reading

1. **Distinguish between sublet and assignment of a lease.**
2. **Describe the rights of the tenant and landlord in subletting.**
3. **Describe the rights of the tenant and landlord when an assignment occurs.**
4. **What is implied if the landlord accepts the rent payments of a tenant who stays in the premises after the lease terminates?**
5. **What is security of tenure? Why has it been included in some of the landlord and tenant *Acts*?**

Rent Controls:

Should they be

eliminated?

In 1975, the federal government imposed wage and price controls in an attempt to control inflation in Canada. The provinces were asked to bring in rent controls to limit rent increases. This measure was designed to fight the war on inflation. Quebec and British Columbia already had such controls. The remaining provinces quickly passed the necessary legislation.

Rent controls were intended as a temporary measure that would be lifted once the battle against inflation was won. In 1978, the federal government suspended wage and price controls. However, only three provinces—New Brunswick, Alberta, and Manitoba—removed rent controls, to the dismay of the landlords and the relief of tenants in other provinces. Other provincial governments were reluctant to abolish rent control because it was a controversial issue that might cost them votes in upcoming elections.

In recent years, governments have become more conservative, and there has been a trend to limit and reduce government involvement in business activities. More provincial governments, like Ontario, are proposing to eliminate rent controls and let the market forces of demand and supply determine rent increases. These proposals have generated considerable controversy. Once governments grant even temporary rights or privileges to certain people or groups, it is difficult to take them back.

On One Side

Landlords oppose rent controls that limit the amount of rent they can charge. They argue that present rates do not cover the cost of repairs, heating, and taxes. Nor do rent increases keep up with mortgage rates, labour costs, and building materials. Moreover, since rent controls limit the return that landlords get on their investment, they find it more profitable to put their money in other business activities that have higher rates of return.

Increasingly, landlords are turning their rental properties into condominiums. These conversions reduce the number of rental apartments available to lower income groups. At the same time, fewer new apartment buildings are being built and governments are being forced to provide rental accommodation to low-income earners either as cooperatives or as subsidized housing. Eventually, there might be only one landlord—the government.

If rent controls were eliminated, the market would determine the levels of rent through

supply and demand. To protect the poor, a "shelter allowance program" could be established. Low-income tenants would pay what they could reasonably afford, and the government would pay the shelter allowance to landlords to make up the difference. Such a program would reduce government involvement in the housing industry, allow landlords to make a fair return on their investments, and encourage construction of new apartment buildings. It would also save taxpayers money and ensure that those who can afford to pay higher rents are not taking advantage of the system.

On the Other Side

Those who support rent controls maintain that controls are necessary to keep landlords from cheating tenants by charging exorbitant rents. Under rent control, government officials rule on the right to increase rents up to the percentage permitted by the government. Landlords who want rent increases above the levels set by the government must appeal to review boards. Stiff fines and legal requirements to reimburse tenants who have been overcharged allow fixed- and low-income tenants to have a decent standard of living.

Almost 12 percent of families that rent spend 50 percent or more on living accommodations. Advocates of rent control say that this figure would increase dramatically if controls were removed. Those who would suffer most would be low-income people who can least afford to pay high rents.

Even with rent controls, tenants are paying a greater percentage of their incomes on rent. Statistics Canada reported that in 1993, 31.5 percent of tenants in the Ottawa-Carleton region spent 30 percent or more of their incomes on rent. This compares with 24 percent in 1983. Imagine what would happen if there were no rent controls! Dan McIntyre of the Ottawa-Carleton Tenants' Association said, "I can't think of anything going up more than rents . . . They are being allowed to increase far faster than incomes are." Figures released by the Ontario Ministry of Housing tend to support him. In 1993, landlords were allowed to increase rents by 4.9 percent, while inflation was only 1.7 percent.

The Bottom Line

Rent controls continue to be a major issue in many provinces. Both sides have associations to protect their interests and present their cases to the government. The mood in many provinces tends toward the elimination of rent controls and less government control of the housing industry. What do you think? Should rent controls be eliminated? You be the judge!

1. **Working in groups as landlords or tenants, develop arguments to either eliminate or support the retention of rent controls. Present the arguments to the class.**

2. **In your opinion, what is the most important argument that each side presents on the issue of rent controls? Which is the most relevant?**

3. a) **Using the resource centre, research the cost of renting a two-bedroom apartment in your area for the years 1975, 1980, 1985, 1990, and 1995. Find out the average annual family income in your province for each of those years. Calculate the percentage of annual income that was required for rent in each year. Present your findings in a graph.**
   b) **Did rent controls influence these figures during this period in your province?**

CHAPTER REVIEW

Reviewing Key Terms

For each of the following statements, indicate the key term being defined:

a) to use one's property free from interference by another party

b) term allowing the landlord to increase the rent to cover increased costs

c) a tenancy created by two or more persons signing a lease

d) a tenancy for a particular period

e) an agreement wherein a person rents premises from the landlord for a term less than that held by the original lessee

f) a person who grants a lease of a property to another person

g) a person who rents property from the owner

h) a term of a contract requiring advance payments to be made if a payment is late

i) occupation of premises against the will of, or without the knowledge of, the owner

Exploring Legal Concepts

1. State 10 things that a person should check about an apartment before signing a lease.

2. In your opinion, should a landlord be able to evict a tenant who has not paid rent on time, or should the landlord have to go before a court to get an eviction order? Justify your answer.

3. Some landlords and some tenants make a video of the apartment on the date that occupancy begins and the day of termination. Why is this a good idea?

4. A student has a lease that states that 30 days' notice is required to terminate the lease. The provincial legislation indicates that a 60-day notice is required. The student gives 30 days' notice, and the landlord demands another month's payment of rent, stating that 60 days is required.

   a) Why should the termination notice be in writing? What should it include?

   b) In this case, is another month's rent due?

5. A tenant has an argument with his landlord and decides to pack up and leave his apartment.

   a) What advantages are there to doing this? What disadvantages?

   b) What must the landlord try to do in this situation?

6. Indicate what you would do as a tenant in each of the following situations:

   a) the landlord refuses to raise the heat above 18°C;

   b) the landlord states that you must leave at the end of your tenancy agreement, but you want to stay;

   c) the landlord states that a security deposit must be paid, equal to one-and-one-half month's rent;

   d) the landlord refuses to fix the stairs leading to your apartment, which are in dangerous disrepair;

e) the landlord decides to raise your rent by an amount greater than that allowed by law;

f) the landlord refuses permission to sublet;

g) the landlord makes frequent unannounced visits to the apartment, even while you are not there.

Applying Legal Concepts

1. White was a tenant for three years in an apartment where the stove and refrigerator were supplied. She asked the landlord, Thomas, for a new refrigerator and, in return, agreed to a rent increase of $20 per month. One $20 payment was made by White. She applied to social services for a $20 increase in benefits to cover the increased rent and was told that the landlord could not increase the rent without giving proper notice under the *Rent Review Act of Prince Edward Island*. She subsequently moved out of the premises, but sought return of her $150 damage deposit plus the $20 that she had paid as an increase in rent for the refrigerator. Thomas counterclaimed for $17 for a broken window and $47 for a new lock set because White wouldn't return her keys. As well, he felt that he was entitled to keep the $20 since he had not increased White's rent for nearly three years. Because White had agreed to pay the additional $20 per month, he did not feel giving notice to the Review Board was required.

   - **Is White entitled to the return of her one-time $20 rent increase that she paid?**

2. O'Brien leased an apartment for the period August 1, 1988, to July 31, 1989. He passed away on January 17, 1989. In late April, the administrator of O'Brien's estate agreed to sublease the apartment to a couple and requested the landlord's consent. The landlord refused. The administrator brought an application to have the landlord approve the proposed sublease on the basis that the landlord had unreasonably withheld consent. The landlord had a uniform policy of maintaining a written waiting list of prospective tenants for apartments in the several buildings he managed. The landlord's position was that, with regard to the waiting-list policy, his refusal to consent to the proposed sublease was not unreasonable. On May 25, the landlord served the administrator with a notice of termination effective July 31, 1989.

   - **Was the landlord unreasonable?**

3. Nuttall was the tenant in Unit 18 of a townhouse complex with her sister and Legault. Legault kept various constrictor snakes, lizards, and tarantulas in the townhouse. One day the reticulated python, which was between 4 to 6 m long and 10 to 15 cm wide, appeared between the window and the screen of the unit. The children sitting below saw the python and were frightened. Evidence was that the python was trying to get out, as the screen was bulging. The landlord then obtained an interim injunction to have the animals removed.

   When she applied for the lease, Nuttall stated that only she and her sister would be occupying the premises. The lease restricted occupancy to two adults and specified that the tenant will not do or permit to be done any act on the premises that will be deemed to be a nuisance or that will cause disturbance or inconvenience to any other tenant. No pets were allowed. Nuttall indicated to the court that when she signed the lease her intention was to house only cats in the premises.

When the landlord investigated the unit, he found that the locks had been altered contrary to the lease. The landlord received dozens of complaints from other tenants who feared for their safety. The *Landlord and Tenant Act* specified that a writ of possession can be issued to the landlord if there is an animal that is inherently dangerous to the safety of other tenants.

- **In what ways has Nuttall breached the lease?**

- **What order did the judge make in regard to the action taken by the landlord against the tenants?**

- **Should the application for a writ of possession be granted?**

4. *Pajelle Investments Ltd. v. Herbold et al.* (1975) Supreme Court of Canada 62 D.L.R. (3rd) 749

The Herbolds, mother and daughter, had rented an apartment in Toronto. The landlord had advertised that the premises were air-conditioned and that there was an indoor swimming pool and sauna bath available. These items were not, however, mentioned in the lease. Some time after the Herbolds moved in, the landlord failed to supply air-conditioning for one month in the summer, and the swimming pool and sauna bath were not usable for nearly five months. The landlord indicated that the facilities in question became unusable because of mechanical breakdown and large sums of money were required for repairs. The Herbolds also contended that the building in which their apartment was located was in a deplorable condition of repair. Other tenants called as witnesses for the landlord countered many of these latter arguments.

The Herbolds filed an affidavit setting out the problems, and the matter was heard by the County Court. It was eventually appealed to the Divisional Court, the Court of Appeal for Ontario, and then to the Supreme Court of Canada.

- **Where would the court look to find the responsibilities of the landlord and tenant regarding repairs?**

- **Should the court grant the Herbolds relief for not having the use of recreational facilities when these items were not specified in the lease? If so, what compensation should be given?**

- **What would be your decision in this case? Why?**

5. *Ozmond v. Young* (1980) Ontario High Court of Justice 28 O.R. (2nd) 225

Ozmond was the landlord of a house that he rented to Young for $630 per month, commencing June 1, 1978. The rent of $630 was payable in advance each month, and Young deposited 12 postdated cheques with Ozmond. On August 11, Ozmond was notified by the bank that the August rent cheque was not payable due to insufficient funds in Young's account. Ozmond went to the house, found nobody there, and could see through the window that there was no significant furniture. He went to the house with a police officer nine days later and entered. They both concluded that the house had been abandoned. The August rent was paid shortly thereafter.

On August 22, Young called to say that he was trying to sublet the house and thought that he could get a subtenant at more than the rent he was paying. The landlord said that he would also advertise, and he took a few people to see the house. Young took Henderson to view the house, and they struck a deal for Henderson to take occupancy on October 1. Young informed Ozmond, at which time Young said, "I guess that means I'll be owing the September rent," and Ozmond agreed.

On September 1, Young's cheque for September could not be paid to Ozmond by the bank for again there were insufficient funds. Fearing that he would not be paid, Ozmond removed Young's furniture from the house, and changed the locks. Young came to ask for his furniture, but Ozmond demanded payment for September. Young refused, saying that he did not owe it. Ozmond sued, seeking the September payment and $362 in expenses. Young counterclaimed to obtain his furniture.

- **Did either the landlord or the tenant take proper steps for terminating the lease?**

- **What acts taken by Ozmond would be considered illegal?**

- **Did any of the acts taken by Young indicate that he had terminated his tenancy before October 1?**

- **In your view, on what date was Young's tenancy terminated?**

- **How could Ozmond get the September rent from Young?**

- **What decision should be given in the case?**

Extending Legal Concepts

1. Now that you have completed this chapter, review the opening article and Something to Think About. Have your answers or opinions changed? Why or why not?

2. Prepare an organizer that shows the rights of the landlord and the rights of the tenant.

3. For each of the following situations, prepare a role-playing situation.

    a) a tenant trying to get the landlord to fix the sink in the bathroom of the apartment;

    b) a landlord trying to make the tenant aware that the surrounding tenants have complained of noise from the apartment;

    c) discrimination by a landlord who is renting an apartment.

4. Write a letter to your landlord to indicate that you wish to end your tenancy on April 30, the end of your one-year lease. Include all information that you think is essential.

5. Assume that you are a college student in your community, and wish to rent an apartment. Prepare a report on how you would proceed to find your apartment. Include in your report at least five advertisements from the newspaper showing apartments for rent. For each apartment, indicate why you would or would not be interested in renting it.

6. Using reference materials in your resource centre, including CD-ROM and the Internet, obtain current information on rental accommodation, rent control, discrimination and/or matters related to tenancy for your province. Write a one-page summary of your findings, and create a poster to display your information.

Researching an Issue

Government Involvement and Personal Property

Historically, a person's home has been looked upon as his or her castle. That is the reason criminal law provides a penalty for anyone who interferes with another's property. In recent years, the government has become more involved with what one does to and in one's house or property. For example, most local governments require maintenance standards be met on the outside of the property, such as cutting grass and making repairs. As well, bylaws usually require smoke detectors. As noted in this chapter, governments are prescribing the amount of rent for buildings. Legislation, such as human rights legislation, even indicates to some extent to whom a landlord must rent accommodation.

Statement

It is appropriate that over time, legislation has shifted from focusing on owner as "king" to owner as responsible landlord.

Point

The government, through bylaws and human rights and landlord and tenant legislation, has involved itself excessively in controlling the use that one may make of one's property.

Counterpoint

Government involvement is not excessive. Legislation is merely to protect the consumer and other residents of the community.

- **With a partner, research this issue and reflect on your findings.**
- **Prepare points on this statement that could be used for a class debate.**
- **Discuss your findings with others in your class.**

Chapter 20

EMPLOYMENT LAW

These are the key terms introduced in this chapter:

adverse effect discrimination

agency shop

agent

arbitrator

binding arbitration

certification

closed shop

collective bargaining

company union

constructive discrimination

discrimination

grievance

harassment

horizontal union

independent contractor

local

lockout

master

open shop

picket lines

poisoned work
  environment harassment

power of attorney

principal

proxy

quid pro quo harassment

servant

shop steward

strike

sympathy strike

union shop

vertical union

wildcat strike

work to rule

Chapter at a Glance

Learning Outcomes

At the end of this chapter, you will be able to

1. distinguish between an employee, an agent, and an independent contractor;
2. discuss common-law duties of the employer and employee;
3. distinguish between provincial and federal jurisdiction over employment;
4. outline various statutory rights of an employee and an employer;
5. outline the prohibited grounds of discrimination in employment;
6. describe how a principal-agent relationship can be formed;
7. discuss the duties of a principal and an agent;
8. describe the process for a union to be certified;
9. compare the rights of the employer and the employee during collective bargaining.

Wrongful Dismissal: Low- and High-Level Employees Treated Equally

Fifty-five-year-old Edna Cronk had worked in Hamilton for Canadian General Insurance Co. for 29 years and was earning $32 000 a year when she was called into her boss's office. There she was informed that her job was being eliminated because of internal reorganization.

Cronk had been working as an assistant surety underwriter, which involved analyzing the financial position of an office-building contractor and determining if it was an insurable risk for a construction project.

She was offered 9 months' pay as severance, but she refused and instead began an action for wrongful dismissal, seeking 20 months' salary as compensation . . . Judge James C. MacPherson of the Ontario Court of Justice ruled that she was entitled to the amount sought because of her age, the lack of work available in her specialized field of commercial insurance and her long years of service with the same company.

MacPherson went against the grain of wrongful dismissal case law. Up to then case law had maintained that the higher the position in the organization, the greater the compensation in wrongful dismissal, the assumption being that senior executives would have a harder time finding a job than more junior employees.

But MacPherson disagreed, stating that because of Cronk's work experience and grade 12 education, she would actually have more difficulty finding something else. "A secretary or cafeteria worker . . . who is fired will probably feel just as terrible as would the president of the same company if he or she were fired."

In fact, Cronk is still unemployed, not able to receive her small pension of $1000 a month until she reaches 60 years of age. She and her husband have had to sell their house and live on his pension.

From: Paul Weinberg, "Wrongful dismissal: low- and high-level Employees treated equally." *Canadian Lawyer*, March 1995. Reprinted with permission of Paul Weinberg.

Something to Think About

- **Would it be more difficult for Cronk to find a job than a senior executive?**
- **Should the amount of notice for dismissal be fixed by statute law for all employees?**
- **Does the law favour the employer or the employee in rights and duties?**

20.1 INTRODUCTION

Employment law is important to us all. Many years of our lives are spent either owning a business and hiring people, or working for someone else. During these years, each of us, or our representatives, will be involved in the negotiation of employment contracts. That process can best be accomplished when both parties are aware of their rights and responsibilities. Conflict between employers and employees usually fluctuates with the state of the economy.

In the early 1990s, Canada's economy was in a downturn. Businesses and governments were downsizing. Many employees were laid off or forced to take a reduction in pay and/or benefits. Governments, caught in a squeeze of high debt payments with less revenue, made many large-scale cutbacks. During this time a lot of discussion took place on the rights of employees. Many of these are outlined below.

20.2 THE EMPLOYMENT CONTRACT

An employment contract must have all the necessary elements that are outlined in Chapters 17 and 18. Many employment contracts for young people working at part-time jobs or for lower wages are informal and usually verbal. Some casual labourers also may have verbal contracts. Other employment contracts are put in writing to protect both parties. If employment is intended to be for longer than one year, the *Statute of Frauds* requires a written agreement.

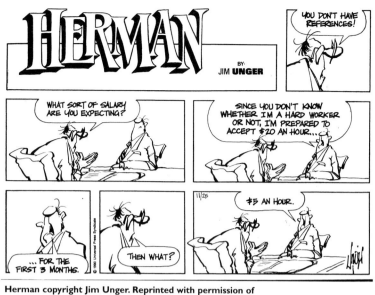

HERMAN

BY: JIM **UNGER**

YOU DON'T HAVE REFERENCES!

WHAT SORT OF SALARY ARE YOU EXPECTING?

SINCE YOU DON'T KNOW WHETHER I'M A HARD WORKER OR NOT, I'M PREPARED TO ACCEPT $20 AN HOUR...

... FOR THE FIRST 3 MONTHS.

THEN WHAT?

$5 AN HOUR.

Herman copyright Jim Unger. Reprinted with permission of *Universal Press Syndicate.* All rights reserved.

Individual and Collective Bargaining

About 60 percent of employment contracts are entered into individually—the employer and employee negotiate the terms of the contract. The remaining 40 percent of contracts are with union members who enter a contract through collective bargaining.

Many employees at the low end of the pay scale and who do not have a union to negotiate on their behalf do not bargain at all. The employer offers a job at a certain pay and with certain benefits, and people apply.

For those who do bargain on their own behalf, three different types of contracts can result:

- the employer and employee relationship;
- the principal and agent relationship;
- the client and independent contractor relationship.

Each of these relationships will be examined in detail.

Common Law, Statute Law, and Collective Bargaining Law

The common law dealing with the employment relationship is for the most part contract law, and it has been developed over time by the courts. Judges resolved disputes over contracts that were not evidenced in writing (verbal contracts). In cases of a written employment contract, courts resolved disputes over implied terms (terms that were not expressly written into the contract, but relied upon by one of the parties as part of the agreement). Courts also helped resolve disputes over the interpretation of express terms in the written contract. Governments have enacted statutes that have modified the common law of employment. The general rule now is that the common law applies only if the statute law is silent on the matter under dispute.

Some of the elements of the employment relationship that are currently controlled by statute law are minimum wage levels; hours of work per day and per week; overtime and vacation pay; and working conditions.

The statute law defines the minimum standard required by law. An employee bargaining for him or herself, or a union bargaining for a group of employees can negotiate to obtain greater benefits than are prescribed by law. These negotiated agreements are the first place an employee should look to answer a question about his or her rights. If the agreement does not deal with the question, then the employee should look to the statute law. If the statute is also silent, then the common law applies. Students should always take care—especially when they are entering verbal employment contracts—to know what their rights are under statute and common law.

Reviewing Your Reading

1. **What type of employment contract must be put into writing?**

2. **Distinguish between individual bargaining and collective bargaining.**

3. **What three types of relationship may arise from individual bargaining?**

4. **What does statute law provide for all workers?**

5. **What three legal forces govern most employment relationships?**

20.3 EMPLOYER AND EMPLOYEE RELATIONSHIP

For many years the relationship of employer and employee was referred to as the law of Master and Servant. The term may appear outdated by present standards, but the employer is still the **master** and the employee, the **servant**. Employees can be directed by their employers as to what work they will do and the manner in which it will be done. Additionally, employees cannot enter into contracts on behalf of their employers. This is important to keep in mind, so that the relationship of employer and employee can be contrasted later with the relationship of principal and agent. Common law and statute law as they apply to the employer-employee relationship are outlined below.

Common Law and Employment

The common law relating to employment developed in England and was inherited by Canada. It is not often referred to in employment disputes now, for disputes can usually be resolved by reference to statute law. However, the common law still imposes certain duties on the employer and employee, which may not be governed in other ways.

In the past, an employee injured at work because of an employer's breach of duty could sue the employer. Today, the employee would receive Workers' Compensation instead.

Duties of the Employer

An employer must

- pay the agreed-upon wage or salary;
- pay for any agreed-upon expenditures made by the employee in the course of duties;
- provide the employee with a safe place to work, and fellow-workers who possess the necessary skills;
- provide work of the type the employee was hired to do, where the job involves a skill;
- allow the employee to moonlight, that is, engage in a second job, provided that the second job is not in competition with the first;
- not assign jobs that are contrary to law, or in violation of the terms of the contract.

Duties of the Employee

An employee must

- be punctual and take only permitted leaves of absence;
- obey legal and reasonable orders;
- be loyal, honest, and competent;
- not be grossly immoral or habitually drunk, on the job or elsewhere.

Apart from the condition of safety imposed upon the employer, employees are considered to accept the normal risks inherent in their occupations. Moreover, regard and care for personal safety are also expected from each employee.

An employee who fails in any of his or her duties is in breach of the employment contract. The employer has the right to declare the contract at an end and to dismiss the employee.

When dismissing an employee where no contract exists, the employer must give a reasonable amount of notice or payment in lieu of notice. The amount of notice required under common law is a "reasonable" notice considering all relevant factors including such matters as years of service, employee's age, availability of similar employment, and employer's financial position. If wrongfully dismissed, or proper notice is not given, the employee can sue for money damages. The court will have to rule if the employee has been dismissed for a just cause, or if improper notice was given. If the court finds in favour of the employee, it will not order that the employee's position be reinstated, except in human rights matters. In many situations, an employer will pay an employee in lieu of giving notice.

An employer is also responsible for any torts that the employee may commit as long as the employee was acting in the course of his or her employment. Thus, an employer is liable to a passer-by who is struck by a piece of scaffolding at a construction site as a result of an employee's negligence.

Statute Law and Employment

The *Constitution Act, 1867,* gives the provinces jurisdiction over civil rights. The right to enter into a contract is considered a civil right; therefore, most statutes relating to employment are provincial. For this reason, the employment law in Canada varies greatly from province to province as discussed below. Federal statutes applicable to employment law only cover those occupations that fall under the federal government's jurisdiction according to the *Constitution Act, 1867,* such as, professions in the post office, in banking, and national defence. When looking for the statute governing employees in a particular occupation, one must know the jurisdiction under which the occupation falls, and whether a special statute is in force. For specific details regarding legislation, contact the provincial Ministry of Labour or the federal Department of Labour.

CASE

T he plaintiff, Gilmour, entered into an agreement with the defendant, Mossop, to be his housekeeper. Mossop's home was a bungalow with a stairway leading from the kitchen into the basement. He owned two house dogs, a Scotch terrier and a Highland terrier. The defendant's married daughter had spent the first two weeks of Gilmour's employment living in the house to explain Gilmour's duties to her. At that time, Gilmour was informed that the dogs were "rather fond of lying on the basement stairs." Gilmour grew attached to the dogs, allowing them to be in the kitchen while she worked.

Mossop, his son, and Gilmour sat down to dinner one evening when Gilmour realized she had forgotten some food that was in the basement. At the top of the stairs, she switched on the basement light which was located on the ceiling at the bottom of the stairs. She then stepped on the Scotch terrier lying on the top step and fell down the stairs, sustaining injuries. She sued her employer.

It was noted at trial that the doorway from the basement led directly into the kitchen, and one of the lights in this room, when turned on, would materially improve the lighting at the head of the stairs. The light was not on when Gilmour fell. There was no handrail on either side of the stairway.

The trial court found in Gilmour's favour, but the decision was reversed on appeal.

Gilmour v. Mossop
(1951)

Supreme Court of Canada
4 D.L.R. 65

1. **According to common law, what responsibilities did Mossop, as employer, have in providing a place to work?**

2. **Did Mossop arrange for Gilmour to be given adequate instructions?**

3. **Were the working conditions which Mossop provided for his employee adequate?**

4. **Why was the original decision reversed on appeal? Do you agree with this judgment?**

Provincial Statutes

Each province has passed numerous *Acts* relating to employment. Some of these *Acts* apply in general, such as *Employment Standards Acts* or *Codes*; others apply to specific occupations, such as teaching, accounting, and medicine. Although employment law varies across Canada, important concerns find expression in each province's statutes. These will be discussed below.

Wages

To ensure an adequate standard of living, each province prescribes a minimum wage for every employee. This minimum wage increases regularly to keep up with cost-of-living changes. Some occupations may be exempt or have special rates applied to them. The various provincial Ministries of Labour have detailed information concerning these occupations.

Canadian Hourly Minimum Wages, November 1995

(for adult workers)

Alberta	5.00
British Columbia	7.00
Manitoba	5.25
New Brunswick	5.00
Newfoundland	4.75
Northwest Territories	6.50
Nova Scotia	5.15
Ontario	6.85
Prince Edward Island	4.75
Quebec	6.45
Saskatchewan	5.35
Yukon Territory	6.72
Federal	4.00

Source: Labour Canada.

An employer is required to give a statement to an employee at the end of each pay period, indicating the pay for the period and explaining all deductions. Payment must be in cash or by cheque. It is illegal to force an employee to accept pay in kind (in the form of the products of the business). Should the employer become bankrupt, the employee still has a claim for the amount earned. A claim should be made to the trustee who is appointed to look after the business as soon as there is a bankruptcy. Some provinces have instituted a fund from which wages earned are paid to those who do not receive them from bankrupt firms.

Time at Work

All provinces have established the 8-hour work day as the normal time period full-time employees will work for their regular rate of pay. All provinces have set maximum hours per week that an employee can be required to work before receiving an overtime rate of pay (usually time-and-a-half). All provinces also set a maximum number of hours in a week that an employee can be required to work for any amount of pay, usually 48, unless a permit is obtained from the Ministry of Labour for extended hours.

All provinces have statutory holidays for which full-time employees must be paid. They include New Year's Day, Good Friday, Victoria Day, Canada Day, Labour Day, Thanksgiving Day, Christmas Day, and Boxing Day. Substitutions can be made so that employees who must work a holiday, such as police officers, medical staff, firefighters, and other emergency personnel, receive an alternative day off. Pay for working a holiday varies—it may be as high as 2 1/2 times the regular hourly rate.

The provisions of the various Sunday shopping laws restrict various businesses from being open to the public on Sunday, and thus employees do not have to work on that day. Employees who do work on a Sunday must be given an alternative day of rest during the week. Legislation in provinces that have Sunday shopping requires that the employee be given a specified number of consecutive hours off, usually 36, during a week-long period. As well, in Ontario, the employee has the right to refuse Sunday work with no reprisal.

With some exceptions, employees are entitled to vacations with pay. An employee must usually work for a year before being eligible for a vacation. Two weeks of annual vacation are given in all provinces except Saskatchewan, which awards three weeks. As a benefit of employment, employees are often given longer vacation terms the longer they work for their employer. Employees are entitled to vacation pay from the date of employment. The pay for a vacation period must be given within a month of the anniversary date of the worker's employment in most provinces, although it is customarily given when the vacation begins. In some provinces, pay can be given instead of an annual vacation. Vacation pay is usually 4 percent of the employee's earnings.

Maternity leave is also granted in each province, without pay, if the employee has worked for a specified period. The length of leave also varies, generally 17 or 18 weeks. A pregnant employee cannot be laid off because of her pregnancy and usually must be reinstated in the same position when she returns. If the mother wishes to return before she has taken the full leave period, she may do so if she has given the employer proper notice of her intention, usually 4 weeks. In addition, any employee who has paid into the Employment Insurance fund is entitled to 15 weeks of employment insurance payment while on maternity leave.

Parental leave is also available. Both the mother and father may apply for it. The mother is usually required to take parental leave immediately after her maternity leave. The father can take the leave immediately after the birth of the baby. In either case, the leave must be taken within a specified time after the birth usually within 9 months. The leave varies by province, but is usually up to 18 weeks. A mother could therefore combine her maternity leave and parental leave and receive a total leave of approximately 9 months. Adoption leave has also been introduced in most provinces. Time limits are the same as for natural parents.

Minimum Age

The age that a person can begin to work full time differs by province, depending on school attendance laws and the type of work. Schooling is generally compulsory until the age of 16. Young people are prohibited from working in some occupations that may be injurious to their lives, health, education, or welfare. In addition, there are restrictions on which hours may be worked, such as school hours and late at night. This legislation is intended to protect minors from exploitation.

Pay Equity

Pay equity works to diminish the disparity between men's wages (higher) and women's wages (lower). Requirements are contained either in the *Human Rights Act* of the province, or in the *Employment Standards Act*. The issue of a wage gap between the two genders is resolved in one of two ways in the legislation. The first is to base the legislation on the principle of "equal pay for equal work." The second, and that used in the *Canadian Human Rights Code* and some provinces, is the principle of "equal pay for work of equal value." The former requires that the employer pay males and females the same amount for substantially the same kind of work—work that requires the same skill, effort, or responsibility and is performed under similar working conditions. "Equal pay for work of equal value" requires payment based on the comparative value to the employer of the jobs being performed. Under the latter system, a ranking of skills needed and responsibilities involved in each task at the job site is required. Each job ranked at the same level receives the same pay, whether a male or female is doing the job.

Did You Know

In 1994, of the people admitted to the bar between 1976 and 1985, 81 percent of the women were earning between $25 000 and $75 000, while 78 percent of the men made between $50 000 and $150 000.

Employment Equity

Employment equity is one of the more contentious issues in labour law. Also known as affirmative action, employment equity is a policy to increase hiring rates for certain target groups—specifically, women, the physically challenged, ethnic minorities, and Native people. It also focuses on eliminating barriers to professional development and training and promotion within the workplace. The federal government has had employment equity legislation in effect for the hiring of public servants since 1986.

Human Rights in Employment

Human rights legislation sets out the principles of equality and provides for freedom from discrimination on the grounds of age, race, gender, religious beliefs, sexual orientation, and physical capabilities.

Discrimination as understood by human rights legislation occurs whenever a person is denied

employment, accommodation, or access to a public facility, among other things, due to personal characteristics. For example, if a man is denied employment as a nursing assistant because the employer believes men "do not make good nurses," the man has grounds for a human rights complaint. This kind of discrimination is termed direct discrimination, and it violates human rights legislation.

When an employer denies work to an otherwise qualified individual on the grounds of personal prejudice against the individual the discrimination is intentional. However, discrimination does not have to be intentional to violate human rights law. For example, an advertisement to recruit police officers could state that applicants have to be a minimum height and weight. Although there may be no intention on the part of the hiring police force to discriminate against anyone, the height and weight requirements would effectively eliminate some people from qualifying for the job. This kind of discrimination

Distribution of Complaints, by Ground of Discrimination, 1991 to 1994

Ground	1991		1992		1993		1994	
	#	%	#	%	#	%	#	%
Sex	237	24	316	24	304	25	373	27
Race/colour	101	10	111	9	71	6	139	10
Disability	313	32	424	33	362	30	420	31
Family/marital status	106	11	134	11	109	9	82	6
Age	88	9	142	11	143	12	154	11
National/ethnic origin	118	12	143	11	101	8	99	7
Religion	17	2	10	1	22	2	37	3
Pardon	4	0	2	0	2	0	4	0
Sexual Orientation	—	—	—	—	100	8	64	5
TOTAL	984	100	1282	100	1214	100	1372	100

Source: Canadian Human Rights Commission.

O'Malley worked for Simpsons-Sears Ltd. as a full-time sales clerk in the ladies' wear department. The store was open Thursday and Friday evenings and Saturdays. The period from Thursday evening to Saturday at closing was described as the "time for selling." Therefore, a condition of employment was that full-time sales staff would work Friday evenings on a rotating basis, and two Saturdays out of three.

O'Malley became a member of the Seventh-Day Adventist Church. A tenet of this faith is that the Sabbath, which extends from sunset on Friday to sunset on Saturday, must be strictly kept. As a result, O'Malley could no longer work Saturdays. She was told she could not stay on as a full-time employee, but that she would be offered any tasks that would accommodate her personal requirements. Simpsons-Sears then offered her part-time work, which came to half her previous number of work hours. She accepted this offer, but brought a complaint to the Ontario Human Rights Commission under the *Human Rights Code*.

The Commission's board of inquiry considered two matters. First, is there discrimination when a policy, such as the one requiring full-time staff to work Saturdays, applies equally to all employees, but adversely affects one or more employees? Second, if there is discrimination, how far must the employer go in accommodating the religious beliefs of the employee to avoid discriminating?

The complaint was dismissed by the board of inquiry. O'Malley's appeal to the Divisional Court and the Court of Appeal of Ontario were subsequently dismissed. Each court held that there must be intent for discrimination to occur. O'Malley appealed to the Supreme Court of Canada, which ruled that intent was not a necessary element of discrimination under the *Human Rights Code*.

Re Ontario Human Rights Commission and Simpsons-Sears Ltd.
(1985)

Supreme Court of Canada
23 D.L.R. (4th) 321

1. **Which of the prohibited grounds of discrimination in employment was at issue here?**
2. **According to the courts, is an employer discriminating if its work policies apply equally to all employees? Do you agree?**
3. a) **Could Simpsons-Sears Ltd. have accommodated O'Malley? How?**
   b) **What problems might this accommodation have caused Simpsons-Sears?**
4. **What does adverse effect discrimination mean?**

that inadvertently has an impact on certain groups in society on the grounds of seemingly neutral requirements is called **adverse effect discrimination**. The accompanying case, *Ontario Human Rights Commission and Simpsons-Sears Ltd.* illustrates adverse effect discrimination.

The prohibited areas of discrimination in employment are covered in the *Canadian Human Rights Act* and the human rights legislation of each province. They apply to matters under federal and provincial jurisdiction, respectively. The human rights statute in each province has primacy over all other provincial statutes. In other words, if there is a conflict between the two statutes, the human rights legislation prevails.

Because discrimination can begin at the hiring stage, each province regulates the type of questions that may be asked during an interview.

Similarly, employment advertisements cannot include qualifications that would discriminate against some potential applicants.

To be non-discriminatory, an employment requirement must have a direct bearing on the ability to do the job. The job requirement may have the effect of eliminating some people as candidates for a job. This is called **constructive discrimination**. However, so long as it is a reasonable and bona fide job requirement, an employer may impose the requirement without contravening human rights laws. For example, a moving company may justifiably not hire people who are not strong enough to do the work. The mover may not place an advertisement for the position requiring applicants to be of a certain height or weight, for these characteristics have nothing to do with strength.

The government has the right to pass employment-equity legislation that might seem discriminatory. For example, a government may initiate a retraining program and restrict it to the unemployed without discriminating against others who might be interested in the program. Or an employer may advertise a job as being open to physically challenged persons only.

Harassment

In recent years, a form of discrimination that has received a lot of focus is **harassment**. It has been defined as ". . . a course of vexatious comment or conduct that is known or ought reasonably to be known to be unwelcome." Harassment often originates from a party who is in a position of power over the person being harassed. Both federal and provincial human rights legislation provide that anyone who has experienced harassment may bring an action against the person responsible, or against the employer for not taking action to prevent harassment. Specifically, the legislation states that every person has the right to freedom from harassment in the workplace by his or her employer, an agent of the employer, or another employee.

Harassment generally falls into one of two categories: *quid pro quo* **harassment** and **poisoned work environment harassment**. *Quid pro quo* is Latin meaning "something for something." This type of harassment occurs when a person in a position of

power uses that position to force others to do things, such as submit to sexual advances, as a condition of keeping a job. In poisoned work environment harassment, employees who differ from the rest by gender, race, religion, or some other characteristic are subjected to hostility or intimidation by others in the workplace.

Termination and Dismissal

Common law requires that the employer or employee give notice if terminating the employment. The amount of notice required varies, but is usually one week's notice for each year of employment up to a maximum of eight weeks. However, if the employee has been with the business many years, is older, or has been in a senior position, the time period required may be much longer. Notice is not required if the job was for a fixed period, if the employee violated the common-law duties of an employee, or if the work has come to an end because of an unforeseeable event. In fact, in recent years, many businesses have dismissed employees and given them pay in lieu of notice to protect the assets of the business or provide a more positive working environment for the remaining employees. Such dismissal has become more common because of business reliance on computers, for the dismissed employee could easily take, alter, or destroy essential data. At times, employees have been called to a meeting, asked to hand in their keys, and been escorted to their offices to pick up their personal possessions.

Where dismissal of large numbers of employees is contemplated, the provinces require that notice also be given to the government so that assistance can be given in relocating employees.

Dismissed employees are entitled to severance pay. The amount varies depending upon the length of employment. It must be paid soon after the date of termination, usually within two pay periods. A person who breaches the employment contract by failing to honour his or her employee duties can be dismissed without notice and is entitled to wages to the date of the dismissal. As noted earlier, an employee can sue for wrongful dismissal or dismissal with improper notice.

In recent years, some employers have forced employees to resign rather than dismissing them. This approach, called constructive dismissal,

Susan Daigle was employed as a receptionist/clerk-typist in the Fire Prevention Division of the City of Fredericton. For financial reasons, it was very important to her to succeed in this position. Daigle's employment was terminated five weeks short of the six-month compulsory probationary period. The reason given was constant spelling and typing errors.

Daigle filed a complaint with the Human Rights commission, alleging discrimination on the basis of gender. She submitted that the unprofessional atmosphere in the workplace, together with sexual harassment, adversely affected her ability to do satisfactory work. She stated that she had been subjected to questions of a personal sexual nature by Keith Hunter, as well as to poking and aggravating conduct.

A board of inquiry noted that the Canadian Human Rights Commission held that any of the following constituted sexual harassment: verbal abuse or threats; unwelcome remarks, jokes, innuendo, or taunting; the display of pornographic or other offensive or derogatory pictures; practical jokes which cause awkwardness or embarrassment; unwelcome invitations or requests, whether indirect or explicit, or intimidation; leering or other gestures; unnecessary physical contact such as touching, patting, pinching, punching, and physical assault.

Case law quoted in the inquiry indicated that using coarse language, showing a pornographic picture, and making sex jokes are not in themselves sufficient for harassment. The incidents must occur with a combination of frequency and offensiveness which warrants the inference that exposure to such conduct in a place of employment constitutes discrimination.

The board found that sexual harassment had not taken place. There was no evidence that the conduct was frequent. Daigle's evidence on the matter was contradicted by a number of witnesses. Moreover, Daigle had actively participated in some of the situations. Evidence justified her dismissal on the grounds of lack of technical ability to fulfill the requirements of the job.

Daigle v. Keith Hunter, the Fredericton Fire Department and the City of Fredericton
(1988)

New Brunswick (Unreported)

1. **Under what circumstances were the use of bad language, showing of pornographic pictures, and making sex jokes considered harassment?**
2. **Why is a board of inquiry used instead of the courts at the initial stage of handling a complaint?**
3. **What factors caused Daigle to lose her case?**
4. **Should employers be held liable if the employees discriminate on the basis of gender or any other grounds? Why or why not?**

employs such tactics as demotion, transfer to less-desirable locations, increasing job pressure, or bypassing the employee for anticipated promotion. An employee who has experienced constructive dismissal has the same legal rights as in wrongful dismissal.

Mandatory retirement, another form of dismissal, is an issue that has been brought before the Supreme Court of Canada. People now live longer due to better living conditions and medical assistance, and many wish, for a variety of reasons, to continue working.

Dickason v. University of Alberta
(1992)

Supreme Court of Canada
2 S.C.R. 1103

Dickason was a full professor at the University of Alberta. She was forced to retire at the age of 65, as provided by a mandatory retirement clause in the collective agreement between the university and its academic staff. She filed a complaint with the Alberta Human Rights Commission alleging that her forced retirement contravened the province's *Individual's Rights Protection Act* by discriminating against her on the basis of her age. Section 11.1 of the *Act*, however, provided that discrimination on a prohibited ground will be permitted if the employer shows that the breach was "reasonable and justifiable in the circumstances." The board of inquiry appointed to hear Dickason's complaint ruled in her favour and ordered that she be reinstated.

The Alberta Court of Queen's Bench upheld the decision, but it was overturned by the Alberta Court of Appeal. Dickason then appealed to the Supreme Court of Canada. The Supreme Court of Canada dismissed the appeal, ruling that the university showed that the practice of mandatory retirement was reasonable and justifiable within the meaning of the *Individual's Rights Protection Act.*

1. **Generally, parties to a contract cannot provide clauses that overrule a statute. The Supreme Court of Canada said that this may not be true in cases where the agreement was freely negotiated by parties with relatively equal bargaining positions. Why would the two groups in this case have relatively equal bargaining positions?**

2. **Why would the university want to have a policy of mandatory retirement?**

3. **In your opinion, should mandatory retirement be permitted?**

Health and Safety Legislation

Each province has legislation, such as an *Occupational Health and Safety Act*, to try to reduce the millions of work days that are lost annually due to job-related injuries and illnesses. The *Acts* specify that the employer is to protect the workers, make sure that the workplace is safe, and provide the workers with the necessary safety training. Employees must follow the safety orders from the employer and must not tamper with safety equipment on the job. Each province provides safety officers to inspect the working conditions in places of work. Directives can be issued to employers to make changes in the workplace, and fines can be imposed for failure to comply. The regulations under the *Act* provide guidelines for special situations, such as the handling of toxic chemicals.

Farcus

by David Waisglass
Gordon Coulthart

WAISGLASS/COULTHART   © 1995 Farcus Cartoons/dist. by Universal Press Syndicate

"That's odd … I don't remember requesting a leave without pay."

Each province also has a *Workers' Compensation Act*, which provides payment to injured workers from a fund paid into by the employers. One provision of the *Act* prohibits the employee from suing the employer due to injury on the job, avoiding lengthy and expensive litigation. The Supreme Court of Canada has ruled that this prohibition against suing does not violate the *Charter of Rights and Freedoms*.

Federal Statutes

The labour legislation enacted by the federal government applies only to those businesses and industries falling under federal jurisdiction according to the *Constitution Act, 1867*. These laws can be further categorized into those applying to industries falling under the *Canada Labour Code* and those applying only to federal public (civil) servants. The laws contained in the *Labour Code* apply to Crown Corporations, as well as to industries that connect one province to another, either by forms of transportation or by physical connections, such as bridges, pipelines, canals, and airfields.

The *Canada Labour Code*

The *Canada Labour Code* is considered the pacesetter for most provincial legislation. The federal government employs people all across Canada. Wages and benefits similar to those received by federal employees are usually sought by provincial employees. Federal laws applying to holidays, discrimination, working conditions, and other areas also set the example for the provinces.

The *Labour Code* is divided into four parts. Most of its provisions are similar to those previously outlined for the provinces. The first section deals with fair employment practices, such as the prohibition of discrimination due to race, national origin, religion, and so on. The second section sets out the standards of employment: wage rates, vacations, hours of work. The third section details the provisions for ensuring that working conditions are adequate. The last section outlines the procedures to be followed in settling industrial disputes. Much of this fourth section will be outlined in our discussion of unions.

Public Servants

The public service (civil service) under the federal government is Canada's largest group of employees. Numbering over 200 000, these people must depend on the federal government to establish legislation that is fair and in accordance with employment standards in private industry. The public service conditions of employment are detailed in the *Public Service Staff Relations Act*. The *Act* is considered to be an advanced piece of legislation in that the employees bargain with the government in a manner similar to that followed by trade unions and, in most areas of government employment, civil servants are allowed to strike. Many people believe that government services, paid for through public taxation, are essential services and therefore public servants should not have the right to strike. While strikes by post-office employees and air-traffic controllers inconvenience the public, the government maintains that the process of collective bargaining is a right to which government employees are just as entitled as employees in private industry.

Reviewing Your Reading

1. What rights does the employee have if the common-law duties of the employer are breached?

2. What rights does the employer have if the common-law duties of the employee are breached?

3. What liability does an employer have regarding torts committed by employees?

4. Distinguish between the jurisdiction that the provincial governments and the federal government have over labour law.

5. How is vacation pay determined? When must it be paid?

6. Outline some restrictions that apply to the hiring of young employees.

7. Distinguish between "equal pay for equal work" and "equal pay for work of equal value."

8. What is constructive discrimination? Give an example.

9. Distinguish between *quid pro quo* harassment and poisoned work environment harassment.

10. What are the two main federal statutes governing labour at the federal level? Whom does each govern?

20.4 *U*NIONS

Early unions protested appalling work conditions—minimal wages and unhealthy and unsafe conditions. Today, unions benefit both employers and employees. Many corporations are so large that it is impracticable to deal with employees individually. Negotiating with one group that represents all the employees is often an advantage, while union members enjoy increased bargaining power and job security.

Types of Unions

There are three types of unions. A **company union** draws its members only from within the company, no matter what their occupation. Clerks, secretaries, drivers, and repairers in a home-heating oil company could form a company union. A **horizontal union** consists of members who are all in the same trade, but work for many different employers across the country, each group forming a **local**—the Painters and Decorators Union is an example. The **vertical union** is the largest and most powerful type. It consists of workers in different trades working for different employers, but all working in the same industry. Examples of such unions are the Mine, Mill and Smelter Workers, the United Steelworkers of America, and the Canadian Autoworkers Union. Many of these Canadian unions are outgrowths of those formed in the United States. Although they are now more independent, they were at one time closely allied to their American counterparts.

Certification of a Union

The *Labour Relations Act* of each province specifies the types of occupations that can organize as a union. Recently, doctors and dentists have been added to the list, since there are now companies that hire doctors or dentists in order to operate a chain of clinics. Each province has set up a Labour Relations Board to control, supervise, and regulate the formation and operation of unions.

A union can be formed from inside or outside a business. If formed from inside, a group of workers usually decides to form a union and begins signing up members of the business according to the type of union being formed. If the union is formed from outside, an existing outside union will approach the workers in an effort to obtain their membership in the union. Thus, if a new car factory were to open, the existing autoworkers union would try to sign up the employees and thereby gain the right to represent them in negotiations with their employer.

To acquire the right to represent employees, the union must apply to the Labour Relations Board for **certification**, that is, official recognition. A union will be successful in obtaining certification if it is able to show that the majority of employees want that union to be their bargaining agent. The union can show majority support by submitting signed membership cards, by a representative vote, or both. If the employer is just starting the business and expects to hire a lot of employees in the near future, the Labour Relations Board may delay the decision to grant or deny the certification until a significant number of the employees have been hired.

An employer may be against the formation of a union, and conflict between the employer and the union organizers might arise during the pre-certification stage. However, the employer cannot threaten or intimidate workers to prevent them from joining a union. Union organizers, similarly, cannot coerce workers into joining the union. Only the power of persuasion may be used to convince the workers that the union will be beneficial to them.

Union Membership

It is unusual for a worker employed in a union-represented business not to belong to the union. Labour law generally permits a **closed shop** to operate, meaning that all employees must belong to the union. An **open shop** contract does not require all workers to be members of the union, but the union conducts a constant drive for membership. Other agreements can be written into the union contract with the employer: a **union shop** permits an employer to hire non-union members, but each employee must join the union within a specified time; an **agency shop** permits non-union workers, but they must still contribute to the union by paying dues. In some areas, workers can pay the dues to a charity rather than to a union that they do not support.

It is not necessary for a union member to actively support the union in any way, other than by following its rules and paying dues. Most union activities are conducted by an elected executive. The general membership is only asked to vote on important issues. In each division or department of a unionized business, there is a **shop steward**, elected by the employees of that division to take any complaints or suggestions before the executive.

A union cannot refuse membership to a worker unless reasonable grounds are proved. According to the *Ontario Human Rights Act*, every person has a right to equal treatment with respect to membership in any trade union, trade or occupational association, or self-governing profession without discrimination because of race, ancestry, place of origin, colour, ethnic origin, citizenship, creed, gender, age, marital status, family status, or disability. The union has a responsibility to "fairly represent" its members since it has the sole right to handle grievances of the employees. Labour Relations Boards have found unions to be negligent when they have not adequately represented their members.

A certified union can lose its right to represent employees. This may occur if employees become dissatisfied with their union. If a majority of employees wish to no longer be represented by the union, the Labour Board will terminate the union's bargaining rights.

An outside union can also try to "raid" an existing union in an attempt to persuade the employees to recognize the outside union as their bargaining agent. In this case, a new vote of the employees would have to take place to decide which union will represent the workers.

Collective Bargaining

The main purpose of a union is to represent its membership in **collective bargaining**, or negotiating, with the employer over such items as benefits and wages, vacations, hours of work, employee training, grievance procedure, dismissal, and working conditions. A recently certified trade union will usually give the employer written notice of its desire to bargain. Once notice has been given, the union and employer must meet within a specified time to begin negotiations. During negotiations, the union presents a request to the employer, outlining the "package" or terms it would like to see in a collective bargaining agreement.

The employer examines the request, discusses it with the union negotiators, then makes an offer. The union negotiators may have the right to accept or refuse such offers on their own. Generally, however, the executive takes the offer to the membership for a vote if it thinks that the offer has a chance of being accepted, or if the employer is making a final offer and the executive wishes to show the solidarity of the membership by voting on an offer they know will be overwhelmingly rejected. During the negotiation procedures, it is required that both sides bargain in good faith. Thus, they cannot hide information from one another or refuse to discuss certain matters. If one side thinks that the other is not bargaining in good faith, it can ask for a ruling from the Labour Relations Board. The board's ruling usually only amounts to just giving the winning side strength in its position.

The procedure for collective bargaining is strictly controlled by legislation. One of the more important provisions allows for the appointment of an outside party, a mediator or arbitrator, to help the parties resolve their dispute.

Mediation and Arbitration

An irresolvable dispute can result in the bargaining parties asking the Labour Relations Board to appoint a mediator. In cases where public welfare is involved because of a strike by workers in an essential service, the government can appoint a mediator on its own initiative. The mediator is usually a person who is experienced in handling labour disputes. Representations are made to the

Lavigne v. Ontario Public Service Employees Union (1991)

Supreme Court of Canada 2 S.C.R. 211

Lavigne was a community college teacher who was required to pay dues to the Ontario Public Service Employees Union under a mandatory check-off clause in the collective agreement. Such a clause meant that the dues were automatically taken off an employee's pay by the employer at pay time and sent to the union. The collective agreement was between the Ontario Public Service Employees Union and the Council of Regents of the college. The automatic payment of dues was authorized by the *Colleges Collective Bargaining Act*. Lavigne objected to certain expenditures made by the union, such as contributions to the New Democratic Party and disarmament campaigns. He therefore applied to have the deductions cease.

The trial judge ruled that the *Colleges Collective Bargaining Act* and the collective agreement were of no force and effect insofar as they compelled Lavigne to pay dues for any purposes not directly related to collective bargaining. He ruled that Lavigne's freedom of association, guaranteed by section 2(d) of the *Canadian Charter of Rights and Freedoms*, was infringed, and that the infringement was not justified under section 1 of the *Charter*. The Ontario Court of Appeal reversed the judgment, ruling that the use of the dues by the union was a private activity by a private organization, and thus the *Charter* did not apply. It also ruled that there was no infringement of Lavigne's freedom of association, since he remained free to associate with others and oppose the union. Lavigne appealed to the Supreme Court of Canada. In its ruling, the Supreme Court of Canada agreed with the trial judge that Lavigne's freedom of association was violated, but found that the violation of association was justified under section 1 of the *Charter*. The Court also ruled that the paying of union dues was not a private activity. The appeal was dismissed.

1. **In what way was Lavigne's freedom of association infringed, according to the trial judge?**

2. **What was the main reason for the Ontario Court of Appeal's reversal of the trial judge's decision?**

3. **Explain what the Supreme Court meant by the ruling that the paying of union dues was not a private activity. On what basis would it make its decision in this case, concerning colleges?**

4. **On what basis would the violation of Lavigne's freedom of association be justified?**

mediator by the two sides, and the mediator then reports to the Board, usually within a specified time period. The recommendations in the report are frequently made public, with the intent of pressuring the two parties to resolve the matter. The government can then set up a formal mediation board that has the right to summon witnesses and examine the employer's business situation. A dispute over how much money an employer could afford, for example, could result in an investigation into the company's financial position.

If both sides reject the mediator's report, the parties can request that an **arbitrator** be appointed. The arbitrator's responsibility is to propose a final agreement. The parties may agree to **binding arbitration**, which means that the arbitrator's decision must be accepted. Binding arbitration is not resorted to very often because it results in a neutral party determining the terms of the contract. This may not resolve many of the inherent problems encountered during the negotiations. It may just put their resolution off to a later date.

Strikes

The ultimate weapon available to a union is the right to **strike**. If collective bargaining, mediation, and arbitration fail, the union is usually then in a legal position to strike. If members walk out in a **wildcat strike**, that is before they are in a legal position to strike, the courts can issue an injunction to prohibit the continuation of such a strike.

Once the union can legally strike, it may set up **picket lines** to make its grievances known to the public and to possibly obtain the support of other unions that may have the same employer. The union hopes that other unions won't cross the picket line to work or to do business with the employer. Other unions might join the picket line or demonstrate solidarity by also striking, which is known as a **sympathy strike**. Although on strike, the union can, however, provide for some employees to remain at work, particularly if valuable equipment or essential services are involved.

During a strike, employees are still legally employees, even though they are not being paid by the company. Occasionally, some workers may not support the union and cross the picket line. Such workers are usually subject to some form of punishment by the union, such as a fine or removal from the union. Many unions build up strike funds or borrow money to provide their striking members with some income. In some provinces, replacement employees can be hired, if the employer can find workers who are willing to cross the picket line.

Picketing must be conducted according to established regulations. Picketers can try to persuade people not to enter or do business with the employer but they cannot use force, block roadways, or commit libel on the placards they carry. The *Criminal Code*, in section 423, prohibits the use of intimidation by way of violence to keep a person from doing anything that he or she has a lawful right to do. In *Harrison v. Carswell* (1976), the Supreme Court of Canada ruled that employees participating in a lawful strike may not picket on private property if the private property owner asks them to leave.

Employees may choose to **work to rule**, which is another form of strike. Under these circumstances, work is carried on by the employees, but the regulations specified for each job are carried out with such exactness and thoroughness that the work is, in effect, slowed down. For instance, if teachers were to strictly follow the terms of their contracts, they could eliminate most of the extra-curricular activities in which they voluntarily participate.

If the employer believes that the strike is illegal or in some way damaging to its equipment or the public, it can seek an injunction that requires the workers to return to work for some period. Similarly, the government can pass legislation forcing the workers to return to work while the contract is under dispute. The legislation may include mandated negotiations, mediation, or arbitration.

Lockout

The employer's weapon comparable to the union strike is the **lockout**: the employer refuses entrance to certain or all employees. This tactic, like strike action, may legally be used only after a given period of time following unsuccessful mediation. It is unusual for lockouts to occur, for if the employees are willing to continue working while their contract negotiations are being carried out, it is usually in the employer's interest to keep the business operating.

Agreement

Once the union and the employer have come to a tentative agreement, the union membership votes on the package. Usually only a simple majority is required for the package to become the formal contract.

Once the contract is in force, however, there still may be many occasions on which one side feels that the other party is not fulfilling its contractual obligations. In this case, the two sides meet and try to resolve the matter; if unresolved, it is referred to arbitration.

Additionally, an individual employee who has a **grievance** (a complaint) can take it to the shop steward, who informs the union executive. The union then meets with the employer to seek resolution of the griever's complaint. If no satisfactory solution can be found by these parties, the contract will provide for some method of arbitration.

K Mart Canada Limited and United Food and Commercial Workers' International Union, Local 1518

(1994)

British Columbia Labour Relations Board

24 C.L.R.B.R. (2d) 1

K Mart applied under the *Industrial Relations Act* of British Columbia to stop their striking employees from handing out leaflets. The leaflets were being handed out at the entrances to various non-unionized K Mart stores on weekends before Christmas. The leaflets referred to the bargaining dispute, bad faith bargaining charges laid against K Mart by the union, and the unfair treatment of women by K Mart. Customers were asked not to spend their Christmas dollars at K Mart. There was no evidence of threats, or of verbal or physical intimidation of customers as they were handed the leaflets.

The union's position was that a prohibition against distributing leaflets contravened section 2(b) of the *Canadian Charter of Rights and Freedoms*, which guarantees freedom of expression. In hearings before two boards, it was ruled that the leaflets were intended to persuade persons not to enter the non-struck K Mart stores and were therefore a form of picketing. As such, it should not be conducted at non-unionized locations. The boards therefore restrained picketing at or near the premises of the non-struck stores. The British Columbia Labour Relations Board overruled this decision.

1. **Why was the union not allowed to distribute leaflets, according to the first two boards?**

2. **Should picketing be allowed at non-unionized outlets of a business that has employees on strike at other outlets?**

3. **Does the prohibition on distributing leaflets interfere with one's right to freedom of expression? If so, can the prohibition be justified under section (1) of the *Charter*?**

Reviewing Your Reading

1. Name and describe the three types of unions.

2. Describe the function of a Labour Relations Board.

3. Describe briefly the steps that a union must follow to become certified. What is the significance of being "certified"?

4. Name and describe the various types of union shops.

5. Describe each step in the collective bargaining process.

6. What is a grievance? What procedures are followed to resolve a grievance?

20.5 PRINCIPAL AND AGENT

An **agent** is a person representing another party, called the **principal**, in business transactions. The agent's purpose is to enter into contracts on the principal's behalf. It is possible for a person to be both an employee and an agent: a chef making pizzas in a take-out restaurant is an employee, but when buying gas for the restaurant's delivery car using the restaurant's credit card, he or she is an agent. Principal-agent relationships may be short term, such as an athlete having an agent negotiate a contract with a team on his or her behalf.

Two examples of principal/agent relationships are insurance agents and stockbrokers. Some of you may already have had an experience with this type of relationship when obtaining automobile

The plaintiff, Higgins, was a real-estate broker in Winnipeg. The defendant, Mitchell, was the owner of a house that she listed with Higgins for sale. Higgins introduced to her a purchaser who was ready, willing, and able to buy the house. The terms of the sale were set out in an unsigned document and given to the owner, Mrs. Mitchell, and her husband. She agreed to these terms after some changes had been made by her husband, one being that possession was to be given on May 1, 1920. A formal agreement was drawn up and sent to Mrs. Mitchell to be signed. Mitchell then insisted that the time for possession be changed to June 1. The purchaser, who was in urgent need of a house, refused to agree to this change, and the sale was called off. The agent, Higgins, sued for his commission and was awarded it by the court.

Higgins v. Mitchell
(1920)

Manitoba Court of Appeal
57 D.L.R. 288

1. **Did Higgins perform the tasks that he, as an agent, was hired to do?**
2. **Mrs. Mitchell changed her mind before signing a formal agreement. Was she bound by her unsigned agreement to sell? Why or why not?**
3. **Why did the court award Higgins his commission, even though the sale was called off?**

insurance. The agent was selling the insurance on behalf of an insurance company, the principal.

Forming a Principal/Agent Relationship

A principal-agent relationship can be formed in the following ways:

Express Contract

A principal and agent could agree in writing, or verbally, on what contracts the agent can enter. An athlete would enter into a contract in writing with an agent. The contract would specify what the agent was to negotiate on behalf of the principal. If the agent enters into contracts on the player's behalf, the player is generally bound by them. An exception occurs if the agent was acting beyond the authority given him or her in the contract with the player and with third party's knowledge.

People can give others a **power of attorney** to act on their behalf. A person on an extended vacation could leave a power of attorney with an agent. The agent could then enter into contracts specified by the power of attorney, such as carrying out emergency repairs on a property. A power of attorney is also given by a **proxy**, that is, a person gives permission to someone to cast a vote on his or her behalf.

Agent by Ratification

An agent by ratification results when a person acts as another person's agent without authority, and the resulting contract is not repudiated by the proposed principal. If your parents go away on holidays and you decide to surprise them by having the broken-down car fixed at their expense at the local garage, you are an agent acting without authority. Your parents may, however, ratify the contract on their return by paying for the repairs.

Agent by Necessity

An agent by necessity results when an agent enters into contracts on behalf of a principal because of an emergency. For example, if your parents are on holidays and the water pipes freeze, burst, and flood the house, you would contact someone to control the damage. You are acting as an agent by necessity, and your parents would be responsible for paying for the costs.

Johnson v. Birkett
(1910)

Ontario Supreme
Court
21 O.L.R. 319

The plaintiff, Johnson, gave instructions to the defendant, Birkett, a stockbroker, to purchase for her 500 shares of Boston Mines Co. Ltd. at one dollar per share. Birkett took the $500 cheque that Johnson gave him and cashed it, but did not use the money to buy the 500 shares for her. He already had an agreement to buy 2000 shares of Boston Mines Co. Ltd. and was going to give Johnson 500 of these shares when the stock was issued. He never delivered the shares to Johnson. Her solicitor wrote to him saying that his authority was revoked and to return the $500. When he did not do so, Johnson took action against Birkett to recover her money. The court awarded Johnson her $500, plus interest, plus costs.

1. **What type of agent had Johnson hired?**
2. **On what grounds did the court make the award?**
3. **Should Birkett be able to sell his own shares to a client? Explain.**

Implied Agency

People can imply by their actions that someone is their agent. A person (the principal) who makes payments on a credit card account for items charged by someone else (the agent) using the card has implied that he or she will also make future payments. To terminate the implied agency relationship, the principal must notify the issuer of the card in writing that he or she will no longer be responsible for charges made on it by the other person.

Principal's Duty to the Agent

The principal, having hired the agent to enter into contracts on his or her behalf, must fulfill certain common-law duties. The principal must pay the agent the agreed fee and any expenses or liabilities incurred by the agent in the performance of his or her duties, unless an agreement states otherwise. Many agents work on a commission basis, so principals must render their account to their agents so that they know the basis for the payment made to them by the principal. If the principal does not make payment of commissions to the agent, the agent has a right of lien on any of the principal's goods or money in his or her possession. As a last resort, the agent could sue the principal for breach of contract.

The principal is liable for any torts that the agent commits while acting in the course of the principal's employment.

Agent's Duty to the Principal

An agent has a strict duty toward the principal who has placed his or her trust in the agent. If there is a written contract between them, it will specify many of the agent's duties. Otherwise, duties are imposed by common law. Agents must be able to carry out their duties according to the skills for which they were hired, and they must perform diligently. If entrusted with money, they must be able to give an account of it. Agents must not sell their own chattels or property to the principal, unless the principal agrees, even if the goods are exactly what the principal wanted. This prevents an agent, such as a buyer for a department store, from starting a personal business which manufactures the same goods that the agent is supposed to buy for the store. Similarly, an agent cannot deal in a line of goods similar to those that the principal provides for him or her to sell, unless the principal agrees.

Reviewing Your Reading

1. **State four ways of forming a principal/ agent relationship.**
2. **What common-law obligations do principals have to their agents?**
3. **What liability do principals have for tortious acts of their agents?**

20.6 INDEPENDENT CONTRACTORS

A person may want to hire an **independent contractor** to do particular jobs for which they have the necessary skills and equipment. The distinction between an employee or agent and an independent contractor is important, for it has implications in tax law, tort law, and labour law. Independent contractors are in business for themselves and may be hired to do such jobs as installing a new kitchen or paving the driveway. Professional services are also provided by independent contractors such as editors.

In recent years, many employers have released employees and hired them back as independent contractors. The employer then does not have to pay Canada Pension Plan, employment insurance, or other benefits for that person. It is estimated that such a move can reduce wage costs by 10 percent, and benefit costs by 18 percent.

Independent contractors control their own work, own or supply their own tools, and can either make a profit or take a loss. They are responsible for obtaining the proper materials to do the job and for directing their own employees. Usually, they are responsible for payment of both. They receive payment from the people who hired them. An independent contractor cannot be held liable by third parties for damages arising from the contractor's wrongdoing. As well, anyone who hires an independent contractor is not liable for injuries suffered by the contractor or the contractor's employees in carrying out the contract.

Reviewing Your Reading

1. **Why would a person want to be an independent contractor instead of an employee?**
2. **Why would a business want a person to be an independent contractor instead of an employee?**

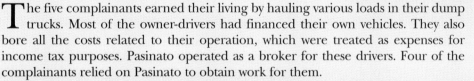

CASE

The five complainants earned their living by hauling various loads in their dump trucks. Most of the owner-drivers had financed their own vehicles. They also bore all the costs related to their operation, which were treated as expenses for income tax purposes. Pasinato operated as a broker for these drivers. Four of the complainants relied on Pasinato to obtain work for them.

Pasinato would phone them the night before a job to indicate where and when to report. Work at the job site would be supervised by the contractor, such as the respondent Adbo, who would indicate where to pick up and deliver loads. Remuneration for any work performed came from Pasinato. The supervisor on the job site and the owner-driver would sign a bill indicating the time worked. Every two weeks the owner-driver would take the bills to Pasinato for payment. There were no deductions from the pay, other than for union dues. Pasinato only appeared on the site from time to time to determine if there were any complaints.

Corrado DiSabatino and Teamsters Union, Local 879 and Adbo Contracting Co. Ltd.
(1977)

Ontario Labour Relations Board
2 C.L.R.B.R. 1

1. **What evidence is there that the owner-drivers were independent contractors?**
2. **What evidence is there that the owner-drivers were employees?**
3. **What difference would it make to the owner-drivers if they were employees rather than independent contractors?**

Should employers be allowed to conduct drug or alcohol tests on workers?

Employee drug testing, a common practice in the United States, has recently been adopted by some Canadian companies and institutions. Safety and security are the reasons cited for such testing. Airline and other transportation companies, for example, perform drug tests on their pilots and other employees to ensure security for their customers.

In 1990, the Toronto-Dominion Bank made it compulsory for newly hired employees to supply samples of urine for drug-testing purposes. Urinalysis tests are used to detect the use of cocaine, cannabis, heroin, or codeine. If drug use is detected, employees are sent for counselling or treatment; those who refuse are fired, as are those who test positive for a third time.

As more companies adopt this policy, however, the question of individual rights must also be considered. In the past few years there have been some seemingly contradictory decisions by human rights commissions on cases involving drug testing of employees.

In 1994, the Canadian Human Rights Tribunal decided that the Toronto-Dominion Bank's drug-testing program did not trespass upon the civil rights of its employees, although it did consider mandatory urinalysis an invasion of privacy.

The Ontario Human Rights Commission decided in 1995 that the substance abuse policy of Imperial Oil discriminated against the civil liberties of Martin Entrop. He was demoted in 1991 after he revealed that he had received treatment for alcoholism in 1984. Entrop maintained that he had not had a drink in seven years at the time of his demotion.

He was later reinstated on the condition that he undergo psychological treatment and provide breath samples at the discretion of the company.

In its decision, the Ontario Human Rights Commission ruled that alcoholism is a disease and is included under the human rights code that protects disabled people from discrimination. These two decisions by different human rights boards seem contradictory, although both appear to emphasize the civil liberties of the individuals involved.

On One Side

The Toronto-Dominion Bank argued that its employees handle huge amounts of money and that drug abusers are often involved with criminals who provide them with drugs. These drugs are expensive, and the bank has a duty to protect the customers' money. It was their position that the *Charter of Rights and Freedoms* should not be used to protect illegal drug users. Mandatory drug testing helps to maintain the values of honesty and trust that are vital to the integrity of the banking industry.

Imperial Oil developed its drug-testing policy because of the 1989 crash of the oil tanker *Exxon Valdez*. The resulting oil spill caused untold damage to the environment and wildlife. Even though the captain of the tanker, a recovering alcoholic, was eventually acquitted of being intoxicated at the time of the accident, the company felt that it was in its best interests to develop a drug-testing policy for its employees to ensure the health and safety of the general public.

Allen King/The Ottawa Citizen

On the Other Side

Alan Borovoy of the Canadian Civil Liberties Association argues that no person "should be required to share urine with a stranger" to obtain employment. He wants governments to make mandatory employee drug testing illegal. Borovoy maintains that "employers are entitled to know information that is relevant to their purposes, but not to conduct inquisitions into an employee's lifestyle and history . . . Such tests are a needless invasion of privacy that will tell you a lot about a person's lifestyle but virtually nothing about an employee's ability to do the job."

Mr. Borovoy's views were supported by the federal Privacy Commissioner (1993) who opposed drug testing in the armed forces and other federal institutions: "Drug testing is a major intrusion that is not offset by any significant benefits."

The Bottom Line

These two human rights cases seem to reflect the efforts of human rights commissions to maintain a balance between protecting society as a whole while at the same time ensuring individual rights and civil liberties. Some believe that companies and institutions have the responsibility and the right to make rules to help create an environment that is safe and secure for everyone. People do not have to apply for jobs if they do not agree with the conditions of employment. They have that choice.

Others agree with the Canadian Human Rights Tribunal's observation that "it is not for the employer to be the trier of fact and the enforcer of the criminal law." What do you think? You be the judge!

1. Are there any circumstances or occupations for which it is either appropriate or necessary for companies to conduct drug tests on their employees?

2. Why do recent decisions by human rights commissions appear to be contradictory?

3. When would drug testing be an invasion of an individual's privacy or an interference with his or her rights?

4. What would be your position if a company informed you that a drug test would be a condition of employment?

CHAPTER REVIEW

Reviewing Key Terms

For each of the following statements, indicate the key term being defined:

a) a settlement of contract negotiations where the two sides are obliged to accept the decision of a neutral third party

b) an employer is able to hire non-union members, but new employees must join the union within a specified time

c) strike that is not legal according to the terms of the contract

d) negotiations carried out by the union on behalf of all its members

e) people who are hired, but who control their own work, own their own tools, and can either make a profit or take a loss

f) a person who has the right to enter into contracts as if he or she were the principal

g) unintentional discrimination which effectively eliminates most members of certain groups

h) discrimination in which an employer may impose a requirement, qualification, or consideration, as long as it is reasonable and bona fide in the circumstances

i) to give someone the right to vote on your behalf

Exploring Legal Concepts

1. In general, statute law has precedent over a contract and common law in labour disputes. Why is this so? Should the rule of *caveat emptor* not apply?

2. From the perspective of (a) the employee, (b) the employer, and (c) the economy, outline the advantages and disadvantages of having a minimum wage.

3. Specify 10 jobs in your community that would be governed by the provincial labour laws, and 10 that would be governed by the federal labour laws.

4. Some jurisdictions have a plan whereby employees are paid their wages for the notice period which their employer was not able to pay due to a variety of reasons, most commonly bankruptcy. The payment is made from the province's revenue. Outline the advantages and disadvantages of such plans.

5. Why does legislation usually require that if an employer is going to lay off a large number of employees, notice of up to six months must be given to the provincial government?

6. What advantages are there to a union in entering into a sympathy strike with another union?

7. The practice of employers releasing employees and then rehiring them as independent contractors to do essentially the same job is costing the government millions of dollars. Should employers have to contribute to the Canada Pension Plan and employment insurance funds for independent contractors?

Applying Legal Concepts

1. In 1994, St. Paul's Hospital dismissed the licensed practical nurse it had employed since 1982. The nurse filed a grievance. Between 1989 and 1994, when she was terminated, she had an unacceptable record of absenteeism. Her head nurse had tried very hard to accommodate her. The griever was a single mother, who had a difficult son and who was having problems in her common-law relationship.

   In the year prior to her dismissal, the common-law relationship ended, her mother was very ill, and there were numerous deaths among her family and friends. It was argued before the labour board that the real cause of the nurse's absences was alcohol and drug addiction and that at the time of her discharge, she had yet to face up to the problem or to take steps to treat it. After her discharge, she had voluntarily sought treatment and was no longer chemically dependent. She had found that she was addicted to alcohol and a prescription drug that had been prescribed in increasingly large doses to help her sleep. She attended both Alcoholics Anonymous and Narcotics Anonymous meetings at least three or four times per week. Her son was no longer living with her, and she promised to attend work when scheduled if she was reinstated.

   The employer's position was that the nurse did not deserve another chance. She had not disclosed her drug and alcohol dependency during meetings with her head nurse. The head nurse was not aware of the griever ever showing signs of intoxication, and dealt with her over six years with compassion and consistently offered assistance. The union indicated at the hearing in March of 1995 that the griever had been released from the detoxification centre in December of 1994, and that it was too soon to say whether the griever had been rehabilitated.

   • **Should the griever be given her job back? Explain your position.**

2. Baker had worked for Burns Foods Ltd. for 40 years, except for a period of military service during the war. He was put in charge of sanitation and night operations, working from 4 p.m. to midnight. He was the senior person on duty during part of his shift, supervising 40 employees. Just before his annual vacation, Baker was advised that his job as supervisor had become redundant. The company offered Baker employment as a beef boner or as part of night security. Neither position was comparable to Baker's job either in status or pay. Neither job was satisfactory to Baker. He received a letter stating that unless he accepted one of the jobs, the company would consider that he had resigned.

   • **Is the company entitled to do this? Explain your answer using legal reasoning.**

3. Meehan and Doherty were employed in a cocktail lounge/supper club. The business was taken over by a new firm. At a staff meeting, the president announced that he had ordered new uniforms for the waitresses. The uniforms included very short pants. Meehan and Doherty wore their uniforms for a number of nights, under protest. One night, they reported for work without them. They were informed that wearing the uniforms was a condition of continued employment. Meehan and Doherty left the premises and did not return. They filed formal complaints with the Human Rights

Commission of New Brunswick, alleging that their employer had discriminated with respect to a condition of employment on the basis of gender.

- **Based on the facts presented, would the commission decide in favour of the employees? Explain.**

4. Goldhawk, the host of a current affairs radio program on the Canadian Broadcasting Corporation, was president of the union that represented writers, journalists, and performers. Under the union's bylaws, the president was also its official spokesperson. In the midst of an election campaign in which free trade was a central issue, Goldhawk wrote an article against free trade in the union newspaper. The CBC was concerned that his article and his public involvement as president of the union violated the CBC's journalistic policy requiring impartiality of journalists. It was agreed that as an interim measure Goldhawk would cease hosting his program until after election day. After the election, the CBC forced Goldhawk to choose between his job as host of a radio program and his role as the president of the union. Goldhawk resigned as union president and resumed hosting his radio program. The union filed a complaint alleging that the CBC had interfered with the activities of a trade union.

- **Did the CBC interfere with the operation of the union? Explain.**

5. *Mossop v. Canada (Attorney General)* (1993) Supreme Court of Canada 1 S.C.R. 556

Mossop, a federal government employee, took a day off work to attend the funeral of the father of a man he described as his lover. The two men had known each other for over 10 years and resided together in a jointly owned and maintained home. They shared the day-to-day developments in their lives and maintained a sexual relationship. Each had made the other the beneficiary of his will.

The collective agreement between the Treasury Board and Mossop's union provided for up to four days' leave upon the death of a member of an employee's "immediate family," a term defined as including a common-law spouse. The term common-law spouse was restricted to a person of the opposite sex. The day after the funeral Mossop applied for bereavement leave pursuant to the collective agreement, but his application was refused. He filed a grievance, but it was rejected. He subsequently filed a complaint with the Canadian Human Rights Commission against his employer and his union.

The Human Rights Tribunal concluded that a discriminatory practice had been committed contrary to the *Canadian Human Rights Act*, which prohibited discrimination on the basis of "family status." The *Canadian Human Rights Act* had been changed by Parliament in 1983 to add the phrase "family status" but it refused to add sexual orientation to the list of prohibited grounds of discrimination. It ordered that the day of the funeral be designated as a day of bereavement leave and the collective agreement be amended so that the definition of common-law spouse include persons of the same sex. The Attorney General of Canada applied to the Federal Court of Appeal to have the decision set aside. That court set aside the Tribunal decision, and Mossop appealed to the Supreme Court of Canada.

- **On what basis did Mossop complain to the Canadian Human Rights Commission?**

- **Why would the appeal go before the Federal Court of Appeal?**

- **Parliament, in 1983, had refused to add sexual orientation to the list of prohibited grounds of discrimination. What significance would this have for the Supreme Court of Canada in its deliberations?**

- **Based on the facts presented, would the Supreme Court of Canada rule in favour of Mossop?**

6. *Investors Syndicate Ltd. v. Versatile Investments Inc. et al.* (1983)
   Ontario Court of Appeal 149 D.L.R. (3d) 46

   Darraugh became a sales representative for Investors, a company selling a complete range of financial services. He signed a "Sales Representative's Agreement." It provided that he was to conduct his business as an independent contractor and was to pay all expenses incurred by him in the operation of the business. It also provided that he was to return all items to Investors when he terminated his agreement, and that he was not at any time to use any information acquired by him in a manner derogatory to the interests of Investors.

   When Darraugh decided to retire, he wanted to sell his customer accounts to another Investors' sales representative. He discussed this with his immediate superior, but nothing came of the discussions. He eventually contacted Musselman, a previous sales representative, who had left and set up Versatile Investments Inc. Two of Versatile's sales representatives eventually agreed to buy the customer accounts from Darraugh. Darraugh also gave them letters of introduction to his customers. Investors sued, stating that Darraugh had breached his agreement.

   - **In reality, was Darraugh an independent contractor, an agent, or an employee?**

   - **Darraugh's defence was that the agreement with Investors was in restraint of trade. Did the agreement with Investors prevent Darraugh from conducting his business freely?**

   - **Was Investors relying on the contract, on statute law, or on common law to prevent its representatives from selling customer accounts?**

   - **Should Investors succeed in its breach of contract action against Darraugh?**

Extending Legal Concepts

1. Now that you have completed this chapter, review the opening article and Something to Think About. Have your answers or opinions changed? Why or why not?

2. With the class, brainstorm a list of survey questions to elicit responses concerning attitudes on the influence of unions in our society. Prepare a final survey and distribute it to people in your school and/or community. Prepare a written report, summarizing the survey results. Include visuals to enhance your report.

3. This chapter has been written in general terms to cover all of Canada. Obtain a copy of the legislation in your province that applies to labour law, including labour relations, employment standards, and human rights. For each of the areas covered in the text, prepare summaries that show the specifics for your province.

4. Assume a position on one of the following topics and write a letter to your local member of the provincial legislature outlining your views:

   a) the right to strike for essential services workers

   b) employment equity

   c) the right to hire replacement employees during a strike

   d) the minimum wage for students

5. With a partner, brainstorm a list of questions that you as an employer would ask someone applying for a clerical position. Examine your list to see if any of the questions are discriminatory. Change partners and role-play the interview.

Researching an Issue

Employment Equity

As the ethnic diversity of a company's client base increases, the employer benefits from having employees that reflect the same diversity. This is especially true for large corporations and financial institutions, which have voluntarily instituted employment equity policies. Some people believe that employment equity will occur naturally through societal changes. Others maintain that employment equity will only occur if mandated.

Statement

Legislation should be introduced that mandates targets for hiring and promoting people from designated groups.

Point

Visible minorities and women cannot rely on the goodwill of employers to police themselves on employment equity. Without legislation, preference will be given to white male applicants for employment and promotion to senior positions.

Counterpoint

Employment equity discriminates against candidates who may be more qualified but are not members of the target group. Emphasis should be on merit and equality of opportunities for all candidates.

- **With a partner, research this issue and reflect on your findings.**
- **Prepare points on this statement that could be used for a class debate.**
- **Discuss your findings with others in your class.**

THE PEOPLE, THE LAND, AND THE LAW

CAREERS

Introduction

In recent years, considerable effort has gone into making Canada's justice system more accessible to the general public. Yet, there will be occasions when the expertise of a lawyer will be needed. Lawyers are trained professionals who can advise people on legal matters generally, and act as their advocates in legal proceedings.

In Focus: LAWYER

Many lawyers are self-employed. Others work in Crown prosecutor offices, corporate law firms, government departments, or large business enterprises. Lawyers often specialize in a particular area of law: corporate law, criminal law, personal injury claims, family and estate law, immigration law, labour law, and so on. While salaries for beginning lawyers are generally modest—in the $38 000 range—prominent lawyers can command very high incomes.

Education and Other Qualifications

If it is your ambition to be a lawyer, you must finish two to three years of an undergraduate program at a recognized university, before applying to law school.

To be a successful law school applicant you must have excellent marks from your earlier studies. Upon completing law school, which typically takes three years, you will be required to article with a law firm. This apprenticeship phase of your career will end when you pass the bar examinations set by the law society of your province or territory. After being "called to the bar" you will be issued a licence to practise law in that province or territory.

Responsibilities

As a lawyer, you will be responsible for advising your clients of their legal rights and duties, and for answering legal questions in general. You may find yourself pleading their cases before courts of law, tribunals, or administrative boards.

You will also assist your clients in drawing up legal documents such as contracts, wills, separation agreements and divorce papers, and real estate transactions. Your clients may call upon you to assist in negotiating out-of-court settlements, or to act as executor of a will, trustee, or guardian in family matters. If you work as a prosecutor, you will represent the Crown in court proceedings.

Work Environment

As a practising lawyer, your work will be very demanding. Your clients will expect high level of quality and will not tolerate mistakes. Your workdays will not follow a routine and often they may be long and arduous. You will rely on your support staff to maintain an organized schedule and allow efficient use of your time. You will use your social skills to establish effective, trusting relationships with your clients. If you are self-employed, you will have to develop business contacts and build a clientele.

Do You Fit the Job?

As a lawyer you will have to possess a thorough understanding of the law, be able to analyze complex situations, and be capable of making wise decisions based on good judgment and knowledge of facts. You should be persuasive, capable of working effectively under difficult conditions and the pressure of meeting deadlines.

$\mathcal{P}$ROFILE: David Nahwegahbow

David Nahwegahbow grew up on the Whitefish River Reserve on Manitoulin Island in Georgian Bay. During high school he primarily took technical subjects until grade 12, when he added a full academic program to his course of studies. About this time, Mr. Nahwegahbow began thinking about a law career, as a way for him to help advance the cause of Native rights.

After two years as an Arts student at Carlton University, Mr. Nahwegahbow entered law school where he spent three years completing his law degree. During this time, he acted as a special assistant to the president of the National Indian Brotherhood—now the Assembly of First Nations—where he gained a Native perspective on constitutional issues.

Mr. Nahwegahbow articled with William T. Badcock, a Native lawyer. After completing his bar admission requirements, he set himself up in independent practice, in a partnership with a friend from law school. He is proud of the fact that he has always been self-employed, and that he has had the initiative to take risks in his career to preserve his independence.

At first, Mr. Nahwegahbow pursued a general law practice in order to gain a broad range of experience. However, gradually he began to specialize in the area of aboriginal and treaty rights. Today, he spends most of his time acting for Native persons charged with offences involving such rights, or representing Native groups pursuing land claims cases.

Mr. Nahwegahbow's greatest satisfaction as a lawyer comes from achieving justice for Native people. He is committed to winning in this cause, and will not settle for less, or compromise his principles to attain a result.

Questions and Activities

1. Visit the career centre at your school and examine the calendars from several Canadian universities that have schools of law. Study the sections of these calendars pertaining to the law schools, and compare tuition fees, entrance requirements and courses of study.

2. As part of a career exploration activity, contact a local law firm and arrange to "job shadow" a lawyer for a period of one to three days.

3. During a courtroom visit, make mental notes on the performance of the lawyers you observe. Afterwards, decide which qualities are the most crucial for lawyers who do courtroom work.

LAW AND THE ENVIRONMENT

These are the key terms introduced in this chapter:

absolute liability offence

biosphere reserve

contaminants

deleterious substance

endangered species

environment

environmental audit

environmental impact
  assessment

Montreal Protocol

Priority Substances List

regulatory offence

strict liability offence

sustainable development

Chapter at a Glance

Learning Outcomes

At the end of this chapter, you will be able to

1. identify major legal, social, and economic issues related to protecting the environment;
2. recognize the areas of tort law that are applied to environmental disputes;
3. explain the advantages and limitations of using civil remedies to protect the environment;
4. discuss the purpose of the *Canadian Environmental Protection Act* and review its provisions for achieving compliance;
5. describe the process of environmental impact assessment as it is practised in Canada;
6. discuss laws in Canada related to parks and endangered species;
7. discuss why international cooperation is required to achieve global solutions.

With its seizure of the Spanish trawler *Estai* in international waters on March 9 [1995], Canada served notice that it considers its own rights to the contested Grand Banks fishery to be paramount. The seizure provoked outrage on the far side of the Atlantic, where European Union Fisheries Commissioner Emma Bonino accused Canada of launching a "wave of terror." At the same time, evidence that the *Estai* had netted immature turbot far smaller than any regula-

Who Owns the Sea?

tion permits prompted Newfoundland Premier Clyde Wells to brand the vessel's crew as "environmental criminals."

The bellicose rhetoric finally cooled somewhat last week when Canadian officials, after charging the *Estai* with a variety of offences and accepting a $500 000 bond from its owners, released the ship. But the *Estai's*

departure from the St. John's, Newfoundland, Harbour last Thursday did nothing to resolve the underlying conflict. Indeed, a United Nations-sponsored gathering of maritime nations, which is scheduled to resume on March 27, is likely only to amplify debate over the question at the heart of the matter: who owns the oceans anyway?

From: Chris Wood, "Who owns the sea?" *Maclean's*, March 27, 1995. Reprinted with the permission of *Maclean's*, of Maclean Hunter Publications Limited.

Something to Think About

- What prompted Canada to seize the *Estai*? Do you agree that Canada's actions were justified?

- What do the expressions "wave of terror" and "environmental criminals" tell you about response to this incident in Spain and Canada? Why do you think Bonino and Wells chose the words they did?

- In what different ways might law be used to protect the environment?

21.1 INTRODUCTION

The *Estai* incident brought a long-simmering dispute to a crisis point. On April 16, 1995, after a Canadian warship was ordered to the disputed area, the five-week "fish war" ended. Canada and the 15-member nations of the European Union signed an agreement under which (1) strict annual quotas for turbot were set, and (2) independent observers were to be placed on board all fishing vessels off the coast of Newfoundland to enforce conservation rules. Canada was given the authority to conduct more thorough inspections of foreign ships at sea and in port.

People have looked to the natural environment as a source of seemingly unlimited resources to be exploited for economic growth. Exploitation of such natural resources has enabled Canada to become one of the wealthiest countries in the world today. However, this high standard of living

has not been achieved without cost. Rapid expansion of industry, fuelled by population growth and strong consumer demand, and supported by the introduction of powerful new technologies, has put enormous stress on the environment.

In its broadest sense, the term **environment** refers to the total surroundings that encompass any individual or thing. The environment occupied by human beings is made up of physical elements—such as water, land, and the atmosphere; biological elements—including all living organisms; and social and cultural elements.

We are only beginning to appreciate the complexity of our natural surroundings. As our understanding of our environment has broadened and evolved, major changes have occurred in our environmental laws and in our approaches to environmental law.

One can draw a link between the goal of environmental protection and the goal of **sustainable development**, that is, "development that meets the needs of the present without compromising the ability of future generations to meet their needs." Sustainable development is not easy. We must revise our thinking, and we must exchange the values of consumerism for the values of conservationism. Our resources are finite, and the environment can only absorb so much waste.

This chapter will identify some of the major environmental problems and examine the main areas of Canadian law that deal with the environment. Efforts to achieve international cooperation on global environmental issues will also be explored.

21.2 THE ENVIRONMENT AT RISK

The human "population explosion," combined with rising material expectations, have produced consumption rates that are rapidly depleting the world's supply of natural resources. Industries that use these resources produce chemical and biologically active **contaminants** on a vast scale. Indeed, there is hard evidence that pollutants have been affecting the ecosphere since the late nineteenth century.

Forests. The annual harvest of wood in Canada has been rising steadily. As a result, wilderness areas are disappearing at an increasing rate, and Canada is running out of old-growth forests. Reforestation practices, such as vast plantings of just one kind of tree for commercial purposes instead of replacing the variety of species that were cut, do not generate new forests. Moreover, questionable logging practices have contributed to the erosion of forest soils and the destruction of fish and wildlife habitats. The building of massive hydro-electric dams has caused the flooding of vast areas of forest land.

Did You Know

Environmental groups in the United States and Europe have mounted advertising campaigns condemning the practice of clear-cutting in Canada's forests in an effort to dissuade tourists from visiting here.

Soil. Valuable layers of topsoil in Canada are being eroded by water and wind. The decline of organic matter in cultivated soil and the demands of modern agriculture have led to a dramatic increase in the use of chemical fertilizers, herbicides, and pesticides. As a result, fragile ecological balances are being disturbed. In some areas, excessive irrigation has caused harmful accumulation of salts in soil.

Landfill sites are filling up rapidly with garbage. The situation is worsened by the growing presence of toxic substances and non-biodegradable materials, such as plastics, in domestic wastes. Moreover, seepage from these sites can contaminate ground water reserves that many Canadians depend on for drinking water.

Air. Vehicle exhaust and smoke and gas emissions from industries are choking the air with smog, aggravating respiratory problems of urban dwellers. Pollutants from waste disposal sites and manufactured products also contribute to air pollution. Global warming, ozone depletion, and acid rain are three concerns that stem from the pollution of the atmosphere.

Water. Pollution of streams and rivers by sewage and industrial wastes is making it increasingly difficult for communities to meet their needs for safe drinking water. Rivers and streams carry pollutants into lakes and coastal waters where they cause harm to local ecosystems.

Millions of fish have suffocated due to oxygen depletion. This fish-kill results from a process called *eutrophication*, in which high concentrations of nutrients, such as phosphates, stimulate excessive algae growth, resulting in a decrease of oxygen in the water.

The closing of public beaches and swimming areas has become common because of high coliform bacteria counts caused by raw or partially treated sewage.

Draining wetlands to accommodate urban growth and agriculture has resulted in the loss of wildlife habitats. Oil spills have fouled fragile seabottoms and shorelines. Contamination of river estuaries contributes to the decline in population of fish species already threatened by overfishing. In deep areas of the ocean, pollution results from the dumping of highly toxic substances. We are only now beginning to understand the dangers of this practice.

Scientists estimate that *acid rain*, caused by the burning of fossil fuels, has killed life in approximately 14 000 lakes and has harmed many thousands of other lakes in Canada. Acid rain is also harming Canada's forests, causing forest dieback in some areas.

Toxic Substances. Toxic contaminants that enter the food chain and eventually find their way into our bodies are causing increasing concern. These very dangerous substances, the by-products of industrial activity, include polychlorinated biphenyls (PCBs), dioxins, mercury, and heavy metals such as arsenic, lead, and cadmium. Scientists have linked human exposure to these substances to cancer, heart disease, damage to the central nervous system, birth defects, and learning disabilities. In many instances, the destructive effects are passed on from one generation to another.

Toxic compounds have already affected many wildlife populations causing thyroid dysfunction in birds and fish; decreased fertility in birds, fish, and mammals; decreased hatching success in birds, fish, and turtles; and unusual birth deformities in birds and fish.

Global Problems

Pollution does not respect national boundaries. Winds, ocean currents, and human transportation systems have carried pollutants to all corners of our planet. The crisis we face is of global dimensions. The stresses on the environment are becoming so great that the world's basic life-support systems may be on the verge of breaking down.

Ecologists have described rain forests as the "lungs of the world," due to their enormous capacity to take in carbon dioxide and release oxygen. Currently, these forests are being destroyed at an alarming rate—to supply industry with raw wood and to make land available for settlement and agriculture. Although rain forests cover only 7 percent of Earth's surface, they are home to 50–80 percent of the world's plant and animal species. More species become extinct each day.

The burning of wood wastes that often accompanies the destruction of rain-forest areas contributes to the atmosphere's already heavy carbon dioxide burden, which comes mainly from the use of fossil fuels. Many scientists believe that the rise in CO_2 levels is causing a *greenhouse effect*: increasing levels of carbon dioxide trap more heat in the atmosphere, resulting in a trend toward global warming.

This process is accelerated by rising levels of methane gas produced by a growing livestock population and the presence of chlorofluorocarbons (CFCs), which are found in refrigerators, air conditioners, and aerosol sprays. Some scientists predict that the average world temperature will rise by as much as 2°C to 5°C by the middle of the next century. A global warming trend would be of particular significance to Canada as it is thought that the greatest effects would be felt between 30 and 60° latitude. Coastal flooding, caused by a rise in the sea level due to melting of the world's ice caps, would displace huge numbers of people throughout the world and destroy large areas of valuable farmland.

In the early 1980s, British scientists, conducting atmospheric research in Antarctica, detected the first hard evidence of ozone depletion. They found that a massive hole had developed in the *ozone layer* over the South Pole. More recently, a much smaller hole has been found developing each spring over the North Pole.

Scientific studies have linked CFCs to the thinning of the ozone layer. Ozone blocks ultraviolet radiation from reaching Earth's surface. As the ozone layer becomes depleted, the occurrence of skin cancers and eye cataracts is expected to rise; phytoplankton, upon which all marine life depends, is expected to diminish. Lower yields of major food crops, such as wheat, rice, corn, and soybeans, are predicted as a result of reductions in photosynthesis, and it is thought that the immune systems of humans might be weakened.

Did You Know

From 1983–1991, the number of Canadians suffering from the two most common forms of skin cancer increased by 135 percent. During the same period, the number of cases of malignant melanoma, a potentially fatal skin cancer, also rose dramatically.

Disasters

Disasters have heightened international concerns about the environment. The effects of a 1970 heavy-oil spill from the *Arrow* tanker in Chedabucto Bay, Nova Scotia, were still visible in 1995, 25 years later!

In 1989, the oil tanker, *Exxon Valdez*, ran aground at the entrance to Prince William Sound, spilling a full cargo of Alaskan crude oil. Although Exxon spent $1.3 billion (U.S.) on clean-up operations, studies have shown that the effects of the spill are still being felt. Reproductive defects have been detected in sea birds and other aquatic life.

Another disaster occurred in 1993, when an American oil tanker sank off the Shetland Islands near Scotland. These are only three of hundreds of oil spills that occur around the world every year. Indeed, the U.S. National Academy of Science has estimated that 6 million tonnes of petroleum flood into the world's oceans every year, adding to an estimated 400 million tonnes of dissolved petroleum and 700 000 tonnes of tarballs that are already there.

On April 26, 1986, an explosion at a nuclear reactor in Chernobyl, Ukraine, triggered a nuclear meltdown. Over 11 tonnes of radioactive debris were released into the atmosphere, with catastrophic results. During the next 10 days, clouds from Chernobyl deposited contaminants from Scandinavia to Greece. Government authorities have declared over 2600 km^2 of land surrounding

Did You Know

During the summer of 1994, major ruptures in sections of the Usinsk-Kharyaga pipeline northeast of Moscow resulted in a spill estimated between 100 000 and 270 000 tonnes of crude oil.

the ruined reactor an uninhabitable "Dead Zone." In the first eight years following the accident, over 8000 people died from radiation-induced diseases. One estimate puts the eventual toll at 39 000 cancer deaths alone. Abnormally high numbers of birth defects have also been reported.

It is clear that more than just the immediate disaster areas are affected, and high-profile disasters such as those mentioned above create a public awareness of environmental issues. If there is a positive side, it is that almost all environmental laws arise as a political response to the pressure of public awareness and opinion.

Reviewing Your Reading

1. a) **List environmental problems in Canada associated with the land, the air, and the water.**

   b) **What dangers are posed by toxic substances?**

2. a) **Identify three global environmental problems occurring in the atmosphere.**

   b) **Note three recent environmental disasters that happened outside Canada.**

3. **Define "acid rain," "greenhouse effect," and "ozone depletion."**

21.3 COMMON-LAW REMEDIES

As you learned in Unit 3, a tort is a civil wrong or injury, other than a breach of contract, for which the injured party or plaintiff may seek damages from the wrongdoer. In some situations, the plaintiff may apply to the courts for an injunction to prevent anticipated harm or to end a continuing wrong. Tort law, in its capacity to protect private rights, can be and has been used to protect the environment.

Consider the example of a pulp mill that is sued successfully by a group of farmers for interfering with their right to unpolluted water. The damages awarded will compensate the plaintiffs for any loss or harm, thus protecting their private interests. The damage award may also act as a deterrent to other pulp mill owners.

In Chapter 12, you learned that torts include negligence, private and public nuisance, trespass to land and to people, and strict liability. Some situations involving environmental abuse also result in civil suits. In *Kerr et al. v. Revelstoke Building Materials Ltd.* (1976), noxious substances, fly ash, and sawdust from a nearby timber mill forced Mr. and Mrs. Kerr to close their motel. They sued in trespass and were granted $30 000 in damages. In another case, *Friesen et al. v. Forest Protection Limited* (1978), Mr. and Mrs. Friesen were caught in a cloud of a pesticide being sprayed by an airplane on a neighbouring field. They sued in trespass and nuisance. The court awarded them $1328.20 plus their legal costs. Not all civil suits involving environmental abuse are successful, however.

There are several advantages to seeking tort-law remedies to environmental disputes. Individuals may act privately against polluters without having to persuade the government to act. Also, the courts will order that successful plaintiffs be reimbursed for losses suffered. Finally, it may be possible to obtain a permanent injunction to stop a polluter.

However, there are also disadvantages. The legal costs of bringing a civil action are very high. The expense of providing expert witnesses, who are often required in environmental cases, is prohibitive for most individuals. The length of time before a case can be brought to trial may be unacceptably long. The requirement that a plaintiff have a property interest in the land being affected by pollution denies the use of civil remedies to many persons concerned with protecting the environment.

It is also often difficult to prove that a polluter's activities are directly linked to the harm and that such harm was reasonably foreseeable. For example, it may be difficult to show that a causal link exists between cancer, which may take years to develop after exposure to a contaminant, and emissions from a particular factory. Similarly, legal problems are created by the fact that environmental damage is usually the result of a combination of actions of many individual tortfeasors (wrongdoers) over considerable time.

Perhaps the greatest limitation is that the most widespread pollution problems—especially those that are global in nature—cannot be addressed effectively through the common law. Problems caused by the greenhouse effect and ozone

CASE

Palmer et al. v. Nova Scotia Forest Industries

(1983)

2 D.L.R. (4th) 397

The plaintiffs had applied to the courts for a permanent injunction restraining Nova Scotia Forest Industries from spraying parts of Nova Scotia with phenoxy herbicides (2,4–D and 2,4,5–T). The purpose of the spraying was to suppress the growth of broad-leaf plants and hardwoods, thereby promoting the rapid growth of coniferous trees.

The two main issues to be decided in the case were (1) whether the plaintiffs were pursuing a proper action in accordance with Civil Procedure Rules and case law, and (2) whether a permanent injunction should be granted to restrain the proposed spraying.

On the first issue, the judge ruled that the action was proper. He agreed that the plaintiffs had the right to pursue the action collectively. In fact, he said, this was preferable to several individuals pursuing their own separate actions against the defendant.

The Civil Procedure rule applying here required *numerous* persons having the same interest in the proceeding. The judge noted that the "numerous persons" requirement had obviously been met. He also found that the plaintiffs shared several interests. They had a common grievance—the allegation of a serious risk to their health, the source of their grievance was common—the proposed spraying, and they sought the same remedy—an injunction to restrain the spraying.

On the second and the far more important issue, the judge ruled against granting a permanent injunction. In his written judgment, he listed the legal causes of action brought by the plaintiffs, and then dismissed each in turn:

- Breach of the *Fisheries Act* —The judge observed that the accepted rule was that civil consequences of breach of statute should be subsumed in the law of negligence. In the present case, negligence was neither pleaded nor proven.
- Private Nuisance—The judge noted that interference with a person's enjoyment of land must be material or substantial to give rise to an action in nuisance. In the present case, the allegation was that if 2,4–D and 2,4,5–T got to the plaintiffs' lands, their health would be put seriously at risk.

  The judge agreed that if a significant risk to health would result from the spraying, this would substantially interfere with the plaintiffs' enjoyment of their lands. The threat of such nuisance would argue in favour of the granting of a permanent injunction. However, based on his interpretation of the scientific evidence presented at trial, the judge concluded that the actual risk to the plaintiffs' health would be negligible or non-existent.
- Trespass to Land—The judge observed that trespass to land does not require proof of damage. However, in the present case no trespass had been proved as probable to occur. In other words, the judge accepted the argument that the spray would likely remain confined to the land belonging to Nova Scotia Forest Industries.
- The Rule in Rylands and Fletcher—The judge declared that no basis had been established for the application of this rule as he had found that the substance was not dangerous and was unlikely to escape to the plaintiffs' lands.
- Riperian Rights and the Right to Uncontaminated Groundwater—The judge stated that since no significant risk to health had been proved, there was no need for him to consider these matters.

1. Why did the plaintiffs launch a court action against Nova Scotia Forest Industries? What was the basis of their case?

2. According to the judge's decision, when are class actions appropriate?

3. On what main grounds did the judge find in favour of the defendants?

4. Do you agree with the court's suggestion that substances sprayed into the air were "unlikely to escape to the plaintiffs' lands"? Explain.

5. During the trial, a considerable body of conflicting scientific evidence was brought before the court. How might this have affected the judge's task?

depletion cannot be solved by private individuals claiming in the courts that they are the victims of torts. These problems require governmental action and international cooperation.

Reviewing Your Reading

1. a) What are the advantages to seeking tort law remedies to environmental disputes?

   b) What are the disadvantages to this approach?

2. a) What is an injunction?

   b) In what types of situations is an injunction the best remedy?

3. Explain how a damage award can be used as a deterrent.

4. Give your own examples of environmental abuse illustrating negligence, trespass, and strict liability.

21.4 CONSTITUTIONAL JURISDICTION

Under the *Constitution Act, 1867*, the power to pass laws relating to the environment is divided between the federal and provincial governments. The provincial governments have, in turn, delegated some of their law-making authority to municipal governments.

The federal government derives its jurisdiction over environmental matters through a number of exclusive powers. Navigation and shipping, seacoast and inland fisheries, canals, harbours, rivers, and lake improvement, federal works and undertakings, and trade and commerce are the most notable powers. Another is the residual power available under the "peace, order, and good government" clause. These powers allow the federal government to pass environmental laws that have a national dimension and deal with a national concern. The regulation of atomic energy and the control of toxic pollution are two examples.

The provinces and territories have jurisdiction over property and civil rights, the management and sale of public lands, and local and private matters. This gives them considerable authority over land use and development of natural resources and allows provincial governments to pass wide-ranging environmental laws.

Sometimes, divisions of responsibility between departments within the same governmental level, or among the different levels of government, overlap or are unclear. Confusion and complexity on environmental issues result. This has led to calls for constitutional reform, but observers believe that change will not be achieved easily. They point out that two seemingly contradictory interests must be reconciled: The federal government must be given enough authority to represent Canada effectively at the international level and to set national environmental standards. At the same time, local and provincial and territorial interests must be recognized and protected, particularly those relating to employment and economic development, to preserve national unity.

The chart shows when some of the major federal and provincial laws were enacted and when some of the agencies and treaties dealing with the environment were established.

Chronology of Canadian Environmental Laws and Treaties

1868	*Fisheries Act*	1975	*Environmental Contaminants Act*
1909	*Boundary Waters Treaty*		*Ocean Dumping Control Act*
	(Canada–United States)		*Environmental Assessment Act* (Ontario)
1911	*National Parks Act*	1985	Amendments to
1916	*Migratory Birds Convention*		*Canada Water Act*
	(Canada–United States)		*Clean Air Act*
1946	*Atomic Energy Control Act*		*Canada Shipping Act*
1957	*Canada Water Act*		*Fisheries Act*
	Canada Shipping Act		*Northern Inland Waters Act*
	Northern Inland Waters Act		*Pest Control Products Act*
1971	*Clean Air Act*		*Environmental Contaminants Act*
	Environment Canada	1988	Amendments to *National Parks Act*
	(federal department)	1989	*Canadian Environmental Protection Act*
1972	*Great Lakes Water Quality Agreement*	1992	*Canadian Environmental Assessment Act*
	(Canada–United States)		Canadian Environmental Assessment
	Pest Control Products Act		Agency
1973	*Canada Wildlife Act*	1992	*Convention on Biological Diversity*

CASE

R. v. Fowler
(1980)

**Supreme Court
of Canada
2 S.C.R. 213**

Fowler was originally charged under section 33(3) of the *Fisheries Act*, which states "No person engaging in logging, lumbering, land clearing, or other operations, shall put knowingly, or permit to be put, any slash, stumps, or other debris into any water frequented by fish or that flows into such water, or on the ice over either such water, or at a place from which it is likely to be carried into such water."

Fowler operated a logging business on the coast of British Columbia. Logs being removed from the forest had been dragged across a small stream, leaving debris in the water. This stream, which flowed into the ocean, was used for the spawning and rearing of salmon. At trial in provincial court, no evidence was presented showing that the debris had harmed the salmon in any way.

Fowler was acquitted at trial. The decision was reversed at the County Court, and a further appeal at the Court of Appeal was dismissed. Fowler then appealed to the Supreme Court of Canada.

The Court restored the trial judgment and indicated that "subsection 33(3) makes no attempt to link the proscribed conduct to actual or potential harm to fisheries. It is a blanket prohibition of certain types of activity, subject to provincial jurisdiction, which does not delimit the elements of the offence so as to link the prohibition to any likely harm to fisheries. Furthermore, there was no evidence before the Court to indicate that the full range of activities caught by the subsection do, in fact, cause harm to fisheries . . . The prohibition in its broad terms is not necessarily incidental to the federal power to legislate in respect of seacoast and inland fisheries and is *ultra vires* of the federal Parliament."

1. With what offence was Fowler charged?

2. What dangers are posed to fish when logging debris is deposited in streams?

3. What does the term *ultra vires* mean? On what basis did the Court declare subsection 33(3) to be *ultra vires*?

Reviewing Your Reading

1. Give two main constitutional sources of the federal government's authority to make laws with respect to the environment.

2. Jurisdiction over what three areas gives the provinces authority to pass laws protecting the environment?

21.5 ENFORCEMENT OF REGULATORY LAWS

The various environmental statutes that have been introduced in Canada impose a vast network of regulations designed to protect the environment. At the same time, these laws recognize that a degree of environmental pollution is necessary for the economy to function to meet the material needs of Canadians. The task has been to find an acceptable balance.

With some important exceptions, the **regulatory offences** that are defined in Canada's environmental laws bring relatively minor penalties that do not carry the stigma associated with a criminal conviction. They are either **strict liability offences** or **absolute liability offences** (see Chapter 3), requiring only proof of *actus reus*. In the case of strict liability offences, due diligence can be offered as a defence. However, such a defence is not available to someone charged with an absolute liability offence.

Recently, there has been a trend at both the federal and provincial levels of government toward creating tougher penalties for those who violate environmental laws. This has given these penalties, which include huge fines, a kind of "quasi-criminal" quality. The *Canadian Environmental Protection Act* goes so far as to define certain acts as indictable offences.

The basic premise behind the environmental statutes that appeared in the 1970s and 1980s was

that we should stop believing that our natural environment has an unlimited capacity to absorb our wastes. These "clean-up" laws were designed to prohibit or minimize discharge of wastes. At the same time, through careful management, we can rely upon the *absorptive capacity* of the environment to dilute and cleanse limited amounts of pollutants with minimal risk of lasting harm.

A common feature of these laws is the use of permits. Industries wishing to discharge wastes must first obtain a permit from the appropriate government agency. Applicants must outline the system of pollution control they intend to use. Permits are then issued. The permits set limits based on the amounts of pollutants government officials have determined are safe to discharge. The following examples are typical of these earlier laws.

The *Canada Shipping Act*

The *Canada Shipping Act* regulates activities that could result in pollution. Specifically, the *Act* prohibits commercial ships and pleasure craft that operate in Canadian waters from discharging certain pollutants. Regulations cover the discharge of wastes and substances such as oil, arsenic, lead, and mercury. Severe penalties are imposed on those who violate regulations, including fines up to $1 million and/or terms of imprisonment not exceeding three years.

The *Act* sets out the factors to be considered by the courts when determining the punishment for violators: the actual harm caused, the cost of clean-up, any remedial action taken by the offender after the violation to reduce harm, whether the offence was deliberate or accidental, evidence of negligence or lack of concern, and finally, precautions taken by the offender to avoid the offence in the first place.

The *Fisheries Act*

The *Fisheries Act* applies to both inland and coastal waters. It forbids the depositing or discharge of

R. v. Catlender
(1959)

British Columbia Magistrate's Court
29 W.W.R. 401

The chief mate of the *Kiaora* was charged under the Oil Pollution Prevention Regulations of the *Canada Shipping Act* which states, "No person shall discharge or allow to escape from a ship into the inland, minor or other waters of Canada any oil or oily mixture that fouls the surface of the water."

Under the chief mate's direction, the *Kiaora* had been discharging bunker fuel into storage tanks on shore by means of hoses attached to the ship. At the end of this operation, the chief mate had ordered that the hoses be winched back aboard ship, knowing that the hoses contained residual amounts of oil. This oil had spilled out onto the water as the hoses were being drawn in.

The chief mate was convicted of the charge and fined $250. The judge in the case noted that the chief mate was the only person in charge of the unloading operation, and that the shore party did not fall within the scope of the *Act's* regulations. The chief mate had also failed to take precautions to prevent or minimize the escape of oil.

1. **With what offence was the chief mate of the Kiaora charged?**
2. **Why had the chief mate been singled out in this case?**
3. **Suggest other kinds of situations to which the regulation involved in this case might apply.**

deleterious substances in waters where fish might be found, or into places where the substance could eventually enter the water. "Fish" includes all aquatic animals. The *Act* defines a deleterious substance as "(a) any substance that, if added to water, would degrade or alter the quality of that water so that it is rendered harmful to fish, and (b) any water that contains a substance in such quantity or concentration that it would, if added to water, degrade the quality of the water and, therefore, cause harm to fish."

Examples of such substances are Bunker "c" oil, diesel fuel, wood preservatives, sewage, and sediments. Enforcement measures include fines and court orders prohibiting activities likely to result in further offences. A spill that continues for several days can lead to the imposition of multiple charges under the *Act*.

Section 41(3) of the *Fisheries Act* provides expressly for a defence of due diligence. "It is sufficient proof of the offence to establish that it was committed by an employee or agent of the accused whether or not the employee or agent is identified or has been prosecuted for the offence, unless the accused establishes that the offence was committed without his knowledge or consent and that he exercised all due diligence to prevent its commission."

If a construction proposal or project seems likely to lead to a deposit or discharge of deleterious substances, the Minister may demand to see the plans. The Minister may then order that the project be modified or abandoned. Where officials suspect that an existing operation is in violation of regulations, the Minister may demand that company representatives produce the information necessary to assess the situation.

Provincial *Environmental Protection Acts*

All provinces have enacted laws that regulate the discharge of contaminants. Many of these laws are patterned after the *Ontario Environmental Protection Act* and contain the following common components. Each has a section that

- defines key terms, such as "environment," "contaminants," and "adverse effect";
- states the general purpose or purposes of the *Act*;
- prohibits the discharge of contaminants without formal approval;

The accused was charged with two offences under section 33(2) of the *Fisheries Act*, namely that it "did permit the deposit of a deleterious substance into water frequented by fish, to wit the Table River . . ." The charges arose out of the construction of a railway line.

At trial, the Crown presented evidence that conservation officers had observed that a clear freshwater creek became muddy and silty as it passed through the defendant's construction site on its way to the Table River. Analysis of water samples taken above and below the construction site showed that siltation in the creek increased 3000-fold as it passed through the site. A similar situation was found to exist at a construction site on a creek nearby. An aerial photograph taken a few days after the sampling showed the water entering the Table River from one of these streams to be apparently silty.

The defence argued successfully that the Crown had not proven beyond a reasonable doubt that the silt deposited by the defendant in the two creeks had reached the Table River. It noted that the creeks had to travel almost 1.5 kilometres from the point where the downstream samples were taken to the Table River. It suggested that a marine biologist, who had testified for the Crown, had ventured beyond his area of expertise when he offered opinions on natural filtration systems in creeks. Further, the defence asserted that the Crown's evidence did not eliminate the possibility that silt from the construction sites had been filtered out by natural processes occurring in the creeks. Finally, the defence said, there was no evidence in the aerial photo that the silt shown entering the Table River was attributable to the defendant's construction activity.

R. v. British Columbia Railway Company (1983)

British Columbia Provincial Court (Unreported)

1. **Does section 33(2) of the *Fisheries Act* create a crime or an offence? Explain.**
2. **Must both *actus reus* and *mens rea* be proved?**
3. **How does the dictionary define "deleterious"?**
4. **What, if any, substance is being released by the company?**
5. **What doubts did the defence attempt to raise about the Crown's case?**
6. **How might the Crown have strengthened its case?**

- sets out types of enforcement orders that can be issued under the *Act*;
- gives the Minister responsible for the *Act* the authority to exempt an applicant from the *Act's* regulations;
- sets out offences or infractions.

The *Canadian Environmental Protection Act*

Beginning in the late 1980s, a new generation of environmental laws began to appear in Canada. Their primary objective is the control of persistent toxic wastes. They reflect scientific findings on hazardous contaminants and recognize the need for cooperation among provincial, federal, and international governments.

The single most important piece of legislation in Canada dealing with toxic wastes is the *Canadian Environmental Protection Act*, commonly known as *CEPA*. This *Act* sets out a comprehensive framework to protect Canadians from harm caused by toxic substances and to prevent potential or actual environmental problems from developing. The

CASE

R. v. Consolidated Maybrun Mines Ltd.
(1992)

Ontario Court
(Provincial Division)
76 C.C.C. (3d) 94

The defendants owned an inactive copper and gold mine in Northern Ontario. They were charged under section 146(1a) of the Ontario *Environmental Protection Act* with four counts of refusing to comply with a director's order.

During an inspection of the mine site, officials of the Ministry of the Environment had found eight transformers leaking polychlorinated biphenyl (PCB). After 20 months of unsuccessful attempts to persuade the company to rid the site of the PCB contamination, the director issued an order under section 17(1) of the *Act*. The order required the company to secure the site within seven days, construct a storage area to house the leaking transformers, clean concrete stained by the PCB spillage, and bag, drum, and store any PCB contaminated soil.

The company secured the site, but not within the seven days specified, and ignored the other provisions of the order. The Crown then laid the charge under section 146(1a) of the *Act*.

At trial, the Provincial Offences Court judge found that the director did not have "reasonable and probable grounds," as required in the *Act,* for issuing an order on three of the four counts. He did convict the defendants of failing to bag, drum, and store contaminated soil; and fined the company $5000, and fined a leading company official $500. Both the Crown and the company launched appeals.

The appeal court ruled that the trial judge had exceeded his authority when he ruled on whether the director had "reasonable and probable grounds" for issuing an order. The proper procedure would have been for the defendants to appeal the director's order to the Ontario Environmental Appeal Board. It was up to the board, not the courts, to determine what constituted "reasonable and probable grounds."

The appeal court found that section 146(1a) did not violate section 7 of the *Canadian Charter of Rights and Freedoms* because it had not created an absolute liability offence as claimed by the defendants. Rather, it had created a strict liability offence, leaving it open to defendants to avoid liability by establishing the defence of due diligence.

The company had acted with due diligence in securing the site, even though they had exceeded the seven-day period. The company had not acted with due diligence to comply with the director's order to bag, drum, and store PCB contaminated soil. Therefore the conviction on this count stood.

The heaviest burden of the fines should fall on the leading company official because he was the controlling mind of the company and was the main reason behind the company's failure to comply with the director's order. The appeal court ordered the official and the company to pay fines of $4500 and $450, respectively.

1. **Why did the director decide to issue an order against Consolidated Maybrun Mines Ltd.?**

2. **What was the decision of the trial judge in this case?**

3. **How do strict liability and absolute liability offences differ?**

4. **Which side did the judgment of the appeal court most favour? Explain.**

5. **Explain the term "controlling mind."**

6. **The appeal court shifted the burden of the fines from the company to the leading company official. Do you see any significance in this? Explain.**

Act attempts to accomplish this by setting up a process for identifying toxic substances; regulating their production, use, and disposal; and detecting violations and punishing violators. Environment Canada and Health Canada together develop *CEPA* regulations and guidelines and Environment Canada administers the *Act*.

CEPA defines a substance to be toxic if it is entering or may enter the environment in a quantity or concentration or under conditions that

- have or may have an immediate or long-term harmful effect on the environment;
- constitute or may constitute a danger to the environment on which human life depends;
- constitute or may constitute a danger in Canada to human life or health.

CEPA gives the federal government authority to control all stages of the "life cycle" of toxic substances, including their development and manufacture, transportation, storage and use, and eventually disposal as waste. The *Act* includes provisions for regulating fuels and components of fuels such as lead additives, controlling sources of air pollution, limiting the use of nutrients, such as phosphates, and managing the dumping of wastes at sea.

Priority Substances List

An advisory panel is currently revising a **Priority Substances List** that identifies substances that should be assessed immediately. Such substances include those that

- are poisonous and pose a severe threat,
- will persist in the environment for a long time,
- are known to accumulate in the food chain,
- are used in considerable quantities and have the potential to cause serious damage if accidentally released, or
- are already known to be causing environmental damage.

Under *CEPA*, no new substance may be used in Canada until it has been properly assessed. Previously, a substance was presumed to be safe until proven otherwise. Now industries or businesses must convincingly establish safety. Controls may be imposed on any substance found to be toxic. A Ministerial order can ban the substance entirely, a list of safety regulations can be imposed, or a permit can place limits on quantities.

Enforcement and Compliance

The federal government has established an Enforcement Policy that sets out a complete strategy for achieving compliance with *CEPA*. Compliance requires that regulations, Ministerial orders, and permit requirements made under *CEPA* be observed.

CEPA seeks compliance in two ways. The first is through promotion, that is, by providing information, consultation, and technical assistance, and by helping with the development of new technology. The second is through enforcement, that is, by conducting inspections and investigations, and by introducing measures to compel compliance.

To promote compliance, Environment Canada distributes information about *CEPA*, and the regulations, guidelines, and codes of practice developed under the *Act*. Environment Canada is also expected to make available information about court actions arising from enforcement of *CEPA*. Finally, industries are being encouraged to conduct their own **environmental audits**, that is, internal assessments by company personnel, to determine whether company operations are in compliance with *CEPA*.

Enforcement activities include regular monitoring of Canada's air, water, soil, and marine environments, and the conducting of inspections and investigations by Environment Canada officials. Inspections are undertaken to verify compliance with *CEPA*; investigations are done in cases of suspected violations.

Responses to Violations. Possible responses for dealing with violators range from the relatively mild to the very severe. Official warnings, either verbal or written, are given in situations where actual or potential harm caused by a violation is minor. Inspectors also issue directions for emergency measures to end the unauthorized release of a substance and to protect human life and the environment. Failure to obey a direction will result in prosecution of the violator. Inspectors have the authority to take direct action to deal with a crisis if the violator does not comply with a direction.

CEPA gives the Minister of the Environment the authority to call for immediate action in connection with two kinds of violations. An order may prohibit activities involving substances new to Canada that have not been assessed properly for their toxicity. A recall order may also be issued

R. v. Aqua Clean Ships Ltd.
(1994)

British Columbia Provincial Court
12 C.E.L.R. 241

The defendants operated an incinerator in Vancouver harbour for disposing of wastes from ships. The incinerator was located on a floating barge. The defendants were charged under the *Canadian Environmental Protection Act* with (1) loading a substance onto a barge for the purpose of dumping, and (2) with dumping refuse into the sea, in contravention of the *Act*.

Section 66(1)(a) of the *Act* defines dumping as "the deliberate disposal at sea from ships, aircraft, platforms, or other anthropogenic structures, including disposal by incineration or other thermal degradation, any substance . . ." Section 67(2) of the *Act* states that dumping may be done in accordance with a permit granted under the *Act*.

The defendants had held a permit that expired on June 17. Environment Canada officials had advised them that the permit would not be renewed until they had demonstrated they could meet new guidelines respecting air emissions from incinerators. Shortly after, the defendants applied for a permit for conducting a test burn to find out whether their equipment could meet the guidelines. The permit was received in August.

An inspection on July 7 revealed that incineration had taken place aboard the barge from July 5 to July 7. The two charges were then laid.

The trial judge convicted the defendants on the "dumping" charge, rejecting the defendants' claim that they had merely been "curing" their equipment using natural gas. He accepted the evidence showing that the defendants had been incinerating small amounts of waste paper and shipboard wastes, and since they did not have a permit to do so, they were in violation of the *Act*.

However, the judge dismissed the charge of loading a substance onto a barge for the purpose of dumping, declaring that there was insufficient evidence that the waste loaded onto the barge on July 5 was intended for incineration during July 5 to July 7.

1. **What events led to the laying of charges against Aqua Clean Ships Ltd.?**

2. **a) On what charge was Aqua Clean Ships Ltd. convicted? Explain.**

   b) Why did the judge dismiss the second charge?

---

requiring that a toxic substance or product be removed from the marketplace. In either case, the order may be followed by formal prosecution of the violator.

Prosecution is the most severe response inspectors may take for violators of *CEPA*. This may occur in situations where loss of human life has occurred or a serious risk has been posed to the environment or human life or health. Prosecution may also occur where the alleged violator deliberately provided false information about a substance, obstructed an inspection, interfered with a seized substance, concealed or attempted to conceal information about an offence, or did not take the required measures to comply with an inspector's direction or Minister's order.

The final decision on whether to proceed with a prosecution rests with the Attorney General of the affected province. Enforcement officials with Environment Canada recommend to Crown prosecutors the penalties that they should request at court.

Penalties. Those convicted of the most serious offences under *CEPA* face the possibility of harsh punishment as criminals.

Penalties include fines of up to $1 million a day and imprisonment for up to five years or both. *CEPA* also authorizes the courts to order polluters to pay the cost of cleaning up pollution they have caused, or to notify at their own expense those unfavourably affected by their activities. A company may have to relinquish any profits gained from engaging in a prohibited activity, or pay for research into how to dispose of the particular unauthorized substances.

No other environmental statute in Canada provides for such harsh penalties. However it is revealing that to date relatively few prosecutions have been launched under *CEPA*, and the severest penalties have not been imposed.

CEPA has its share of critics. In July 1994, the Standing Committee on Environment and Sustainable Development was designated by the House of Commons as the committee responsible for conducting a review of the *Act*. In its report, the committee concluded:

> If *CEPA* is to tackle the environmental problems facing Canadians today, it must be changed. *CEPA* does not address enough of these problems. Action under *CEPA* has been unacceptably slow in assessing toxic substances. Enforcement under *CEPA* has been inconsistent and disappointing. Fundamentally, *CEPA* focuses on the wrong issues. By emphasizing the control of specific substances, *CEPA* promotes "react and cure" strategies which do not address the root causes of polluting behaviour and do not work toward preventing pollution in the first place.

It will be interesting to see what amendments are made to *CEPA* to address these concerns.

Reviewing Your Reading

1. Distinguish between "absolute liability" offence and "strict liability" offence.

2. Define "due diligence" and "deleterious substance."

3. List the six components common to provincial laws regulating the discharge of wastes.

4. Define "toxic substance" as set out in *CEPA*.

5. Distinguish between "promotion" and "enforcement" as strategies for achieving compliance with *CEPA*.

6. a) Briefly describe the four main responses provided in *CEPA* for dealing with alleged violators.

b) In what kinds of situations will prosecutions be launched for violations of *CEPA*?

c) What are the harshest penalties available upon conviction for an offence under *CEPA*?

21.6 *E*NVIRONMENTAL IMPACT ASSESSMENT

Perhaps the most significant recent development in the field of environmental protection has been the move toward the use of **environmental impact assessments** (EIAs). Environmental impact assessment has been defined as "the official appraisal of the likely effects of a proposed policy, program, or project on the environment; alternatives to the proposal; and measures to be adopted to protect the environment."

Examples of projects in Canada that have been subjected to EIAs include dams, pipelines, mining and industrial developments, offshore drilling, nuclear power plants, highways and railways, and harbours and airports. The *Canadian Environmental Assessment Act* defines an "environmental effect" as

1. any change that the project may cause in the environment, including any effect of any such change on health and socio-economic conditions, on the physical and cultural heritage, on the current use of lands and resources for traditional purposes by aboriginal persons, or on any structure or site or thing that is of historical, archaeological, paleontological, or architectural significance, and

2. any change to the project that may be caused by the environment, whether any such change occurs within or outside Canada.

In 1991, the Canadian Council of Ministers of the Environment approved a set of principles for conducting environmental impact assessments. These principles emphasized

- the building in of cost-effectiveness and consistency in the environment assessment process,
- assessing environmental impacts before any irreversible decisions are made,

Looking Back

In Canada, environmental impact assessment officially began in 1973 when the federal government adopted an EIA and review process for projects undertaken by federal departments and agencies, or which involved federal property or funds. Within a few years, many of the provinces had passed EIA laws of their own. In 1984, the federal government introduced a new, two-stage environmental assessment and review process (EARP) consisting of an initial "self-assessment" phase and a "public review" phase.

In practice, this meant that any federal department or agency contemplating a new undertaking now had to screen the project for its potential effect on the environment. The new rules required that it arrive at one of four decisions:

- The project had little or no environmental impact and could proceed without modification.
- The environmental impact was not adequately known and further study in this area was required before the project could be properly assessed.
- The environmental impact was unacceptable and the project should be abandoned or significantly modified.
- The project had potentially major environmental impact that might raise considerable public concern and therefore it should be referred to an independent panel for review.

The department or agency then had to send its decision to the Federal Environmental Assessment Review Office (FEARO) for scrutiny, and for publication to allow public response.

The Beaufort Sea Project illustrates the "public review" phase of the process. The Beaufort Sea, located in the western Arctic, is home to more than 30 000 people, many of whom are Inuit. In the 1970s, many geologists thought that the region might contain large quantities of oil and natural gas, and companies were eager to begin exploring for these resources.

From 1980 to 1984, an independent Environment Assessment panel headed by Justice Thomas Berger carried out an extensive review of proposed oil and gas development. For three years, the panel of seven members travelled throughout the region that borders the Beaufort Sea and held consultations with 29 potentially affected communities.

In its final report, the panel recommended that future development take the form of relatively small, phased-in projects, to be closely controlled and monitored. It advised that ice-breaking tankers for transporting oil and natural gas should not be used at their current stage of technology. The panel also endorsed the idea that the local communities should have a major role in managing the effects of any development, and that they should gain long-term benefits from these developments.

The federal Department of Public Works launched a study into the feasibility of linking New Brunswick and Prince Edward Island with a fixed crossing. In accordance with the Environmental Assessment and Review Process Guidelines Order, a general environmental evaluation was conducted. As well, three proposals for a bridge were chosen for specific consideration.

A public review panel reviewed the general concept of a fixed link, but not the three proposals. The panel recommended against a fixed link due to anticipated negative environmental effects.

A government inter-departmental committee studied the matter further and concluded that one of the specific proposals—a bridge—could be built with little environmental impact. A company was chosen to construct and operate the bridge.

Friends of the Island Inc. then brought an application to prevent the project from proceeding on the grounds that environment assessment and review guidelines had not been properly followed, and that to discontinue the ferry service would contravene the terms under which Prince Edward Island joined Canada. Subsequently, the Department of Public Works was ordered not to begin work on the bridge project until a proper environmental assessment had been carried out.

Government officials undertook an evaluation and initial assessment of the proposed bridge. Their findings indicated there were no significant environmental concerns. The Minister of Public Works concluded that a full public review of the proposal was unnecessary in light of the report's findings and the apparent lack of public concern. Friends of the Island Inc. challenged his decision in court.

The court held in favour of the Minister, declaring that the Minister had the discretionary power to decide against a public review, that the evaluation and assessment of the specific bridge proposal had more than met the requirements of the assessment and review guidelines, and that no significant environmental effects had been found.

Friends of the Island Inc. v. Canada (Minister of Public Works)
(1993)

11 C.E.L.R. 253

1. **What position did the Friends of the Island Inc. take on the building of a fixed link?**

2. a) **What opportunity for public involvement was provided by the assessment process set up by the government officials?**

    b) **What faults did the Friends of the Island Inc. find with this process?**

3. a) **How did the judge rule in this case? Explain.**

    b) **Do you agree with his ruling? Why or why not?**

- giving the public access to information and creating opportunities for public involvement in the process,
- early identification of issues to ensure that they are properly addressed,
- the proponent's responsibility to pay all costs related to the preparation of an environmental assessment,
- making allowance in the process for the use of innovative procedures such as mediation,
- the necessity for federal-provincial and interprovincial cooperation on environmental assessment.

The *Canadian Environmental Assessment Act*

The *Canadian Environmental Assessment Act, 1992* (proclaimed into law in 1994), maintains most of the elements of EARP which it replaced. It incorporates many of the principles approved in 1991 by the Council of Ministers of the Environment. Finally, the *Act* has expanded the scope for public participation by emphasizing the role of public reviews and by introducing mediation as an option.

The purpose of the *Act* is to

- ensure that the environmental effects of projects receive careful consideration before responsible authorities take actions in connection with them;
- encourage responsible authorities to take actions that promote sustainable development and thereby achieve or maintain a healthy environment and a healthy economy;
- ensure that projects that are carried out in Canada or on federal lands do not cause significant adverse environmental effects outside the jurisdictions in which the projects are carried out; and
- ensure that there be an opportunity for public participation in the environmental assessment process.

Section 16(2) of the *Canadian Environment Assessment Act* declares:

16.

(2) Every assessment of a project by a review panel, or every mediation, shall include a consideration of the following factors:

(a) the purpose of the project;

(b) alternative means of carrying out the project that are technically and economically feasible and the environmental effects of such alternative means;

(c) the need for, and the requirements of any follow-up program in respect of the project;

(d) the capacity of renewable resources that are most likely to be significantly affected by the project to meet the needs of the present and those of the future.

Where a project is referred to a review panel for assessment, the Minister of the Environment must ensure that persons appointed to the panel "are unbiased and free from any conflict of interest relative to the project." The review panel must make certain that all relevant information obtained is made available to the public and that proper public hearings are held. Review panels have the authority to summon persons as witnesses to give verbal or written evidence or to produce documents or anything else deemed necessary for conducting the assessment.

Where the Minister is considering mediation, the interested parties must first be identified and then agree to participate in the mediation, before it can proceed. If the mediation process breaks down, the Minister can terminate the mediation and refer the matter to a review panel.

The decision to proceed with a project rests with the "responsible authority" for the project, such as a particular department of government. The decision to proceed cannot be made until the responsible authority receives the assessment report from the review panel or mediator and duly considers its findings and recommendations. The *Act* states that the responsible authority may proceed where the project is not likely to cause significant adverse environmental effects or where likely significant adverse environmental effects can be justified.

Reviewing Your Reading

1. Define "environmental impact assessment." Why are environmental impact assessments necessary?

2. a) List the kinds of changes the *Canadian Environmental Assessment Act (CEAA)* defines as "environmental effects."

   b) Give your own examples of "environmental effects" to illustrate the meaning of this term.

3. Summarize the stated purposes of the *CEAA*.

4. a) What four factors must be considered, according to the *CEAA,* when an environmental assessment is undertaken?

   b) What two approaches for conducting environmental assessments are set out in *CEAA*?

21.7 PARKS AND ENDANGERED SPECIES

The primary motive behind the creation of Canada's first national park was the desire for profit. In 1883, the government of John A. Macdonald created Banff National Park at the urging of the Canadian Pacific Railway, which was eager to exploit the tourist potential of the Banff hot springs. Canada now has more than 30 national parks, covering approximately 2 percent of its territory. Other protected areas, comprising 5 percent of Canada's landmass, include national wildlife areas, migratory bird sanctuaries, ecological reserves, provincial parks, provincial wildlife management areas, and wilderness areas.

Today, Canadians hold essentially two visions of parks:

- as tourist playgrounds offering recreational and commercial opportunities;
- as sanctuaries essential to the preservation of natural habitat and wildlife.

This dual purpose, which is reflected in the *National Parks Act*, presents a problem. Many species require large habitats free of any or most human activity to ensure their survival. It may not be possible to open parks to the public and still ensure that natural environments are preserved for these species.

Section 5(1) of the *National Parks Act* addresses this issue, requiring a "management plan" for each national park. The plan must include a zoning scheme based on the following categories of land use:

Zone I (Special Preservation)—areas requiring the highest level of ecological protection with very limited human access permitted.

Zone II (Wilderness)—areas that are to be maintained in a wilderness state with limited numbers of visitors and no motorized access.

Zone III (Natural Environment)—low-density outdoor activities with some motorized access.

Zone IV (Outdoor Recreation)—a broad range of educational and recreational facilities permitted, with motorized access.

Zone V (Park Services)—includes town centres.

Canada's parks attract visitors from around the world. This creates a dilemma. As the number of visitors to parks increases, more roads, trails, townsite development, campgrounds, and recreation facilities are required. This means more sewage and garbage. The presence of more and more people and the development required to accommodate them directly threatens the fragile ecosystems that the parks are supposed to preserve. Banff National Park is a good example. The city of Banff and surrounding areas have been transformed by an economic boom that has lasted for several years. Banff's rapid growth has put considerable pressure on the natural environment and raised concern for the preservation of the wildlife.

Did You Know

Canada's park service is considering a policy of making people responsible for paying the cost of their own rescue operations when engaging in activities such as hiking, skiing, climbing, and kayaking.

Resource extraction, mainly mining and logging, is another concern. It has been estimated that less than 50 percent of provincial parkland in Canada is protected in law from resource extraction.

Canada's parks face external threats as well. Air and water pollution originating from outside park boundaries often enters parks. Particularly damaging are acid rain and water-borne pollution from local communities and nearby industries. Logging activities in areas bordering parks can affect water quality through soil erosion. Hunters sometimes use logging roads to gain illegal access to parks. Perhaps the most serious problem posed to parks by these external threats is that they may imperil intact but vulnerable ecosystems existing within the parks, thereby endangering the very survival of certain wildlife species.

The extinction of species is not new to this planet. Scientists estimate that over 90 percent of the species that have inhabited Earth since life first appeared no longer exist. During the last few decades the accelerated rate of extinction, which some scientists estimate to be between 100 and 1000 times the natural rate, can be attributed almost entirely to human activity. The main causes are the fragmentation and loss of natural habitat

Dated 1-18-96. By permission of Johnny Hart and Creators Syndicate, Inc

due to economic activities, overhunting and harvesting of species, and pollution of the air, rivers, lakes, and coastal waters. Although Canada, because of its northern location, is home to fewer species than countries in the tropics, the World Wildlife Fund has designated 255 species here as either threatened or **endangered species**.

Environmentalists have called on the federal and provincial governments to expand considerably the amount of land allocated specifically to habitat and wildlife protection. Both levels of government have made some progress in this direction.

One obstacle has been the high cost of acquiring new parkland. For example, South Morseby National Park cost the federal government $106 million when it was created in 1988: $50 million went to the British Columbia Government, which owned the land; $26 million went to compensating forest companies that held logging rights to the land; and the remainder went to park costs.

Another obstacle has been public opposition—often from residents of communities dependent upon resource-based industries, but also from large business interests. Parks "lock up" valuable natural resources. Creating new parks can eliminate potential job opportunities and cause loss of jobs for some types of occupations. Some of the bitterest and most emotionally charged confrontations in Canada in recent years have been between environmentalists campaigning to have a particular area declared a wilderness sanctuary, and forestry workers fearing for their jobs.

The 1993 protests in British Columbia, over the provincial government's decision to allow mixed use of land in Clayoquot Sound, offer a dramatic example and raise a number of legal and moral questions.

Reviewing Your Reading

1. **What percentage of Canada's land mass has been designated as "protected areas"?**

2. **a) What dual purpose do parks attempt to serve?**

   b) What kinds of threats face fragile ecosystems located within parks?

3. **What are the primary causes of the extinction of species in the world today?**

4. **Identify two main obstacles to the creation of new parks.**

21.8 *T*HE GLOBAL VIEW

Canada's international efforts to protect the environment involve multinational treaties, programs, and conferences. Canada has played an active role in international efforts to devise ways of addressing environmental issues.

In the early 1990s, Canada and the United States negotiated an agreement aimed at protecting both countries from transboundary air pollution. Canada had campaigned hard for this agreement because studies had shown that approximately half of the acid rain falling on Canada was being caused by sulphur dioxide emissions in the United States. The agreement created a bi-national forum for reporting and verifying progress on air quality issues.

Under a United Nations' program called "Man and the Biosphere," Canada has designated several sites as **biosphere reserves**, that are intended to conserve threatened ecosystems and to preserve irreplaceable genetic material. In 1992, Canada signed the *Convention on Biological*

Diversity, committing itself to enacting a federal endangered species Act, a promise it has yet to fulfill. Canada has also signed the Convention on International Trade in Endangered Species.

In 1987, Canada joined 23 other countries in signing the ***Montreal Protocol*** *on Substances That Deplete the Ozone Layer.* By 1994, 133 countries had signed this pact. The signatories have agreed to implement domestic regulations to gradually phase out the consumption and production of CFCs, halons, and other ozone-depleting substances. Canada is meeting its commitments through regulations introduced under the *Canadian Environmental Protection Act.*

Perhaps the largest international meeting to date on the global environment was the Earth Summit held in Rio de Janeiro in 1992. Approximately 30 000 people, representing 100 countries, attended this 12-day event. Their argumentative mood was a sign of deep rifts that separate the nations.

Evidence was offered that global warming was occurring and that the main culprit was carbon dioxide emissions. Reportedly, the industrialized nations of Europe, North America, and the former Soviet Union were producing 70 percent of these emissions. Delegates were called upon to agree to a rapid and significant decrease in CO_2 production.

The United States stood alone among the wealthy, industrialized countries, by refusing to agree to significantly reducing its carbon dioxide output. It argued that the measures necessary to achieve a major reduction in emissions would be too costly. Poorer countries indicated that they would be willing to lower their CO_2 emissions if the wealthy countries offered sufficient financial and technical assistance. Eventually, 24 of the participating nations agreed to a number of modest goals they were to achieve by the end of the century.

In April 1995, representatives from 130 nations met in Berlin in an attempt to achieve further progress on CO_2 reduction. While delegates reported some progress, it was clear that the desire of countries such as the United States, Canada, Australia, and Japan to protect their economies continued to block a significant breakthrough.

Reviewing Your Reading

1. **What is the purpose of a "biosphere reserve"?**
2. a) **What global problem did the *Montreal Protocol* address?**

   b) **What obstacles have slowed efforts to reduce global CO_2 emissions?**

Issue

Civil Disobedience:

Is it a necessary

component of justice?

Civil disobedience is the refusal to obey civil laws in an effort to change legislation. This disobedience is usually nonviolent and may take the form of protests and demonstrations, roadblocks and sit-ins. Participants in these activities are willing to accept the penalties, such as fines or imprisonment, for breaking the law. They believe that by attracting public attention and creating an awareness of their cause the government will be forced to take positive action to correct a situation that they feel is wrong.

The objective of recent acts of civil disobedience in Canada has been to protect the environment and natural resources. In the summer of 1993, demonstrators violated a court order by blocking a logging bridge to prevent loggers from entering Clayoquot Sound on Vancouver Island in British Columbia. This area contains one of the last temperate rain forests in Canada, and the protestors used civil disobedience to try to protect the trees, wildlife, fish, and rights of the people living in this area.

In the same year, on the East coast of Canada, 100 fishing boats illegally held a Russian fishing boat at bay off the coast of Nova Scotia, blocking its attempt to unload 12 000 tonnes of cod at a fishing plant. The six-day blockade was to protest foreign fleets, which had been overfishing the cod and threatening the livelihood of fishers in Nova Scotia.

On One Side

Those who support civil disobedience argue that it is a necessary component of justice. While the democratic process of drafting, passing, and implementing legislation is an important one in our society, it is also a lengthy one. If citizens wait for legislation to evolve through due process, resources like the cod and areas like Clayoquot Sound will be long gone before there are laws in place to protect them. Acts of civil disobedience, they argue, are also important in our society in that they create public awareness of situations that require immediate attention.

On the Other Side

Opponents of civil disobedience feel these actions threaten the freedoms of all Canadians and should not be tolerated. They want the government and the courts to take stronger action against those who deliberately break the law and impose hardship on other law-abiding citizens. They point out that Canada is a democracy where the majority rules. If special interest groups feel their needs and objectives are being ignored, they have the right to try to convince others of the legitimacy of the viewpoint through legal means.

The Bottom Line

The debate over the value and necessity of acts of civil disobedience is ongoing. Can civil disobedience be justified as a necessary component of justice? Or is the democratic process the only valid process for changing legislation? Where do you stand on this issue? You be the judge!

To protest overfishing, a fleet of small fishing boats formed a blockade around a Russian freighter in Shelburne, Nova Scotia.

1. What other conflict resolution strategies might be more effective than civil disobedience as a way to get laws changed?

2. Use your resource centre to answer the following about either the Clayoquot Sound or the Nova Scotia incident.
   a) What incidents led up to the protest?
   b) What penalties, if any, were imposed on the participants?
   c) What results, if any, did their actions have on changing legislation?

3. Research another incident of civil disobedience in Canada (preferably in your province) and write a summary of your findings.

CHAPTER REVIEW

Reviewing Key Terms

For each of the following statements, indicate the key term being defined:

a) an internal assessment conducted by a company to determine whether its operations are in compliance with the Canadian Environmental Protection Act

b) the policy of meeting the needs of human society in the present without impairing the ability of future generations to meet their needs

c) a wrongful act for which the defence of due diligence can be put forward by the defendant

d) an area designated by the UN to be a special protected area to conserve a threatened ecosystem

e) a special list identifying new compounds that should be assessed immediately for their toxicity

f) any material that, upon being added to water, renders the water harmful to fish

g) the total surroundings that encompass any individual or thing

Exploring Legal Concepts

1. Why is international cooperation required for solving many environmental problems?

2. Explain the term "absorptive capacity." Show how the environmental statutes that appeared in Canada in the 1970s and 1980s reflect the premise that the environment has an absorptive capacity.

3. The *Canadian Environmental Assessment Act* states that once an assessment has been conducted, the "responsible party" may proceed with a project where "the project is likely to cause significant adverse environmental effects" if these effects "can be justified in the circumstances." What circumstances might justify allowing a project to proceed where it is known that adverse environmental effects may occur?

4. What criticisms have been made of *CEPA*? Propose two changes you would make to *CEPA* to address these criticisms.

5. Review the provisions in *CEPA* and *CEAA* that provide opportunities for the public to participate in environmental affairs.

Applying Legal Concepts

1. *340909 Ontario Limited v. Huron Steel Products (Windsor Inc. and Huron Steel Products)* (1990) 73 O.R. (2d) 641

   Soon after Huron Steel Products installed a new 800-tonne press at its Windsor, Ontario, stamping plant in 1979, Douglas Kenney complained to both the company and the Ministry of the Environment. As president of a corporation called 340909 Ontario Limited, which owned a building near the plant, he was concerned that the noise and vibrations resulting from the press's operations were causing his tenants to leave and making it difficult to rent apartments.

Mr. Justice Potts found that Huron Steel's operations unreasonably interfered with its neighbour's use and enjoyment of its property, thus constituting a nuisance. He awarded $71 427 damages for lost rental revenue and reduction in the value of the apartment building. He also ordered that if Huron Steel failed to complete remedial work within four-and-a-half months, it would be prohibited from operating its press.

- **What prompted the plaintiff to sue Huron Steel Products?**

- **Why did the court find in favour of the plaintiff?**

- **What damages did the court award the plaintiff? How was this amount calculated?**

- **What further court action did the defendant face if it did not remedy the problem within a specified time?**

2. *R. v. Bata Industries Ltd.* (1993) Ontario Provincial Court General Division 14 O.R. (3d) 354

The company, which operated a shoe manufacturing plant, was charged under section 16(1) of the *Ontario Water Resources Act* with allowing a discharge of pollutants into the environment. Two directors of the company were charged under section 75(1) of the *Act* with failing to take reasonable care to prevent contamination of the environment.

Investigators had found drums and barrels on the plant site containing chemical wastes. Many of the containers were in a state of disrepair and were foaming and leaking their contents. Tests at the site showed that contamination of ground water would result from chemical spills.

The company and the directors were found guilty of the charges. The company was fined $120 000 and the directors were fined $12 000 each. In deciding on the sentences, the court had considered the following: the area affected was not special or unique in any way; the damage was repairable and confined to a small area; the company had not deliberately disregarded the law and had taken full responsibility for cleaning up the site; and the directors had shown some remorse. On the other hand, the court wanted to set a penalty that would be harsh enough to deter others from committing similar violations. Also, the directors had not shown up at the hearing.

- **What charges did the courts rule on in this case? What decisions did the courts render?**

- **What general factors did the courts consider in determining the penalties?**

- **What is your opinion of the decision of the directors not to attend the hearings?**

3. *Canada (Environment Canada) v. Canada (Northwest Territories Commissioner)* (1994) Northwest Territories Court 1 W.W.R. 441

The defendant, the Northwest Territories Commissioner, was charged by Environment Canada with three counts of depositing a deleterious substance into the water, contrary to section 36(3) of the *Fisheries Act*. The defendant owned and operated a sewage lagoon located just outside of town. In June 1991, heavy runoff during a period of high temperatures had caused the dike around the lagoon to fail, and the sewage in the lagoon had emptied into a nearby inlet.

The defendant was convicted on all three counts. A scientific test had demonstrated that the effluent was lethal to fish in the inlet. Also, the defendant failed to establish the defence of due diligence.

The defendant was responsible for the operation of the lagoon. It had set up safety guidelines, which it had then failed to follow. It had not carried out regular inspections of the site even though the dike containing the sewage had failed several times in the past, usually during spring runoff. A major construction project near the lagoon had significantly altered the surrounding terrain and had changed drainage patterns.

- **Who were the opposing parties in this case?**

- **What event had resulted in the charges being laid?**

- **Explain the defence of due diligence.**

- **How did the judge rule in this case? Explain.**

4. *R. v. Northwood Pulp Timber Ltd.* (1992) British Columbia Provincial Court 9 C.E.L.R. 289

The company, which operated a pulp mill on the Fraser River, was charged with three offences under the *Waste Management Act*. During a partial shutdown of the mill, tests by company workers had shown that toxin levels in effluent from the plant were exceeding permit levels. As well, total suspended solids in the effluent were found to be exceeding permit levels. Prior to this event, the Ministry of the Environment had directed the company to find an alternative to the practice of discharging sludge, a by-product of the pulp-making process, directly into the river.

The court dismissed two of the charges and granted a stay of proceedings on the third. Although the Crown had proved the *actus reus* of each offence, the company had established the defence of due diligence. The evidence showed that the company's effluent treatment and monitoring system was extensive and thorough, the problem was not foreseeable, and the company had acted in good faith in reporting the excessive levels to the government and in working to find their cause.

Also, at the time the company had been told to stop dumping sludge no alternative technology was available to deal with the problem. Meanwhile, the company had been making every effort to develop a process that would meet the new government requirement.

The court found that the Ministry had acted unfairly and oppressively, and that the prosecution of the charge was so offensive that it constituted an abuse of the process.

- **With what offences was Northwood Pulp Timber Ltd. charged?**

- **Why did the company's defence of due diligence succeed?**

- **What criticism did the court make against the Ministry of the Environment in this case? Suggest the larger implications of this decision.**

Extending Legal Concepts

1. Prepare a research report for presentation to class on one of the following topics. Use information in your school resource centre and computer data bases. Be sure to explain how environmental laws relate to the topic.

   - International efforts to reduce atmospheric pollution: A story of success or failure?

   - The collapse of the Atlantic fisheries: Who is to blame?

   - The Hibernia Project: Are the potential benefits worth the risk to the environment?

   - Canada–U.S. efforts at restoring the Great Lakes ecosystem: An example of international cooperation.

   - The cancellation of the Kemano Completion Project in British Columbia: Weighing the costs and benefits.

2. Working in groups of four, arrange a visit to a local industry. (Alternatively, write to a major industry for the information.) Find out what environmental laws and regulations most affect the company's operation, and what measures the company has put in place to bring it into compliance with these laws and regulations. If possible, find out the cost to the company of implementing these measures.

3. Compare the environmental policies of the major political parties in your province. Identify the parts of each party's policy with which you most agree and most disagree. Be prepared to defend your choices.

4. Organize a panel discussion for your school or class around some aspect of the law and environmental protection. Invite representatives from government, political parties, and activist groups to participate on the panel.

Researching an Issue

The Role of the Public

Many people in Canada are passionately concerned about the protection of the environment. They have shown their concern by expressing their opinions in letters to newspapers, joining activist groups, and even participating in protests. In short they have shown a willingness to get directly involved.

Statement

Canadian environmental law gives environmental activists useful tools for protecting the environment.

Point

Laws such as the *Canadian Environmental Assessment Act* and the use of environmental impact assessments have made possible direct public input into the decision-making process.

Counterpoint

Canada's environmental laws and policies show a strong bias toward allowing economic growth even at the cost of further harm to the environment.

- **With a partner, research this issue and reflect on your findings.**
- **Prepare points on this statement that could be used for a class debate.**
- **Discuss your findings with others in your class.**

Chapter
22

THE LAW AND NATIVE PEOPLES

These are the key terms introduced in this chapter:

aboriginal title	First Nations	non-registered Indians
alienate	Indian	off-reserve Indians
assimilate	Indian treaty	registered Indians
band	indigenous	reserve
Certificate of Possession	Inuit	reserve land
comprehensive claims	Métis	specific claims
enfranchised	numbered treaties	treaty Indians

Chapter at a Glance

Learning Outcomes

At the end of this chapter, you will be able to

1. identify legal distinctions existing among Canada's aboriginal peoples;
2. identify the purpose and provisions of the *Indian Act*;
3. explain the status of the *Indian Act* in relation to other statutes;
4. review the history of treaty making in Canada up to and including the numbered treaties, and make a legal assessment of these treaties;
5. analyze and assess the legal arguments for and against recognition of aboriginal title;
6. list the aboriginal rights being claimed by Native peoples;
7. describe the modern-day process of negotiating land claims agreements;
8. explain the relationship of the present Constitution to aboriginal and treaty rights;

After warnings over the past decade that Canada's Indian reserves are a powder keg waiting to explode, there are signs the summer of 1995 will be remembered as the year when the fuse was lit.

Across the country, unrest in aboriginal communities is marking these hot months. During a season usually best known in Indian country for travelling pow-wows and family bush outings, violence and confrontation are leaving an ugly stain.

- Last week, the military was forced off its Ipperwash, Ontario, base by a breakaway group of Indians.
- A month-long protest, which ended last weekend, over salmon fishing on New Brunswick's Miramichi River could have turned violent after self-proclaimed warriors joined the fray.
- Road blockades at two different Indian communities

Ready to Explode

in British Columbia produced tense moments, including an incident at Adams Lake where an off-duty police officer was threatened at gunpoint.

- There has been significant unrest at Oka, the modern reference point for aboriginal militancy. This time, Quebec police and part of the Kanesatake community joined forces to try to wipe out a lucrative cash crop of marijuana.
- In Ottawa, tax protesters who occupied a government office in Toronto earlier this year are now occupying an island in the Ottawa River.

The causes of the unrest on reserves—which just about

every aboriginal leader agrees have only begun—have some similarities, no matter where they start up.

And Indian leaders say nothing is likely to change as a result of federal Indian Affairs Minister Ron Irwin's proposal this week to give municipal-type powers to aboriginal governments. The most common thread of unrest is a growing frustration and impatience with the provincial and federal governments. Expectations have been raised among the aboriginal population during the past five years and many are reaching the conclusion that the politicians—both Indian and non-Indian—cannot deliver.

From: Jack Aubry, "Ready to explode." *The Ottawa Citizen*, August 12, 1995. Reprinted with permission of *The Ottawa Citizen*.

Something to Think About

- **What is the cause of unrest on Canada's Indian reserves?**
- **Could alternative dispute resolution methods be used effectively in these situations? Why or why not?**
- **Is adopting a militant approach an effective way to settle Indian claims?**

22.1 *I*NTRODUCTION

Aboriginal peoples are the **indigenous** inhabitants of an area. That is, they are the descendants of those who first occupied a land or were found by colonial powers to be in possession of a territory. In Canada, the terms "aboriginal" and "Native" are used interchangeably.

In this chapter, you will examine the law as it applies to the Native peoples of Canada. In the

1990s, the relationship Native people have with Canadian law and the justice system is an uneasy one. These tensions are rooted in an unhappy and troubled history.

Native peoples have occupied the North American continent for at least 12 000 years—perhaps as long as 30 000 years. At the time Europeans began establishing their first permanent settlements, not one of the regions the colonial powers wanted to occupy was completely uninhabited.

Two main objectives of the European powers were to **alienate** or remove Native peoples from their traditional lands, and to encourage their **assimilation** into European society. The purpose behind this was to make it possible for Europeans to settle peacefully in North America.

Contact between European and aboriginal cultures had profound and often devastating effects on the Native peoples. Native populations were ravaged by diseases against which they had no natural resistance. They soon found themselves linked economically with the new arrivals. Their cultures were eroded. Major social problems resulted from these changes. These effects continue to be felt and are particularly evident among young Native people today.

The approach taken in this chapter reflects the view that the study of the law and Native peoples should not be done in a strictly legalistic way. It is important to have some sense of the historical, cultural, political, and economic context within which laws operate. One must also be aware that this area of the law is constantly changing. These changes mark progress that is slowly being made toward the creation of a new and more just relationship between Canada and its first peoples.

Did You Know

The United Nations declared 1995–2005 to be the Decade of the World's Indigenous People. This followed the United Nation's Year of Indigenous People in 1993.

22.2 CULTURAL AND LEGAL DISTINCTIONS

When European colonists began arriving in North America in the 1600s, they encountered people who spoke unfamiliar languages and differed greatly in their physical appearance and way of life. We now know that within the boundaries of present-day Canada, there were at least 11 major language groups speaking more than 50 local languages or dialects, and 7 major cultural areas with considerable variation within each.

Non-Native Canadians have often failed to grasp the extent and significance of this diversity. Too often, they resort to using inaccurate, stereotypical images when portraying Native peoples. Conversely, for Native peoples, their sense of identity is strongly influenced by their linguistic and cultural uniqueness.

Legal Distinctions

Complicating the concept of Native identity are divisions based along legal lines. These divisions are important because they ultimately affect the rights and benefits due persons of Native ancestry.

Section 35(1) of the *Constitution Act, 1982*, distinguishes between **Indians**, **Inuit**, and **Métis**, stating that Canada's "aboriginal peoples" include these three groups. Broadly speaking, the term Inuit applies to aboriginal peoples living in arctic and sub-arctic regions north of the tree line. The term Métis has referred historically to the offspring of Native women and French and Scottish fur traders and their descendants but is being used more and more to describe all people of mixed Indian/non-Indian ancestry.

However, the *Constitution Act, 1982*, does not offer a precise definition of who is an Indian, Inuit, or Métis in the legal sense, thus leaving the distinction between "aboriginal peoples" and other Canadians unclear.

Section 91(24) of the *Constitution Act, 1867*, gives the federal Parliament exclusive jurisdiction over "Indians, and Lands reserved for Indians." In 1939, the Supreme Court of Canada ruled that the term *Indian*, as used in the *Constitution Act, 1867*, does apply to the Inuit. However, there has been no ruling on whether the term applies to the Métis as well. How this question is resolved will influence the legal status of the Métis as a distinct group in Canadian society.

The *Indian Act*, which is discussed in detail in the next section, is arguably the most important single piece of legislation affecting aboriginal people in Canada. It applies to persons who are formally registered as "Indians" under the *Act* and affects most Native people living on the 2242 **reserves** scattered across Canada. Native people who are registered are known as **registered Indians**. Those, who for some reason are not registered, are called **non-registered Indians**.

R. v. Perry

[1996]

Ontario Superior Court (Unreported)

Harold Perry, a person of Indian ancestry but not registered under the *Indian Act*, was charged with hunting ducks without a licence. At the time the charges were laid, Ontario had brought in an *Interim Enforcement Policy* that afforded registered Indians with band status some protection from fishing and hunting prosecutions, while the government worked out "management" agreements with Native groups.

At trial, Perry challenged the charges against him on constitutional grounds, arguing that the *Interim Enforcement Policy* unfairly discriminated against him on the basis of his "non-registered" status. The trial judge agreed and dismissed the charges.

The effect of this was to bolster aboriginal hunting and fishing rights in relation to Ontario laws and to extend the *Interim Enforcement Policy* to include Ontario's 125 000 Métis and non-registered Indians. When the Ontario government withdrew the *Policy*, the judge ordered that it be restored.

1. a) **What was the purpose of the *Interim Enforcement Policy*?**

   b) **Why had Perry been charged with a hunting offence despite the existence of this policy?**

2. **What effect might the decision in this case have on aboriginal people outside Ontario?**

Bill C-31, proclaimed into law in 1985, changed the rules governing eligibility for Indian status. It eliminated certain discriminatory features of the *Indian Act* such as the provision that caused Native women to lose their status if they married non-Natives. The number of non-registered Indians is now relatively small, as many who had lost their status prior to the enactment of Bill C-31 successfully applied for reinstatement. The obvious consequence of this is that the number of registered Indians has increased dramatically since 1985.

Bill C-31 also gave Indian bands the option of exercising some control over who could be band members. What this has meant for some newly reinstated Indians is that they have had trouble in gaining membership in an Indian band.

The *Indian Act* defines a **band** as "a body of Indians for whose use and benefit in common, lands, the legal title to which is vested in Her Majesty, have been set apart." There are 607 bands in Canada, which are now commonly referred to by Native people as **First Nations**. A single band might occupy several separate pieces of **reserve land** distributed over a wide area.

Over 200 bands have opted to develop their own membership codes. Bill C-31 declared certain categories of Indian people as automatically entitled to band membership. However, a band may set its own criteria for the admission of new members and even exclude certain classes of registered Indians.

Other legal distinctions are deserving of mention. **Treaty Indians** are persons who are covered by treaties with respect to their aboriginal lands. They enjoy access to specific benefits granted under the terms of the treaties. At present, about one-half of the land making up Canada's 10 provinces is not covered by Indian treaty. However, this situation can be expected to change as treaty negotiations are currently under way in many areas.

People who live away from their reserve for 12 consecutive months or longer are defined as **off-reserve Indians** and lose a number of rights dependent upon residency and band membership.

All these legal distinctions have created a complex and sometimes confusing situation for those trying to determine what rights and benefits are due to persons of Native ancestry. The chart provides a useful summary.

Benefits of Indian Status

The benefits of Indian status are difficult to list completely. This is because some of the benefits are dependent on government policy, and others are dependent on status with a First Nation. Some highlights are listed below.

a) Registered Indians who are members of a First Nation and live on the Nation's reserve
- can vote in First Nation elections and run for office
- can enjoy treaty rights
- are entitled to tax exemptions
- can enjoy rights, such as residence, granted by the First Nation
- are eligible to receive health, educational, and economic development benefits provided by Indian Affairs

b) Registered Indians who are members of a First Nation and live off the Nation's reserve
- may not be able to vote in First Nation elections or run for office
- can enjoy treaty rights
- are entitled to partial tax exemptions, but may not be exempt from provincial sales tax
- have the potential to exercise rights granted by the First Nation
- are eligible to receive some health, educational, and economic development benefits provided by various provincial or federal agencies . . .

d) People without Indian registration who live on the reserve of a First Nation and are members of that First Nation
- can participate in the affairs of the First Nation
- may enjoy only partial treaty rights (still not clear)
- are not entitled to tax exemptions
- can enjoy rights granted by the First Nation such as residence, housing, etc.
- are eligible for some health, educational, and economic development benefits provided by various provincial and federal agencies

Source: *Aboriginal Law Handbook.*

Reviewing Your Reading

1. Prior to their contact with Europeans, did the Native people of what is now Canada share a common language and culture? Explain.

2. Distinguish between "Indian," "Inuit," and "Métis."

3. a) Under the *Constitution Act, 1867*, what level of government was given jurisdiction over Indian affairs?

   b) Within the meaning of this *Act*, to what two groups does the term "Indian" refer? Which group, now excluded, might some day be covered under this term?

4. Distinguish between "registered Indian" and "non-registered Indian."

5. What changes with respect to Indian status were introduced under Bill C-31?

6. What advantage is there for a person of Native ancestry to be a treaty Indian?

7. What rights and benefits does a registered Indian, who is also a member of a First Nation, stand to lose by choosing not to permanently live on a reserve?

22.3 THE INDIAN ACT

The first *Indian Act* was passed by the federal Parliament in 1876. The *Act* was revised extensively in 1880 and underwent further amendments in 1884, 1895, 1906, 1927, 1951, 1970, and 1985. The *Indian Act* sets out the legal requirements for being a status Indian, provides for the administration of Indian reserve lands, and generally regulates the lives of Indians. In effect, the *Act* gives Indians a special legal position in Canadian society, but one that does not necessarily work to their advantage. Although Indians are accorded special benefits and rights, they also face restrictions that are not shared by other Canadians.

The original purpose of the *Indian Act* was to promote a policy of total assimilation. Indian culture was to be gradually eliminated and Indians were to live sheltered, carefully supervised lives on reserves in preparation for taking on the full rights and responsibilities of citizenship. "Protection and advancement" was the slogan of the government department responsible for Indian affairs. The thinking was that, with the loss of most of their traditional lands, Indians had no choice but to undergo a complete change of culture and join the mainstream of Canadian society.

The *Indian Act* has been used to perpetrate a number of serious injustices. Under the first *Indian Act,* Indians lost their status if they became doctors, lawyers, or ministers. Local Indian agents persuaded thousands of registered Indians to give up their status in order to become **enfranchised**, that is, be given the full rights of citizenship. To qualify for enfranchisement, a person had to live off reserve for several years and prove economic self-sufficiency.

In 1884, the *Indian Act* was amended to outlaw the potlatch festival. This deprived the First Nations living in coastal areas of British Columbia the right to hold traditional ceremonies long used to invest new chiefs, honour the dead, and mark other important occasions.

Band Councils

As noted earlier, the *Indian Act* defines a band as a group of registered Indians for whom the federal government has set aside reserved land for their common benefit and use. Bands are legal entities whose authority is derived from the *Act.* Bands may enter contracts, may sue and be sued, and may be held liable for criminal acts. Bands are governed by a chief and band council. The original intention of the *Indian Act* was to replace traditional tribal systems of government, which were often matriarchal (ruled by women) and based on inherited authority, with a system modelled on the parliamentary system.

However, the *Indian Act* does give bands a choice. A band may elect a chief and council by "*Indian Act* declaration," a system that is based on modern, western democratic practices. In this case, the *Act* sets the rules determining who may run for office, who may vote, election procedures, and terms of office. Or a band may follow "band custom" and conduct an election according to long-standing traditions.

It is noteworthy that the *Act* gives the Minister of Indian Affairs the authority to overturn an election held under the *Indian Act* or change a band's election practices to an *Indian Act* election system without its formal consent. The majority of bands in Canada conduct their elections by *Indian Act* declaration.

Law Making

The *Indian Act* gives bands the authority to enact their own bylaws. Such laws are enforceable in Canadian courts. While some bylaws are passed by every person voting on an issue, most bylaws require only that they be passed by majority vote at a band council meeting. The Minister of Indian Affairs can disallow a bylaw within 40 days of it being passed. If the Minister takes no action the bylaw goes into effect. Normally, the penalty for violating bylaws is a maximum fine of $1000 or 30 days in jail or both.

Certain types of bylaws require broader approval from a band. For example, the *Indian Act* authorizes bands to make bylaws prohibiting the sale or manufacture of alcoholic beverages on a reserve, and prohibiting anyone on a reserve from being intoxicated or in possession of alcohol.

The procedure for enacting such bylaws is as follows:

1. A draft bylaw is passed by the majority vote of a band council.
2. A special meeting of band members is called to vote on the draft bylaw.

3. The draft bylaw is approved by a majority of those attending the meeting.
4. The band council meets to pass the approved bylaw.
5. The bylaw is sent to the Minister of Indian Affairs, who has 40 days to disallow it.

A number of bands in Canada have passed such bylaws. Penalties for breaking them can range up to a $1000 fine and/or six months' imprisonment.

Land

Many of the bylaws passed by bands relate to land use. Examples could include bylaws regulating construction of roads and other local works, zoning, surveying, and allotting reserve lands to individuals, and regulation of the construction and repair of buildings. The *Indian Act* attempts to retain the traditional concept of collective ownership and also to provide rights of private ownership. An Indian may obtain a **Certificate of Possession** upon approval of the band council and the Minister of Indian Affairs. This entitles the bearer to occupy and work a piece of reserve land. However, the bearer cannot sell the land, except to another band member. Also, a band may order the removal of a person from his or her land upon approval of the Minister. The Crown holds legal title to all reserve lands in Canada. An Indian band cannot sell land except to the Crown, and only if provisions specified in the *Indian Act* are met.

Education

The first *Indian Act* granted band councils the power to choose the religious denomination of teachers at reserve schools but gave very little other authority over educational matters. The government saw education as a primary means of assimilating Indian children into Canadian society.

In many parts of Canada from the 1920s to the 1960s, Indian children were removed from their parents and educated far from home in residential schools. They were taught little if anything of Native traditions or values and were often punished for speaking their own language. Tragically, many were subjected to physical or even sexual abuse.

The Department of Indian Affairs has moved to transfer powers to administer on-reserve schools to local bands by empowering them to create their own Education Authorities.

Aboriginal leaders see this as an important step toward full Native control of education, but some have expressed concern about the need for better funding.

Did You Know

An accord signed in November 1994 gave Nova Scotia's Micmacs control over the education of their children.

NEWSWORTHY

Band Chiefs Asked to Help Clean Up Indian Act

Indian Affairs Minister Ron Irwin has asked Canada's 600 Native Indian chiefs for help in cleaning up the Indian Act.

Irwin said amending the "offensive" and "intrusive" law, which has governed Indians since Confederation, is only an interim measure that should not last "even another 10 years."

"The Act is colonial and archaic and many of the things in it aren't even followed any more," he said in an interview.

His letter lists four areas that need to be eliminated or changed: ministerial power over bands, implementation of land claim and treaty land entitlement settlements, elections, and length of band council terms, and bylaw enforcement.

From: "Band chiefs asked to help clean up Indian Act," *The Ottawa Citizen*, April 18, 1995. Reprinted with permission of *The Ottawa Citizen*.

Discretionary Powers of the Department of Indian Affairs

The first *Indian Act* gave wide discretionary powers to local Indian agents, who could override the decisions of band councils. These agents were encouraged by their superiors in the Indian Affairs Department to look upon themselves as having a kind of protecting role. The result was that many Native communities came to view agents as autocratic and the source of delay in handling their requests.

The role of Indian agents has diminished significantly, but the Department of Indian Affairs continues to exercise its supervisory powers. Since 1982, for example, Indian Affairs ministers have disallowed almost half of all bylaws passed by band councils. Because these bylaws are made under the authority of a federal statute, they may be overturned by other federal laws. It is not surprising that, at a time when aboriginal peoples are pressing for the right of self-government, they see the *Indian Act* as increasingly oppressive and outdated.

Relationship of the *Indian Act* to Provincial Laws

Section 88 of the *Indian Act* states:

> **88.**
>
> Subject to the terms of any treaty and any other Act of the Parliament of Canada, all laws of general application from time to time in force in any province are applicable to and in respect of Indians in the Province, except to the extent that such laws are inconsistent with this Act or any order, rule, regulation or any bylaw made thereunder, and except to the extent that such laws make provision for any matter for which provision is made by or under this Act.

Put simply, this means that provincial laws apply to registered Indians, unless they conflict with Indian treaties, or the *Indian Act* and other federal "Indian" laws and regulations, and unless they single out Indians as a distinct group. Thus the courts have ruled that provincial hunting regulations do not apply on Indian reserves because they directly affect the use of reserve land, which falls under federal jurisdiction.

Reviewing Your Reading

1. **What was the original goal of the *Indian Act* and what was the underlying rationale for this goal?**

2. **Bands may choose their chief and council by "*Indian Act* declaration," or by "band custom." Distinguish between the two approaches.**

3. **Cite two overriding powers the Minister of Indian Affairs can exercise that can affect band affairs.**

4. **What rights does a Certificate of Possession convey to a bearer?**

5. **What procedure must a band follow if it wants to enact a bylaw prohibiting the possession of alcohol on a reserve?**

6. **Explain in your own words the meaning of section 88 of the *Indian Act*.**

22.4 TREATIES AND TREATY RIGHTS

In the legal sense, **Indian treaties** can be viewed as written agreements, concluded between government officials and a recognizable group of aboriginal people, setting out various terms that the two parties are obliged to honour. The courts have taken the view that these agreements are neither full "international" treaties in the sense of being agreements between *sovereign* nations, nor are they simply domestic contracts. Rather, they are unique documents for which special rules of interpretation and enforcement must be developed.

What of rights guaranteed under treaties? In Canada, rights are generally viewed as individual rights. Treaty rights are different. They are collective rights belonging to a particular group or community, and are enjoyed by all its members.

Looking Back

The earliest treaties in Canada date back to the eighteenth century, when First Nations peoples and Europeans in Quebec and the Maritimes formed political alliances and concluded peace and friendship agreements. Our present treaty system has its roots in the *Royal Proclamation of 1763,* which made the British Crown the exclusive agency of land transfers between Indians and settlers.

The *Proclamation* declared that Indian lands could be surrendered only to the Crown's representatives at public meetings. This meant that direct purchases of land from Indians by private individuals or groups were no longer recognized in law.

It has been argued that the *Proclamation* established the principle that Indian lands could be legally acquired only by treaty and with the full voluntary consent of the First Nations directly affected. Also, it implicitly recognized tribal sovereignty and the aboriginal right of self-government. Others have countered that the *Proclamation* was intended mainly to protect Native people from exploitation by settlers, and in no way recognized or protected the right to self-government.

Numerous land cession treaties were concluded in Upper Canada during the late 1700s. These treaties typically provided for a surrender of small amounts of land in return for a one-time payment of money and goods and an *annuity,* that is, an annual payment in perpetuity.

In the early 1850s, similar agreements were formed on Vancouver Island. Governor James Douglas, acting in his capacity as local head of the Hudson's Bay Company, entered into 14 treaties with First Nations peoples. The Indians surrendered land in exchange for the promise of reserved land and small payments per family.

Significantly, these treaties were not made in the name of the Crown. When Douglas tried to correct this by petitioning the British Government for money to cover the cost of land surrendered, his request was turned down. This was not because the British were against the principle of Crown purchases of land, but because they felt that the colony should pay the cost. As a result of this disagreement, the treaty-making process in British Columbia broke down.

A new type of land agreement appeared with the Robinson treaties of 1850. In 1846, the First Nations of the regions north of Lake Huron and Lake Superior petitioned the Governor General of Canada to halt mining development there until treaties had been concluded. The treaties that were eventually signed dealt with vast tracts of land and formally listed 21 reserves, including details of their size and location. The Robinson treaties were the first to recognize continued hunting and fishing rights. The Robinson treaties were also unique in that the First Nations affected did not surrender and then receive back their reserve lands—they always kept their reserve lands and only ceded their surrounding lands.

At trial, the respondents were found guilty of having in their possession the carcasses of six deer during the closed season without having a valid permit, contrary to the provisions of the *British Columbia Game Act, 1960*. The respondents appealed to the County Court, where their conviction was overturned. The Crown then appealed to the British Columbia Court of Appeal.

The respondents argued that an 1854 agreement between their ancestors and Governor James Douglas for the sale of tribal land to the Hudson's Bay Company gave them the right to hunt for food over this land. They also contended that they possessed an aboriginal right to hunt for food over unoccupied land lying within their traditional hunting grounds.

The Crown insisted that the 1854 agreement created no hunting rights, and even if it did, these rights had been extinguished by section 88 of the *Indian Act*, which had the effect of extending the provision of the *British Columbia Game Act, 1960,* to Indians. This, the Crown contended, was because the agreement in question was not a treaty, but merely an agreement for sale of land.

The appeal court found the agreement to be a treaty within the meaning of section 88, and concluded that the provisions of the *British Columbia Game Act, 1960,* did not extend over the land in question. To quote from the judgment:

"In my opinion, their peculiar rights of hunting and fishing over their ancient hunting grounds, arising under agreements by which they collectively sold their ancient lands, are Indian affairs over which Parliament has exclusive legislative authority, and only Parliament can derogate from those rights." The Crown's appeal to the British Columbia Court of Appeal was dismissed.

1. **With what offence were the respondents charged? What defence did they offer?**

2. **On what basis did the British Columbia Court of Appeal rule that the** *British Columbia Game Act, 1960,* **did not apply to the respondents?**

R. v. White and Bob (1965)

British Columbia Court of Appeal
52 D.L.R. (2d) 481

Post-Confederation Period

Confederation set the stage for the transfer of control over huge territories, known as Rupert's Land, from the Hudson's Bay Company to Canada. This area included the interior plains, the northern part of British Columbia, and northwestern Ontario. It has been argued that at the time of Confederation, Canada assumed a moral and legal responsibility for protecting the interests and well-being of the First Nations. As noted earlier, section 91(24) of the *Constitution Act, 1867,* gave the Government of Canada exclusive law-making authority over aboriginal peoples.

Between 1871 and 1921, the Government of Canada concluded a series of land agreements with the First Nations inhabiting the newly named "Northwest Territory." These agreements are known as the **numbered treaties** and total 11 in all.

The numbered treaties resemble the Robinson treaties, both in terms of their complexity and the size of the land areas involved. For example Treaty No. 11 affects an area of about 963 000 km^2 in size.

Typically, these treaties provided for the granting of reserve lands (on the basis of so many hectares per family) for the exclusive use and benefit of the First Nations signing the treaty; the

R. v. Sikyea
(1964)

**Northwest
Territories
Court of Appeal
43 D.L.R. (2d) 150**

The respondent, a member of Band 84 under Treaty 11 was convicted on a charge of killing a female mallard duck out of season in violation of regulations made under the federal *Migratory Birds Convention Act, 1917*. The respondent was unaware of this restriction and argued that he was protected under the hunting, fishing, and trapping guarantee in Treaty 11.

The trial court fined the respondent $10 and costs. The bird and the respondent's gun were seized. The conviction was appealed, and at a trial *de novo*, the conviction was set aside. The Crown then appealed the case to the Northwest Territories Court of Appeal.

The judgment handed down by the appeal court stated: "It is always to be kept in mind that the Indians surrendered their rights in the territory in exchange for these promises. This 'promise' like any other, can, of course, be breached, and there is no law of which I am aware that would prevent parliament, by legislation properly within section 91 of the *BNA Act*, ch.3, from doing so.

"It is, I think, clear that the rights given to the Indians by their treaties as they apply to migratory birds have been taken away by this *Act* and its regulations. How are we to explain this apparent breach of faith on the part of the government, for I cannot think it can be described in any other terms."

In other words, the court declared that where there was a clear contradiction between a federal statute and an Indian treaty, the statute must prevail.

1. **According to the Court of Appeal, what authority do federal laws have in relation to rights guaranteed in treaties?**

2. **The judgment refers to a "breach of faith" by the federal government. What breach of faith had occurred in the opinion of the court?**

3. **Would the Sikyea decision have been different if, at the time of the trial, aboriginal and treaty rights had been formally protected in Canada's Constitution? Explain.**

building of schools; the furnishing of farm equipment, seed, and livestock; hunting and fishing rights; lump sum cash payments; and annuities (varying from $3 to $12 per member). Chiefs and headmen were given more money than others, sets of clothing every three years, and various other goods. The government promised to provide assistance in time of "famine or pestilence."

A large and growing body of case law now exists on Indian treaties. Among the more significant rulings are that Indian treaties can extinguish aboriginal rights; can preserve aboriginal rights; prevail over provincial laws where there is a conflict; prior to the *Constitution Act, 1982*, were subordinate to federal laws; and following the proclamation of the *Constitution Act, 1982*, can prevail over federal laws.

Indians and federal government officials have often found themselves at odds over the way they view aboriginal treaties. Some writers have suggested that misunderstandings arose originally because First Nations and Europeans held different notions of land ownership and saw their relationship to the land in very different ways. Also, the Indian negotiators of the time found the legalistic language of the written treaty documents almost impossible to interpret and misunderstood what they were agreeing to. Finally, the oral tradition of Native peoples led them to place greater faith in speech making and verbal promises than in written documents.

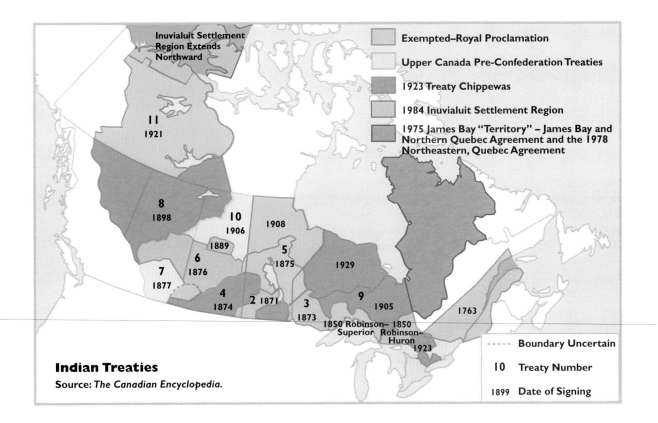

Indian Treaties

Source: *The Canadian Encyclopedia.*

Legend:
- Exempted–Royal Proclamation
- Upper Canada Pre-Confederation Treaties
- 1923 Treaty Chippewas
- 1984 Inuvialuit Settlement Region
- 1975 James Bay "Territory" – James Bay and Northern Quebec Agreement and the 1978 Northeastern, Quebec Agreement

----- Boundary Uncertain
10 Treaty Number
1899 Date of Signing

Inuvialuit Settlement Region Extends Northward

11 1921
8 1898
10 1906
1908
1889
6 1876
5 1875
1929
7 1877
4 1874
2 1871
3 1873
9 1905
1763
1850 Robinson– Superior
1850 Robinson–Huron
1923

In *R. v. Battisse* (1978) 9 C.N.L.P. 429 (Ontario District Court) involving Treaty No. 9, the presiding judge observed:

> When Treaty No. 9 was negotiated, the parties to the agreement were on grossly unequal footing. Highly skilled negotiators were dealing with an illiterate people, who, though fearful of losing their way of life, placed great faith in the fairness of His Majesty, as represented by federal authorities. As a matter of fact, a careful reading of the Commissioners' Reports makes it fairly obvious that the Indians thought they were dealing with the King's personal representatives and were relying on the word of His Majesty rather than officials of Government. . . . As a result, approximately 90 000 square miles [about 233 000 km^2] of resource-rich land was acquired by the Crown, free of any beneficial Indian interest, for an absurdly low consideration (even for that time).

When the last numbered treaty was concluded in 1921, large areas of Canada were still not covered by Indian treaty. Land-cession treaties did not cover the Maritimes, most of Quebec, British Columbia, and the northern territories.

In 1973, the treaty-making process began again following a decision in a landmark case, *Calder et al. v. The Attorney General of British Columbia* where the Supreme Court gave some limited recognition to the existence of aboriginal title. The present-day equivalent of the Indian treaty is the "land claims agreement." The subject of modern Native land claims will be examined later in the chapter.

Reviewing Your Reading

1. How do the courts view Indian treaties?

2. What basic rule did the *Royal Proclamation of 1763* establish regarding the sale of Indian lands?

3. Why did the treaty-making process, begun by Governor James Douglas, come to a halt in British Columbia?

4. a) In 1921, what areas of Canada were still not covered by Indian treaty?

   b) What court decision in 1973 rekindled interest in treaty making? Explain why this court case created this renewed interest.

22.5 Aboriginal Rights

Aboriginal rights are considered "inherent" rights, not rights that are negotiated, as we saw in the instance of treaty rights. Aboriginal rights form an immensely complex area of the law, and despite progress that has been made toward defining their source and content, many issues and unanswered questions remain. Like treaty rights, aboriginal rights are conceived as collective rights belonging to an entire group or community.

The term **aboriginal title** refers to rights created by first occupation and use of the land. Native peoples claim many rights based on aboriginal title, including

- the right to occupy traditional lands and to control and benefit from their resources;
- the right to self-government and to determine what form relationships with Canada's other levels of government will take;
- the right to a Native justice system and control over local law enforcement;
- the right to protect and maintain language and culture;
- the control over social services such as administering education;
- the return of cultural objects from museums and private collections;
- compensation for resources taken without Native consent.

In pressing their claims, aboriginal leaders have used many tactics, including court injunctions and protest actions.

A fundamental issue is determining the source of aboriginal rights. David W. Elliott of the Department of Law at Carlton University has identified three approaches to this question: recognition-based, occupancy-based, and community-based. These approaches are discussed below.

Recognition-based Approach

Using the first approach, the courts have looked for proof of the existence of aboriginal rights through examination of evidence of government recognition of their existence, as seen in laws and Constitutional declarations. In this connection, the *Royal Proclamation of 1763,* is viewed as a primary source of aboriginal rights. Some writers have argued that the *Proclamation* recognizes aboriginal title, but this proposition has been hotly disputed.

Occupancy-based Approach

The recognition-based approach prevailed in the courts until the decision in the *Calder* case in 1973, which signalled acceptance of the occupancy-based approach. This approach rests on the idea that aboriginal rights arise from "common law" recognition of the occupation and use of the land by Native peoples prior to the arrival of Europeans.

As we will later see, perhaps the most important finding in the *Calder* case was the idea that aboriginal title may exist at common law independently of the *Royal Proclamation* or other laws or government actions. In the years following the *Calder* decision, the Supreme Court shed little further light either on the issue of aboriginal title, or on the very important related question of what is the actual content of aboriginal rights. In 1984, new legal ground was broken in the *Guerin* case.

The central question in the *Guerin* case was whether or not the Crown owes aboriginal people a fiduciary duty, or duty of trust. The general rule is that a trust can arise when one party assumes responsibility for the property of another, and exercises control over it. Questions raised by the finding in this case include, "What is the extent of the fiduciary duty owed by the Crown to aboriginal peoples?" and "Is this duty related in some way to aboriginal treaties and land claims agreements?"

The proclamation of the *Constitution Act, 1982,* ushered in a new era in aboriginal law. The Constitutional provisions holding the greatest significance for Native peoples are section 25 of the *Charter of Rights and Freedoms,* and section 35 in Part II of the *Charter.*

Section 25 (see Appendix) recognizes that the protection of individual rights may conflict with the preservation of the collective rights of First Nations and attempts to strike a balance between the two. How the courts interpret this section will have the potential to greatly affect the cause of aboriginal self-government. The topic of self-government is examined later in the chapter.

Section 35 acts to "entrench" aboriginal rights in the Canadian Constitution. However, nowhere does the *Act* define what is meant by "existing rights."

The *Act* also remains silent on other important questions, such as, "Are there circumstances where government laws would prevail over entrenched aboriginal rights, and if so, to what extent?" Finding answers to questions of this nature was apparently for the courts to decide.

Indeed, perhaps the most immediate and significant impact of the *Constitution Act, 1982*, was that it gave the courts a greater role in defining relations between First Nations and the rest of Canada. This is dramatically illustrated in the *Sparrow* case.

35.

(1) The existing aboriginal and treaty rights of the aboriginal peoples of Canada are hereby recognized and affirmed.

(2) In this Act, "aboriginal peoples of Canada" includes the Indian, Inuit, and Métis people of Canada.

(3) For greater certainty, in subsection (1), "treaty rights" includes rights that now exist by way of land claims agreements or so may be acquired.

(4) Notwithstanding any other provision of this Act, the aboriginal and treaty rights referred to in subsection (1) are guaranteed equally to male and female persons.

CASE

The Nisga'a people of northwestern British Columbia claimed in court that they held an unextinguished title to their ancestral lands. The British Columbia Supreme Court and the British Columbia Court of Appeal both found that there was no aboriginal title because the British had no knowledge of the area at the time of the *Royal Proclamation of 1763*. Both courts also found that any aboriginal title that might have existed would have been extinguished by proclamations and laws enacted by the colony of British Columbia.

The Supreme Court of Canada also ruled against the Nisga'a, but on a technicality. The laws of British Columbia required that a fiat, or decree, be issued in cases affecting the Crown's own title to land, and this requirement had not been met in this case. Far more significant, however, was the finding of three of the seven judges that aboriginal title may exist at common law independent of the *Royal Proclamation of 1763* or other government acts. The dissenting judges also found that where aboriginal title had not been extinguished, it might exist wherever land had been occupied and used by aboriginal peoples. They further declared: "The Nishga tribe has persevered for almost a century in asserting an interest in the lands which their ancestors occupied since time immemorial. The Nishgas were never conquered nor did they at any time enter into a treaty or deed of surrender as many other Indian tribes did throughout Canada and in southern British Columbia."

Calder et al. v. The Attorney General of British Columbia
(1973)

Supreme Court of Canada
34 D.L.R. (3rd) 145

1. **On what technical ground did the Nisga'a lose their case?**

2. **Summarize the findings of the three dissenting judges with respect to aboriginal title.**

3. **Show how this case illustrates the "occupancy-based" approach to aboriginal rights.**

4. **Why do you think the federal government decided to press ahead with treaty making even though the Nisga'a lost their case?**

Guerin et al. v. R.
(1984)

Supreme Court of Canada

13 D.L.R. (4th) 321

In 1957, Anfield, the Indian Affairs branch officer for the Musqueam band, negotiated a long-term lease of band land to a local golf club. The *Indian Act* requires that leases or sales of Indian land to non-Indians must have the approval of the Indian Affairs Department. This reflects the federal government's view that it is the trustee in all matters relating to Indian land.

In 1975, the Musqueam band sued the federal government claiming that Anfield had violated his position of trust. They argued that the lease he had negotiated did not contain the terms which they had orally conveyed to him at a special meeting of band members.

The Musqueam band had wanted an initial annual rent of $2900 for 15 years. This was to be followed by 10-year renewal periods with rents to be agreed upon at the time of renewal. The lease that Anfield actually signed provided for renewal periods of 15 years, with increases limited to 15 percent of the previous rental.

The trial judge ruled that there had been a breach of trust and awarded $10 million to the Musqueam band in compensation for the band being bound to an agreement that did not reflect the current value of the land. The Crown appealed, and in 1982 the Federal Court of Appeal overturned the trial court decision, ruling that a relationship of trust in the strict legal sense had not existed.

Upon appeal, the Supreme Court of Canada ruled unanimously in favour of the Musqueam band. It noted that Indians have no choice in their land dealings but to work with representatives of the Indian Affairs Department, and they rely on these officials to represent their interests. By altering the terms of the lease without the band's knowledge or approval, Anfield had failed in his fundamental duties to the Musqueam band. More generally, there had been a breach of a trust obligation by the federal government. This trust arose in part from the Musqueam band's aboriginal title, whether existing, or once existing and now extinguished.

1. **Does the law give Indians an unrestricted right to sell or lease reserve land? Explain.**

2. **Why was the Musqueam band dissatisfied with the agreement Anfield had negotiated?**

3. **Why did the Supreme Court of Canada find in favour of the Musqueam band?**

4. **Suggest how this case might be used to promote the larger cause of aboriginal rights.**

Sparrow, a Musqueam Indian, while fishing for salmon in the Fraser River near Vancouver, was charged under section 61(1) of the *Fisheries Act* with using a drift net longer than permitted by regulations. Sparrow argued that he had an inherent aboriginal right to fish guaranteed by section 35(1) of the *Constitution Act, 1982,* and that the regulations affecting the length of net did not apply to him.

Sparrow was convicted of the charge in provincial court, and the conviction was upheld later in the county court. Sparrow appealed and the case eventually ended up at the Supreme Court of Canada. The Supreme Court found in favour of Sparrow and ordered a retrial. The main elements of the Supreme Court decision are as follows:

- The term "existing rights" in section 35(1) means unextinguished as of April 17, 1982, (the date when the *Constitutional Act, 1982,* came into effect). The test for extinguishment is whether the government's intention to extinguish is clear and plain. The Court found that nothing in the *Fisheries Act* demonstrated such intention with respect to the extinguishment of aboriginal fishing rights.
- Evidence supporting the Musqueams' claim of an aboriginal right to fish was found in the fact that they had lived in the area of the Fraser River as an organized society long before contact with Europeans, and that fishing was and remains important to their way of life.
- The Musqueams' aboriginal right to fish extended to fishing for food and for ceremonial and religious purposes. The Court did not address the question as to whether or not this right extended to commercial fishing.
- Unless there is a compelling reason for passing a law that interferes with an aboriginal right, the law will infringe section 35(1) of the *Constitution Act, 1982,* and will be declared unconstitutional. In the *Sparrow* case, the Court found no such compelling reason.

R. v. Sparrow
[1990]

**Supreme Court
of Canada
1 S.C.R. 1075**

1. **With what offence was Sparrow charged? What legal argument did he offer in his defence?**

2. **What main findings convinced the Supreme Court that the Musqueams enjoyed an aboriginal right to fish?**

3. **What evidence might Sparrow have brought into court to support his claim that the Musqueams had inhabited the Fraser River delta as an organized fishing culture for a very long time?**

Community-based Approach

Our look at the *Sparrow* case affords us a good point of departure for examining the community-based approach to aboriginal rights. This approach is based on the premise that aboriginal rights are constituted from all distinctive community traditions, not simply derived from aboriginal title based on first occupation and use. In other words, aboriginal title is only one aspect of the source and content of aboriginal rights.

Those using this approach seek to establish that aboriginal traditions predate European colonization and continue to be evident in the everyday life of Native communities. These traditions encompass

- religious beliefs and rites,
- economic practices,
- family organization and custom,
- language,
- justice and law enforcement,
- rules of self-government.

The ruling in *R. v. Sparrow* may provide evidence that the courts have moved a little toward accepting the community-based approach in aboriginal rights cases. It is interesting that many First Nations see in this approach support for their claim to the aboriginal right of self-government. However, to date, Canadian courts have not recognized an inherent, common-law right of aboriginal self-government.

CASE

R. v. Noel
[1995]

Northwest Territories Court
4 C.N.L.R. 78

Noel was charged with violating a regulation that created year-round "no shooting zones" in traditional aboriginal hunting areas. At trial, the Crown argued that the regulation was necessary for the protection of public safety. The defence argued that the regulation interfered with an existing aboriginal right to hunt.

The court found in favour of the defence. The regulation was not enforceable against the accused because the "justificatory" standard had not been met.

The trial judge stated that aboriginal people were to be treated in a manner that ensured their rights were taken seriously. In practical terms, this meant that the government should have sought a solution that intruded as little as possible upon the aboriginal right to hunt. To accomplish this, the government should have carried out direct and meaningful discussions with the aboriginal people who would be affected by the regulation.

1. **What did the court decide in this case? Why?**

2. **What broader implications might the decision in this case have in the general area of aboriginal and treaty rights? Suggest one or two hypothetical examples to illustrate your answer.**

Reviewing Your Reading

1. List several of the rights Native peoples claim based on aboriginal title.

2. Distinguish among the recognition-based, occupancy-based, and community-based approaches to defining aboriginal rights.

3. In your own words, briefly explain what sections 25 and 35 of the *Charter of Rights and Freedoms* declare.

4. a) On what aspects of aboriginal life do proponents of the community-based approach focus their attention?

   b) What is their purpose in researching these community traditions?

22.6 LAND CLAIMS

In 1969, the federal government proposed to repeal the *Indian Act*, revoke existing Indian treaties, and turn over responsibility for Indian programs to the provinces. Government proposals of the time rejected the notion of "aboriginal rights" and suggested that Indian claims to the land were "so general and undefined that it is not realistic to think of them as specific claims capable of remedy." In 1973, following the Supreme Court ruling on the *Calder* case, the federal government reversed itself, and brought in a policy for negotiating land claims settlements. This policy recognized two types of claims—specific and comprehensive.

Specific Claims

Specific claims refer to claims that the government did not fulfill lawful obligations to Indians under the treaties, other agreements, or the *Indian Act.* Since 1973, a sizeable number of specific claims have been settled. These include cases where Indian bands have been compensated for lands wrongfully "cut off" from their reserves, and where the federal government has failed to honour the terms of existing treaties.

Comprehensive Claims

Comprehensive claims are based on the concept of continuing aboriginal rights and title that have not been dealt with by treaty or other lawful means. The federal government's acceptance of a comprehensive claim is contingent upon evidence that the "claimant group" has aboriginal title to its traditional lands. A First Nations group making a comprehensive claim must submit a statement of intent declaring that it has never signed a treaty by which it relinquished its aboriginal rights to the land. It must also provide proof of its continuing occupation or use of traditional lands and include a map or detailed description of the territory being claimed. The application is reviewed by the Comprehensive Claims Branch of the Office of Native Claims and then sent to the Department of Justice for legal appraisal.

Acceptance or rejection of a claim is made ultimately by the Minister of Indian and Northern Affairs. Acceptance means only that the federal government recognizes that a claim has merit and is willing to negotiate a settlement.

Participants in the negotiation process include the claimant group, federal negotiators, and representatives of provincial or territorial governments directly affected. The negotiation process has five main stages:

1. Initial negotiation—to identify key issues and to develop a "framework agreement" to direct the overall approach.

2. Substantial negotiation—to produce an "Agreement-in-Principle."

3. Finalization—to formalize a final agreement.

4. Enactment of settlement legislation—to bring the agreement into force.

5. Implementation of settlement legislation—to carry out the agreement.

Once a land claims agreement is fully settled, it comes under the protection of section 35(1) of the *Constitution Act, 1982*. Negotiations on comprehensive claims are complex and often last many years. Issues for negotiation normally include property rights, hunting and trapping rights, financial compensation, the right to representation on local governing bodies, and the right to share in revenues gained from resource exploitation.

The original settlement process required aboriginal groups to accept extinguishment of their aboriginal title before negotiation of a claim could be completed. This precondition, along with other unwelcome features, made the process unacceptable to many First Nations. In 1986, an amended policy that attempted to address earlier criticisms was introduced. The new policy broadened the scope of what was negotiable and removed extinguishment of title as a requirement for settlement. The continuing issue of self-government has held up progress in a number of claims cases. It is likely that this will be a point of contention for years to come.

Major Settlements

In the two decades after 1973, the following comprehensive claims settlements were concluded. With the exception of the first two agreements, all fall geographically within the Yukon Territory or the Northwest Territories.

1975	James Bay and Northern Quebec Agreement
1978	Northeastern Quebec Agreement
1984	Inuvialuit Final Agreement (western Arctic)
1992	Gwich'in Final Agreement (western Arctic)
1993	Nunavut Land Claims Agreement (eastern Arctic)
1993	Council for Yukon Indians Umbrella Final Agreement and four Yukon First Nations Final Agreements
1993	Sahtu Dene and Métis Final Agreement

An interesting feature of the Nunavut Final Agreement is that it called for the division of the Northwest Territories to create a Nunavut Territory. In 1992, a referendum held in the Northwest Territories set the boundary for this new territory. In the same year, a political accord was signed outlining the powers of a proposed Nunavut Territorial Government. The actual divi-

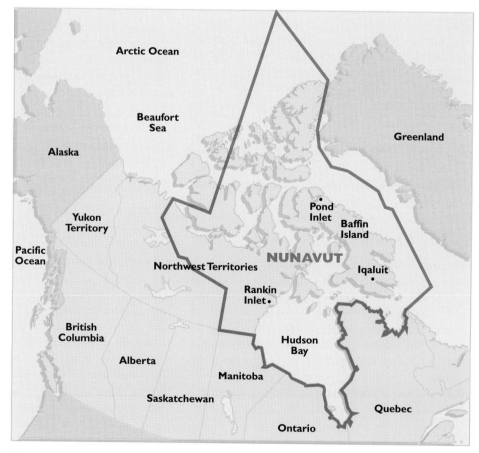

Source: *The Globe and Mail.*

sion of the Northwest Territories is scheduled to take place on April 1, 1999. Iqaluit has been chosen as the capital of the Nunavut Territory.

Land Claims in British Columbia

There are more unsettled comprehensive claims from First Nations in British Columbia than in the rest of Canada combined. From the time of Governor James Douglas's retirement from office in 1864 and up to 1990, the British Columbia government steadfastly refused to recognize the existence of aboriginal land rights. Consequently, no treaty negotiations were possible.

In 1990, British Columbia finally agreed to engage in land claims talks. A task force, representing the province's First Nations and the governments of British Columbia and Canada, was created to define the scope and process of treaty negotiations. The 19 recommendations of the task force presented in 1991 were later endorsed by the federal government.

A key recommendation of the task force was that a treaty commission be created to oversee and facilitate treaty negotiations. This commission was established in 1993, and within a year it had accepted statements of intent from 43 Native groups wanting to negotiate land claims treaties. The commission is prepared to provide mediation services to the parties directly involved in negotiating treaties upon request and makes available loans to Native negotiators to cover their costs. Both the provincial and federal governments are represented at the treaty talks.

On February 26, 1996, after more than 20 years of negotiations, the governments of Canada and British Columbia signed an agreement-in-principle with the Nisga'a, who inhabit the Nass Valley in northwestern British Columbia.

The tentative agreement gives the Nisga'a:

- ownership of 1930 km^2 of land, including timber resources and mineral rights; and the right to harvest a certain volume of timber per year outside the treaty area;
- $190 million to be paid over several years, plus $11.5 million for the purchase of commercial fishing vessels and licences;
- powers of self-government, including the power to tax Nisga'a citizens on Nisga'a land;

- the authority to set up their own police board and system of courts;
- the right to reclaim hundreds of artifacts now held in Canadian museums;
- noncommercial hunting, fishing, and food gathering rights within their traditional territory of 9000 km^2; and participation in wildlife management;
- a guaranteed share of the commercial salmon fishery on the Nass River, in return for agreeing to reduce their constitutionally protected traditional food fishery during low-run years.

Under the agreement, the reserve system is to be abolished on Nisga'a land. The Indian Act will no longer apply to the Nisga'a except for the purpose of determining whether a person is an Indian. Nisga'a who live and work on reserve and purchase goods there will gradually lose the tax exempt status they now enjoy.

The Nisga'a agreement guarantees the general public some access to Nisga'a land for recreational purposes.

The tentative agreement has already been approved in a vote by the Nisga'a people, but still must be ratified by Parliament and the British Columbia legislature.

The agreement has received praise from many non-Native people. However, it has been strongly criticized by others. Opponents of the British Columbia government have declared that the present agreement is not acceptable because it violates the principle of the equality of individuals. Non-Native fishers have voiced strong opposition. Forest companies are worried about the transfer of timber rights to the Nisga'a, which may result in a reduction of timber quotas. All this indicates that the ratification process will be long and difficult.

It is generally accepted that ratification of the Nisga'a deal would set a strong precedent for future land claims settlements in British Columbia. One can only speculate on the effect that a failure to ratify this agreement would have on the larger treaty-making process, in which 48 Native groups are now participating. One thing does seem certain: the final settlement of aboriginal land claims in British Columbia will take many years, even decades, to complete.

Reviewing Your Reading

1. Distinguish between "specific claims" and "comprehensive claims."

2. a) Outline the steps in the process for negotiating comprehensive claims.

   b) What kinds of issues are normally dealt with during treaty negotiations?

3. a) What is the role of British Columbia's treaty commission?

   b) How many Native groups in British Columbia have stated their willingness to enter into treaty negotiations?

   c) What three main parties will be represented at these talks?

4. Which of the provisions of the Nisga'a land claims agreement appear to be most controversial?

22.7 *A*BORIGINAL SELF-GOVERNMENT

The right of self-government has been a recurrent theme in court cases on aboriginal rights, in negotiations on land claims settlements, and in Constitutional talks. Such an interest is understandable. People want to be able to control their own affairs. However, aboriginal people themselves have attached different meanings to the term "self-government." This difference in views is a product of their cultural diversity, varied local and regional needs, historical experience, and personal beliefs.

David W. Elliott, Department of Law, Carleton University, has suggested a number of forms that aboriginal self-government might take. These include the following:

Sovereign Government. The establishment of sovereign aboriginal governments would require the secession of First Nations from Canada and the creation of independent states. This is an extreme solution to be sure, but it is one that is supported by some Native leaders.

Traditional Self-Government. This form of government is based on customs and practices predating European contact. It depends on the voluntary compliance of the aboriginal community to function effectively.

Legislated Self-Government. This is the form of government sanctioned by the *Indian Act.* Although many aboriginal peoples resent this *Act* for the supervisory powers it gives to the Department of Indian Affairs, some bands have taken full advantage of the powers available to them to regulate many areas of community life.

Guaranteed Participation through Negotiation. All the major, comprehensive land claims agreements concluded since 1973 make formal provision for some form of aboriginal representation on local administrative/advisory bodies.

Public Government. Aboriginal people form a majority of citizens in several areas of the country, particularly in the far North. This creates the opportunity for them to determine the outcome of local elections. The newly created territory of Nunavut is made up mainly of aboriginal people, who are in a position to dominate political life there.

Coordinated Ethnic Government. This form of government operates on a two-tiered system. At the reserve level, band councils operate under the authority of the *Indian Act.* At the district level, the same bodies act as district councils with an advisory group that includes non-Natives. Acting in their role as district councils, the band councils exercise delegated provincial powers to provide a wide range of public services.

Judicial Self-Government. This type of government might arise in the event that the courts recognized an inherent right of self-government, or if there were Constitutional recognition of such an inherent right. The courts would ultimately determine the form and powers of such governments.

The topic of aboriginal self-government poses several important questions. What limits should there be on the authority of aboriginal governments? How can the interests of non-Native people affected by aboriginal governments best be protected? Should aboriginal governments be able to infringe on individual rights protected under the *Charter of Rights and Freedoms*? Finally, how should aboriginal governments be financed?

Since the proclamation of the *Constitution Act, 1982*, Native peoples have pressed their demand that the Canadian Constitution be amended to entrench the right of aboriginal self-government. The failure of the Meech Lake Accord in 1990 was due, in part, to Manitoba M.L.A. Elijah Harper's refusal to support it. Harper spoke for many Native people when he criticized the Accord for its failure to address aboriginal demands.

In 1992, the Charlottetown Accord attempted to make amends by proposing entrenchment of an aboriginal right of self-government and offer-ing Native peoples a veto in regard to Constitutional changes directly affecting them. However, these proposals came to nothing when the Canadian people turned down the Accord in a referendum.

Reviewing Your Reading

1. Distinguish between the different forms of aboriginal self-government.

2. Account for the wide diversity of views held by Native peoples on aboriginal self-government.

3. Review sections 25 and 35 of the *Charter*. What aboriginal rights are entrenched in the Canadian Constitution?

Should aboriginal people have their own system of justice?

Aboriginal people make up about 3.6 percent of Canada's population, yet they account for 12 percent of male and 17 percent of female convicts serving sentences of two years or more. Clearly, something must be done to reduce the overwhelmingly disproportionate rate at which they are incarcerated.

In recent years, several countries, including Canada, have been considering giving aboriginal peoples their own system of justice. Canada has been experimenting with aboriginal justice. In some communities, aboriginal police officers have replaced local police authorities. These officers have a better understanding of Native offenders and their lives, and they can deal with the situations more effectively.

Experiments have also included penitentiary ceremonies to help aboriginals. The Stony Mountain Penitentiary in Manitoba has four sweat lodges at the far end of the exercise yard. In these round, tentlike structures, aboriginal prisoners gather once a week to participate in the spiritual program of sweat-lodge ceremonies. According to the prison's warden, the healing process works. He has seen prisoners who have participated in the program completely changed.

Since fines and imprisonment have not been an effective deterrent to Native offenders, the Native peoples in some Canadian communities have looked to their traditions to rehabilitate lawbreakers. Native justice emphasizes treatment and healing through sentencing circles and healing circles, instead of imprisonment.

In a sentencing circle, the offender is brought before victims and their families, friends, family members, band elders, witnesses, lawyers, and the judge to discuss sentencing. Everyone has an equal say in the sentencing. While the setting is more relaxed than a courtroom, the encounter between victim and victimizer can be especially intense. The sentence could range from doing community work to banishment to the woods for a set period of time. There the offender must live off the land as his or her ancestors did to be spiritually cleansed and rehabilitated.

In *R. v. Cheekinew*, Mr. Justice Grotsky noted that to qualify for a sentencing circle, the accused, at the very least, must be eligible for either a suspended sentence, an intermittent sentence, or a short term of imprisonment coupled with a probation order; genuinely contrite; supported in the request for a sentencing circle by the community in which he or she lives; and honestly interested in turning his or her life around.

A healing circle is an alternative to traditional punishment. If an offender pleads guilty and agrees to participate in a healing circle, the sentence is usually suspended. The offenders must meet with the victims, their families, and other offenders and work with them to share their experiences and finally to seek forgiveness for the wrongdoings. The guilty parties must also take courses in anger management.

According to defence counsel Gord Coffin in Whitehorse, "It is very much harder for a lot of people to bare their soul in front of people who know them. It is easy to stand up in front of a judge and blame the system—it's harder to do that in the community you have harmed."

One Manitoba community reports that, in nine years, of the 52 offenders there have been only two repeat offenders. The apparent success

A sweat-lodge ceremony at Stony Mountain Penitentiary.

On the Other Side

Reports from a Manitoba inquiry and from the Law Reform Commission of Canada support the idea of a separate aboriginal justice system. Canada's criminal justice system has not solved the problems encountered in aboriginal communities. Rates of suicide, alcoholism, crime, and imprisonment have never been higher among the aboriginal peoples.

Those who support aboriginal justice claim that many Natives turned to alcohol and drugs to block out painful memories of degradation and sexual abuse. Criminal activity followed, taking them in and out of jail. Instead of incarceration, these offenders need to reconnect with themselves and their people through a healing process.

Associate Chief Provincial Court Judge Murray Sinclair agrees. In the 1991 *Aboriginal Justice Inquiry* report, he advocates the use of healing circles. Judge Sinclair calls Canada's treatment of the aboriginal peoples by the justice system "an international disgrace" and has called for a separate aboriginal justice system. As he puts it, "They have paid the price of high rates of alcoholism, crime, and family abuse."

The Bottom Line

Aboriginal self-government and a separate justice system seem to coincide. Aboriginals have different needs and concerns. They are striving to meet them in a new and daring manner. Perhaps with more authority and responsibility they will be able to solve their unique problems more effectively. What do you think? You be the judge!

of the healing circle has encouraged other communities to experiment with similar programs.

On One Side

Some Canadians oppose the concept of a separate Native justice system. They believe that all Canadians should be treated in the same manner under the criminal justice system. Since the *Charter of Rights and Freedoms* guarantees equal treatment to all Canadians, there should be no problem. Members of aboriginal communities should not be treated differently. As Canadians, they must obey the laws of the land.

Others argue that a separate justice system for Native peoples will lead to lobbying by other ethnic groups for their own separate justice systems. Denying these factions could lead to resentment, but agreeing to them could lead to chaos in the Canadian justice system.

1. **Explain the functions of the sweat-lodge ceremonies and healing and sentencing circles. How do they relate to Native justice?**

2. **Write a speech that either supports or argues against a separate system of aboriginal justice in Canada. Give your speech to the class.**

3. **Explain the link between aboriginal self-government and aboriginal justice. Do you think that one is possible without the other?**

4. **Should healing circles and sentencing circles be considered for non-Native offenders? Explain.**

CHAPTER REVIEW

Reviewing Key Terms

For each of the following statements, indicate the key term being defined:

a) descendants of those who first occupied a land

b) a distinct group of Native people for which reserve land has been set aside for their common benefit

c) rights created by the first occupation and use of the land

d) land agreements concluded between 1871 and 1921 pertaining to First Nations of the Northwest Territory

e) people of mixed Indian/non-Indian ancestry

f) land set aside for the common use of an Indian band, the title to which is held by the Crown

g) claims related to the failure of the federal government to fulfill lawful obligations owed under treaties

h) a document that entitles the bearer to occupy and work a piece of reserve land

i) to absorb one group into the culture and ways of another group

Exploring Legal Concepts

1. Many aboriginal leaders have called for the return of cultural and religious objects now in museums and private collections.
   a) Suggest reasons why First Nations peoples want these objects returned to them.
   b) What legal obstacles might stand in their way?
   c) Can you recall other instances where Native protests have had a religious aspect? If so, give details of the protests.

2. Prepare a list of the different legal distinctions that exist among Canada's aboriginal people.

3. a) The *Indian Act* has been criticized for denying the First Nations control over their own affairs. Identify at least three provisions of the *Act* that would seem to bear out this view.
   b) Note two limitations the *Indian Act* imposes on the buying and selling of reserve land. Suggest why these limitations have been put in place.

4. Compare the positions legal experts have taken with respect to the significance of the *Royal Proclamation of 1763* to aboriginal rights.

5. Suggest reasons for the very different views Native people and federal officials have taken regarding the numbered treaties.

6. What would be the legal consequence of entrenching an aboriginal right of self-government into the Canadian Constitution?

Applying Legal Concepts

1. Steven Point, a registered Indian, was charged under the local *Highway Traffic Act* with a speeding offence. Point argued that the *Act* did not apply to him because the speeding incident had occurred on the reserve where he lived, and provincial traffic laws had no force on reserve or treaty land.

- **Do provincial traffic laws have force on reserve or treaty lands? Justify your answer.**

- **Give examples of instances where provincial laws would not necessarily apply to registered or treaty Indians.**

2. Edward Grant and Rose Mitchell were found by provincial park authorities living in a small, roughly-built cabin on park land. They were charged under provincial park regulations with cutting trees in a park and constructing a permanent dwelling therein without a permit.

At trial, Grant and Mitchell explained that they had built their cabin for shelter while they hunted for food in the park. They argued that as treaty Indians their right to hunt was protected in law, and that since the province permitted limited hunting in the park to non-aboriginals, their aboriginal hunting rights extended to the park.

- **With what offences were Grant and Mitchell charged? What defence did they offer for their actions? Do you think their defence would succeed? Why or why not?**

- **Would it make any difference to the outcome of this case if the Crown could show that Grant and Mitchell had not engaged in hunting and had had no intention of doing so?**

- **Would it make any difference to the outcome if the Crown could show that Grant and Mitchell's main interest in hunting was to obtain animal parts for sale to foreign buyers?**

3. *R. v. Sioui et al.* (1990) Supreme Court of Canada 70 D.L.R. (4th) 427

The four respondents were convicted of cutting trees, camping, and making fires in places not designated in Jacques Cartier Park contrary to regulations under Quebec's *Park Act*. The respondents argued that they were protected by treaty rights found in a document signed by British general James Murray. The document stated:

These are to certify that the CHIEF of the HURON Tribe of Indians, having come to me in the name of His Nation, to submit to His BRITANNIC MAJESTY, and make Peace, has been received under my Protection, with his whole Tribe; and henceforth no English Officer or party is to molest, or to interrupt them in returning to their Settlement at LORETTE; and they are received upon the same terms with the Canadians, being allowed the free Exercise of their Religion, their Customs and Liberty of trading with the English: —recommending it to the Officers commanding the Posts, to treat them kindly.

The Supreme Court of Canada found in favour of the respondents, declaring:

> The 1760 agreement was a treaty because of its intention to create obligations, and its tone of solemnity. The treaty rights under the treaty had never been extinguished. No documents or other clear evidence had been produced in court to prove otherwise. The guarantees in the treaty prevailed over *Park Act* regulations. The important test here was whether the guarantees were consistent with the general purpose of the *Park Act,* and the court found this to be the case.

- **With what offences had the respondents been charged? What legal defence did they offer?**

- **Briefly, why did the Supreme Court find in favour of the defendants?**

- **Does the treaty define a particular geographic area within which its terms are to have force? Does this make it similar to, or different from, the numbered treaties?**

4. *MacMillan Bloedel Ltd. v. Mullen et al.* (1985) British Columbia Court of Appeal 61 B.C.L.R. 145

MacMillan Bloedel, a lumber company, obtained a licence from the British Columbia government to log Crown land on Meares Island. Local Indian bands applied to the British Columbia Supreme Court for an injunction to prevent logging. They argued that they held aboriginal title to Meares Island and consequently the logging licence was of no legal effect.

The trial judge ruled that an injunction was not warranted. He did not accept that the Indian bands held aboriginal title, which he said had been extinguished at the time British Columbia joined Confederation in 1871. Since no serious legal question was at issue, an injunction was not justified.

The bands appealed this decision to the British Columbia Court of Appeal where three of the five judges found that the band's claim to aboriginal title had raised a serious legal question which deserved to be considered in court. They reversed the decision and awarded an interim injunction preventing logging operations until the bands' land rights were decided.

- **On what legal ground did the Indian bands apply for an injunction?**

- **What reasons did the Court of Appeal give for awarding an injunction?**

- **Of what practical value would injunctions such as the one awarded in the Meares Island case be to Indian groups pursuing land claims?**

Extending Legal Concepts

1. Following formal debate procedures, conduct a debate on one or more of the following topics.

   BE IT RESOLVED THAT

   - Rejecting the aboriginal claim of an inherent right of self-government would perpetuate a glaring injustice.

   - The *Indian Act* should be abolished.

   - Native people are justified in using road blockades as a tactic in pursuing settlement of their land claims.

- If Quebec were to declare its independence, the aboriginal peoples of northern Quebec would have the right to determine whether or not their ancestral lands remained part of Canada.
- Land claims agreements should be rejected if they violate the principle that all citizens should enjoy the same rights.

2. Prepare a research paper on one of the following topics. Be sure to include your thesis statement in your introduction.
   - The Mackenzie Valley Pipeline Inquiry and the Protection of Aboriginal Rights
   - The Oka Crisis of 1990
   - The Nunavut Land Claims Agreement
   - The Gustafsen Lake Stand-off of 1995
   - Ipperwash on the Edge—1995

3. Find out the position of the government of your province or territory on aboriginal land claims and self-government. Compare that point of view with that held by local aboriginal groups and/or the federal government.

4. Invite a spokesperson to your class from a local band council or other aboriginal organization to discuss his or her views on local aboriginal issues.

5. Conduct a study of a nearby First Nation reserve, focusing on the history of Native occupation and use of the land. Include a description of the main elements of the traditional culture and identify cultural traditions that are still observed.

Researching an Issue

Land Claims
Current efforts to settle aboriginal land claims have stirred strong feelings among Canadians. Concerns have been expressed about the cost of settlements and the disruption they may cause to the lives of non-aboriginal people.

Statement
Land claims settlements can benefit both aboriginal and non-aboriginal people, and provide a firm foundation for approaching present and future problems.

Point
Existing land claims settlements in places such as Alaska and New Zealand offer encouraging evidence that it is possible to negotiate agreements that benefit all groups in society.

Counterpoint
The possibility of failed negotiations is very real, and there are many obstacles that will make it particularly difficult to achieve fair and lasting treaties in Canada.

- **With a partner, research this issue and reflect on your findings.**
- **Prepare points on this statement that could be used for a class debate.**
- **Discuss your findings with others in your class.**

ENTERING AND LEAVING CANADA

These are the key terms introduced in this chapter:

asylum
Convention refugee
departure order
deportation order
designated class refugees
displaced persons
emigration
employment authorization
entrepreneur
exclusion order
extradition
family business class
family class
head tax

immigrant
Immigration and Refugee
  Board
Immigration Visa and Record
  of Landing
independent class
investor
job skills
landed immigrant
landing
landing tax
naturalization
passport
permanent resident

point system
port of entry
refugee
refugee claims officer
refugee class
selective immigration
senior immigration officer
student authorization
ultra vires
Undertaking of Assistance for
  Family Class
visitor's visa

Chapter at a Glance

Learning Outcomes

At the end of this chapter, you will be able to

1. describe the main events in the history of immigration to Canada;
2. summarize the history of Canadian immigration law and policy;
3. discuss the main provisions of the *Immigration Act, 1976*;
4. distinguish among the different categories of visitors and immigrants, as defined in the *Immigration Act, 1976*;
5. describe the "point system" for selecting immigrants;
6. explain the term "Convention refugee";
7. explain how refugee claims are decided in Canada;
8. describe the appeal procedures available for challenging the decisions of immigration officials;
9. list the legal matters that should be attended to when planning a trip abroad;
10. identify and discuss the key issues in Canadian immigration law.

Canadians have adopted an unrealistic attitude of "zero tolerance" toward mistakes and abuses in the immigration system, says the head of the Immigration and Refugee Board.

The resulting demands to overhaul or scrap the system are an overreaction that amount to "throwing the baby out with the bath water," Nurjehan Mawani said in an interview.

"If you want a system which is foolproof, then you cannot take a chance. So you either won't let anybody in or you remove everybody," Mawani said. "Haven't we as Canadians decided there is a balance here?"

The system has been rocked recently by a series of horror stories—including two foreign criminals who managed to avoid

Perfection in Refugee System Unrealistic, Board Head Says

deportation and went on to become involved in high-profile murders, and a rapist who was deported, returned illegally, and then claimed refugee status.

The information [that] board members rely on in deciding whether to accept a refugee claim or to overturn a deportation order is not always complete or easy to obtain. Refugees, for instance, commonly flee with false identity papers or arrive with no papers at all.

Seeking information from the authorities in the claimant's home country is not necessarily trustworthy and could endanger the claimant's life.

"Ultimately, it's a human being judging another human being. So long as we as human beings are fallible, some mistakes will occur," said Mawani. "It's like trying to play God."

Unfortunately, Mawani said, the relentless media focus on the handful of horror stories has tainted Canadians' view of the entire system.

From: Joan Bryden, "Perfection in refugee system unrealistic, board head says." *Southam News/The Vancouver Sun*, October 15, 1994. Published by *Southam News* as it appeared in *The Vancouver Sun*.

Something to Think About

- **Why does Nurjehan Mawani believe that it is impossible to eliminate all mistakes and abuses from Canada's immigration system?**
- **What criticism does Mawani have of Canada's news media? Do you agree with this view? Why or why not?**
- **Canada accepts about 200 000 new immigrants a year. Do you support this level of immigration, or would you raise or lower it? Why?**

23.1 INTRODUCTION

Canada is very much a nation of newcomers. In the twentieth century, over 10 million immigrants have come to Canada from all over the world. They have had a profound effect in shaping Canadian society and culture. For these reasons, questions related to immigration have generated much public interest and impassioned debate.

Like all countries, Canada has immigration laws that regulate who may enter and who may be

ordered to leave. These laws also set out the procedures to be followed in such situations. This chapter will outline the history of Canadian immigration and government immigration policy, current immigration laws, and some contentious issues related to immigration.

Some legal aspects regarding travel and **emigration** to other countries will also be examined.

23.2 LOOKING BACK: NEW ARRIVALS AND IMMIGRATION POLICY

Pre-Confederation

Archaeological evidence suggests that the earliest people to reach North America arrived between 15 000 and 20 000 years ago by way of a natural land bridge connecting Siberia and Alaska. Successive waves followed. By the time of the first European contact, the continents of North and South America were occupied by many peoples with distinctly different beliefs, languages, and ways of life. It is interesting to consider that the cultural diversity that characterizes Canada today was very much evident among First Nations peoples before the arrival of Europeans.

New France (1600–1760)

Following the establishment of the first French colonies in North America—in Acadia and on the St. Lawrence River—the population grew very slowly. One historian has estimated that of the 27 000 people who came to New France between 1608 and 1760, only about 10 000 stayed. Explanations for the slow immigrant population growth vary. French government policy decreed that all immigrants had to be Catholic, thereby barring French Protestants from New France, but this fact alone does not explain the low immigration numbers. By 1759, the population of New France totalled approximately 75 000. The isolation of this population from France for the next half century contributed to the emergence of a strong sense of separate identity and cultural solidarity.

Did You Know

Louis XIV arranged the transport of some 800 women, known as *filles du roi*, to New France as prospective brides to boost population growth.

Post-Conquest Period (1763–1815)

In the years following the British conquest, most immigrants who came to settle in what is now Canada arrived from the Thirteen Colonies (now the United States): 7000 New Englanders moved into Nova Scotia, 60 000 Loyalists fled the United States at the end of the American Revolution, and several thousand Americans came north in search of land during the 1790s. In 1815, the population of Lower Canada had reached 335 000, 90 percent of whom were French speaking, while the population of Upper Canada was only 95 000.

Toward Confederation (1815–1867)

This period of rapid growth was marked by dramatic changes in immigration patterns. In 50 years, more than a million British immigrants came to British North America.

Most eventually moved to the United States, but their impact in what is now Canada was still considerable. By 1867, British immigrants—English, Scots, Welsh, and Irish—and their descendants formed a majority in all British colonies except Quebec, and even there the British population grew to 25 percent of the whole. Their sense of belonging to a common British culture and their desire to maintain imperial ties with Great Britain led them to support Confederation, which they saw as a way of strengthening the British connection.

Did You Know

During the 1840s, famine in Ireland, caused by the failure of the potato crop, brought nearly 100 000 Irish to Canada.

From Confederation to World War I

Under section 95 of the *Constitution Act, 1867*, immigration was made a shared responsibility of the federal and provincial governments. However, the federal government was given virtually a free hand in this area until after World War II.

Entry of immigrants was relatively unrestricted from 1867 to 1895, with some notable exceptions.

Criminals, persons with certain physical and mental disabilities, and those identified as "paupers," "destitutes," or "vagrants" were denied.

Then, in 1885, Parliament imposed a $50 **head tax** on every Chinese person wishing to enter Canada. This tax was increased to $500 in 1903. In 1914, a $200 **landing tax** was added to further discourage Chinese immigration. These measures were introduced in response to political pressures from people in British Columbia who feared that continued Chinese immigration would threaten their jobs.

The Laurier Era (1896–1911)

Clifford Sifton, Minister of the Interior of the new Laurier government, launched an aggressive campaign to attract immigrants to the Canadian West. He brought in a policy of **selective immigration**, which continues to be a central principle of Canada's immigration laws.

Sifton wanted to attract British and American farmers to settle in the prairies. The government focused its promotional efforts on those countries, offering free land for homesteading. When "desirable" immigrants failed to respond, Sifton turned his attention to potential immigrants in eastern and southern Europe.

In 1910, the federal Parliament passed a new *Immigration Act* that specifically excluded three classes of "undesirable" immigrants:

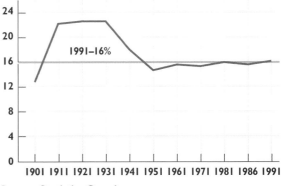

Immigrants as a Percentage of Canada's Population, 1901–1991

Source: Statistics Canada.

- those considered to be physically, morally, or mentally unfit;
- those belonging to nationalities thought unlikely to assimilate;
- those thought likely to settle in cities and contribute to unemployment.

In the same year, a regulation was introduced requiring all Asian immigrants to travel to Canada by direct continuous journey from their homelands. This requirement effectively barred persons from India from which there was no direct travel at the time. When the courts declared this regulation to be ***ultra vires*** (not valid), the federal government enacted other regulations barring the entry of Asians.

1914–1945

World War I brought immigration to Canada to a virtual standstill. In 1917, the Department for Immigration and Colonization was created in anticipation of high levels of immigration at the end of the war, but the expected wave did not materialize. A list of "preferred" and "non-preferred" countries continued to favour British and American immigrants and to block immigrants from Asia. The *Chinese Immigration Act* of 1923 effectively ended immigration from China. In the next 25 years, only eight Chinese immigrants were permitted to enter Canada.

During the 1930s, Jews escaping persecution in Nazi Germany were often refused entry to Canada on the grounds that their presence would upset Canada's ethnic balance. They were forced to return to Europe where many later perished during the Holocaust.

Post-War Period: 1945–1967

In 1947, Prime Minister Mackenzie King announced a new immigration policy that would attract new immigrants for the purpose of sustaining economic growth. A careful selection process would ensure that the number of new immigrants would not exceed what he termed the "absorptive capacity" of the country. Particular preference would be given to sponsored relatives and **displaced persons**, refugees who had lost everything in the war and were without a home.

King bluntly declared that it was not a "fundamental human right" of all foreigners to immigrate to Canada. Only persons whom the government regarded as "desirable future citizens" would be admitted. King considered large-scale immigration of non-white people as undesirable because he believed it would fundamentally change Canada's ethnic composition and give rise to social and economic problems.

The years following World War II saw a new wave of immigration from Europe. About one-third of the many thousands who came were of British origin. Others were Italian, Dutch, German, and Polish—mostly people seeking escape from the dreadful economic conditions that were a result of the war.

1967 Immigration Policy

In the mid-1960s, Canada's immigration policy underwent a fundamental change. Many racially discriminatory policies were abandoned.

A 1966 government White Paper argued for selective immigration based solely on education and skill. It reasoned that Canada's industrialized economy needed large numbers of trained immigrants to ensure future growth. In 1967, the government eliminated race or nationality as a basis for selecting immigrants. As a result of the new regulations, large numbers of immigrants from Africa, Asia, Latin America, and the Caribbean began arriving in Canada for the first time.

Immigrant Population by Place of Birth and Period of Immigration, 1991

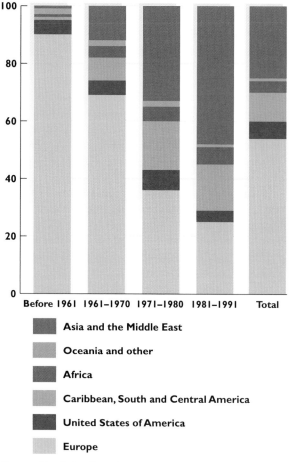

Legend:
- Asia and the Middle East
- Oceania and other
- Africa
- Caribbean, South and Central America
- United States of America
- Europe

Source: Statistics Canada.

Reviewing Your Reading

1. List the different periods in Canada's immigration history. For each period, note the kinds of immigrants who came to Canada.

2. Refer to the line graph on p. 611. Give reasons for the escalation in immigration between 1901 and 1911.

3. Compare the immigration policies of Clifford Sifton, Mackenzie King, and the 1967 immigration policy.

4. a) Refer to the bar graph above. What trends in immigration patterns does the bar graph reveal?

   b) Considering *all* immigrants living in Canada in 1991, where were most born?

23.3 *The Immigration Act, 1976*

The *Immigration Act, 1976,* proclaimed into law in April 1978, established the basic legal framework for immigration to Canada that exists to this day. In section 3, the fundamental objectives of Canada's immigration were spelled out for the first time.

3.

(a) to support the attainment of such demographic goals as may be established by the Government of Canada from time to time in respect of the size, rate of growth, structure, and geographic distribution of the Canadian population;

(b) to enrich and strengthen the cultural and social fabric of Canada, taking into account the federal and bilingual character of Canada;

(c) to facilitate the reunion in Canada of Canadian citizens and permanent residents with their close relatives from abroad;

(d) to encourage and facilitate the adaption of persons who have been granted admission as permanent residents to Canadian society by promoting cooperation between the Government of Canada and other levels of government and non-government agencies in Canada with respect thereto;

(e) to facilitate the entry of visitors into Canada for the purpose of fostering trade and commerce, tourism, cultural and scientific activities, and international understanding;

(f) to ensure that any person who seeks admission to Canada on either a permanent or temporary basis is subject to standards of admission that do not discriminate on grounds of race, national or ethnic origin, colour, religion, or sex;

(g) to fulfill Canada's international legal obligations with respect to refugees and to uphold its humanitarian tradition with respect to the displaced and the persecuted;

(h) to foster the development of a strong and viable economy and the prosperity of all regions in Canada;

(i) to maintain and protect the health, safety, and good order of Canadian society; and

(j) to promote international order and justice by denying the use of Canadian territory to persons who are likely to engage in criminal activity.

Among the highlights of the *Act* was the provision that the federal government would set immigration levels annually after consultation with the provinces and "such persons, organizations, and institutions as the Minister deems appropriate." This was recognition of the fact that immigration affects different parts of Canada in different ways.

The main parts of the *Act* deal with who can enter Canada and who can be excluded or expelled, and related appeal procedures.

Entry into Canada

Under the *Act,* all persons coming to Canada must apply for entry at a designated **port of entry** such as a border crossing, international airport, seaport, or railway station. There they are subject to an examination by an immigration officer. Canadian citizens and permanent residents can enter Canada upon producing necessary proof, such as a passport, birth certificate, or naturalization papers. Visitors and immigrants must satisfy specific requirements set out in the *Immigration Act* before they are allowed entry.

Visitors

In the strict legal sense, visitors are persons lawfully in Canada for temporary purposes. The main classes of visitors are tourists, students, temporary workers, and business persons.

Under the *Immigration Act,* visitors can be ordered out of the country for any one of several reasons. These include violating the terms of one's visa, committing a serious criminal act, engaging in subversive activities or being identified as a possible security risk, and entering Canada illegally.

Tourists

Canada is known around the world as a tourist destination and it is not surprising that tourists are the most common type of visitor to Canada. With the exception of citizens of certain countries—such as Great Britain, the United States, Australia, New Zealand, and Japan—tourists must obtain a **visitor's visa** prior to coming to Canada. Applicants for a visitor's visa must show that they have enough money to support themselves and any accompanying family dependants during their stay. They are also asked to give information about persons they will be visiting here, and the purpose and length of their visit.

An immigration officer, if suspicious of the stated reasons for the visit, may bar entry to the country. For example, an officer may conclude that a person's real purpose is to seek work in Canada. Persons entering as tourists are not permitted to work nor to attend educational institutions.

Students

Every year, large numbers of young people travel to Canada to attend school on **student authorizations**. Applicants must apply for their authorization at any Canadian embassy or consulate. They must show proof that they have already been accepted as students by an educational institution in Canada. They must also show proof that they have already paid one year's tuition fees, and that they have enough money for living expenses while in Canada and for transportation home when leaving Canada.

Temporary Workers

Certain visitors may enter Canada to work on a temporary basis. Most have to go through a lengthy process to obtain authorization. However, persons performing particular types of work are exempted from this requirement. These include diplomats and United Nations personnel, members of allied armed forces, crew members of ships and airplanes, athletes participating in international sporting events, performing artists, and foreign news correspondents on assignment.

Those who do not fall into one of the exempted categories must find a prospective employer in Canada willing to apply for a work permit, known as an **employment authorization**, on their behalf. Governmental approval will be given to an employer to hire a foreigner for temporary work only after attempts by Employment and Immigration Canada to find a suitable Canadian citizen or landed immigrant for the job have proven unsuccessful.

Business Visitors

The 1989 Free Trade Agreement concluded by Canada and the United States has created a more open border between the two countries. U.S. citizens may now enter Canada to perform specified kinds of business activities as long as they are done on a temporary basis only.

Immigrants

The *Immigration Act, 1976,* defines an **immigrant** as "a person who seeks landing." **Landing** means "lawful permission to establish permanent residence in Canada." **Landed immigrants** are persons who have been allowed to enter the country to establish permanent residence, and are referred to in the *Act* as **permanent residents**.

After living in Canada for three years, permanent residents can apply to become citizens through a process known as **naturalization**. The advantages of becoming a Canadian citizen are many and include: the right to vote and run for public office; the right to travel on a Canadian passport and to re-enter Canada after a trip abroad; access to certain jobs that require Canadian citizenship; and certain property rights available only to persons who are Canadian citizens.

The *Immigration Act, 1976,* divides immigrants into three main categories: **family class, independent** (or economic) **class**, and **refugee class**. These classes reflect basic values we hold as Canadians: the importance we give to family unity, our desire for a high standard of living, and our pride in our humanitarianism.

Family Class

Under this category, Canadian citizens or permanent residents can sponsor the immigration of "family class" relatives to Canada provided that requirements specified in the *Act* are met. Sponsors have considerable, ongoing financial obligations to the relatives they sponsor. They must be willing and able to provide for housing, food, clothing, medical care, and other expenses to ensure that the sponsored relatives do not become a financial burden on Canada. This commitment is formally made in a document known as an **Undertaking of Assistance for Family Class**, which requires sponsors to declare their willingness to provide assistance for as long as 10 years.

The number of persons someone is permitted to sponsor is directly tied to one's income level; failure to meet a minimum annual income requirement will exclude a person as a sponsor entirely.

Applications to sponsor a family class member must be made in Canada. The sponsoring relative must be at least 19 years of age. Normally, the sponsored relative must be living outside Canada at the time the application is made. Family class members include

- the sponsor's spouse or the person to whom the sponsor is engaged to marry;
- the sponsor's unmarried children who are under 19; or, if over 19 dependent on their parents and in full-time attendance at school;
- the sponsor's parents and grandparents within certain restrictions;
- unmarried orphans under the age of 19 who are the brothers, sisters, nieces, nephews, or grandchildren of the sponsor;
- any child under the age of 19 whom the sponsor has legally adopted, or orphaned or abandoned children whom the sponsor intends to adopt.

In addition, one relative of any age or relationship may be sponsored if the sponsor's other family class relatives—in or outside Canada—are dead or are ineligible for immigration.

Brothers or sisters of the sponsor can come to Canada under the family class, but only through their parents, and only if they meet certain

CASE

The appellant had sponsored an application for landing on behalf of his parents and three sisters. The application was refused on the ground that the appellant lacked the means to fulfill the requirements of his undertaking of assistance. The appellant agreed that he could not meet the conditions of his undertaking, but he asked the Immigration Appeal Board to grant him special relief on the ground that he had been seeking to improve his family's economic circumstances. He pointed to the fact that his father and sisters were unemployed and lived in a city where the unemployment rate was higher than 70 percent.

The Immigration Appeal Board rejected the appeal noting that most immigrants are motivated to come to Canada out of a desire to improve themselves economically. The law provided for the granting of relief, but only in unusual or compelling circumstances. The situation of the appellant's relations was similar to that of many immigrant families, and therefore the appellant should not expect to attract special relief.

Abdul Rafeek Latiff v. Ministry of Employment and Immigration (1986)

Immigration Appeal Board No. 85-9019

1. Why did immigration officials reject the application for landing?
2. a) On what ground did the appellant ask that special relief be granted?
   b) Why did the Immigration Appeal Board reject the appeal?

requirements (see rules for a sponsor's children). Otherwise they will have to apply on their own under another immigrant category.

Since 1991, DNA testing has been used in Canada in hundreds of immigration cases to prove that a familial relationship exists. Typically, these cases involve family-class applicants from developing countries where, due to the unavailability of proper identification papers, persons have been unable to establish that they are biologically related to their sponsor.

Immigration Canada has established strict requirements for testing procedures to reduce the possibility of fraud. Records show that in 90 percent of cases to date, the DNA test establishes that a familial relationship does exist.

Related to the family class is the **family business class**, which was created to allow relatives to immigrate to Canada to join small family businesses, thereby promoting family unification. Such businesses must be legitimate and have been operating successfully for at least a year prior to the application. Most important, it must be demonstrable that the nature of the job opening to be filled—particularly the need for trust—makes the hiring of a family member the most logical choice.

Independent Class

Independent class applicants must be at least 19 years old and must apply on their own behalf at a Canadian embassy or consulate outside Canada. Successful applicants are issued a document called an **Immigration Visa and Record of Landing**, to be given to immigration officials upon their arrival in Canada. Those who are accepted have the right to bring their spouse and dependent children with them to Canada.

Independent class applicants can be further subdivided into four groups: workers whose applications are based on their job skills, entrepreneurs, self-employed persons, and investors.

The Point System

Established in 1967, the **point system** is used by immigration officers to assess all independent class applicants. Under this system, applicants are awarded points according to how they measure up in the following categories:

- *Education*: Persons with post-secondary education receive the greatest number of points, for example, 15 points are currently awarded for a first-level university degree. Persons who have not completed secondary school receive zero points. Starting in 1996, applicants also receive points for recognized trade skills and apprenticeship training.

- *Specific vocational training*: This refers to training received in apprenticeship programs, vocational schools, and technical institutes. The training is measured against Canadian standards. Amendments to the *Immigration Act* made in 1993 substantially increased the maximum number of points available under this category.

- *Experience*: The work experience must relate to the job area one is applying within. Applicants whose jobs required longer training receive more points than others who may have worked the same amount of time but whose jobs required less training. As of 1996, applicants must have a full year of work experience within the past five years, related to one's job area.

- *Occupational demand*: Points are based on what the federal government perceives to be the current demand in Canada for a particular occupation or skill. Adjustments to the point values of the occupations listed are made several times a year.

- *Arranged employment*: A person who can show proof in writing of a good job offer will receive maximum points. However the federal government must be satisfied that there are no Canadians available to fill this job. Under new rules that went into effect in 1996, the number of points available in this category was reduced significantly.

- *Designated occupations*: Occupations in high demand are identified through joint consultation between the federal and provincial governments. Numbers of job openings in "designated occupations" are calculated for each province and quotas or "targets" are then set.

- *Age*: Prior to 1996, maximum points were given to persons between the ages of 21 and 44. Currently only people under 35 years get points for their age.

- *Knowledge of English and French*: Applicants who are fluent in both English and French receive the most points. Separate point totals are calculated for proficiency in speaking, reading, and writing. In 1996, the point share of this category rose from 14 percent of all points to 20 percent.
- *Personal suitability*: Points are awarded according to the immigration officer's subjective assessment of an applicant's adaptability, motivation, and resourcefulness. In 1996, points awarded in this category increased from 9 percent of all points to 16 percent.
- *Levels control*: This allows the government to regulate the flow of immigrants in a given year. If the numbers appear to be high, the points awarded in this category might be reduced to slow the flow of immigrants.

The number of points an independent class applicant requires is determined by which of the following subgroups the applicant falls into:

Worker whose application is based on job skills. Applicants must get at least 70 points to qualify for immigration. Whether an application is accepted depends primarily on the applicant's **job skills** and the current demand for these skills in Canada.

Entrepreneur. Regulation 2(1) of the *Immigration Act, 1976,* defines an **entrepreneur** as an immigrant who:

(a) intends and has the ability to establish, purchase, or make a substantial investment in a business or commercial venture in Canada that will make a significant contribution to the economy and whereby employment opportunities will be created or continued in Canada for one or more Canadian citizens or permanent residents, other than the entrepreneur and his dependents, and

(b) intends and has the ability to provide active and ongoing participation in the management of the business or commercial venture.

Entrepreneurs need only 25 points to qualify for immigration. However, candidates must also present a detailed business proposal to federal and provincial authorities and convince them that they possess the financial resources, expertise, and experience to make the proposed venture work. Typically, an applicant is required to make a minimum investment of $150 000. Each province has established its own set of guidelines for prospective entrepreneurs that reflect local economic conditions and government priorities.

Self-employed. Self-employed applicants include owners of family businesses, artists and musicians, lawyers and engineers, and professional athletes. Professionals, such as doctors, must meet all local training and licensing standards before they can apply for visas. Applicants will be turned down if they will require additional training in Canada to meet licensing standards. They need a total of 70 points to qualify for immigration, including 30 "bonus points" awarded for presenting a convincing business proposal to immigration officials.

Investor. An **investor** is defined in section 2(1) of the *Immigration Act, 1976,* as an immigrant who:

(a) has successfully operated, controlled, or directed a business,

(b) has made a minimum investment since the date of the investor's application for an immigrant visa as an investor, and

(c) has a net worth, accumulated by the immigrant's own endeavours.

Investors, like entrepreneurs, need only 25 points to qualify for immigration. Investment funds must be committed at the time an application to immigrate is made. In Ontario, Quebec, and British Columbia, applicants must have a minimum net worth of $500 000 of which they must invest $350 000 or more in a government-approved business venture for at least five years. In all other provinces, the minimum investment is $250 000. The applicant must show that the business venture will maintain or create jobs for Canadians.

Investors are not required to participate in the daily management of the business venture. The ventures themselves can be set up by Canadians and then offered to potential immigrants.

Refugee Class

In recent times war, political strife, and natural disasters have made millions of people refugees. The displacement of Kurds in northern Iraq during the 1990 Gulf War, the tribal massacres in Rwanda in 1994, and famine in Somalia are all-too-familiar examples. Throughout our own history, many people migrating to Canada have been refugees, fleeing circumstances such as loss of homeland, political and religious persecution, and racial discrimination.

Today, Canada's treatment of refugees is a topic of heated debate. To understand the current situation, one must look back to the period immediately following World War II, which saw countless people displaced from their homelands. Article One of the 1951 UN Convention Relating to the Status of Refugees defined a **refugee** as a person who

> as a result of events occurring before 1 January 1951 and owing to well-founded fear of being persecuted for reasons of race, religion, nationality, membership of a particular social group, or political opinion, is

> outside the country of his nationality and is unable or, owing to such fear, is unwilling to avail himself of the protection of that country; or who, not having a nationality and being outside the country of his former habitual residence as a result of such events is unable or, owing to such fear, is unwilling to return to it.

The 1951 Convention went on to state that its provisions would not apply to persons who had committed a "crime against peace, a war crime, or a crime against humanity," or who had committed a "serious non-political crime outside the country of refuge prior to his admission to that country as a refugee." A 1967 UN Protocol expanded the definition of "refugee" by deleting time and geographic limitations. The United Nations' declarations and recognition of Canada's obligation to assist refugees are incorporated into the *Immigration Act, 1976*.

Although there was no special provision in its immigration laws for refugees prior to this *Act*, Canada did honour its international commitments by opening its doors to several refugee groups:

Alexander Kats, centre, a Russian concert pianist, his wife Rimma, and son Emil left Russia in 1991 and received refugee status in Israel. From there they came to Canada and applied for refugee status. Even though Alexander and Rimma had guaranteed paying jobs, they were faced with deportation. Officials later allowed them to stay. Why did the government first deny their application for refugee status?

political refugees from the Hungarian uprising of 1956 and the Soviet invasion of Czechoslovakia of 1968, Asians expelled from Uganda in 1972, and refugees from Southeast Asia following Communist victories there in the mid-1970s.

The *Immigration Act, 1976*, recognizes two classes of refugees: **Convention refugees**, persons who comply with the UN Refugee Convention definition on p. 618, and **designated class refugees**, persons in refugee-like situations who are accorded the opportunity to settle in Canada because they are displaced or persecuted or both. Designated class refugees can be anyone to whom Canada wants to grant refugee status, usually done on humanitarian grounds.

Claimants seeking to enter Canada as Convention refugees must establish that they have a "well-founded" fear of being persecuted. This requires that a fear of persecution exists in their minds and that this fear is based on credible facts. Claimants who can show that there is a real risk that they will be subjected to persecution now or in the foreseeable future will be accepted into Canada as refugees. Once a refugee claim has been approved, a refugee may apply to become a permanent resident.

Claims for refugee status arising from natural disasters or poor living standards will normally be rejected. This will also be the case where claimants have not taken advantage of a reasonable "internal flight alternative" available to them within their own country.

The Federal Court of Appeal has ruled that a person must pursue the option of seeking refuge in another part of his or her own country unless it is "objectively unreasonable" to do so. It is not enough to argue that one has no friends or job prospects in a particular region. However, if a person faces the risk of great danger or undue hardship in travelling to that region, then flight to Canada is deemed an acceptable course of action.

According to section 2(e) of the *Immigration Act, 1976*, a claimant who has been declared a Convention refugee may lose that status if the reasons for the person's fear of persecution cease to exist.

CASE

Upon arriving in Canada from Peru, the applicant claimed to be a Convention refugee on the ground of his well-founded fear of being persecuted for reasons of "membership of a particular social group." This fear stemmed from an incident that had initially involved his father.

The applicant's father had been attacked and robbed by a group of persons that included a member of Peru's Civil Guard. After refusing to drop charges against this group, the father's life had been threatened. He subsequently fled from Peru. The Civil Guard then detained, beat, and threatened the applicant, who was later unable to conduct his normal business.

The Immigration Appeal Board ruled that the phrase "membership of a particular social group" should be given a wide interpretation to include family membership so that individuals whose fear of persecution was not based on religious, political, or racial ties could be recognized as Convention refugees. The Immigration Appeal Board also found that the applicant was a credible witness and that violation of human rights by the police and military were still occurring in Peru. On these grounds, the applicant was determined to be a Convention refugee.

Richard Cid Requena-Cruz v. Ministry of Employment and Immigration
(1986)

Immigration Appeal Board No. 83-10 559

1. **On what basis had the appellant claimed to be a Convention refugee?**
2. **How did the ruling of the Immigration Appeal Board extend the meaning of "membership of a particular social group"?**

The process by which a claim for Convention refugee status is decided follows these steps:

1. Upon entering Canada, a person makes a claim to be a Convention refugee to an immigration officer. The immigration officer is required to immediately refer the refugee claim to a **senior immigration officer** (SIO).

2. The SIO determines whether the claimant is "eligible" to make a refugee claim. The claim will be rejected if the SIO finds that the claimant

   • has refugee status in another country,
   • is a previously rejected claimant,
   • has been convicted of a serious crime,
   • is a known war criminal or is considered to be a security threat.

   If the SIO finds the claimant to be ineligible, the person will be refused entry to Canada.

   The federal government has still not put into effect a controversial section of the *Act*. Under this section, claimants arriving in Canada from "third countries," designated by Canada to be safe, could be returned there without Canadian authorities examining their claims. For example, a refugee who travelled to Canada by way of Great Britain—a so-called "safe third country"—would not be permitted to enter Canada. The underlying argument is that refugees should seek **asylum** (refuge) in the first safe country they reach. They do not have the right to shop around from country to country to satisfy a personal preference. Critics counter that the "third country" rule could put legitimate refugees at risk because a third country might deport refugees to their homeland, who have been turned away by Canada.

   In March 1995, Canada and the United States were in the process of finalizing an agreement that would require refugee complainants to request asylum in whichever of the two countries they reached first. It was estimated that this proposal would reduce by one-third the number of refugee claims being made in Canada. Persons coming from Central and South America particularly would be affected. The current rules permit asylum seekers to travel to Canada by way of the United States and claim refugee status here. The proposed accord would close this door.

3. Once eligibility is established, the SIO refers the refugee's case to the Convention Refugee Determination Division (CRDD) of the Immigration and Refugee Board for a full hearing. The claimant outlines his or her case in a formal document and submits it to the CRDD.

4. Prior to the full hearing, an immigration official known as the refugee claims officer may "concede" before a member of the Immigration and Refugee Board that the claimant appears to be a Convention refugee and recommend that the claim be "fast tracked" or expedited. A short meeting would then be held to confirm that the claimant is indeed a Convention refugee.

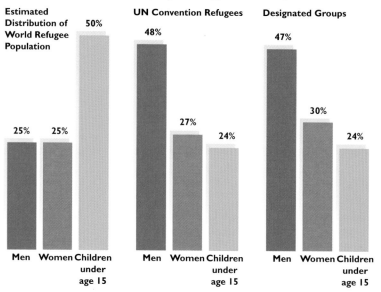

Percentage Distribution of Refugees Entering Canada as Permanent Residents, by Refugee Status, 1981–1991

Estimated Distribution of World Refugee Population — Men 25%, Women 25%, Children under age 15 50%

UN Convention Refugees — Men 48%, Women 27%, Children under age 15 24%

Designated Groups — Men 47%, Women 30%, Children under age 15 24%

Source: Statistics Canada.

5. If a claimant is not referred to the expedited procedure, then a full hearing is held before a panel consisting of two members and with a new refugee claims officer. The **refugee claims officer** examines the claimant, any witnesses, and documentary evidence. The hearing is not intended to have the formal, adversarial atmosphere of a trial; rather the aim is to bring forward all available evidence. If the facts are unclear, the claimant is given the benefit of the doubt. If just one member rules in favour of the claimant, the claimant will be accepted as a refugee and may apply for permanent resident status. If both members rule against the claimant, the claimant will be required to leave Canada. A unanimous decision of the two-member panel is required in circumstances where there is evidence that

- the claimant has disposed of personal identity papers without any valid reason;
- in the period since making a claim, the claimant has visited the country from which he or she has allegedly fled;
- the country from which the claimant has fled respects human rights.

In March 1995, Immigration and Refugee Board Chairperson Nurjehan Mawani announced a number of changes to the refugee determination process. These changes support the conception of the Refugee Division as a "special board of inquiry." Greater emphasis is now placed on information gathering and analysis to promote just and efficient processing of claims. The role of the refugee claims officer has been enhanced to support information gathering and analysis. The reforms are intended to enable early identification of the key issues in claims to allow more focused hearings.

Did You Know

For the year ending December 31, 1994, 22 006 refugee claims were referred to the Immigration and Refugee Board. Of those, 21 666 claimants received decisions: 15 224 were favourable; 6442 were not.

Amendments to the *Immigration Act, 1976*, provide severe penalties for persons helping to bring illegal immigrants into Canada. Penalties include fines of up to $500 000 and prison terms of up to 10 years for persons who organize, induce, aid, or abet groups of 10 or more illegal immigrants to enter Canada. Persons who instruct others in how to make false or misleading statements to claim refugee status can be fined up to $10 000, imprisoned up to five years, or both.

Recent Changes to Immigration Policy

In November 1994, the Minister of Immigration announced a new immigration policy for Canada that was to be phased in over the next 10 years. To begin, the immigration level for 1995 was to be cut by as much as 50 000 from that of the previous year. The following were also proposed:

- A requirement that persons sponsoring family class immigrants post a surety bond to cover possible future costs their relatives might pose to Canada's social system.
- Greater value to be placed on level of education, fluency in English and French, and work skills of prospective immigrants to "increase the economic benefits of immigration."
- Reducing the proportion of immigrants belonging to the family class in favour of independent class immigrants. In particular, making it more difficult for parents and grandparents to be sponsored.

Reaction to the announcement varied. Immigration analysts predicted that the changes would mean fewer skilled immigrants coming from Hong Kong and China, and proportionally more immigrants arriving from the Philippines and India, where the language of commerce is English.

Some commentators argued that the new policy reflected what the majority of Canadians wanted. Others criticized the new policy, saying that it went against the promises the Liberals had made during the 1993 election campaign and discriminated against applicants from certain countries. Still others contended that the proposals would have a different impact on regions and that this was an argument in favour of more provincial control over immigration policy.

In February 1995, the Finance Minister brought down a budget aimed at substantially reducing the federal government's annual deficit. One provision of the budget directly affected would-be immigrants—the introduction of a $975 landing fee for adult immigrants to help defray the cost of processing their admission. Some immigration advocates likened the fee to a "head tax" and said that low-income families from poor countries would be unfairly burdened by it.

In November 1995, the Minister of Immigration set the immigration level for 1996 at between 195 000 and 220 000 people, marginally higher than the numbers projected for the year 1995. Independent class immigrants were to make up about one-half the 1996 quota. Immigration officials projected the total number of immigrants to Quebec for 1995 at 24 000, or 40 percent below quota.

Refusal of Entry, Removal after Entry, and Appeals

The *Immigration Act* sets out who may not enter Canada and who may be ordered to leave, removal procedures, and avenues of appeal for those wishing to challenge decisions of immigration officials.

Certain types of persons will automatically be refused entry to Canada. Inadmissible persons include non-Canadian citizens who are suffering from illnesses that pose a public danger or may place an undue financial burden on health services; those who lack the funds to support themselves; and convicted criminals or those who pose a risk of committing serious crimes. Potential or known terrorists and persons who have been convicted of war crimes are also inadmissible.

To determine whether a prospective immigrant falls into the inadmissible class, immigration offi-

NEWSWORTHY

Bureaucratic Red Tape Traps Popular Grandpa

He escaped the war in El Salvador, only to end up in the middle of the drug scene on Vancouver's East Hastings Street. Now Salomon Gonzalez is facing what seems to him the most mystifying foe of all—Canadian immigration department red tape.

After three years in Canada, the 68-year-old grandfather is facing deportation. Immigration has rejected his refugee application and is trying to send him back to El Salvador on the grounds that the civil war in that Central American country is over and he is no longer in danger.

Gonzalez, a former union official in El Salvador, said all he wants to do is live out his years baby-sitting his grandchildren in Vancouver.

As for the immigration department's contention that El Salvador is safe: "The men with the guns [the death squads] are still there. People still die. I am afraid, so dangerous."

His son and daughter-in-law were given refugee status and are now Canadian citizens.

Only a week ago, friends and community groups held a tamale dinner and passed around the hat so Gonzalez, who is on welfare, could pay the $500 immigration fee to apply to remain in Canada on humanitarian and compassionate grounds.

But this week he was told he can't apply until he pays the new $975 landing fee, imposed retroactively by federal Finance Minister Paul Martin as a deficit buster in the federal budget only two weeks ago.

When he first came to Vancouver, Gonzalez took English lessons in a storefront school on East Hastings, dodging the drug dealers to get to class.

From: Robert Sarti, "Bureaucratic red tape traps popular grandpa." *The Vancouver Sun*, March 13, 1995. Reprinted with permission—*The Vancouver Sun*.

1. On what grounds did the immigration department decide that Salomon Gonzalez should be deported? Do you agree with this policy?

2. What was the basis of Gonzalez's appeal against his deportation order?

Couple Can Sponsor Retarded Son in India

A couple who left their retarded son behind in India because they were not allowed to bring him to Canada have now won permission to sponsor his immigration.

Ajit Singh Bhullar and his wife, Harbhajan Kaur, of Abbotsford, came to Canada in 1985 and became seasonal farm workers.

They originally applied to immigrate in 1980 with their son Harshvinderjit Singh Bhullar, then 17, but were turned down because the teenager was medically inadmissible.

According to documents filed at the father's recent appeal to sponsor his son, the immigration department concluded the son was mentally retarded and would need family help for life.

The department added that should family assistance break down, "institutional care would be required, which would place excessive demand on health and social services in Canada."

Several years after this refusal, the couple was allowed to immigrate here, sponsored by a daughter living in Merritt, because they had dropped their son from their application and left him in India in the care of elderly relatives.

The senior Bhullar, who works seasonally on farms and lives on unemployment benefits for the rest of the year, has returned to India three times, in 1989, 1992, and 1994, to make care arrangements for his son.

In 1991, his sponsorship application for his son was turned down by the immigration department on the grounds—once again—that the son would place excessive demands on Canada's health and social services if family assistance broke down.

In Bhullar's appeal hearing last December, there was evidence the extended family here has the financial ability to look after the man and help him find a job. There was also evidence that several farms in B.C. have already offered him jobs picking fruit and vegetables.

Allowing the appeal so that Bhullar senior can sponsor his son, immigration and refugee board member Des Verma concluded there are compassionate and humanitarian grounds for his decision.

From: Moira Farrow, "Couple can sponsor retarded son in India." *The Vancouver Sun*, March 17, 1995. Reprinted with permission—*The Vancouver Sun*.

1. **Why did the immigration department refuse the application of Harshvinderjit Singh Bhullar.**

2. **What reasons did the refugee board member give for allowing the appeal?**

cers will conduct a security check with police authorities in the applicant's country of permanent residence. An applicant will also have to go through a complete medical exam that meets Canadian standards while still outside Canada. Immigration visas will be refused to persons who do not pass these checks.

Immigration officials may refuse entry due to missing or incomplete documents, membership in an inadmissible class, or inability to establish a credible basis for a claim to refugee status. Persons who are refused admission must be offered the opportunity to depart voluntarily.

Persons who commit a minor infraction of immigration rules, such as overstaying their visit, may be issued a **departure order**. This will require that they leave Canada on or before a certain date. However, if they do not leave by that date, the departure order becomes a **deportation order**. Deportation orders are issued to persons who have committed a very serious violation of immigration rules. Normally, deported persons will never be allowed to return to Canada.

Persons who arrive at a port of entry and are found to be in violation of immigration rules may

Man, 84, Accused of War Crimes

The federal government has accused an 84-year-old Toronto man of participating in the execution of Jews in German-occupied Latvia during the Second World War.

Documents filed Monday in Federal Court identify Erichs Tobiass as one of four suspected war criminals Ottawa is trying to deport for hiding their Nazi past when they came to Canada.

The immigration department began formal proceedings against Tobiass to strip him of his Canadian citizenship.

The documents allege Tobiass was a member of the Latvian security police, or Arajs Kommando, between 1941 and 1943 and participated "in the execution of civilians during that time."

They also claim Tobiass was a member of the German security police, the Waffen SS, between 1943 and 1945.

The government says Tobiass obtained Canadian citizenship "by false or by knowingly concealing material circumstances."

Justice Minister Allen Rock has said war crime investigators have evidence against at least 12 suspects, but will pursue four cases first to clarify legal principles and establish precedents.

From: Man, 84, Accused of War Crimes *Southam News/Edmonton Journal*, March 21, 1995. Published by *Southam News* as it appeared in *The Edmonton Journal*.

1. **Why did the immigration department decide that Erichs Tobiass should be deported?**

2. **What difficulties might one encounter in trying to prove that someone is a war criminal?**

---

be issued an **exclusion order**. Exclusion orders can be issued for relatively minor infractions such as not being in possession of a valid passport or a proper visa. Persons who leave Canada under an exclusion order will not be permitted to enter Canada for a period of one year.

Before a deportation order or an exclusion order is carried out, the immigration department must conduct a removal inquiry to determine whether a removal is justified. Removal inquiries are conducted by an adjudicator. They resemble court proceedings, except that the rules of procedure and evidence are not as formal. Also, the person who is the subject of the hearing cannot refuse to testify. The alleged infraction that is the subject of the inquiry may have occurred while the person was in or outside Canada.

Appeals of decisions for removal are heard by the Appeal Division of the Immigration and Refugee Board. If an appeal is lost at the Immigration and Refugee Board, a person can apply to the Federal Court, Trial Division, for a judicial review of the case, but only on a point of law or of jurisdiction. Appeals are not available to visitors. If the Federal Court allows the application, it will be sent back to the Immigration and Refugee Board for a hearing.

Reviewing Your Reading

1. **What classes of persons have an automatic right to enter Canada?**

2. **Note three reasons for which visitors can be ordered out of Canada.**

3. **What requirements must be met to obtain**
   a) a student authorization?
   b) an employment authorization?

4. **a) Distinguish among "family class," "independent class," and "refugee class" immigrants.**
   b) For which class of immigrants do DNA tests hold the most importance? Explain.

5. **What obligations must sponsors of family class immigrants be prepared to honour?**

6. Distinguish among "self-employed," "investor," and "entrepreneur," as defined in the *Immigration Act*.

7. According to the United Nations definition, what kinds of people are considered refugees?

8. Define the terms "internal flight alternative" and "third country rule" as they apply to refugees.

9. What is the role of the senior immigration officer and the refugee claims officer in the refugee-determination process?

10. What types of persons are automatically refused entry to Canada?

11. a) Distinguish among a "departure order," a "deportation order," and an "exclusion order."

    b) What avenues of appeal are available to people ordered to leave Canada?

23.4 LEAVING CANADA

Most people leave Canada by choice, usually to visit places on business or as tourists, but sometimes to seek a new life elsewhere. A small number leave against their will, as a result of decisions of immigration officials or judicial bodies.

If you travel outside Canada, you will want to take note of the following.

Passports

Most countries require a **passport** upon arrival at a port of entry. Canadian citizens can apply for a passport in person at a local passport office or by mail. A passport is a highly valuable document. A lost or stolen passport should be reported to the local police and to the nearest Canadian consulate or embassy as quickly as possible. Replacement will require proof of identity and citizenship, such as a citizenship card, a birth certificate, or an expired passport.

Visitor's Visa

A visitor's visa can be a document or a stamped passport authorizing visitation for a specified period of time. A visitor's visa can also be given verbally as is done between Canada and the United States. Visa regulations vary from place to place. In some instances it may be necessary to apply for a visa well in advance of arrival. Some countries deny entry if a passport contains visa stamps from countries with which they are at war or have poor relations.

International Driver's Licence

Some countries require an International Driver's Licence for the operation of a motor vehicle. Applicants must be at least 18 years of age. Normally, such licences are valid for one year. Other countries will accept a current driver's licence issued by the province of residence.

Insurance

Medical emergencies and theft are common risks associated with foreign travel. In the event of illness or injury, Canadians are protected to some extent under their province's medical insurance plan. It is advisable to check the provisions of the provincial plan to determine if additional medical insurance coverage should be purchased from a private insurance carrier.

Many household policies cover damage and loss or theft of belongings when one is outside Canada. Again, it is advisable to check existing coverage.

Travellers, when purchasing an airline ticket or passage aboard a ship, may also purchase "cancellation insurance" to protect themselves from financial loss in the event that an emergency interrupts their travel plans.

Travelling Abroad

It is important to obey the laws of any country. Travellers, like residents, are subject to the justice system of the host country. Compared with Canada, the laws, the penalties for breaking them, trial and appeal procedures, and the treatment of those who are imprisoned may vary. Some countries offer very little in the way of civil rights protection.

Travellers commonly face situations that may lead them into trouble. Submitting to temptations to smuggle contraband goods such as gems or antiquities, or accepting money to illegally transport drugs are extremely foolish. In some countries drug smuggling carries the death penalty. Black marketeers often offer more attractive exchange rates for foreign currency than those offered by legitimate currency exchanges, but again this poses the risk of criminal prosecution.

Canadians who find themselves in legal difficulties should contact the nearest Canadian consulate or embassy as soon as possible.

Canadians who commit crimes in other countries and return home before they are caught may face **extradition**, i.e., the "handing over by one state or country to another of people accused of crimes." This is a complex area of the law, and successful extradition will depend on such factors as whether an extradition treaty exists between Canada and the other country; whether the alleged offence is considered a crime in Canada; what possible punishment might befall a person who is found guilty; and, generally, whether Canada and the other country have sharply different political ideologies and judicial systems.

Emigration from Canada

As noted earlier, many immigrants who came to Canada in the 1800s stayed only for a short time before moving on to the United States. This has been a continuing theme in Canada's history. Today, the United States is home to large numbers of expatriate Canadians, with California and Florida being particularly popular places to live.

Better economic opportunities have attracted businesspeople, entertainers, professional athletes, academics, and doctors to the United States. This talent "drain" from Canada is a source of concern to many.

Recently, a new phenomenon has been seen: young Canadians whose parents immigrated to Canada from Western Europe after World War II have been leaving Canada to settle in Europe. Again, most often the reason is economic opportunities not available in Canada. But for some, the motivation comes from uncertainties over Canada's future. Most of those leaving are well-educated and highly skilled, the kind of people that Canada has been working hard to attract as immigrants.

Reviewing Your Reading

1. **Distinguish between a "passport" and a "visitor's visa."**

2. **Note three precautions travellers abroad should generally observe.**

3. **What is the most common reason that Canadians emigrate?**

23.5 THE IMMIGRATION DEBATE: POINTS OF CONTENTION

The current debate over immigration has tended to focus on the following questions.

Is the Immigration System Open to Abuse?

Critics of Canada's immigration system have charged that many people abuse the present system. They contend that persons applying for refugee status are often "economic refugees" who are seeking to "jump the queue" ahead of legitimate applicants trying to immigrate to Canada through proper channels. The immigration and refugee boards in particular have come under the close scrutiny of some critics who have accused board members of incompetence and soft-heartedness. They point to the relatively high acceptance rates of refugee claims in Canada compared with rates in other countries, and the fact that some criminals and other dangerous persons have been allowed into Canada as Convention refugees.

Another concern relates to immigrants who have been ordered deported because they have committed crimes. Failure to enforce their deportation orders before subsequent violent crimes have been committed by these people has led to a public outcry.

Some critics have suggested that immigration officials responsible for investigating, detaining, and removing offenders are undertrained, and overwhelmed by the number of deportation orders they must enforce. In response, in 1994, the Minister of Immigration set up a special group of investigators, including RCMP officers and immigration officials, to locate foreign criminals in Canada and process them for removal.

Do the Economic Costs of Immigration Outweigh the Benefits?

Recent trends have prompted debate over whether the economic costs associated with immigration are beginning to outweigh the benefits.

- During the past decade, a growing proportion of immigrants have been entering Canada under the family class, where levels of education and job skills tend to be lower. Generally, the demands of this group for social services are higher than those from the independent class.
- Ontario and British Columbia are receiving a disproportionate share of immigrants to Canada. In 1993, Ontario received 133 665 immigrants and British Columbia received 45 546. In the first nine months of 1994, these provinces received 90 000 and 39 000, respectively. A large majority of these new Canadians settled in major urban centres such as Toronto and Vancouver, placing stress on the social services available in these communities and burdening the taxpayers of these provinces.
- A large proportion of immigrants to Canada are not proficient in English or French. This is particularly true of immigrants arriving from Hong Kong, India, Taiwan, and China. As a consequence, the cost of English as a Second Language instruction has risen dramatically, particularly in Metropolitan Toronto and Greater Vancouver.
- In addition to English-language training, new arrivals require other forms of support such as job-related training and orientation to Canadian customs and government services to ease their adjustment to life in Canada. In smaller communities, it is much harder to provide this support and the barriers of isolation are harder to break down.

These developments have led some people to question current immigration policy. In response, it is worth remembering that Canada has always sought to attract immigrants who are financially secure or highly skilled, i.e., persons readily able to find employment, and this is certainly no less true today. Yet, this very fact begs a number of questions: Should economic cost-benefit analysis be the sole driving force of immigration policy? Is consideration of the long-term economic benefits of immigration being neglected in favour of the debate over short-term costs? How might Canada's federal system be changed to ensure that the costs and benefits of immigration are equally shared among Canadians? Finally, and perhaps most important, how does one ensure that the full measure of credit is given to the many, different ways immigrants have enriched Canada?

Most Canadians acknowledge that immigration is necessary to ensure Canada's future security and prosperity. At the same time, the questions of how many and who should be accepted into Canada will continue to stir debate. The reason is simple: at the heart of these questions lie competing visions of Canada and the issue of our own national identity.

Reviewing Your Reading

1. **According to critics, what are two ways Canada's immigration system is commonly abused?**

2. **Note two types of economic costs associated with getting immigrants settled in Canada.**

3. **Explain how immigration policy and population trends are interlinked.**

Multiculturalism:

Does it foster hostility

toward immigrants?

Canada has become one of the most multicultural countries in the world. Over one million immigrants and refugees enter Canada every four years. Many of these people are attracted to Canada because of its reputation as a country that respects and encourages cultural diversity. While many new Canadians adopt some of the values common to Canadians, they often continue to feel a strong attachment to their homeland and to their traditional customs and values.

These attachments are quite evident in some urban areas—in neighbourhoods where immigrants from a particular country have settled in large numbers. Retail outlets sell goods from the homelands, professional services are offered in the language, and billboards, advertisements, and even street names appear in that language. Some Canadians are uncomfortable with these visible displays. For other Canadians, they generate suspicion and hostility rooted in racial prejudice.

Community debates on immigration policy are often disguised debates over multiculturalism. Opposition to high immigration levels may stem from the fact that the largest number of immigrants entering Canada today are coming from "non-traditional" areas. People from these countries differ in skin colour, language, custom, and belief from those who led Canada into Confederation in 1867. This shift may have triggered fears in the descendants of these "founding groups" for their place in Canadian society.

At the extreme, these negative feelings are used by radical white supremacist organizations to promote their hatred of minority groups. They appeal to the insecurities and prejudices of bigots and the unemployed, recruiting white urban youth into their organizations. These hate groups distribute messages that call for the persecution and expulsion of various religious, racial, and other targeted groups.

Canada does not tolerate hate and violence against minority groups. The *Criminal Code* makes it illegal to deliberately promote "hatred" on the basis of religion or race. A new law, Bill C-41, has toughened this

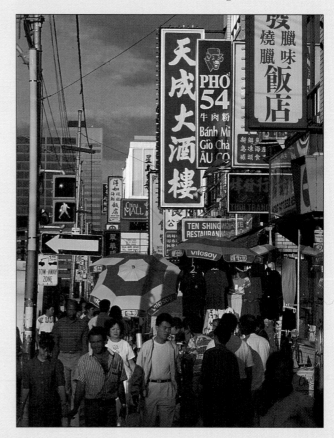

law and increased the penalties for crimes motivated by hatred because of the victim's gender, race, religion, or sexual orientation.

On One Side

Those who call for the complete assimilation of immigrants regard multiculturalism as a divisive force that is weakening Canada. They feel that all newcomers should assimilate into the mainstream of Canadian society. They are critical of cultural differences and feel that customs such as keeping women subservient to men and using physical punishment to discipline children should not be tolerated in Canada.

Some people even feel the immigrants deserve the hatred of white supremacists. They claim that by asserting their differences, the immigrants are inviting the hostility of radical groups.

On the Other Side

Supporters of multiculturalism respect this diversity of new Canadians. They feel that the celebration of their various cultures makes Canada a richer and more interesting country. They consider suggestions that the assimilation of immigrants will deter those who foster hate crimes as ludicrous. Assimilation does not change physical differences.

Bill C-41 reflects how seriously the Canadian government and people view hate-motivated crimes. Legislation like this sends a clear message to those who are intolerant and act on their bigotry. It also emphasizes this country's respect for the diversity of minority cultural groups.

The Bottom Line

It is important that all Canadians feel that they belong in their community. For some people this means retaining some traditional customs. At the same time, these displays of tradition may make long-time residents of the same community feel uncomfortable. Does multiculturalism enrich the community? Or does it foster hostility toward immigrants? What do you think? You be the judge!

1. **What is multiculturalism? How do you react to it?**

2. **How can the government's policy of multiculturalism be connected to prejudice and racism in Canada?**

3. **Who are white supremacists and what are their beliefs? Do they represent a danger to other Canadians?**

4. **What laws exist to control the promotion of hatred in Canada? Are they adequate or should they be changed?**

CHAPTER REVIEW

Reviewing Key Terms

For each of the following statements, indicate the key term being defined:

a) work permit issued to temporary workers

b) a person who leaves his or her homeland because of a well-founded fear of persecution

c) the formal process by which an immigrant becomes a citizen of another country

d) the leaving of a homeland with the intention of becoming a permanent resident of another country

e) handing over, by one state to another, of a person accused of a crime

f) a document served upon persons who have committed very serious violations of immigration rules

g) an immigrant who agrees to commit a large sum of money to a business venture in Canada as a condition of acceptance

h) a place such as an international airport where a person can formally request to enter a foreign country

i) immigrants who require a sponsor as a condition of their entry into Canada

j) a stamp placed in a passport authorizing entry

Exploring Legal Concepts

1. Canada formally adopted a policy of selective immigration during the early 1900s. Compare how this policy was applied during the Laurier era and in the period since the proclamation of the *Immigration Act, 1976.*

2. How might Canada be affected in the long term if the federal government moved to severely reduce immigration from its current levels?

3. Review the objectives of Canada's immigration policy, as set out in the *Immigration Act, 1976.* Identify the three objectives you see as being the most important. Restate these objectives in your own words.

4. Speculate on the purpose behind the creation of the "entrepreneur" and "investor" classes of immigrants.

5. What is the policy of requiring sponsors of family members to sign an Undertaking of Assistance? Do you agree with this policy? Why or why not?

6. Distinguish between "extradition" and "deportation." Suggest two circumstances in which Canada might refuse a request for extradition.

7. What two main screening methods are used by immigration officials to identify "undesirable" immigrants?

8. Identify three world figures who would likely be declared inadmissible to Canada. Justify your choices.

Applying Legal Concepts

1. *Awale v. Canada (Ministry of Employment and Immigration)* (1994) Fed. T.D. Doc. No. A-1083-92

   Awale, an applicant for refugee status, was a citizen of Somalia and a member of a little known clan. This clan was distinguishable from other clans in Somalia partly by their lighter skin colour.

   The applicant claimed that he and his family were subject to harassment by the other clans on the basis of their clan membership. He cited examples of harassment that he and his relatives had already experienced. The Immigration and Refugee Board accepted the subjective component of Awale's case—that he genuinely feared persecution because of his clan membership. However it found no objective evidence supporting his claim that his clan was being singled out for discrimination. Indeed, the only piece of documentary evidence presented by Awale dealt with persecution of other clans in Somalia and made no reference to his clan.

   - **What part of the applicant's case did the Immigration and Refugee Board accept? On what ground did it fail?**

   - **What additional kinds of evidence might have helped the applicant's case?**

2. *Thirunavukkarasu v. Canada (Ministry of Employment and Immigration)* (1993) [1994] 163 N.R. 232 (I.A.B.)

   Thirunavukkarasu, a claimant for refugee status, was a citizen of Sri Lanka and a Tamil, an ethnic minority concentrated in northern Sri Lanka. For years, a bitter conflict has been waged between Tamil revolutionaries and the Sri Lankan government. The Immigration and Refugee Board accepted that the claimant faced serious risk to his life in the north of Sri Lanka. However it refused his claim for refugee status on the basis that there was an internal flight alternative (IFA) available to him in the southwest part of the country. Thirunavukkarasu appealed the decision. At the appeal hearing, the appeal board raised the following points:

   - The burden of proof with respect to an IFA is on the claimant.
   - The claimant must take advantage of an IFA if it is not objectively unreasonable to do so.
   - The claimant must show that there is a serious possibility of persecution in the area alleged to constitute an IFA.
   - The claimant has the right to adequate notice that an allegation of an IFA will be raised at an IRB hearing.

   During the hearing, reports from Amnesty International were presented in support of Thirunavukkarasu's case. The reports spoke of several violent incidents in which Tamils in the southwest were persecuted by the Sri Lankan government in retaliation for the activities of Tamil terrorist groups. The appeal board overruled the original decision and granted the claimant refugee status.

   - **Why did the Immigration and Refugee Board reject Thirunavukkarasu's claim?**

   - **What did the claimant have to do to convince the appeal board to overrule the IRB's decision?**

3. *Taei v. Canada (Ministry of Employment and Immigration)* (1993)
19 Imm. L.R. (2d) 187

The applicant applied to the courts to obtain an order requiring immigration authorities to process his application for landing as a permanent resident. The applicant had arrived in Canada in 1989 and had made a successful application for refugee status.

Shortly after, he was charged with aggravated assault, attempted murder, and extortion—charges that were still pending at the time of his application for landing. The immigration department had refused to process his application until the criminal charges were disposed of in criminal court. On the landing question, the courts found that the right to presumption of innocence required only that the immigration department stay the applicant's request to be admitted. The stay would continue until the criminal charges had been decided. If the applicant was acquitted on all charges, then immigration authorities should proceed with granting admission. If the applicant was found guilty, then the applicant would have disqualified himself from landing.

• **What case was the applicant attempting to argue?**

• **To what extent was the applicant successful in winning his case? How was he unsuccessful?**

4. *Rambharose (Litigation Guardian of) v. R.* (1994) Fed T.D. Doc. No. T-167-93
The plaintiff was born in Canada shortly after his parents arrived here from Trinidad in 1988. His mother had not obtained an immigrant visa prior to appearing at a Canadian port of entry. Later, her application for Convention refugee status was rejected, as were two attempts to be accepted for landing on humanitarian and compassionate grounds.

When a removal order was issued against his mother, the plaintiff applied to the courts to stay its execution. The plaintiff argued that removal of his mother from Canada would violate his rights under the *Canadian Charter of Rights and Freedoms*. Either he would be forced to leave Canada to be with his mother, or be separated from her. The courts sided with the plaintiff, declaring that the plaintiff would suffer irreparable harm if he were separated from his mother at such a tender age. And as a Canadian citizen, he had a right to remain in Canada. Consequently, the courts ordered that the removal order against his mother be stayed.

• **Would the case presented by the plaintiff have been possible if he had been born outside Canada? Explain.**

• **What "irreparable harm" might the plaintiff have suffered if he had been separated from his mother?**

5. *Cheung v. Canada (Ministry of Employment and Immigration)* (1993)
Federal Court of Appeal 153 N.R. 145
When Ting Ting Cheung gave birth to her second child in China in 1987, she came to the attention of the local Family Planning Bureau. Faced with the prospect of forced sterilization under China's one-child policy, she came to Canada and applied for refugee status. The court considered two questions in deciding her case. First, do women in China who have more than one child and are faced with forced sterilization, constitute a "social group"

within the definition of Convention refugee? Second, did forced or strongly coerced sterilization, in the context of China's one-child policy, constitute persecution? On the first question, the court found that the following criteria provided a useful test:

(1) a natural or non-natural group of persons with (2) similar shared background, habits, social status, political outlook, education, values, aspirations, history, economic activity, or interests, often interests contrary to those of the prevailing government, and (3) sharing basic, innate, unalterable characteristics, consciousness, and solidarity or (4) sharing a temporary but voluntary status, with the purpose of their association being so fundamental to their human dignity that they should not be required to alter it.

The court found that such women did constitute a social group, but that only those women who had a well-founded fear of persecution could claim refugee status. On the second question, the court found that forced sterilization was a violation of articles 3 and 5 of the *Universal Declaration of Human Rights* and constituted persecution. The court therefore declared the applicant, Ting Ting Cheung, to be a Convention refugee.

- **Explain why the court found the applicant to be a Convention refugee.**

- **Can you think of groups that might use the test devised by the court in this case to argue that they constitute a "social group" within the definition of a Convention refugee?**

Extending Legal Concepts

1. Many provincial leaders are calling for the decentralization of Canada's federal system.

   a) What advantages do you see in giving the provinces more control over immigration policy?

   b) What disadvantages do you see in giving the provinces more control?

   c) What course of action do you recommend? Why?

2. a) Using the current "point system" as your guide, identify the attributes that would make a prospective immigrant to Canada a highly desirable candidate. What attributes would make a prospective immigrant undesirable as a candidate?

   b) Measure your own attributes against the standards set out in the point system. Imagine that you are an immigrant wanting to enter Canada under the "independent" class. Give an assessment of your chances of being accepted for landing.

3. Refer to the bar graph on p. 620.

   a) What does the graph reveal about the make-up of the world's refugee population?

   b) How does Canada's refugee population differ from the world's refugee population?

   c) What factors might account for this difference?

4. With a partner, visit a local community organization that provides support services to recent immigrants. Find out their view on what kinds of support recent immigrants need most and how these needs are being met.

5. Talk to a local group involved in sponsoring refugees to Canada. Find out how the group became involved in such work and the experiences they have had in helping refugees.

6. Interview a person who immigrated to Canada to learn about his or her immigrant experience.

7. Compare the immigration policies of Canada's major political parties.

8. Interview a lawyer who works with new immigrants to find out the most common problem they encounter when dealing with Canada's court system.

Researching an Issue

The $975 Landing Fee
In 1995, the federal government announced its intention to introduce a $975 landing fee for adult immigrants. This was one of several measures intended to reduce the government deficit.

Statement
The landing fee has been strongly criticized by some immigrant spokespersons for causing undue hardship to low-income immigrants.

Point
Immigrants should be expected to pay at least part of the cost of government services related to their coming to and settling in Canada.

Counterpoint
Immigrants benefit Canada economically and in other ways. Imposing such a fee may dissuade highly desirable immigrants from coming to Canada.

- **With a partner, research this issue and reflect on your findings.**
- **Prepare points on this statement that could be used for a class debate.**
- **Discuss your findings with others in your class.**

APPENDIX

Constitution Act, 1982
Schedule B
Part I

CANADIAN CHARTER OF RIGHTS AND FREEDOMS

Whereas Canada is founded upon principles that recognize the supremacy of God and the rule of law:

Guarantee of Rights and Freedoms

Rights and Freedoms in Canada

1. The *Canadian Charter of Rights and Freedoms* guarantees the rights and freedoms set out in it subject only to such reasonable limits prescribed by law as can be demonstrably justified in a free and democratic society.

Fundamental Freedoms

Fundamental Freedoms

2. Everyone has the following fundamental freedoms:

✓ **(a)** freedom of conscience and religion;

(b) freedom of thought, belief, opinion and expression, including freedom of the press and other media of communication;

(c) freedom of peaceful assembly; and

(d) freedom of association.

Democratic Rights

Democratic Rights of Citizens

3. Every citizen of Canada has the right to vote in an election of members of the House of Commons or of a legislative assembly and to be qualified for membership therein.

Maximum Duration of Legislative Bodies

4. (1) No House of Commons and no legislative assembly shall continue for longer than five years from the date fixed for the return of the writs at a general election of its members.

Continuation in Special Circumstances

(2) In time of real of apprehended war, invasion or insurrection, a House of Commons may be continued by Parliament and a legislative assembly may be continued by the legislature beyond five years if such continuation is not opposed by the votes of more than one-third of the members of the House of Commons or the legislative assembly, as the case may be.

5. There shall be a sitting of Parliament and of each legislature at least once every twelve months.

Annual Sitting of Legislative Bodies

Mobility Rights

6. (1) Every citizen of Canada has the right to enter, remain in and leave Canada.

Mobility of Citizens

(2) Every citizen of Canada and every person who has the status of a permanent resident of Canada has the right

Rights to Move and Gain Livelihood

(a) to move and take up residence in any province; and

(b) to pursue the gaining of a livelihood in any province.

(3) The rights specified in subsection (2) are subject to

Limitation

(a) any laws or practices of general application in force in a province other than those that discriminate among persons primarily on the basis of province of present or previous residence; and

(b) any laws providing for reasonable residency requirements as a qualification for the receipt of publicly provided social services.

(4) Subsections (2) and (3) do not preclude any law, program or activity that has as its object the

Affirmative Action Programs

amelioration in a province of conditions of individuals in that province who are socially or economically disadvantaged if the rate of employment in that province is below the rate of employment in Canada.

Legal Rights

Life, Liberty and Security of Person

7. Everyone has the right to life, liberty and security of the person and the right not to be deprived thereof except in accordance with the principles of fundamental justice.

Search or Seizure

8. Everyone has the right to be secure against unreasonable search or seizure.

Detention or Imprisonment

9. Everyone has the right not to be arbitrarily detained or imprisoned.

Arrest or Detention

10. Everyone has the right on arrest or detention

(a) to be informed promptly of the reasons therefor;

(b) to retain and instruct counsel without delay and to be informed of that right; and

(c) to have the validity of the detention determined by way of habeas corpus and to be released if the detention is not lawful.

Proceedings in Criminal and Penal Matters

11. Any person charged with an offence has the right

(a) to be informed without unreasonable delay of the specific offence;

(b) to be tried within a reasonable time;

(c) not to be compelled to be a witness in proceedings against that person in respect of the offence;

(d) to be presumed innocent until proven guilty according to law in a fair and public hearing by an independent and impartial tribunal;

(e) not to be denied reasonable bail without just cause;

(f) except in the case of an offence under military law tried before a military tribunal, to the benefit of trial by jury where the maximum punishment for the offence is imprisonment for five years or a more severe punishment;

(g) not to be found guilty on account of any act or omission unless, at the time of the act or omission, it constituted an offence under Canadian or international law or was criminal according to the general principles of law recognized by the community of nations;

(h) if finally acquitted of the offence, not to be tried for it again and, if finally found guilty and punished for the offence, not to be tried or punished for it again; and

(i) if found guilty of the offence and if the punishment for the offence has been varied between the time of commission and the time of sentencing, to the benefit of the lesser punishment.

Treatment or Punishment

12. Everyone has the right not to be subjected to any cruel and unusual treatment or punishment.

Self-Crimination

13. A witness who testifies in any proceedings has the right not to have any incriminating evidence so given used to incriminate that witness in any other proceedings, except in a prosecution for perjury or for the giving of contradictory evidence.

Interpreter

14. A party or witness in any proceedings who does not understand or speak the language in which the proceedings are conducted or who is deaf has the right to the assistance of an interpreter.

Equality Rights

Equality Before and Under Law and Equal Protection and Benefit of Law

15. (1) Every individual is equal before and under the law and has the right to the equal protection and equal benefit of the law without discrimination and, in particular, without discrimination based on race, national or ethnic origin, colour, religion, sex, age or mental or physical disability.

Affirmative Action Programs

(2) Subsection (1) does not preclude any law, program or activity that has as its object the amelioration of conditions of disadvantaged individuals or groups including those that are disadvantaged because of race,

national or ethnic origin, colour, religion, sex, age or mental or physical disability.

Official Languages of Canada

Official Languages of Canada

16. (1) English and French are the official languages of Canada and have equality of status and equal rights and privileges as to their use in all institutions of the Parliament and government of Canada.

Official Languages of New Brunswick

(2) English and French are the official languages of New Brunswick and have equality of status and equal rights and privileges as to their use in all institutions of the legislature and government of New Brunswick.

Advancement of Status and Use

(3) Nothing in this Charter limits the authority of Parliament or a legislature to advance the equality of status or use of English and French.

Proceedings of Parliament

17. (1) Everyone has the right to use English or French in any debates and other proceedings of Parliament.

Proceedings of New Brunswick Legislature

(2) Everyone has the right to use English or French in any debates and other proceedings of the legislature of New Brunswick.

Parliamentary Statutes and Records

18. (1) The statutes, records and journals of Parliament shall be printed and published in English and French and both language versions are equally authoritative.

New Brunswick Statutes and Records

(2) The statutes, records and journals of the legislature of New Brunswick shall be printed and published in English and French and both language versions are equally authoritative.

Proceedings in Courts Established by Parliament

19. (1) Either English or French may be used by any person in, or in any pleading in or process issuing from, any court established by Parliament.

Proceedings in New Brunswick Courts

(2) Either English or French may be used by any person in, or in any pleading in or process issuing from, any court of New Brunswick.

20. (1) Any member of the public in Canada has the right to communicate with, and to receive available services from, any head or central office of an institution of the Parliament or government of Canada in English or French, and has the same right with respect to any other office of any such institution where

(a) there is a significant demand for communications with and services from that office in such language; or

(b) due to the nature of the office, it is reasonable that communications with and services from that office be available in both English and French.

(2) Any member of the public in New Brunswick has the right to communicate with, and to receive available services from, any office of an institution of the legislature or government of New Brunswick in English or French.

21. Nothing in sections 16 to 20 abrogates or derogates from any right, privilege or obligation with respect to the English or French languages, or either of them, that exists or is continued by virtue of any other provision of the Constitution of Canada.

22. Nothing in sections 16 to 20 abrogates or derogates from any legal or customary right or privilege acquired or enjoyed either before or after the coming into force of this Charter with respect to any language that is not English or French.

Minority Language Educational Rights

23. (1) Citizens of Canada

(a) whose first language learned and still understood is that of the English or French linguistic minority population of the province in which they reside, or

(b) who have received their primary school instruction in Canada in English or French and reside in a province where the language in which they received that instruction is the language of the English or French linguistic

Communications by Public with Federal Institutions

Communications by Public with New Brunswick Institutions

Continuation of Existing Constitutional Provisions

Rights and Privileges Preserved

Language of Instruction

minority population of the province, have the right to have their children receive primary and secondary school instruction in that language in that province.

Continuity of Language Instruction

(2) Citizens of Canada of whom any child has received or is receiving primary or secondary school instruction in English or French in Canada, have the right to have all their children receive primary and secondary school instruction in the same language.

Application Where Numbers Warrant

(3) The right of citizens of Canada under subsections (1) and (2) to have their children receive primary and secondary school instruction in the language of the English or French linguistic minority population of a province

(a) applies wherever in the province the number of children of citizens who have such a right is sufficient to warrant the provision to them out of public funds of minority language instruction; and

(b) includes, where the number of those children so warrants, the right to have them receive that instruction in minority language educational facilities provided out of public funds.

Enforcement

Enforcement of Guaranteed Rights and Freedoms

24. (1) Anyone whose rights or freedoms, as guaranteed by this Charter, have been infringed or denied may apply to a court of competent jurisdiction to obtain such remedy as the court considers appropriate and just in the circumstances.

Exclusion of Evidence Bringing Administration of Justice into Disrepute

(2) Where, in proceedings under subsection (1), a court concludes that evidence was obtained in a manner that infringed or denied any rights or freedoms guaranteed by this Charter, the evidence shall be excluded if it is established that, having regard to all the circumstances, the admission of it in the proceedings would bring the administration of justice into disrepute.

General

25. The guarantee in this Charter of certain rights and freedoms shall not be construed so as to abrogate or derogate from any aboriginal treaty or other rights of freedoms that pertain to the aboriginal peoples of Canada including

(a) any rights or freedoms that have been recognized by the Royal Proclamation of October 7, 1763; and

(b) any rights or freedoms that now exist by way of land claims agreements or may be so acquired.

Aboriginal Rights and Freedoms not Affected by Charter

26. The guarantee in this Charter of certain rights and freedoms shall not be construed as denying the existence of any other rights or freedoms that exist in Canada.

Other Rights and Freedoms Not Affected by Charter

27. This Charter shall be interpreted in a manner consistent with the preservation and enhancement of the multicultural heritage of Canadians.

Multicultural Heritage

28. Notwithstanding anything in this Charter, the rights and freedoms referred to in it are guaranteed equally to male and female persons.

Rights Guaranteed Equally to Both Sexes

29. Nothing in this Charter abrogates or derogates from any rights or privileges guaranteed by or under the Constitution of Canada in respect of denominational, separate or dissentient schools.

Rights Respecting Certain Schools Preserved

30. A reference in this Charter to a province or to the legislative assembly or legislature of a province shall be deemed to include a reference to the Yukon Territory and the Northwest Territories, or to the appropriate legislative authority thereof, as the case may be.

Application to Territories and Territorial Authorities

31. Nothing in this Charter extends the legislative powers of any body or authority.

Legislative Powers not Extended

Application of Charter

32. (1) This Charter applies

(a) to the Parliament and government of Canada in respect of all

Application of Charter

matters within the authority of Parliament including all matters relating to the Yukon Territory and Northwest Territories; and

(b) to the legislature and government of each province in respect of all matters within the authority of the legislature of each province.

Exception

(2) Notwithstanding subsection (1), section 15 shall not have effect until three years after this section comes into force.

Exception Where Express Declaration

33. (1) Parliament or the legislature of a province may expressly declare in an Act of Parliament or of the legislature, as the case may be, that the Act or a provision thereof shall operate notwithstanding a provision included in section 2 or sections 7 to 15 of this Charter.

Operation of Exception

(2) An Act or a provision of an Act in respect of which a declaration made under this section is in effect shall have such operation as it would have but for the provision of this Charter referred to in the declaration.

Five Year Limitation

(3) A declaration made under subsection (1) shall cease to have effect five years after it comes into force or on such earlier date as may be specified in the declaration.

Re-enactment

(4) Parliament or a legislature of a province may re-enact a declaration made under subsection (1).

Five Year Limitation

(5) Subsection (3) applies in respect of a re-enactment made under subsection (4).

Citation

34. This Part may be cited as the *Canadian Charter of Rights and Freedoms*.

Citation

A

abduction the kidnapping or illegal taking of a person, often a child

abet to encourage, incite, or set another on to commit a crime

aboriginal title rights created by first occupation and use of the land

absolute discharge a sentence whereby the accused is discharged rather than convicted, even though the charge is proven, or the plea is guilty

absolute liability a criminal offence in which intent is assumed to be present and need not be proven

absolute privilege a defence against defamation for statements made in legislative or court proceedings

absolute sale transfer of title to goods from seller to buyer in return for money

accelerated review review by the parole board for the release of an offender who has either committed a non-violent offence or a drug offence where the judge did not set parole eligibility at one-half of the sentence, and who has served one-third of the sentence

acceleration clause a clause in a rental contract that makes the rent for a specified number of months due immediately if one month's payment is overdue

access the right of the noncustodial parent to visit his or her child, and to make inquiries about the child's health, welfare, and education

accessory after the fact a person who receives, comforts, or assists another person for the purpose of escape, knowing that the person is party to an offence

accused a person charged with a crime

act a written law, formally passed by either Parliament or a provincial legislature

Act of God an unpredictable, uncontrollable event caused by the forces of nature

actus reus Latin phrase meaning "a wrongful action"

adjournment putting off to another time

administrative law the decisions of government agencies and boards and the law that regulates them

administrator/administratrix a man/woman appointed by the court to administer a deceased person's estate when there is no will

adoption a legal process in which a couple or, a single person, raises a child born to another as their own child

adultery voluntary sexual intercourse by a married person with a person other than the offender's spouse

adversary system a contested action, in which each party presents its case to the court

adverse effect discrimination intentional or unintentional discrimination which appears to be neutral, but effectively discriminates against most members of a group

affinity a relationship created by marriage

affirmation a solemn declaration by a witness that he or she will tell the truth

age of majority the age at which a person has the ability to undertake a legal obligation, 18 or 19, depending on the province

agency shop a business that permits non-union workers, though still requiring them to pay dues

agent a person empowered to act on behalf of another

aggravated assault assault wherein bodily harm occurs, including the wounding, maiming, and/or disfiguring of the victim; the most severe form of assault

aggravated sexual assault assault involving sexual activity, and the wounding, maiming, and/or disfiguring of the victim; the most severe form of sexual assault

aid to help, assist, or facilitate the commission of a crime

alibi a defence that places the accused at the relevant time in a different place than the scene of the crime

alienate to estrange or divert Native people from their traditional lands and culture

allurement something that is inviting or luring to young children; for example, a swimming pool or bells on an ice cream truck

alternative dispute resolution a term for processes such as mediation, negotiation, arbitration, and settlement designed to resolve or settle disputes without formal trials

alternative measures program an agreement between a young offender and authorities wherein the young offender admits to having done something wrong and then does something to make up for the wrong; is an alternative to a Youth Court trial

amelioration make better or improve

amending formula a procedure to amend or change Canada's Constitution without the involvement of the British Parliament

annulment the declaration that a marriage is void, or has never existed

anti-social act conduct that is not acceptable to society

appeal to seek a different decision in a higher court

appearance notice a legal document stating that the person to whom it is issued is alleged to have committed a criminal offence, and requiring that person to appear in court at a specified time

appellant a private person chosen, by the parties to a labour dispute for the purpose of hearing their arguments, and giving a judgment

arbitration a process for resolving disputes between persons through a third party whose decision is final and binding

arbitrator a private person chosen by the parties to a dispute for the purpose of hearing their arguments, and giving a judgment

arraignment the reading of the charge by the court clerk to the accused

arrest to deprive a person of his or her liberty by legal authority so that he or she may answer to a criminal charge

arson intentionally or recklessly causing damage by fire or explosion to property

artistic merit the benefit to society that a creation has

assault (1) a tort causing the victim to reasonably fear that bodily harm may occur; (2) the threat of actual physical contact without consent

assault causing bodily harm assault involving a weapon or threat of a weapon or an imitation, or assault in which the victim's health or comfort is threatened; the second form of assault

assignment the transfer of a right under a contract to another person

assimilate to make Native people become like Europeans in customs and viewpoint

assizes trials held before travelling judges

asylum a place of refuge

attempt to have intent to commit an offence, and to do or omit to do anything for the purpose of carrying out the intention

automatism actions performed by an individual who is not conscious of what he or she is doing; for example actions performed while sleepwalking or concussed

autrefois acquit French phrase meaning "formerly acquitted"

autrefois convict French phrase meaning "formerly convicted"

B

bail the process whereby an accused person is released pending trial

balance of probabilities the degree of proof in a civil action; a greater likelihood

band a body of Native people for whom lands were set aside for their use and benefit in the *Indian Act*

banns of marriage a church proclamation of an intended marriage; an option to a marriage licence in some provinces

bars to divorce reasons for the court not to grant a divorce; see collusion, condonation, and connivance

barter to trade by exchanging goods or services without money

battery intentional physical contact harmful or offensive to another person; the completion of an assault

beneficiaries persons who receive benefit from a trust or a will; also called heirs

best interests of the child the criteria used for a judge to determine custody of and access to a child or children

bigamy the state of being married to two persons at the same time

bill a proposed law; a draft of an act or statute

binding arbitration the terms of a negotiated settlement are imposed on labour and management by a neutral third party; the arbitrator, to resolve a dispute

binding-over the requirement by a judge of a person to keep the peace and be of good behaviour

biosphere reserve areas designated for the conservation of threatened ecosystems and the preservation of irreplaceable genetic material; program instituted by the United Nations

birth parent a child's natural or biological mother or father

bonding a form of insurance guaranteeing the honesty of a person handling money or other valuables

breach failure to observe a law or to perform an obligation owed under a contract

breach of condition failure to perform a major or very important part of a contract, entitling the injured party to treat the contract as ended

breach of contract failure to perform an obligation owed to another under a contract

breach of warranty failure to perform a minor term of a contract, entitling the injured party to damages only

break and enter to enter another's premises without permission by breaking or opening anything that is closed; also called burglary

Breathalyzer an approved instrument, as listed in the *Criminal Code,* that analyzes a person's breath to measure the concentration of alcohol in the person's blood

British North America Act Canada's first Constitution: an Act of the British Parliament that brought the Dominion of Canada into being on July 1, 1867

business assets see non-family assets

bylaws written laws formally passed by a municipality

C

Cabinet a political body comprised of the Prime Minister or Premier and Ministers of the Crown who make and determine the direction of government policy

capacity (1) the ability to understand the nature and effect of one's acts; (2) the legal ability to enter a contract on one's own behalf

capital punishment to receive the death penalty for committing a crime

care to be concerned with, and to attend to, the needs of oneself or another; watchful attention; the opposite of negligence or carelessness

case law the decisions of judges, in contrast to statute law, recorded in reports to form precedents

causation the fact of being the cause of something that happened; an important principle in law of negligence

caveat emptor Latin phrase for "Let the buyer beware."

Certificate of Possession a certificate that entitles the bearer to occupy and work a piece of reserve land

certification official recognition of a union by a labour relations board as the bargaining agent for a group of employees

challenge (for cause) the challenging of the suitability of a juror on the grounds of lack of qualifications, lack of impartiality with regard to the Crown and the accused, or knowledge of the case

child abuse any form of cruelty to a child's physical, mental, or moral well-being

circumstantial evidence all evidence of an indirect nature

citation a reference to the source of a law case as found in reports

civil law (1) another term for private law governing the relationship between individuals; (2) the legal system of Quebec, based on Roman law, as distinct from English common law

civil rights rights guaranteed by the *Bill of Rights* and *Charter of Rights and Freedoms*

claim a legal document in a civil action outlining the plaintiff's case against the defendant

clerical mistake an error caused by a clerk or an employee; an example of a unilateral mistake

closed shop a business in which all employees must belong to the union

Code of Hammurabi a set of nearly 300 laws recorded by Hammurabi, the king of Babylon, nearly 4000 years ago; earliest codification of laws

codicil an addition or change made to a will by its maker

codification the process of assembling any system of law into one body of statutes or a single statute; for example, the Code of Hammurabi or the *Criminal Code of Canada*

cohabitation agreement a domestic contract between two unmarried people, who are living together, providing for the governing of their property and obligations to each other

collateral relatives persons not in a direct line of descent to an inheritance; for example, the deceased's parent, brother, sister, and so on

collective bargaining negotiation done by a union on behalf of all its members concerning wages, hours, and other conditions of employment

collusion the act of spouses lying to or deceiving the court in order to get a divorce; a bar to divorce

colour of right anything that serves to indicate a person has true ownership of something

common law (1) law that relies on court decisions for its authority and recorded in case law reports, as distinct from statute law; (2) the law that developed in English courts, as distinct from French civil law; (3) law that is common to all people

common-law marriage a relationship in which two persons live together as husband and wife without being legally married

common mistake a misunderstanding that arises when both parties entering a contract are in error over the same fundamental fact

community service order a sentencing option whereby a judge instructs an offender to do some specific work in the community under supervision

community tolerance what the community would accept others being exposed to on the basis of the degree of harm that may flow from such exposure

company union a union that draws its members from within one company only

compensation something given to make amends for a loss; for example, damages to an injured plaintiff

complainant the assaulted person who files a complaint

conciliation a meeting between opposing parties in an attempt to settle a dispute in a friendly way

concurrent sentence the serving of two or more sentences at the same time

condition an essential term of a contract

conditional discharge a discharge with certain conditions, such as probation, attached; if conditions are violated, offender can be brought back to court and given the original sentence on the charge

condonation the art of one spouse forgiving an act, such as adultery, committed by the other spouse, that would constitute a ground for divorce; a bar to divorce

confession an acknowledgment in words by the accused of the truth of all or part of the charge against him or her

connivance the act of encouraging a spouse to commit an unlawful act, such as adultery; a bar to divorce

consanguinity a relationship by blood

consecutive sentence the serving of two or more sentences one after the other

consent free and voluntary agreement

consideration something of value exchanged between the parties to a contract

conspiracy planning and acting together for an unlawful purpose

Constitution Act, 1867 formerly the *British North America Act, 1867;* distributes legislative powers between federal and provincial governments

Constitution Act, 1982 Canada's Constitution, which includes the *Charter of Rights and Freedoms* and an amending formula.

constitutional law the body of law that deals with the distribution or exercise of powers of government

constructive discrimination the right to discriminate as long as it is bona fide in the circumstances

consummation validation of a marriage by sexual intercourse between spouses

contaminants substances that pollute ecosystems on a vast scale; for example, exhaust, smoke, and gas emissions

contempt of court any act that is calculated to embarrass, hinder, or obstruct a court in its administration of justice, or lessen its dignity

contingency fee system arrangement between lawyer and client in which the lawyer will be paid a percentage of whatever sum of money is awarded to the client at trial

contract a legally binding agreement enforceable at law

contract law that branch of private or civil law that deals with the making and enforcing of agreements between individuals

contract under seal a written contract in formal language, signed and witnessed, and with a red seal to signify serious intent

contributory negligence negligence on the part of the victim that contributes to his or her own injury or loss; a partial defence to negligence

controlled drugs drugs legally prescribed by doctors; listed in Schedule G of the *Food and Drug Act*

Convention refugee a definition assigned to a refugee in Article One of the 1951 UN Convention

cooling-off period a length of time given to allow a buyer the opportunity to cancel a contract with an itinerant seller without giving any reason

co-respondent a co-defendant; the person charged with adultery with the respondent in a divorce action

correctional services government agencies responsible for probation services and the incarceration and supervision of inmates and their parole

counterclaim a defendant's claim in a civil action in response to the plaintiff's related claim; action between two opposing parties

counter-offer a response to an offer that varies or qualifies the original offer and brings it to an end

credibility the fact or quality of having one's evidence believed

Criminal Code of Canada a statute containing the main criminal offences of Canada, the rules for prosecuting and appealing them, and the penalties that apply to each offence

criminal law the body of public law that declares acts to be crimes and prescribes punishments for those crimes

criminal negligence wanton or reckless disregard for the lives and safety of other persons; may involve the operation of a motor vehicle, or may cause bodily harm or death

Crown attorney prosecutor in criminal matters on behalf of the Crown and society; an agent of the Attorney General

Crown wardship order a court order whereby the Crown becomes the legal guardian of a child in need of protection

cruelty (mental or physical) intentional infliction of physical or mental suffering by one spouse on the other; a ground for divorce

culpable homicide blamable or criminal homicide, such as murder, manslaughter, infanticide

custody (1) the care and control of a child awarded by a court to one of the parents in a divorce proceeding; (2) actual imprisonment or physical detention of an offender

D

damages money awarded by the court to a plaintiff for a wrong or loss suffered

damages (exemplary) money that a defendant must pay the plaintiff for pain and suffering, loss of enjoyment of life, and future monetary loss; is not an exact dollar value and requires judicial discretion

damages (nominal) a small sum of money awarded to a plaintiff who has won an action but has not suffered substantial harm or loss

damages (non-pecuniary) money for financial losses such as loss of future earnings and cost of future care; part of general damages

damages (punitive) money to be paid to a plaintiff for the purpose of punishing the defendant for an uncaring or violent act; intended to act as a deterrent

damages (special) money paid to a plaintiff for specific out-of-pocket expenses

dangerous offender a person who has committed serious personal injury involving the use or attempted use of violence, and

who is sentenced to an indeterminate sentence

day parole release of an offender into the community under specific conditions and supervision for the day, with reincarceration at night

decree of nullity a court order granted for an annulment

defamation uttering or publication of false and malicious statements injurious to a person's fame, reputation, or character; see also libel and slander

default judgment a decision made in the plaintiff's favour when the defendant does not dispute the plaintiff's claim within the required time

defence (1) a reason or set of circumstances that might relieve a defendant of liability; (2) a defendant's response to a plaintiff's claim

defendant (1) the party being sued in a civil action; (2) the party being charged in a criminal offence

deleterious substance substance that degrades or alters the quality of water, thereby causing harm to fish

demerit points points taken away from a licenced driver for various driving offences; can lead to licence suspension

departure order an order issued by immigration officials to people who have committed a minor infraction of immigration rules to leave Canada by a certain date

deportation the action of expelling someone to his or her country of origin

deportation order a departure order issued by immigration officials to persons who have committed a very serious violation of immigration rules

designated class refugees persecuted and/or displaced refugees who are given the opportunity to settle in Canada

detention the act of keeping someone in custody; an enforced delay

deterrence something that serves to discourage a person from doing something; a sentencing objective

differential treatment intentional discrimination

direct evidence evidence given by a person who witnessed the event in question, or which cannot be disproved by any other fact

directed verdict judge's direction to the jury, after the Crown presents its evidence, to find the accused not guilty due to the fact that the Crown has not proven its case

discharge (1) the methods by which a legal duty or obligation may be ended; (2) a sentencing option

discharge (conditional) a discharge with certain conditions, such as probation, attached; violation of conditions can result in sentencing on the charge

disclaimer clause a clause in a contract denying that guarantees or other promises have been made to the buyer; see also exemption clause

discrimination to show a difference based on a prejudice

displaced persons refugees who have lost everything in war

disposition a sentence handed down for a young offender

distribution clauses instructions in a will detailing the division of property among the next-of-kin

diversion (1) the practice of keeping a convicted offender out of the prison system by imposing a sentence not involving incarceration; (2) a warning given by a peace officer, instead of a charge, to keep a person from entering the criminal process

diversion programs sentences that keep offenders out of prison; for example, suspended sentences and probation

divorce the legal dissolution of a marriage

divorce judgment the court order issued at the end of a divorce action

domestic contract a cohabitation agreement, marriage contract, or separation agreement between two spouses; provides for the governing of their property and obligations to each other

dominant party the party in a position of power over another

double doctoring the criminal offence of trying to obtain the same narcotic prescription from different doctors; also called prescription shopping

double jeopardy prohibition against being tried for the same offence twice

dual procedure offence an offence punishable as either summary or indictable at the option of the Crown; a hybrid offence

due diligence a defence that the accused took reasonable care not to commit the offence or that the offence was committed in the honest belief by the accused that his or her actions were innocent

due process an orderly proceeding, wherein a person is served with notice, and has an opportunity to be heard and to enforce and protect his or her rights before the court

duress the threat or use of violence by one party that forces another to do something against his or her will

duty counsel lawyer who is on duty at a police station or court room, to give legal advice to those arrested and/or brought before the court

duty of care the obligation that is required to ensure that others are not harmed by one's actions

E

economic class a category of immigrants identified in the *Immigration Act, 1976*; also called independent class

emigration leaving one's own country to settle in another

empanelling the selection of a jury

employment authorization a work permit obtained by a prospective employer to allow a foreigner to work in Canada temporarily

employment equity a program or law intended to help a particular group of people, the passing of which might be considered discriminatory under usual circumstances

employment law that branch of private or civil law that outlines the rights and obligations of employers and employees; also called labour law

endangered species wildlife threatened to become extinct owing to destruction of their natural habitats

enfranchised to be given full rights of citizenship

enterprise crime proceeds of crime involving illegal stock exchange transactions and drug trade offences

enticing wrongfully soliciting, procuring, attracting, or alluring

entrapment the action of inducing a person into committing an offence

entrenched a right that can only be changed by an amendment to the Constitution

entrepreneur a category under the point system that requires an applicant to present a business plan and invest a minimum of $150 000 as a condition of immigration

environment the total surroundings that encompass any individual or thing

environmental audit internal assessment by company personnel to determine whether the company operations are in compliance with the *Canadian Environmental Protection Act*

environmental impact assessment (EIA) an official appraisal of a program or project to determine potential effects on the environment, alternatives, and measures to protect the environment

equalization payment a payment in cash or property made by the spouse with the greater net family property to the other spouse to make the division of property more equitable upon separation or divorce

equity law administered according to principles of fairness or justice, rather than by following the strictly formulated precedents of common law

escalation clause a clause in a rental contract that provides for automatic rent increases if

taxes, utilities, and other such variables increase

escorted absence absence from an institution for an inmate, under the direct supervision of a parole officer, correctional service staff member, or citizen volunteer

essential requirements the rules about legal capacity or ability to marry under the federal government's authority

euthanasia the act of painlessly putting to death persons suffering from incurable and disabling diseases as an act of mercy

eviction order a court order to cease use of rented property

Examination for Discovery a civil pre-trial process to disclose evidence and relevant documents and to reach agreement on certain issues to be presented at trial

examination-in-chief the first questioning of a witness

examination of the debtor a process in which a defaulting debtor's financial ability to make payments of a judgment is examined by a judge

exclusion order an order issued at port of entry to persons found in violation of immigration rules, such as not having a valid passport

exculpatory confession a denial by the accused of the truth of the charge

execution (1) the process of enforcing or carrying out a judgment; (2) the completion of the formalities necessary to give validity to a will

executor/executrix a man/woman named in a will to carry out the provisions of the will

exemplary damages money awarded to a plaintiff, as a deterrent, for the purpose of punishing the defendant for an uncaring or violent act; also called punitive damages

exemption clause in contract law, a clause protecting a party from liability; see also disclaimer clause

express condition an essential term of a contract clearly outlined by the manufacturer of the object for which the contract is made

express contract an oral or written contract in which the terms and conditions are clearly defined and understood by the parties

express warranty a clear and open promise that goods or services will meet a certain standard

extradition the surrender of a person by one country to another by international agreements; often occurs when an abducted child and parent are sent back

F

factum a statement of facts, summarizing both sides of a case, for an appeal

fair comment a defence for defamation wherein the defendant shows that the comments were made without malicious intent

false imprisonment unlawful physical restraint or detention

false pretences representation of a matter of fact that is known by the person making it to be false and made with a fraudulent intent to induce the person to whom it is made to act on it

family asset property owned by one or both spouses ordinarily used or enjoyed by the spouses and/or their children; normally divided equally between spouses upon separation

family business class a category of immigration related to family class that allows relatives to immigrate to Canada to join small family businesses

family class a category of immigrants identified in the *Immigration Act, 1976*

family law that branch of private or civil law dealing with all matters pertaining to the family

fault a failing in a legal responsibility; a wrongdoing or neglect of duty

federalism a form of government in which each member agrees to subordinate its own power to that of the central authority in common affairs

feudalism a political, social, and economic system prevalent in Europe between the ninth and fifteenth centuries that was based on the relationship between lord and vassal

fine option program a sentencing option that allows offenders to earn credit for doing community work; an option to paying a fine

first-degree murder planned and deliberate murder, or the murder of a law enforcement official, or murder resulting from the commission of various crimes particularly offensive to society

First Nations the 607 bands of Native peoples in Canada

fixed-term tenancy a tenancy that expires on a specific date without any further notice being required by either party

forensic science science dealing with the application of medical science to law

foreseeability the ability of a reasonable person to anticipate or expect what might occur as a result of his or her actions

formal requirements provincial requirements for performing legal marriage ceremonies; also see solemnization of marriage

foster home the home of an existing family into which a young offender may be placed for rehabilitation for some period; a form of open custody

franchise the right to vote

fraud intentional deception resulting in loss or injury to another

fraudulent misrepresentation an untrue statement concerning facts, made with the knowledge that it is false and with the intention of deceiving the party to whom it is made

free pardon a remission of punishment under which the person granted a pardon is considered not to have committed the offence for which he or she has been convicted

freedom the power to act without arbitrary interference by an individual or the state

French *Civil Code* the basis of the law in Quebec, based on the *Napoleonic Code*

full disclosure the reporting of the true cost of borrowing money, quoted as an annual percentage and as a dollar amount, to give consumers an opportunity to compare credit terms

full parole release of an offender into the community under specific conditions and supervision

future consideration valuable consideration exchanged in a contract under which one or both parties promise to do something later; for example, buying goods on credit

G

garnishment a process in which a defendant's money or goods in the hands of a third person are attached by a plaintiff to settle an unpaid judgment

general damages money that the defendant must pay the plaintiff for pain and suffering, loss of enjoyment of life, and future monetary loss; is not an exact dollar value and requires judicial discretion

general intent a criminal offence that does not require an intentional unlawful action, but only that a wrongful act was committed

generous access very regular visiting time a child spends with the non-custodial parent; also called reasonable access

genocide extermination of a defined group of people

grievance a complaint made by an employee, the union, or management when it is thought that the collective agreement is not being followed

group home a home, operated by a non-profit agency and run by a professional staff, into which young offenders are placed for rehabilitation for some period; a form of open custody

gross negligence a very high or extreme degree of negligence

guarantee (1) a promise to answer for the debt of another; (2) a promise that goods and

services meet a certain standard; also called a warranty

guardian a person appointed to care for another person, and his or her affairs and property

guardian ad litem a person who represents a minor who is being sued

H

habeas corpus a court document that requires the determination of whether a person is being legally detained

harassment unwelcome actions or conduct toward another

head tax a $50 tax imposed by Parliament in 1885 on every Chinese person wishing to enter Canada; increased to $500 in 1903

hearsay evidence evidence not proceeding from the personal experience or knowledge of a witness

heir one who inherits or is entitled to inherit another's property

holograph will a will written in the testator's own hand and not witnessed by others

homicide causing the death of another human being

honest mistake the defence that the offender truthfully did not know that a criminal wrong was committed

horizontal union a union whose members all work in the same trade but for many different employers

House of Commons the elected Members of Parliament in Ottawa

human rights rights that protect one from discrimination by other individuals in certain areas of his or her life

hung jury a jury that cannot come to a unanimous decision in a criminal case

hybrid offence an offence that is punishable as an indictable or summary offence at the option of the Crown

I

immigrant a person who seeks landing, as defined in the *Immigration Act, 1976*

Immigration and Refugee Board (IRB) a federal body that acts as an independent court to hear appeals of immigrants and refugees

Immigration Visa and Record of Landing a document issued to successful independent class applicants from a Canadian embassy or consulate outside Canada

implied condition a term in a contract that is not clearly outlined, but rather assumed by buyer and seller

implied contract a contract that is suggested or understood without being openly and specifically stated; the opposite of an express contract

implied warranty a promise that a seller may not have made but which legislation says must be included in the contract

impotence inability to consummate the marriage and ground for annulment

in camera Latin phrase meaning "in private"; refers to matters heard in a courtroom from which the spectators have been excluded

incarceration imprisonment or confinement

incest sexual intercourse between a man and woman related to each other by degrees of affinity and consequently that prohibits marriage

inculpatory confession a statement that incriminates the person giving it

independent class a category of immigrants identified in the *Immigration Act, 1976*; also called economic class

independent contractor a person hired to carry out a specific task who works without direction from the party that did the hiring

indeterminate sentence a term of imprisonment during which a convicted person may be released on parole at any time; often used for dangerous offenders

Indian treaties written agreements between government officials and aboriginal peoples, setting out various terms and obligations

Indians aboriginal peoples

indictable offence a severe criminal offence, for which the Crown proceeds by indictment; carries a correspondingly severe penalty

indigenous originating in a particular country

infant a person under the age of majority; also called a minor

infanticide the killing of an infant, shortly after birth, by its mother as a result of the effects of giving birth or of post partum depression, causing a disturbed mind

information a written complaint, made under oath, stating that there is reason to believe that a person has committed a criminal offence

informed consent an agreement that a patient gives for a medical procedure after all the risks are disclosed

inherent defects an intrinsic fault or problem that results in the spoilage or deterioration of goods during transit

injunction a court order directing a person to do or not to do something

innocent misrepresentation an untrue statement concerning facts, made in the honest belief that it is true

intent (1) something planned or intended; intentionally causing a wrongful consequence; (2) a person's state of mind, in which the person desires to carry out a certain action and can foresee the results

intentional discrimination to have discrimination as a purpose

intermittent sentence a sentence served, at the judge's discretion, on weekends or at night to allow the offender to maintain a job; only imposed for sentences of less than 90 days

intestate the condition or state of dying without a will

intra vires Latin phrase meaning "within the powers"; within the authority of the government to pass a law

Inuit aboriginal people living in arctic and sub-arctic regions

investor a category under the point system that requires an applicant to invest money in a business venture that will create jobs for Canadians as a condition of immigration

invitation to sexual touching a new criminal offence that involves inviting or inciting a person under 14 to touch another person's body directly or indirectly

invitee any person on the premises for a purpose other than a social visit, such as students, customers, and patrons

itinerant seller a seller who does not have a permanent business location; a door-to-door seller

J

job skills capacity for employment; an important consideration in the acceptance or rejection of a person applying for immigration

joint custody a court order that gives both parents full legal responsibility for the major decisions affecting their child

joint legal custody a custody order in which the children spend equal, or nearly equal, time with both parents

joint physical custody a custody order in which the children remain with one parent, while the other parent has generous access, but both parents still responsible for the major decisions affecting their children

joint tenancy the purchase of land wherein two or more persons make the purchase together, each having an undivided interest

judiciary the judges of the courts of law

jurisdiction authority or power to do something, such as make laws

Justinian Code a code of law put into writing under Justinian, Emperor of Rome, during the fifth and sixth centuries

K

kind payment in the form of goods, produce, or services, instead of money

knowledge to know certain facts, which provide the necessary *mens rea* for an offence

L

labour law that branch of private or civil law that outlines the rights and obligations of employers and employees; also called employment law

landed immigrants people who have been allowed to enter Canada to establish permanent residence; also called permanent residents

landing lawful permission to establish permanent residence in Canada

landing tax a $200 tax added to head tax in 1914 to further discourage Chinese persons wishing to enter Canada

lapse the termination of an offer or a right; to no longer be in effect

laundering a criminal offence involving the seizure of money or property obtained from the commission of *Narcotic Control Act* offences

law a rule to govern action; rules of conduct, established by government, for society to follow and obey

lease a contract between a landlord and tenant for the rental of property

LeDain Commission a royal commission appointed to study the non-medical use of drugs in the 1960s

legal object a lawful purpose or reason

legal tender forms of legal payment; money

lessee the tenant of rented premises

lessor the owner of rented premises

letters probate the formal authority giving an executor complete control to carry out the provisions of a person's will

liability legal responsibility for a wrongful action

libel defamation in printed or permanent form, such as pictures, printed words, signs, or video

licensee a person who enters another's premises for non-business purposes; for example, a friend or visitor

limitation of liability the lessening or reduction of an obligation to do something provided for in a contract; see also disclaimer clause and exemption clause

lineal descendants a person in direct line of descent to receive an inheritance; the deceased's spouse, children, and so on

line-up a group of people who are lined up by the police, to enable a witness to a crime to specify the person that he or she witnessed committing it

liquidated damages a reasonable amount of damages, agreed upon in advance by the parties to a contract, to be paid by the party causing any breach of contract that may occur

litigants the parties involved in a civil action; the plaintiff and the defendant

litigation a lawsuit; the act of bringing a civil dispute to court for resolution

litigation guardian see *guardian ad litem*

lobbyist a person who presents the opinions of the group that he or she represents to the government

local a branch of a labour union

lockout an employer's refusal to open the workplace to the employees, in the event of a labour dispute

M

malice desire to harm another; active ill will

mandatory supervision the early release, because of good behaviour, of an inmate who has served two-thirds of his or her sentence, to be supervised by a parole officer

manslaughter homicide that is committed in the heat of passion by sudden provocation, unlike murder, that is planned and deliberate

marriage the voluntary union of a man and a woman for life to the exclusion of all others

marriage breakdown a basis for divorce on the ground that the marriage is no longer functioning; the only valid ground for divorce in Canada today

marriage contract a domestic contract between a man and a woman who are married and living together providing for the governing of their property and obligations to each other

master a person who hires another to work under his or her direction; an employer

material fact a fact that induces a person to enter a contract

material risk any significant or major risk or problem that could occur in any proposed medical treatments

material witness a person whose evidence is important in a court of law

matrimonial home the home in which the spouses live during their marriage

matrimonial property property owned by the spouses during their marriage; also called marital property

mediation attempt by a third person to get two opposing parties to come to an agreement

"meeting of the minds" a valid offer and acceptance in a contract; see also offer and acceptance

mens rea Latin phrase meaning "a guilty mind"

merchantable quality marketable condition; suitable for sale

Métis people of mixed aboriginal and non-aboriginal ancestry

minor a person under the age of majority; also called an infant

mischief destruction or damage of property; interference with the lawful use or enjoyment of property

misrepresentation a statement made that conveys a false impression; may be innocent or intentional

mistake an error concerning the existence of the subject matter of a contract, or the identity of a marriage partner, or the nature of a marriage ceremony

mitigation of loss a requirement that a person seeking to recover damages for a breach of contract must try to reduce the losses arising from the breach

molesting improperly or indecently interfering with a person; first level of sexual assault

monogamy the concept of being married to only one spouse at a time

Montreal Protocol an agreement signed in 1994 among 133 countries to gradually phase out substances that deplete the ozone layer

mosaic law a code of laws set out in the first five books of the Old Testament, as established under Moses, in approximately 1400 B.C.

motor vehicle any vehicle drawn, propelled, or driven by any means other than muscular power; includes automobiles, motorcycles, snowmobiles, boats and aircraft

murder planned, deliberate homicide; of two classes, first and second degree

N

Napoleonic Code a code of civil law drawn up by Napoleon Bonaparte, and adopted in France in 1804; the basis of the civil law in Quebec today

narcotic any substance listed on the schedule in the *Narcotic Control Act* or anything that contains any substance included in the schedule

naturalization a process whereby permanent residents of three years or longer can apply to become citizens

necessaries goods or services provided for the health and welfare of a person, such as food, clothing, shelter, medical care, and education

necessity a defence that indicates the accused had no other alternative to the action taken

negligence a person's failure to exercise reasonable care, which results in injury to another

negotiation an informal and voluntary civil dispute resolution process between the parties involved without the involvement of a third party

net family property the net value of a spouse's assets, less any debts, at the date of separation; see also equalization payment

next friend an adult who represents a minor in a civil action

no-fault insurance insurance that is paid to the injured party promptly by the insurer, regardless of who is at fault in an accident

nominal damages a small sum of money awarded to a plaintiff who has won a civil action but has not suffered substantial harm or loss; money awarded for a moral victory

non est factum Latin phrase meaning "It is not my deed"; a denial that a document was properly executed by the one who executed it, based on ignorance of the nature of the contract

non-culpable homicide death caused by complete accident or in self-defence

non-family asset items such as stocks, bonds, investments, and other business assets retained by the spouse who owns them and not divided equally between spouses upon separation

non-necessaries goods and services that are not essential for a person, especially a minor

non-pecuniary losses damages awarded for such intangibles as loss of enjoyment of life, pain and suffering; part of general damages

non-registered Indians Native people who for one reason or another are not registered

notwithstanding clause a provision making a law valid, even though it contradicts some other law

nuisance an unreasonable interference with the right of others to enjoy their property

numbered treaties a series of 11 land agreements made by the federal government with First Nations

O

oath a solemn promise or statement that something is true

occupier an occupant, including both property owners and renters

occupiers' liability responsibility of occupiers towards persons who come onto property and might be injured

off-reserve Indians treaty Indians who live off the reserve for 12 consecutive months or longer

offer and acceptance a proposal that expresses the willingness of a person to enter into a contract, followed by the assent to that offer by words or conduct; a "meeting of the minds"

offer to lease an offer by a prospective lessee to a lessor to enter into a tenancy agreement

offeree the person to whom an offer is made

offeror the person who makes an offer

omission failure to do something

onus responsibility to prove something in a court of law

open custody detention of a young offender in a special home or wilderness camp with limited, supervised access to the community

open shop a business that allows employees to join a union if they wish, but non-union workers are not required to pay dues

opinion evidence evidence of what a person thinks in regard to facts in dispute

ordinary pardon a remission of punishment under which the person granted the pardon is considered guilty, but is forgiven by the Crown and released

out-of-court settlement an opportunity to resolve a civil dispute to each party's satisfaction before proceeding to trial

P

Parliament the highest national law-making body in Canada

parole early release of an inmate from prison on certain conditions to be followed; available after serving one-third of sentence or seven years, whichever is less

parolee an inmate released on parole

passport a document that indicates country of citizenship

past consideration consideration for services that have been performed; not valuable consideration for legally enforcing a contract

patriation to return to one's own country; for example, the patriation of Canada's constitution from England in 1982

pecuniary loss damages awarded for financial losses such as loss of future earnings and cost of future care; part of general damages

penology the study of the reform and rehabilitation of offenders and the management of prisons

peremptory challenge the challenging of the suitability of a juror for no reason

performance the fulfillment of an obligation or a promise, as in the completion of a contract

periodic tenancy a tenancy renewed weekly, or at some other regular interval, either by express agreement or by implication, as by payment of rent

perjury the act of knowingly giving false evidence in a judicial proceeding, with intent to mislead

permanent residents landed immigrants who have been allowed to enter Canada to establish permanent residence

petition for divorce the legal document that begins a divorce action

petitioner the plaintiff in a divorce proceeding; the spouse who begins the divorce action

picket lines demonstrations in which striking workers present their views in public by blocking access to the employer's business

placement the process of selecting adoptive parents with whom to place a child

plaintiff the party suing in a civil action

plea bargain process in which the Crown and the accused "make a deal," usually resulting in the accused pleading guilty to a lesser charge in return for a lower penalty than would be received if found guilty of the original charge

pleadings written statements exchanged between the parties

in a civil action outlining the details of each party's case

point system a system whereby independent applicants are awarded points according to certain categories to qualify for admission as immigrants

poisoned work environment to have a group harass another person, due to gender, race, religion, or some other characteristic

polygraph test a process in which a person is asked various questions, and a lie-detector machine measures changes in the blood pressure, respiration, and pulse rate to indicate whether the truth is being told

port of entry place of entry into Canada, such as an international airport, a seaport, or a railway station

possession in possession of a narcotic without legal permission; a hybrid offence

power of attorney a document authorizing another to act as a person's agent

precedent the legal principle in which court cases with similar facts result in similar decisions; also known as *stare decisis*

pre-disposition report a report prepared by a youth probation officer at a judge's request before sentencing the young offender

prejudice a preconceived opinion

preliminary hearing a hearing held to determine if there is sufficient evidence to justify a trial

prescription acquisition of a personal right to use a road, water, or air by reason of continuous usage

prescription shopping see double doctoring

present consideration valuable consideration exchanged at the formation of a contract, usually in the form of money for goods or services

pre-sentence report a report prepared for the court prior to the sentencing of an accused which sets out the accused's background

presumption of death certificate a court document that allows a surviving spouse, whose spouse has been absent for at least seven years and is presumed dead, to remarry

pre-trial conference a meeting of the parties in a civil action with a judge to clarify and narrow the issues in dispute prior to trial

prima facie on the face of something; something presumed to be true unless disproved by some evidence to the contrary

principal a person who employs another to act as his or her agent

principle of totality concept that a person who has committed several violations of the same offence should not receive an oppressively long prison term

Priority Substance List a list of toxic substances compiled by the *Canadian Environmental Protection Act*

private law all law relating to interaction between persons, as distinct from public law; also called civil law

private nuisance a nuisance that concerns an individual or a few persons only

privilege an exemption from liability for the speaking or publishing of defamatory words concerning another

privileged communications a communication that cannot be required to be presented in court as evidence

probate to establish the validity of a will

probation a sentencing option whereby a convicted person may be released instead of imprisoned, on the condition that he or she must be of good behaviour and must follow whatever conditions are imposed by the judge; common for first offenders

probation order an order by a court allowing a person to live in the community under the supervision of a probation office, instead of serving a term of imprisonment

procedural law the body of law that prescribes or outlines the method of enforcing rights and obligations

proclamation date the date on which a piece of legislation comes into effect

procuring obtaining, as in obtaining a person for prostitution

prohibited weapons weapons that are illegal and may not be kept by anyone, such as a switchblade knife and sawed-off shotgun

property law that branch of private or civil law that deals with ownership, rights, and interests in property

provocation any action or words that might cause a reasonable person to behave irrationally or to lose self-control

proximate cause the primary or moving cause of another's injury; the one that sets the other causes in operation

proxy a document empowering a person to vote in the place of another person

public law all law dealing with relations between an individual and the state

public nuisance a nuisance that concerns an indefinite number of persons or all residents in a community

public policy the belief that no person can lawfully do what tends to injure the public or go against the public good

public service the employees of a government, specifically the federal government

punitive damages money awarded to a plaintiff, as a deterrent, for the purpose of punishing the defendant for an uncaring or violent act; also called exemplary damages

Q

qualified privilege a defence against defamation enjoyed by persons who are required to express opinions; for example, reporters, employers, and teachers

quasi-criminal law an offence against certain provincial laws; not part of federal criminal law

quid pro quo **harassment** harassment in which a person wants someone to exchange something in return for a favour; to give something for something

quiet enjoyment the right of a tenant to use rented premises free from interference by another person

R

random virtue testing the practice of investigating an individual for drug offences without having reasonable or probable grounds for doing so

ratification the act of approving or confirming a contract that would otherwise be voidable; the opposite of repudiation

read down a court decision that indicates that a law is generally acceptable, but is unacceptable in the case before the court

reasonable access when the time spent with the non-custodial parent is flexible and regular

reasonable person the standard used in determining whether a person's conduct in a particular situation is negligent

rebut (rebuttal) to present evidence that counteracts or disproves evidence given by the adverse party

recidivism relapse into crime; the return to prison of criminal repeaters

recklessness a state of mind that pays no regard to the probable or possible injurious consequences of an act

recognizance with surety a document signed by a person acknowledging that he or she is alleged to have committed an offence and will be required to appear in court; payment is made by another person on behalf of the accused

recognizance without surety a document signed by a person acknowledging that he or she is alleged to have committed an offence and will be required to appear in court; payment is made by the accused

reconciliation the renewal of a friendly and marital relation between spouses; a procedure for trying to save a marriage

refugee a person who is persecuted or fears persecution in his or her homeland and seeks protection in another country

refugee claims officer a federal official who considers claims for Convention refugee status

refugee class a category of immigrants identified in the *Immigration Act, 1976*

registered Indians status Indians outside treaty areas

regulations rules made under the authority of a statute by the department or ministry responsible for carrying out the statute

regulatory offence offences as defined in Canada's environmental laws that carry relatively minor penalties; can be strict liability offences or absolute liability offences

rehabilitation the restoration of a person to good physical, mental, and moral health through treatment and training; a sentencing objective

remand to put off to a later date

remission the act of forgiving part of a prison sentence, usually for good behaviour

remoteness lack of close connection between a wrong and an injury that prevents the injured party from claiming damages from the wrong-doer; the opposite of proximate cause

repeal to withdraw or abolish a law

report a book containing the decision of the courts for certain cases

repudiation the act of rejecting or disclaiming a contract to avoid being liable; the opposite of ratification

res ipsa loquitor rule of evidence whereby negligence of the wrongdoer may be inferred from the fact that an accident happened; the act speaks for itself

rescission the cancellation or revocation of a contract

reserve lands areas set aside for aboriginal people covered by treaties

resocialization the process of preparing a person to allow him or her to function adequately in society when released from prison; see also rehabilitation

respondent (1) the party in an action who opposes the appeal; (2) the defendant in a divorce action

restitution the act of making good; the act of returning that which was taken unlawfully from a person

restraint of trade the limiting of competition in business; makes a contract void if restraint is unreasonable or against public policy

restricted drugs illegal drugs not used for medical purposes, such as LSD and MDA

restricted weapon a weapon for which a permit is required, such as a firearm or semi-automatic weapon

retribution a deserved penalty for a wrong or crime; vengeance; a sentencing objective

revocation the cancellation of an offer by the offeror or before acceptance

revoke to cancel, annul, or take back

right something that has been granted by legislation or regulation

right of distress a landlord's right to seize a tenant's property if rent is in arrears; now abolished in residential tenancies

right of lien the right to hold the property of another as security for an obligation or debt until it is paid

riots an unlawful assembly that has begun to disturb the peace tumultuously

roadside screening test a demand that a driver suspected of consuming alcohol breathe into an approved device

robbery theft accomplished by means of force or fear

Royal Assent the monarch's signature, required to formally pass an *Act*; now given by the Governor General

Royal Prerogative of Mercy the right of the monarch to reduce a criminal sentence imposed on a convicted person, or the Cabinet's right to grant a pardon

Rule of Law the fundamental principle that neither the individual nor the government is above the law; society is governed by law that applies equally to all persons

rule of precedent the legal principle whereby court cases with similar facts result in similar decisions; also known as *stare decisis*

S

search a police procedure, to look for evidence that may be used in a court of law

search warrant a document issued by a justice or judge to peace officers of a territory giving them the right to search a specific location, at a specific time, for a specific reason

second-degree murder murder that is not first-degree murder

secure custody detention of a young offender in a youth detention centre with bars on the windows and locks on the doors

security deposit a deposit made at the beginning of a tenancy

security of tenure the right of a tenant to remain in rented premises and not be asked to leave without a valid reason

segregation the act of keeping an inmate in prison apart from other inmates; placing dangerous offenders in prison to protect society; a sentencing objective

selective immigration a policy instituted by Clifford Sifton, Minister of the Interior in Wilfrid Laurier's government, to attract a certain type of immigrant to Canada

self-incrimination behaviour, such as the giving of evidence, that indicates one's guilt

self-sufficiency the intent of the *Divorce Act* that each spouse has an obligation to support himself or herself within a reasonable period of time after a divorce

Senate the second federal legislative body, after the House of Commons, whose members are appointed rather than elected; also called the Upper House

senior immigration officer a federal official who reviews refugee eligibility

sentence the judgment of the court after a criminal is convicted

separate property property owned by a married person in his or her own name during marriage

separation a partial dissolution of a marriage in which the spouses no longer live together as husband and wife

separation agreement a domestic contract between a separated couple outlining the

distribution of property and obligations to each other

sequestered a jury that is prevented from interacting with non-jurors and kept together until a decision is reached

servant a person hired by a master to carry out a job under the master's direction; an employee

sexual assault parallels the three forms of assault and accentuates the violent nature of these crimes; combines former offences of rape and indecent assault

sexual interference a new criminal offence that involves direct or indirect touching of a person under 14 for a sexual purpose

shop steward a person nominated by the union members to represent them

show-cause hearing a hearing before a judge wherein the Crown or the accused must show cause as to why the accused should be detained or released, pending trial

show-up the appearance of an accused before a witness to see if the witness recognizes the accused as being the one who committed the alleged offence

siblings brothers and sisters and stepbrothers and stepsisters living together

similar fact evidence evidence that the accused had previously committed a similar offence

simple contract a contract, either express or implied, oral or written, not under seal

slander verbal statements that defame or injure another's reputation

sole custody a court order that gives the legal guardianship of a child to one parent only; the opposite of joint custody

solemnization of marriage the various steps and preliminaries, including the ceremony, leading to marriage; under provincial jurisdiction

soliciting communicating with another person for the purpose of prostitution

special damages money awarded to a plaintiff for specific out-of-pocket expenses

specific claims claims made by Native people for lawful obligations to Indians under the treaties, other agreements, or the *Indian Act* that the government did not fulfill

specific intent a criminal offence which requires an intentional unlawful action

specific performance a court order that requires a person to do something previously promised in a contract

specified access the time a child spends with the non-custodial parent as specified by the court, such as certain holidays, weekends, and precise times

spousal support financial assistance paid by one spouse to another after a marriage breakdown; see also self-sufficiency

spouses a husband or wife; a partner in a marriage

standard of care the degree of caution expected of a reasonable person when carrying out an action that involves risk of harm to others

stand-aside the process wherein a prospective juror who is not selected when first brought forward may later be selected

stare decisis Latin phrase meaning "to stand by previous decisions"

Statement of Claim a legal document filed by the plaintiff to initiate a civil action; also called Writ of Summons

statement of defence a legal document for higher courts outlining the defendant's response and defence to the plaintiff's claim

station-in-life social standing or rank

statute an *Act* passed by a governing body

statute law all law passed by Parliament or a provincial legislature

Statute of Westminster an *Act* passed in 1931 in England, giving Canada specific rights concerning law-making

statutory release release of an inmate from an institution as required by a statute

stay of proceedings a court order to stop a judicial proceeding, with no further action until the occurrence of some event

stereotyping applying characteristics assumed to belong to one member of a group to all members of that group

sterility inability to have children; not a ground for annulment

strict liability (1) imposed in tort law when a lawful activity exposes others to harm or risk, even though there is no fault on the wrongdoer's part; (2) criminal liability based on simple negligence

strike a work stoppage by union members to enforce their contract demands

strike down a court decision stating that a law is no longer in effect

student authorization a document that allows a young person

from another country to enter Canada to attend school

sublet the process of finding a third party to take over the remaining time on a rental lease

subpoena a court document ordering the appearance of a person in court for a specific purpose, usually as a witness

substantial performance the completion of all essential elements of a contract, though not of a few minor or unimportant details

substantive law that part of law that creates, defines, and regulates rights and obligations

summary conviction offence a fairly minor criminal offence tried summarily, or immediately, without a preliminary hearing or a jury

summation the recapitulation or summing up of key arguments by legal counsel at the end of a trial

summons (1) an order to appear in criminal court; (2) an order to a defendant requesting him or her to appear for trial to defend a plaintiff's claim

supervised access time a child spends with the non-custodial parent at specified times and in the presence of a supervisor to guard against possible harm to the child

supervision order a court order allowing a child in need of protection to remain in his or her home under professional supervision

supremacy highest authority or power

surety a person who pays money on behalf of another released on bail

surrebuttal to present evidence that counteracts or

disproves evidence given by the adverse party

suspended sentence a judgment wherein sentencing is put off until a later date, and if the offender meets certain conditions, will not occur at all

suspension a sentencing option involving the removal of privileges, such as driving or attending school

sustainable development using resources to meet the present needs of society with regard to conserving for future generations

sympathy strike a strike by employees of one union to show support for another union that is on strike

T

telewarrant a warrant obtained by a peace officer, via telephone communication with a justice or judge, giving the officer the right to conduct a search

temporary absence absences from an institution granted to an offender for medical, administrative, community service, family contact, and personal development rehabilitative reasons

temporary wardship order a court order transferring custody of a child to a child protection agency on a temporary basis

tenancy the renting of land, or a building, or a portion thereof

tenancy at sufferance an arrangement wherein a person occupies premises against the will of, or without the knowledge of, the owner

tenancy at will an arrangement wherein a landlord permits a tenant to stay in the rented premises, but reserves the right

to ask the tenant to leave without giving notice

Ten Commandments one of the main parts of Mosaic law

tender years doctrine a principle whereby custody of a young child, under the age of seven, was usually awarded to the mother; has been replaced by the "best interests of the child" doctrine

theft taking another's property with the intent to deny the owner the use and enjoyment of the goods

theft over stealing of goods valued over $5000

theft under stealing of goods valued under $5000

third-party liability insurance compulsory automobile insurance for all licensed drivers; involves three parties when claim is made

title right of ownership to goods or property

tort a civil wrong or injury, other than breach of contract, for which the injured party may seek damages from the wrongdoer

tort law that branch of private or civil law that deals with a wrong committed by one person against another, other than a breach of contract, for which the court will apply a remedy

trafficking a criminal offence involving the manufacture, sale, giving, or sending of illegal drugs to another person

treaty Indians status Indians who are covered by treaties with respect to their aboriginal lands

trespass to enter another's property without consent

trespasser a person who enters another's property without consent

trial by jury a trial in which the innocence or guilt of the accused is determined by peers

trial by ordeal a trial in which the innocence or guilt of the accused is determined by the ability to withstand an ordeal

trial *de novo* Latin phrase for "a new trial"; a new trial or retrial in which the whole case is retried as if no previous trial had occurred

truth an established or verified fact; the best defence against defamation

U

ultra vires Latin phrase meaning "beyond the power"; beyond the authority of a government to pass a law on a specific topic; to make null and void

unconditional acceptance an acceptance made without any changes to the original offer; the opposite of a conditional acceptance or counter-offer

unconscionable judgment a decision considered grossly or shockingly unfair

under seal (contract) a written contract in formal language, signed and witnessed, and with a seal to signify serious intent

undertaking a court document signed by a person indicating that he or she understands that he or she has been charged with a criminal offence, that he or she must attend a court at a specified time, and that he or she must follow any conditions laid down by the judge

Undertaking of Assistance for Family Class a document completed by sponsors declaring they are willing to provide assistance to sponsored family class immigrants for as long as 10 years

undue influence improper, unlawful pressure applied by one person to another in order to benefit the one who pressures, as in the signing of a will or contract

unescorted absence the temporary release of an inmate on humanitarian or medical grounds without an escort

unilateral mistake a mistake made by one party to a contract

unintentional discrimination see adverse effect discrimination

union an organization whose purpose is to represent and negotiate for the employees of a particular company or industry

union shop a business in which each employee must join the union within a specified time after being hired

unlawful assembly three or more persons who, with intent to carry out any common purpose, assemble in such a manner or conduct themselves to cause persons to fear that they will, or will cause others to, disturb the peace tumultuously

V

valid contract a contract having legal force and recognized by law

venue location

verdict the formal decision made by a jury

vertical union a union whose members work in different trades and for different employers but in the same industry

vicarious liability holding a blameless person responsible for another's actions; for example, an employer for an employee's harmful actions

victim impact statement a statement from the victim, describing the effect of the offence on his or her life, used by a judge as a factor in sentencing an accused

visitor's visa a document that people from some countries must obtain before visiting Canada

void without legal force; invalid

void contract a contract having no legal force and unenforceable in a court of law

voidable contract a contract that may be valid or void at the option of one or both parties

voir dire a trial within a trial to decide upon the admissibility of evidence

voluntary assumption of risk the legal principle that a plaintiff may not recover for an injury to which he or she consents; a partial defence to negligence

W

warrant for arrest a document issued by a justice or judge to peace officers of a territory giving them the right to arrest an accused and bring him or her before the court

warranty another name for a guarantee

weapon anything used or intended for use in causing death or injury to another person

wildcat strike an illegal strike

wilful blindness to decline to make some inquiry, knowing the need to do so, because the person does not wish to know the truth

will a legal document indicating property division and distribution after a person's death

work release an offender is released into the community to work on a paid or voluntary basis

work to rule to follow exactly one's job description as a form of expressing dissatisfaction, usually with the employers' position in collective bargaining

Writ of Summons the legal document that initiates a civil action; see also Statement of Claim

Y

young offender a person, at least 12 and under 18, who breaks the criminal law

INDEX

Barter, 484
Battered spouses, 135, 144–45
Battery, 322
　defences against, 328–31
　medical, 322–23, 324
Beneficiaries of will, 427, 434
Bets and wagers, 478
Bicycle helmets, mandatory
　(research issue), 289
Bigamy, 354
Bill, 21
Bill of Rights (1960), 30–31, 32
Binding arbitration, 536
Binding-over, 156
Biosphere reserve, 572
Birth parent, 415
Blood contamination (issue),
　312–13
Blood samples, 224, 226
Blood tests as marriage
　requirement, 361
Blood-alcohol level, 222–23
Bonding, 171
Breach of condition, 480
Breach of contract, 480–84
　damages, 480–82, 483
　government cutbacks (issue),
　　492–93
　limitation of actions, 484
　mitigation of loss, 481–82
　remedies, 480–84
Breach of warranty, 480
Breaking and entering, 62, 67, 68,
　71, 74, 191–92
Breathalyzer tests, 224, 225
　research issue, 235
British North America Act (1867), 19
Burden of proof, 297, 301
Business assets, 378–79
Bylaws, 20, 21, 331, 332

C

Cabinet, 21
Canada Labour Code, 533
Canada Shipping Act, 561
*Canadian Environmental Assessment
　Act,* 568
*Canadian Environmental Protection
　Act,* 561, 563, 565–67
Canadian law, development of,
　14–16
Canadian Standards Association
　(CSA), 487

Capacity to contract, 448, 460–63
　developmentally challenged or
　　impaired, 463
　minors, 460–63
Capacity to make a will, 428
Capacity to marry, 353, 354
Capital punishment, 161–62
Case law, 15–16
Causation, 182, 294–95, 296
Caveat emptor, 472
Certificate of Divorce, 364
Certificate of Possession, 586
Certification of unions, 534
Challenge of jury list
　for cause, 123
　peremptory challenge, 123–24
Character evidence, 131
Charge to the jury, 142
Charitable donations, 458
Charter of Rights and Freedoms, 10, 30,
　31, 32–46, 64, 67, 593, 635–39
　effect on individuals and society
　　(issue), 50–51
　illegally obtained evidence, 135
　limitation of rights under,
　　32–34, 44–45
　resolving infringements of,
　　44–46
　rights and freedoms under,
　　36–44
Child abuse, 166, 165, 411–14
　central registry, 413
　damages for, 414
　reporting, 412
"Child of the marriage," 408–409,
　410
Child pornography, 198, 199
Child protection laws, 411, 412
Child support, 384–85, 408–409,
　410–11
Child Support Guidelines Project,
　411
Children
　abuse of *see* Child abuse
　best interests of, 398, 399, 401,
　　403, 405, 406, 412, 413
　committing torts, 321
　corruption and abandonment
　　of, 199
　custody of, 398, 399–404
　guardian for, 431
　historical background, 399
　negligence and, 299–301
　and poverty (issue), 420–21
　trespassing, 291, 310

as witnesses, 127, 128, 131
Circle sentencing, 153, 602
Circumstantial evidence, 125
Citation, 16
Citizen's arrest, 91, 323
Citizens' rights on arrest, 94, 96,
　132
Civil courts, 267–68
　trial procedures in, 268, 270–72
Civil disobedience (issue), 574–75
Civil law, 10–12, 14, 62
　compared with criminal law, 269
　main purpose, 265
Civil rights, 30–46
　Bill of Rights (1960), 30–31, 32
　*Charter. See Charter of Rights and
　　Freedoms*
　on detention and arrest, 92–96,
　　132
　distinguished from human
　　rights, 46
　limits to, 32–34, 44–45
Claim, 270
Class action suit, 268, 558
Closed shop, 535
Co-respondent, 364
Cocaine, effects of, 230
Code of Hammurabi, 12–13
Codicil to a will, 431–32
Codification, 12
Cohabitation agreement, 390, 391
Collateral relatives, 438
Collective bargaining, 535
Collusion, 366
Colour of right, 191
Common law, 15, 16
　and employment, 524–25
Common-law relationships, 353
　inheritance, 389
　rights of partners, 375, 387–90
Community service order, 158
Community tolerance, 198
Company unions, 534
Compensation, 156, 266, 274
　from young offenders, 246
　other sources, 279–81
Competition Act, 450, 451, 471, 478
Complainant, 185
Conciliation, 48
Concurrent sentence, 159
Conditional discharge, 155
Conditions
　express, 485
　implied, 485–89
Condonation, 366–67

M

Magna Carta, 18
Malice, 337
Malpractice insurance, 280, 305, 318
Manslaughter, 182–84
Manufacturer's liability, 292–93
Marijuana, effects of, 230
Marriage
  defined, 351
  essential requirements, 352, 353–57
  formal requirements, 352, 357–61
  historical background, 353
Marriage breakdown, 365
  see also Property division on marriage breakdown
Marriage ceremony, 352, 359
Marriage contract, 351, 390, 391
Marriage licence, 358
Married Women's Property Act (U.K., 1882), 376
Master, 524
Material fact, 472
Material risks, 306–307
Material witness, 108
Matrimonial home, 351, 378
Matrimonial property, 378
  division on marriage breakdown, 377–82, 396
Mediation, 282, 283
  for custody and access problems, 407
  of divorce, 367
  issue, 22
  of labour disputes, 535–36
Medical negligence, 305–307
  contaminated blood raises issue, 312–13
  punishment for (research issue), 318
"Meeting of the minds," 450
Mens rea, 67–68, 70–72, 74
  intent, 67, 68, 70–71
  knowledge, 71
  motive, 71
Mental capacity for marriage, 353, 354
Mental cruelty, 365
Mental disorder as defence, 135–37, 139
Mental fitness
  at time of offence, 136

to stand trial, 136
Mental suffering, 325–26
Merchantable quality, 487
Métis, 582
  see also Native peoples
Minority language education rights, 43–44
Minors
  and contracts, 460–63
  defined, 268
  see also Age; Child; Children; Young offenders
Mischief, 200
Misleading advertising, 450–52, 471
Misrepresentation, 472, 473
  of age, 462
  innocent or fraudulent, 472
Mistake, 321
  clerical, 474
  common, 473
  of fact, 141
  regarding marriage, 355
  unilateral, 474–75
Mitigation of loss, 481–82, 510
Mobility rights, 40–41
Molesting, 186
Monitoring of non-dangerous offenders, 156, 157–58
Monogamy, 354
Montreal Protocol, 573
Mosaic law, 13
Motive, 71, 321
Motor vehicle
  accident, 278
  dangerous operation, 220, 221, 227
  defined, 220
  impaired driving *see* Impaired driving
  liability insurance, 279–80
  negligence, 301–305
Multicultural heritage rights, 44
Multiculturalism (issue), 628–29
Murder, 181–82
  capital or non-capital, 161
  first-degree and second-degree, 181–82
  parole for offenders, 169, 170
  penalty for young offenders, 253

N

Name change upon marriage, 361
Napoleonic Code, 14, 15

Narcotic Control Act, 212–18
  excerpted, 217
  penalties, 214
Narcotic, defined, 213
National Parole Board, 168, 171
Native peoples
  aboriginal rights, 44, 592–97
  aboriginal title, 592–96
  contact with European settlers, 582
  cultural diversity, 582, 610
  justice system (issue), 602–603
  land claims, 597–600, 607
  legal distinctions, 582–84
  recent confrontations, 581
  self-government, 600–601
  treaty system, 587–91
  see also Indian Act; Indians
Naturalization, 614
Necessaries, contracts for, 460, 463
Necessity, 135, 331, 539
Negligence, 290–318
  children and, 299–301
  contributory, 298
  defences to, 297–99
  elements of, 291–97
  gross, 302
  medical *see* Medical negligence
  motor vehicles, 301–305
  seat belts, 304, 305
Negotiation, 48, 282, 283
Net family property, 378
Next friend, 268
No-fault divorce, 365
No-fault insurance, 280
  fraud and (issue), 284–85
Nominal damages, 276
Non est factum, 474–75
Non-culpable homicide, 181
Non-necessaries, 461–62, 463
Non-pecuniary losses, 274, 275
Non-registered Indians, 582, 584
Nonfamily assets, 378–79
Notice to creditors, 434, 435
Notwithstanding clause, 34, 35, 43, 639
Nuisance, 331–33, 557, 558
Numbered treaties, 589–91
Nunavut Territory, 598

O

Oath, 127
Obscenity, 197–99
Occupational Health and Safety Acts, 532–33

CREDITS

Unit Openers: Unit One, Courtesy of the House of Commons, Ottawa; Unit Two, Rick MacWilliam/The Edmonton Journal; Unit Three, P. Irish/The Toronto Star; Unit Four, C-OOO-11765-150/Comstock; Unit Five, Moe Doiron/Canapress; Unit Six, Chuck Stoody/Canapress

Chapter 1

3, Courtesy Federal Court of Canada; 6, Al Harvey/The Slide Farm; 7, Ontario Ministry of Transportation; 14, Reprinted with permission of Bob Thaves; 19, Canapress; 23, Reprinted with permission of Ed Hore

Chapter 2

31, Canapress; 33, Courtesy of the Supreme Court of Canada

Chapter 3

59, Courtesy of C. Silverberg; 62, Reproduced with permission of the Minister of Supply and Services Canada, 1995. Taken from Justice Canada, Criminal Code of Canada, Section 348; 65, Reprinted with permission of Ed Hore; 66, Reproduced with permission of the Minister of Supply and Services Canada, 1995. Taken from Justice Canada, Criminal Code of Canada, Section 334; 81, Reprinted with permission of The Toronto Star Syndicate

Chapter 4

91, Reproduced with permission of the Minister of Supply and Services Canada, 1995. Taken from Justice Canada, Criminal Code of Canada, Section 494 (1) and (2); 110, R. Bull/The Toronto Star

Chapter 5

134, Reproduced with permission of the Minister of Supply and Services Canada, 1995. Taken from Justice Canada, Criminal Code of Canada, Sections 34 (1) and (2), and 35; 136, Reproduced with permission of the Minister of Supply and Services Canada, 1995. Taken from Justice Canada, Criminal Code of Canada, Section 2

Chapter 6

151, Tibor Kolley/The Globe and Mail, Toronto; 155, Reprinted by permission: Tribune Media Services; 173, Chuck Stoody/Canapress

Chapter 7

181, Reproduced with permission of the Minister of Supply and Services Canada, 1995. Taken from Justice Canada, Criminal Code of Canada, Section 229; 183, Reproduced by authority of the Minister of Industry, 1996, Statistics Canada, Canadian Crime Statistics, 1993, Catalogue 85-205, Figure ; 186, Reproduced by authority of the Minister of Industry, 1996, Statistics Canada, Canadian Social Trends, Spring 1985, Catalogue 11-002E;188, Reproduced with permission of the Minister of Supply and Services Canada, 1995. Taken from Justice Canada, Criminal Code of Canada, Section 276 (3)(a) to (h); 189, Courtesy the West End Creche/Reprinted by permission of Lisa Herman; 193, Reproduced with permission of the Minister of Supply and Services Canada, 1995. Taken from Justice Canada, Criminal Code of Canada, Section 342; 194, Reproduced with permission of the Minister of Supply and Services Canada, 1995. Taken from Justice Canada, Criminal Code of Canada, Section 223; 200, Reproduced with permission of the Minister of Supply and Services Canada, 1995. Taken from Justice Canada, Criminal Code of Canada, Sections 219 and 430; 201, CanadaWide; 205, Chuck Stoody/Canapress

Chapter 8

214, Reproduced with permission of the Minister of Supply and Services Canada, 1996. Taken from Justice Canada, Criminal Code of Canada, Section 4(3); 217, Reproduced with permission of the Minister of Supply and Services Canada, 1996. Taken from Justice Canada, Narcotic Control Act, Section 10; 222, Reproduced by authority of the Minister of Industry, 1996, Statistics Canada, Canadian Crime Statistics, 1993, Catalogue No. 85-205, Figure 29; 222, Reproduced with permission of the Minister of Supply and Services Canada, 1996. Taken from Justice Canada, Criminal Code of Canada, Section 253; 224, Courtesy Metropolitan Toronto Police; 229, Courtesy MADD Canada; 224, Reproduced with permission of the Minister of Supply and Services Canada, 1996. Taken from Justice Canada, Criminal Code of Canada, Section 254; 230, Reproduced by authority of the Minister of Industry,1996, Statistics Canada, Canadian Crime Statistics,1993, Catalogue No. 85-205, Figure 27

Chapter 9

242, Reproduced with permission of the Minister of Supply and Services Canada, 1996. Taken from Justice Canada, the Young Offenders Act, Section 56(2); 245, Reproduced with permission of the Minister of Supply and Services Canada, 1996. Taken from Justice Canada, the Young Offenders Act, Section 16(2); 247, Reproduced with permission of the Minister of Supply and Services Canada, 1996. Taken from Justice Canada, the Young Offenders Act, Section 23(1); 248, Courtesy Ministry of the Attorney General, Communications and Education Branch, British Columbia; 250, Reproduced by authority of the Minister of Industry,1996, Statistics Canada, Canadian Crime Statistics,1993, Catalogue No. 85-205; 255, Al Harvey/The Slide Farm

Chapter 10

263, Courtesy of Minori Arai; 266, Tony Freeman/Photo Edit; 283, Courtesy of Law Now, Legal Resource Centre, Faculty of Extension, University of Alberta and Conflict Management Services, Calgary, Albterta; 284, J. Goode/The Toronto Star

Chapter 11

298, Paul Chaisson/Canapress; 302, Al Harvey/The Slide Farm; 309, Tony Costa Photo; 312, Division of HIV/AIDS, Surveillance Bureau of HIV/AIDS and STDs

Chapter 12

328, AP Photo/David Boe/Canapress; 333, C000-09614-089/Comstock; 336, Reprinted with the permission of Bill Bierman; 340, Leader-Post photo by Don Healy

Chapter 13

349, Courtesy of Samantha Morgan; 352, Reproduced by authority of the Minister of Industry, 1995, Statistics Canada, Canadian Social Trends, Summer 1992, Catalogue No. 11-008E; 358, Courtesy Vital Statistic Office, Alberta; 359, L.D. Gordon/Image Bank; 361,© 1995 Washington Post Writers Group; 365, Reproduced with permission of the Minister of Supply and Services Canada, 1995. Taken from Justice Canada, Divorce Act, 1985, Sections 8(1) and (2); 366, Reproduced by authority of the Minister of Industry, 1995, Statistics Canada, Catalogue Nos. 84-212, 94-213, 82-552, 89-502 and 84-205; 368, Dave Chan/*The Citizen*, Ottawa, Canada

Chapter 14

382, Courtesy Province of British Columbia; 391, Jose L. Pelaez/First Light; 393, Jeff Smith/The Image Bank

Chapter 15

408, Reproduced with the permission of the Minister of Supply and Services Canada, 1995. Taken from Justice Canada, Divorce Act, 1985, Section 2(1); 410, Jacques Boissinot/Canapress; 413, Reprinted with permission of the Province of British Columbia-Queen's Printer; 416, Reprinted by permission of the Southam Syndicate, copyright 1995; 419, Al Harvey/The Slide Farm

Chapter 16

428, StarPhoenix Photo-Peter Wilson; 436, Courtesy Multiple Organ Retrieval and Exchange Programme of Ontario; 441, courtesy Carswell Legal Publishing

Chapter 17

445, Courtesy of William Siemens; 448, Billy E. Barnes/Photo Edit; 453, Harris, L.S., *North Shore, Lake Superior*. National Gallery of Canada, Ottawa. Reprinted with permission of Mrs. Elizabeth Anne Harris and Mrs. Margaret Knox; 455, Michael Newman/Photo Edit; 465, Canapress

Chapter 18

478 © Letraset; 482, Lismer, A., *A September Gale*. National Gallery of Canada, Ottawa; 485, Dana White/Photo Edit; 487, Canadian Standards Association; 488, Mas Kikuta; 493, Winnipeg Free Press; 509, Reproduced with permission Queen's Printer for Ontario, 1994—Residential Rent Regulation Act of Ontario, Section 100

Chapter 19

514, P. Power/The Toronto Star

Chapter 20

526, Labour Canada; 528, Bachmann/Photo Edit 528, Reproduced with the permission of the Minister of Supply and Services Canada, 1995. Taken from the Canadian Human Rights Commission, Prohibited Grounds of Discrimination in Employment, Table 3

Chapter 21

551, Courtesy of David Nahwegahbow; 575, Canapress

Chapter 22

584, *Aboriginal Law Handbook* by Shin Imai, Katherine Logan, and Gary Stein (Toronto: Carswell, 1993). Reprinted by permission of Carswell—a Division of Thomson Canada Limited; 587, Reproduced with the permission of the Minister of Supply and Services Canada, 1995. Taken from Justice Canada, Indian Act, Section 88; 591, Used by permission of McClelland & Stewart, Toronto; 591, *Aboriginal Law Handbook* by Shin Imai, Katherine Logan, and Gary Stein (Toronto: Carswell, 1993). Reprinted by permission of Carswell—a Division of Thomson Canada Limited; 593, Reproduced with the permission of the Minister of Supply and Services Canada, 1995. Taken from Justice Canada, Constitution Act, Section 35; 598, Reprinted with permission, The Globe and Mail, Toronto; 601, Canapress; 603, Peter Moon/The Globe and Mail,Toronto

Chapter 23

611, Glenbow Archives, Calgary, Alberta; 611, Reproduced by authority of the Minister of Industry, 1995, Statistics Canada, Canadian Social Trends, Catalogue No. 11-008E; 612, Reproduced by authority of the Minister of Industry, 1995, Statistics Canada, Canadian Social Trends, Catalogue No. 11-008E; 613, Reproduced with the permission of the Minister of Supply and Services Canada, 1996; 618, Copyright United Nations. All United Nations rights reserved. Reprinted with permission of the United Nations; 618, P. Gower/The Toronto Star; 620, Reproduced by authority of the Minister of Industry, 1995, Statistics Canada, Canadian Social Trends, Catalogue No. 11-008E; 628, Ken Straiton/First Light

Appendix

635–39, Reproduced with the permission of the Minister of Supply and Services Canada, 1996. Taken from Justice Canada, Constitution Act, 1982, Charter of Rights and Freedoms